M & E PROFESSIONAL STUDIES

Written by a team of practising lecturers and prepared under t
leading partnership of London accountancy tutors, the *M & E Pr*
been specially designed to meet the course needs of professional
the examined subjects at appropriate professional, degree and diplor

With carefully structured and thoroughly up-to-date contents, n
chapter progress tests based on the text, a large number of practice examination questions and suggested answers, a glossary of the more difficult key terms, and a very comprehensive index. An extensive programme of classroom testing, student surveys and independent assessment has been completed in relation to this series prior to publication.

With twenty substantial texts in the series, *M & E Professional Studies* constitutes a major contribution to business education, and will enable students throughout the English-speaking world to gain the syllabus-related depth of knowledge and practice necessary to ensure a successful examination result.

SERIES EDITORS

Emile Woolf

Emile Woolf first qualified in 1961 and joined the London Office of Deloitte Haskins & Sells. Since 1964 he has played a major part in pioneering accountancy education first at Foulks Lynch and the London School of Accountancy, and then as founder and Chairman of the Emile Woolf Colleges in London and overseas. In 1984 he became a partner in Kingston Smith & Co with special responsibility for technical standards and training. He is an established author, and a regular contributor to numerous professional and student journals and magazines in the UK and overseas. In 1980 he received the Distinguished Services Award for Authorship at Hartford University, Connecticut, USA. Recently he was commissioned by the ACCA to produce a series of audio cassetts and workbooks for students throughout the world. Between 1973 and 1979 he was also an Examiner for the ACCA in Advanced Auding and Investigations. Emile Woolf lectures regularly on accountancy, financial and economic matters in Ireland, the UK, USA, Trinidad, Jamaica, Singapore, Hong Kong, Malaysia, Nigeria, Ghana and elsehwere. He also conducts seminars on financial management topics for industrial and commercial clients as well as for professional accountancy firms.

Suresh Tanna

Suresh Tanna graduated in 1971 in chemical engineering from Edinburgh University. Following a career in business management he qualified as a chartered accountant in 1978. In 1981 he joined Karam Singh in setting up the city Accountancy Centre, which merged with the Emile Woolf Schools in March 1983, and he is now a Director of Studies on ACCA courses, and Financial Director of the enlarged FACT Group. He specialises in accounting, advanced accounting practice and advanced financial accounting.

Karam Singh

After a period of project planning with Burmah Oil as a graduate chemical engineer, Karam Singh obtained his MBA from the Liverpool Business School whilst also engaged in part-time consultancy work for clothing manufacturers and retailers and research at a P & O subsidiary. In 1971 he joined the London accountancy firm of Harmood Banner and Company which later merged with Deloittes. He qualified as a chartered accountant in 1974, and lectured for several years at the London School of Accountancy and the North East London Polytechnic. In 1981 he joined Suresh Tanna in the formation of the City Accountancy Centre, where he began to develop study material geared for in-school and home studies students. At present he is Principal Lecturer for the FACT schools for Level 2 ACCA courses, specialising in quantitative analysis. He has contributed numerous articles to the various professional and students' journals.

Contributing authors

The titles in this series have been prepared under the Series Editorship of Emile Woolf, Suresh Tanna and Karam Singh in conjunction with the staff and tutors of the FACT Organisation, 23 Hand Court, High Holborn, London WC1V 6JF. All contributors and authors are practising lecturers with many years' experience of teaching accountancy at all levels.

M & E PROFESSIONAL STUDIES

ADVANCED TAXATION

Third Edition

Doug Beardon MA FCA FCCA SCollP
Principal Lecturer in Taxation,
North East London Polytechnic

and other members of the EW FACT taxation staff

Series Editors
Emile Woolf FCA FCCA FBIM
Suresh Tanna BSc(Hons) FCA
Karam Singh BTech MBA FCA

ME

PITMAN PUBLISHING LIMITED
128 Long Acre, London WC2E 9AN

A Longman Group Company

First published in Great Britain 1985
Second Edition 1986
Third Edition 1986

British Library Cataloguing in Publication Data
Beardon, Doug
Advanced taxation.—3rd ed.—
(M & E professional studies, ISSN0266–8475)
1. Taxation—Great Britain
I. Title
336.2′00941 HJ2619

ISBN 0–7121–0689–8

Printed and bound in Great Britain
at The Bath Press, Avon

Preface

Written by renowned taxation tutors and drawn together by experienced editors also well known for their business studies lecturing, this textbook incorporates subject matter on all the main taxation areas. It is arranged in a logical sequence and concludes with a large number of questions and answers, all of examination standard, to test your knowledge. Much effort has been expended on making this book as simple to use as possible and to that end a lengthy index and table of cases have been included.

The book opens with a discussion of income tax, detailing its history and development. The basic rules are then explained, covering the most important areas, e.g. Schedule D Cases I and II, capital allowances, losses, etc., and incorporating the provisions introduced in the Finance Act 1986. The theory explained in the text is immediately supported by numerous examples.

Corporation tax, unlike income tax, is a relatively new imposition dating from 1965. As such it is precisely defined in the statutes and is easier to follow than other taxes. The section on corporation tax attempts to approach the subject by considering the general principles, pointing out that since its beginning corporation tax has had income tax principles grafted onto it. The problem of liability to corporation tax as encountered over issues of "residence" and "chargeability" is discussed and at an early stage the student is introduced to computational problems specifically related to the calculation of corporation tax liabilities for all types of company. The imputation system of corporation tax is also considered at an early stage. This is seen as the application of ACT to qualifying distributions, and the discussion gives the student the opportunity to consider the effect of ACT on distribution policy and its uses once paid. Several special sections introduce the student to the issue of losses within single as well as groups of companies, and the final chapters of the section discuss such issues as the problems of investment and overseas companies. The majority of companies within the UK are classified as close companies and these chapters consider the meaning and effect of such a classification. Throughout the section the overlap between this area of corporation tax and other taxes such as capital gains tax and inheritance tax is fully considered. Throughout the corporation tax chapters special emphasis is placed on explaining and illustrating elementary planning techniques so that the reader can approach the whole subject from a critical as well as an arithmetical viewpoint. Finally, throughout, the text of this section takes into account the provisions of the Finance Act 1986.

The following section of the book considers capital gains tax. A large number of examples illustrate the various points of law and also reflect the changes brought about by the Finance Act 1986. The next section on value added tax (VAT) contains chapters on all aspects of the subject, from its history through to appeal procedures, and is again in line with the provisions of the latest Finance Act. The final section of the book deals with inheritance tax.

Contents

Table of Cases

Cases recorded in the text are reproduced here with cross-references to help you pin point where they occur.

The following abbreviations are used for the case sources: AC = Appeal Cases; All ER = All England Reports; All ER Rep = All England Reports reprints; KB = Kings Bench; QBD = Queens Bench Division; SCR = Court of Session (Scotland); STC = Simon's Tax Cases; TC = Tax Cases; TLR = Times Law Reports.

1 History and Administration of Taxation

1.0 INTRODUCTION

Income tax in its present form was introduced by William Pitt the younger in order to provide funds for the Napoleonic wars. It superseded an ineffective system of direct taxation largely based on property, e.g. the Window Tax. It remained at extremely low rates, rarely more than 5p in the pound, up to the end of the nineteenth century. It was originally intended to be a temporary measure only, but with the expansion of national income, receipts from the tax even at the low level of rates then in force proved too attractive to dispense with altogether. Over the years a marginal rate of 1p in the pound has crept up to one of 60p in the pound today!

All the other taxes are far more recent in origin. Corporation Tax and Capital Gains Tax were introduced in the Finance Act 1965; Value Added Tax and Capital Transfer Tax in the Finance Acts 1972 and 1975 respectively.

In addition to the taxes considered above both central and local government have other ways of raising revenue. These include customs duties, local and water rates, social security contributions, car taxes etc. Whether these are "taxes" in the true sense of the word is open to debate.

This manual is concerned with two major areas of tax:

(a) Direct Taxes - Income Tax, Corporation Tax, Capital Gains Tax and Inheritance Tax;

(b) Indirect Taxes - Value Added Tax.

Direct Taxes are administered by the Board of the Inland Revenue; Value Added Tax by the Commissioners of Customs and Excise.

2.0 THE ORGANISATION OF THE INLAND REVENUE

The Queen in Parliament

Chancellor of the Exchequer

Treasury

Board of Inland Revenue

Divisional Structure

Management | Technical | Finance | Other Divisions:

Policy

Statistics

Fig.1

2.1 THE QUEEN IN PARLIAMENT

Tax law is derived from a number of Acts of Parliament. These include:

(a) Income and Corporation Taxes Act 1970;

(b) Capital Allowances Act 1968;

(c) Taxes Management Act 1970;

(d) Capital Gains Taxes Act 1979;

(e) Value Added Taxes Act 1983;

(f) Inheritance Tax Act 1986;

(g) Annual Finance Acts.

Each year the tax proposals included in the budget become the subject of the annual Finance Act. This also empowers the Government to tax income, as the power to levy income tax must be renewed annually. The Provisional Collection of Taxes Act 1968 enables the Government to collect income tax on the basis of the budget resolution between the beginning of a fiscal year - 6th April - and the time that the Finance Act becomes law by the following 5th August.

In addition to the above, there are other sources of "legislation" deriving from the Inland Revenue directly. Whilst these have no legal effect they assist in the smooth running of the system. Critics however point out that it is undesirable that the Revenue can operate a quasi-legislative function in a largely unsupervised way. These sources include:

(a) Extra-statutory concessions - these mitigate a charge to tax despite the operation falling within the provisions of a taxing statute;

(b) Statements of practice - these broadly state how the Inland Revenue view the tax treatment of a particular operation;

(c) Advance rulings and clearances - these allow the Inland Revenue to comment on the tax implications of a particular transaction. The clearance procedure is specifically provided to avoid subsequent difficulties where a transaction, e.g. a demerger, can have dramatic tax implications if not carried through in the right form.

2.2 THE CHANCELLOR OF THE EXCHEQUER

He is responsible to Parliament for the conduct and efficiency of the Inland Revenue. He reviews all proposals for legislation and through the Treasury may issue instructions to the Board of Inland Revenue concerning the administration of the Revenue service. He is assisted by the Financial Secretary to the Treasury.

2.3 THE COMMISSIONERS OF INLAND REVENUE

The Commissioners of Inland Revenue, known as the CIR, are full time civil servants responsible to the Chancellor of the Exchequer. They consist of a chairman, two deputy chairmen, two Directors General and two other commissioners. The junior commissioners normally have a specific executive function within the Revenue such as responsibility for the establishment etc. The functions of the Commissioners are:

(a) to implement all Acts of Parliament relating to the Inland Revenue;

(b) to give advice and information to the Chancellor of the Exchequer and the Treasury concerning Revenue matters. In particular to provide statistical information;

(c) to exercise overall control of the various divisions of the Inland Revenue Service.

2.4 THE MANAGEMENT DIVISION

This is the largest division of the Inland Revenue. It is concerned with all aspects of the functional operations of the Revenue including personnel and training, general organisation and the operation of income and capital taxes. The UK is divided into approximately 600 districts each under the charge of a district inspector - often a law graduate with an expert knowledge of taxation.

The size of the district offices varies from a small country district to the large "London Provincial" offices responsible for several million taxpayers. Special offices deal with civil servants and members of the armed forces. The functions of the Inspector of Taxes include:

(a) to issue return forms;

(b) to receive and examine completed returns;

(c) to obtain additional information if required;

(d) to make assessments;

(e) to receive notices of appeal against assessments;

(f) to negotiate settlements;

(g) to represent the Revenue at appeal hearings;

(h) to make repayments;

(i) to conduct correspondence and liaise with taxpayers generally as regards their taxation liabilities.

In recent years there has been considerable activity in the ascertainment and prevention of tax evasion. Whilst much of the work in this area is dealt with in the district offices, specialist units also make significant contributions. These include:

(a) the Enquiry and Investigation Offices which deal with cases of fraud;

(b) Special Offices which deal with types of case which a district could find difficult to manage;

(c) Audit Units dealing with PAYE compliance etc.

2.5 THE TECHNICAL DIVISION

This deals with the technical operation of the Revenue. It formulates advice on the operation of legislation and the prevention of elaborate tax avoidance schemes.

2.6 THE FINANCE DIVISION

This division deals with the accountancy of the Inland Revenue, including the collection of tax, estimates of tax yields and the payment of Revenue salaries and expenses. It operates as far as the collection is concerned through a number of collection offices.

2.7 INTERPRETATION OF TAX LEGISLATION

In many cases tax legislation is difficult to understand and, in some cases, almost incomprehensible. Rules of statutory interpretation have been evolved, and in these the courts have tried to blend consistency with the recognition that the taxing Acts are a rather special form of statute demanding a strict or predictable form of interpretation. Over the years certain broad principles have been laid down:

(a) The words of the Act must be given their natural meaning.

The taxpayer, when interpreting the taxing statutes is entitled to assume a literal construction of the provisions in the Act even in those cases where the result is unusual. In **Rennell v. IRC (1962)**, Lord Justice Donovan said:

> "Nevertheless in the end, one simply has to look at the words of the statute and construe them fairly and reasonably, and, if such a construction yields anomalous results in particular cases, it is a commonplace that they must be accepted, whether it be the Crown or the taxpayer who is thereby advantaged."

(b) Where there is doubt as to meaning of a statutory provison, the taxpayer must be given the benefit of the doubt.

This principle states that where there is doubt, the taxpayer must be the one to benefit from it. In **IRC v. Ross and Coulter (1948)**, Lord Thankerton observed:

"...if the provision is reasonably capable of two alternative meanings then the courts will prefer the meaning more favourable to the subject."

(c) The tax must be clearly imposed on the taxpayer by the terms of the statute.

This principle establishes that an individual cannot be liable to tax unless the words of the taxing statute unambiguously impose the tax upon him. In **Ayrshire Employers Mutual Insurance Association Limited v. IRC (1946)**, Lord Normand stated:

"In the end, I seem to be driven to the last refuge of judicial hesitation when faced with a difficulty of interpretation, the doctrine that no tax can be imposed on the subject without words in an Act of Parliament clearly showing an intention to lay a burden upon him..."

(d) There is no equity in taxation.

Lord Cairns, LC in **Partington v. Attorney General (1869)** said:

"...because, as I understand the principle of all fiscal legislation, it is this: if the person sought to be taxed comes within the letter of the law he must be taxed, however great the hardship may appear to the judicial mind to be."

This leads to the presumption that the courts will adopt a literal approach to the interpretation of tax statutes without speculating on the probable opinions or motives of those who drafted the legislation, and without attempting to remedy deficiencies in drafting:

"It is not the function of the court to give words a strained and unnatural meaning which, had the legislature thought of it, would have been covered by appropriate words."

per Lord Simmonds in **IRC v. Wolfson (1949)**.
Nor will the courts attempt to deal with suggestions that they should exercise a moral judgment. This, according to Lord Normand in **Vestey's Executors v. IRC (1949)**, would have been an undesirable first step down a very slippery slope.

"...the court will not stretch the terms of taxing statutes in order to improve on the efforts of Parliament and to stop gaps which are left open by the statutes. Tax avoidance is an evil, but it would be the beginning of a much greater evil if the courts were to subject to taxation people of whom they have disapproved."

In recent years the House of Lords has considered as a aid to interpretation the substance of the transaction. Although it can be said that the controversy of form over substance and vice versa is really concerned with the interpretation of the transaction as opposed to the interpretation of the statute, it is nevertheless of valid interest.

In looking towards the substance of a transaction, the courts take an overview of the intention and effects of a transaction rather than looking merely towards the relevant documentation. In the late nineteenth and early twentieth centuries there were several cases which intimated that this was the correct approach e.g. **A-G v. Partington (1869)** and **Secretary of State for India v. Scoble (1903)**. Later cases, in particular **IRC v. Duke of Westminster (1936)** 19 TC 490 have disagreed with this approach:

" If all that is meant by the doctrine (the substance) is that having once ascertained the legal rights of the parties you may disregard mere nomenclature and decide the questions of taxability and non-taxability in accordance with the legal rights, well and good...If, on the other hand, the doctrine means that you may brush aside deeds, disregard the legal rights and liabilities arising under a contract between parties and decide the question of taxability or non-taxability upon the footing of the rights and liabilities of the parties being different from what in law they are, then I entirely dissent from such a doctrine."

per Lord Russell of Killowen.

In the case of **IRC v. Plummer (1979)** it was held that separate transactions which are interlinking and mutually interdependent can be considered as a whole:

"The plan now involved was explained by the brokers in great detail and its intended accomplishment set out, with timetables in almost military precision. This...entitles and requires us to look at the plan as a whole. It does not entitle us to disregard the legal form and nature of the transactions carried out."

per Lord Wilberforce.

The cases of **WT Ramsay Ltd. v. IRC (1981)** and **IRC v. Burmah (1982)** have extended this position still further. It appears that although an avoidance scheme consists of documentation and transactions which are genuine per se it will not preclude a different finding as to the effects of the scheme as a whole particularly when the following features are present:

"(i) On completion of the scheme the taxpayer is in the same financial position as he was at the beginning;

(ii) The clear and stated intention of the parties is that the scheme should proceed through its various steps to completion;

(iii) The taxpayer is not required to use his own money for the purpose of the scheme;

(iv) The whole and only purpose of the scheme is the avoidance of tax."

per Lord Wilberforce.

This emphasis on a new and radical approach was formalised by the House of Lords in **Furniss v. Dawson (1984)**. Broadly, in this case Dawson wished to sell shares to a UK company (WB Ltd.); to defer a liability to CGT the shares were first sold to a newly incorporated Isle of Man company (G Ltd.), in return for shares in that company. The Isle of Man company then sold the shares to WB Ltd. Throughout, the price charged and paid for the shares was £152,000. As a result of this:

(a) there was no liability to CGT on the disposal to G Ltd. - share for share exchange;

(b) there was no liability on the disposal from G Ltd. to WB Ltd. bought and sold for £152,000.

In the judgment of Lord Brightman:

"The whole process was planned and executed with faultless precision. The meetings began at 12.45 p.m. on 20th December at which time the shareholdings of the operating companies were still owned by the Dawsons...they ended with the shareholdings in the ownership of Wood Bastow."

His Lordship held that the courts could ignore the parts of the operation which has no commercial purpose. Thus by excluding G Ltd. the position was a simple sale by the Dawsons to Wood Bastow Ltd.

Many commentators have stated that the **Furniss v. Dawson** decision raises more questions than it resolves, in particular:

(a) Will the presence of a commercial motive exclude the principle and what, in any case, is a commercial motive?

(b) Can the taxpayer apply the Ramsay principle against the Revenue?

(c) How will the principle operate when there is an express statutory defence?

The danger of these cases in the matter of interpretation is that an even greater level of judicial discretion has been introduced into the law. The fact that the transactions fall within the letter of the law will not preclude the court from ignoring this and looking to the end effect.

3.0 RETURNS AND ASSESSMENTS

A person chargeable to tax must make a return of his income and capital gains to the Inland Revenue. Even if he is not sent a return form he must notify the Revenue if he has received any income within one year from the year of assessment in which it is received. A year of assessment runs from 6th April to the following 5th April; the year from 6th April 1986 to 5th April 1987 is known as the year 1986/87. A return must include a declaration by the person making it that it is, to the best of his knowledge and belief, complete and correct and it must be submitted to the Inspector of Taxes 30 days after issue though in practice further time is allowed. Where the taxpayer's only income is from an employment, the Inspector may not issue him with a return form each year and in this case the taxpayer should ensure that the Inspector knows immediately about any changed circumstances.

Companies must make returns in respect of their accounting periods.

Assessments to tax are made by the Inspector of Taxes. They must show the following:

(a) the type and amount of income assessed,

(b) the date issued, and

(c) the time limit for making appeals.

The taxpayer may request the Inspector to send a copy of any assessment to his agent. Estimated assessments may be made when no return of income is submitted to the Inspector or where he is not satisfied that the return is full or complete.

A person who has been assessed to tax may apply for relief against any over-assessment due to an error or mistake in any return made to the Inland Revenue. This must be claimed within six years from the end of the relevant year of assessment. No relief is available if the income was assessed in accordance with the law existing at the time of assessment.

4.0 APPEALS

If a taxpayer objects to the amount of income assessed upon him, he can appeal against it. Appeals are initially heard by either the General or the Special Commissioners. To be effective the appeal must be:

(a) in writing, stating the grounds of the appeal,

(b) signed by the taxpayer or his agent,

(c) lodged within 30 days of the date of issue of the assessment.

A late appeal may be accepted by the Inspector if there is reasonable excuse for the delay. If he does not accept it, it must be referred to the Commissioners for their decision.

4.1 THE GENERAL COMMISSIONERS

The General Commissioners are appointed locally for divisions. They are appointed by the Lord Chancellor and in some ways, such as non-payment for services, resemble the lay magistrates. They generally have no special qualifications in tax or accounting and a clerk, often a local solicitor or accountant is appointed to assist them and to deal with the administrative arrangements. The quorum required to hear an appeal is at least two Commissioners.

4.2 THE SPECIAL COMMISSIONERS

The Special Commissioners are full-time civil servants appointed by the Lord Chancellor. They consist of barristers or solicitors with considerable experience of Revenue law. Certain appeals such as those against capital transfer tax assessments can only be heard by them. The normal quorum is one Commissioner unless the Presiding Commissioner decides otherwise.

Whilst Special Commissioners go on circuit to major provincial towns, their base is London and most appeals can be heard there if desired.

Appeals are normally heard by the General Commissioners unless they involve difficult questions of law when they are usually brought before the Special Commissioners. Appeals can, by agreement, or by direction, be transferred from one body to another.

4.4 THE CONDUCT OF AN APPEAL BEFORE THE COMMISSIONERS

At the hearing of the appeal before the Commissioners, the taxpayer may be represented by either a solicitor, barrister or member of an incorporated body of accountants. The onus of proof is on the taxpayer and he or his representatives will be asked to make the opening address and to call and examine his witnesses who may be cross-examined by the Inspector or the other representative of the Revenue. The Revenue then present their case and witnesses who are available for cross-examination by the taxpayer. The Commissioners may examine witnesses on oath and may impose penalties for non-attendance. After hearing all the evidence, the Commissioners may retire to consider their decision. The Inspector of Taxes may not retire with them. The Commissioners decide by a majority and if evenly divided the practice is to discharge the assessment. The Commissioners have no power to award costs.

4.5 APPEALS TO THE COURTS

Appeals fall into two main classes, fact or law; a Commissioners' determination on a question of fact is normally final. The taxpayer or the Revenue may appeal to the High Court on a question of law. This right can only be exercised if the party concerned expresses dissatisfaction immediately upon receiving the Commissioners' decision. The procedure is initiated by giving notice in writing to the clerk to the Commissioners within 30 days after the decision requesting a case to be stated for the opinion of the High Court. The fee for this is £25. Once the case has been stated it must be sent by the appellant to the High Court within 30 days of receipt. The appeal will be heard in due course in the Chancery Division by a single judge. The court may confirm, amend or reduce the assessment as appropriate, it may also award costs. Further appeals lie to the Court of Appeal (Civil Division) and thence, with leave, to the House of Lords. Under certain circumstances it is possible to take appeals directly from the High Court to the House of Lords, omitting the Court of Appeal.

2 Income Tax

1.0 LIABILITY TO INCOME TAX

Broadly, Income Tax is chargeable on:

(a) All persons resident in the UK whether British subjects or not, and whether or not their income is derived from inside or outside the UK;

(b) Non-residents to the extent that they derive income from any property, trade, profession, vocation or employment in the UK.

Certain income derived from the UK may be exempt from UK tax in the hands of a non-resident, either under UK law (e.g. s.99 TA 1970) or under the terms of a double tax agreement.

The following are not liable to Income Tax:

(a) limited companies - they are chargeable to corporation tax;

(b) Ambassadors, High Commissioners and Ministers of any foreign state, together with their staff;

(c) visiting armed forces and staffs of allied headquarters;

(d) officials of the United Nations;

(e) agents for Commonwealth Countries;

(f) approved pension funds;

(g) certain organisations such as charities, hospitals, trade unions etc, on specific types of income;

(h) pensions received by war widows;

(i) capital gains.

2.0 INCOME LIABLE TO INCOME TAX

All income is liable to income tax with the exception of the following:

(a) National Savings Bank Ordinary Account interest not exceeding £70;

(b) National Savings Certificate interest;

(c) SAYE interest;

(d) certain benefits in kind to employees, other than directors, earning less than £8,500 pa provided the benefit cannot be converted into money or money's worth;

(e) certain scholarships;

(f) death grant, maternity grant and child benefit;

(g) certain supplementary benefit and family income supplements;

(h) wound and disability pensions;

(i) War Widows' pensions;

(j) annuities to holders of the George Cross, Victoria Cross, Edward Medal or Albert Medal, and additional pensions payable to the holders of such awards.

3.0 THE SCHEDULAR SYSTEM

Income is classified according to its source under one of six schedules. Certain of these schedules are sub-divided into cases. Each schedule has its own rules as to the calculation of income and the deduction of expenses. The schedules are mutually exclusive which means that the Inland Revenue cannot assess to tax under one schedule which properly belongs to another **(Fry v. Salisbury House Estate Ltd. (1930))**.

The income liable under the various schedules can be summarised as given in Fig.2.

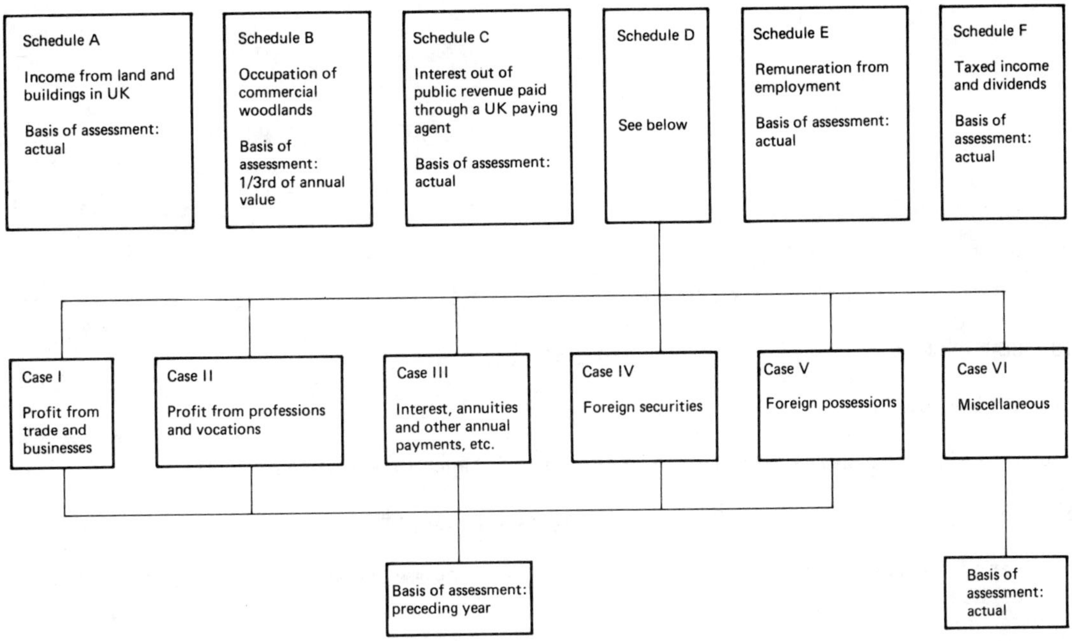

Fig.2 Summary of the Schedules and Cases

3 Income from Real Property

1.0 SCHEDULE A

1.1 INCOME LIABLE

Annual profits or gains arising in respect of land in the UK including:

(a) rents received from land and unfurnished property;

(b) rent charges, wayleaves, ground rents and income from the letting of sporting rights;

(c) other receipts from land including premiums and similar receipts.

1.2 BASIS OF ASSESSMENT (TA 1970, s.72)

The basis of assessment is the income which the landlord is entitled to receive in the fiscal year, irrespective of whether he receives it or not. To mitigate possible hardship the landlord will not be assessed:

(a) when he has taken all reasonable steps to recover the rent from the tenant, and still has not succeeded,

(b) when he has waived the rent to avoid hardship to the tenant and has not received any consideration for making the waiver.

Where rent is subsequently received after relief has been given, the Revenue must be notified within six months and the assessment will be amended (TA 1970, s.87).

Where rent has been paid in advance and the property is sold, the advance rent will be apportioned between buyer and seller (TA 1970, s.86).

<u>Illustration</u>
A let property for the first time on 24th June 1986. He has agreed a rent of £1,000 per annum payable by the tenant either:

(a) Annually in advance,
(b) Annually in arrears,
(c) Quarterly in advance, on the usual quarter days,
(d) Quarterly in arrears, on the usual quarter days.

The usual quarter days are:

24th June, 29th September, 25th December, 25th March.

Advise A in respect to the 1986/87 liability.

	(a)	(b)	(c)	(d)
	£	£	£	£
24th June 1986	1,000	-	250	-
29th September 1986	-	-	250	250
25th December 1986	-	-	250	250
25th March 1987	-	-	250	250
	1,000	-	1,000	750

1.3 DEDUCTIBLE EXPENSES

To be deductible espenses must generally satisfy three basic criteria:

(a) they must relate to the property;
(b) they must relate to the period of ownership;
(c) they must be reflected in the rent.

In detail, the expenses that may be deductible include:

(a) interior and exterior repairs and redecorations. This only gives relief for current dilapidations and not for expenditure incurred on remedying preacquisition defects (TA 1970, s.72(2));

(b) the upkeep of gardens;

(c) the wages of porters, cleaners and persons concerned in estate management;

(d) insurance premiums, and valuation fees for insurance;

(e) rates and rents payable to a superior landlord;

(f) the cost of rent collection, but not rents stolen by an agent;

(g) capital allowances on plant and machinery used in the maintenance and repair of the property;

(h) payments of other services and amenities to tenants, of a revenue nature;

(i) legal and accountancy costs for preparing accounts and tax computations.

Loan or mortgage interest for the purchase or improvement of the property is not treated as an expense in arriving at the assessment but as a deduction from the assessable income.

To be allowed, the property must be let at a commercial rent for more than 26 weeks out of any 52 week period falling wholly or partly in the fiscal year, and during any period in which it is not let it must be either:

(a) occupied by the landlord as his main residence; or
(b) available for letting; or
(c) be incapable of being let because of repairs etc.

The interest payable may be relieved not only against the assessable income that it relates to but also against income from other properties, including those let furnished. Unrelieved interest may be carried forward to be offset in future years (FA 1974, Sch. 1).

Expenses are deductible in the fiscal year in which they are paid (TA 1970, s.72).

Illustration

On 1st December 1985 B purchased a freehold block of flats for £200,000. All the flats were let through letting agents on monthly tenancies at rack rents. All rents had been paid to 30th November 1985 prior to the purchase. In the period to 5th April 1987 his receipts and payments were:

	1st Dec 1985 to 5th April 1986 £	Year ended 5th April 1987 £
Receipts:		
Rents	4,760	14,950
Wayleaves	3	10
Contributions from tenants towards repairs	-	642
	4,763	15,602
Payments:		
Agents` commission (10% on rents)	476	1,495
Repairs and maintenance	218	1,748
Caretaker's wages	260	780
Outgoings on caretaker's flat	85	270
Insurance and incidentals (all allowable)	162	225
Construction of swimming pool - 31st May 1986	-	1,600
Rates on outbuildings	14	44
Purchase of motor mower - 1st January 1986	160	-
Professional charges	1,242	123
Mortgage interest	1,800	5,400
	4,417	11,685

	1st Dec 1985 to 5th April 1986 £	£	Year ended 5th April 1987 £
(1) Rents received comprised:			
Rent owing at beginning of period	-		240
Rents due	5,000		15,520
	5,000		15,760
Less: Rent owing at end of period	240	540	
Rents lost through defaulting tenants.		270	
			810
	4,760		14,950

(2) Repairs and maintenance were made up as follows:

Garden maintenance	40	120
Lift maintenance	36	108
Normal decorations and incidental repairs	142	420
Asphalting drive (in April 1986), (the drive was in a dangerous state at the time of purchase)	-	1,100
	218	1,748

(3) The contributions from tenants towards repairs were deposits against work to be done in the summer of 1987.

(4) Professional charges comprised:	£	£
Legal charges re defaulting tenant	-	50
Accountancy	37	42
Valuation for insurance purposes	-	31
Valuation for mortgage	1,205	-
	1,242	123

(5) The swimming pool was constructed at the request of the tenants who agreed to higher rents having regard to this facility. HM Inspector of Taxes admitted a claim for capital allowances on 50% of the cost.

You are required to compute the amount of the Schedule A assessment for 1985/86 and 1986/87 making such assumptions as you consider necessary.

Schedule A assessments	1985-86		1986-87	
	£	£	£	£
Rents receivable		5,000	15,520	
Less: Irrecoverable			270	
				15,250
Wayleaves		3		10
		5,003		15,260
Less: Expenses:				
Repairs and maintenance	218		648	
Insurance and incidentals	162		225	
Agents' commission	476		1,495	
Caretaker's wages	260		780	
Outgoings on caretaker's flat	85		270	
Rates on outbuildings	14		44	
Professional charges	37		123	
Capital allowances	80	1,332	220	3,805
Schedule A		3,671		11,455
Mortgage interest deducted from Schedule A assessments		1,800		5,400
		1,871		6,055

Capital allowances are claimed as follows:

	£	£
1985/86		
Motor Mower - cost	160	
FYA - 50%	80	80
	80	===
1986/87		
Swimming Pool ½ x £1,600	800	
	880	
WDA - 25% x 880	220	220
		===
c/f	660	
	===	

No allowance can be given for expenditure unless incurred.

1.4 CLASSIFICATION OF LEASES

There are two main classifications of leases:

(a) leases at a full rent;
(b) leases at a reduced rent.

Leases at a full rent
These can be defined as leases from which, taking one year with another, the landlord expects to recover his expenses. There can be two types of lease at full rent:

(a) landlord repairing lease - a lease under which the landlord is required to maintain the property;

(b) tenant repairing lease - a lease under which the tenant is responsible for all or substantially all the repairs to the property.

Leases not at a full rent
These are defined as leases from which taking one year with another the landlord does not expect to recover all the expenses relating to the lease.

The reason for the subdivision of leases relates to relief for excess expenses.

1.5 RELIEF FOR EXCESS EXPENSES

Relief for excess expenses depends on the type of lease:

(a) Landlord repairing lease (LRL)
Surpluses and deficits on individual leases are pooled. Overall surpluses are assessed, overall deficits are carried forward to offset against future surpluses in the pool.

(b) Tenant repairing leases (TRL)
Each lease is treated individually, surpluses are assessed; a deficit is either:

(i) carried forward against a surplus under the same or future leases of the same property.

(ii) set against available surpluses in the pool of landlord repairing leases of the same or future fiscal years.

(c) Leases at a reduced rent (LRR)
Each lease is treated individually: surpluses are assessed, deficits are carried forward and offset against future surpluses under the same lease.

Illustration
C had several properties. You are provided with the following information for the fiscal year 1986/87:

Property	Type	Profit	Loss	Loss b/f
		£	£	£
A	LRL	500		
B	LRL		120	
C	TRL	190		30
D	TRL		170	
E	LRR	60		80
F	LRR	15		

Losses brought forward in the pool of LRL are £100.

Schedule A assessable income 1986/87

	£	£	£
LRL			
A	P 500		
B	L (120)		
		380	
Loss b/f		(100)	
		280	
TRL			
C	P 190		
Loss b/f	(30)		160
D		L (170)	
			110
LRR			
E	P 60		
Loss b/f	(80)		
	c/f (20)		
F			15
			£285

In general it will be advantageous to offset the loss on any TRL against profits in the pool of LRL to obtain the earliest possible relief.

1.6 VOID PERIODS

There may be periods during the ownership of property where expenses are incurred but no income is being received. Relief is available to a landlord for this expenditure provided it is incurred in a void period. A void period occurs when the property is not occupied and which either:

(a) begins with the acquisition of the property and is followed by a lease at a full rent; or

(b) follows a lease at a full rent.

A lease at a full rent may be either landlord or tenant repairing.

Expenses incurred in a void period may be offset against income from the property in the fiscal year in which they are paid. Excess expenses may be carried forward and offset against further income from a lease at a full rent.

It is important to appreciate that a period of landlord occupation in the void period or the presence of a lease at a reduced rent may negate the deduction of expenses in the void period.

1.7 PREMIUMS (TA 1970, s.80)

(a) General

A premium receivable by the landlord under a lease granted not assigned for a term not exceeding 50 years is treated as additional rent and taxable in the fiscal year in which it is received. The amount taxable is the amount of the premium less a deduction of 2% of the premium for each year of the life of the lease other than the first. Only complete years of the life of the lease are taken into account.

Illustration

D grants to E a lease for ten years on payment of a premium of £5,000.

	£
Premium	5,000
Less: 2(10 - 1)% x £5,000	900
	4,100

(b) Duration of the lease (TA 1970, s.84)

Whilst there is normally no doubt as to the duration of the lease TA 1970, s.84 provides that full account may be taken of commercial reality. Thus where the landlord grants a lease which is likely to terminate before the end of its life either:

(i) because of a premature right of formal determination by the landlord; or

(ii) because of an informal right as, for example, having the right to increase the rent tenfold every five years but allowing the tenant to surrender the lease if wished;

then the duration of the lease will be from granting to the earliest date on which it is likely to be determined (which is generally the earliest possible date).

Illustration

F grants to G a lease for 60 years on payment of £10,000. The lease can be terminated at the landlord's option at the end of the 7th or 35th year.

	£
Premium	10,000
Less: 2(7 - 1)% x £10,000	1,200
	8,800

(c) Premiums paid by instalments

Where a premium is received by instalments, and provided that the taxpayer can satisfy the Revenue that it would cause him undue hardship to pay tax on the whole premium at once, the taxpayer may pay the tax by instalments over a period not exceeding:

(i) eight years, or
(ii) the period during which the instalments are received, if less.

(d) Other forms of premium

As a result of the high liability to tax on premiums, attempts were made to avoid tax by either giving the premium a different name or putting it into a form other than cash.

(i) A payment for the variation of the terms of a lease will be treated as a premium. The "duration" of the lease is the period for which the variation is effective.

Illustration

H grants to J a lease for ten years. The terms are that J uses the property for offices. H grants to J a licence to use part of the building for industrial purposes for a period of four years on payment of £1,000.

	£
Premium	1,000
Less: 2(4 - 1)% x £1,000	60
Assessable	940

(ii) A requirement of the lease that the tenant carries out capital work on the property, the cost of which would not have been allowed as a Schedule A if incurred by the landlord, will mean that the landlord is deemed to have received a premium. The value of the premium is the difference between the values of the reversionary interest:

(1) assuming that the lease did not require the carrying out of the capital work, and
(2) assuming that it did require the carrying out of the work.

The valuations are to be made as at the date the lease was granted.

Illustration

C grants to D a lease for 16 years. A condition of the lease is that D will erect an extension to the office. It is estimated that this will increase the value of the landlord's reversion by £10,000.

	£
Premium	10,000
Less: 2(16 - 1)% x £10,000	3,000
Assessable	7,000

(iii) Where the terms of a lease permit the lessee to surrender it on payment of a lump sum, that sum is treated as a premium when received by the landlord. The "duration" of the lease is the period of the lease from the date of surrender to the normal expiry date.

Illustration

E had a lease of 40 years under which he paid F his landlord £1,000 pa rent in in arrears on 31st December annually. He found alternative premises at a rent of £200. On 31st December 1987 he paid F £5,000 to terminate the lease. It then had 30 years to run.

Premium	5,000
Less: 2(30 - 1)% x £5,000	2,900
Assessable	2,100

(e) Relief for premiums paid

There are two basic forms of relief for a premium paid on the granting of a lease:

(i) against trading profits or rents received if a sublease is granted;
(ii) against premiums received if a sublease is granted.

Calculation of relief:

(i) Against trading profits and rents received:

$$\frac{\text{Premium assessed on superior landlord}}{\text{Duration of the lease}}$$

(ii) Against premiums received on a sublease:

$$\text{Premium assessed on superior landlord} \times \frac{\text{Duration of sublease}}{\text{Duration of head-lease}}$$

Illustration

G grants to H a lease for 20 years on payment of a premium of £10,000.

The amount of relief that H can get by deduction against trading profits (if he occupies the premises himself) or against rents received (if he grants a sublease) is:

Premium assessed on superior landlord:

		£
Premium		10,000
Less: 2(20 - 1)% x £10,000		3,800
		6,200
Relief 6,200/20	=	310 pa

Alternatively, if H grants to J a six-year sublease for a premium of £6,000, the relief is:

	£
Premium received	6,000
Less: 2(6 - 1)% x £6,000	600
	5,400
Less: £6,200 x 6/20	1,860
Assessable	3,540

If the deduction for the premium paid exceeds the premium received the excess may be offset against rents received from the sublease. Thus if the premium received on the sublease was only £1,000 the position would be:

	£
Premium received	1,000
Less: 2(6 - 1)% x £1,000	100
	900
Less:	1,860
Assessable	-

Relief against any annual rents received.

£960/6 = £160 pa

It appears that where a sublease is granted at both a premium and a rent, the offset is first against the chargeable amount of the premium received and secondly against any rents.

Where only part of premises are sublet, an appropriate part of any premium paid may be deducted. In general, floor area is an appropriate criterion to apply.

(f) Relief for tax payable on premiums received (TA 1970, s.85 and Sch. 3)
To avoid the very high tax charge which would result from including the whole of the assessable premium in the income of the year of receipt, "top-slicing" relief is available. This involve a hypothetical averaging of the premium received over the years to which it relates following the sequence:

(i) find the chargeable amount of the premium received;

(ii) divide it by the duration of the lease; the resulting figure is described as the annual equivalent:

(iii) find the tax on the annual equivalent treating it as the top slice of the individual's income and making all deductions such as charges and personal allowances first of all from other income;

(iv) multiply the tax so found by the duration of the lease and the resulting figure represents the tax due on the premium.

Illustration

In 1986/87 A grants a ten-year lease of a property to B for a premium of £40,000. A's other income is:

Trading profits	11,000	
Unearned income	12,000	
Mortgage interest paid	2,000	(not under MIRAS)

A is entitled to a married personal allowance of £3,655.

	£	£	£	£
Trading profits		11,000		
Unearned income	12,000			
Less: Mortgage interest	2,000			
		10,000		
		21,000		21,000
Premium			40,000	
Less: 2(10 - 1)%			7,200	
				32,800
				53,800
Less: Personal allowances		3,655		3,655
		17,345		50,145
Tax:				
£				
17,200 @ 29%		4,988		
145 @ 40%		58		
17,200 @ 29%				4,988
3,000 @ 40%				1,200
5,200 @ 45%				2,340
7,900 @ 50%				3,950
7,900 @ 55%				4,345
8,945 @ 60%				5,367
		5,046		22,190
Annual equivalent		5,046		22,190
$\frac{£32,800}{10}$ =	3,280			
Additional tax thereon:				
£				
2,855 @ 40%	1,142			
425 @ 45%	191			
	1,333			
1,333 x 10		13,330		
		18,376		22,190

Thus the tax savings obtained by claiming top slicing relief will be £22,190 - £18,376 = £3,814

An alternative method of presentation is:

	£
Tax liability	22,190
Less: Top slicing relief	3,814
	18,376

It can be seen that the aim of the top-slicing calculation is to effect a theoretical spreading of the chargeable amount over the duration of the lease. In strict logic, it would be appropriate to calculate a separate liability for each fiscal year involved - however, the Revenue make the calculation using only the facts of the fiscal year in which the premium is received. This may enable the tax payable on the premium to be substantially reduced:

(1) by arranging for the premium to be received in a year in which there is little other income;

(2) by creating a loss and making a claim under TA 1970, s.168 to offset it against the other income including the annual equivalent of the premium. Thus if in the above example capital allowances of £25,000 had been claimed on plant and machinery for use in the trade the result could be:

	£	£
Schedule DI	11,000	
Capital allowance	25,000	
Loss	(14,000)	
Other income:		
Unearned income		10,000
Annual equivalent of premium received		3,280
		13,280
s.168 relief	13,280	(13,280)
		NIL

Thus tax on the annual equivalent is nil and 10 x NIL = NIL. There will be no charge to income tax on the premium and tax of £13,330 will be saved.

(g) Date of payment of the tax

The tax due under Schedule A is payable on 1st January in the year of assessment. Provision is made for the assessment to be based initially on the income of the preceding year with a revision to the actual assessable income once the final details are known. If the income of the preceding year includes rents in respect of properties now sold or premiums in respect of leases, these may be eliminated by the Inspector provided that an application is made prior to 1st January.

Where rents are paid to an agent, the agent will be responsible for accounting for tax to the Revenue. There are powers in TA 1970, s.70 which allow the Revenue to direct the lessee of a property to pay part or all of the rent due, to the Revenue on account of the tax liability of the landlord.

2.0 SCHEDULE D CASE VI - INCOME FROM FURNISHED LETTINGS

2.1 INCOME LIABLE

Income from furnished lettings is assessable under Schedule D Case VI. The computation follows the same general structure as for Schedule A except that income should strictly be calculated on the accruals basis. In practice, however, the Schedule A entitlement basis is commonly used. The expenses deductible will include:

(a) repairs
(b) rents payable
(c) rates
(d) management and letting expenses
(e) insurance
(f) capital allowances on furniture etc

As an alternative to claiming capital allowances the taxpayer may claim a deduction for wear and tear based on a fixed percentage of the gross rents, which is normally ten per cent.

An Inland Revenue Statement of Practice of October 1977 indicates that rates or other payments for services which are normally a tenant's burden should be deducted from the rent, in arriving at the allowance for wear and tear.

Illustration

D owns a house in Ramsgate which he lets furnished at £50 per week. During 1986/87 he incurred the following expenses:

	£
Rates	420
Outside painting	210
Furniture repairs	40
Commission	250
Garden upkeep	300
Insurance: Building	25
Contents	70
Accountant's fee	30

The Schedule D Case VI assessable income is as follows:

	£	£
Rent £50 x 52		2,600
Less: Rates	420	
Exterior painting	210	
Furniture repairs	40	
Garden upkeep	300	
Insurance: (£25 + £70)	95	
Commission	250	
Accountancy	30	
Wear & tear 10% x £2,180	218	
		1,563
Case VI		1,037

Where the taxpayer wishes, he may, by election made within two years of the end of the year of assessment, have the income from the property split - the rent applicable to the structure being assessed under Schedule A and that applicable to the contents under Schedule D VI. Expenses will be split in an appropriate manner.

Thus if D has unrelieved losses in 1986/87 from unfurnishyed property let at a full rent, amounting to £400, he should elect to split his Case VI assessment, in order to maximise the use of such losses. For this purpose the rent is agreed as £2,080 relating to the building and £520 relating to the contents. The computation is then:

		Building		Contents	
		£	£	£	£
Rent			2,080		520
Less:	Rates	420		-	
	Exterior painting	210		-	
	Furniture repair	-		40	
	Garden upkeep	300		-	
	Insurance	25		70	
	Commission	200		50	
	Accountancy	24		6	
	Wear and tear	-		218	
			1,179		384
			901		136
Less:	Loss under Schedule A		400		
	Schedule A		501	Case VI	136

Where the letting of the property involves a considerable degree of service the profits may be treated as earned income assessable under Schedule D Case I.

2.2 DATE OF PAYMENT

The tax due is payable on 1st January in the year of assessment. Similar provisions apply to the making of estimated assessments and subsequent revision to actual as for Schedule A.

2.3 FURNISHED HOLIDAY LETTINGS S50 + Sch 11 FA 1974

General

Income from furnished holiday accommodation is assessable under Schedule D VI, subject to the right of the landlord to elect that the proportion of rent attributable to the structure be assessed under Schedule A. In most cases it was assessable on the recipients as earned income. However the case of Griffiths v. Jackson (1983) held that even if organised on proper business lines this type of activity could not constitute a trade. Amendments in s.50 FA 1984 effective from 6th April 1982 (individuals), 1st April 1982 (companies) now permit such an activity to be treated as a trade whilst leaving the income assessable under Schedule D VI.

To qualify for this treatment, the lettings must be on a commercial basis and:

(a) the property must be available as holiday accommodation for at least 140 days in the fiscal year and be actually let for at least 70 days;

(b) for a period of at least 7 months (including the period in (a)) it is not normally in the same occupation for a continuous period exceeding 31 days.

It is possible to average the letting periods of two or more units of accommodation in order to achieve the aggregate of 70 days per unit required under (a) above. A claim must be made within two years of the end of the year of assessment or accounting period in the case of a company.

Illustration

A, an individual, has three flats in Hastings which are available for letting throughout the fiscal year 1986/87. The periods of holiday letting in that year are:

Flat 1 150 days
Flat 2 80 days
Flat 3 40 days

At present flat 3 would not qualify as it has not been let for at least 70 days. If, however, A elects no later than 5th April 1989 the periods of letting can be averaged, i.e.

150 + 80 + 40 = 270 ÷ 3 = 90 days

therefore all the properties qualify as furnished holiday accommodation.

The tests mentioned above to determine whether a property qualifies for relief will be made by reference to a year of assessment. On a commencement, however, the tests will be applied to the twelve month period starting with the date on which it was first let furnished, and in the year of cessation the relevant period will be the twelve months ending on the date on which it ceased to be let furnished.

Illustration

B acquired furnished holiday accommodation on 30th June 1986 and let it furnished for the first time on 1st September 1986. To qualify the relevant periods are:

1986/87	1.9.1986 - 31.8.1987
1987/88	6.4.1987 - 5.4.1988
1988/89	6.4.1988 - 5.4.1989 etc.

For a company the conditions must normally be satisfied for the accounting period.

Advantages

If the conditions are satisfied the following advantages are available:

(a) Expenditure is allowable if it satisfies the Schedule D I expenses rules; the full range of loss reliefs available for a normal trade are generally available;

(b) the profits are treated as earned income, qualify for retirement annuity relief and have the tax paid in two equal instalments on 1st January in, and 1st July following, the year of assessment;

(c) relief is available for pre-trading expenditure;

(d) capital allowances are available;

(e) for CGT purposes, the following reliefs are available:

(i) rollover;
(ii) "retirement";
(iii) gifts;
(iv) relief for losses on loans to trades.

Specific rules deal with the situation where holiday accommodation becomes the taxpayer's private residence.

3.0 SCHEDULE B

3.1 OCCASION OF CHARGE

Tax is levied under Schedule B on the occupier of woodlands situated in the UK, managed on a commercial basis and with a view to the realisation of profit. Where the use of woodlands takes place after 13th March 1984, the occupier would exclude people whose physical presence is mainly for the purpose of cutting down the trees and removing the timber or clearing the land for replanting.

3.2 THE NORMAL BASIS OF ASSESSMENT

The assessment is based on one-third of the annual value of the property. The annual value is the rent that would have been received had the land been let in its natural state (i.e. without the timber), with the landlord paying repairs and insurance and the tenant paying rates. There is no additional charge to tax on the sale of timber.

3.3 THE ALTERNATIVE BASIS - THE CHARGE UNDER SCHEDULE D CASE I

The occupier of woodlands may elect within two years from the end of the year of assessment to be assessed under Schedule D Case I instead of Schedule B. Once the election has been made it continues until there is a change of occupier. Under normal circumstances a taxpayer would be advised to elect to be assessed under Schedule D Case I whilst the timber is growing, thus obtaining capital allowances on plant, utilising any losses against other income.

Once the timber is ready for sale the woodlands should be transferred to another occupier such as a close relative or a controlled company thus achieving a change of occupier so that the assesment may revert to a Schedule B basis.

Where instead of merely being sold, the timber is processed, the profits may be treated as trading income assessable under Schedule D Case I and not Schedule B. Thus in IRC v. Williamson Bros (1949) an occupier who cut down timber and made it into furniture was held to be carrying on a trade assessable under Schedule D Case I.

3.4 POINTS FOR CONSIDERATION

Woodlands not only possess income tax advantages but other benefits accrue in the areas of capital gains tax and inheritance tax. This favourable tax climate may well continue for some while in the future (it has been recommended that they be exempt from any potential wealth tax.) It should always be remembered however that:

(a) timber is a very long term investment;

(b) the tax position may change;

(c) timber is also prone to external factors; these can include fire, damage and disease, all of which, rather like the Inland Revenue, are no respecters of persons.

4 Income from a Trade or Profession – Schedule D Cases I and II

1.0 WHICH CASE?

Schedule D Case I assesses the profits of a trade carried on in the UK or elsewhere. Case II charges income tax on the profits of a profession or a vocation. A profession was defined by Scrutton LJ in **IRC v Maxse (1919)** as an occupation requiring either purely intellectual skill or manual skill directed by the intellectual skill of the operator. A vocation was described by Denman J in **Partridge v. Mallendaine (1886)** as the way in which a person passes his life. A dramatist, jockey and a racing tipster have all been held to be carrying on a vocation.

2.0 THE MEANING OF TRADE

The term trade is not precisely defined. TA 1970, s.526(5) provides that it includes:

"every trade, manufacture, adventure or concern in the nature of trade".

In general, judicial definition adds very little to this unsatisfactory state of affairs. **In Erichsen v. Last (1881)** Sir George Jessel MR said:

"There is not, I think, any principle of law which lays down what carrying on a trade is. There are a multitude of things which together make up the carrying on of trade, but I know of no one distinguishing incident, for it is a compound fact made up of a variety of incidents".

In **Ranson v Higgs (1974)** Lord Reid said that the word is used to denote:

"Operations of a commercial character..."

Broadly the question of whether a trade is carried on is one of fact. This means that the courts will be unwilling to interfere with the findings of the Commissioners unless there are overriding reasons for doing so. In reviewing the relevant case law it is important to appreciate that many of the cases were decided before the introduction of capital gains tax. Before 1965 there was not any liability to tax on long term capital gains and thus if the Revenue wanted to assess a particular profit it was income tax or nothing. It is fair to say that had there been a capital gains tax always in operation, many of the cases on trading would never have been heard.

In 1955 the Royal Commission on Taxation attempted to classify trading under a number of indicators or "badges" of trading. It is opportune to use these as main headings in reviewing the relevant case law:

(a) The subject matter of the realisation

In general any item can be bought or sold but some items are more likely to be dealt in in the course of trade than others.

In **Rutledge v IRC (1929)** the taxpayer, whilst in Germany on business, purchased one and quarter million toilet rolls. Shortly after his return to England he sold them making a profit of £10,000. Held to be trading.

In **Martin v. Lowry (1927)** an agricultural machinery merchant purchased from the Government its entire stock of aircraft linen amounting to almost 45 million yards. He had hoped to sell the linen to manufacturers but instead was forced to sell it through an extensive retail operation direct to the public. He made a profit of almost £2,000,000. Held to be trading.

(b) The length of the period of ownership

An item purchased as an investment is often held for a long period of time. Items bought as trading stock are generally intended to be kept for as short a period of time as possible.

In **Wisdom v. Chamberlain (1969)** the taxpayer had, with borrowed money, purchased silver bullion as a hedge against a possible devaluation. After about a year he sold it making a profit, after expenses, of approximately £48,000. Held to be trading, per Harman LJ:

> "this was a transaction entered into on a short term basis for the purpose of making a profit ... and if that is not an adventure in the nature of trade, I do not really know what is".

(c) The frequency of a number of similar transactions

Broadly, the more often that a taxpayer has entered into a particular transaction, the greater the presumption of trading. In **J Bolsom & Son Ltd. v. Farrelly (1953)**, Harman J said:

> "A deal done once is probably not (trading). Done three or four times it usually is".

In **Pickford v. Quirke (1927)**, the taxpayer was one of a syndicate who purchased the shares of companies, liquidated them and sold the assets at a profit. The taxpayer had entered into four transactions each resulting in a profit. Held to be trading.

(d) Supplementary work

Whether the transaction is trading or capital may depend on the way in which the product was handled or treated by the taxpayer.

In **Cape Brandy Syndicate v. IRC (1921)**, three individuals in the wine trade purchased 10,000 gallons of South African brandy. This was blended, bottled and sold to over 100 separate purchasers over a period of about 18 months. Per Rowlatt J, they had

> "... bought it with a view to transport it, with a view to modify its character by skilful manipulation, by blending with a view to alter..."

In **IRC v. Livingston (1927)**, a syndicate purchased a cargo vessel with a view to converting it into a steam drifter and selling it at a profit. They had never previously done this. Held to be trading.

(e) Circumstances responsible for the realisation

> "Some explanation such as a sudden emergency or opportunity calling for ready money, negatives the idea that any plan of dealing prompted the original purchase".
>
> Royal Commission on Taxation, 1955

There have been few cases on this point. In **Page v. Pogson (1954)** the taxpayer built a house for himself and sold it six months after completion. He then built another one but had to sell it when his employment moved to another part of the country. Held by the Commissioners to be trading and Upjohn J felt unable to reverse their finding whilst doubting whether he would have reached that conclusion himself.

(f) Intention

Intention to trade is clearly trading. Intention to make a profit may not necessarily be so.

In **IRC v. Reinhold (1953)** the taxpayer bought four houses admittedly for resale. Held not to be trading. Per Lord Keith:

> "It is not enough for the Revenue to show that the subjects were purchased with the intention of realising them some day at a profit. This is the expectation of most, if not all, people who make investments."

Conversely, the intention not to make a profit will not necessarily mean that a trade is not being carried on.

In **Grove v. YMCA (1903)** the canteen of a YMCA made a surplus. The organisation was a non-commercial one. Held the profits were trading profits.

The fact that the profits are to be used for a particular purpose or even applied to the common good will not mean that they escape tax, **Mersey Docks & Harbour Board v. Lucas (1883)**.

The question of whether a trade is being carried on or not, often in the minds of the Revenue, will depend on the results of the transaction. In **Salt v. Chamberlain (1979)** a number of speculative transactions in investments by an individual was not held to be the carrying on of a trade, thus denying him loss relief against income.

3.0 SPECIAL TYPES OF TRADING

3.1 MUTUAL TRADING

A basic rule of taxation is that a person cannot trade with himself. That means for example, that if a person decorates a room and as a reward to himself pays himself £10 for doing it, that amount is not taxable income. This concept, called the "mutuality principle", also applies to the situation where two or more persons join together in some form of association e.g. a sports or social club and contribute to a common fund for their joint benefit. Any surplus received by the members on division of the fund is free of tax, as it is really nothing more than a return to the members of the association of their own money. Where the mutual association trades with outsiders, the amount of profits relating thereto will be taxable (**NALGO v Watkins (1934)**). Similarly, mutuality must be genuine, the courts will not recognise elaborate shams designed to avoid tax (**Fletcher v. Income Tax Commissioner (1972)**).

3.2 ILLEGAL TRADING

In general the profits from illegal activities are liable to tax. In **Partridge v. Mallandaine (1886)** the profits of a bookmaker from illegal betting contracts were taxable and in **Mann v. Nash (1932)** the profits of illegal fruit machines were similarly charged. One important factor may be that where there is, for example, a burglary then the "profits" would not be chargeable as there would be a civil liability to restore the goods to their rightful owner. If there is no obligation on or ability of the person who receives these profits to restore them to the persons from whom they derive, then he will not be able to rely on their incidental illegality to avoid tax.

4.0 THE COMPUTATION OF ASSESSABLE PROFITS

4.1 GENERAL

Accounts of both individuals and companies will need to be "adjusted" in order to arrive at the taxable profit. Certain income is not assessable to income tax and certain expenses are not allowable. Some items, such as a proportion of the premium paid on the acquisition of a lease, are allowable even though they are not an expense incurred in the particular accounting period.

4.2 INCOME NOT TAXABLE UNDER SCHEDULE D CASES I AND II

(a) Income taxable under another Schedule or Case. Income from property would be taxed under Schedule A; income received as enterprise allowances from 18th March 1986 is taxable under Schedule D Case VI;

(b) Income which has already suffered tax by deduction at source such as dividends and certain interest payments;

(c) Income not liable to tax at all. This very restricted class comprises certain compensation payments and other isolated non-trading receipts.

In **Murray v. Goodhews (1976)**, Watneys, the brewers, did not renew the tenancies of the tenants of a number of public houses that they owned and in order to protect their good name paid compensation to the tenants. It was not held to be a trading receipt as it was in the form of a testimonial or payment for other personal qualities. In **McGowen v. Brown and Cousins (1977)**, however, a payment to an estate agent for the loss of the opportunity to earn professional fees was held to be taxable, notwithstanding that it was made in consequence of a moral rather than a legal obligation.

A payment made to a trader for agreeing not to carry on his trade may be capital (as in **Higgs v. Olivier (1952)** where Sir Laurence Olivier was paid £15,000 not to make any films for an 18 month period) or revenue, as in **Thompson v. Magnesium Elektron Ltd. (1944)**, where ICI sold chlorine cut-price and made a capital payment to Magnesium Ltd. to prevent them making their own chemicals, which would compete with those of ICI.

4.3 THE CALCULATION OF INCOME AND POST-CESSATION RECEIPTS

Income is normally included in the accounts and taxed on the accruals basis. Thus a trader will be taxed on the amounts earned in the accounting period rather than on the amounts actually received. In the case of certain professions (particularly barristers), the Inland Revenue may allow profits to be calculated on the basis of the actual cash received in the accounting period provided that the person concerned undertakes to render bills promptly. This basis will not normally be allowed for the early years on a commencement or for the last year. Once an assessment for one of the intervening years has been made on the cash basis, the Inland Revenue cannot adjust it to an earnings basis **(Rankine v. IRC (1952))**.

If after a taxpayer has ceased to trade he receives income which was omitted from his last accounts either because they were prepared on a cash basis or because the debtors were incorrect, such income is assessable as earned income under Case VI. Post-cessation expenses may be deducted from such income, as may any unused losses or capital allowances of the trade. If the taxpayer wishes he can elect to have such income, which is received during the six years following cessation, added to his last profit.

If the taxpayer was born before 6th April 1917 and was carrying on trade before 18th March 1968 (the profits of which were on a cash basis) the net amount of the post-cessation receipt is reduced by a fraction, according to age, which is 1/20th if he was born before 6th April 1917 but not before 6th April 1916. In other words the income is reduced by 5% for each year that the taxpayer's age exceeded 51 years on 6th April 1968 up to 75% if he was over 65 on that date.

4.4 ALLOWABLE AND DISALLOWABLE EXPENDITURE

Certain expenditure is specifically allowed or disallowed by statute. Other expenditure has been found to be allowable or disallowable through the procedure of being tested in the courts.

The basic rule for the deductibility of expenses is contained in TA 1970 s.130 - the Schedule D I and II expense rule. It states that no expenditure shall be allowed which is not:

> "wholly and exclusively laid out or expended for the purposes of the trade, profession or vocation".

In **Strong & Co. of Romsey v. Woodifield (1906)** Lord Davy said that it was not just sufficient that the expense was incurred for the purposes of the trade. It must be incurred:

> "for the purpose of enabling a person to ... earn profits".

The words "wholly and exclusively" are interpreted strictly. In **Mallalieu v. Drummond (1983)**, a lady barrister bought dark clothing for her use in court. If she had not worn suitable clothing she would not have been allowed to appear as an advocate. This was held not to be enough, she needed the clothes for other purposes. Per Lord Brightman:

> "it is inescapable that one object ... was the provision of clothing she needed as a human being."

Where expenditure is incurred exclusively for business purposes but gives a coincidental private advantage to the trader then it will not necessarily preclude the exclusivity of the business purpose.

Certain items of expenditure have detailed rules:

(a) Appropriations of profit including:

(i) transfers to reserve;

(ii) salaries of a proprietor or partner;

(iii) interest on capital

are not allowed.

In **Owen v. Southern Railways of Peru (1956)** the company made reserves for compensation due to their Peruvian employees on the termination of their contracts. Held that there was no rule of law prohibiting the deduction of a potential future liability but it must be a "measured provision" rather than a "rough reserve".

(b) UK income tax on profits is not allowable.

(c) VAT will be allowable as a trading expense when it cannot be recovered because the trader is exempt or partly exempt or where he is not liable to VAT because of the smallness of his turnover.

(d) Depreciation is not an allowable deduction for tax purposes. It is replaced by a standardised depreciation known as capital allowances.

(e) The cost of maintaining a trader's family or of providing them with private accommodation or services is disallowed TA 1979, s.130(6).

Wages or salaries paid to his family will be disallowed to the extent that they exceed a reasonable commercial rate.

In **Copeman v. Flood (1941)** a pig breeder paid salaries to his son and daughter of approximately £2,500 per annum each. They were in their late teens or early twenties. Held that the Revenue could enquire as to whether they were wholly and exclusively incurred.

Goods taken by a trader from stock must be charged at full retail price.

In **Sharkey v. Werhner (1956)** Lady Zia Werhner owned a stud farm assessed as a trade and also racing stables which were admitted to be purely recreational. She transferred five horses from the stud to the stables. Held that the transfer should be at market value.

In **Mason v. Innes (1967)** the author Hammond Innes transferred the copyright in an unpublished novel as a gift. Held that **Sharkey v. Werhner** only applied to stock in trade and that the rights in a novel could not be so classified.

(f) Capital expenditure is not allowable whilst revenue expenditure is.

In **British Insulated and Helsby Cables v. Atherton (1926)** Lord Cave said:

> "When expenditure is made, not once and for all, but with a view to bringing into existence an asset or advantage for the enduring benefit of a business, I think that there is very good reason to treat such expenditure as capital".

Thus a lump sum payment of £30,000 to form the nucleus of a pension fund was held to be capital expenditure.

The courts tend to look to an identifiable asset test - is there an asset in existence for which a payment was made?

In **Associated Portland Cement Manufacturers Ltd. v. Kerr (1945)**, lump sum payments were made to retiring directors on condition that they would not compete with the business. Held to be capital - the right of non-competition was being acquired.

Particular difficulty is often experienced in relation to repairs. In **Lurcott v. Wakeley and Wheeler (1911)**, Buckley LJ said:

> "Repair is restoration by renewal or replacement of subsidiary parts of a whole. Renewal ... is the reconstruction of the entirety".

In **O'Grady v. Bullcroft Main Collieries (1932)**, a chimney used to carry away smoke and fumes from a furnace became unsafe. A new one was built. Held to be capital; the chimney was not part of the factory but an entirety on its own. (There was no evidence that the old chimney had been pulled down).

In **Samuel Jones & Co. (Devondale) Ltd. v. IRC (1951)** a chimney which was part of the main factory was dangerous. It was therefore demolished and replaced. Held to be repairs; it was only a replacement of part of the factory.

In **Phillips v. Wheldon Sanitary Potteries Ltd. (1952)** a substantial amount of expenditure on one large job was held to be capital and thus the question of repair or renewal often appears to depend on the size and importance of the work carried out. One large job may be capital whilst a succession of smaller jobs may be revenue.

When an asset is acquired which requires substantial expenditure to be incurred on it before it can be used in the trade, this expenditure will be capital.

In **Law Shipping Co. Ltd. v. IRC (1924)** a trader purchased a ship in a severe state of disrepair. Considerable expenditure had to be carried out to obtain the Lloyds Certificate of Seaworthiness. Held that to the extent that this related to remedying pre-acquisition defects it was capital expenditure.

In **Odeon Associated Theatres v. Jones (1971)** the taxpayer acquired a cinema in 1945. Owing to the war it was in a state of disrepair and because of postwar restrictions it had been impossible to carry out work immediately. Some years later renovation work was carried out and the Revenue claimed that the cost of the work needed to remedy defects existing at the time of purchase were capital. Held they were revenue. The factors influencing this decision and distinguishing it from the **Law Shipping** case were:

(i) the cinema was in use throughout the state of disrepair; the ship could not be used;

(ii) the purchase price of the cinema had not been reduced by the amount of any disrepair;

(iii) accountancy evidence was produced in the **Odeon** case that the charge to revenue was in accordance with the principles of commercial accountancy.

There appears to be some practical doubt about the precise extent of the **Odeon** decision.

Amounts paid to get rid of an unsatisfactory employee are revenue expenditure but if coupled with a non-competition covenant they are capital. A lump sum for the surrender of a lease is capital expenditure.

(g) A charge for bad debts will be allowed provided it is for:

(i) a trade debt written off, or

(ii) a specific provision against trade debts.

Staff bad debts will not normally be allowed unless they result from the carrying on of the taxpayer's trade.

Bad debts written off but subsequently recovered, and reductions in a provision for specific doubtful debts, will be taxable as trading receipts.

<u>Illustration</u>

A provides you with the following bad debts account:

	£	£		£	£
Trade debts written off		500	Provisions b/f:		
Provisions c/f:			Specific	100	
Specific	150		General	200	
General	300				300
		450	Profit and loss account		650
		950			950

The charge for tax purposes should be:

	£
Trade debts written off	500
Increase in specific provision	50
	550
Already allowed	650
Should be allowed	550
Increase taxable profit by	100

No allowance is given for the increase in the general provision.

Illustration

B also provides you with the following bad debts accounts. He is a toy manufacturer.

	£	£		£	£
Trade debts written off		600	Provisions b/f:		
Loan to member of staff written off		200	Specific	200	
Provisions c/f:			General	250	
Specific	150				450
General	300		Trade debts recovered		100
		450	Loan to customer recovered		50
			Profit and loss account		650
		1,250			1,250

The charge for tax purposes will be:

	£	£
Trade debts written off		600
Less: Decrease in specific provision	50	
Trade debt recovered	100	
		150
		450
Already allowed		650
Should be allowed		450
Increase taxable profit by		200

No allowance is given for the loan to the staff member as the business of B is not to make loans. Similarly, there is no charge in respect of the loan to the customer now recovered as, when it was incurred, it was not allowed as a bad debt.

The expenses of trade debt collection are allowable. Defalcations of an employee are generally allowable but not those of a person having control such as the proprietor or director.

In **Curtis v. Oldfield (1925)** the managing director of a company used cash of the company to pay bills relating to his personal expenditure.

Held the loss was not allowable but per Rowlatt J, losses due to the dishonesty "of the subordinates" would be allowed.

(h) Subscriptions to trade associations are allowable, provided that the association has entered into the usual agreement with the Revenue to pay tax on its excess income. Charitable subscriptions, apart from small amounts to local charities, are not allowed. Direct donations to a political party are not allowable.

(i) Entertaining expenditure is not allowable unless it was incurred in entertaining:

(i) staff,

(ii) a customer who is not ordinarily resident in the UK,

(iii) the agent, who is himself not ordinarily resident in the UK, of a customer in (ii) above.

Such expenditure may be incurred by the proprietor or a member of his staff. The cost of a gift is also disallowed unless:

(i) it bears a prominent advertisement for the donor, and

(ii) the total value of such gifts in the year to any one customer does not exceed £10. Gifts of food, drink, tobacco are not allowed. The cost of trade samples, mainly for advertisement, is allowable.

Gifts to charities are not subject to the above restrictions, however, the expenditure must still satisfy the "wholly and exclusively" condition.

(j) Legal and professional fees are normally allowable when they are connected with the following:

(i) renewal of leases with a life of less than 50 years (short leases);

(ii) the preservation of existing trading rights,

(iii) successfully refuting an allegation of breach of contract,

(iv) termination of an onerous trading contract,

(v) audit and accountancy fees,

(vi) contracts of employment for staff.

They are not normally allowable when they relate to:

(i) acquiring a new asset or a new right,

(ii) professional and legal services in relation to a tax appeal or investigation, **Smith's Potato Estates v. Bolland (1948)**,

(iii) preparing a partnership agreement.

Fines, costs and other penalties incurred for breaches of the law are not allowed. Where, however, they are paid on behalf of an employee and assessed on him as a benefit under Schedule E they will be treated as an allowable expense to the employer. Civil penalties, default interest, etc, incurred because of VAT expenses are not allowed.

(k) The cost of hiring a motor car is restricted to the amount obtained by the formula:

$$\text{Hire charge} \times \frac{£8{,}000 + \frac{1}{2}(\text{Retail price of car} - £8{,}000)}{\text{Retail price of car}}$$

Illustration

C rented a car for £2,000 per annum. The retail price was £13,000.

$$\text{Amount allowable} = £2{,}000 \times \frac{£8{,}000 + \frac{1}{2}(£13{,}000 - 8{,}000)}{£13{,}000}$$

$$= £2{,}000 \times \frac{£10{,}500}{£13{,}000}$$

$$= £1{,}616$$

The amount that must be disallowed is £384.

(l) Payments of fees to obtain and renew patents are allowable.

(m) Payments for technical education of staff are allowable.

(n) Remuneration of employees, and contributions to approved pension funds are allowable.

Where sole traders, partnerships or companies make the services of an employee available to charity, the expenditure attributable to the employee's employment is deductible as a Schedule D Case I or II expense. The secondment must be of a temporary nature.

(o) The cost of a shop front is capital; the cost of replacing it is revenue. (Any improvement element on a replacement would be capital).

(p) Payments made under deduction of tax are not allowable deductions. Where appropriate, however, they can be treated as a charge on the taxpayer's total income. This will be dealt with later.

(q) Incidental costs incurred in obtaining loan finance will be allowable. The costs referred to are expenditure on fees, commissions, advertising, printing etc., wholly and exclusively incurred for the purpose of obtaining finance, whether obtained or not, or providing security for it, or repaying it. This does not include stamp duty. The finance must be by way of a qualifying loan or the issue of qualifying loan stock. For this purpose "qualifying" means that the interest on the loan or loan stock is deductible for income tax or corporation tax purposes. For corporation tax purposes loan stocks which carry the right of conversion into ordinary shares or other non-qualifying loan stocks will be treated as qualifying, providing the conversion rights are not exercised within three years of the date of issue.

If the conversion rights are exercised within the three year period then no part of the expenses of the issue will be allowed. If some of the rights are exercised within this period and some not then the expenses qualifying for relief are proportionately reduced.

(r) Expenditure incurred for the purposes of a trade before the trade commences will be allowable as a deduction where it is incurred not more than three years before commencement. It is treated as a loss incurred on the first day of trading.

(s) For the fiscal year 1985/6 and subsequent years, a person carrying on a trade or profession can claim a deduction from his total income of 50% of the final Class 4 National Insurance Contributions. No relief is available for the flat rate class 2 contributions.

4.5 THE FORMAT OF THE COMPUTATION

The format of the computation is demonstrated below. It commences with the net profit and proceeds to adjust it for tax purposes. The final figure of adjusted profits represents the amount of trading profits liable to tax.

Illustration

H Beech, who has carried on a manufacturing business for many years makes up his accounts to 31st December each year. The following is a summary of his profit and loss account for the year to 31st December 1985:

	£		£
Salaries and wages	12,320	Gross profit	30,160
Rates and insurance	850	Bank interest	60
Light and heat	750	Profit on sale of car	40
Repairs	650	Dividend received (excluding tax credit)	45
Motor car expenses	280		
Bank interest	170		
Loan interest	240		
Bad and doubtful debts	150		
General expenses	1,630		
Management salary: H Beech	1,200		
Net profit	12,065		
	30,305		30,305

Particulars of the accounts were as follows:

	£
Repairs:	
Additional toilet facilities for staff	200
Redecorations	400
Overhaul of machinery	50
	650
General expenses:	
Printing and stationery	250
Legal costs: Debt collections	25
Agreements with staff	30
Loan agreement	28
Accountancy and audit fee	320
Annual payment under deed of covenant to trade benevolent association (gross)	35
Subscription: Trade association	20
Donation: Spastics Society	15
Entertaining and gifts	907
	1,630

Entertaining expenses and gifts were made up as follows:

	£
Entertaining: UK customers	300
Foreign customers	400
London agent of foreign firm	25
Christmas gifts to London agent of foreign firm	20
Gifts of wine to UK customers	162
	907

The copy of the bad and doubtful debts account was:

	£		£
Trade debtors w/o	120	Balance 1st January 1985:	
Loan to customer w/o	80	Specific debt reserve	115
Balance 31st December 1985:		2% of debtors	200
Specific debt reserve	150	Debt recovered (previously charged and allowed for, Case I)	20
2% of debtors	135	Profit and loss account	150
	485		485

It has been agreed that one-third of the use of the car is for private purposes.

H BEECH

Computation of Adjusted Profit for the year ended 31st December 1985

	£	£
Net profit per accounts	12,065	-
Management salary: H Beech	1,200	
General expenses:		
Annual payment under deed of covenant	35	
Entertaining other than foreign customers (£907 - £400)	507	
Bad and doubtful debts (Note 1)	15	
Motor car expenses (one-third)	93	
Repairs: Additional toilet facilities	200	
Donation to Spastics Society	15	
Bank interest (assessable under Case III)		60
Dividend received		45
Profit on sale of car		40
	14,130	145
	145	
Schedule D I adjusted trading profits	13,985	

Note 1

	£
Doubtful debts:	
Trade debts written off	120
Increase in specific provision	35
	155

	£
b/f	155
Less: Debt recovered	20
Allowable	135
Already allowed	150
Add back	15

5.0 THE BASIS OF ASSESSMENT

5.1 THE NORMAL BASIS (TA 1970,s.115)

The normal basis of assessment for Schedule D Cases I and II is the accounting period of twelve months ended in the preceding year of assessment. Thus to find the profits that are assessable for a particular fiscal year it is necessary to find an accounting period of twelve months ended in the preceding fiscal year.

Illustration
G makes up accounts as under:

Year ended 31st December 1986
Year ended 31st December 1987

The adjusted profits of these years will be assessed for the fiscal years, 1987/88 and 1988/89 respectively. The year ended 31st December 1986 is said to be the basis period for 1987/88 and the year ended 31st December 1987 is the basis period for 1988/89.

5.2 THE BASIS OF ASSESSMENT ON THE COMMENCEMENT OF A TRADE

Special rules apply on the commencement of a business.

The normal basis TA 1970,s.116

Year of assessment	Assessable Profit
First year	Profits from date of commencement to 5th April following.
Second year	Profits of the first twelve months trading.
Third and subsequent years	Profits of the accounting period of twelve months ended in the preceding year of assessment.

Any apportionment of profits is made on a strict time basis.

Illustration
H commenced trading on 1st July 1984 and made up accounts to 30th June, each year. The profits, as adjusted for tax, were as follows:

Year ended 30th June	£
1985	4,800
1986	6,000
1987	9,800

The assessments will be:

		£
1984/85	(year in which trade commenced) 1st July 1984 to 5th April 1985 $\frac{9}{12}$ x £4,800	3,600 =====
1985/86	First 12 months trading 1st July 1984 to 30th June 1985	4,800 =====
1986/87	Preceding year basis Year ended 30th June 1985	4,800 =====
1987/88	Preceding year basis Year ended 30th June 1986	6,000 =====
1988/89	Preceding year basis Year ended 30th June 1987	9,800 =====

The revised basis TA 1970,s.117

As the first three assessments are based on the profits of the first accounting period, it might prove a considerable disadvantage where the profits of that period were materially higher than those in future accounting periods. It is therefore provided that the taxpayer has the right to have the assessments for the second and third years of assessment calculated by reference to the actual profits of those years - TA 1970,s.117. The election, which must be made within 7 years of the end of the second year of assessment, covers both second and third years. It may be revoked within 6 years of the end of the third year of assessment.

Illustration

If H in the above example made an election under TA 1970,s.117 for the second and third years, the assessments would become:

		£
1985/86	6th April 1985 to 5th April 1986 $\frac{3}{12}$ x £4,800 + $\frac{9}{12}$ x £6,000	5,700
1986/87	6th April 1986 to 5th April 1987 $\frac{3}{12}$ x £6,000 + $\frac{9}{12}$ x £9,800	8,850
		14,550 ======

In this case, it will not be beneficial to make the s.117 election.

	Normal £	Revised £
1985/86	4,800	5,700
1986/87	4,800	8,850
	9,600 =====	14,550 =====

If, when trying to find the assessment of the third fiscal year, there is no accounting period of 12 months ended in the preceding year of assessment, the normal practice of the Inland Revenue is:

(a) if the first accounting period is less than 12 months, reassess the profits of the first 12 months of trading;

(b) if the first accounting period exceeds 12 months, assess the last 12 months of the first accounting period.

Illustration

J commenced a music shop on 1st October 1985 and decided to make accounts to 30th June 1986. The results adjusted for income tax were as follows:

		£
9 months ended	30th June 1986	1,800
Year ended	30th June 1987	1,200
Year ended	30th June 1988	1,500

The assessments for the first 3 fiscal years would be:

Original assessment	£	Revised assessment	£
1985/86 1.10.85 to 5.4.86			
$\frac{6}{9}$ x £1,800	1,200		1,200
1986/87 1.10.85 to 30.9.86 (first 12 months)		6.4.86 to 5.4.87	
£1,800 + $\frac{3}{12}$ x £1,200	2,100	$\frac{3}{9}$ x £1,800 + $\frac{9}{12}$ x £1,200	1,500
1987/88 1.10.85 to 30.9.86 (first 12 months reassessed)		6.4.87 to 5.4.88	
	2,100	$\frac{3}{12}$ x £1,200 + $\frac{9}{12}$ x £1,500	1,425
	4,200		2,925

In this case the taxpayer will be advised to have his profits assessed on an actual basis.

Illustration

K commenced trade as a builder on 1st October 1985 and decided to make accounts to 31st December 1986 with the following adjusted results:

		£
15 months to	31st December 1986	20,000
Year ended	31st December 1987	16,800
Year ended	31st December 1988	18,000

The assessments are:

Original assessment	£	Revised Assessment	£
1985/86 1.10.85 to 5.4.86 $\frac{6}{15} \times £20,000$	8,000 =====		
1986/87 1.10.85 to 30.9.86 $\frac{12}{15} \times £20,000$	16,000	6.4.86 to 5.4.87 $\frac{9}{15} \times £20,000 + \frac{3}{12} \times £16,800$	16,200
1987/88 1.1.86 to 31.12.86 $\frac{12}{15} \times £20,000$	16,000	6.4.87 to 5.4.88 $\frac{9}{12} \times £16,800 + \frac{3}{12} \times £18,000$	17,100
	32,000 ======		33,300 ======

In this case there will be no revision to actual.

Where, in the fourth fiscal year, there is still no accounting period of twelve months ended in the preceding year of assessment, the normal practice of the Revenue will be to re-assess the profits of the last twelve months of the first accounting period.

Illustration

L commenced to trade on 1st January 1986 and made up accounts to 30th June 1987 and thereafter annually. The adjusted profits are:

	£
18 months to 30th June 1987	9,000
Year ended 30th June 1988	12,000

The assessments on the normal s.116 basis are:

		£
1985/86	1.1.86 to 5.4.86 $\frac{3}{18} \times £9,000$	1,500 =====
1986/87	1.1.86 to 31.12.86 $\frac{12}{18} \times £9,000$	6,000 =====
1987/88	1.7.86 to 30.6.87 $\frac{12}{18} \times £9,000$	6,000 =====
1988/89	1.7.86 to 30.6.87 $\frac{12}{18} \times £9,000$	6,000 =====

5.3 ASSESSMENTS ON THE CESSATION OF A TRADE (TA 1970,s.118)

As with a commencement, there are special rules of assessment on the cessation of a trade.

Year of assessment	Assessable Profits
Ultimate year	Profits from 6th April preceding discontinuance to the date of discontinuance.
Penultimate year	Normal (preceding year) basis
Pre-penultimate year	Normal (preceding year) basis

Illustration

M ceased business on 30th September 1987 after trading for many years and making accounts up to 30th September each year. The assessable profits for recent years had been:

Year ended 30th September	£
1984	9,600
1985	12,000
1986	18,000
1987	16,800

	£
1987/88 (ultimate year) 6th April 1987 to 30th September 1987 $\frac{6}{12}$ x £16,800	8,400 ======
1986/87 (penultimate year) Year ended 30th September 1985	12,000
1985/86 (pre-penultimate year) Year ended 30th September 1984	9,600
	21,600 ======

Just as when a taxpayer commences to trade he pays tax on the same profits more than once, so when he ceases some profits will not be taxed at all. In the above illustration M would not pay tax on the profit for the year ended 30th September 1986 of £18,000 plus the time apportioned profit for the six months to 5th April 1987 of £8,400. However, the Revenue have rights when there is a cessation of trade, similar to those of the taxpayer on commencement. If the total assessments on an actual basis for the penultimate and pre-penultimate years is greater than those on the normal basis, they may adopt actual.

In the case of M, the Revenue would adopt an actual basis for 1986/87 and 1985/86 which in total amounts to £32,400 - greater than the preceding year basis total of £21,600:

	£
1987/88 (ultimate year) As before	8,400 ======
1986/87 (penultimate year) 6th April 1986 to 5th April 1987 $\frac{6}{12}$ x £16,800 + $\frac{6}{12}$ x £18,000	17,400
1985/86 (pre-penultimate year) 6th April 1985 to 5th April 1986 $\frac{6}{12}$ x £18,000 + $\frac{6}{12}$ x £12,000	15,000
	32,400 ======

5.4 SHORT PERIODS OF TOTAL TRADING

Where the total period of trading is so short that there is liable to be a clash of interest between the taxpayer's right of election on commencement and the Revenue's obligation to revise on cessation, the actual basis always takes priority. This will mean that where the total period of trading covers five or fewer fiscal years then assessments will be on an actual basis throughout.

5.5 CHANGE OF ACCOUNTING DATE

For the normal preceding year basis to apply, certain conditions must be complied with in relation to each accounting period:

(a) it must be a twelve month period;

(b) it must end in the year preceding the year of assessment;

(c) it must be the only accounting period ending in that year.

Where these rules are not complied with, the Revenue, have the right to select any period of twelve months that ends in the year preceding the year of assessment and to base the assessment on the profits of those twelve months. The Revenue will adopt this procedure every time the rules are not complied with. They also have the statutory right to determine the profits of another twelve month period corresponding to the earliest period of twelve months they have had to determine. It should be noted that this second statutory right, to compute the profits of a corresponding period, will amend an assessment for which there is already an otherwise acceptable twelve month accounting period ended in the year preceding the year of assessment.

This statutory procedure, if applied rigidly, is arbitrary in result and can be distinctly advantageous to either the taxpayer or the Revenue. To avoid inequity the Revenue have adopted a code of practice whereby they seek to average profits actually made over the years of assessment affected. Although the code of practice is not statutory, it has received judicial approval in the case of **IRC v. Helical Bar Ltd. (1972).**

The calculations on a change of accounting date can be best explained by an example.

Illustration

O Bow made up accounts to 30th September each year until 30th September 1986 when it was decided for stock taking reasons to prepare accounts to 30th June in future. The adjusted trading profits were:

	£
Year ended 30.9.1984	20,000
Year ended 30.9.1985	39,000
Year ended 30.9.1986	24,000
9 months ended 30.6.1987	16,000

Step 1

Allocate the basis periods to fiscal years:

Year to 30.9.84	£20,000	-	1985/86
Year to 30.9.85	£39,000	-	1986/87
Year to 30.9.86	£24,000	-	1987/88
9 months to 30.6.87	£16,000	-	1988/89

It can be seen that there will be difficulties with the fiscal year 1988/89 as there is no accounting period of twelve months ended within the preceding year of assessment. There will be the need to make up a new basis period for that fiscal year and the normal practice of the Revenue will be to select a twelve month period ended on the new permanent accounting date.

1988/89	£
12 months to 30.6.87	
$\frac{3}{12}$ x £24,000	6,000
9 months to 30.6.87	16,000
	22,000

Step 2
Find whether there is a missing year. On occasions, because of the timing of the changed accounting date, a fiscal year drops out with no basis period. The calculations will be shown in a later example; however, the test is whether the fiscal years in Step 1 follow sequentially. Here they do - there is no missing year.

Step 3
Find the corresponding period. This is a period of twelve months immediately preceding the earliest new basis period. In this example it is the twelve months to 30th June 1986.

Corresponding period:

	£
12 months to 30.6.86	
$\frac{3}{12}$ x £39,000	9,750
$\frac{9}{12}$ x £24,000	18,000
	27,750

Step 4
Find how many fiscal years have been affected by the calculations in Steps 1 to 3 above. A fiscal year is affected if any of the profits of its basis period have been used.

In Step 1 the profits that have been used are:

(a) £16,000 - nine months to 30th June 1987, thus 1988/89 affected.

(b) Part of £24,000 - twelve months to 30th September 1986, thus 1987/88 affected.

In Step 3 the profits that have been used are:

(a) Part of £24,000 - twelve months to 30th September 1986, thus 1987/88 affected.

(b) Part of £39,000 - twelve months to 30th September 1985, thus 1986/87 affected.

Thus the fiscal years affected are:

1988/89, 1987/88 and 1986/87

Expressed in months this gives 36 months.

Step 5

Find how many accounting periods have been affected, by the calculations in Steps 1 to 3. Again, an accounting period is affected if any of the profits of that period have been used. Thus the accounting periods affected are:

twelve months to 30th September 1985
twelve months to 30th September 1986
nine months to 30th June 1987

Expressed in months - a total of 33 months.

Step 6

Find out the total profits of the accounting periods in Step 5.

	£
12 months to 30.9.85	39,000
12 months to 30.9.86	24,000
9 months to 30.6.87	16,000
	79,000

Step 7

Find the revised profits of the fiscal years affected. Here there are three fiscal years affected - a total of 36 months; however, there are profits of 33 months only. These need to be upgraded to 36 months. Perform the calculation:

$$\frac{\text{Fiscal years}}{\text{Accounting periods}} \times \text{Profits}$$

	£
$\frac{36}{33} \times £79,000$	86,182

Step 8

This represents the total profits of the three fiscal years 1986/87, 1987/88 and 1988/89. One of these years will be the variable year. This will be the fiscal year for which the corresponding period could have formed a basis period. The corresponding period - the twelve months to 30th June 1986 - could form a basis period for 1987/88; this is the variable year.

Deduct the "fixed" assessments for the other two years:

	£	
1986/87	39,000	
1988/89	22,000	
		61,000
This could be assessed for 1987/88	c/f	25,182

Step 9 b/f 25,182

For this figure to be assessed for 1987/88 it must satisfy the intermediacy test. If it does not the Revenue will not allow the averaging formula to be used. It will satisfy the test if it lies between:

(a) the original assessment for 1987/88 - £24,000

and

(b) the profits of the corresponding period - £27,750.

In this case the test is satisfied.

Step 10

	£
Deduct the original assessment for 1987/88	24,000
Potential additional assessment	1,182

Any adjustment to the original assessment will only be made by the Revenue if it is material. It will be immaterial where it is both:

(a) less than £1,000 and also

(b) less than ten per cent of the average of the original assessment of the variable year and the assessment of the next following fiscal year.

Here, the adjustment is material as it exceeds £999 and therefore it is not necessary to perform part (b). If this were done, however, the calculation would be:

	£
1987/88 original assessment	24,000
1988/89 assessment	22,000
	46,000
Average	23,000
10% thereof	2,300

The final assessments will be:

	£
1985/86	20,000
1986/87	39,000
1987/88	25,182
1988/89	22,000

Illustration

Basil made up accounts to 30th September until he decided to change to 31st March. His adjusted results for tax purposes were:

	£
Year ended 30.9.1984	2,000
Year ended 30.9.1985	3,750
Year ended 30.9.1986	1,500
6 months to 31.3.1987	500
Year ended 31.3.1988	1,800

Step 1

Allocate the accounting periods to fiscal years:

	£	
Year ended 30.9.84	2,000	1985/86
Year ended 30.9.85	3,750	1986/87
Year ended 30.9.86	1,500	1987/88
6 months to 31.3.87	500	1987/88
Year ended 31.3.88	1,800	1988/89

There will be difficulties in the year 1987/88 as although there is an accounting period of twelve months ended in the preceding year of assessment 1986/87 it is not the only accounting period ended in that year. It will therefore be necessary to make up a new basis period of twelve months ended on the new permanent accounting date.

1987/88

	£
12 months to 31.3.87	
$\frac{6}{12}$ x £1,500	750
6 months to 31.3.87	500
	1,250
	=====

Step 2

There is no missing year.

Step 3

The corresponding period is the year to 31st March 1986.

	£
$\frac{6}{12}$ x £3,750	1,875
$\frac{6}{12}$ x £1,500	750
	2,625
	=====

Step 4

Fiscal years affected:

Step 1	1987/88
Step 3	1987/88 and 1986/87

Two fiscal years - 1986/87 and 1987/88 - equals 24 months.

Step 5

Accounting periods affected:

	£
12 months to 30.9.85	3,750
12 months to 30.9.86	1,500
6 months to 31.3.87	500
30 months	

Step 6

Profits of those accounting periods	5,750

Step 7

	£
$\frac{24}{30}$ x £5,750	4,600

Step 8

Deduct assessments for the fixed fiscal year (the variable year will be 1986/87 as it is the fiscal year for which the corresponding period could have formed a basis period).

1987/8	1,250
Possible assessment 1986/87	3,350

Step 9

This passes the intermediacy test as it lies between:

		£
(a)	the original assessment for 1986/87, and	3,750
(b)	the profits of the corresponding period	2,625

Step 10

Deduct the existing 1986/87 assessment	3,750
Possible reduction in assessment	(400)

As this is less than £1,000 it satisfies the first test of immateriality. The second test is whether it is also less than ten per cent of the average of:

	£
1986/87 original assessment	3,750
1987/88 assessment	1,250
	5,000
Average	2,500
10% thereof	250

Here it exceeds £250 and therefore the difference is material; the Revenue will revise the 1986/87 assessment to £3,350.

The final assessments will be:

	£
1985/86	2,000
	=====
1986/87	3,350
	=====
1987/88	1,250
	=====
1988/89	1,800
	=====

Illustration

K made up accounts as under:

		£
Year ended	28.2.1985	9,000
Year ended	28.2.1986	8,400
Year ended	28.2.1987	7,200
16 months ended	30.6.1988	12,000

Step 1

Allocate the accounting periods to fiscal years:

		£	
Year to	28.2.1985	9,000	1985/86
Year to	28.2.1986	8,400	1986/87
Year to	28.2.1987	7,200	1987/88
16 months to	30.6.1988	12,000	1989/90

Make up a new basis period for 1989/90.

12 months to 30.6.1988

$\frac{12}{16}$ x £12,000 £9,000

======

Step 2

Here there is a missing year and it will be necessary to make up another new basis period for 1988/89. Following the normal practice of the Revenue, this will be the twelve months immediately preceding the first new basis period.

1988/89

Twelve months to 30.6.1987

	£
$\frac{8}{12}$ x £7,200	4,800
$\frac{4}{12}$ x £12,000	3,000
	7,800
	=====

Step 3
The corresponding period is the year to 30th June 1986.

	£
$\frac{8}{12}$ x £8,400	5,600
$\frac{4}{12}$ x £7,200	2,400
	8,000

Step 4
Fiscal years affected:

Step 1	1989/90
Step 2	1988/89 and 1987/88
Step 3	1987/88 and 1986/87

4 fiscal years affected - 1989/90; 1988/89; 1987/88 and 1986/87 - equal to 48 months.

Step 5
Accounting periods affected:

	£
12 months to 28.2.1986	8,400
12 months to 28.2.1987	7,200
16 months to 30.6.1988	12,000
40 months	

Step 6
Profits of those accounting periods 27,600

Step 7

	£
$\frac{48}{40}$ x £27,600	33,120

Step 8
Deduct fixed assessments:

	£	
1989/90	9,000	
1988/89	7,800	
1986/87	8,400	
		25,200
Possible assessment 1987/88		7,920

1987/88 will be the variable year - it is the fiscal year for which the corresponding period could have formed a basis period.

Step 9
This passes the intermediacy test as it lies between:

		£	£
(a)	the original assessment for 1987/88	7,200	
(b)	the profits of the corresponding period	8,000	

Step 10

Deduct the existing 1987/88 assessment	7,200
Possible increase in assessment	720

As this is less than £1,000 it again satisfies the first test of immateriality. The second test is whether it is also less than ten per cent of:

	£
1987/88 original assessment	7,200
1988/89 assessment	7,800
	15,000
Average	7,500
10% thereof	750

As the possible additional assessment is less than £750 it will be immaterial and no adjustment will be made by the Revenue. The final assessments will be:

	£
1985/86	9,000
1986/87	8,400
1987/88	7,200
1988/89	7,800
1989/90	9,000

5.7 DATE OF PAYMENT

Tax due under Schedule D Cases I and II is due in two equal instalments on 1st January in the year of assessment and 1st July following the end of the year of assessment. This makes the choice of a suitable accounting date important and in general it is more beneficial to have an accounting period ending just after the end of a fiscal year rather than on or just before the end of the year. Assuming that there are two alternative year end dates - 31st March or 30th April, the following points are relevant:

(a) the choice of the 30th April year end date gives the longest period of "credit" for the payment of tax. The year to 30th April 1987 would be assessed for the fiscal year 1988/89 and tax would be paid on:

1st January 1989
1st July 1989

Periods of credit of 20 months and 26 months respectively. Conversely if accounts were made up to 31st March 1987 the assessment would be for the year 1987/88 with payment due on:

1st January 1988
1st July 1988

(b) A 30th April year end date will give a reasonably long period of time for the finalisation of accounts before submission to the Inland Revenue.

(c) On cessation there will be a "drop out" resulting in profits being earned which are not liable to tax. A 30th April accounting date will normally result in a far greater drop out period than one ending on 31st March.

As can be seen in the second example dealing with changes in accounting date substantial tax savings may occur. This technique may not only be used to mitigate a tax liability but also to change an accounting date to an earlier part of the fiscal year and so secure the advantages referred to above.

6.0 STOCK RELIEF

Stock relief for individuals was first introduced by F (no 2) A 1975, Sch.10 and applied to periods of account ending in the fiscal year 1974/75. Although amended by the provisions of FA 1976, Sch.5 the principle of the relief remained unaffected. The main change brought about by FA 1981,s.35 and Sch.9 and 10 was the basis of calculation of the relief. While the old relief (i.e. the F (no 2) A 1975, Sch.10 and FA 1976, Sch.5 relief) was based on the increase in the actual value of stock and work in progress during the period of account, subject to a deduction of a percentage of the relevant income, the new relief (i.e. that introduced by FA 1981) was determined by reference to movements in the "all-stocks" index during the period of account as applied to the closing stock value of the previous period. However, many of the provisions relating to the old relief were carried through, largely unchanged, to be used with the new relief. Stock relief has been abolished with effect for periods of account beginning after 12th March 1984, though provisions relating to its use in loss claims still remain and are dealt with in the section on losses.

7.0 RELIEF FOR FARMERS (FA 1978,s.28)

7.1 NATURE OF RELIEF

Where an individual has been carrying on a trade of farming or market gardening in the UK, he may claim to have the adjusted profits from that trade for any two consecutive years of assessment averaged, so that the profits for each year equal one half of the aggregate profits for the two years.

The first years for which the provisions relate are 1977-78 and 1978-79. Relief will not be applicable if either year is the year of assessment in which the trade commenced or ceased, neither will relief be given in respect of any year which is before a year for which a claim has already been made,

To qualify for full relief the profits of one of the years must not exceed 70% of the profits of the other. Profits are defined as the Schedule D Case I assessment for the year of assessment before:

(a) any deduction for losses;

(b) any deduction or addition for capital allowances or balancing charges;

Illustration

D has been a farmer for many years and his adjusted profits for years ended 31st March 1987 and 31st March 1988 were £14,000 and £6,000 respectively. Capital allowances for 1987/88 are £1,600 and for 1988/89 £6,000. He has no other income.

Without an average claim the net assessments will be:

		£		£
Adjusted profit	1987/88	14,000	1988/89	6,000
Less: capital allowance		1,600		6,000
		12,400		NIL

Personal allowances for 1988/89 will be lost.

If an averaging claim is made the assessments become:

		£
1987/88	$\frac{(£14,000 + £6,000)}{2}$	10,000
Less: capital allowances		1,600
		8,400
1988/89		10,000
Less: capital allowances		6,000
		4,000

Thus preserving some personal allowances.

Where one of the years concerned has a "Nil" profit, because of an adjusted Schedule D Case I loss, the profit of that year is treated as Nil.

Illustration

R has been a farmer for many years and has adjusted results for the years ended 31st May 1987 and 31st May 1988 of £17,000 profit and £8,000 loss. Before averaging, the assessments will be:

1988/89	£17,000
1989/90	Nil

after averaging they will be:

1988/89	£ 8,500
1989/90	£ 8,500

Loss relief will be available for the £8,000 loss in the normal way. If s.168 relief is claimed it would be against the profits of 1988/89.

1988/89		£
DI	Year to 31.5.1987	8,500
s.168 relief	Year to 31.5.1988	(8,000)
		500

Successive claims to relief will give the effect of giving a moving average on a two-year basis. If in the first illustration D had profits of £20,000 for the year ended 31st March 1989 and a further claim was made, the assessments would become:

1988/89

DI $\frac{(£10,000 + £20,000)}{2}$ = £15,000

1989/90

DI = £15,000

7.2 MARGINAL RELIEF

If the profits of one year exceed 70%, but do not exceed 75% of the other year, a marginal relief is available. This does not provide full averaging but does allow some of the profits of one year to be charged to tax in the other. This is computed as under:

$$3(PH - PL) - \frac{3PH}{4}$$

where PH is the higher profit
PL is the lower profit.
The resulting figure is deducted from the higher profit and added to the lower.

Illustration

S had been a farmer for many years and had adjusted profits of £30,000 and £22,000 for the years ended 30th September 1985 and 30th September 1986.

The assessments are:

1986/87 £30,000
1987/88 £22,000

£22,000 is more than 70% of £30,000 but not more than 75% of £30,000.

Marginal relief gives:

$$3(£30,000 - £22,000) - \frac{3}{4} \times £30,000$$

£24,000 - £22,500 = £1,500

The assessments become:

1986/87 (£30,000 - £1,500) = £28,500
1987/88 (£22,000 + £1,500) = £23,500.

7.3 EFFECTS OF CLAIM

Any adjustments made under these provisions have the effect of substituting the average assessment for all purposes of income tax except that:

(a) any loss for a particular period of account will still qualify for relief in the normal way (see 7.1 above);

(b) for the purposes of TA 1970,s.118 (adjustment of assessments on discontinuance of trade) the averaging adjustment will be ignored;

(c) where a claim for averaging has been made, and either one or both of the years concerned are subject to an adjustment for any other reasons, the averaging claim will be treated as not having been made. It may, however, still be possible to make an averaging claim on the basis of the revised figures for the years concerned;

(d) whilst averaging can substantially reduce a tax liability it can also have the undesirable effect of accelerating the payment of tax; this potential danger should always be borne in mind.

7.4 TIME LIMITS

Any claim must be made by notice in writing to the Inspector of Taxes not later than two years after the end of the second year of assessment.

8.0 RETIREMENT ANNUITIES

These are in effect pensions for the self employed and those not in pensionable employment.

8.1 BASIC CONDITIONS

(a) The annuity must be made with a person carrying on a life assurance business in the UK.

(b) The annuity must not normally commence before the recipient reaches the age of 60 nor later than the year in which he reaches 75.

(c) Should he die, the agreement must not provide for more than an annuity, which must not exceed the original annuity, payable to a surviving spouse or a return of premiums with reasonable interest.

These conditions may be varied with the agreement of the Revenue. Once the premium is paid, it is effectively lost until the date of payment of the annuity as the annuity contract once made is incapable of commutation, surrender or assignment. It is possible to use the policy as "security" for loans to be repaid out of part of the proceeds of the policy.

Retirement annuity contracts can be very tax efficient, in particular:

(a) within the limits described below the premiums attract relief at the individual's highest rates of tax;

(b) the pension when received is classed as earned income;

(c) part of the capital fund provided under the policy can be commuted into a tax free lump sum and can be used to repay a mortgage etc;

(d) the income earned on the invested fund up to retirement is normally exempt from tax.

8.2 NET RELEVANT EARNINGS

The limit for retirement annuity relief is 17½% of the individual's net relevant earnings (NRE). There is no limit to the amount of relief that can be obtained.

NRE are income from non-pensionable employments or from a trade or profession but specifically excluding income received as the controlling director of an investment company. Capital allowances and losses must be deducted; trade charges need only be deducted if they exceed other income.

Illustration

B has the following income assessable for 1986/87:

	£
Schedule D I profits	8,000
Earnings as hot-dog seller - non pensionable	2,000
Earnings as Polytechnic lecturer	6,000
Director's fees as the controlling director of an investment company	1,000

Capital allowances for the year are £400; there are unrelieved s.171 losses of £700.

The computation of NRE would be:

	£	£	£
Schedule D I		8,000	
Less: Losses brought forward	700		
Capital allowances	400		
		1,100	
			6,900
Earnings as hot-dog seller			2,000
			8,900
The maximum annuity that can be paid is 17½% thereof			1,558

8.3 UNUSED RELIEF

As from 1980/81, any relief not used during the last six years may be carried forward and used to cover any qualifying premiums paid in excess of the limit for a year after 5th April 1980, unused relief for earlier years being taken before that for later years.

This means that where in past years the retirement annuity premiums are less than 17½% of relevant earnings, the difference - called the unused relief - may be carried forward and used to justify the deduction of a premium paid greater than the 17½% limit.

Thus, if in the year 1980/81 the maximum possible premium was £3,000 but A only paid £1,900, there is unused relief of £1,100 which may be carried forward for the next six years - up to 1986/87 and used to cover a larger premium. If in 1983/84, A had NRE of £10,000 and paid a retirement premium of £2,500:

	£	£
NRE		10,000
17½% thereof	1,750	
Retirement annuity paid	2,500	
Normally offset would be restricted to £1,750, however, as A has unused relief of £1,100 brought forward from 1980/81 he may use £750 of it to cover the excess premium and therefore offset the whole		2,500
		7,500

The following is a pro forma of an unused relief calculation.

Year	NRE	17½% thereof	RAP paid	Unused Relief	Total Unused Relief
	£	£	£	£	£
1980/81	6,000	1,050	750	300	300
1981/82	8,000	1,400	1,400	-	300
1982/83	10,000	1,750	1,350	400	700
1983/84	9,000	1,575	1,275	300	1,000
1984/85	12,000	2,100	1,500	600	1,600
1985/86	21,000	3,675	2,675	1,000	2,600

If in 1986/87, the NRE are £12,000 and the retirement annuity premiums paid are £3,000, the position is:

	£	£
NRE		12,000
17½% thereof	2,100	
RAP paid	3,000	
All these may be offset using firstly the £2,100 allowance of the year and then the unused relief from past years on a FIFO basis. Thus £900 of unused relief will be taken, identified as under: 1 £300 from 1980/81 2 £400 from 1982/83 3 £200 from 1983/84		3,000
		9,000

There is an element of carry-back in the new system. Where a taxpayer pays a retirement annuity premium in a year of assessment, he may elect to carry all or part of it back into the immediately earlier year of assessment. If there are no relevant earnings in that year, the premiums may be treated as being paid in the year before that.

Illustration

X pays a retirement annuity of £4,000 per annum by four quarterly payments of £1,000. His net relevant earnings are:

1986/87	£30,000
1987/88	£20,000

	1986/87	1987/88
	£	£
17½% NRE	5,250	3,500
Premiums paid	4,000	4,000
Unused relief	1,250	
		500

X may elect before the end of the year of assessment in which the payment is made to relate back up to £1,250 of the amount paid in 1987/88 into 1986/87 thus maximising the offset in that year. It is possible to relate back part of a premium.

It is appreciated that it would be possible to bring forward the 1986/87 unused relief into 1987/88 and so obtain a full deduction of the 1987/88 premium. In this case, however, relating a premium back will obtain relief at a higher marginal rate of tax.

Where an assessment is finalised more than six years after the end of the relevant year of assessment, retirement annuity premiums which are paid within six months of finalisation may be offset against the relevant earnings of the year in which they are paid. This would prevent the loss of any unused relief which is normally lost after six years.

For taxpayers born before 1934, the relief is extended as under:

Year of birth	Percentage of NRE
1916 - 1933	20
1914 or 1915	21
1912 or 1913	24
1910 or 1911	26½
1908 or 1909	29½
1907 or earlier	32½

9.0 THE VALUATION OF STOCK

Trading stock can be valued on either a global or piecemeal basis at the lower of cost or market value. Where a trade is discontinued, stock can be valued on one of two bases:

(a) where it is sold or transferred for valuable consideration to a person carrying on a trade in the UK who can deduct the cost as an expense for tax purposes, the stock is to be valued at sales price. To counter what appears to be an easy avoidance device it will be appreciated that the closing stock of one trade will be the opening stock of the successor;

(b) in all other cases stock is to be valued at the open market price at the date of discontinuance.

10.0 SUCCESSIONS AND EXTENSIONS

A trader may carry on more than one trade and it is a question of fact whether a trader who starts a new activity expands his existing trade or starts a new one. The position is of some importance. If a new trade is started then the commencement trade the profits will start to be taxed on a normal preceding-year basis. In **Scales v. George Thompson & Co. Ltd. (1927)** Rowlatt J said:

> "the real question is, was there any interconnection, any interdependence, any unity at all...".

Illustration

A is a fishmonger. His profits for recent years have been:

	£
Year to 31.12.1985	10,000
31.12.1986	15,000
31.12.1987	14,000

On 1st January 1987, A acquired a fish and chip restaurant next door to his existing premises. The profit of that restaurant for the year to 31st December 1987 was £12,000.

If the acquisition is treated as the start of a new business:

	Continuing trade P/Y		New trade commencement		Total
		£		£	£
1986/87	Year to 31.12.85	10,000	1.1.87 - 5.4.87	3,000	13,000
1987/88	Year to 31.12.86	15,000	1.1.87 - 31.12.87	12,000	27,000
1988/89	Year to 31.12.87	14,000	Year to 31.12.87	12,000	26,000
					66,000

If it is treated as the expansion of an existing business:

		£		£	£
1986/87	Year to 31.12.85	10,000			10,000
1987/88	Year to 31.12.86	15,000			15,000
1988/89	Year to 31.12.87	14,000	Year to 31.12.87	12,000	26,000
					51,000

Once both trades are on the P/Y basis then they may be merged if they are absorbed together, otherwise they are kept separate for assessment capital allowances and losses.

Where a person succeeds to a trade by acquisition from its former owner there will be a cessation on that latter person. He will not be able to transfer across unused losses to the new owner. A succession must be distinguished from an expansion of an existing business by the purchase of assets from another trader which in general will not mean the start of a new trade (unless the assets are used in a totally different business). Very often the distinguishing factor between acquisition of assets and the acquisition of an entire business is the treatment of goodwill.

Where two businesses merge and the proprietors agree to carry on in partnership then both businesses will normally cease and a new combined one will be considered to have commenced. This may be avoided by a continuation election under s.154(2) TA 1970.

5 Capital Allowances

1.0 GENERAL

Depreciation of fixed assets is not an allowable deduction for taxation purposes. It is replaced by capital allowances which are a standardised system of depreciation for taxation purposes. Capital allowances are available in respect of the following categories of assets:

(a) plant and machinery,

(b) industrial buildings and hotels,

(c) agricultural buildings and works,

(d) patents,

(e) mines and oil wells,

(f) scientific research,

(g) know-how,

(h) cemeteries and crematoria,

(i) dredging.

Items (e), (h) and (i) are not covered in these notes.

Capital allowances are normally given in respect of assets owned on the last date of an accounting period. For an individual they are not given for the accounting period, but for the fiscal year for which the accounting period is the basis period. Thus the capital allowances based on the assets owned by a trader in the year ended 31st December 1985 will be given for the fiscal year 1986/87, for which the year ended 31st December 1985 is the basis period.

In general an asset will qualify for capital allowances when the expenditure is incurred. This is the date on which the obligation to pay is unconditional irrespective of the date of payment though if the payment date is more than four months after the above date the expenditure will be treated as having been incurred on that later date.

Assets acquired before the commencement of trade will be deemed to have been acquired on the first day of trading. The rate of first year or initial allowances, where appropriate, will, however, be determined by the date on which the expenditure is incurred.

1.1 RELIEF FOR ALLOWANCES

Relief for capital allowances can be given in two ways:

(a) in taxing the trade, or

(b) by discharge or repayment of tax.

1.2 RELIEF GIVEN IN TAXING THE TRADE (CAA 1968,s.70)

In this case, the allowances are given as a deduction against the Schedule D Case I assessment. If they exceed the assessable income they can be used in a loss claim or carried forward without time limit and offset against future assessable profits of the same trade.

1.3 RELIEF GIVEN BY DISCHARGE OR REPAYMENT OF TAX (CAA 1968,s.71)

Relief in this case is given primarily from a specific class of income. If the allowances exceed the income, they may be carried forward and offset against income of the same class in future years without time limit. The main allowances dealt with in this way are:

(a) agricultural buildings allowances;

(b) allowances on certain leased assets.

<u>Illustration</u>

A is a farmer. His adjusted profits are:

	£	£
Year ended 31st December 1985	2,000	
Year ended 31st December 1986	14,000	

Agricultural buildings allowances are:

	£
1986/87	7,800
1987/88	3,000

1986/87			
Year ended 31.12.1985 DI		2,000	
ABA 1986/87		7,800	
		NIL	5,800 c/f
1987/88			
Year ended 31.12.1986 DI		14,000	
ABA 1986/87 brought forward	5,800		
1987/88	3,000		
		8,800	
		5,200	

Where the allowances exceed the specific class of income from which they are deducted, the taxpayer may elect to offset the excess against the other income of the fiscal year to which the allowances relate. As no specific order of deduction is laid down in s.71 the excess allowances can be deducted:

(a) from unearned income

(b) from earned income

if so desired.

Illustration

A's other income for the fiscal year 1986/87 was:

	£
Salary as journalist	10,000
Dividends (gross)	9,000

The excess allowances for 1986/87 may be offset against the other income of that year as under:

	Earned		Unearned
	£	£	£
Salary	10,000		
Dividends			9,000
s.71 Relief for excess allowances			(5,800)
	10,000		3,200
		13,200	

Before 1984/85 this order of offset would have resulted in a saving of investment income surcharge.

Where the excess allowances exceed the other income of the fiscal year to which they relate or exceed the other income of that year, the excess may be carried forward into the next fiscal year and offset against:

(a) income of the specific class,

(b) the other income.

If there are still excess allowances they may be carried forward without time limit against income of the specific class only. Where in the next fiscal year there are also similar capital allowances the order of utilisation is:

(a) capital allowances brought forward,

(b) capital allowances of that year.

Illustration

Information as before except that the ABA of 1986/87 were £70,000. The other income of 1987/88 was identical to 1986/87.

1986/87	£	£
DI - year ended 31.12.1985	2,000	
ABA 1986/87	70,000	(68,000)
	NIL	
Other income:		
Salary	10,000	
Dividends	9,000	
	19,000	
s.71 Relief for excess allowances	(19,000)	19,000
	NIL	(49,000)
1987/88		
DI - year ended 31.12.1986	14,000	
ABA brought forward	(14,000)	14,000
	NIL	(35,000)
Other income as above	19,000	
s.71 Relief for excess allowances	(19,000)	19,000
	NIL	(16,000)

The £16,000 may be carried forward and offset against future agricultural income <u>only</u>. The ABA of 1987/88 may either be:

(a) carried forward against future agricultural income, or

(b) offset against other income of 1988/89 with any excess carried forward.

An election to offset against other income must be made within two years of the end of the year of assessment for which relief is claimed.

2.0 PLANT AND MACHINERY

2.1 THE MEANING OF PLANT AND MACHINERY

There is no definition of plant and machinery in the Taxes Acts. The first definition was given in 1887 by Lindley, LJ in **Yarmouth v. France** (a workmen's compensation case) when he said,

> "... in its ordinary sense (plant) includes whatever apparatus is used by a business man for carrying on his business - not his stock in trade ... but all goods and chattels, fixed or movable, alive or dead which he keeps for permanent employment in his business".

This definition is wide and a number of cases have excluded specific items from relief. In general, if the item is of a durable nature, it may be plant, so in **Caledonian Railway Co. v. Banks** (1880), railway engines and carriages were held to be plant as were shoemaking knives and lasts in **Hinton v. Maden and Ireland Ltd (1959)**. However in **Earl of Derby v. Aylmer (1915)**, stallions for stud purposes were held not to be plant and in **Norman v. Golder (1944)** similar treatment was applied to the human body.

The definition of plant is not however restricted to items used physically. In **Munby v. Furlong (1977)** the law books of a barrister were held to be plant; they were, per Fox J:

> "... part of the apparatus used by a professional man for carrying on his profession".

According to Lord Denning, they were part of "the intellectual storehouse" of a professional man.

More recent cases have drawn a distinction between an asset with which the business is carried on and the setting in which it is carried on. In **Dixon v. Fitch's Garage Ltd. (1975)**, Brightman J said:

> "The proper test is whether the canopy had a functional purpose to enable the taxpayer company to perform the activity".

It was not...

> "... whether the item in question is commercially desirable or necessary to enable the taxpayer to sell his (product)".

This concept has been approved by Lord Reid in **IRC v. Barclay Curle & Co.Ltd. (1969)**. In **St. Johns School v. Ward (1975)**, Templeman J applied the functional test in considering the tax status of a prefabricated building at a school used to accommodate a chemistry laboratory and held that as the building had no function to perform other than to shelter the pupils they could not qualify as plant and machinery. This may be contrasted with **Cooke v. Beach Station Caravans Ltd. (1974)** where Megarry J held that a swimming pool in a caravan park qualified as plant:

> "Nobody could suggest that the principal function of the pool was merely to protect the occupants from the elements ... (it) is part of the means whereby the trade is carried on and not merely the place at which it is carried on".

One particular difficulty in trying to draw a distinction between plant and setting is that the terms are not mutually exclusive. Electrical wiring and fittings have often been victims of this difficulty. The Revenue generally refuse to allow wiring as plant whilst light fittings will not be plant unless they are of a specialised nature-**Cole Brothers Ltd. v. Phillips (1980)** - a matter which must be judged on the facts of the particular case.

Details of specific cases are:

Held to be plant and machinery:	
The law books of a barrister	**Munby v. Furlong (1977)**
A swimming pool and paddling pool together with the appropriate landscaping	**Cooke v. Beach Station Caravans Ltd.(1974)**
Grain silos including bins and chutes	**Schofield v. R & H Hall Ltd. (1975)**
Decorative screens placed in the windows of a building society's offices	**Leeds Permanent Building Society v. Proctor (1982)**
Movable partitioning	**Jarrold v. John Good & Sons Ltd. (1963)**

Held not to be plant and machinery:

Prefabricated buildings used as a laboratory and gymnasium	**St. John's School (Mountford and Knibbs) v. Ward (1975)**
A canopy over the forecourt of a petrol station (The correctness of this decision has been recently doubted in **Cole Brothers Ltd. v. Phillips**, per Lord Hailsham LC).	**Dixon v. Fitch's Garage Ltd. (1975)**
A ship used as a floating restaurant	**Benson v. Yard Arm Club (1979)**
A stand for spectators at a football stadium	**Brown v. Burnley Football and Athletic Club (1980)**

2.2 THE GENERAL SCHEME

(a) Pooling

Unless the plant comes within one of certain special cases, expenditure on plant acquired after 26th October 1970 is pooled.

The exceptions are expenditure on:

(i) motor cars, where expenditure incurred on or after 1st June 1980;

(ii) motor cars costing more than £8,000 (£5,000 for acquisitions on or before 12th June 1979 and £4,000 before 7th April 1976);

(iii) plant with an element of private usage, by the proprietor;

(iv) certain plant which is leased and where the expenditure is incurred before 1st April 1986.

Apart from items (i) and (iv) these will be treated individually with each asset forming a separate pool. Items (i) and (iv) will form a combined but separate pool.

Motor cars acquired before 1st June 1980 and not in a separate pool because of private use or cost were included in the general plant pool.

(b) Allowances available

The allowances available for assets acquired after 26th October 1970 are:

(i) In the year of acquisition - a First Year Allowance (FYA) at the following maximum rates:

Expenditure incurred between 27.10.70 and 19.7.71	60%
Expenditure incurred between 20.7.71 and 21.3.72	80%
Expenditure incurred after 22.3.72 up to 13.3.84	100%
Expenditure incurred between 14.3.84 and 31.3.85	75%
Expenditure incurred between 1.4.85 and 31.3.86	50%
Expenditure incurred from 1.4.86	NIL.

Where capital expenditure is incurred after 13th March 1984 the 100% FYA is still available, if it is made in pursuance of a contract agreed on or before 13th March 1984, where the expenditure is incurred before 1st April 1987.

FYA will not be available:

(1) on motor cars (not lorries), capable of private use other than those:

(a) of a type unsuitable, and not commonly used as private vehicles, or

(b) provided wholly or mainly for a trade of public hire or conveyance;

(2) where motor cars are hired out or leased as part of such a trade; first year allowances will only be available to the lessor:

(a) where the lessee will be using the vehicle to carry freight, or the vehicle is of a type not normally used as a private vehicle;

(b) where the vehicle is not normally hired to the same person for 30 or more consecutive days and the total number of days in any twelve-month period that the vehicle is used by the same person is less than 90.

(c) where the vehicle is hired to disabled persons in receipt of mobility allowance.

For capital expenditure payable on or after 21st November 1983, the first year allowance will also be available if the vehicle is hired to persons in receipt of a war pensioner's inability supplement.

(3) on assets acquired when the buyer and seller are "connected persons" unless the asset has not been used before;

(4) on expenditure in a period related to the permanent discontinuance of the trade.

First year allowances are available to the owner of plant and machinery provided that the items belong to him at some time in the respective basis period.

The rates of FYA above are maximum rates; a claim can be made for any amount up to the maximum.

(ii) In subsequent years, or in the current year when a first year allowance is not available, writing down allowances (WDA) are available at the rate of 25% on the balance of the amount in the pool at the beginning of the accounting period, less the disposal proceeds of any plant sold etc. in the accounting period. In the case of motor vehicles costing £8,000 or more the annual writing down allowance is restricted to £2,000 per annum.

Where assets are acquired on hire purchase, the full cost of the asset will qualify for capital allowances immediately provided the asset is brought into use.

Where a trader has previously acquired an asset for non-trading purposes and subsequently commences to use it in the trade, he will be deemed to have acquired it at its market value in the basis period in which it was first used in the trade. Only WDA will be available thereon.

2.3 DISPOSALS OF PLANT

Where plant is disposed of in the accounting period, the disposal value (or original cost if the disposal value exceeds the original cost of the asset) must be deducted from the balance in the pool at the beginning of the accounting period. Disposal value means the following:

(a) where the sale is between unconnected persons, the sale proceeds;

(b) where the sale proceeds are less than the open market value, the open market valuation unless:

 (i) the buyer will be claiming capital allowances on the expenditure, or

 (ii) a charge will arise under Schedule E, when the actual sales proceeds, irrespective of market value, will be used;

(c) where the asset is lost or destroyed, the compensation or scrap value received.

If the sale proceeds exceed the balance of expenditure in the pool there will be a profit known as a balancing charge. This will be assessed as a trading receipt. There will, of course, be no unrelieved expenditure in the pool on which writing down allowances may be claimed.

Where the asset forms a pool on its own, on its disposal there will be a profit or a loss. The profit will be a balancing charge (described above), and the loss a balancing allowance. A balancing allowance is given as a capital allowance of the year.

The cost of assets less the capital allowances given on them to date is known as the tax written-down value. This is normally described as the tax written down value at 5th April in the fiscal year for which the allowances are given. Thus if A makes up accounts to 31st December 1986, the capital allowances based on that year are the allowances for 1987/88 and the tax written down value is that at 5th April 1988.

2.4 EXPENDITURE QUALIFYING AS PLANT AND MACHINERY

Certain expenditure, although not strictly incurred on plant and machinery, qualifies for capital allowances as if it was so incurred. The various items include:

(a) fire safety expenditure incurred from 1st June 1972.

(b) industrial building heat insulation expenditure incurred from 13th November 1974.

(c) sports stadium expenditure, to comply with a safety certificate, incurred from 31st July 1975.

2.5 SPECIMEN CAPITAL ALLOWANCES COMPUTATION

		Pool			Separate pools		Total allowances
		General	Cars and leased assets	Car with private use	Car costing >£8,000	Car costing >£8,000	
	£	£	£	£	£	£	£
Brought forward		x	x	x	x	x	
Non-qualifying additions and expenditure on which FYA not claimed		x	x				
		x	x				
Disposal proceeds of assets		(x)	(x)		(x)		
		x	x		BC/BA x ===		
Writing down allowances		(x)	(x)	(x)		(x)Restricted	x
		x	x	x		x	x
Assets qualifying for first year allowances	x						
Less: Already included above	(x)						
	x						
First year allowances	(x)	x	x	x			x
		x ===	x ===	x ===		x ===	x
Less:Private use reductions							(x)
							x
Add balancing allowances							x
Total Allowances Claimed							x ===

Leased assets acquired after 31st March 1986 will normally enter the general pool. There are limited exclusions including assets leased to non-residents etc.

2.6 ASSETS WITH AN ELEMENT OF PRIVATE USE

It has already been mentioned that expenditure on assets with an element of private use (almost invariably motor cars) forms a separate pool of expenditure. In addition the capital allowances must be restricted by the amount of the private use. The amount deducted from the value of the asset, resulting in the tax written down value, remains the same; the amount of the restriction is only deducted from the total allowances column. This only applies to private use by the proprietor; if the private use is by an employee full allowances will be given.

Illustration

B makes up accounts to 31st October annually. In the year to 31st October 1986 he bought a car costing £5,000. Private use was agreed at 20% per annum.

		Car £	Total Allowances £
1987/88	(Year ended 31.10.1986)		
	Cost	5,000	
	WDA	1,250	1,250
		3,750	
	Less: Private element - 20%		250
			1,000
1988/89	(Year ended 31.10.1987)		
	WDA 25%	937	937
		2,813	
	Less: Private element - 20%		187
			750
1989/90	(Year ended 31.10.1988)		
	WDA	703	703
		2,110	
	Less: Private element - 20%		141
			562

Should the car now be sold for £2,650 in the year to 31.10.89 there will be a balancing charge:

1990/91	(Year ended 31.10.1989)	
	WDV b/f	2,110
	Sales proceeds	2,650
	Balancing charge	540

To avoid an element of double taxation, this will be reduced by applying the private use percentage:

	£
Balancing charge	540
Less: 20% thereof	108
	432

This will be assessed as a trading receipt of the fiscal year 1990/91 (based on the year to 31st October 1989). In no case can the balancing charge exceed the allowances actually given.

In certain cases the element of private use can vary each year. If in the illustration the private use element was:

1987/88	20%
1988/89	50%
1989/90	30%

the abbreviated computation would be:

Year	Cost £	Restrict for private use	Allowance given £
1987/88			
31.10.86	5,000		
WDA	1,250	-20%	1,000
	3,750		
1988/89			
31.10.87			
WDA	937	-50%	468
	2,813		
1989/90			
31.10.88			
WDA	703	-30%	492
	2,110		1,960

Should the car now be sold, again for £2,650, the calculation of the restricted balancing charge is more complex. It is multiplied by the fraction:

$$\frac{\text{Allowance actually given}}{\text{Allowances that could have been given}}$$

	£
WDV (as above)	2,100
Sales proceeds	2,650
Balancing charge	540

Restricted to: $\dfrac{1,960}{1,250 + 937 + 703} \times 540 =$ 366

An alternative calculation to achieve the same adjustment is to restrict the balancing charge by the average business use:

$$540 \times \frac{0.8 + 0.5 + 0.7}{3} = \underline{\underline{360}}$$

If there is a balancing allowance it will be similarly restricted.

For accounting periods ended after 31st March 1985, first year and writing down allowances will be limited to expenditure on plant which is wholly and exclusively incurred for the purposes of the trade. Where the plant is used for other purposes, i.e. there is some private use, then as before it will be deemed to be used in a separate trade (the notional trade), placed in a separate pool and have any capital allowances restricted by reference to the non-business use as previously.

Where the plant was originally used wholly for the purposes of the trade and is then only partly used for trading purposes, it will be transferred from the general pool to a separate pool at market value. The writing down allowances will be restricted in the same way as before. This transfer is made at the beginning of the period in which the change of use occurred.

Illustration

X, a trader, bought a typewriter on 1st June 1985 for £1,000. It was wholly used for trading purposes up to 31st December 1986. On 1st January 1987 X started to use it privately. It was agreed that the private use was 50% and that the market value at the date of transfer was £600. Accounts are prepared to 31st December throughout and the tax written down value in the pool at 5th April 1986 was £8,000.

1986/87

Year to 31.12.1985		Pool	Typewriter	Allowances
		£	£	£
Brought forward		8,000		
WDA		2,000		2,000
		6,000		
Typewriter	1,000			
FYA - 50%	500			
		500		500
		6,500		2,500

1987/88

Year to 31.12.1986	Pool	Typewriter	Allowances
WDA	1,625		1,625
	4,875		

1988/89

Year to 31.12.1987	Pool	Typewriter	Allowances
Transfer to separate pool	(600)	600	
	4,275	600	
WDA	1,069	150	1,219
c/f	3,206	450	
Less: Private use - ½			75
			1,144

Illustration
Kings and Lynne are partners in a manufacturing business, sharing profits and losses equally. After the capital allowances given in the 1985/86 assessment on the firm's profits, the brought-forward figures of assets at 5th April 1986 were:

	£
Plant	27,300
Volvo motor car used by Lynne partly for private purposes	1,125

In the year ended 31st December 1985, the following movements in assets took place:

Additions	£
Pre 1.4.1985	
(i) A new grinder was purchased for	4,000
Post 31.3.1985	
(ii) A second-hand weighing machine was purchased for	800
(iii) A motor lorry was bought on hire purchase. The cash price was £13,000, hire purchase charges £1,500. A deposit of £1,800 was paid followed by 36 equal monthly instalments commencing on 15th July 1985.	
(iv) A Rolls Royce for Kings costing There was no private use.	22,000
(v) A second-hand hoist was acquired from Lynne's brother costing	3,000
(vi) A new car was purchased for the use of the sales manager. The private use was agreed at 25%.	6,000
(vii) A second-hand Ferrari was purchased for Lynne's use to replace the car sold - cost Private use was agreed at 30%	9,000

Disposals	£
(i) Plant acquired second-hand in 1973 was sold and realised	50
(ii) A lathe acquired in 1978 for £1,200 was sold and realised	1,500
(iii) The car used by Lynne was sold for £1,400. It was acquired in 1982 for £2,666 and the personal usage element was agreed at:	

1983/84	1/4
1984/85	1/3
1985/86	1/5

Calculate the capital allowances for 1986/87.

		Pool		Separate Pools			
				Lynne's Cars		Kings	Total
		General	Cars and leased assets	Volvo	Ferrari	Rolls-Royce	Allowances
Year ended 31.12.85		£	£	£	£	£	£
1986/87							
brought forward		27,300		1,125			
Non-Qualifying Additions:							
Rolls-Royce						22,000	
Hoist		3,000					
Sales Manager's Car			6,000				
Ferrari					9,000		
		30,300	6,000	1,125	9,000	22,000	
Disposal Proceeds of Assets sold	£						
Plant	50						
Lathe (restricted to cost)	1,200						
		1,250					
Lynne's car				1,400			
		29,050		275			
WDA		7,263	1,500		(Rest) 2,000	(Rest) 2,000	12,763
		21,787	4,500		7,000	20,000	
Qualifying additions							
Pre 1.4.1985							
Grinder	4,000						
FYA - 75%	3,000	1,000					3,000
Post 31.3.1985							
Lorry	13,000						
Weighing machine	800						
	13,800						
FYA - 50%	6,900	6,900					6,900
		29,687	4,500		7,000	20,000	22,663
Less: Private use - Lynne							600
							22,063

The balancing charge will be assessed as under:

Lynne's Volvo

	£		£
Cost	2,666		
WDA 1983/84	666	- 1/4 166	500
	2,000		
WDA 1984/85	500	- 1/3 166	334
	1,500		
WDA 1985/86	375	- 1/5 75	300
	1,125		1,134
	=====		=====

$$275 \times \frac{1,134}{666 + 500 + 375} = £202$$

If it is decided not to claim FYA on the expenditure in the accounting period then the whole of that expenditure will enter the pool, before deducting disposal proceeds of assets sold and will therefore qualify for WDA. Reducing the claim to FYA in this way can also reduce a balancing charge.

Illustration

Y bought plant for £3,000 on 30th June 1985. He also sold plant for £4,000 on 30th April 1985. Accounts were prepared to 31st December 1985 and tax written down value of plant brought forward in the pool at 5th April 1986 was £1,000.

If FYA are claimed:

1986/87 Year to 31.12.1985	£	£	£
b/f		1,000	
Disposal proceeds		4,000	3,000 BC
			=====
Additions	3,000		
FYA	1,500	1,500	1,500
			=====
c/f		1,500	
		=====	

Therefore, a net tax charge on £1,500.

If FYA are not claimed:

1986/87 Year to 31.12.1985	
b/f	1,000
Additions on which FYA not claimed	3,000
	4,000
Disposal proceeds	4,000
	-
	=====

No balancing charge.

If first year allowances are only claimed on part of the additions the items on which it is not claimed will again enter the pool before deduction of disposal proceeds. Thus if a trader has additions in the year to 31st March 1986 of £12,000 but only wants FYA of £4,500 then, with a FYA rate of 50%, FYA will be claimed on £4,500 x 100/50 = £9,000. The balance of £3,000 will enter the pool and may qualify for WDA.

2.7 REDUCTION OF ALLOWANCES

In certain cases a trader's profit may be very small and deduction of the full amount of capital allowances may result in a situation where he is unable to obtain full relief for his personal allowances. In such a situation he has the option of not claiming some or all of his FYA or WDA. If he does this, he cannot reclaim them in a subsequent year. Thus if he acquires an item of plant for £1,000 and only claims a 50% FYA on £500, he cannot make up the balance of FYA in a later year.

Illustration

C makes up accounts to 31st December 1985, and for that year has adjusted profits of £4,000. He has qualifying expenditure in the pool of £3,500, brought forward, and buys a lathe on 30th June 1985 for £2,400. He is married.

If he claims all his capital allowances the position will be:

1986/87	£	£	£	£
Schedule D Case I profits				4,000
Less: Capital allowances:				
Pool b/f		3,500		
WDA - 25%		875	875	
		2,625		
Lathe	2,400			
FYA 50%	1,200	1,200	1,200	
				2,075
		3,825		
				1,925
Less: Personal allowances				3,655
				NIL

Personal allowances lost £1,730

As personal allowances cannot be carried forward, C should consider making a reduced claim. The revised computation could appear as under:

	£	f	£
Schedule D Case I profits			4,000
Less: Capital allowances:			
Pool b/f		3,500	
No WDA		-	
		3,500	
Lathe	2,400		
FYA (restricted)	345	2,055	345
		5,555	
			3,655
Less: Personal allowances			3,655
			NIL

This is only one possible answer; it is possible to reduce the claim to WDA and claim no FYA, or even to claim part of both allowances.

2.8 ELECTION FOR TREATMENT AS A SHORT LIFE ASSET

Short life plant, i.e. that which the trader intends to sell or scrap within 5 years of acquisition, may be excluded from the pool where it is acquired after 31st March 1986. Certain types of plant will not qualify for this treatment; they include:

(a) ships;

(b) cars but not vans;

(c) certain leased assets;

(d) plant with an element of private use.

All short life assets are deemed to be used in a separate trade and therefore will be in individual pools. If the asset is sold or scrapped within 5 years the notional separate trade is deemed to have been discontinued and there will be a balancing charge or allowance. A similar treatment is applied when there is the commencement of part private use.

If at the end of the 5 year period the asset has not been sold or scrapped it will be transferred to the general pool at its tax written down value. An election to 'depool' short life assets must be made within 2 years of the end of the accounting period in which the assets are acquired.

Illustration

In the year to 31st December 1986 A bought the following items of plant:

		£
1.2.1986	Printing machine	20,000
1.6.1986	Computer	10,000
1.11.1986	Grinder	8,000

The balance in the pool at 5th April 1987 was £6,000. An election was made to treat the computer and grinder as short life assets. The computer was sold for £4,000 in the year to 31st December 1989.

		Pool	Short Life Pools		Allowances
1987/88			Computer	Grinder	
Year to 31.12.1986	£	£	£	£	£
b/f		6,000			
Additions:					
Printing machine	20,000				
Computer			10,000		
Grinder				8,000	
Allowances:					
WDA - 25%		1,500	2,500	2,000	6,000
		4,500	7,500	6,000	
FYA - 50%	10,000	10,000			10,000
		14,500			16,000

		Pool	Short Life Pools		Allowances
			Computer	Grinder	
		£	£	£	£
	b/f	14,500	7,500	6,000	
1988/89					
Year to 31.12.1987					
WDA - 25%		3,625	1,875	1,500	7,000
		10,875	5,625	4,500	
1989/90					
Year to 31.12.1988					
WDA - 25%		2,719	1,406	1,125	5,250
		8,156	4,219	3,375	
1990/91					
Year to 31.12.1989					
DP			4,000		
			BA 219		219
WDA - 25%		2,039		844	2,883
		6,117		2,531	3,102
1991/92					
Year to 31.12.1990					
WDA - 25%		1,529		633	2,162
		4,588		1,898	
1992/93					
Year to 31.12.1991					
Transfer to general pool		1,898		(1,898)	
		6,486		-	
WDA - 25%		1,622			1,622
c/f		4,864			

Where a short life asset is sold to a connected person it will normally be transferred at market value. Where they jointly elect, however, it can be transferred across at tax written down value with the person acquiring it stepping into the shoes of the vendor as far as the 5 year period is concerned.

2.9 CAPITAL ALLOWANCES FOR FIXTURES

In **Stokes v. Costain (1984)** the Court of Appeal held that fixtures in a building inserted by the lessee did not qualify for capital allowances as they became landlord's fixtures and thus did not 'belong' to the taxpayer lessee as required by FA 1971. For expenditure incurred after 11th July 1984 it is now provided that where a person who has an interest in land incurs capital expenditure on plant or machinery and that subsequently becomes a landlord's fixture, then the fixture is deemed to belong to that person with the interest in the land (i.e. normally the tenant). Where expenditure has been incurred by the landlord, who subsequently grants a lease on the property, the lessor and lessee may elect to transfer the right to receive allowances to the lessee.

3.0 INDUSTRIAL BUILDINGS

3.1 DEFINITION

An industrial building includes:

(a) a building used in a manufacturing trade, mining, oil exploration or fishing;

(b) warehouses for the storage of stock to be used in the manufacturing trade, deriving from the manufacturing trade or included as work in progress and buildings used for the repair or maintenance of goods in such a trade;

(c) canteens or other buildings provided for the welfare of employees engaged in a trade in (a) above;

(d) sports pavilions in any trade;

(e) certain hotels.

3.2 CASE LAW

Bourne v Norwich Crematorium Ltd. (1967)
A crematorium was held not to be an industrial building as it did not subject the human body to an industrial process.

Buckingham v Securitas Properties Ltd. (1980)
A building used for breaking down bulk cash into individual wage packets did not qualify as an industrial building.

3.3 THE QUANTUM OF RELIEF

Relief is only available for the cost of construction, which does not include the cost of the land, but includes the cost of foundations etc. Where a building includes a non-qualifying part, such as offices or showrooms, that part will not qualify for relief unless the cost of that part, exclusive of land, does not exceed 25% of the cost of the whole of the structure, exclusive of land. Prior to 16th March 1983 the relevant percentage was 10%. There is no marginal relief; it is all or nothing.

Illustration
A erects an industrial building, the cost of which is as follows:

	£
Land	40,000
Factory block	35,000
Canteen	6,000
Digging foundations	4,000
Sales office	10,500
	95,500

The cost of the sales office will qualify for industrial buildings allowance (IBA) as it does not exceed 25% of the cost of the total structure:

£10,500 < 25% of £55,500

If, however, the cost of the sales office were £16,000, it would not qualify for IBA as the cost would exceed the 25% limit:

£16,000 > 25% of £61,000 (i.e. £55,500 + £5,500)

Where a building is purchased <u>before</u> it has been used as an industrial building, the purchaser will receive IBA on:

(a) the full purchase price, if the building is purchased from a builder in the normal course of business;

(b) the lower of the full purchase price or the vendor's original cost of construction, if the building is purchased other than from a builder.

The allowances available consist of:

(a) Initial allowances, and

(b) Writing down allowances.

(a) <u>Initial allowances</u>
These are given on the cost of the structure, less any government or local authority grants or sums received from a landlord, excluding regional development grants. It is given for the fiscal year for which the accounting period in which the expenditure is incurred forms the basis period. The building does not have to be in use to qualify for initial allowance. The rates are:

<u>Expenditure incurred</u>

8.4.59 to 16.1.66	5%
17.1.66 to 5.4.70	15%
6.4.70 to 21.3.72	30%
22.3.72 to 12.11.74	40%
13.11.74 to 10.3.81	50%
11.3.81 to 13.3.84	75%
14.3.84 to 31.3.85	50%
1.4.85 to 31.3.86	25%
From 1.4.86	NIL

An individual or a company may take a smaller amount of initial allowance other than the above maxima.

Where capital expenditure is incurred after 13th March 1984 but before 1st April 1987, the 75% initial allowance is still allowed, if it is made in pursuance of a contract agreed on or before 13th March 1984.

(b) <u>Writing down allowances</u>
WDA are available provided that:

(i) the building is in use at the end of the basis period, and

(ii) the person claiming the allowances has the relevant interest.

The rates are:

Expenditure incurred:

6.4.1946 to 5.11.1962	2% on cost
6.11.1962 onwards	4% on cost.

Both of these allowances are straight line which means that the building has a definite life for tax purposes - 50 years for pre-6th November 1962 expenditure and 25 years for post-5th November 1962 expenditure. No writing down allowance is available after the end of the 50th or 25th year of ownership of a building and the total allowances cannot exceed the total qualifying cost of the building, which means in practice that where initial allowances have been claimed, allowances often cease much earlier.

For the purpose of calculating allowances, each new building or addition to a building is treated as a separate item.

The relevant interest is the freehold or the leasehold interest that the person incurring the expenditure has in the property. For a subsequent purchase to obtain capital allowances he must obtain the relevant interest. The term is interpreted strictly; in **Woods v Mallen Engineering Ltd. (1983)** the grant of a sublease for three days shorter than the term of the original lease was not treated as a transfer of the relevant interest as the new lease was not identical with that of the person originally incurring the expenditure. It can be seen therefore that if a person owning the freehold of a property incurs expenditure qualifying for IBA and subsequently grants a lease to another manufacturer, the purchaser will not be able to qualify for IBA even though he pays a premium to the vendor as he will not have the same relevant interest (i.e. the freehold interest) as the person who erected the building had at the time he incurred the expenditure.

To alleviate this problem FA 1978,s.37 provides that where a person with the relevant interest in an industrial building grants a long lease to another then the vendor and the purchaser may jointly agree that this can be treated as the transfer of the relevant interest and thus the lessee will qualify for capital allowances in respect of the expenditure incurred by the landlord.

Illustration

B acquired a factory new on 1st June 1961 at a cost of £50,000 including land costing £10,000 and offices which cost £4,500. On 1st September 1968 he had an extension built at a cost of £15,000. He sold the factory and extension on 1st June 1987 for £100,000 (exclusive of land) of which £90,000 was attributable to the original factory and included £6,000 for the office. Bird makes his accounts to 31st December each year.

Original Factory	£	Extension	£
Cost	50,000	Cost	15,000
Less: Land	10,000		
	40,000		
Less: Office (being more than 10% of £40,000)	4,500		
	35,500		

1962/63	£	1969/70	£
IA - 5%	1,775	- 15%	2,250
WDA - 2%	710	- 4%	600
c/f	2,485		2,850

	£	£		£	£
b/f	2,485	35,500		2,850	15,000
1963/64 - 1987/88			1970/71 - 1987/88		
WDA 25 x £710	17,750		18 x £600	10,800	
		20,235			13,650
Residue of expenditure		15,265			1,350

3.4 SALE OF A BUILDING

On the disposal of an industrial building, there will be a balancing charge or allowance. This is found by deducting the disposal proceeds of the structure only, (or market value if the disposal is other than at open market value) from the tax written down value, known in this case as the 'residue of expenditure'. A balancing charge cannot exceed the allowances given and no balancing adjustment will arise if the building is sold after the end of its 'tax life' i.e. after 50 or 25 years from the date of first use. Any costs of demolition are added to the residue of expenditure before calculating the balancing adjustment.

	£	£
Residue of expenditure	15,265	1,350
Disposal proceeds £(90,000 - 6,000)	84,000	10,000
Balancing charge	68,735	8,650
Restricted to	20,235	

3.5 ALLOWANCES AVAILABLE TO A SUBSEQUENT PURCHASER

A subsequent purchaser of a used industrial building will, provided that he uses it as an industrial building, be able to claim capital allowances. The only capital allowance available is a writing down allowance calculated by using the formula:

$$\frac{\text{Residue of expenditure plus any balancing charge or less any balancing allowance}}{\text{Tax life of building less period of previous ownership from first use}}$$

No initial allowance is available. In the illustration, the allowance available to a subsequent purchaser would be:

	£	£
<u>Original factory</u>		
Residue of expenditure	15,265	
<u>Add</u>: Balancing charge	20,235	
	35,500	
$\frac{£35,500}{50 - 26}$ =		1,479
<u>Extension</u>		
Residue of expenditure	~~2,550~~ 1350	
<u>Add</u>: Balancing charge	~~7,450~~ 8650	
	~~10,000~~ 10,000	
$\frac{£10,000}{25 - 18\ 9/12}$ =		1,600
		3,079

In most cases, the numerator will be equal to the lower of the sales proceeds or the original cost for capital allowance purposes.

3.6 NON-INDUSTRIAL USE

If at the end of the basis period the building is not in industrial use or being used for non-industrial purpose no WDA will be available unless the period of non use is merely temporary. Where there is a period of non-industrial use, notional WDAs, i.e. allowances calculated but not deducted from profits, will be deducted from cost in arriving at the residue of expenditure. In finding the balancing charge or allowance the calculations will differ depending upon whether the building is sold for more or less than the original cost.

(a) Sale for more than cost

The balancing adjustment will be calculated as under:

	£	£
Cost		x
Less: IBA for periods of industrial use	x	
Notional WDA for periods of non-industrial use	x	
		x
Residue of expenditure		x
Disposal proceeds		x
Balancing charge		x

The balancing charge will be restricted to the allowances actually given.

Illustration

Anton bought a factory on 15th December 1978 for £10,000 exclusive of land. He used it for non-industrial purposes throughout the period 7th November 1980 to 18th March 1982. He sold it on 15th December 1986 for £11,000 exclusive of land. Accounts are made up to 31st December throughout.

		£	£
1979/80	Year ended 31.12.78		
	Cost		10,000
	IA - 50%	5,000	
	WDA - 4%	400	
			5,400
			4,600
1980/81	Year ended 31.12.79		
	WDA 4%		400
			4,200
1981/82	Year ended 31.12.80		
	Notional WDA (buildings not in use at end of basis period)		400
			3,800
1982/83	Year ended 31.12.81		
	Notional WDA (buildings not in use at end of basis period)		400
c/f			3,400

		£
b/f		3,400
1983/84 to 1986/87	Years ended 31.12.82 to 31.12.85 WDA - 4% x 4 years	1,600
	Residue of expenditure before sale	1,800
1987/88	Year ended 31.12.86 Sale of building - proceeds	11,000
		9,200

The balancing charge will be limited to the allowances given:

£5,400 + £400 + £1,600 — £7,400

The allowances available to a subsequent purchaser would be:

	£
Residue of Expenditure	1,800
Balancing charge	7,400
	9,200
÷ (25 — 8)	541 p.a.

(b) Sale for less than cost

The balancing adjustment would be:

	£	£
Cost		x
Less: IBA for periods of industrial use	x	
Notional WDA for periods of non-industrial use	x	
		x
Residue of expenditure		x
Cost		
Less: Sales proceeds		x
Net cost		x
Less: Proportion attributable to non-industrial use:		
Net cost x $\frac{\text{Period of non-industrial use}}{\text{Period of ownership from first use}}$		x
Adjusted net cost		x
Less: Allowances actually given		x
Balancing charge (or Balancing allowance)		x

Example

B makes up accounts to 31st December annually. On 30th June 1973 he acquired a factory from a builder at a cost of:

	£
Land	50,000
Building	150,000
	200,000

It was first brought into use on 31st December 1973. It was out of industrial use for the period from 1st August 1978 to 31st January 1980. On 31st December 1987 the factory was sold for £30,000 (excluding land).

		£	£
1974/75	Year to 31.12.73 - Cost		150,000
	IA - 40%	60,000	
	WDA - 4%	6,000	
			66,000
			84,000
1975/76 to 1978/79	Years 31.12.74 to 31.12.77 WDA - 4% x 4		24,000
			60,000
1979/80	Year to 31.12.78 Notional WDA - 4%		6,000
			54,000
1980/81	Year to 31.12.79 Notional WDA - 4%		6,000
			48,000
1981/82 to 1987/88	Years 31.12.80 to 31.12.86 WDA - 4% x 7		42,000
	Residue of expenditure		6,000

	£
Cost	150,000
Disposal proceeds	30,000
	120,000
Less: Proportion attributable to non-industrial use - 1½/14	12,857
Adjusted net cost	107,143
Less: Allowances actually given	132,000
Balancing charge	24,857

Allowances available to subsequent purchaser:

	£
Residue of expenditure	6,000
Balancing charge	24,857
	30,857
But restricted to cost to subsequent purchaser	30,000
÷ 25 − 14	2,727 p.a.

3.7 MANNER OF MAKING ALLOWANCES

Where the industrial building is used by a trader, the allowances will be given against the Schedule D Case I assessments - i.e. in taxing the trade. If the building is leased, then the lessor will receive the allowances by discharge or repayment of tax against any rental income. In the case of leased industrial buildings any balancing charge will be assessed under Schedule D Case VI.

3.8 HOTELS

IBA can be claimed in relation to a 'qualifying hotel' as if it were an industrial building or structure.

The allowances available are:

(a) Initial Allowance:

Expenditure incurred	from 12.4.1978 to 31.3.1986	20%
	after 31.3.1986	NIL

(b) Writing down allowance:
4% straight line.

A 'qualifying hotel' is an hotel the accommodation in which is in a building or buildings of a permanent nature and which complies with the following requirements:

(a) that it is open for at least four months in the season (April to October);

(b) that during the time when it is open in the season:

(i) it has at least ten letting bedrooms;

(ii) the sleeping accommodation offered at the hotel consists wholly or mainly of letting bedrooms; and

(iii) the services provided for guests normally include the provision of breakfast and an evening meal, the making of beds and the cleaning of rooms.

A letting bedroom is defined as a private bedroom available for letting to the public generally and not normally in the same occupation for more than one month.

In determining whether the hotel is qualifying, the various conditions must be satisfied for the twelve months prior to the end of the basis period for which allowances are claimed. Thus if C makes up accounts as under, the relevant periods will be:

Year ended 31.12.1985	1.1.85 - 31.12.85
18 months to 30.6.1987	1.7.86 - 30.6.87

Any building (whether or not on the same site as any other part of the hotel) which is provided by the person carrying on the hotel for the welfare of workers employed in the hotel and which is in use for that purpose, is treated as included in a 'qualifying hotel'. However, where a qualifying hotel is carried on by an individual, (whether alone or in partnership), any accommodation which, during the time when the hotel is open in the season, is normally used as a dwelling by that person or by any member of his family or household must be excluded from relief.

3.9 INDUSTRIAL AND COMMERCIAL BUILDINGS IN ENTERPRISE ZONES

Expenditure on the construction of an industrial building or a qualifying hotel, or a commercial building or structure, will qualify for industrial building allowances if, at the time the expenditure was incurred, the site of the building is in an enterprise zone. The expenditure must have been incurred within ten years of the site having been included in the zone.

A commercial building is one which does not already qualify for relief, which is used for the purposes of a trade, profession or vocation, or in any case is used as an office, excluding any building in use as or as part of a dwelling house.

The initial allowance available is up to 100% subject to the right of reducing the claim to a lesser amount; a straight-line writing down allowance of 25% is available on the balance of expenditure (if any).

3.10 ASSURED TENANCIES

Capital allowances are available to a company who incurs expenditure on dwellings let at freely negotiated rents that are not subject to the Rent Acts. The allowances are available for expenditure incurred between 10th March 1982 and 31st March 1987.

The allowances are:

(a) Initial allowance
Expenditure incurred from:

10.3.82 to 13.3.84	75%
14.3.84 to 31.3.85	50%
1.4.85 to 31.3.86	25%
From 1.4.86	NIL

(b) WDA is 4% straight line.

Allowances may be claimed on expenditure on the buildings. There is no provision for any disclaimer.

The expenditure that qualifies for relief is a maximum of £60,000 per dwelling in Greater London or £40,000 per dwelling elsewhere. Expenditure incurred in erecting a block of flats is apportioned rateably. Relief is given by discharge or repayment of tax against rental income.

3.11 SPREADING OF EXPENDITURE UNDER CERTAIN CONTRACTS

In view of the phasing out of FYA and initial allowances by reducing the rate of allowances over a number of years, taxpayers may enter into contractual agreements in earlier years and have the contracts completed in later years. Any deposits, or partial payments made when the contract is signed may attract a higher rate of FYA, or initial allowance, than the payments of the remaining amounts when the contract is completed. Such schemes will enable the taxpayer to accelerate payments and take advantage of higher rates of FYA or initial allowances on at least part of the cost of capital expenditure before they are reduced or phased out and by the time they take delivery of the assets to complete the contract.

Anti-avoidance provisions prevent the above situation by spreading the expenditure over the period from the agreement date to the completion date of the contract.

Contracts entered into between 14th March 1984 and 31st March 1986 (inclusive) are caught by these provisions.

The capital expenditure that is deemed to be incurred for the period 1st April 1984 to 31st March 1985 (financial year 1984) is determined by taking a fraction of the total contract price. The fraction is determined by taking the number of complete months after the agreement date of the contract but within the FY 1984, and dividing it by the number of complete months from the agreement date of the contract to the completion date or 31st March 1987 if earlier.

For the financial year 1985, the fraction is twelve divided by the number of complete months from the agreement date of the contract to the completion date or 31st March 1987 if earlier. Where the agreement date is within the financial year 1985, then the numerator in the fraction for FY 1985 will be the number of complete months from the agreement date to 31st March 1986.

Hire purchase contracts on plant and machinery are not affected by these anti-avoidance provisions.

Illustration

P entered into a contractual agreement to purchase plant and machinery on 31st January 1985. He paid the full contract price of £75,000. The completion date of this contract is 30th June 1986 when the plant and machinery would be delivered.

The amount of expenditure which has been allocated to the financial year 1984 is:

$$\frac{2}{17} \times £75,000 = £8,824$$

This amount of £8,824 will qualify for the maximum FYA of 75%.

The amount of expenditure which has been allocated to the financial year 1985 is:

Balance of expenditure deemed to be incurred on 1st April 1985

$$£75,000 - £8,824 = \underline{£66,176}$$

Allowed in FY 1985 $\frac{12}{17} \times £75,000 = \underline{£52,941}$

This amount of £52,941 will qualify for the maximum FYA of 50%.

The remaining amount of the expenditure of (£75,000 - £8,824 - £52,941 = £13,235) has been allocated to the period after 31st March 1986. Therefore no first year allowance will be available on this amount.

4.0 AGRICULTURAL BUILDINGS AND WORKS

4.1 EXPENDITURE INCURRED PRIOR TO 1ST APRIL 1986

4.1.1 GENERAL

This is an allowance given to the owner or tenant in respect of expenditure incurred on the following:

(a) construction or extension of farmhouses and farm cottages;

(b) construction of farm or forestry buildings including intensive rearing houses;

(c) drainage, sewerage and land reclamation works, erection of fences and installation of gas and electricity services, etc.

Any grants received must be deducted from the cost of the works before claiming allowances. In respect of expenditure on the farmhouse, no more than one-third of the cost qualifies for relief.

4.1.2 ALLOWANCES AVAILABLE

(a) Initial allowance of 20%. This allowance is available only in respect of expenditure incurred after 11th April 1978 - before that date only writing down allowances were available.

(b) WDA of 10%. This is a straight-line allowance, calculated on the expenditure incurred, and given until the allowances equal the expenditure.

Unlike other types of allowances, these allowances are given in the fiscal year following the year to 31st March in which the expenditure was incurred.

Illustration

J makes up accounts for the year to 31st December 1985. In that year he incurs the following expenses:

		£
(a)	Additions to barn on 31.1.85 (a grant of £2,000 was received)	8,000
(b)	New bathroom for farmhouse on 10.4.85	1,500

Capital allowances can be claimed as under:

	£	£	£	£
1985/86				
Expenditure to 31.3.1985				
Additions to barn	8,000			
Less: Grant	2,000			
		6,000		
Initial allowance - 20%	1,200			
WDA - 10%	600			
		1,800		1,800
		4,200		
1986/87				
Expenditure to 31.3.1986				
New bathroom (1/3 x £1,500)			500	
Initial allowance - 20%	100			
WDA - 10%	50			
			150	150
WDA on barn		600		600
Carried forward		3,600	350	750

Note the first WDA is available in the same year as the initial allowance.

To avoid the problems associated with allocating expenditure incurred in an accounting period to different fiscal years for the purpose of determining the allowances, an individual taxpayer may agree with the Inspector to substitute his own accounting year date for 31st March.

Where the individual does not claim the initial allowance, the WDA of 10% is given for each of the ten years in the normal way. The individual may claim part of the initial allowance in which case the WDA's are given at the 10% rate until the expenditure has been relieved.

Illustration
M makes up accounts to 30th April 1983 and during the year he incurs expenditure of £25,000 on new cowsheds, on the 15th January 1983.
He can claim initial allowance and writing down allowances as follows:

		£
1983/84	Initial 20% of £25,000	5,000
	Writing down 10% of £25,000	2,500
		7,500
		=====
1984/85	Inclusive writing down	
1990/91	(each year)	2,500
		=====

Alternatively, if M decided to claim 5% initial allowance:

		£
1983/84	Initial 5% of £25,000	1,250
	Writing down 10% of £25,000	2,500
		3,750
		=====

		£
1984/85 to	Writing down 10% of £25,000	
1991/92	(each year)	2,500
1992/93	Writing down (balance of expenditure)	1,250

4.1.3 MANNER OF GIVING ALLOWANCES

Agricultural buildings allowances are given against agricultural income, any excess being carried forward against the same income for future years. Alternatively the taxpayer may elect under CAA 1968,s.71 to have the excess offset against other income. The time limit for this claim is two years after the end of the year of assessment.

4.1.4 SALE OF AGRICULTURAL BUILDINGS

On the sale of an agricultural building there is no balancing adjustment. The transferee will obtain the allowance for the remaining part of the original writing down period and in the fiscal year of transfer any allowance will be apportioned.

Illustration
Following the first Illustration in section 4.1.2, if J sold his barn to S on 30th June 1987 for £9,000, for the fiscal year 1987/88 the allowance would be split between them by reference to the respective periods of ownership in the year to 31st March 1988.

	£
J	
3/12 x £600	150
S	
9/12 x £600	450
	600
	===

S will continue to get capital allowances of £600 per annum for the next five years.
Where the person incurring the expenditure on agricultural buildings etc. is the tenant and the tenancy comes to an end the remaining allowances will pass as under:

(a) if there is an incoming tenant and he makes any payment to the outgoing tenant in respect of the relevant expenditure then the remaining allowances will go to the incoming tenant;

(b) in any other case e.g. when no payment is made or another tenancy is not granted, the allowances will pass to the immediate landlord.

4.2 EXPENDITURE INCURRED AFTER 31ST MARCH 1986

4.2.1 GENERAL

For expenditure incurred after 31.3.1986 there are detailed changes to the legislation many of which are similar to the procedures already applied to industrial buildings. Broadly allowances will be given on capital expenditure as in 4.1.1 above where the person incurring the expenditure has a major interest in the property. A major interest is:

(a) a freehold interest, or

(b) a lease.

4.2.2 ALLOWANCES AVAILABLE

A writing down allowance is given at 4% per annum straight line over a period of 25 years. The allowance is first given for the fiscal year for which the accounting period forms a basis period. As with the previous legislation, allowances are only given on a maximum of 1/3 of the cost of expenditure on the farmhouse. Where the expenditure consists of payments under a contract entered into on or before 13th March 1984 and the expenditure is incurred before 1st April 1987 the old allowances apply.

Illustration
K makes up accounts to 31st March 1987. In that year he spends £20,000 on a new barn.

		£
1987/88	Year to 31st March 1987	
	Cost	20,000
	WDA - 4%	800
	c/f	19,200

4.2.3 MANNER OF GIVING ALLOWANCES

ABA on expenditure incurred after 31st March 1986 is normally given in taxing the trade and can thus qualify for S.168 relief unless the property is subject to a lease where the allowances will continue to be given by discharge or repayment of tax primarily against agricultural or forestry income.

4.2.4 SALE OF AN AGRICULTURAL BUILDING etc.

If an asset on which ABA has been claimed is sold before having been brought into use, then there will be a clawback of any WDA previously claimed. The person acquiring the relevant interest in the property will be able to claim WDA on the lower of:

(a) Cost to the original owner, or
(b) price paid by the subsequent purchaser.

Where a person disposes of his interest in the property to another during the tax life, it is possible to have two differing treatments:

(a) No balancing adjustment;

(b) a balancing adjustment.

If no claim is made for a balancing adjustment on disposal, the purchaser of the relevant interest steps into the shoes of the vendor and becomes entitled to receive the WDA for the remainder of the building's tax life. If the disposal occurs in the middle of a fiscal year, the allowances will be apportioned on a time basis between vendor and purchaser in the same way as before.

Where it is desired to have a balancing adjustment, then a balancing charge or allowance is calculated in the normal way. The subsequent purchaser can obtain a writing down allowance by using the formula:

$$\frac{\text{Residue of expenditure plus any balancing charge or less any balancing allowance}}{\text{Tax life of the asset less any previous period of ownership}}$$

Illustration

L makes up accounts to 31st March annually. On 1st April 1987 he acquires a barn for £10,000. On 1st April 1990 he sells it to M for £9,000. A claim is made to treat the sale as a balancing event.

		£
1988/89	Year to 31st March 1988	
	Cost of barn	10,000
	WDA	400
		9,600
1989/90	Year to 31st March 1989	
	WDA	400
		9,200
1990/91	Year to 31st March 1990	
	WDA	400
		8,800
1991/92	Year to 31st March 1991	
	Disposal proceeds	9,000
	Balancing charge	200

Allowances available to M:

$$\frac{£8,800 + £200}{25 - 3} = £409 \text{ p.a.}$$

An election to treat the disposal as a balancing event must be made within two years of the end of the year of assessment in whose basis period the event occurs. A company must make the election within two years of the end of the relevant accounting period. When the event is a sale, the election must be made jointly by buyer and seller otherwise, e.g. in the case of destruction etc. of the asset, the election need only be made by the former owner.

5.0 PATENTS

5.1 EXPENDITURE INCURRED BEFORE 1ST APRIL 1986

5.1.1 GENERAL

There are two basic types of expenditure on patents:

(a) the cost of creating a patented process:
this is treated as a revenue expense and deducted from trading profit;

(b) the cost of purchasing patent rights;

these attract capital allowances.

5.1.2 ALLOWANCES AVAILABLE

The allowance is a WDA given over 17 years if a new patent, or its life if that is a shorter period.

Illustration
Y acquires the rights to two patents:

(a) a new one costing £34,000;

(b) one with ten years to run also costing £34,000.

Allowances available:

(a) £34,000/17 = £2,000 per annum

(b) £34,000/10 = £3,400 per annum

Where the owner of the patent rights is a trader, the writing down allowance can be given against trading profits. If he is not a trader, it can only be given against patent income, any excess being carried forward and relieved when such income is available.

Illustration
Z is a pensioner who receives a state retirement pension of £2,000 per year. To provide for his retirement, he acquires the rights to a revolutionary process. The patent has ten years to run and cost £20,000. His income from the royalties is:

1984/85	£1,400
1985/86	£3,000

		£	£	£
1984/85	Patent royalties	1,400		
	WDA £20,000/10	2,000		
	c/f	600		
	Pension			2,000
	Total income			2,000

		£	£	£
1985/86	Patent royalties		3,000	
	WDA brought forward	600		
	for the year	2,000		
			2,600	
				400
	Pension			2,000
	Total income			2,400

5.1.3 SALE OF A PATENT

The sale of a patent can be either total or partial:

(a) Partial sale

The sale proceeds of the part sold are deducted from the written down value brought forward. A new WDA is then calculated by dividing the remaining figure by the residual life of the patent.

Illustration

In 1986/87 Z sold part of his patent for £4,000.

	£
WDV brought forward (£20,000 - £4,000)	16,000
Less: Partial sale proceeds	4,000
	12,000
WDA 1986/87 and subsequent years: £12,000/8	1,500
	10,500

(b) Total sale

The sale of the whole of the patent will give rise to a balancing charge or allowance. The balancing charge cannot exceed the allowances actually given. The balancing charge will be assessed as a trading profit where the owner is a trader. If the patent is held as an investment the charge will be assessed under Schedule D Case VI.

Illustration

In 1987/88 Z sold the remainder of the patent for £15,000.

		£
1987/88	WDV brought forward	10,500
	Sales proceeds	15,000
	Balancing charge	4,500

Where the patent is sold for more than its original cost, the balancing charge will be restricted to the allowances given and there will be an additional charge to income tax on the excess of sales proceeds over original cost. This sum is assessable under Schedule D Case VI and provided the vendor is a UK resident, is spread equally over the year of receipt and the five successive years. Alternatively, the taxpayer may, by election within two years of the end of the year of receipt, be assessed on the whole amount in the year of receipt.

Illustration

If Z sold the remainder of the patent rights for £18,000 instead of £15,000, the calculation would be:

		£
1987/88	WDA brought forward	10,500
	Sales proceeds	18,000
		7,500
	Balancing charge (restricted to allowances given £2,000 + £2,000 + £1,500)	5,500
	Capital profit	2,000

The capital profit will be divided by six and assessed in six equal sums for the years 1987/88 to 1992/93 inclusive.

Where patent royalties are received by the person who created the patent, they are classed as earned income.

5.2 EXPENDITURE INCURRED AFTER 31ST MARCH 1986

5.2.1 GENERAL

Expenditure on the acquisition of patent rights incurred after 31st March 1986 is dealt with in a similar way to expenditure on plant and machinery.

5.2.2 ALLOWANCES AVAILABLE

There is a writing down allowance of 25% on the reducing balance in the pool of expenditure incurred after 31st March 1986. The format of the computation is:

Tax written down value in pool b/f	x
Add: Expenditure on patent rights in the basis period	x
	x
Less: Disposal proceeds of patent rights disposed of in the period	(x)
	x
WDA at 25%	(x)
c/f	x

Illustration

A bought patent rights for £50,000 on 30th June 1986. He made up accounts to 31st December annually. A is a trader.

		£
1987/88	Year to 31st December 1986	
	Cost of patent	50,000
	WDA - 25%	12,500
	c/f	37,500

In the year to 31st December 1987 A acquired rights to a further patent with 10 years to run for £12,000

1988/89	Year to 31st December 1987	
	TWDV b/f	37,500
	Additions	12,000
		49,500
	WDA - 25%	12,375
	c/f	37,125

5.2.3 SALE OF A PATENT

Where a patent rights are sold, the disposal proceeds will be deducted from the pool as in 5.2.2 above. Under no circumstances can disposal proceeds exceed cost. Any capital profit is dealt with as in 5.1.3 above.

In the year to 31st December 1988 A sold the rights to the first patent for £14,000 and acquired rights to a further patent with 2 years to run for £6,000.

		£
1989/90	Year to 31st December 1988	
	TWDV b/f	37,125
	Additions	6,000
		43,125
	Disposal proceeds	14,000
		29,125
	WDA - 25%	7,281
	c/f	21,844

A balancing charge will arise if the disposal proceeds of sales exceed the balance in the pool.

There will be a balancing allowance where:

(a) the disposal proceeds of the remaining patent rights is less than the balance in the pool;

(b) the life of the last patent remaining in the pool comes to an end and it is not renewed;

(c) there is the cessation of the trade.

In the year to 31st December 1989 A sold the second patent for £20,000. The third patent expired on 31st October 1990.

		£
1990/91	Year to 31st December 1989	
	TWDV b/f	21,844
	Disposal proceeds of patent 2 £20,000 but restricted to	12,000
		9,844

1991/92	Year to 31st December 1990	
	As the last patent has expired there will be a balancing allowance of	9,844
		======

There are restrictions on the cost of the patent qualifying for allowances where the patent has been acquired from a connected person or where it appears that the obtaining of capital allowances is the sole or main purpose of the acquisition.

6.0 SCIENTIFIC RESEARCH

6.1 GENERAL

Expenditure on scientific research can consist of capital and revenue expenditure on pure research or contributions to research establishments or universities. Scientific research is defined as activities in the fields of natural or applied science for the extension of knowledge. No allowance is normally given on land acquired after 31st March 1985.

6.2 ALLOWANCES AVAILABLE

The whole of the expenditure, whether capital or revenue, is treated as a deduction in the year in which it is made. It is given in taxing the trade.

6.3 SALE OF AN ASSET

Where the capital asset ceases to belong to the trader, the disposal proceeds, or open market value if more, up to the amount of the original expenditure, are treated as a trading receipt accruing at the time of sale.

7.0 KNOW-HOW

7.1 EXPENDITURE INCURRED BEFORE 1ST APRIL 1986

7.1.1 GENERAL

Know-how is defined as any industrial information and techniques of assistance in:

(a) manufacturing or processing goods or materials;

(b) working or searching for mineral deposits;

(c) agricultural, forestry or fishing operations.

7.1.2 ALLOWANCES AVAILABLE

A WDA of 1/6th of the cost of the know-how is available. It is given first for the fiscal year for which the accounting period in which it was acquired forms the basis period and for the following five years.

7.1.3 DISPOSAL OF KNOW-HOW

The disposal of know-how can take two forms:

(a) a sale independent of the trade;

(b) a sale with the trade or part of the trade.

(a) A sale independent of the trade

The proceeds of sale will be treated as a trading receipt or assessed under Schedule D Case VI if sold by a non-trader. The vendor will continue to receive his WDA (even though he may no longer own the asset); the purchaser may receive WDA on the cost of the know-how.

(b) A sale together with the trade

This will be treated as a sale or purchase of goodwill and therefore cease to be within the charge to income tax (it will be liable to capital gains tax). The purchaser will not get any capital allowances on the cost; the vendor will get a balancing allowance equal to the unallowed capital allowances.

Alternatively an election can be made by both parties in writing within two years to substitute the treatment described in (a) above.

7.2 EXPENDITURE INCURRED AFTER 31ST MARCH 1986

Expenditure incurred after 31st March 1986 is treated in a similar way to that of patent rights except that on a disposal the entire disposal proceeds (not just restricted to cost) are included in the capital allowance computation.

8.0 THE BASIS PERIODS FOR CAPITAL ALLOWANCES

8.1 NORMAL BASIS

The basis period determines when the capital allowances are given and against which profits they are available for set-off. It follows, therefore, that the capital allowances basis period is derived from the basis period for adjusted profits under Schedule D Cases I and II. In fact, with the exception of commencements, cessations and changes of accounting date, the basis periods are identical.

If a taxpayer has made his accounts to 31st December 1986, the profit shown by them will be assessed in 1987/88. The basis period for calculating capital allowances deductible in arriving at the net income for 1987/88 will be 1st January 1986 to 31st December 1986, the accounting period. Capital allowances will be calculated after including all new assets acquired during that year and after excluding all assets sold during it.

Where WDA is claimed it will be reduced proportionately if the basis period is less than twelve months in length.

8.2 COMMENCEMENT

On a commencement there will be an overlap of basis periods. Where there is such an overlap, it will be allocated to the earliest basis period. This will ensure that expenditure will qualify for allowances as early as possible.

Illustration

X commenced trading on 1st January 1985 and made his first acounts to 31st December 1985 and thereafter annually.

The basis period will be:

1.1.85 | 31.12.85 | 31.12.86 | 31.12.87 | 31.12.88

1984/85 | adds | WDA for 3 months
1.1.85 5.4.85

1985/86 | adds | WDA for 12 months
1.1.85 6.4.85 31.12.85

1986/87 | | WDA for 12 months
1.1.85 31.12.85

1987/88 | Additions | WDA for 12 months
1.1.86 31.12.86

Thus in the fiscal year 1984/85, FYA etc. will be due on all expenditure between 1st January 1985 and 5th April 1985 and WDA for three months only as the basis period is only three months.

In 1985/86 FYA etc. are due on expenditure in the period from 6th April 1985 to 31st December 1985 and as the basis period (ignoring the overlap) is twelve months in length a full WDA will be available.

In 1986/87 no FYA or initial allowances are available as all expenditure in the basis period has qualified for relief already, either in 1984/85 or in 1985/86. A full WDA will be available.

If an election were made under TA 1970,s.117 the basis period would become:

1.1.85 | 31.12.85 | 31.12.86 | 31.12.87 | 31.12.88

1984/85 | adds | WDA for 3 months
1.1.85 5.4.85

1985/86 | Additions | WDA for 12 months
6.4.85 5.4.86

1986/87 | Additions | WDA for 12 months
6.4.86 5.4.87

1987/88 | | WDA for 12 months
1.1.86 31.12.86

1988/89 | | | WDA for 12 months
1.1.87 31.12.87
6.4.87

In this case the claim to capital allowances will be accelerated and by the end of the third year 1986/87 allowances will have been claimed on all additions up to 5th April 1987. There will be no additions in 1987/88 as expenditure in the basis period from 1st January 1986 to 31st December 1986 will already have qualified for allowances in 1985/86 or 1986/87 though full WDA are available. In 1988/89 capital allowances are available on expenditure incurred in the period 6th April 1987 to 31st December 1987 together with a full WDA on the balance brought forward.

Capital expenditure incurred before the commencement of trade is treated as having been incurred on the first day of trading.

Illustration

R commenced in business on 1st January 1984 and his profits, adjusted for income tax purposes, were:

1st January to	31st May 1984	£ 4,975
Year ended	31st May 1985	£ 7,416
Year ended	31st May 1986	£12,120

The following assets, on which capital allowances were claimed in full, were acquired as shown:

Item	Date of Purchase	Cost
		£
Plant and machinery	1st January 1984	1,825
Motor car (used 1/4 privately)	28th February 1984	1,200
Plant and machinery	15th June 1984	2,180
Motor car (used entirely for business purposes)	31st December 1984	640
Office furniture	1st June 1985	250
Motor van	31st July 1985	900

You are required to compute the Schedule D Case I assessments for the years 1983/84 to 1986/87 and the capital allowances for those years.

S·117

The assessments are:		Normal	Revised
		£	£
1983/84	3/5 x £4,975	2,985	
		=====	
1984/85	1st 12 months	9,301	
	Actual		8,170
1985/86	1st 12 months reassessed	9,301	
	Actual		11,335
		18,602	19,506
		=====	======

No revision to actual.

The basis periods will be:

```
|__________________|____________________|___________________|
1.1.84          31.5.84              31.5.85             31.5.86

1983/84     |    FYA     |
            1.1.84    5.4.84

1984/85     |____________|    FYA    |
            1.1.84    6.4.84     31.12.84

1985/86     |       NO FYA           |
            1.1.84               31.12.84

1986/87                  |________|    FYA   |
                     1.6.84    1.1.85    31.5.85
```

Capital Allowances:

1983/84 Additions	Pool General	Pool Cars	Motor Car		Allowances
	£	£	£		£
1.1.84	1,825				
28.2.84			1,200		
FYA 100%	1,825				1,825
	———				
WDA				Private use	
25% x 3/12			75	- (1/4)19 = 56	56
			1,125		1,881
					=====
1984/85 Additions					
15.6.84	2,180				
31.12.84 (car)		640			
FYA 75%	1,635			Private use	
WDA 25%		160	281	- (1/4)70 = 211	2,006
	545	480	844		
1985/86					
WDA 25%	136	120	211	- (1/4)53 = 158	414
	409	360	633		
1986/87					
WDA 25%	102	90	158	- (1/4)39 = 119	311
	307	270	475		

8.3 CESSATION

In the case of a taxpayer who ceases to trade, there will be a gap between basis periods. This gap will be allocated to the penultimate or prepenultimate years as appropriate.

Illustration

Y makes up accounts to 30th September annually and ceases to trade on 30th September 1987. Assuming a normal basis the basis periods would be:

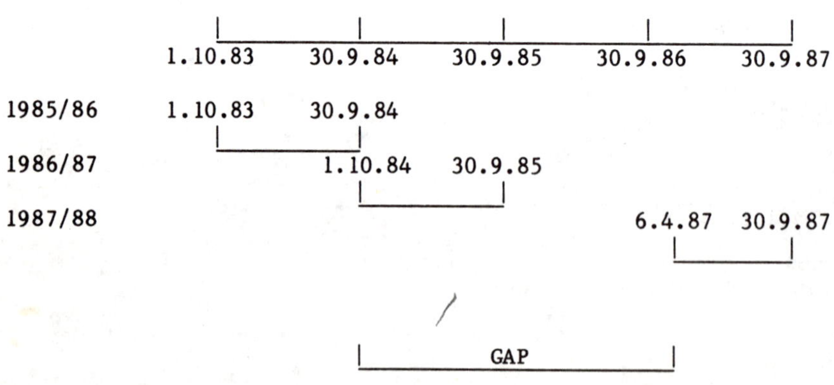

Applying this rule, the above basis period becomes:

1985/86	1.10.83	to	30.9.84
1986/87	1.10.84	to	5.4.87
1987/88	6.4.87	to	30.9.87

and any asset purchased between 1st October 1984 and 5th April 1987 will be included before calculating 1986/87 allowances. Although the basis period is two-and-a-half years, only twelve months WDA is given.

If adjustment under s.118 is made, the assessment basis periods are:

1984/85	1.10.82	to	30.9.83
1985/86	1.10.83	to	5.4.86
1986/87	6.4.86	to	5.4.87
1987/88	6.4.87	to	30.9.87

Expressed diagrammatically as follows:

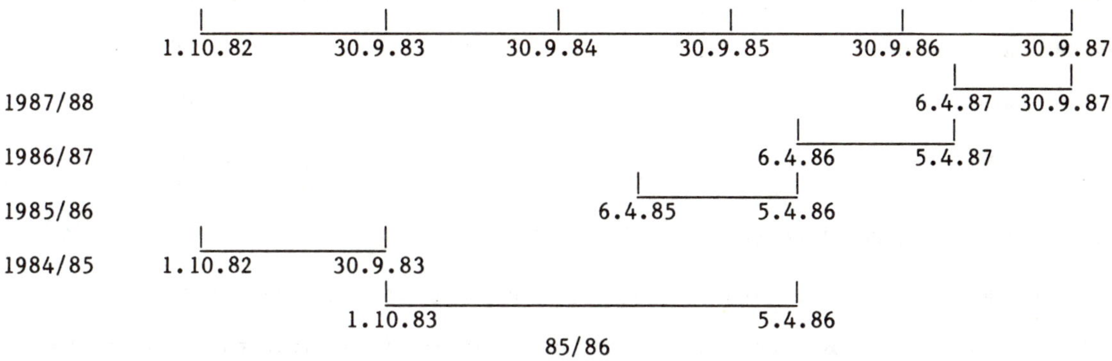

Where the gap arises because of a cessation the somewhat complicated position can be expressed as follows:

(a) if adjustment is <u>not</u> made under s.118 for actual, the gap forms the end of the basis period for the penultimate year of assessment;

(b) if adjustment is made under s.118 for actual, the gap forms the beginning of the prepenultimate year of assessment.

On a cessation the Revenue decide whether or not to revise the assessments without taking into account the effect of capital allowances.

When a trader ceases, there will normally be no FYA, initial allowances or WDA available for the last fiscal year. At the end of the last period of trading all plant and machinery not sold must be valued and an overall balancing charge or allowance calculated. If demolition costs are incurred in removing machinery, they are added to the balance in the pool and decrease the amount of the balancing charge or increase the balancing allowance. Items taken over by the trader will be included at their proper market value.

<u>Illustration</u>
D ceases trading. At the beginning of the final period he has:

Balance in pool b/f	£3,000
Motor car	£2,000

In the final period he buys a machine, which he uses in his trade, for £500; he sells most of the plant for £1,500. At the end of the accounting period the value of the remaining plant is £600 and D takes over the car at £1. Its proper market value is £1,000. The cost of demolishing part of the plant was £100.

		Pool	Motor Car	Total Allowances
	£	£	£	£
WDV b/f		3,000	2,000	
Additions: Machine	500			
Demolition costs	100			
		600		
		3,600		
Less: Disposal proceeds of plant		1,500		
		2,100		
Valuation of remainder		600	1,000	
Balancing allowance		1,500		1,500
Balancing allowance			1,000	1,000
Total allowances				2,500

8.4 CHANGE OF ACCOUNTING DATE

On a change of accounting date the rules for ascertaining the basis periods are:

(a) if there is an overlap, the common period always falls into the earliest basis period;

(b) if there is a gap, the missing period always falls into the later basis period.

Illustration

O decided to change his accounting date, his accounting periods are:

Year ended	30.9.1986
Year ended	30.9.1987
9 months to	30.6.1988

This is similar to an earlier illustration.
The basis periods will be:

1989/90	1.7.1987 - 30.6.1988
1988/89	1.10.1986 - 30.9.1987
1987/88	1.10.1985 - 30.9.1986

Expressed diagrammatically as:

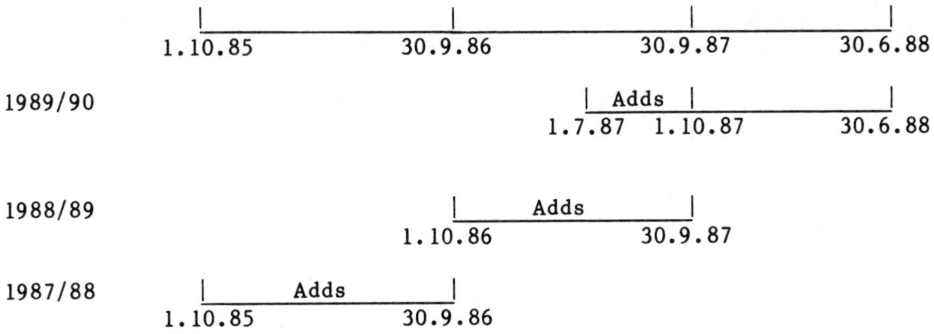

WDA for twelve months throughout.

As can be seen, the period 1st July 1987 to 30th September 1987 is common to the years 1988/89 and 1989/90. It will therefore be allocated to the earliest basis period. The basis periods for capital allowances will be:

1989/90	1.10.1987 - 30.6.1988
1988/89	1.10.1986 - 30.9.1987
1987/88	1.10.1985 - 30.9.1986

<u>Illustration</u>

B makes up accounts as under:

Year ended	30.9.1986
Year ended	30.9.1987
6 months ended	31.3.1988

Again this is similar to an earlier illustration.

The basis periods would be:

1988/89	1.4.1987 - 31.3.1988
1987/88	1.10.1985 - 30.9.1986

Expressed diagrammatically as:

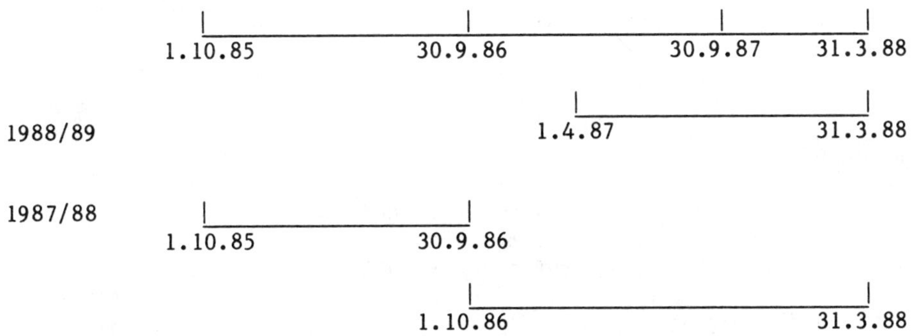

As there is a gap of six months, this is allocated to the later period. The basis periods for capital allowances are therefore:

1988/89	1.10.1986 - 31.3.1988
1987/88	1.10.1985 - 30.9.1986

WDA is for twelve months throughout.

6 Losses

1.0 GENERAL

A trading loss can be relieved in four main ways:

(a) by carry forward and offset against future trading profits - TA 1970,s171;

(b) by offset against total income liable to income tax of the fiscal year in which the loss was incurred, and if claimed, the following year - TA 1970,s.168;

(c) by offset against income received from a limited company when the business producing the loss has been incorporated - TA 1970, s.172;

(d) by carry back where the loss arises on a commencement or on a cessation - FA 1978,s.30, TA 1970,s.174.

2.0 CARRY FORWARD (TA 1970,s.171)

A trading loss can be carried forward and offset against the first available profits of the same trade, profession or vocation carried on by the same owner without time limit. A formal claim to obtain relief under this section must be made within six years of the end of the year of assessment for which relief is claimed.

Illustration

A had the following results:

Year ended 30.6.1985	Loss	£6,000
Year ended 30.6.1986	Profit	£4,000
Year ended 30.6.1987	Profit	£1,000

			£
1986/87	Year ended 30.6.85 (Loss c/f £6,000)	DI	Nil
1987/88	Year ended 30.6.86	DI	4,000
	Less: s.171 relief		(4,000)
			NIL

	(Loss c/f £2,000)		£
1988/89	Year ended 30.6.86	DI	1,000
	Less: s.171 relief		(1,000)
	(Loss c/f £1,000)		NIL

It is important to appreciate that once a claim is made under s.171 the loss must be offset against the earliest available future trading profit, even if this results in a possible loss of personal allowances.

3.0 OFFSET AGAINST OTHER INCOME - TA 1970,s.168

3.1 GENERAL - THE CONCESSIONAL BASIS

Instead of carrying a loss forward, a taxpayer may elect to offset it against other income of the fiscal year in which it was incurred and the next following fiscal year. Normally, for s.168 the year 'in which the loss was incurred' will be the fiscal year in which the accounting period producing the loss ends. Thus if B makes a trading loss in the year ended 31st December 1986 it will be incurred in 1986/87 and s.168 relief may be claimed in 1986/87 and 1987/88. A s.168 claim is voluntary and can be made for the first year, the first and second years, or the second year. The time limit for making the claim is two years from the end of the year of assessment for which relief is claimed, thus in the above, the time limits would be:

1986/87	-	5th April 1989
1987/88	-	5th April 1990

The claim against other income under s.168 is for two years only; any unrelieved losses go forward under s.171.

Illustration

B makes up accounts to 30th June, each year. He provides you with the following information; he has no other income.

Year ended 30.6.1985	Profit	£ 6,000
Year ended 30.6.1986	Loss	£10,000
Year ended 30.6.1987	Profit	£ 5,000

First year of s.168 claim - 1986/87	£	£
1986/87		
Sch. D Case I		
Year ended 30.6.1985		6,000
Sch. D Loss		
Year ended 30.6.1986	(10,000)	
s.168 claim	6,000	(6,000)
	(4,000)	NIL
1987/88		
Sch. D Case I		
Year ended 30.6.1986		NIL
(No s.168 claim)		
c/f	(4,000)	

	£	£
b/f	(4,000)	
1988/89		
Sch. D Case I		
Year ended 30.6.1987		5,000
s.171	4,000	(4,000)
	-	1,000
	=====	=====

3.2 ORDER OF SET-OFF

Where a claim is made under s.168 to offset the trading loss against other income, the offset is made in the following order:

(a) against the loss-maker's earned income

(b) against the loss-maker's unearned income

then

(c) against the spouse's earned income

(d) against the spouse's unearned income

The claim is made against the whole of the lossmaker's earned and unearned income then against the whole of the spouse's earned and unearned income. However, a claim can be made which excludes the whole of the spouse's income. This is to avoid the waste of personal allowances, which cannot be carried forward, or transferred to another taxpayer.

Illustration

C advises you of the following income:

Trading profit (loss):

Year ended 31.3.1986	£ 6,000
31.3.1987	£(12,000)

Other income:

Self - unearned	£1,000 pa
Wife - earned	£1,600 pa
- unearned	£3,000 pa

Personal allowances are £5,200 per annum.

(1) Assuming the claim does not exclude the wife's income:

	£	£
1986/87		
Mr C		
Schedule D Case I		
Year to 31.3.1986	6,000	
Unearned income	1,000	
		7,000
Mrs C		
Earned income	1,600	
Unearned income	3,000	
		4,600
c/f		11,600

	£	£
b/f		11,600
Loss - Year ended 31.3.1987	(12,000)	
s.168 relief	11,600	
		(11,600)
s.168 c/fwd.	400	-

Personal allowance lost £5200

1987/88	£	£
Mr C		
Schedule D Case I		
Year to 31.3.1987	NIL	
Unearned income	1,000	
		1,000
Mrs C		
Earned income	1,600	
Unearned income	3,000	
		4,600
		5,600
s.168 relief - balance		(400)
		5,200
Less: Personal allowances		5,200
		-

(2) Assuming wife's income excluded from claim:

1986/87	£	£
Mr C		
Schedule D Case I		
Year to 31.3.1986	6,000	
Unearned income	1,000	
		7,000
Loss - year ended 31.3.1987	(12,000) ~~(10,000)~~	
s.168 relief	7,000	
		(7,000)
	(5,000)	-
Mrs C		
Earned income	1,600	
Unearned income	3,000	
		4,600
		4,600
Less: Personal allowances		5,200
		-

1987/88	£	£
Mr C		
Schedule D Case I		
Year to 31.3.1987	Nil	
Unearned income	1,000	
		1,000
Less: s.168 relief		(1,000)
		-
Mrs C		
Earned income	1,600	
Unearned income	3,000	
		4,600
		4,600
Less: Personal allowances		5,200
		-

Balance of loss carried forward to be relieved under s.171 of (£12,000 - £7,000 - £1,000) = £4,000.

Thus by excluding the spouse's income from the claim and making the maximum use of personal allowances the same result is obtained in both cases for the years 1986/87 and 1987/88 but there is still a balance of loss carried forward for future relief.

A working wife is entitled to a wife's earned income relief (WEIR) of the lower of:

(a) her earned income, or

(b) £2,335.

If the husband makes an s.168 claim and extends it to the wife's income it will be offset against her earned income first and this may reduce the entitlement to WEIR.

Illustration

D has the following income for 1986/87:

	£
Self:	
Trading Profits - year to 31.12.85	5,360
Wife:	
Salary	2,360
Rents	3,800

There is a loss of £6,700 for the year to 31st December 1986.

Personal allowances are:

Married	£3,655
WEIR	£2,335

If the loss claim is extended to the total income:

86/87

	£	D Earned Income £	Mrs D Earned Income £	Mrs D Unearned Income £
Schedule DI -				
Year ended 31.12.85		5,360		
Salary			2,360	
Rents				3,800
Loss - Year ended 31.12.86	(6,700)			
s.168 relief	6,700	(5,360)	(1,340)	
		NIL	1,020	3,800
			4,820	
Personal allowances:				
Married	3,655			
WEIR restricted to	1,020			
			4,675	
Taxable			145	

If the loss claim is restricted to the husband's income:

	£	£	£	£
Schedule DI		5,360		
Salary			2,360	
Rents				3,800
		5,360	2,360	3,800
Loss as before	(6,700)			
s.168 relief	5,360	(5,360)		
Loss c/f S.171	(1,340)	Nil	6,160	
Personal allowances:				
Married	3,655			
WEIR	2,335			
			5,990	
Taxable			170	

Thus by utilising the WEIR further losses are available for future relief.

It is vitally important to appreciate that the claim is against the whole of the lossmaker's earned and unearned income and then (if appropriate) the spouse's earned and unearned income. In particular it is not possible to claim just enough relief to utilise the whole of the personal allowances.

3.3 SUCCESSIVE LOSSES

Where losses are sustained in successive years, the balance of any loss not relieved under s.168 in the first year will be relieved in the second year in priority to the loss of that second year. This will enable relief for the loss of the second year to qualify for s.168 relief in the subsequent year of assessment.

Illustration

E has the following income:

Trading results - Year ended 31.12.85	-	£ 2,000	profit
31.12.86	-	£(10,000)	loss
31.12.87	-	£ (1,000)	loss
31.12.88	-	£ 5,000	profit

He has investment income of £1,000 per annum.

Loss relief is to be claimed as early as possible.

	£	£
1986/87		
DI - Year to 31.12.85		2,000
Investment income		1,000
		3,000
Loss - Year to 31.12.86	(10,000)	
s.168 relief	3,000	(3,000)
	(7,000)	Nil
1987/88		
DI - Year to 31.12.86		Nil
Investment income		1,000
		1,000
s.168 relief	1,000	(1,000)
		Nil
c/f s.171	(6,000)	
1988/89		
DI - Year to 31.12.87		Nil
Investment income		1,000
		1,000
Loss - Year to 31.12.87	(1,000)	
s.168 relief	1,000	
		(1,000)
		Nil
1989/90		
DI - Year to 31.12.88		5,000
s.171 relief		(5,000)
		Nil
Investment Income		1,000
		1,000

In the year 1987/88 it was possible to claim s.168 relief for both losses:

	1986/87	1987/88	1988/89
Year to 31.12.86	1st year	2nd year	
Year to 31.12.87		1st year	2nd year

Priority has to be given for the second year claim of the 1986 loss.

If, however, the investment income of 1987/88 had been £10,000, relief for both losses would have been available:

1987/88	£	£
DI		Nil
Investment Income		10,000
		10,000
s.168 relief		
Loss - Year to 31.12.86	(7,000)	
Year to 31.12.87	(1,000)	
		(8,000)
		2,000

3.4 THE DEDUCTION OF CHARGES

Charges on income are deducted before giving loss relief. FA 1971,s.34(2) gives the taxpayer almost complete freedom to deduct charges from income in the most beneficial way.

Where mortgage interest is paid under the MIRAS scheme, basic rate tax will already have been deducted before payment. If charges are deducted from income as well, it would be possible to obtain double relief for the interest paid. In this case it will be necessary to account to the Revenue for the excess basic rate tax deducted, on the interest. Where there are unrelieved personal allowances, these may be deducted from the excess interest paid and only basic rate tax on the balance needs to be accounted for to the Revenue.

Illustration

F, a married man, has the following income for 1986/87:

Trading profits - Year ended 31.12.85	£3,000
Dividends	£3,000 gross

He pays mortgage interest under the MIRAS scheme of £1,200 gross - £852 net.

There is a loss of £1,800 for the year ended 31st December 1986.

1986/87	£	£
DI - Year to 31.12.85		3,000
Dividends		3,000
		6,000
Less: Charges		1,200
Loss - Year to 31.12.86	(1,800)	4,800
s.168 relief	1,800	(1,800)
		3,000
Less: Personal Allowances		
MA		3,655
		NIL

	£	£
Charges paid under MIRAS		1,200
Less: Excess PA		655
		545
Account to Revenue for 29% x £545		158
But tax credits repayable on dividends 29% x £3,000		870
Due to Revenue as above		158
Repayment due		712

3.5 THE UTILISATION OF CAPITAL ALLOWANCES AND STOCK RELIEF

(a) Capital Allowances - TA 1970,s.169

TA 1970,s.169 provides that capital allowances can be used to augment a loss or to convert a profit into a loss. The capital allowances used are those relating to the basis period which produced the loss. Thus, if a loss was incurred for the year ended 30th September 1986 it could be augmented by the capital allowances for 1987/88 - based on the assets owned at the end of the year to 30th September 1986.

Illustration

E had alternatively (a) a trading loss of £400 or (b) a trading profit of £400 for the year to 31st December 1987. The capital allowance computation for 1988/89 showed allowances of £1,000.

	(a) £	(b) £
Trading loss - year ended 31.12.1987	400	
Schedule D Case I assessment 1988/89		400
Capital allowances	1,000	1,000
Loss relief available on	(1,400)	(600)

In both cases the first year for loss relief under s.168 will be 1987/88.

Illustration

F is a bachelor. He gives you the following details regarding his trading income; he has no other income.

Year ended 31.12.1984	Profit	£4,000
Year ended 31.12.1985	Loss	£3,000
Year ended 31.12.1986	Profit	£6,000

Capital allowances:

1985/86	£1,900
1986/87	£1,500
1987/88	£1,000

He wishes to claim relief under s.168.

	£	£
1985/86 Year ended 31.12.1984		
Schedule D Case I		4,000
Less: Capital allowances		1,900
c/f		2,100

	£	£
		2,100
Trading loss - year ended 31.12.85	(3,000)	
Add: Capital allowances 1986/87	(1,500)	
	(4,500)	
s.168 relief	2,100	(2,100)
		NIL
Carried forward trading loss	(2,400)	

1986/87		
Year ended 31.12.1985		
Schedule D Case I		NIL
1987/88		
Year ended 31.12.1986		
Schedule D Case I		6,000
Less: Capital allowances 1987/88		1,000
		5,000
Less: s.171 loss brought forward	2,400	(2,400)
		2,600

In certain cases, it may be beneficial to restrict a claim to capital allowances to obtain maximum loss relief.

Illustration

G, a married man, has income in 1986/87 of £8,000. For the year ended 31st December 1986 he makes a trading loss of £4,200. The written down value of plant and machinery at 5th April 1986 was £3,200 and in the year to 31st December 1986 he bought plant costing £6,000 on 28th February 1986.

1986/87	£	£	£	£
Income				8,000
Loss - Year to 31.12.86			(4,200)	
Capital allowances 1987/88				
b/f	3,200			
WDA	800	800		
c/f	2,400			
FYA - 50%		3,000	(3,800)	(8,000)
				-

Personal allowances £3,655 lost.

To ensure no loss of personal allowances, the claim to capital allowances should be restricted to:

1986/87	£	£	£	£
Income				8,000
Loss - Year to 31.12.86			(4,200)	
Capital allowances 1987/88				
b/f		3,200		
WDA		145	(145)	
		3,055		
Plant	6,000			
No FYA to be claimed		6,000		4,345
c/f		9,055		3,655
PA		=====		3,655
				NIL
				=====

(b) Stock Relief FA 1976, Sch.5 para 6

Stock relief could also be used to augment a loss or to convert a profit into a loss. The amount of stock relief which could be so used was that for the basis period which produced the loss, i.e. if a loss were incurred for the year to 31st March 1984 it could be augmented by the stock relief for 1984/85 which is based on the stock relief for the period of account to 31st March 1984.

Illustration

H had a trading loss of £10,000 for the year to 30th November 1984. The stock relief available for 1985/86 amounted to £3,000. He has two alternatives with regard to making a claim under s.168.

(a) he may make a claim restricted to the trading loss of £10,000 or

(b) he may make a claim including stock relief.

	£
Trading loss	10,000
Stock relief	3,000
	13,000
	======

If there are capital allowances available which could be used to augment the loss, a claim to include stock relief in the calculation of the loss may only be made if a claim is also made to include capital allowances. This is to prevent the claimant from seeking to utilise stock relief in priority to capital allowances, since there are restrictions on the carry-forward of utilised stock relief given for periods of account ended on or after 14th November 1980 but no such restrictions on the carry forward of unutilised capital allowances.

Illustration

If, in addition to the stock relief, H had capital allowances of £2,000 for 1985/86, there would be three alternatives to the claim he could make:

(i) the claim could be restricted to the trading loss £10,000

(ii) the amount claimed could be increased by the capital allowances:

	£
Trading loss	10,000
Capital allowances	2,000
	12,000

(iii) the amount claimed could be further increased by the stock relief:

	£	£
Trading loss		10,000
Capital allowances	2,000	
Stock relief	3,000	
		5,000
		15,000

(c) Order of utilising the loss etc.
Where a loss is offset against income it is deemed to be utilised in the following order:

(i) Trading losses

(ii) Capital allowances

(iii) Stock relief.

Illustration
X has traded for many years. He provides you with the following information.

Year to:	Profit (loss)	Capital Allowances	Stock Relief
	£	£	£
31.12.1982	8,000	2,000	1,000
31.12.1983	(6,000)	4,000	2,500
31.12.1984	9,000	4,000	3,500

He has other income of £2,000 per annum; loss relief is to be claimed as soon as possible.

			Loss Analysis		
			Loss	CA	SR
	£	£	£	£	£
1983/84					
DI - Year to 31.12.82		8,000			
Less: CA	2,000				
SR	1,000				
		3,000			
		5,000			
Other income		2,000			
c/f		7,000			

			Loss Analysis		
			Loss	CA	SR
	£	£	£	£	£
b/f		7,000			
Year to 31.12.83					
Loss	6,000		6,000		
CA	4,000			4,000	
SR	2,500				2,500
	(12,500)				
s.168	7,000	(7,000)	(6,000)	(1,000)	
	(5,500)		NIL	3,000	2,500
		NIL			
1984/85					
DI - Year to 31.12.83		NIL			
Other income		2,000			
		2,000			
s.168 relief	2,000	(2,000)		(2,000)	
	(3,500)			1,000	2,500
		NIL			

Where losses etc. are carried forward the order of offset is:

(1) current year capital allowances

(2) current year stock relief

(3) capital allowances brought forward from years of assessment not earlier than the year for which the basis period ended on or after 14th November 1980

(4) new stock relief brought forward using relief for later years before that for earlier years

(5) capital allowances brought forward from years earlier than (3)

(6) old stock relief

(7) trading losses under s.171.

Thus in the above illustration:

			CA	SR
1985/86	£	£	£	£
DI		9,000		
<u>Less</u>: CA	4,000			
SR	3,500			
		7,500		
		1,500		

	£	£	CA £	SR £
b/f		1,500		
Loss b/f	(3,500)		1,000	2,500
s.171 relief	1,500	(1,500)	(1,000)	(500)
c/f	(2,000)		NIL	2,000
		NIL		
Other income		2,000		
		2,000		

Illustration

Accounts are prepared by P to 31st July. At 1st August 1983 the following were being carried forward:

	£
Trading losses	5,000
Unused capital allowances (including £2,000 for the year to 31st July 1983 - the remainder relating to 1978)	4,000
Unused old stock relief	3,000
Unused new stock relief	2,500

A trading profit of £12,000 arose in the year to 31st July 1984, and the capital allowances and stock relief for 1985/86 were £1,500 and £2,000 respectively.

The trading profits chargeable in 1985/86 must be reduced in the following manner:

	£	£
Chargeable profits		12,000
Less: (a) current capital allowances	1,500	
(b) current stock relief	2,000	
(c) capital allowances re year to 31.7.1982	2,000	
(d) new stock relief b/fwd	2,500	
(e) capital allowances - earlier years	2,000	
(f) old stock relief	2,000	
		12,000
		NIL

Unused reliefs at 31st July 1984 comprise:

	£
Old stock relief	1,000
Trading losses	5,000

The order of setoff is important as the carry forward of new scheme stock relief is restricted to six years. Stock relief given for periods of account ended before 14th November 1980 can be carried forward indefinitely.

3.6 RESTRICTIONS ON CLAIMING RELIEF

Relief under s.168 will not be given where:

(a) the trade, profession or vocation was not being carried on on a commercial basis and with a view to the realisation of profit - TA 1970,s.170;

(b) in the case of farmers and market gardeners, if in the five preceding years of assessment, trading losses were incurred. Section 168 relief may however be given in the sixth year, if the Revenue are satisfied that the farming etc. activities in that year are being carried on in a way which might reasonably be expected to produce profits in the future - TA 1970,s.180.

Relief for the loss will therefore be restricted to a carry-forward under s.171.

3.7 SECTION 168 RELIEF - THE STRICT BASIS

Up to this stage, the method of allocating losses for relief under s.168 has been on the concessional basis. This is commonly used as a simple effective way of allocating the loss. In strictness however the loss available for relief should be calculated by splitting the taxpayer's results to obtain the actual loss of the actual fiscal year - TA 1970,s.127. This will often involve the amalgamation of profits and losses.

Illustration

L made up accounts to 30th June annually; his results were:

Year ended 30th June 1984	Profit	£6,000
Year ended 30th June 1985	Profit	£5,000
Year ended 30th June 1986	Loss	£8,000
Year ended 30th June 1987	Profit	£2,000

The amount available for s.168 relief in the fiscal year 1985/86 will be:

			£	
6.4.1985 -	30.6.1985 -	3/12 x £5,000	1,250	P
1.7.1985 -	5.4.1986 -	9/12 x £8,000	(6,000)	L
			(4,750)	

This is then available for relief against the assessment for 1985/86

	£
1985/86 Schedule D Case I - Year to 30.6.84	6,000
s.168 relief	(4,750)
	1,250

For the year 1986/87 the amount available for relief will be:

			£	
6.4.1986 -	30.6.1986 -	3/12 x £8,000	(2,000)	L
1.7.1986 -	5.4.1987 -	3/12 x £2,000	1,500	P
			(500)	

This can then be relieved:

	£
1986/87 Schedule D Case I - Year to 30.6.85	5,000
s.168 relief	(500)
	4,500

It is important to appreciate that the amalgamation of profits and losses to find the net losses of the various fiscal years is a memorandum calculation only and does not mean that part of the loss is unrelieved. To the extent that loss relief is not available under s.168 it will be available under s.171. Thus:

	£	£
Loss - Year ended 30.6.86		(8,000)
Available - s.168 1985/86	4,750	
1986/87	500	
		5,250
Available for carry forward - s.171		(2,750)

The strict basis will be applied:

(a) in the commencing three fiscal years of the business (and following years until a profit is made);

(b) in the ultimate year;

(c) when the taxpayer wishes to use it. This will normally be so where the taxpayer wishes to relieve the loss in an earlier fiscal year than would be available under the concessionary basis.

4.0 RELIEF FOR TAXED PAYMENTS (TA 1970, s.173)

When a taxpayer pays a charge under deduction of tax which is made wholly and exclusively for the purposes of a trade and, because of an insufficiency of income, becomes liable to an assessment under s.53, the amount of that assessment can be carried forward under s.173 and relieved against future trading profits in subsequent years.

Illustration

G advises you of the following results:

	£
Trading results	
Year to 31.12.1985	400
Year to 31.12.1986	200
Schedule A income assessable 1986/87 and 1987/88	300

She pays patent royalties under deduction of tax of £1,000 (gross) for the fiscal year 1986/87.

		£	
1986/87			
Schedule D Case I		400	
Schedule A		300	
s.53 assessment (Note 1)		300	c/f s.173 £300
	c/f	1,000	

		£	
	b/f	1,000	
Less: Patent royalties		(1,000)	
Total income		-	

1987/88		
Schedule D Case I	200	
s.173 relief	200	c/f s.173 £100
	-	
Schedule A	300	
Total income	300	

Note 1 - As the patent royalties exceed income liable to tax by £300 (£400 + £300 - £1,000) the s.53 assessment will be in the sum of £300.

5.0 LOSSES ON A COMMENCEMENT

5.1 A LOSS IN THE FIRST ACCOUNTING PERIOD FOLLOWED BY A PROFIT IN THE SECOND - THE RULE IN IRC v. SCOTT-ADAMSON (1932)

When this situation occurs and the first accounting period is less than twelve months, it will be necessary to amalgamate together profits and losses to find the assessments. When the profits exceed the losses the net profit will be assessed. When the losses exceed the profits the assessment will be nil. Each time that the loss is amalgamated with a profit, that part of the loss is deemed to have been used.

Illustration

M commenced trading on 1st January 1986 and makes up accounts to 30th September annually. His results adjusted for tax purposes were:

				£	£
9 months to	30.9.1986	£1,800	Loss		
Year ended	30.9.1987	£2,000	Profit		
1985/86	1.1.1986 - 5.4.1986 :	3/9 x £1,800	Loss		NIL
1986/87	1.1.1986 - 31.12.1986:				
	1.1.1986 - 30.9.1986		Loss	(1,800)	
	1.10.1986- 31.12.1986 Profit 3/12 x £2,000			500	NIL
1987/88	1.1.1986 - 31.12.1986 : as before				
	1.1.1986 - 30.9.1986		Loss	(1,800)	
	1.10.1986- 31.12.1986 Profit 3/12 x £2,000			500	NIL
1988/89	Year to 30.9.1987			2,000	
	Less: Loss b/f not yet utilised £(1,800 - 500 - 500)			(800)	
					1,200

5.2 A PROFIT IN THE FIRST ACCOUNTING PERIOD FOLLOWED BY A LOSS IN THE SECOND

In this case it will again be necessary to amalgamate profits and losses if the first accounting period is less than twelve months. The difference between this and the **Scott-Adamson** principle is that, provided that the loss used in aggregation is that of the same period of time, then no matter how many times it is aggregated with a profit to find an assessment, it is only treated as having been used once.

Illustration

N commenced to trade on 1st January 1985, adjusted results are:

9 months to 30.9.1985	Profit	£2,400
12 months to 30 9.1986	Loss	£1,800
12 months to 30.9.1987	Profit	£1,600

		£		£
1984/85				
1.1.1985 - 5.4.1985			Profit	800
				=====
1985/86				
1.1.1985 - 31.12.1985				
1.1.1985 - 30.9.1985	Profit	2,400		
1.10.1985 - 31.12.1985				
Loss 3/12 x £1,800		(450)		
		______		1,950
				=====
1986/87				
1.1.1985 - 31.12.1985				
1.1.1985 - 30.9.1985	Profit	2,400		
1.10.1985 - 31.12.1985				
Loss 3/12 x £1,800		(450)		
		______		1,950
				=====
1987/88				
12 months to 30.9.1986				NIL
				=====
1988/89				
12 months to 30.9.1987	Profit	1,600		
Loss brought forward		(1,350)		
		______		250
				=====

The loss for the year to 30th September 1986 is divided into two periods:

1.10.1985 - 31.12.1985	- 3/12 x £1,800	=	£ 450
1.1.1986 - 30.9.1986	- 9/12 x £1,800	=	£1,350

The period 1st January 1986 - 30th September 1986 has not been used in aggregation and can therefore be carried forward intact. The fact that the period 1st October 1985 to 31st December 1985 has been used twice is immaterial.

As an alternative to the normal basis of assessment, treatment under s.117 may be claimed.

		£	£	
1984/85				
as before			800	Profit
				======
1985/86				
6.4.1985 - 30.9.1985				
6/9 x £2,400	Profit	1,600		
1.10.1985 - 5.4.1986				
6/12 x £1,800	Loss	(900)	700	Profit
				======
1986/87				
6.4.1986 - 30.9.1986				
6/12 x £1,800	Loss	(900)		
1.10.1986 - 5.4.1987				
6/12 x £1,600	Profit	800		NIL
				======
1987/88				
Year to 30.9.1986				NIL
				======
1988/89				
Year to 30.9.1987		1,600		
Loss not used in aggregation b/f £(1,800 - 900 - 800)		(100)		
				1,500
				======

The comparative position will therefore be:

	Normal basis s.116	s.117
	£	£
1984/85	800	800
1985/86	1,950	700
1986/87	1,950	-
1987/88	-	-
1988/89	250	1,500
	4,950	3,000
	=====	=====

So far the loss has been relieved in aggregation i.e. in finding the assessment, with any unused loss being carried forward under s.171 for offset against future trading profits. The taxpayer, if he wishes may also claim relief under TA 1970, s.168 or under FA 1978,s.30 for the loss. In both cases, the amount that will qualify for relief will be calculated on the strict basis. Where a claim has been made in this way then the amount of loss used will reduce the loss available for aggregation in later fiscal years.

Illustration

The results of M are:

9 months to 30.9.1986	£1,800	Loss
12 months to 30.9.1987	£2,000	Profit

M claims relief under s.168; he has abundant other income.

				£	£
1985/86	1.1.1986 - 5.4.1986				
	3/9 x £1,800 = £(600) available				
	on a strict basis for s.168 relief				NIL
					=====
	(£600 used against other income).				
1986/87	1.1.1986 - 31.12.1986:				
	1.1.1986 - 30.9.1986		Loss	(1,800)	
	Less: relieved under s.168			600	
				(1,200)	
	1.10.1986 - 31.12.1986				
	3/12 x £2,000			500	
					NIL
					=====
	s.168 claim on strict basis:				
	6.4.1986 - 5.4.1987				
	6.4.1986 - 30.9.1986				
	6/9 x £1,800		Loss	(1,200)	
	1.10.1986 - 5.4.1987				
	6/12 x £2,000		Profit	1,000	
	s.168 claim			(200)	
				=====	
1987/88	As before				
	1.1.1986 - 31.12.1986:				
	1.1.1986 - 30.9.1986		Loss	(1,200)	
	1.10.1986 - 31.12.1986				
	3/12 x £2,000			500	
					NIL
					=====
	No s.168 relief available				
	Loss carried forward			1,800	
	Less: 1985/86 s.168	600			
	1986/87 aggregation	500			
	1986/87 s.168	200			
	1987/88 aggregation	500			
				1,800	
				NIL	
				=====	
1988/89	Year ended 30.9.1987				2,000
					2,000
					=====

In this last example, the amount of loss and the relief obtained were identical. It may be possible to obtain more relief than the amount of loss.

Illustration

N commenced to trade on 1st May 1985 and made up accounts as follows:

8 months to 31.12.1985	£(2,000)	Loss
Year to 31.12.1986	£ 3,600	

		£	£
1985/86			
1.5.1985 to 5.4.1986			
8 months to 31.12.1985		(2,000)	
3 months to 5.4.1986			
3/12 x £3,600		900	
			NIL
1986/87			
1.5.1985 to 30.4.1986			
8 months to 31.12.1985		(2,000)	
4 months to 30.4.1986			
4/12 x £3,000		1,200	
			NIL
1987/88			
Year to 31.12.1986			3,600
Loss c/f		(2,000)	
Less: Used in aggregation:			
1985/86	900		
1986/87	1,200		
		2,100	
			NIL
			3,600

The amount of loss claimed under s.168 can be augmented by capital allowances and stock relief.

It can be seen that problems in aggregation have been caused by a combination of profits and losses and a first accounting period of less than twelve months in duration. It follows that there will be no difficulties:

(a) if the first accounting period is twelve months or more in length; or

(b) if both the first and second accounting periods produce losses.

6.0 FURTHER RELIEF FOR LOSSES IN EARLY YEARS OF TRADE (FA 1978,s.30)

From the year 1978-79 onwards, an individual who incurs a loss in his trade, profession or vocation in the year of assessment in which the trade etc. commenced or in any of the three succeeding years of assessment, may claim to carry the loss backwards to set against his income for the three years of assessment prior to that in which the loss was incurred. The set off is on a FIFO basis, i.e. relieving the earliest year first.

Any relief available under s.168 or s.171 remains available, relief under s.30 being an alternative. It is not possible to have relief for the same loss more than once. The claim for relief under s.30 must be made within two years of the end of the year of assessment in which the loss arose. For a claim to be valid the trade must have been conducted on a commercial basis and with a reasonable expectation of profit.

To prevent loss relief being manufactured by transferring trades between spouses, it is provided that no relief can be given for any loss incurred later than the third year of assessment following that in which the first spouse started to trade.

As mentioned above s.30 is an alternative claim to s.168 or s.171. The taxpayer can claim whichever relief he wishes and if the loss exceeds relief under a given loss-relieving section, then the remainder is available for relief under another; partial claims however cannot be made - **Butt v. Haxby (1983).**

Illustration

P, who was an employee of a company manufacturing breakfast cereals, resigned on 31st May 1987, to become a freelance cornflake salesman. His income has been as follows:

		£
Salary	1984/85	6,000
	1985/86	7,000
	1986/87	7,500
	2 months to 31.5.87	1,000
Adjusted Schedule D Case I Loss		
	Year to 31.5.88	6,000
	Year to 31.5.89	12,000

Assessment - normal basis

1987/88	1.6.87 - 5.4.88	NIL ===
1988/89	1.6.87 - 31.5.88	NIL ===
1989/90	Year to 31.5.88	NIL ===
1990/91	Year to 31.5.89	NIL ===

Loss available for relief calculated on the strict basis:

		£
1987/88	1.6.87 - 5.4.88	
	10/12 x £(6,000)	(5,000) =====
1988/89	6.4.88 - 5.4.89	
	2/12 x £(6,000)	(1,000)
	10/12 x £(12,000)	(10,000)
		(11,000) ======

There will presumably be no advantage in claiming s.168 relief in 1987/88 as personal allowances will cover the other income.

Assuming s.30 relief is claimed the position will become:

	Income	s.30 Relief 1987/88	s.30 Relief 1988/89	Taxable
	£	£	£	£
1984/85	6,000	5,000	-	1,000
1985/86	7,000	-	7,000	-
1986/87	7,500	-	4,000	3,500
1987/88	1,000	-	-	1,000
		5,000 =====	11,000 =====	

As with relief under s.168 it is possible to augment or create losses by deduction of capital allowances.

7.0 THE CARRY FORWARD OF A LOSS WHERE A BUSINESS IS TRANSFERRED TO A LIMITED COMPANY (TA 1970,s.172)

When a sole trader or partnership transfers a business to a limited company there will be a cessation. However, provided:

(a) the business was transferred mainly for shares in the company, and

(b) the business transferred continue to be carried on by the company,

any trading losses unrelieved may be carried forward and offset against income received from the company during any fiscal year throughout which the shares continue to be held by the individual. The losses are offset in the following order:

(a) against earned income i.e. directors' salaries and fees, then

(b) against other income received from the company such as dividends.

Revenue practice is to give relief when at least 80% of the shares are held by the claimant.

Relief is expressed to be in accordance with s.171 which will mean offset against the first available income received from the company. Relief must be claimed within six years of the end of the relevant year of assessment.

Illustration

K decides to incorporate her business on 31st March 1986 and transfers her business on that day to K Ltd. At the time of transfer there were unrelieved losses of £2,400. Income received from the company in the year 1986-87 consisted of:

Director's fees	1,800	
Dividends (net)	710	
Relief will be given as under:	£	£
1986/87		
Schedule E - Director's fees	1,800	
s.172 relief	(1,800)	
		-
Dividends received	710	
Tax credit 29/71	290	
	1,000	
s.172 relief - balance	(600)	
		400
		400

8.0 TERMINAL LOSSES (TA 1970,s.174)

8.1 GENERAL

On the permanent discontinuance of any trade, profession or vocation, any loss incurred in the twelve months preceding discontinuance may (so far as it is unrelieved) be carried back and offset against adjusted trading profits of the three preceding years of assessment on a LIFO basis. It is not necessary to take terminal loss relief if another form of relief can be claimed such as s.168. If part is claimed under s.168, the balance can be dealt with in a terminal loss claim.

8.2 CALCULATION OF TERMINAL LOSS

A terminal loss normally consists of four main elements:

(a) the loss arising in the last fiscal year;

(b) the capital allowances of the last fiscal year, if any;

(c) the balance of the loss (if any) arising in the remainder of the twelve months preceding discontinuance;

(d) the lower of:

 (i) a proportion of the capital allowances of the fiscal year preceding discontinuance, or

 (ii) the amount of the capital allowances for that year unrelieved.

In finding items (a) and (c) it may be necessary to amalgamate profits and losses. If the net result is a profit then it is included as 'Nil'; it does not reduce the loss claim.

<u>Illustration</u>
H made up accounts to 31st December each year until 31st December 1987, when he ceased to trade. His adjusted results and capital allowances were:

Years ended:		£
31.12.1983	Profit	1,900
31.12.1984	Profit	1,200
31.12.1985	Profit	600
31.12.1986	Profit	400
31.12.1987	Loss	1,800

Capital allowances:

1984/85	£100;	1985/86	£300;
1986/87	£200;	1987/88	£600.

In this case, there will be no revision to actual by the Revenue as profits are on a declining trend.

<u>Calculation of Terminal Loss:</u>		£
(a)	The loss of the last fiscal year 1987/88: 6.4.1987 - 31.12.1987	
	9/12 x £1,800	1,350
(b)	Capital allowances of the last fiscal year - 1987/88	600
(c)	The balance of the loss arising in the remainder of the 12 months preceding discontinuance - 1.1.1987 - 5.4.1987	
	3/12 x £1,800	450
	c/f	2,400

		£
	b/f	2,400
(d) The lower of:		
(i) a proportion of the previous year's capital allowances: 1.1.1987 - 5.4.1987 = 3/12 x £200 =	£50	
	===	
(ii) capital allowances unrelieved	£Nil	
	===	
(all offset against 1986/87 assessment)		Nil
		2,400

<u>Loss relieved</u>:

	1984/85	1985/86	1986/87
	£	£	£
DI	1,900	1,200	600
<u>Less</u>: Capital Allowances	100	300	200
	1,800	900	400
Terminal Loss Relief	1,100 (3)	900 (2)	400 (1)
	700	NIL	NIL
	=====	=====	===

A repayment of tax will occur where the tax due on the revised assessment differs from that originally.

If instead of H's last accounting period being to 31st December 1987 it was to 30th September 1987, the calculation of the terminal loss would be as under:

		£	£
(a)	Loss 6.4.1987 - 30.9.1987		
	6/9 x £1,800		1,200
(b)	Capital allowances 1987/88		600
(c)	Balance of loss 1.10.1986 - 5.4.1987		
	3/12 x £400	100 P	
	3/9 x £1,800	600 L	
			500
(d)	Capital allowances 1986/87		Nil
			2,300
			=====

In (c) profits and losses are aggregated to give a smaller loss. Had the figures been reversed i.e. 100 L
600 P
the amount included in the computation would have been NIL.

8.3 THE INCLUSION OF s.53 ASSESSMENTS

Where there are s.53 assessments in respect of trade charges which cannot be relieved because of the cessation of trade, they may, to the extent that they are paid in the year of assessment falling into the last twelve months trading, be included in the terminal loss computation. Thus two additional elements may appear in the terminal loss computation:

(a) the s.53 assessment on unrelieved retainable trade charges of the ultimate fiscal year

(b) a proportion of any similar assessment of the penultimate fiscal year.

Illustration

J ceased trading on 30th June 1986 having previously made up accounts to 31st December. His trading results, adjusted for tax purposes, were:

Year ended 31.12.1982	Profit	£3,600
Year ended 31.12.1983	Profit	£2,400
Year ended 31.12.1984	Profit	£ 600
Year ended 31.12.1985	Loss	£ 720
1.1.1986 to 30.6.1986	Loss	£3,000

Capital allowances:

1983/84	£1,000
1984/85	£ 400
1985/86	£ 350
1986/87	£ 700

J paid £400 (gross) per annum under deed of covenant to a trade association on 1st May each year. He has no other income; s.168 relief is not claimed.

Calculation of Terminal Loss:		£	£
(a)	1986/87 - loss 6.4.1986 - 30.6.1986		
	3/6 x £3,000		1,500
(b)	1986/87 - Capital allowances		700
(c)	1986/87 - s.53 assessment Covenant paid 1.5.1986		400
(d)	1985/86 - loss 1.7.1985 - 5.4.1986		
	6/12 x £720	360	
	3/6 x £3,000	1,500	
			1,860
(e)	1985/86 - Capital allowances lower of 9/12 x 350	262	
	or		
	unrelieved allowances of 1985/86	NIL	NIL
(f)	1985/86 - Proportion of s.53		
	Assessment:		
	Schedule D Case I	600	
	Less: Capital allowances	350	
	c/f	250	4,460

		£	£
	b/f	250	4,460
s.53 Assessment		150	
		400	
Less: Charge		400	
		-	
9/12 x £150			112
			4,572

When the terminal loss is carried back for relief the charges must be deducted in priority to terminal loss relief.

	1983/84	1984/85	1985/86
	£	£	£
Schedule DI	3,600	2,400	600
Capital Allowances	1,000	400	350
	2,600	2,000	250
Trade charges	400	400	400
	2,200	1,600	NIL
Terminal Loss Relief	(2,200)(2)	(1,600) (1)	
	NIL	NIL	

The balance of the terminal loss relief will be lost.

As already mentioned, it is possible to claim s.168 relief instead of terminal loss relief if the taxpayer wishes. If in 1986/87 J had other income of £1,000 he could claim s.168 relief against that income. The amount of the loss to be included in the terminal loss computation would then be:

		£
Loss	1986/87	(1,500)
Less:	Relieved s.168	1,000
		(500)

If there are non-trade charges in the carry back period, they will reduce the amount of the terminal loss to be carried back into an earlier period. If it is possible both trade and non-trade charges may be offset against other income rather then trading income (FA 1971,s.34(2)). This will increase the trading income available to cover terminal loss relief.

Illustration

P has a terminal loss of £(20,000). It can be carried back into the fiscal years 1984/85, 1985/86 and 1986/87. Details for those years are as under:

Assessable trading profits:

1984/85	£14,000
1985/86	£ 6,000
1986/87	£ 3,000

Other income:

1984/85	£ 2,000
1985/86	£ 520

Patent royalties and deeds of covenant to charity of £500 and £30 respectively are paid annually:

	1984/85	1985/86	1986/87
	£	£	£
Schedule DI	14,000	6,000	3,000
Less: charges	-	10	530
	14,000	5,990	2,470
Terminal loss relief	(11,510)	(5,990)	(2,470)
	2,490	NIL	NIL
Other income	2,000	520	
Less: charges	530	520	
	1,470	NIL	
TOTAL INCOME	3,960	NIL	NIL
Terminal loss			(20,000)
Less: Relieved			2,470
			(17,530)
Less: Reduction for non-trade charges deducted			30
Relieved	(11,510)	(5,990)	(17,500)

Note: In 1985/86 the non-trade charges have been deducted from the unearned income first to prevent any restrictions of the terminal loss available for carry back into 1984/85.

9.0 RELIEF FOR LOSSES ON SHARES IN UNQUOTED TRADING COMPANIES

FA 1980,s.37 provides that where a person subscribes for shares in an unquoted trading company and makes a capital loss on a disposal at arm's length it is possible to offset that loss against income.

The loss is calculated as for CGT purposes and may be offset against income in:

(a) the fiscal year in which disposal takes place; and

(b) the next fiscal year.

The order of offset is as for s.168; however, s.37 takes priority over s.168.
A qualifying trading company is an unquoted company which:

(a) is a trading company at disposal or which ceased to be such a company not more than three years before such a disposal;

(b) is resident in the UK;

(c) has traded for at least six years prior to the date of disposal, subject to certain conditions.

Companies which trade in stocks and shares, land or commodity futures or has not traded with a reasonable expectation of profits are not eligible for relief. The disposal must be at arm's length or by way of a distribution in a winding up or by a deemed disposal under CGTA 1979,s.22.

If the subscriber for shares is an investment company, then it may offset the loss against the other income in the same way as a loss under s.177(2).

If relief cannot be claimed under s.37, then normal CGT relief is available.

7 Partnerships

1.0 DEFINITION

Partnership is the relationship which subsists between two or more persons carrying on business in common with a view to profits. To be taxable a partnership must exist in fact, the existence of a partnership agreement will not be conclusive if the facts clearly show that the partnership is non-operative in practice. In **IRC v. Williamson (1928)** Lord President Clyde said:

> "...you do not constitute or create or prove a partnership by saying that there is one".

In **Fenstone v. Johnson (1940)** the taxpayer wished to acquire some property but lacked the necessary finance. He agreed with another person that the other would provide finance and assist in the development. The agreement stated that there was to be no partnership and described the other's share as a fee. Held there was a partnership.

A partnership agreement is not effective for tax purposes prior to the date of execution unless a partnership de facto existed prior to that date.

In **Waddington v. O'Callaghan (1931)** W, a solicitor, told his son on 31st December 1928 that he intended taking him into partnership as from that date. On 11th May 1929 the agreement was executed expressing to have effect from 1st January 1929. Held that the facts showed that no partnership was contemplated until the deed was executed.

2.0 ASSESSMENT

Although the partnership is assessed in the partnership name, the liability to tax of the partners is joint **(Harrison v. Willis Bros (1966))**. Thus if one partner is unable to pay the tax on his apportioned share of the profits, the Revenue can proceed against the other partners. The precedent acting partner is responsible for returning to the Inland Revenue the total profits of the partnership and each individual partner must return his share on his own tax return.

3.0 THE APPORTIONMENT OF THE ASSESSMENT

As already mentioned the business is the unit of assessment and it is therefore the adjusted profits of the partnership that will need to be apportioned between the partners. Like any trader the profits available for division can take one of three main forms:

(a) interest on capital;

(b) salaries;

(c) residual profits.

The first two items will have already been added back in arriving at the adjusted profit. The basic rule for the allocation of profits between the partners is that they will be divided between them in accordance with the profit sharing arrangements of the fiscal year for which the accounting period forms the basis period. Thus the adjusted profits of the year ended 31st December 1985 will be divided between the partners in accordance with the profit sharing arrangements of the period 6th April 1986 to 5th April 1987 - the fiscal year for which those profits are assessed. As can be appreciated, a change in the profit sharing arrangements can mean a different allocation of profits for accounts purposes than that applying for tax. When this occurs one partner will compensate the other for any increase or reduction in his liability.

Illustration

A, B and C are in partnership sharing profits equally; as from 6th April 1986 they decide to share profits 3:2:1.

The adjusted profits for the year to 31st December 1985 are £9,000.

For tax purposes the profit of £9,000 will be divided between the partners in accordance with the profit sharing arrangements of the fiscal year for which it will be assessed i.e. 1986/87.

	Total	A	B	C
1986/87	£	£	£	£
Profits	9,000	4,500	3,000	1,500
	=====	=====	=====	=====

Assuming a basic rate of tax of 29% and no personal allowances the appropriate adjustment between partners would be:

	A	B	C
	£	£	£
Per accounts	3,000	3,000	3,000
For taxation	4,500	3,000	1,500
	(1,500)	-	1,500
	=====	=====	=====
@ 29%	(435)		435
	===		===
In current accounts	Cr		Dr

Where it is necessary to apportion the adjusted profits, a strict time basis is applied.

Illustration

The facts are as in the above Illustration except that the partners changed their profit sharing arrangements on 30th June 1986.

1986/87	Total £	A £	B £	C £
6.4.86-30.6.86				
3/12 x £9,000	2,250	750	750	750
1.7.86-5.4.87				
9/12 x £9,000	6,750	3,375	2,250	1,125
	9,000	4,125	3,000	1,875

Where the partners receive interest on capital and salaries, these receive priority in the apportionment of the profits.

Illustration

A and B had the following annual profit sharing arrangements up to 30th September 1987:

	Salaries £	Interest on Capital £
A	1,000	500
B	500	400

Until this date they shared residual profits and losses equally. From 1st October 1987 they divided profits as under:

	Salaries £	Interest on Capital £
A	2,000	300
B	1,000	300

As from this date, residual profits are to be shared 2:1. The adjusted profits for the year to 30th June 1986 were £6,000.

		Total £	A £	B £
1987/88				
6.4.87-30.9.87				
6/12 x £6,000	= £3,000			
Salaries		750	500	250
Interest		450	250	200
Balance		1,800	900	900
		3,000	1,650	1,350
1.10.87-5.4.88				
6/12 x £6,000	= £3,000			
Salaries		1,500	1,000	500
Interest		300	150	150
Balance		1,200	800	400
		3,000	1,950	1,050
TOTAL		6,000	3,600	2,400

Where salaries and interest on capital exceed the adjusted profits, they are nevertheless given in full, even though this will have the effect of creating a negative balance. This negative balance is divided between the partners in the same way as a positive balance would have been.

Illustration

A, B and C have the following profit sharing arrangements:

	Salaries	Interest on Capital	Balance
	£	£	
A	2,000	500	3
B	2,000	300	2
C	1,000	200	1

The adjusted profit for the year ended 30th June 1986 was £4,500.

	Total	A	B	C
	£	£	£	£
1987/88				
Salaries	5,000	2,000	2,000	1,000
Interest	1,000	500	300	200
	6,000	2,500	2,300	1,200
Balance	(1,500)	(750)	(500)	(250)
	4,500	1,750	1,800	950

Although the profits may be said to consist of salary, interest on capital etc., they are all assessed under Schedule D Case I or II. There is no assessment of the salary under Schedule E or the interest under Schedule D Case III.

In certain cases the allocation of a negative balance to one partner may result in his share of profit being turned into a loss. The Inland Revenue will not allow one partner loss relief when the overall result of the partnership is a profit. The notional loss must be apportioned to the remaining partners in proportion to their respective shares of profit as determined before making any adjustment for the loss.

Illustration

X, Y and Z have the following profit sharing arrangements:

	Salaries	Balance
	£	
X	2,000	3
Y	2,000	2
Z	500	3

The adjusted profit for the year ended 30th April 1986 was £2,500.

	Total	X	Y	Z
	£	£	£	£
1987/88				
Salaries	4,500	2,000	2,000	500
Balance	(2,000)	(750)	(500)	(750)
	2,500	1,250	1,500	(250)
Z's "loss" divided £1,250:£1,500		(114)	(136)	250
	2,500	1,136	1,364	-

A similar procedure would apply when one partner has a profit and the others losses.
Where a partner is entitled to a guaranteed share of profits, any deficiency in his allocation of profits will be given to him and divided between the remaining partners in the proportion in which they share the residual profits.

Illustration
A, B and C share profits 3, 2 and 1 after salaries of £3,000, £2,000 and £2,000 respectively. As from 1st January 1987, C is to have a minimum share of partnership income of £4,000. The adjusted profits for the year ended 31st December 1986 are £10,000.

	Total	A	B	C
	£	£	£	£
1987/88				
Salaries	7,000	3,000	2,000	2,000
Balance	3,000	1,500	1,000	500
	10,000	4,500	3,000	2,500
Adjustment to bring C up to minimum share dividend 3:2		(900)	(600)	1,500
	10,000	3,600	2,400	4,000

It will be noted that the new arrangement covers the fiscal year 1987/88, and therefore C will be assessed on his share of profits under the new arrangements. For accounts purposes however there was no guaranteed share for the year ended 31st December 1986.

4.0 CAPITAL ALLOWANCES

When capital allowances are due to the partnership, they will be deducted from the assessment before division between the partners. Where a partner has capital allowances due to him personally - for example, for the business use of his private car - they are deducted from his individual share of profits.

5.0 PERSONAL ALLOWANCES

Once the partnership assessment has been divided between the partners, each partner may deduct from his share the personal allowances etc. to which he is entitled. If one partner has an excess of personal allowances they may not be transferred to another partner.

Illustration
A and B are trading in partnership as nurserymen sharing profits and losses in the ratio of 2:1 after charging B a salary of £6,000. For the year ended 31st December 1985 the partnership had an adjusted profit of £42,000.
Neither partner has any other income and their entitlements to personal allowances are as follows:

A - Married
B - Unmarried, supporting his widowed mother who has no income apart from her state retirement pension. In 1986/87 he paid a mortgage interest of £900 gross. MIRAS does not apply.

	£	Total £	£	A £	£	B £
1986/87 Year to 31.12.85						
Salary		6,000				6,000
Balance		36,000		24,000		12,000
		42,000		24,000		18,000
Charges		900				900
		41,100				
						17,100
Personal allowances						
MA	3,655		3,655			
SA	2,335				2,335	
DRR	100	6,090		3,655	100	2,435
		35,010		20,345		14,665

Tax						
	31,865 @ 29%	9,241	17,200 @ 29%	4,988	14,665 @ 29%	4,253
	3,000 @ 40%	1,200	3,000 @ 40%	1,200		
	145 @ 45%	65	145 @ 45%	65		
		10,506		6,253		4,253

6.0 PARTNERSHIP CHARGES

Where a partnership pay annual charges, such charges are divided between the partners on the same basis as they agree to share residual profits. For tax purposes the charges are taken into account in the fiscal year in which they are paid and the basis for division is the profit sharing arrangement of that fiscal year.

Illustration

A and B are in partnership sharing profits and losses equally to 31st December 1986 and thereafter 2:1. Their profit and loss account for the year ended 31st December 1986 was as under:

	£	£		£
Office expenses		6,000	Trading profit	12,000
Annuity to wife of retired partner		600		
Balance: A	2,700			
B	2,700	5,400		
		12,000		12,000

The annuity was an amount of £100 per month and commenced on 1st July 1986.

	£
Adjusted profit:	5,400
Per accounts	600
Add: annuity	6,000

Divided:	Total	A	B
1987/88	£	£	£
Profit	6,000	4,000	2,000
Less: Charges 1987/88	1,200	800	400
	4,800	3,200	1,600

7.0 CHANGES IN THE PARTNERSHIP

7.1 ASSESSMENTS

Whenever there is a change in the partnership, either by one partner being admitted or another leaving, retiring or dying, there is a deemed cessation and recommencement for tax purposes even though there is no physical break in the trade. As a result it is necessary to treat the old partnership as having ceased on the date of the change and a new partnership as having immediately commenced (TA 1970, s.154(1)). This will necessitate the application of the cessation and commencement provisions of the Taxes Act.

Illustration

X and Y make up accounts to 31st December annually. On 1st October 1985 Z was admitted as a partner. The adjusted profits of the firm were:

	£
31st December 1982	8,000
31st December 1983	10,000
31st December 1984	12,000
31st December 1985	9,000
31st December 1986	11,000
31st December 1987	14,000
31st December 1988	16,000
31st December 1989	20,000
31st December 1990	15,000

The old partnership is deemed to have ceased on 30th September 1985 and a new partnership commenced on 1st October 1985.

Old Partnership (X and Y)

1985/86

6.4.85-30.9.85

6/12 x £9,000 £4,500

1984/85

P.Y. (year to 31.12.1983) £10,000

£18,000

1983/84

P.Y. (year to 31.12.1982) £8,000

Revised s.118

		£		
1984/85				
9/12 x £12,000	=	9,000		
3/12 x £ 9,000	=	2,250	£11,250	
				£21,750
1983/84				
9/12 x £10,000	=	7,500		
3/12 x £12,000	-	3,000	£10,500	

FA 1985 introduced amendments to the legislation dealing with partnership changes whenever there is an admission or retirement of a partner to or from an existing partnership on or after 20th March 1985. Whilst the normal cessation rules will apply to the old partnership, the assessments for the first four fiscal years of the new partnership will be calculated on an actual basis. The assessments for the fifth and sixth years will be on the preceding year basis unless the partnership elects to have those assessed on an actual year basis also. Thereafter the preceding year basis applies.
In the preceding example the assessments on the new partnership would be:

		£	£
1985/86	1.10.85-5.4.86		
	3/12 x £9,000	2,250	
	3/12 x £11,000	2,750	
			5,000
1986/87	6.4.86-5.4.87		
	9/12 x £11,000	8,250	
	3/12 x £14,000	3,500	11,750
1987/88	6.4.87-5.4.88	10,500	
	9/12 x £14,000	4,000	14,500
	3/12 x £16,000		
1988/89	6.4.88-5.4.89	12,000	
	9/12 x £16,000	5,000	17,000
	3/12 x £20,000		
1989/90	Year to 31.12.1988		16,000
1990/91	Year to 31.12.1989		20,000

or actual for 1989/90 and 1990/91 if appropriate.

If the partners wish, they may avoid the s.154(1) treatment of cessation and recommencement by making an election under TA1970, s.154(2). If such an election is made, there is no deemed cessation and the assessments continue on the normal preceding year basis throughout. The conditions for a valid election are:

(a) it must be made in writing to the Inspector of Taxes within two years of the change;

(b) it must be signed by all the partners of both the old and the new firm (if one is dead, his personal representative will sign);

(c) there must be at least one partner common to both old and new partnerships.

An election made may be revoked within the time limit.
A comparison of the assessments will be:

	s.154(1)	s.154(2)
	£	£
1983/84	10,500	8,000
1984/85	11,250	10,000

	4,500	12,000
1985/86	5,000	
1986/87	11,750	9,000
1987/88	14,500	11,000
1988/89	17,000	14,000
1989/90	16,000	16,000
1990/91	20,000	20,000
	110,500	100,000

The basis of assessment for the first six years of the new partnership will not apply where:

(a) a sole trader takes in one or more partners, or

(b) a partnership of not more than two loses a partner.

In these cases the normal rules of cessation and commencement apply. Thus if the above illustration Y had left the partnership rather than Z joining it, the position would be:

1985/86	1.10.85-5.4.86	£	
	3/12 x £ 9,000	2,250	
	3/12 x £11,000	2,750	
			£5,000
1986/87	First 12 months		
	3/12 x £ 9,000	2,250	
	9/12 x £11,000	8,250	
			£10,500
1987/88	PY (year to 31.12.1986)		£11,000

or s.117 if appropriate.

Where there are successive changes in the partnership it is possible that a later change may have an effect on a partner who has left the partnership at an earlier date.

Illustration

X, Y and Z have been in partnership for many year sharing profits one-half, one-third and one-sixth after allowing Z a salary of £1,500. They made their accounts up to 30th November each year and the results, adjusted for tax purposes, of recent years, have been:

		£
Year ended:	30.11.83	6,360
	30.11.84	7,740
	30.11.85	8,400
	30.11.86	7,200
	30.11.87	6,300

X retired on 30th November 1985 and Y and Z continued in business sharing profits equally, without either partner drawing a salary, until 1st December 1986 when M was admitted to the partnership receiving a salary of £1,000 and one-sixth of the profit while Y and Z continued to share the balance equally. On the retirement of X an election was made for continuation, but no such election was made on the admission of M.

Assessment up to X's retirement		Total	X	Y	Z
		£	£	£	£
1984/85 (y/e 30.11.83)					
Salaries		1,500			1,500
Balance (3:2:1)		4,860	2,430	1,620	810
		6,360	2,430	1,620	2,310
		=====	=====	=====	=====
1985/86 (y/e 30.11.84)					
To X's retirement					
6.4.85 to 30.11.85					
8/12 x £7,740 =	£5,160				
	======				
Salary		1,000			1,000
Balance (3:2:1:)		4,160	2,080	1,387	693
		5,160	2,080	1,387	1,693
		=====	=====	=====	=====
Assessment on Y and Z only:					
1985/86 from X's retirement					
1.12.85 to 5.4.86					
4/12 x £7,740		2,580		1,290	1,290
		=====		=====	=====

Because no election was made when M was admitted to the partnership and 1st December 1986 falls in the tax year 1986/87 the partnership will be deemed to be discontinued on that date and the Schedule D Case I assessments then become:

Original Assessment	£	Final Assessment	£
1984/85 y/e 30.11.83	6,360	6.4.84 to 5.4.85	
		8/12 x £7,740 + 4/12 x £8,400	7,960
1985/86 y/e 30.11.84	7,740	6.4.85 to 5.4.86	
		8/12 x £8,400 +4/12 x £7,200	8,000
	14,100		15,960
	======		======

1986/87 6.4.86 to 30.11.86 8/12 x £7,200 £4,800

The Revenue will revise the penultimate and prepenultimate years onto an actual basis.

As a result of the revision of the penultimate and prepenultimate years onto actual it will be necessary to revise the division of assessments for 1984/85 and 1985/86 between the partners and raise additional assessments on all individuals who were partners during those years, including X.

	Total £	X £	Y £	Z £
1984/85				
(6.4.84-5.4.85)				
Salaries	1,500			1,500
Balance (3:2:1)	6,460	3,230	2,154	1,076
	7,960	3,230	2,154	2,576
	=====	=====	=====	=====
1985/86				
(6.4.85-30.11.85)				
8/12 x £8,000				
Salaries	1,000			1,000
Balance (3:2:1:)	4,333	2,167	1,444	722
	5,333	2,167	1,444	1,722
	=====	=====	=====	=====
(1.12.85-5.4.86)				
4/12 x £8,000	2,667	-	1,333	1,334
	=====		=====	=====

7.2 EFFECTS OF A CHANGE IN PARTNERSHIP

(a) <u>Capital Allowances</u>
On a s.154(1) cessation, all assets on which capital allowances have been claimed will be treated as though they were transferred to the new partnership at market value. Alternatively, an election may be made by the successor and predecessor (if they are connected persons) to transfer the assets at tax written-down values.

If a s.154(2) election is made the capital allowances computation continues on the normal basis throughout.

(b) <u>Losses</u>
Where there is a s.154(1) cessation, a retiring partner may claim terminal loss relief, but this is not available to the continuing partners. If there have been losses before the cesssation, then the continuing partners may carry forward their shares of loss against future profits. This will also apply to their shares of unused capital allowances. A new partner may claim s.30 relief in respect of losses in the first four fiscal years. This is not available to continuing partners, or where a continuation election has been made.

8.0 PARTNER'S LOANS TO THE PARTNERSHIP

Interest paid on a loan by a partner to the firm, as distinct from interest paid on capital, is treated as unearned income.

9.0 PARTNERSHIP LOSSES

Where a partnership makes a loss it will be necesary to divide the adjusted loss between the partners. As a partnership is a collection of individuals, each may choose the relief that he requires for his share of the loss. There are two basic methods of apportioning the loss:

(a) <u>Relief under s.168 (normal basis)</u>
The adjusted loss is divided between the partners <u>in accordance with their profit sharing arrangements of the fiscal year in which the accounting period producing the loss ends</u>.

(b) Relief under s.171

The adjusted loss is divided between the partners in accordance with their profit sharing arrangements of the acounting period producing the loss.

The results of (a) and (b) will only differ if the profit sharing between partners alters during the basis periods.

Each partner may claim the loss relief that he requires and the total relief granted to a partner may not be less than is available under s.171.

Illustration

A and B make up accounts to 31st December 1986. Their profit and loss account for that year is as below:

		£	£			£	£
Trade Expenses			6,000	Trading profit			1,000
Salaries:	A	2,000		Loss:	A - 2/3	6,000	
	B	2,000			B - 1/3	3,000	
			4,000				9,000
			10,000				10,000

As from 1st January 1987 they decided to share profits equally, salaries as before. Both claim relief under s.168.

The adjusted loss is:

	£
Loss for the year	(9,000)
Less: Salaries	4,000
	(5,000)

Its apportionment under s.168 would be:

	Total	A	B
6.4.86-31.12.86	£	£	£
9/12 x (5,000) = (£3,750)			
Salaries	3,000	1,500	1,500
Balance	(6,750)	(4,500)	(2,250)
	(3,750)	(3,000)	(750)
1.1.87-5.4.87			
3/12 x (£5,000) = (£1,250)			
Salaries	1,000	500	500
Balance	(2,250)	(1,125)	(1,125)
	(1,250)	(625)	(625)
	5,000	(3,625)	(1,375)

and under s.171 it would be:

Salaries	4,000	2,000	2,000
Balance	(9,000)	(6,000)	(3,000)
	(5,000)	(4,000)	(1,000)

As A cannot get less relief that he would have been entitled to receive under s.171 he will receive loss relief of £4,000 in total. Only £3,625 of this relief however will be available under s.168, the balance will be given under s.171. Thus the total loss relief that could be given is £5,375.

If the s.168 claim is computed on a strict basis, it will still be divided as in (a) but the loss will be that of the tax year (or years) of loss found by aggregating parts of accounting periods.

In the case of B maximum loss relief will be under s.168. If relief is claimed under s.168 of £900 then relief under s.171 will be restricted to £100 - (£1,000 - £900). If relief is claimed under s.168 of £1,200, no further relief will be due as the loss relief claimed under s.168 exceeds the maximum of £1,000 available under s.171.

Illustration

A,B and C are in partnership sharing profits and losses 4:3:3 respectively. Results for recent years have been:

Year ended 30.11.1984	19,500
30.11.1985	(48,000)
30.11.1986	36,000

A retires on 30th November 1985 and D is admitted with a profit share of 40%, the other partners remaining as before. An election is made under s.154(2); loss relief under s.168 is claimed on a strict basis.

	Total	A	B	C	D
1984/85	£	£	£	£	£
6.4.84-30.11.84					
8/12 x £19,500	13,000	5,200	3,900	3,900	
1.12.84-5.4.85					
4/12 x £(48,000)	(16,000)	(6,400)	(4,800)	(4,800)	
	(3,000)	(1,200)	(900)	(900)	
1985/86					
6.4.85-30.11.85					
8/12 x £(48,000)	(32,000)	(12,800)	(9,600)	(9,600)	
1.12.85-5.4.86					
4/12 x £36,000	12,000		3,600	3,600	4,800
	(20,000)	(12,800)	(6,000)	(6,000)	4,800
		2,478	1,161	1,161	(4,800)
Eliminate D					
	(20,000)	(10,322)	(4,839)	(4,839)	NIL

If a partner wishes to augment a trading loss by the addition of stock relief for the purposes of a s.168 claim, all other persons who were partners at any time in the period from the end of the year of loss and the time of making the claim must give written consent.

For chargeable periods beginning after 19th March 1985 any loss allocated to a limited partner will be restricted as far as the offset under s.168 TA 1970 is concerned, for any year of assessment to the amount of the partner's contribution to the partnership trade at the end of that year.

The amount of the partner's contribution is the aggregate of the amount he has contributed as capital and which he has not withdrawn, together with the amount of that partner's share of the profits or gains of the trade, which he has not received in money or money's worth.

10.0 PARTNERSHIP TERMINAL LOSSES

Where there is a cessation or deemed cessation (as in s.154(1)) of a partnership, terminal loss relief is available.

11.0 PARTNERSHIP RETIREMENT ANNUITIES

11.1 GENERAL RULES

Where annual payments are made under the terms of a partnership agreement for the benefit of a former partner, who has retired because of old age or ill-health, or to his widow on his death, they may be treated as earned income in the hands of the recipient. To qualify in full they must not exceed 50% of the average of the former partner's profit share in the best three out of the last seven complete years of assessment in which he was required to devote substantially the whole of his time to the partnership.

Where the annuity exceeds the limit the excess will be treated as unearned income.

For the remaining partners who pay the annuity, relief will be available as a charge on income in their total income computation, thereby reducing their liability to higher rate tax where applicable. It should be noted that the charge will not reduce their income liable to investment income surcharge, except and to the extent that it is treated as unearned income in the hands of the former partner.

FA 1982 provided with retroactive effect that the profit shares used in the computation may be indexed upwards by increases in the Retail Price Index between December in the relevant fiscal year and December in the final year.

Illustration

Chalk and Clease traded together as grocers for many years until Chalk retired on 1st April 1980. Partnership profits, as adjusted for tax purposes, before capital allowances and stock relief have been:

		£
Year to 31st March	1973	5,000
	1974	6,000
	1975	7,000
	1976	4,000
	1977	8,000
	1978	7,000
	1979	9,000
	1980	10,000

Profits had been divided equally until 31st March 1976 whereafter Chalk took 4/10ths and Clease 6/10ths. When Chalk retired no election was made under TA 1970, s.154(2) and so the assessable profits are:

	Assessment	Chalk	Clease
	£	£	£
1973/74	5,000 PY	2,500 (1/2)	2,500 (1/2)
1974/75	6,000 PY	3,000 (1/2)	3,000 (1/2)

1975/76	7,000 PY	3,500 (1/2)	3,500 (1/2)
1976/77	4,000 PY	1,600 (4/10ths)	2,400 (6/10ths)
1977/78	7,000 Actual	2,800 (4/10ths)	4,200 (6/10ths)
1978/79	9,000 Actual	3,600 (4/10ths)	5,400 (6/10ths)
1979/80	10,000 Actual	4,000 (4/10ths)	6,000 (6/10ths)

The RPI for relevant years is:

December 1973	110.7
December 1974	116.9
December 1975	146.0
December 1976	168.0
December 1977	188.4
December 1978	204.2
December 1979	239.4
December 1980	275.6
December 1981	308.8
December 1982	319.6
December 1983	327.6
December 1984	341.5
December 1985	360.4

Index Chalk's share:

	£		£
1973/74	$2,500 \times \frac{239.4}{110.7}$	=	5,406
1974/75	$3,000 \times \frac{239.4}{116.9}$	=	6,143
1975/76	$3,500 \times \frac{239.4}{146.0}$	=	5,739
1976/77	$1,600 \times \frac{239.4}{168.0}$	=	2,280
1977/78	$2,800 \times \frac{239.4}{188.4}$	=	3,558
1978/79	$3,600 \times \frac{239.4}{204.2}$	=	4,221
1979/80	4,000	=	4,000

The three largest years are:

	£
1974/75	6,143
1975/76	5,739
1973/74	5,406

17,288 ÷ 3 = £5,762
=====

50% thereof = £2,881
=====

Thus if Chalk receives an annuity of £5,000 per year it will be classified as:

	£
Earned income	2,881
Unearned income	2,119
	5,000

11.2 INDEX-LINKED ANNUITIES

Traditionally, annuities were fixed sums of money paid annually, but with the recent emphasis on the effects of inflation many annuities are now inflation adjusted, allowing for predetermined increases in the annuity or index-linking them.

As from the fiscal year 1980/81 it is possible to increase the amount of a retired partner's annuity that qualifies as earned income, by reference to the Retail Prices Index. If the index for the month of December immediately preceding the year of assessment shows an increase over the index for the month of December in the year of assessment in which the partner retired, the limit that qualifies as earned income can be increased by the same percentage increase in the index.

Illustration

Assuming circumstances as in the previous illustration, Chalk retired in the year 1979/80 and for 1986/87 the December falling in the previous year will be 31st December 1985 and the indices therefore show:

December 1985	360.4
December 1979	239.4
An increase of	121.0

As a percentage increase this is 121.0/239.4 i.e. 50.5%.

Thus for 1986/87 the amount of annuity that can be regarded as earned income can be increased by a similar percentage:

£2,881 x 150.5% = 4,336

An alternative way of achieving the same calculation is:

$$\text{Original limit for annuity} \times \frac{\text{index of December prior to year of assessment}}{\text{index of December in year in which retirement occurred}}$$

$$£2,881 \times \frac{360.4}{239.4} = 4,336$$

12.0 PARTNERSHIP SERVICE COMPANIES

A partnership may set up a service company to own assets of the partnership and to provide services to the partnership. In return, the company charges fees to the partnership which will be deducted as an expense in the partnership accounts. By doing this profits can be removed from the partnership and sheltered within the company. If the company is small within the terms of s.95 FA 1972 profits not exceeding £100,000 will only be charged at 29%. The retained profits may be taken out by means of dividend or salary in years in which other income is low. Doing this effectively will depend on the profit uplift applied to the charge from the company to the partnerships. If this exceeds 5-15% then the Revenue may seek to disallow some of the charge in the partnership's computation as not having been incurred wholly and exclusively for the purposes of the trade (**Stephenson v Payne, Stone, Frazer & Co 1967**).

In the opening years of a partnership this can be very advantageous as whilst the expense will be allowed several times in the case of the partnership it will only be taxed once in the company. Whilst the service company will normally be close there will be no apportionment problems unless it receives property or investment income. A point that must be borne in mind however is that the excess profits removed into the company will be liable to corporation tax 9 months after the end of the company's accounting period. This is disadvantageous compared to the much longer period that might be available within the partnership before the payment of income tax.

13.0 SLEEPING PARTNERS

When a partner acts in a "sleeping" role, his share of the partnership profits is classed as unearned income.

14.0 AVERAGING CLAIMS FOR FARMING PARTNERSHIPS

The averaging rules for individuals apply to trades carried on by partnerships in much the same way subject to the following modifications:

(a) the averaging calculation is applied to the partnership assessment, not to the individual partner's share of that assessment,

(b) any claims must be made jointly by all the partners,

(c) if on a partnership change an election under TA 1970, s.154(2) is made (continuing basis), any claim for averaging must be made jointly by all parties who were engaged in the trade at any time during the two year period.

8 Investments

1.0 GENERAL

Most taxpayers have some investments. The income from investments is classified as unearned income and for many years was liable to an additional tax if it exceeded given limits. This additional charge has now been abolished.

Certain investments, e.g. in land, have already been considered but there are many others some of which offer particular tax advantages in terms of tax free income or which are designed to encourage investment in growing companies.

2.0 TAX EFFICIENT INVESTMENTS

Certain investments are tax efficient because income or capital gains arising from them is wholly or partly tax free. These investments include:

2.1 NATIONAL SAVINGS CERTIFICATES

These can be purchased in various denominations and are redeemable at a premium over cost price. After the end of a fixed period of time, often 5 years, the certificate can be redeemed and the premium will be exempt from all taxes. This can be very advantageous to higher rate tax payers; a tax free yield of 10% grossing up at 60% to the equivalent of 25%. If the certificate is held for a shorter period of time a reduced premium will be paid. Each issue of savings certificates is subject to a maximum holding; the premium on certificates held in excess of the maximum is fully taxable.

Indexed linked savings certificates provide an alternative option. They will rise in value in line with the retail price index and again the increase in value is free of all taxes. There are limits on the amount of each issue that can be held.

2.2 NATIONAL SAVINGS BANK ORDINARY ACCOUNTS

The first £70 of annual interest in an NSB ordinary account is free from income tax.

2.3 PREMIUM BONDS

Whilst no interest is paid on these bonds, they qualify for prizes in a monthly draw. The prizes are exempt from all tax and if desired, the bonds can be repaid at par.

2.4 SAVE AS YOU EARN

SAYE schemes are offered by the national savings movement and building societies. The national savings movement requires monthly savings which accumulate towards the purchase of an annual certificate which if held for a fixed period of time gives a tax free yield. The building societies operate a similar monthly savings plan. Whilst both types of investment produce tax free yields, the yields are maximised if the investment is held for a fixed period of time.

2.5 GILT EDGED SECURITIES AND CORPORATE BONDS

Capital gains, often representing an element of accrued income, are exempt.

2.6 PERSONAL EQUITY PLANS

With effect from 1st January 1987, individuals may make investments in personal equity plans [PEP]. These are intended, through certain tax concessions, to encourage wider share ownership.

The schemes are open to individuals aged 18 or more who are resident and ordinarily resident in the UK. They may invest up to £2,400 per year with an authorised PEP manager who will invest the money in equities dealt in on a recognised stock exchange or on the USM. Provided that the investment is retained for two years any reinvested income will be free of tax (the PEP manager recovering the tax credit on income from the Inland Revenue) and there will be no liability to capital gains tax on any capital gains.

Whilst the minimum period of ownership to qualify for tax concessions is two years there is no maximum period of time during which the PEP can be maintained in its tax-free state. If the investment is withdrawn within the two year period then any income or gains will be assessed in the normal way.

The managers of the PEP scheme will act on the instructions of the individual investor as to choice of investments and period of retention. Investments can be bought and sold within the two-year qualifying period without a tax charge.

Whilst there are tax advantages as far as exemption from tax of any accumulated income and capital gains, there is no tax relief for the payments made into the PEP.

3.0 SCHEDULE D CASE III - INCOME ASSESSABLE

(a) Under Schedule D Case III there is assessed any interest, annuity or other annual payment. In particular there is assessed: interest not already taxed at source, including certain bank interest, interest on certain Government securities such as three and half per cent War Loan and interest received on deposits in the National Savings Bank.

In respect of interest on deposits in the NSB the first £70 interest received on deposits in the Ordinary Department is exempt from tax. Where husband and wife have a joint account the first £140 interest is exempt.

<u>Illustration</u>
A husband and wife receive the following interest on their deposits in the Ordinary Account of the NSB:

Husband	£80
Wife	£60

The amount assessable will be:

	Husband	Wife
	£	£
Interest	80	60

Exempt	70	70
	10	-

There is no transfer of the balance of the wife's exemption to the husband. If, however, they had a joint account all the interest would have been exempt.

As from 6th April 1985 interest paid by banks and similar institutions on relevant deposits will be paid net of basic rate tax under a composite rate scheme. The recipient of the interest will be liable to tax on the gross amount and will be able to deduct the tax credit against a tax liability. He will not be able to recover the tax credits by repayment.

A relevant deposit is basically one made with a bank by an individual, a partnership being a collection of individuals. A person not ordinarily resident in the UK may make a declaration to that effect to the bank and the interest will continue to be paid gross. The person concerned must undertake to notify the bank of any changes in his circumstances. Interest paid to charities, clubs, companies and other persons not being individuals will remain gross.

The following are excluded from being relevant deposits:

(i) deposits held by a UK resident bank at an overseas branch;

(ii) interbank loans;

(iii) time deposits of at least £50,000 (or the foreign currency equivalent) the terms of which prevent part withdrawals and prohibit repayment within 28 days;

(iv) bank certificates of deposit of at least £50,000 with a term of at least 28 days.

(b) Discounts on Treasury Bills;

(c) Small maintenance payments paid under the order of a UK court for the benefit of:

(i) a separated or divorced spouse;

(ii) a person aged under 21.

Payment to a spouse or former spouse or to any person under 21 years for his own benefit, maintenance or education must not exceed £48 per week or £208 per month.

Payments to a person for the benefit, maintenance or education of another person aged under 21 years must not exceed £25 per week or £108 per month.

(d) Sickness and disablement benefits received from insurance companies and friendly societies for periods in excess of one year;

(e) Income from deep discount securities. This will be taxable under Schedule D Case IV if they are deep discount foreign securities.

3.1 SCHEDULE D CASE III BASIS OF ASSESSMENT

3.1.1 NORMAL BASIS

The normal basis of assessment is the income arising in the preceding year of assessment. Income arises when it becomes under the control of the recipient such as being credited to a bank deposit account. Accrued interest is not assessable and each individual investment is regarded as a separate source of income.

Illustration
In the years to 5th April 1986 and 1987 X received the following:

	£	£
£1,000 3½% War Loan		
Interest payable 1st May and 1st November		
National Savings Bank Ordinary Account Interest:		
30th June 1985		44
31st December 1985		39
Assessable: 1986/87		
War Loan Interest		35
NSB Interest	83	
Less:	70	
		13
		48

Income received from small maintenance payments is always assessed on actual basis; the person making such payments may treat them as a charge on income.

3.1.2 COMMENCEMENT

On the commencement of a new source of interest the following rules apply:

First year - the actual income arising in that year.
Second year - the actual income of the second year.
Third and subsequent years - the income arising in the preceding year of assessment.

In the third year the taxpayer may elect to substitute the actual income of that year if it is advantageous to him. The election must be made within six years of the end of the third year of assessment.

Illustration
A made a loan to his friend B on 1st July 1984 and the following interest was paid to him:

	£		£
December 1984	70	June 1986	170
June 1985	145	December 1986	120
December 1985	160		

A
Schedule D Case III Assessments

Original		£	Revised	£
1984/85	Actual	70		
1985/86	Actual £(145+160)	305		
1986/87	Preceding year	305	Revised to actual at taxpayer's option	290
1987/88	Preceding year	290		

Therefore, the taxpayer will revise the assessment of 1986/87 on to an actual basis.

Where income first arose on 6th April in the first year of assessment, the preceding year basis will first apply to the second year of assessment as will the taxpayer's right to revise the actual.

3.1.3 CESSATION

On the cessation of a source the assessment will be adjusted as under:

Ultimate year - the actual income arising from 6th April to cessation.
Penultimate year - the income arising in the preceding year of assessment.

The Revenue must adjust the assessment of the penultimate year on to an actual basis if it is to their advantage.

Illustration

B had a special investment account with the National Savings Bank for many years. On 31st December 1986 he decided to close the account. The interest credited was as follows:

	1983	1984	1985	1986
	£	£	£	£
June	500	580	690	835
December	520	630	760	620

Schedule D Case III Assessments

	Original	£	Revised	£
1984/85	Preceding year £(500 + 520)	1,020		
1985/86	Preceding year £(580 + 630)	1,210	Revised to actual by Revenue	1,450
1986/87	Actual	1,455		

Therefore the Revenue will revise the 1985/86 assessment on to an actual basis.

Where a source fails to produce income for six separate years of assessment the taxpayer may, by election made within two years from the end of the six year period, treat the source as if it had ceased at the date on which it last produced income. When it again produces income it will be assessed as if it were a new source.

4.0 THE RULE IN HART v. SANGSTER (1957)

It was held in **Hart v. Sangster** that each deposit in a bank deposit account represented a separate source of income and that each withdrawal represented the cessation of a source. To prevent the difficult situation that could arise if this was applied strictly the Revenue only apply the rule to large deposits and withdrawals. To prepare a computation it is essential to divide the deposits and withdrawals into separate columns and to deal with each deposit or withdrawal individually, on a first in, first out basis.

Illustration

A paid £10,000 into a National Savings Bank special investment account in 1963 and the interest was credited to his current account each half year. On 31st December 1984 he withdrew £5,000 and on 30th June 1986, he closed the account. Interest paid to A in recent years was:

	£		£
31st December 1981	370	30th June 1984	370
30th June 1982	380	31st December 1984	350
31st December 1982	400	30th June 1985	180
30th June 1983	420	31st December 1985	190
31st December 1983	400	30th June 1986	170

	£5,000 Withdrawn 1984 £	£		£5,000 Withdrawn 1986 £	Total £
1983/84					
P/y $\frac{1}{2}$ x £(380 + 400)	390 ===				
Revised					
$\frac{1}{2}$ x £(420 + 400)	410 ===				
I.R. to actual		410 ===	P/y $\frac{1}{2}$ x £(380 + 400)	390 ===	800 ===
	£	£		£	£
1984/85					
Actual $\frac{1}{2}$ x £(370 + 350)		360 ===	P/y $\frac{1}{2}$ x £(420 + 400)	410 ===	770 ===
1985/86			P/y $\frac{1}{2}$ x £(370 + 350)	360 ===	
			Actual £(180+190)	370 ===	
			I.R. to actual		370 ===
1986/87			Actual		170 ===

5.0 THE DEDUCTION OF INCOME TAX AT SOURCE (TA 1970,s.52 and 53)

Income tax at the basic rate is normally deducted from certain annual payments. These are:

(a) any annuity or annual payment other than interest - mostly from deeds of covenant (mortgage interest on a qualifying loan is paid net under the MIRAS Scheme);

(b) patent royalties;

(c) certain mining rents and royalties.

Where the payment is made out of income liable to tax the payer may deduct tax from it at the basic rate in force at the due date of payment irrespective of when it was paid (TA 1970,s.52). The payment when grossed up is treated as a charge on the income of the payer and reduces his total statutory income. To avoid obtaining double relief for the charge, the tax deducted is added to the individual's tax liability.

Illustration

X, a single man, has Schedule D Case I assessable income of £3,000 for 1986/87. He makes an annual payment of £400 from which he deducts income tax at 29% - £116.

	£	£	£
DI			3,000
Less: Annual payment:			
net paid to recipient		284	
+ tax deducted		116	
			400
			2,600
Less: Personal allowances			2,335
			265
Income tax: £265 @ 29%	77		
Add: tax deducted from deed of covenant	116		
1986/87 liability	193		

Where the annual payments made under deduction of tax exceed the taxpayer's income brought into charge to tax, the payer must deduct tax at the basic rate in force at the date the payment was made and must inform the Revenue which will raise an assessment under TA 1970,s.53 to recover the tax. The procedure of raising the assessment under s.53 is to give the taxpayer the opportunity of appealing against it. As, however, the normal rule is that income tax is only payable on income it means that the s.53 assessment is treated as notional income.

Illustration

The facts are as in the previous illustration except that Mr. X has no income for 1986/87.

As he has no income the income tax deducted from the annual payment will be paid over to the Revenue by means of the s.53 assessment.

	Income	Tax due
	£	£
Schedule D I	NIL	NIL
s.53 Assessment	400	116
	400	116
From this can be deducted the annual payment of	400	
To give total statutory income of	NIL	
and the £116 tax due on s.53 assessment is satisfied by paying to the Revenue the tax deducted from the annual payment		116
		NIL

Where there is some income then the s.53 assessment can be reduced.

Illustration

The facts are as in the first Illustration in this section, except that Mr X has Schedule D Case I assessable income of £160.

Of the annual payment of £400, £160 is paid out of income and the rest out of capital. There will therefore be a s.53 assessment on £400 - £160 = £240.

6.0 SCHEDULE D CASE VI

This is charged on a wide variety of miscellaneous receipts including:

(a) furnished lettings;

(b) certain balancing charges;

(c) capital profits on patent rights;

(d) sub-underwriting commissions;

(e) isolated commissions;

(f) casual authorship;

(g) certain introduction fees;

(h) certain post-cessation receipts.

The income assessable is that arising in the year of assessment.

If losses are made on Schedule D Case VI transactions they may be deducted from other Schedule D Case VI income of the year of assessment and the balance may be carried forward against future Schedule D Case VI income from any source. They may not be offset against general income.

7.0 TRUSTS AND SETTLEMENTS

7.1 INCOME SETTLEMENTS

(a) Deeds of Covenant

Deeds of covenant are a means of settling income on an individual or organisation for a specified period without having to lose control of the capital.

In order to be allowed for tax purposes the deed of covenant must satisfy the following conditions:

(i) it must be capable of exceeding six years (three years for covenants to charities in respect of payments made after 5th April 1980);

(ii) it must be irrevocable;

(iii) it must not be for the benefit of the infant unmarried children of the settlor.

Most deeds of covenant are only eligible for relief from income tax at the basic rate which is given by retention of the tax deducted at source. There is normally no benefit in entering into a deed of covenant unless the beneficiary is able to reclaim the tax deducted and retained by the covenantor.

The deeds of covenant which are allowable for higher rate taxes are:

(i) all deeds entered into before 7th April 1965 provided they are payable to a named individual who is not, at the time of payment, either a servant, employee or agent of the covenantor;

(ii) deeds entered into after 6th April 1965 only if they are:

(1) entered into under a partnership deed for the benefit of a

former partner or his widow;

(2) entered into in connection with the acquisition of a business;

(3) entered into in accordance with a settlement arising from divorce or separation.

(iii) deeds of covenant payable to charities.

To decide whether a covenant is capable of exceeding six years (or three years if appropriate) the relevant date is that on which the deed is signed and not that of the first payment. Thus if the deed contains a provision for seven annual payments but is signed after the first payment is made it may be invalidated. **(IRC v. Trustees of the Hostel of St. Luke)**

(b) Life Interests and Life Tenants

Another form of income settlement is obtained where a person settles property for life or a period of time determined by reference to the life or lives of identifiable persons, so that those persons can enjoy that property or the income therefrom during the period specified. The person able to enjoy the income is known as the life tenant and his right to the income is known as a life interest.

The life tenant is deemed to have received the income arising from the trust property the moment it is received by the trustees, irrespective of when and how much of it they released to the life tenant. The extent of the life tenant's liability to income tax is determined by the income of the trust, or his share of the income if there is more than one life tenant, after payment of the trustees' expenses properly attributable to income.

7.2 SETTLEMENTS OF CAPITAL

A settlement of capital may be:

(a) Absolute - where the capital becomes the property of the beneficiary as soon as the trust is created and the trustees' actions are treated as those of the beneficiary. Any income arising under the trust is taxed as the income of the beneficiary immediately, even if it is not distributed to him.

(b) Contingent - here the capital will not vest in the beneficiary unless a specified event happens, e.g. when he attains the age of 25 years or earlier marriage. In such circumstances only income actually distributed to the beneficiary is considered as his.

(c) Discretionary - in this case the treatment is somewhat similar to the contingent settlement except that the distribution of income and capital is totally at the discretion of the trustees and the trust terms are such that the settlement is likely to continue for many years.

Where a distribution is made out of a trust it will be considered as being made net of tax and must be grossed up for inclusion in the recipient's taxable income. The rate at which the grossing up takes place is dependent upon the type of settlement involved. Any income arising to trustees under a discretionary or accumulation trust is liable to additional rate tax at 16% as well as the basic rate of tax. In such circumstances the grossing up rate will be 45% for 1986/87 - 29% basic rate tax and 16% additional rate; in all other cases the rate will be 29% basic rate only.

As regards the trust, all income received is liable to tax in the normal way either by deduction at source or by direct payments by the trustees. As indicated above, there is a liability to additional rate tax in the case of discretionary etc. trusts.

The trustees are required to make a return annually to the Revenue of the income and charges of the trust and from this will be calculated the liability of the trust to tax.

Illustration

The AB Will Trust consists of the following assets:

House let since 1965 at £900 per annum, the tenant paying the rates and being responsible for internal repairs. During 1986/87 the landlord paid £90 for external decorations and £30 management expenses.

£6,000 9% Treasury Stock 1994 (bought 6th May 1973, interest payable 17th May and 17th November).

8,000 shares in C Ltd of 25p each, fully paid, on which a dividend of 2.5p per share was paid on 3rd June 1986.

Lloyds Bank deposit opened 1st January 1975) on which the interest received has been:

1984/85 - £35; 1985/86 - £38; 1986/87 - £31

The trust expenses, other than those in respect of the house, payable out of income, amount to £50 per annum.

The net income of the trust for the year ended 5th April 1987 was fully distributed to the two beneficiaries, who are joint life tenants. (The trust is not discretionary).

THE AB WILL TRUST
Statement of Trust Income

	£p	£p	Income Tax Due £p
House - rent		900	
Less: repairs	90		
management expenses	30	120	
		780.00	226.20
£6,000 9% Treasury Stock 1994		540.00	156.60
Dividend from C Ltd	200.00		
Tax credit at 29/71	81.69	281.69	81.69
Lloyds Bank deposit interest		43.66	12.66
		1,645.35	477.15
Less: Income tax		477.15	
		1,168.20	
Less: Trustees' expenses		50.00	
Net income available for division		1,118.20	

The certificate issued by the trustees to each of the beneficiaries will be as follows:

Certificate of Deduction of Tax - R 185 E

Gross amount of beneficiaries' share of trust income	Amount of income tax suffered thereon by the trust	Amount of net payment actually made to beneficiaries
(1)	(2)	(3)
£p	£p	£p
787.46	228.36	559.10

Notes: (1) The income tax column includes all the liability of the trust, not just the tax suffered by deduction.

(2) If a statement of trust income is not required the beneficiaries' gross share can be calculated as follows:

	£
Net income from house	780.00
9% Treasury Stock	540.00
Dividend from C Ltd	281.69
Deposit interest	43.66
	1,645.35
Less: Trustees' expenses: £50 x 100/71	70.43
	1,574.92 ÷ 2 = £787.46

The trustees' expenses must be grossed up as they are paid out of net income.

Where the trustees of a settlement make a payment out of the capital of the trust, this must be grossed up at the appropriate rate of tax and the tax accounted for to the Revenue under TA 1970,s.53.

Illustration

The trustees of the XYZ Settlement receive taxed dividends of £355 net. They are obliged to pay an annuity to Miss X of £1,000 per annum net. Any difference between the income and the annuity can be made up out of capital.

The income of the Trust is:	£	£
Gross	500	
Tax @ 29%	145	
		355 net
To make up the difference		645 is required from capital
		1,000
Tax of 29/71 of £645 =		263.45 is required to be paid under s.53

7.3 SETTLEMENTS ON CHILDREN

Where a settlement is created by a parent in favour of the infant, unmarried child of the settlor then the distributed income is for tax purposes treated as the income of the parent. An infant child is one aged under 18 and includes the adopted, illegitimate or stepchild of the settlor. To avoid this, an accumulation and maintenance settlement may be created. In this type of settlement, income is accumulated and distributed only on the occurrence of a certain event, often when the child marries after reaching the age of 18 or attains a certain age. Whilst retained income is liable to basic and additional rate tax in the hands of the trustees it will not be assessable on the parent unless the income is distributed.

8.0 LIFE ASSURANCE

Prior to FA 1984 life assurance policies were extremely attractive investments. Not only did the premiums payable attract tax relief, up to certain limits, but income and gains received by the insurance company on the policy investments also attracted a favourable rate of tax. Insurance policies taken out after 13th March 1984 will not qualify for relief on the premiums paid though the favourable tax rates applying to income and capital gains still remain.

8.1 RELIEF FOR POLICIES TAKEN OUT PRE 14.3.1984

A deduction of 15% is made from the qualifying premiums. The taxpayer pays the net premium to the life assurance company which then recovers the deduction from the Inland Revenue.

Illustration
C took out a qualifying life assurance policy in 1980; he pays a premium of £100 per year before relief.

	£
Gross premium	100
Tax relief	15
Paid to assurance company	85

The tax relief must not exceed 15% of the greater of 1/6 of total statutory income or £1,500.

Illustration
D has the following income for 1986/87

	£
Salary	10,000
Dividends gross	6,000

He pays mortgage interest of £1,600 gross and life assurance premiums of £2,250 after tax relief.

	£
Salary	10,000
Dividends	6,000
	16,000
Mortgage interest	1,600
Total statutory income	14,400

Life assurance relief available on the greater of

			£
(a)	1/6 x £14,400	=	2,400
	or		
(b)	£1,500		

As the gross premiums are £2,250 x 100/85 = £2,647

relief has been overclaimed on £2,647 - £2,400 = £247 and relief of £247 x 15% = £37 will be clawed back.

To obtain relief for pre 14.3.1984 policies it was necessary for them to be qualifying policies, broadly the conditions were:

(a) the policy should be on the lives of the taxpayer or his spouse;

(b) the maturity date should be at least 10 years from the date the policy was taken out;

(c) the premiums have to be paid at annual or shorter intervals and not vary excessively from year to year.

Where a qualifying policy is varied after 13th March 1984 it will cease to qualify for relief.

8.2 RELIEF FOR LATER POLICIES

No tax relief is given on policies taken out after 13.3.1984 but the income of the life assurance company still qualifies for tax exemptions.

8.3 SURRENDERS OF POLICIES

Where a policy is surrendered there may be a charge to tax. If the policy is a qualifying policy a surrender within 4 years will involve a clawback of all or part of the life assurance relief given as under:

Time of surrender	Clawback of total premiums	Restricted to surrender value less the following percentage of premiums paid to date
Years 1 and 2	15%	85%
3	10%	90%
4	5%	95%

Any clawback will be deducted by the life assurance company which will account for it to the Inland Revenue.

<u>Illustration</u>
D took out a qualifying life assurance policy and paid premiums of £3,000 gross. After 30 months he surrendered the policy and received £2,800 before any deduction.

The clawback will be the lower of:

		£
(a)	10% x £3,000	300
(b)	£2,800 - (90% x 3,000)	100

The surrender of a life assurance policy within 10 years can give rise to a liability to higher rate tax on any excess of surrender proceeds over premiums paid. Any excess is subject to top slicing relief as under:

(a) Find the profit;

(b) divide it by the life of the policy (complete years only);

(c) find the tax on the annual equivalent in (b) above treating it as the top slice of taxable income of the fiscal year in which surrender occurs;

(d) multiply the tax so found by the number of complete years.

Illustration

E has an income for 1986/87 of £20,000 after all deductions and personal allowances. In that year he surrenders a qualifying life assurance policy on its 6th anniversary. The surrender value was £8,000 and the premiums paid £6,200.

Gain on policy surrendered:

			£
Surrender value			8,000
Premiums paid			6,200
			1,800
Annual equivalent £1,800 ÷ 6 =			300
Taxable income			20,000
		£	
Tax -	£17,200 @ 29%		4,988
	£ 2,800 @ 40%		1,120
			6,108
	- On annual equivalent		
	£200 @ 40%	80	
	£100 @ 45%	45	
	£300	125	
	Less: Basic rate tax		
	£300 @ 29%	87	
		38 x 6	228
			6,336

A similar treatment applies to non-qualifying policies and investment and property bonds. The latter are single premium policies which aim to give a substantial capital profit over a fixed term. They often include the right of a policyholder to make partial surrenders. These will be tax free if they do not exceed 5% of the original investment per year. This is calculated on a cumulative basis and if they do, the excess is charged to tax in the year the event occurs. At the end of the fixed term of the policy partial withdrawals are included in finding the overall profit.

9.0 PURCHASED ANNUITIES

A person can make a lump sum purchase of an annuity. This will guarantee a payment on a regular basis for a fixed period of time, often for the recipient's life. The payment received from the assurance company will consist of a repayment of capital and an interest payment on the remainder of the investment. The amount of the capital element is fixed by the Inland Revenue, subject to appeal, and is tax free. The income element will be subject to basic rate tax prior to receipt by the annuitant.

10.0 ENTERPRISE FUNDING

10.1 GENERAL

In recent years, a number of incentives have been given to encourage investment in new or existing enterprises. They can be loosely classified as:

(a) Reactive incentives

(b) Pro-active incentives.

Reactive incentives take the form of relief given for a loss. They include relief for losses on shares subscribed for in a qualifying trading company s.37, FA 1980, relief for losses incurred by an individual in the first 4 years of trading s.30, FA 1978 and relief for losses made on loans and guarantees to traders.

Proactive incentives are relief given at the time of the investment irrespective of the outcome. They can include regional development grants, the enterprise allowance, personal equity plans and the business expansion scheme.

10.2 RELIEF FOR INVESTMENT IN CORPORATE TRADES - THE BUSINESS EXPANSION SCHEME

10.2.1 GENERAL

This relief is designed to encourage investment in unquoted companies. It is unusual in as much as it allows a deduction from income in order to acquire a capital investment. The relief is available from the fiscal year 1983/84 to qualifying individuals who subscribe for eligible shares in a qualifying company which either carries on a qualifying trade or which intends to carry on such a trade within 2 years from the date of issue of the shares.

10.2.2 DEFINITIONS

(a) Qualifying individuals

An individual will qualify if he is resident and ordinarily resident in the UK at the time the shares were issued and he is not connected with the company at any time during the qualifying period which commences with the incorporation of the company (or two years before the share issue if later) and ends five years after the share issue. Crown employees working abroad are treated as resident and ordinarily resident for BES relief.

He will be connected with the company if he or an associate is:

(1) an employee of the company;

(2) a partner of the company;

(3) a director of the company, unless no payment is received from the company other than reasonable expenses or normal dividends on the shares issued;

(4) entitled to possess either directly or indirectly more than 30% of the share capital or voting rights.

(b) Eligible shares

These are new ordinary shares which carry no preferential rights to dividends etc. for the period of five years from the date of issue.

(c) Qualifying company

This is a company which:

(1) is incorporated and resident in the UK;

(2) exists wholly or substantially for the purpose of carrying on a qualifying trade;

(3) is not the subsidiary of another or which has its own subsidiary, unless the subsidiary would itself qualify for relief;

(4) is unquoted (this excludes USM companies);

(5) has all its shares fully paid up.

(d) Qualifying trades

These must be bona fide trades carried on commercially and with a view to profit. It will not qualify if it is a trade consisting of:

(1) dealing in land, commodities or shares;

(2) dealing in goods other than in the course of wholesale or retail distribution, dealing in collectible items normally held as investments is excluded where the company holds stocks for excessive periods of time;

(3) banking, insurance or money lending;

(4) providing legal or accountancy services;

(5) property development.

The trade must be carried on commercially through the relevant period which commences at the date on which the shares are issued and ends normally three years afterwards.

Relief is not available for shares issued after 18th March 1986 in companies which are substantially 'land backed'. These are companies which in the relevant period have more than 50% of their net assets in land.

10.2.3 RELIEF AVAILABLE

The maximum relief available to an individual is £40,000 in any one year of assessment. The minimum investment in a company qualifying for relief is normally £500. Husband and wife are treated as one person. There is no resriction on the number of shares issued which qualify for relief though no individual must hold more than 30% (see above).

Illustration

X, Y and Z make the following investments in qualifying companies in 1986/87:

	Alpha Ltd	Beta Ltd
	£	£
X	200	400
	===	===

No relief is available as the investment in either company is not at least £500.

	£	£
Y	400	11,000
	===	======

Relief is available in respect of the investment in Beta Ltd. The investment in Alpha Ltd is under the £500 limit.

	£	£
Z	15,000	30,000
	======	======

Overall relief will be restricted to a maximum of £40,000.

The relief is given as a personal allowance; this gives a potential 60% rate of relief.

Illustration

X has the following income for 1986/87:

Earned	£25,000
Unearned	£24,000

He is married and pays mortgage interest of £2,000 (not under MIRAS).

He makes a qualifying investment of £12,000.

1986/87	£	£
Earned income		25,000
Unearned income	24,000	
Less: Mortgage interest	2,000	
		22,000
		47,000
Less: Personal allowances:		
MA	3,655	
Business Expansion Relief	12,000	
		15,655
		31,345
		======

Tax:

£			£
17,200	@	29%	4,988
3,000	@	40%	1,200
5,200	@	45%	2,340
5,945	@	50%	2,972
31,345			11,500

10.2.4 WITHDRAWAL OF RELIEF

Relief will be withdrawn if during the relevant period - five years from the date of issue of the shares - either:

(a) the shares are disposed of; or

(b) value is withdrawn from the company.

10.2.5 DISPOSAL OF SHARES

On a sale of shares the relief given will be clawed back via a Schedule D Case VI assessment. For disposals by way of gift the relief is totally withdrawn. For all other disposals the relief is reduced by the amount of the consideration received. Where there has been more than one qualifying subscription for shares of the same class, disposals will be matched in a FIFO basis. Where the shares have been sold after five years, there will be no withdrawal of relief.

For CGT purposes, any excess of disposal proceeds over cost will be assessed as a capital gain. If the shares are sold at a loss, the amount of the loss will be reduced by any amount on which relief has been obtained under the Business Expansion Scheme.

Illustration

Y subscribed £10,000 for qualifying shares obtaining relief at 75%. After 5 years they were sold for:

(a) £14,000

(b) £7,000

As the disposal took place after five years there will be no clawback of Business Expansion Relief. The CGT position (ignoring indexation) would be:

	(a)	(b)
	£	£
Disposal proceeds	14,000	7,000
Cost	10,000	10,000
Chargeable gain	4,000	
Loss		(3,000)
Less:Relief obtained under Business Expansion Scheme		10,000
Allowable loss		NIL

If the disposal had taken place within five years, Business Expansion Relief would have been withdrawn on:

(a) £10,000 @ 75% = £7,500

(b) £ 7,000 @ 75% = £5,250

The CGT position for (a) would have been the same; for (b) it would be:

	£
Disposal proceeds	7,000
Cost	10,000
	(3,000)
Less:Business Expansion Scheme relief (£10,000 - £7,000)	3,000
Allowable loss	NIL

10.2.6 VALUE WITHDRAWN

If the investor receives value from the company within five years of the issue of the shares, relief will be withdrawn to the extent of the amount received. Value received can include:

(a) repayment of loans;

(b) redemption of share capital;

(c) payments for forgiveness of debts;

(d) provision of benefits;

(e) transfers at an undervalue.

9 Schedule E

1.0 SCOPE

Tax is charged under Schedule E on the 'emoluments of an office or employment'.

1.1 DEFINITIONS

'Emoluments'

These include all salaries, wages, fees, benefits, perquisites and profits whatsoever.

'Office'

An office is a position existing independently of the incumbent. The Archbishop of York holds an office.

'Employment'

Employment exists where there is a legal relationship of master and servant. This may be evidenced by a contract of employment or may be implied by conduct.

Whether the taxpayer is employed or self-employed is sometimes a matter of some difficulty to decide.

In **Stevenson Jordan and Harrison Ltd v. Macdonald & Evans Ltd (1952)**, Lord Denning looked to the place of the person in the organisation of the 'employer' and implied that if he occupied an integral part of that organisation then his relationship was more likely to be that of an employee and not that of an independent self-employed contractor.

In **Fall v. Hitchen (1973)** a professional ballet dancer worked under contract at Sadlers Wells. His contract was a full time one and prohibited him from undertaking other duties without the consent of his employer. Held that the contract was one of service rather than one of services.

In deciding whether a person is employed or self-employed the following may be taken into account:

(a) whether the person provides own equipment;

(b) whether he can delegate his work to a third party;

(c) the degree of freedom that he possesses in deciding where and when the work is performed;

(d) what financial risk he undertakes;

(e) whether he can profit by sound management.

2.0 INCOME ASSESSABLE

2.1 GENERAL

The income assessable under Schedule E is that earned in the year of assessment. It is not necessary for the amount to be paid over to the recipient; a credit entry in a personal ledger account is sufficient. The assessable income can include:

(a) wages and salaries;

(b) pensions from approved superannuation schemes, the State or any other source including a voluntary pension;

(c) other social security benefits, including retirement pensions, unemployment, widow's pension and child's special allowance. Sickness, and maternity benefits, attendance allowance and death grant are not taxable.

To be liable to tax, the emoluments must derive from the office of employment. In **Hochstrasser v. Mayes (1959)** Upjohn J said:

> "... the payment must be made in reference to the services the employee renders by virtue of his office and it must be something in the nature of a reward for services past, present or future."

The payments taxable are not merely those such as salaries and wages but can also include payments by way of bonus or appreciation for services.

In **Moorhouse v. Dooland (1955)** the taxpayer was a professional cricketer. Under the club rules, he was entitled to talent money and a public collection whenever he produced a particularly meritorious performance. In the 1951/52 season he so qualified on eleven occasions. Held the proceeds of the public collections were taxable. They were a contractual right and therefore an emolument of the employment.

In **Seymour v. Reed (1927)** the taxpayer was again a professional cricketer and in 1920 was awarded a benefit which meant he was entitled to a public collection and the proceeds of one of the home matches. Held not taxable. The awards were not contractual and were in the form of an appreciation for past services.

Certain principles can be drawn from these and similar cases:

(a) if the entitlement to a payment is contractual it is strong grounds for considering it to be an emolument **(Moorhouse v. Dooland)**;

(b) recurrence may be an important factor **(Seymour v. Reed)**.
In **Moore v. Griffiths (1972)**, Bobby Moore received a payment from the Football Association in recognition of England's victory in the 1966 World Cup. Held not taxable. The payment was intended to mark a great sporting achievement. It was 'one-off' and unlikely to be repeated;

(c) if the payment is made as a result of the office or employment the identity of the payer is irrelevant.
In **Blakiston v. Cooper (1909)** a vicar of a parish received the customary Easter offering from the parishioners. Held taxable. The payment was made in respect of the services performed as incumbent of a parish; the fact that the payment was voluntary and not made by the employer was irrelevant.
However, payments made as a mark of personal esteem may not be taxable even if made by the employer. In **Ball v. Johnson (1971)** an award made to a bank clerk for passing the Institute of Bankers' examinations was held not to be taxable.

2.2 BENEFITS

As already mentioned the emoluments assessable under Schedule E include benefits in kind. This term includes many items such as free holidays, housing and the private use of a firm's car. For the assessment of benefits, employees fall into two classes.

(a) Non P11D Personnel

These are:

(i) Employees earning less than £8,500 per annum;

(ii) Directors who are full-time working directors, do not have a material interest in the company, and who earn less than £8,500 per annum.

(b) P11D Personnel

These are:

(i) Directors, other than those in (ii) above;

(ii) Employees earning £8,500 or more per annum.

A full-time working director is one required to devote substantially the whole of his time to the service of the company in a managerial or technical capacity.

A person will have a material interest if together with his associates he can control more than 5% of the ordinary share capital of the company. The meanings of 'associates' and 'ordinary share capital' are as for Corporation Tax.

Where a person is employed by more than one employer each employment will be considered separately. However, where there are two or more employments with the same employer, including the situation where there are employments with several companies within the same group, they will be considered as one in deciding whether the individual has reached the £8,500 limit.

2.3 TREATMENT OF BENEFITS FOR LOWER PAID (NON P11D) EMPLOYEES

The basic rule for the taxability of benefits for this group of employees is that the benefit must be capable of cash convertibility.

In **Tennant v. Smith (1892)** the taxpayer was a senior employee of the Bank of Scotland in Montrose. He was required to live over the bank and could not leave his accommodation for substantial periods without the consent of his employers. He was not allowed to sublet the accommodation or use it other than for his employer's business. Held he was not assessable in respect of the benefit of his occupation of the premises. Per the Earl of Halsbury LC the benefit is,

> " ... not income unless it can be turned into money."

If the benefit is capable of cash conversion then the quantum will be the cash into which it could be converted.

In **Wilkins v. Rogerson (1961)** an employer arranged for all the employees to purchase at his expense a suit, overcoat or sports jacket up to a maximum cost of £15. Held to be taxable. The item of clothing was the employee's property and therefore capable of cash conversion. The quantum of the benefit was, however, only the second-hand value of the suit £5.

Certain benefits may be received which are not capable of cash conversion, for example, if an employer pays a fine of an employee. Where the employer pays for an item which is the legal liability of the employee it is taxable irrespective of any cash convertibility.

In **Nichol v Austin (1935)** the taxpayer's contract of service provided that he should reside in his own house but that his employers should pay all expenses including rates, insurance, heating and maintenance of the house and gardens. Held that the payments constituted money's worth and were therefore taxable.

2.4 BENEFITS - DIRECTORS AND THOSE EMPLOYEES EARNING OVER THE INCOME LIMIT (P11D EMPLOYEES)

Members of this class of taxpayer are liable to tax in respect of any benefit provided by the employer. The value of the benefit is the cost to the employer. In deciding to which class of taxpayers the person belongs all emoluments received by the employee are aggregated with the benefits valued as if they were received by a higher paid employee. No expenses are deducted.

Benefits received by this class of employee must be returned on form P11D. Dispensations from the completion of all or part of the return may be given by the Revenue. If the dispensation is given the expenses and benefits will be disregarded in determining whether the £8,500 limit has been reached.

It is not necessary for the benefit to be provided to the employee direct, it will be taxable upon him if it is provided to a member of his family or household. The family includes a spouse, parents, sons or daughters and their spouses. Neither is it necessary that the employee should be the exclusive recipient of the benefit. It is enough if it is made available to him and he does not disclaim it. Also, the fact that he would have spent less on the benefit had he provided it himself is irrelevant.

In **Rendell v. Went (1964)**, a company director was charged with dangerous driving. The potential penalty, if he were convicted, was a term of imprisonment. The company did not wish to lose his services and employed legal representatives to defend him. Held he was liable to tax on the amount of the services provided. The fact that they also benefited his employers was immaterial.

2.5 SPECIAL CLASSES OF BENEFITS

(a) Motor Cars:

The benefit of the use of a car depends upon the nature of its use:

(i) The 'Perk' Car

This is a car provided for the use of an employee or director where the business use is insubstantial. This is where the business mileage is not more than 2,500 per annum. Also where any second cars are provided, the 'perk car' rules apply to such cars irrespective of business use.

The benefit of a perk car is one and a half times cost price calculated in the same way as for a business car together with any appropriate petrol and other benefits.

(ii) The Business Car

Where the use of the car for business purposes is not insubstantial (i.e. the car is not regarded as a 'perk' car) the value of the benefit is established by reference to Tables which are updated periodically, and which are indicated below. If the business mileage exceeds 18,000 annually, the benefit is reduced by one-half.

Table 1
Cars with original market value of up to £19,250

Cylinder in cubic centimetres	Age at end of year of assessment Under 4 years	4 years or more
	£	£
1,300 or less	450	300
1,301 - 1,800	575	380
1,801 or more	900	600

Table 2
Cars with original market value up to £19,250 but with no cylinder capacity

Original market value	Age at end of year of assessment Under 4 years	4 years or more
	£	£
Less than £6,000	450	300
£6,000 - £8,499	575	380
£8,500 - £19,250	900	600

Table 3
Cars with original market value more than £19,250

Original market value	Age at end of year of assessment Under 4 years	4 years or more
	£	£
£19,251 - £29,000	1,320	875
more than £29,000	2,100	1,400

The calculation of the benefit is as under:

Benefit per table		x
Less: Period of unavailability (see below)	x	
Private contribution for use of car	x	
	—	x
Assessable benefit		x
		=

The car will not be available on a day when it was not available for the employee to use or was incapable of being used provided in the last case that the period in which it was incapable of being used exceeded 30 consecutive days. This restriction also applies to fuel benefits.

There will also be an additional fuel benefit if <u>any</u> fuel is made available for the employee's private use. It will be made available if:

(a) any liability for the supply of fuel is discharged;

(b) a voucher or credit token is used to obtain fuel;

(c) a sum is paid for expenses in providing fuel.

If the car has travelled over 18,000 business miles per annum the scale is reduced by one half. The scale charge will be reduced to nil where:

(a) the fuel is only provided for business use, or

(b) the employee makes good the whole of any private fuel used.

Partial contribution towards private usage of fuel cannot be deducted. The amount of the benefit for 1986/87 is listed below:

Table 1
Cars with cylinder capacity

Cylinder capacity in cubic centimetres	Cash equivalent
1,300 or less	£450
1,301 - 1,800	£575
1,803 or more	£900

Table 2
Cars with no cylinder capacity

Original market value	Cash equivalent
Less than £6,000	£450
£6,000 - £8,499	£575
Over £8,499	£900

Where other expenses are reimbursed to the employee, there may be an additional benefit in respect of these expenses. As from 1983/84 these will only be treated as an additional benefit if they are round sum allowances.

Illustration

B has the use of a Silver Shadow Rolls Royce which cost £20,000 in 1972 and has a cylinder capacity of 7,941 cc. It was acquired by his present employers in 1975 for £10,000. In the year ended 5th April 1987 the running costs of the car were:

Paid directly by employer:

Tax	£ 85
Repairs	£300
Petrol (business use)	£600

Reimbursed to employee:

Insurance	£200
Private petrol	£140

It is estimated that of the total mileage of 20,000, 5,000 relates to business. B contributes £100 towards private use of the car. In the year, the car was involved in a serious accident and as a result was incapable of use for 49 consecutive days.

		£	£
Benefit per table		875	
Less: Period of inactivity	49/365	117	758
Petrol benefit per table		900	
Less: Period of inactivity	49/365	121	779
			1,537
Less: Private contribution towards use of car			100
			1,437

Note: Private contributions towards petrol could not be deducted. The provision of a chauffeur would be an additional assessable benefit.

(iii) The Pool Car
Where the car is a 'pool' car there will be no assessable benefit. To qualify, the following conditions must be satisfied:

(1) it must be available to two or more persons;

(2) it must not normally be kept overnight at or near the residence of the employee concerned;

(3) private use must be incidental.
Regular travel between home and work would not be considered incidental.

(b) Accommodation

Where accommodation is provided for any category of employee there is an assessable benefit. This is equal to the higher of either the gross annual value for rateable purposes, or the rent paid by the employer.

There is an additional charge levied where an employee is taxable in respect of an occupation benefit and the cost of the accommodation (including improvements) exceeds £75,000. This charge is calculated as:

Cost of providing the accommodation - £75,000 x Appropriate percentage

The appropriate percentage is the official rate of interest as applied to beneficial loans - presently 12%.

The benefit can be reduced by any private contribution.

Illustration

A had the use of a company flat in 1986/87 which had a rateable value of £800. It cost £240,000 to his employers. He contributes £2,000 per annum for the use of the flat.

		£
Annual value		800
Additional charge		
£240,000 - £75,000 =	£165,000	
12% thereof		19,800
		20,600
Less: Contribution		2,000
		18,600

There is no assessable benefit either, on the annual value, rent or additional charge when the employee's (whether higher or lower paid) occupation is 'representative'. This is:

(i) where it is necessary that the employee should reside in the accommodation to properly perform his duties, or

(ii) where it is customary to provide employees of a particular class with accommodation to enable them to more effectively perform their duties, or

(iii) where the premises are provided to counter a threat to the personal security of the employee.

The concept of representative occupation under (i) and (ii) above will also apply to full-time working directors who do not have a material interest. Other directors are generally liable in full.

Where the services are provided in connection with the accommodation there is an assessable benefit on the recipient. This applies whether or not the occupation is representative though if it is, no charge will be made for rates. A charge can therefore arise in respect of the following:

(i) lighting, heating and cleaning;

(ii) repairs, other than structural repairs, maintenance and decoration;

(iii) the provision of furniture, calculated as 20% of cost.

However, where the occupation is representative, the charge in respect of these services must not exceed a limit. This limit is 10% of the employee's total emoluments (excluding the above, and as reduced by other allowable expenses, capital allowances and pension or retirement annuity contributions), less any sum made good by the employee.

Illustration

C receives a salary of £8,500 from his employer together with a company car the assessable benefit of which is £400. He pays 10% of his basic salary to an approved pension scheme. He also occupies a company house and it is agreed that the ~~accommodation~~ occupation is representative. In 1986/87 his employers pay the following expenses:

	£
Rates	290
Light and heat	350
Redecoration	220
Wages of cleaner	250
Benefits assessable:	
Light and heat	350
Redecoration	220
Wages	250
	820

		£
Salary		8,500
Car benefit		400
		8,900
<u>Less</u>: Pension scheme contributions		850
		8,050
Accommodation benefit as above	£820	
* restricted to 10% x £8,050		805
		8,855

Where employees receive bed and board accommodation as part of their overall job package there will generally be no benefit in respect of lower paid employee as the benefit will not be capable of cash conversion. For higher paid employees, the benefit will be the cost to the employer of providing such accommodation.

(c) <u>Loans (P11D employees only)</u>
Where a director or employee (or his relative) has a loan from the employer and it is wholly or partly written off, the amount written off is a taxable benefit. There will be no benefit where the taxpayer can show that he is charged to tax elsewhere, e.g. as a participator in a close company, or where the loan was made to a relative and he can show that he received no benefit through it being written off.

When a loan is made to an employee at a favourable rate of interest, the difference between the interest charged and that calculated by using an official rate is a taxable benefit but only if the difference exceeds £200. There is no liability where the interest would, if paid, have been allowed as a deduction for income tax purposes.

The benefit will be either calculated on an informal or a formal basis:

(i) <u>Informal</u>:

$$\frac{\text{Balance of loan at beginning of fiscal year} + \text{Balance of loan at end of fiscal year}}{2} = \text{Average Loan}$$

* If the scheme is unapproved the employees contributions will not be tax deductible & also the employers contributions towards the scheme 9.9 will be an additional benefit in kind. This rule applies to both lower & higher paid employees.

Average Loan x official rate of interest	x
Less: Payment made	x
Benefit	x

(ii) Formal:
Interest is calculated on a day to day basis.

The official rate of interest was 15% up to 5th October 1982 and 12% thereafter.
Either the taxpayer or the Revenue can elect for the interest calculation to be on the formal basis.

Illustration
B had a balance on his loan account from his employer of £20,000 at 6th April 1986. He repaid £8,000 on 1st December 1986. The loan agreement with his employer provides that he is to be charged interest at 2% on the balance at the beginning of the fiscal year.

Informal basis: £

$$\frac{20{,}000 + 12{,}000}{2} = £16{,}000$$

	£
£16,000 x 12%	1,920
Less: Interest paid	400
	1,520

Formal basis: £

	£
$£20{,}000 \times \frac{239}{365} \times 12\%$	1,571
$£12{,}000 \times \frac{126}{365} \times 12\%$	501
	2,072
Less: Interest paid	400
Benefit	1,672

If the loan was for a qualifying purpose no charge would be made.

(d) Other assets provided
Where other assets which remain the property of the employer are provided for the use of the employees or directors there is a benefit equal to the greater of:

(i) 20% of the market value when they were made available as a benefit; and

(ii) the cost of hiring or leasing the asset.

For assets which were provided up to the 5th April 1980 the rate was 10%.
In both cases the amount of the benefit is reduced by the contribution made by the employee.

Illustration

C, a higher paid employee, has the use of a suit of clothes provided by his emnployer. It cost his employer £250.

Benefit - 20% x £250 = £50.

If it had been hired by his employers for £80 per year, the benefit would be the greater of:

£50 or £80 = £80

Where the asset is given or sold to the employee then the benefit is the greater of:

Market value at date of disposal	x
Less: Price paid by employee	x
	x
OR	
Original market value @ date of gift.	x
Less: Already assessed on employee	x
	x
Less: Price paid	x
	x

Illustration

If after two years' use the suit was sold to C for £15 when its market value was £25, the benefit would be:

	£
Market value at disposal	25
Less: Price paid	15
	10
Original market value	250
Less: Assessed 2 x £50	100
	150
Less: Price paid	15
	135
The greater is	135

(e) Vouchers etc.

The provision of cash or non-cash vouchers is treated as an assessable emolument to both higher and lower paid employees. For cash vouchers the amount assessable is the cash into which it is convertible and for non-cash vouchers the benefit is the cost to the employer, less any amount made good by the employee.

Non-cash vouchers can include cheque vouchers and transport vouchers but exclude luncheon vouchers of a value of not more than 15p per day.

The provision of a credit token and any goods received by using the token are an emolument. A credit token is defined as any card, token, document etc. given to a person, which agrees to provide money, goods or services on credit.

A claim may be made to reduce the amount of the benefit by any genuine business expense.

(f) Scholarships

A scholarship awarded as a result of a directorship or higher paid employment, will be subjected to income tax as a benefit in kind under Schedule E.

If the scholarship is not awarded as a result of such employment, no taxable benefit would arise if not more than 25% of such scholarship payments are made by reason of the employment. The 25% limit would include lower paid employees in receipt of such benefits but who are not taxed thereon as a benefit in kind.

(g) A summary of benefits is shown overleaf.

2.6 BONUSES

Where a bonus is paid by the employer there are three possible ways of assessing it.

(a) The earnings basis

This applies to the strict concept that the emoluments assessable are those earned in the year of assessment irrespective of when they are paid.

(b) The accounts basis

This basis charges the bonus to tax in the fiscal year in which the accounting period to which the bonus relates, ends.

(c) The receipts basis

This basis charges the bonus to tax in the fiscal year in which it is paid.

Of the three methods (a) is statutorily correct and should be applied when no other basis is mentioned. The third basis is only normally used in connection with small amounts such as Christmas Boxes etc.

Illustration

C received a bonus of £1,000 on 1st May 1986 in respect of his employer's year to 31st December 1985.

Earnings basis:

	£
Applicable to 1984/85 3/12 x £1,000	250
Applicable to 1985/86 9/12 x £1,000	750
	1,000

Accounts basis:

Accounting period ended in 1985/86	£1,000

Receipts basis:

Bonus paid in 1986/87 assessed 1986/87	£1,000

2.5(g) Benefit Summary

Type	Non-P11D Personnel	P11D Personnel
Luncheon vouchers	No benefit up to 15p per day	No benefit up to 15p per day
Meals in subsidised canteen	No benefit	No benefit where meals available to all members of staff
Use of car:		
(1) Insubstantial use	(No benefit in respect of capital value,	(i) Charge at 150% of scale
(2) Substantial use	(possible benefit for private running (costs reimbursed, e.g. private petrol	(ii) Charge as scale
(3) Pool cars	(No benefit	(iii) No benefit
Accommodation	Annual value assessable Excluding representative accommodation	Annual value assessable Excluding representative accommodation (Directors with material interest may be taxed in full
Running costs of accommodation	Normally not taxable	Taxable benefit as above
Private medical insurance	Not taxable	Taxable benefit equal to cost to employer
Private use of company assets	No benefit	Taxable benefit
Removal expenses	No benefit where required by employer to move elsewhere	No benefit where required by employer to move elsewhere
Beneficial loans	No benefit	Taxable benefit
Cash vouchers	Taxable benefit equal to cash benefit of voucher	Taxable benefit as before
Non-cash vouchers including travel and cheque vouchers	Taxable benefit equal to expense incurred in providing voucher	Taxable benefit as before
Scholarships for children of employee	Not assessable	Taxable benefit

Expenses reimbursed by an employer will in general be an allowable deduction for the employee and any question of disallowance will be dealt with in the employer's accounts. If the employee receives a "round sum" allowance this will normally be considered to be emoluments of the employee and he will be responsible for claiming the amount spent which is allowable under the Schedule E expense rule. The employer will obtain full deduction for the whole of the lump sum.

3.0 EXPENSES

Where the director or employee incurs expenses in connection with his employment he can claim a deduction from his Schedule E assessable emoluments. The conditions that must be satisfied are laid down by TA 1970,s.189.

> "If the holder of an office or employment is necessarily obliged to incur and defray out of the emoluments thereof the expenses of travelling in the performance of the duties of the office or employment or of keeping and maintaining a horse to enable him to perform the same, or otherwise to expend money wholly, exclusively and necessarily in the performance of the said duties, there may be deducted from the emoluments to be assessed the expenses so necessarily incurred and defrayed."

As can be seen the Schedule E expenses rule is extremely strict: it divides expenses into two broad categories:

(a) travelling expenses;

(b) other expenses.

3.1 TRAVELLING EXPENSES

These will only be allowed as a deduction if they are incurred 'in the performance of the duties of the office or employment'.

In general the costs of travelling from home to work are not allowable. In **Ricketts v. Colquhoun (1926)** the taxpayer was Recorder of Portsmouth and regularly travelled from his home in London to hold Quarter Sessions. He was assessable under Schedule D Case II in respect of his London practice and under Schedule E in respect of his office of Recorder. Held the costs of travelling to Portsmouth were not allowed:

(a) they were not incurred in the performance of his duties which did not start until he arrived at Portsmouth;

(b) they were not incurred necessarily - a Recorder <u>could</u> have lived at Portsmouth.

In **Owen v. Pook (1969)** it was held that travel expenses from one place of work to another are generally deductible, and that in certain circumstances one place of work may be the taxpayer's home. Dr. Owen was a medical pracitioner in Fishguard who held a part-time medical appointment at a hospital in Haverfordwest. At certain times he would be on standby duty and was required to be available by telephone. If called he would give advice and instructions and if necessary come out to the hospital. He was responsible for the patient immediately he received the telephone call. He claimed a deduction for travelling expenses between his home and the hospital. Held the expenses were allowable: he started work when he received the telephone call and travelling to the hospital was in the performance of his duties.

3.2 OTHER EXPENSES

These will only be allowed if they are incurred 'wholly, exclusively and necessarily in the performance of the duties'.

The test is strict and disallows many expenses.

In **Brown v Bullock (1961)** a bank manager employed in the West End of London sought to deduct the subscription to a London club where he met clients rather than seeing them in his office. Held that the expenses were not allowable; they were not necessary - he could have seen his clients at the bank.

The requirement of an employer that the employee incurs expenditure is not necessarily a criterion of deductibility. In **Brown v Bullock** the requirement to join the club was 'virtually a condition of the bank manager's appointment' yet it was not enough. Per Donovan LJ

> " ... the test is not whether the employer imposes the expense but whether the duties do".

Thus in **Griffiths v. Mockler (1953)**, a major in the army was obliged to join the officers' mess and would have been subject to disciplinary action if he had not joined. Held that the expenses were not in the performance of his duties.

In **Humbles v. Brooks (1962)** a history teacher attended part-time lectures in order to improve his background knowledge. Held that the expense was not allowable; it was not incurred in the performance of the duties.

In **Newlin v. Woods (1966)** an employee was frequently obliged to work unsocial hours and bought a record player and records in order to stimulate his performance whilst working late at night. Held not allowed; it was not necessarily incurred in the performance of the duties. Per Cross J:

> "... it may well be that he was stimulated to work better by hearing good music, just as others may be stimulated to work better by drink..."!

Other cases of interest are:

Blackwell v. Mills (1945) A student employee required to attend part-time classes for a degree was not allowed to deduct expenses;

Sanderson v. Durbridge (1955) A clerk obliged to work in the evenings could not deduct the excess cost of a meal.

In certain cases clothing and food allowances may be negotiated by trade unions; fees paid to professional bodies may be allowed.

With effect from 1987/88, donations to charities up to £100 per year will be allowed as a Schedule E deduction, subject to conditions.

3.3 THE EXPENSES CLAIM

To comply with the strict requirements of the law it is necessary to add all the assessable emoluments together and deduct from the expenses incurred. An example appears in the personal computation section of this book.

4.0 WAGES IN LIEU OF NOTICE

These are generally not taxable, but see section 6.0 below.

5.0 WORKERS SUPPLIED BY AGENCIES

When a worker is employed through an agency and renders services to a client which are subject to supervision, direction or control by the client or the agency, he will be treated as assessable under Schedule E. This will not apply to:

(a) entertainers or fashion models;

(b) home workers, or

(c) construction sub-contractors.

The person paying the remuneration, normally the agency, must deduct tax under PAYE and account for it to the Revenue.

6.0 PAYMENTS ON REMOVAL OR RETIREMENT FROM OFFICE

Where an employee receives a lump sum on removal or retirement from his office or employment it is liable to tax under Schedule E. It is treated as earned income received at the date of removal or retirement and must be notified by the payer to the Revenue within 30 days of the year of assessment in which the payment is made.

6.1 DEDUCTIONS

Although such a lump sum is liable to tax under Schedule E, there are several exemptions and reliefs which remove many payments from liability to tax, or otherwise reduce the tax payable. For payments received after 5th April 1981 the basic exemption is £25,000.

Illustration

D retired on 31st December 1986, having been employed by Global Company for the past 40 years. On retirement he received a lump sum payment of £40,000.

The amount that will be taxable is:

	£
Lump sum received	40,000
Less: exemption	25,000
Chargeable lump sum	15,000

Where any of the duties constitute 'foreign service' i.e. where such service would not have been liable to tax under Schedule E Case I, any sums chargeable can be reduced, or further reduced, by the fraction:

$$\frac{\text{foreign service}}{\text{total service}}$$

If in the above Illustration D spent eight years abroad of the total period of service the amount assessable would be further reduced:

	£
After exemption	15,000
Less: 8/40 x £15,000	3,000
	12,000

If the foreign service proportion is sufficiently high, the whole of the lump sum will be exempt. For this exemption, it must be shown that the foreign service comprised either:

(a) three-quarters of the entire service; or

(b) where total service exceeds 10 years, the whole of the last 10 years; or

(c) where total service exceeds 20 years, one-half thereof, including any 10 of the final 20 years.

When a redundancy payment is received under the Redundancy Payments Act 1965, it is exempt from tax in the hands of the recipient. However, the maximum available exemption of £25,000 is reduced by such a payment.

Where the compensation payment is contractual and not ex gratia it will be fully taxable as a payment for services under TA 1970,s.181 and no deduction can be claimed therefrom.

In **Dale v. de Soissons (1950)** the contract of employment specified payments to be made in the case of the contract terminating before the end of its full term. The payment was held to be fully taxable, as an emolument.

6.2 TOP SLICING

To avoid the high effective rate of tax that would be payable if the chargeable amount of the lump sum was assessed in one year, 'top slicing' relief may be claimed. Under the original legislation, the rules for determining the 'top slicing' relief involved complex calculations, and there was a distinction between the treatment of payments on removal from office, and other payments. The new top slicing relief is greatly simplified and there is no longer a distinction between the treatment of the different types of payment.

The steps are:

(a) find the tax on the other income;

(b) find the tax on the chargeable lump sum treating it as the top slice of earned income but making the following reductions of the tax charged:

  (i) from the first £25,000 - one-half

  (ii) from the next £25,000 - one quarter

  (iii) from any excess - Nil.

Illustration

D retired on 31st December 1986 and received a lump sum retirement payment of £80,000. During 1986/87 he had other earned income of £14,500 and investment income of £6,000. He is a married man, but his wife has no income.

		£	£	£
	Earned income		14,500	
	Investment income		6,000	
			20,500	
	Personal allowance		3,655	
			16,845	
Tax:	£16,845 @ 29%			4,885
Lump sum		80,000		
Less: Exempt		25,000		
	Chargeable	55,000		
First	£25,000			
Tax:	£ 355 @ 29%	103		
	£3,000 @ 40%	1,200		
	£5,200 @ 45%	2,340		
	£7,900 @ 50%	3,950		
	£7,900 @ 55%	4,345		
	£ 645 @ 60%	387		
	£25,000	12,325 - ½ (6,163) =		6,162
Next	£25,000	c/f		11,047

			b/f	12,325	(6,163)	11,047
Tax:		60%		15,000	-1/4(3,750) =	11,250
Next	£ 5,000					
	=======					
Tax:		60%		3,000	NIL	3,000
				30,325	9,913	______
Total tax liability for the year				______	______	25,297
						======

This may alternatively be expressed as:	£
Tax on whole income	
Normal	4,885
On lump sum	30,325
	35,210
Less: Top slicing relief	9,913
	25,297
	======

7.0 THE BASIS OF ASSESSMENT

7.1 THE CASES

Liability to tax under Schedule E is under one of three cases:

(a) Case I
This applies where the employee is resident and ordinarily resident in the UK. The total emoluments earned by such a person will be liable to tax unless:

(i) the duties are performed wholly or partly outside the UK when certain deductions may be allowed; or

(ii) the emoluments are 'foreign emoluments', when other deductions may be available. Note however that foreign emoluments in respect of duties performed wholly outside the UK are excluded from Case I.

(b) Case II
This applies where the employee is not resident in the UK or, if resident, not ordinarily resident in the UK. The emoluments for duties performed in the UK are taxable under this Case, subject to any deduction for 'foreign emoluments'.

(c) Case III
This applies to the emoluments of employees resident in the UK which are not already liable under Cases I or II. This Case covers income earned abroad from a non-resident employer which is remitted to the UK. A charge under Case I or II supersedes one under Case III.

7.2 FOREIGN EMOLUMENTS

'Foreign emoluments' mean earnings of an employee not domiciled in the UK from a non-resident employer. When the duties are performed in the UK a deduction may be made from the emoluments assessable. If the duties are performed outside the UK only remittances are taxable. To qualify for the deduction for 1984/85 and subsequent years, the employee must be in the employment of the non-resident employer at some time between 6th April 1983 and 13th March 1984 and must continue the employment from 1984/85.

Employees who enter into foreign employment before 1st August 1984 by way of an agreement before 14th March 1984 will still be entitled to a deduction.

The deduction of 50% will be reduced to 25% for 1987/88 and 1988/89. It will be abolished from 6th April 1989.

The 25% deduction from foreign emoluments for employees who have been resident in the UK for nine out of the previous ten fiscal years has been abolished from 1984/85.

7.3 DEDUCTIONS FROM THE EMOLUMENTS OF AN EMPLOYEE RESIDENT AND ORDINARILY RESIDENT IN THE UK

When the taxpayer is resident and ordinarily resident in the UK certain deductions can be made from his assessable emoluments where the duties of the employment are performed wholly or partly outside the UK.

If they are performed wholly or partly outside the UK where the employee is abroad for a continuous period of 365 days a deduction of 100% is made from the emoluments assessable. Visits to the UK will not break the continuity of the period of absence provided they do not exceed 62 consecutive days or more than one-sixth of the total period whether continuous or not. Days of arrival are treated as days in the UK but not days of departure.

7.4 CALCULATION OF THE DEDUCTION

Where a taxpayer is absent for 365 days the period of return to the UK can be not more than 60 days (1/6 x 365) and as they do not exceed 62 days they may be continuous.

Where the taxpayer has regular visits back to the UK it is not possible to consider the period as a whole. It must be divided into qualifying periods of:

(a) period overseas;

(b) period in UK;

(c) period overseas.

At the end of each period the conditions must be satisfied if the taxpayer wishes to qualify for the 100% deduction i.e.:

(a) the period in the UK must not exceed 62 continuous days, and

(b) must not exceed one-sixth of the total period.

Illustration

D goes abroad for 100 days, returns to the UK for 20 days and then goes abroad for a further 60 days.

Overseas	100 days
UK	20 days
Overseas	60 days
	180 days x 1/6 = 30

The period qualifies as the days in the UK do not exceed one-sixth of the total. Although it is not yet possible to claim the 100% deduction it is possible to extend the qualifying period.

After the 60 days abroad he returns to the UK for a further 40 days and then goes abroad for a further 150 days.

Overseas	100 days
UK	20 days
Overseas	60 days x 1/6 = 30
UK	40 days
Overseas	150 days
	370 days x 1/6 = 61

It is now possible to qualify for the 100% deduction. All the conditions are satisfied - there is no continuous period of 62 days and the days back in the UK do not exceed one-sixth of the total period.

If the second period in the UK was one of 45 days, then the 100% deduction would not have been available:

Overseas	100 days
UK	20 days
Overseas	60 days
UK	45 days
Overseas	150 days
	375 days x 1/6 = 62

The period in the UK is 65 days which exceeds one-sixth of the total period. The 100% deduction will now be lost.

It is important to appreciate that the period cannot be looked at as a whole but will be divided up into qualifying periods.

Thus if in the above example the structure of UK visits was:

Overseas	100 days
UK	40 days
Overseas	60 days
UK	20 days
Overseas	150 days
	370 days

although the total visits to the UK do not exceed one-sixth of the total period it will not be possible to qualify for the 100% deduction.

Overseas	100 days
UK	40 days
Overseas	60 days
	200 days x 1/6 = 33 days

The first period will not qualify as the period of return to the UK exceeds the maximum available.

It is possible at that stage to abandon the first period abroad and attempt to build up another qualifying period commencing with the second trip:

Overseas	60 days
UK	20 days
Overseas	150 days
	230 days x 1/6 = 38 days

This does qualify but as it is not 365 days then no deductions are available.

The various percentage reductions are made to the emoluments of a qualifying period, which need not necessarily be co-terminous with a year of assessment. Thus if A who receives a salary of £12,000 per annum goes to work abroad on 1st July 1985 returns on 1st August 1986 and then works abroad again for the month of January 1987, his assessable emoluments will be:

	£	£
<u>1985/86</u>		
UK duties - 6.4.85 to 30.6.85		
86/365 x £12,000		2,827
Overseas duties - 1.7.85 to 5.4.86		
279/365 x £12,000	9,173	
Less: 100%	9,173	
		NIL
		2,827
		=====
<u>1986/87</u>		
Overseas duties - 6.4.86 to 31.7.86		
117/365 x £12,000	3,847	
Less: 100%	3,847	
		NIL
UK duties - 1.8.86 to 31.12.86		
153/365 x £12,000		5,030
Overseas duties - 1.1.87 to 31.1.87		
31/365 x £12,000		1,019
No deduction as less than 365 days		
UK duties - 1.2.87 to 5.4.87		
64/365 x £12,000		2,104
		8,153
		=====

The deduction is applied to the average emoluments of the fiscal year. It may be possible to establish with the Inland Revenue a higher figure to which the deduction is to be applied where clearly a higher salary is paid for the overseas duties. The deduction is also applied to benefits etc. Where the benefits clearly relate wholly to the overseas period they will qualify for a full 100% deduction. Where they clearly relate to the period of UK duties then they will not normally qualify for any deduction.

The rules for expenses for employees working abroad are:

(a) the expenses of travelling to and from the overseas employment are allowable together with the costs of travelling between one overseas employment and another. The expense must be borne by the employer or by the employee and reimbursed. Similar relief is available to UK employees who perform part of their duties abroad. Where the employee performs part of his duties in the UK and part abroad, there is no limit to the number of trips abroad, the travel expenses of which are allowed, provided that the duties can only be performed abroad and that the journey is made solely for that purpose;

(b) expenses of board and lodging are allowed if:

(i) borne by the employer, or

(ii) borne by the employee and reimbursed by the employer.

No allowance is available if the costs were borne by the employee with no reimbursement;

(c) family travel for the spouse or children is allowed if they are paid or reimbursed as in (b) above. Relief is however, only available if the taxpayer is absent for a continuous period of at least 60 days and is restricted to two return journeys by the same persons in a fiscal year. Accommodation provided by the employer is assessable.

Similar relief is also available for UK domiciles working in the UK provided that they were not:

(a) resident in the UK in either of the two fiscal years immediately preceding their arrival in the UK, or

(b) were not in the UK for any purpose at any time during the two years preceding the date of arrival.

Provided that the expense is borne by the employer or borne by the employee and then reimbursed by the employer travelling expenses will not be assessed where they relate to:

(a) journeys between the country of his normal residence to the UK and back in order to perform his UK duties;

(b) where he has been in the UK for a continuous period of 60 days or more family visits as in (c) above.

The reliefs are limited to a period of five years from the date of the employee's arrival in the UK.

8.0 PAYE

8.1 GENERAL

Most of the tax levied under Schedule E is collected by the Pay As You Earn (PAYE) system which is operated by employers. Regulations issued in 1981 require that tax on the cash equivalent or car benefits, and petrol, etc., will be collected under the PAYE system as from 6th April 1982. The main documentation and tables are as under:

8.2 TAX TABLES

There are two sets of tax tables used:

(a) Free Pay which by use of a code number allocates the employee's entitlement to personal allowances over the year. Thus an employee paid weekly will receive 1/52nd of his total allowances for that tax year (known as free pay). If he is paid monthly 1/12 of the total allowances will be deducted from his monthly salary before computing the tax payable. In finding the code number the last digit of the total allowances is omitted, so that a person with allowances of £2,335 will have a code number of 233. Each code number is followed by a letter L, H or T. 'L' shows that the recipient receives the lower rate of personal allowance and 'H' the higher rate. This enables alterations in personal allowances to be effected speedily. Where a taxpayer does not wish his or her marital status to be known, the code 'T' is given. When an employee commences work and has no code number he is taxed using an emergency code number. This gives him the basic single person's personal allowance. This will be amended once he has completed a return form and submitted it to the Revenue.

(b) Taxable Pay which gives the total tax due on the total remuneration to date less the appropriate proportion of the personal allowances.
Table B shows the tax payable on pay falling into the basic rate band; the table D shows the tax chargeable on pay falling into the higher rate bands.

8.3 TAX RECORD SHEETS

These record the details of gross pay, free pay, taxable pay and tax due, week by week throughout the year. They also record additional information such as the employee's code number and national insurance number.

8.4 FORM P45

This form is used when an employee leaves and shows his total gross pay, taxable pay, tax deducted and code numbers in accordance with the tax record sheet which is retained by the former employer. It also shows the week or month up to which entries have been made on the tax record sheet and enables the new employer to continue deducting tax in the correct manner.

8.5 YEAR END PROCEDURES

At the end of the tax year the employer must provide each employee with a form P60 setting out his gross pay during the year and the total tax deducted therefrom. If the employee considers he has been overtaxed he can apply to his Income Tax District for a formal assessment under Schedule E using the form P60 as evidence of the tax suffered during the year.

The employer must also send to the Inland Revenue a form P35 showing details of the total tax due to the Inland Revenue no later than 14 days after the end of the relevant fiscal year. This will be accompanied by a year end return for each employee on form P14 (this is normally a copy of the P60) together with forms P9D (a return of taxable benefits received by non PIID (lower paid) employees) and PIID where appropriate.

9.0 PENSION SCHEMES

Pension schemes can be either approved or unapproved. If the scheme is approved, valuable benefits are available. These are:

(a) the employee's contribution, not exceeding 15% of remuneration, is allowed as a deduction;

(b) the employer's contributions are an allowable trade expense and are not treated as benefits accruing to the employees;

(c) the pension once received is classified as earned income;

(d) the income of the pension fund itself attracts certain tax exemptions.

To obtain these benefits the Pension Scheme must be approved by the Revenue. Before approval can be obtained certain conditions must be satisfied:

(a) the scheme must be established by Trust Deed and must provide retirement benefits for employees and their dependants;

(b) the employer must be resident in the UK and must contribute to the scheme which must be administered by a UK resident administrator (often a bank or insurance company);

(c) benefits which must commence between the ages of 60 and 70 for each man and 55 to 70 for women must not exceed one-sixtieth of the average of the total remuneration of the last three years' service paid for each year of employment up to a maximum of 40 years. Any widow's benefit must not exceed two-thirds of this figure;

(d) commutation of part of the pension is allowed provided that it does not exceed three-eighths of the average of the total remuneration of the last three years' service for each year of employment. In no case can it normally exceed one and a half times the average remuneration described above;

(e) there can be no refund of employer's contributions.

The Revenue can agree to vary certain of these conditions.

If the scheme is unapproved then employees' contributions are now allowable as a Schedule E expense and the employer's contributions are taxable as a benefit in kind of the employee.

10.0 SHARE OPTION AND INCENTIVE SCHEMES

10.1 GENERAL

Share option and incentive schemes have been operated by companies for many years. Legislation introduced in the early 1970s made them unfashionable by subjecting profits to income tax. More recently the trend has been to provide relief for 'approved' schemes.

10.2 UNAPPROVED SCHEMES

Schemes designed purely for one sector or group of employees in general fall outside the approved schemes. They fall into two main groups.

Share options TA,s.186

An employee is liable to income tax under Schedule E on any benefit derived from a share option scheme in the tax year in which the option is exercised. The benefit is calculated by deducting the market value of the shares, at the time the option is exercised, the price paid for the shares by the employee and the price paid for the option (if any). If the right to exercise the option is capable of being exercised more than seven years after grant, there may be a charge to tax on the grant of the rights. Where bonus or rights issues are received, they are deemed to be acquired at the date of the original acquisition.

In addition to the above a liability will arise on the final sale of the share-holding. The amount assessed under Schedule E is treated as an addition to the cost of acquiring the shares.

Where, under an option scheme, the employee has acquired shares which have subsequently fallen in value, he may have an agreement with his employer to sell his shares back at not less than that which he paid for them. This is termed a 'Stop Loss' agreement. Where such an arrangement applies it will be considered as being equal to the making of a loan which is then written off and a liability will result under Schedule E.

Share incentive schemes - FA 1972,s.72

Where an employee or director acquires shares as the result of an opportunity offered to him as a result of his office or employment there will be a liability to tax under Schedule E on the difference in value between that at the date on which the shares are acquired and their value at the earliest of:

(a) the date of disposal;

(b) the date on which they are no longer subject to any restrictions not applicable to shares issued generally;

(c) the expiration of seven years from acquisition.

Illustration
A acquired 1,000 shares in Alpha Ltd. - his employer - on 1st January 1978 as a result of an opportunity available to all employees. The cost was £2,000. He sold the shares on 1st January 1988 for £15,000. The value on 1st January 1985 was £10,000.

	£
1984/85 (7 years after acquisition)	
Value at 1.1.85	10,000
Cost	2,000
Liable under Schedule E	8,000

Any subsequent increases in value will be liable to Capital Gains Tax.

	£
Disposal proceeds	15,000
Value at 1.1.85	10,000
Capital gain (subject to indexation)	5,000

If the shares had been acquired at 1.1.1978 at a value lower than their market value there would be an additional charge to income tax under s.186.

10.3 APPROVED SCHEMES

There are three main schemes. The first was introduced under the provisions of FA 1978 and the initial scheme was followed by variants firstly under the SAYE provisions and then in FA 1984 by a scheme which though approved is not entirely open to all employees.

Approved profit-sharing schemes - FA 1978,s.53
Provided approval is obtained from the Inland Revenue, employees may acquire shares in their employing companies without any charge arising under Schedule E.

An approved scheme is one where the company provides trustees with cash to acquire shares in the company which they then appropriate to employees. The scheme must be open to all employees, and the shares must be fully paid - irredeemable and not subject to special restrictions. The shares may be quoted or unquoted.

The maximum annual value of shares appropriated to an employee must not exceed the greater of:

(a) £1,250, or

(b) 10% of salary, exclusive of benefits of the current or preceding year (if greater) up to a maximum of £5,000.

The participant must be bound by contract to allow the trustees to retain the shares for a period of retention. This will end at the earlier of:

(a) the second anniversary of appropriation of the shares to the trustees;

(b) the date of the participant's death;

(c) the date on which the participant reaches pensionable age.

If the shares are sold either during the period of retention or within the next three years tax will be charged under Schedule E on a percentage of the share valuation at the date of appropriation:

Period held	Percentage
During period of retention	100%
2 but less than 4 years	100%
4 but less than 5 years	75%

The 100% or 75% charge will be reduced to 50% if the employee ceases to be employed because of retirement, redundancy or injury.

If the disposal proceeds are less than the value on appropriation, the percentage charge will be applied to the disposal proceeds.
There will be a liability to CGT on the difference between the value on appropriation and the disposal proceeds.

Illustration
X had appropriated to him shares worth £1,000 under an approved profit-sharing scheme. He sold them after 4½ years for:

(a) £1,800;

(b) £800.

Sale for £1,800

Schedule E charged on 75% x £1,000	=	£750
		====
CGT liability on £1,800 - £1,000 (subject to indexation)	=	£800
		====

Sale for £800

Schedule E charged on 75% x £800	=	£600
		====
Capital loss of £1,000 - £800	=	£200
		====

Where the shares sold have been acquired on various dates, they will be identified on a FIFO basis for the purpose of ascertaining the Schedule E charge. For capital gains tax purposes, the normal rules will apply.

To avoid difficulties with private companies whose articles of association have required members of the company who are employees to sell their shares on leaving employment provisions have been introduced in FA 1986 which allow for approval for profit sharing schemes operating this restriction provided that:

(a) the disposal consideration must be in cash;

(b) the formula for calculating it must be specified in the articles;

(c) the formula must not discriminate between employee and non-employee shareholders.

FA 1986 has also allowed Workers Co-operatives to set up approved profit sharing schemes using redeemable shares, broadly under same conditions as normal approved schemes.

Under the provisions of FA 1980,s.47, employees may participate in approved share option schemes conducted through the medium of an SAYE contract. Broadly, ordinary shares may be acquired from the proceeds of SAYE savings contracts up to a maximum monthly contribution of £100. The price of the shares must be fixed at the time that the employee obtains the option and must represent no less than 90% of the value of the shares at that time. The option will be exercised when the SAYE contract matures and the employee will not be liable to income tax under s.186 on any profit made on the grant or exercise of the option. To be approved the scheme must be open to all employees and provide that the option cannot normally be exercised within three years of the date of the grant.

In general, the existing rules for share option schemes provide that there will be a liability to Schedule E tax on the difference between the market value of the shares at the time the option was exercised and the amount paid for them. Provisions have now been introduced in FA 1984 which avoid this charge in respect of approved schemes.

Obtaining approval

Application may be made to the Board of Inland Revenue to approve a share option scheme under the new rules. The Board may withdraw approval where it appears that the conditions are no longer satisfied. Appeals against the Board's decisions may be made to the Special Commissioners.

Conditions

In general, the scheme must provide that options can only be granted to full-time directors or qualifying employees of a participating company. They must be required to work for the company for at least 25 or 20 hours per week respectively. A person who leaves employment may exercise it subsequently and the personal representatives of a deceased employee may exercise it within 12 months of his death.

No options may be granted to an employee or director if he has, or had within the preceding 12 months a material interest (more than 10% of the ordinary share capital) in a close-company whose shares might be acquired under an approved scheme.

The shares to be acquired under an approved scheme may be those in:

(a) the company granting the option; or

(b) its holding company; or

(c) in certain conditions, a consortium owning company.

The shares must be quoted or unquoted or be in a company controlled by a quoted company, fully paid up and not redeemable. The price to be paid for the shares must be stated when the option is granted and must not be manifestly less than their market value at the date the option was granted. The scheme must limit the value of the shares available to the employee under unexercised options to the greater of:

(a) £100,000; or

(b) four times the remuneration (excluding benefits, etc.) of the fiscal year for which the limit needs to be ascertained, e.g. because new options are to be issued; or

(c) four times the remuneration of the preceding fiscal year.

Share options granted under the scheme must not be transferable. The option must be exercised not less than three or more than ten years after granting and not less than three years after the owner last exercised an option under the scheme.

Tax treatment

When the options are granted, there will be no liability under Schedule E except in the unusual circumstances where the price paid for the shares is less than their market value at the time the option was granted. When the option is exercised there will again be no liability provided that the scheme remains approved at that time. On disposal of the shares there will be a liability to CGT on the difference between the amount paid for the shares and the disposal proceeds.

11.0 SUB-CONTRACTORS IN THE CONSTRUCTION INDUSTRY

Where a sub-contractor is providing labour on hire for use in the construction industry he must receive his payments from the main contractor after deduction of tax at 29% unless he holds an exemption certificate (form 714). An exemption certificate will only be issued by the Revenue if the sub-contractor can show that he had paid his past tax liabilities when they fell due and completed all the Income Tax Returns etc. which were required. If he had not been asked to complete any tax returns the Revenue must be satisfied that he would have completed them had he been required to do so.

Where the sub-contractor has been given an exemption certificate he must provide the main contractor with a receipt for payments received on a specially provided form (form 715) and he will receive these payments gross. The main contractor must forward all the forms 715 received by him together with a return showing the name and exemption certificate number of each sub-contractor; this must be done quarterly.

If the sub-contractor does not have an exemption certificate and thus suffers deduction at source he must obtain a certificate of deduction of tax (form SC 60) whenever he stops working for a specific main contractor. The main contractor is required to account for the tax deducted on a monthly basis in much the same way as for PAYE.

To obtain a certificate applicants must:

(a) have been employed or self-employed for the previous three years;

(b) have complied with obligations under the Taxes Acts for the previous three years and the relevant National Insurance Acts for the same period.

In addition:

(a) the business must be carried on mainly through a separate business bank account;

(b) proper records must be kept;

(c) the business must be carried on from the proper premises with proper equipment, stock and other facilities;

(d) if required by law, the firm's name must be registered under the Registration of Business Names Act 1916.

The new provisions regarding exemption certificates also apply to limited companies and agencies which supply construction workers.

Special regulations are in force for school and college leavers and others offering a guarantee.

10 Personal Computations

1.0 GENERAL

Once the income of an individual has been ascertained it can be accumulated into a personal computation and the final amount of tax payable calculated. The personal computation basically divides into four main stages:

(a) the amalgamation of income to arrive at statutory income;

(b) the deduction of charges from statutory income;

(c) the granting of personal reliefs;

(d) the calculation of tax payable.

2.0 THE AMALGAMATION OF INCOME

Total income will include not only income which has not suffered tax at source but also that which has already had basic rate tax deducted. This income can include:

(a) building society interest and certain bank interest;

(b) dividends; and

(c) certain interest payments received from companies, national and local government.

This 'taxed' income must be 'grossed up' before being brought into the tax computation. The amount of the basic rate tax already deducted is allowed as a credit against the final tax liability. If the final tax liability is less than the tax deducted at source the excess will be repaid, but not to the extent that the tax deducted represents the tax credit on building society or certain bank interest received.

The tax credit in respect of this income can only be offset against a tax liability, it can never be repaid in cash.

In setting out a computation it is advisable to group the income under four heads:

(a) Earned Income
Husband
Wife

(b) Unearned Income
Husband
Wife

3.0 THE DEDUCTION FROM INCOME OF CHARGES AND EXPENSES

3.1 GENERAL

Certain payments can be deducted from an individual's total statutory income before charging it to tax. Other payments can only be deducted from specific types of income.

3.2 CHARGES DEDUCTIBLE FROM SPECIFIC TYPES OF INCOME ONLY

(a) Schedule E expenses - from Schedule E income.

(b) Pension scheme contributions and retirement annuity payments - from the income to which they relate.

(c) Section 171 losses - from trading profits of the same trade.

(d) Certain interest on loans to acquire land - from the income from that land only (see below).

3.3 CHARGES DEDUCTIBLE FROM STATUTORY INCOME

These can consist of two broad types:

(a) interest payable;

(b) charges paid under deduction of tax.

3.4 INTEREST PAYABLE

In order to qualify for relief from income tax on the loan interest paid, the loan must have been used for one of the following purposes, within a reasonable time (twelve months) of the loan being raised:

(a) To purchase or improve the taxpayer's main residence or that of his separated or former spouse or that occupied rent free by a dependent relative of himself or his spouse but only to the extent that the loan or loans do not exceed £30,000. The house must be in the UK or Eire and occupied by the taxpayer within one year of acquisition to qualify, though this period may be extended by the Revenue. The taxpayer's main residence is ascertained by fact and not by election.

If the taxpayer is moving he may during a bridging period have two loans running - one on the old property and one on the new. The taxpayer will continue to obtain interest relief on the old property as long as the total of old and new loans does not exceed £30,000. The Revenue may extend this period. The MIRAS scheme (Mortgage Interest Relief at Source) applies to loans of up to £30,000.

(b) To purchase or improve property acquired for letting at a commercial rent. The property must be let for more than 26 weeks in any year and must be available for letting during the remainder of the time unless it is occupied as the taxpayer's main house or is uninhabitable due to repairs. The interest can only be set against letting income from property, any excess being carried forward for future relief.

(c) To purchase an annuity, provided the taxpayer is over 65 and the loan is secured on his own home. No relief is available for interest paid on a loan in excess of £30,000.

(d) To introduce capital into a partnership. For interest paid prior to 11th March 1981 on such loans, it was a requirement that the partner should be an active member of the partnership.

(e) To pay capital transfer tax or inheritance tax before the grant of representation.

(f) To purchase plant and machinery for use in an employment or partnership. The item must qualify for capital allowances and the interest is only allowable for three years from the end of the fiscal year in which the loan was received.

(g) To contribute capital to industrial co-operatives.

(h) To invest in an employee controlled company. This is one where more than 50% of both:

  (i) the issued ordinary share capital; and

  (ii) the voting power;

are owned by full time employees of the company or their spouses. An employee together with his spouse cannot hold more than ten per cent of the ordinary share capital or the voting rights of the company. If the employee's spouse is also an employee of the company, no account will be taken of the spouse's shareholding in the company in determining the ten per cent limit. Each of them will have a separate ten per cent limit.

(i) Persons taxable under Schedule D Case I or II or Schedule E may obtain relief on the interest paid on a loan to purchase property whilst living in job-related accommodation. The property must have been used by the borrower as a residence at the time the interest is paid. Where interest is paid within twelve months of the loan, then the accommodation must be used by the borrower at some time within the twelve month period.

This relief is also given where the borrower intends to occupy the accommodation as his only or main residence in due course.

The limit on the amount borrowed for which this relief is available is £30,000.

Accommodation is job-related where the borrower or his spouse is required under contract to carry on a trade, profession, vocation or employment in premises provided by another person. They must also live on those premises. The contract must have been entered into at arm's length.

Accommodation is not job-related where the borrower or his spouse live in accommodation where the agreement is entered into with a company in which the borrower, his spouse or his business partner have a material interest.

(j) To purchase ordinary shares in or to make a loan to a close company provided that when the interest is paid the person concerned has either:

  (i) a material interest (more than five per cent of the ordinary share capital) in the company; or

(ii) works full time as a manager or director of the company and also is a shareholder in the company.

If interest is paid by a trader on an overdraft or loan for use in his business that interest will be allowed as a trading expense.

All these charges are allowable as a deduction for both basic and higher rates of tax. Subject to the previous paragraph no relief is available for bank overdraft interest.

3.5 CHARGES PAID UNDER DEDUCTION OF TAX

There are a number of types of payment which fall into this category such as payments under deed of covenant, maintenance payments, patent royalties etc. These are all paid under deduction of tax and are known as retainable charges.

Before they are deducted in the personal computation it is necessary to gross the payment. Most of these charges are allowed for basic and higher rates of tax. Special rules apply to deeds of covenant, which will be allowed as a deduction for higher rate tax only if they satisfy the following conditions:

(a) if the deed of covenant arose in connection with the acquisition of a business;

(b) if the payment under covenant is made to a former partner or the widow of a former partner;

(c) if the payment is under a deed between husband and wife after their divorce or permanent separation;

(d) if the deed of covenant was entered into before 7th April 1965 and is not, at the time of payment, for the benefit of:

(i) an employee or agent;

(ii) an infant unmarried child of the covenantor.

The payment under this exception must be to a named individual.

(e) if the deed of covenant is paid to a charity. Following FA 1986 deeds to a charity are exempt up to any amount.

Deeds of covenant are only effective for tax purposes where they are for a period which is capable of exceeding six years, or three years where they are made to a charity.

MIRAS (Mortgage Interest Relief at Source) was introduced as from 1983/84. Before then, all interest paid to building societies was paid gross. Now if a qualifying borrower pays relevant loan interest to a qualifying lender then he may deduct basic rate tax before paying the interest. Where relief is due at the higher rates, this will still be given by adjusting the code number. A qualifying lender can recover from the government any tax deducted by the borrowers. The system applies to loans of up to £30,000, and if the loan exceeds this figure interest will still be gross unless the lender agrees that interest on the first £30,000 of a loan can be paid net and the rest gross. As from 6th April 1987 this treatment will be applied to all new loans.

A qualifying borrower is basically an individual who pays relevant loan interest apart from an individual whose income from employment is exempt from tax in the UK e.g. a diplomat.

A qualifying lender includes banks, building societies, local authorities and others designated by the Treasury.

Relevant loan interest is interest to purchase or improve the taxpayer's only or main residence in the UK or to purchase an annuity by a taxpayer aged 65 or more secured on his house; 3.4 (a) and (b) above.

Where the borrower or lender consider they are no longer qualifying, or where the interest no longer is relevant loan interest the Inland Revenue must be informed.

3.6 THE DEDUCTIBILITY OF RETAINABLE CHARGES

It has already been mentioned that:

(a) all retainable charges are paid after deducting basic rate tax; and

(b) they are allowable as a deduction from basic or basic and higher rates of tax at the gross figure.

Clearly, unless measures were taken to prevent it, the taxpayer could possibly get substantial tax savings out of paying a retainable charge. By, for example, paying patent royalties of £71 net in the fiscal year 1987/87 he could:

		£
(a)	Get relief for tax at up to 60% on the gross amount of £100	60
(b)	Retain the basic rate tax of 29%	29
		89

To ensure that this situation does not apply it is necessary to ensure that credit is given to the Revenue for the £29 basic rate tax deducted and retained. This is normally done by increasing the tax liability by the amount of the basic rate tax retained.

Illustration

A, a bachelor, has an earned income in 1986/87 of £4,000 and pays a charge of £300 from which he deducts tax at source of £87. His liability to income tax is:

	£
Earned Income	4,000
Less: Charge	300
	3,700
Less: Personal allowance	2,335
	1,365
Income tax @ 29% on £1,365	396
Add: Income tax retained	87
	483

An alternative way of dealing with it is to ignore the charge altogether.

Illustration

	£
Facts as before	
Earned Income	4,000
Less: Personal allowance	2,335
	1,665

	£
Income tax @ 29% on £1,665	483
Add: Income tax retained	-
	483

It can thus be seen that no tax saving is achieved by paying a retainable charge and obtaining relief at the basic rate only.

Of the two methods, that shown in the first Illustration should be used as it gives the correct figure of total income (see below).

Where the charge is allowable at the higher rates of tax, the calculation would appear as under:

Illustration

B, a married man with no children or other dependants, is in receipt of the following income in 1986/87:

	£
Earned	11,700
Unearned (gross)	11,000

He pays a charge, which is allowable as a deduction when computing the higher rate tax liability of £1,500, of which he retains £435 income tax by deduction at source.

	£
Earned income	11,700
Unearned income	11,000
	22,700
Less: Allowable charge (gross)	1,500
	21,200
Less: Personal allowance	3,655
Taxable Income	17,545

	£
Income tax:	
£	
17,200 @ 29%	4,988
345 @ 40%	138
17,545	5,126
Add: Basic rate tax retained on charge	435
	5,561

If the charge were not allowed at the higher rates the calculation would be:

Taxable Income (as above)		£17,545
	£	£
Income tax		5,126
Add: Basic rate tax on charge paid	435	
Benefit of higher rates £1,500 @ (40-29)%	165	
		600
		5,726

This recognises that, by deducting the charges in the computation, relief has been given at the higher rates; the basic rate element has already been dealt with.

3.7 THE OFFSET OF CHARGES

FA 1971,s.34(2) gives the taxpayer the right to offset charges on total income to his greatest advantage.

Statutory income (i.e. income from all sources as computed in accordance with the rules and schedules of income tax) less charges gives Total Income.

4.0 PERSONAL RELIEFS

4.1 GENERAL

These are granted for the year of assessment and are treated as a deduction from total income. If they exceed this, the surplus cannot be carried forward.

4.2 PERSONAL ALLOWANCES

(a)	Married allowance	1986/87	£3,655
		1985/86	£3,455
		1984/85	£3,155

This is given to a husband living with his wife or, if she is not living with him, wholly maintaining her and not getting income tax relief for any alimony or maintenance paid. In the year of marriage this allowance is proportionately reduced.

(b)	Single allowance	1986/87	£2,335
		1985/86	£2,205
		1984/85	£2,005

An individual resident in the UK irrespective of age, who is not married, is entitled to a single personal allowance.

4.3 WIFE'S EARNED INCOME RELIEF

Where a married woman is in receipt of earned income she is entitled to a further allowance of the smaller of the amount of her earned income of £2,335 (1985/86 £2,205). The following income, although classified as earned income does not attract WEIR:

(a) national insurance benefits other than a retirement pension received from her own contributions;

(b) any other form of pension income received in respect of a husband's services or contributions.

Illustration

Mrs D receives the following income:

	£
Salary	400
Dividends - gross	200

She will be entitled to WEIR of £400.

If her salary was £3,000 the WEIR would be £2,335.

4.4 DEPENDANT RELATIVE RELIEF

If the taxpayer is maintaining a dependant relative who is incapacitated by old age or infirmity or is the taxpayer's widowed mother or mother-in-law irrespective of age or state of health, he may claim dependant relative relief of £100.

In theory the amount of the maintenance must be a minimum of £100 and must be a voluntary contribution. However, if the amount of the contribution is less than £100, the relief is given, by Revenue concession, up to the amount contributed by the taxpayer. If the relative resides with the taxpayer no further contribution is necessary.

If the dependant's income exceeds the basic social security retirement pension the relief is reduced by the excess.

Where the relief is claimed by a single woman it is increased to £145 provided she contributes that amount in maintenance or has the relative living with her. The allowance can be split where more than one person contributes.

4.5 ADDITIONAL PERSONAL ALLOWANCE

Relief may be claimed for any year of assessment where the claimant has at least one 'qualifying' child resident with him during part or all of the year. The child does not necessarily have to be the taxpayer's own child, but the relief will not be available where at the beginning of any particular year the child is over the age of 18 years.

The claimant may be either:

(a) a widow, widower, or other person not eligible for the married person's allowance (other than by reason of any election);

(b) a married man whose wife is incapacitated physically or mentally throughout the tax year.

The amount of the allowance is £1,320 (£1,250 for 1985/86) irrespective of how many qualifying children there are. A qualifying child is one who is:

(a) born in the year of assessment; or

(b) under 16 at the beginning of that year; or

(c) 16 or over at the beginning of that year and who is receiving full-time education;

(d) and is:

  (i) a child of the claimant, or

  (ii) under 18 and maintained by him at his own expense.

4.6 HOUSEKEEPER RELIEF

This relief is only available to a widow or widower who has a relative resident with him as housekeeper. If there is no relative willing or able to act as housekeeper the taxpayer may employ a resident housekeeper on a formal employer/employee relationship. If the housekeeper is a relative and is married, no higher personal allowance in respect of the marriage will be allowed. The allowance is £100.

4.7 DAUGHTER'S AND SON'S SERVICES

Any taxpayer who is incapacitated by infirmity or old age and in consequence is compelled to rely upon help provided by his son or daughter, who resides with and is maintained by him, may claim this relief; it is a substitute for housekeeper relief. The allowance is £55.

4.8 BLIND PERSON'S ALLOWANCE

A registered blind person may claim this relief, of £360. If the taxpayer and his wife are both registered blind persons, relief of £720 may be claimed.
The son's or daughter's services relief cannot also be claimed.

4.9 LIFE ASSURANCE RELIEF

Prior to the fiscal year 1979/80, income tax relief in respect of premiums paid on certain life assurance policies was given against the income tax liability of the payer. For 1979/80 and subsequent years, tax relief is given by a reduction of 15% on the premium payable. The assurance company will then recover this 15% from the Inland Revenue. It does not affect the calculation of the income tax liability of an individual except where there is disallowable relief.
The amount of premiums payable on which relief is available is restricted to the greater of:

(a) £1,500; or

(b) one sixth of total income.

For assurance policies made after 13th March 1984, the 15% relief is withdrawn. For policies already in existence prior to 13th March 1984, the 15% relief continues to be available on premiums paid after this date.

5.0 THE CALCULATION OF TAX

5.1 INCOME TAX

This is calculated at varying rates starting with a lower rate of 29% and moving through the basic and higher rates to a top rate of 60%. A table of rates for 1986/87 is as under:

Band of Taxable Income	Amount	Rate	Tax on Band	Cumulative Tax
£	£		£	£
0-17,200	17,200	29%	4,988	4,988
17,201-20,200	3,000	40%	1,200	6,188
20,201-25,400	5,200	45%	2,340	8,528
25,401-33,300	7,900	50%	3,950	12,478
33,301-41,200	7,900	55%	4,345	16,823
over 41,200		60%		

6.0 THE FORMAT OF THE COMPUTATION

A suggested layout of a personal computation is as under:

	£	£
Earned income:		
Husband	x	
Wife	x	
		x
Unearned income:		
Husband	x	
Wife	x	
		x
		x
Less: Charges		x
Total income		x
Less: Personal allowances		x
Taxable income		x
Income Tax		x
Add: Tax on MIRAS Interest		x
Tax borne		x
Less: Tax credits		x
Tax payable by direct assessment		x

This recognises the fact that, unless a special election is made, a husband and wife are one taxable entity, their income will be jointly assessed to tax, and the husband will be responsible for the tax on both his and his wife's income.

<u>Illustration</u>

Ben, a married man, has the following income for 1986/87:

Self:	Salary	£20,000
Wife:	Salary	£ 2,500
	Schedule A	£ 4,500

	£	£
Earned income: Self		20,000
Wife		2,500
		22,500
Unearned income: Wife		4,500
		27,000
Allowances: Married	3,655	
Wife's earned income	2,335	
		5,990
		21,010
Income tax due:		
29% on £17,200		4,988
40% on £ 3,000		1,200
45% on £ 810		364
		6,552

7.0 THE TAXATION OF HUSBAND AND WIFE

7.1 JOINT ASSESSMENT

For taxation purposes, husband and wife are considered basically as one taxable unit.

Illustration

A.Ford is a sales director employed at a salary of £16,000 per annum plus commission (on sales) which amounted to £2,250 in the year to 5th April 1987. He contributes 10% of his basic salary to his employers' approved superannuation fund.

His employers provide him with a car for which he contributes £200 for private use; his business mileage totalled 2,000 in the year to 5th April 1987. His employers reimburse all other expenses for which he submits approved vouchers.

There is no private petrol paid by his employers.

In the year ended 5th April 1987 the company made a return of expense payments as follows:

	£	£	£
Car: 150% of Table benefit: £1,400 x 150%		2,100	
Less: private contribution		200	1,900
Reimbursed expenses:			
Travelling and hotel expenses in UK		674	
Entertaining UK customers		341	
Agreed business proportion of home telephone		24	
			1,039
			2,939
Subscriptions:			
Club	26		
Professional bodies	16		
British United Provident Association	84		
		126	
Fares and hotel expenses, sales tour to Austria		328	
			454
			3,393

His wife has been a freelance photographer since before their marriage; her adjusted profits have been:

Year to 31st December 1985	£5,580
Year to 31st December 1986	£4,692

The other income of Mr and Mrs Ford has been:

		Years ended 5th April	
		1986	1987
		£	£
Ford:	Dividends received	1,134	1,775
	National Savings bank ordinary account interest (account opened June 1985)	90	79
Wife:	Interest on 3½% War Loan (paid gross)	1,400	1,400
	Dividends received	2,320	4,260
Ford pays interest on a mortgage (under MIRAS)		475(gross)	492(gross)

You are required to calculate the income tax liability for 1986/87.

<u>Earned income</u>:				
<u>Mr.Ford</u>:	£	£	£	£
Salary			16,000	
Commission			2,250	
Benefits		1,900		
Car				
Reimbursed expenses:				
Travelling, etc.	674			
Entertaining	341			
Home telephone	24	1,039		
Subscriptions:				
Club	26			
Professional bodies	16			
BUPA	84	126		
Fares and hotel		328	3,393	
			21,643	
Less: Expenses Claim:				
Reimbursed expenses		1,039		
Subscriptions to professional bodies		16		
Fares and hotel expenses		328		
			1,383	
			20,260	
Less: Pension scheme contributions -			1,600	
10% x £16,000				18,660
<u>Mrs Ford</u>:				
Profits - year ended 31.12.1985				5,580
				24,240
<u>Unearned income</u>:				
<u>Mr Ford</u>:				
Dividends		1,775		
+ Tax credit 29/71		725		
			2,500	
NSB interest £(79-70)			9	
(2nd year - actual)			2,509	
<u>Mrs Ford</u>:				
War Loan		1,400		
Dividends	4,260			
+ Tax credit 29/71	1,740			
		6,000		
			7,400	
			9,909	
Less: building society interest paid			492	
				9,417

Total income			33,657
Less: Allowances:			
Personal allowance		3,655	
Wife's earned income relief		2,335	
			5,990
Taxable income			27,667

Income Tax:

£			£
17,200 @ 29%			4,988
3,000 @ 40%			1,200
5,200 @ 45%			2,340
2,267 @ 50%			1,133
27,667			9,661
Tax deducted on mortgage interest			143
			9,804
Less: Tax Credits:			
Mr Ford		725	
Mrs Ford		1,740	2,465
			7,339

In normal circumstances a husband is liable for the tax on his wife's income.

7.2 SEPARATE ASSESSMENT OF HUSBAND AND WIFE (TA 1970 s.38)

A husband or his wife can make a claim for separate assessment. It does not reduce the joint taxation liability, but makes the wife legally responsible for payment of her apportioned share of the joint liability. An election, which can be made by either husband or wife, must be made within the period 6th January to 5th July in the first year of assessment to which it relates. It continues in force until revoked by the person originally making it.

The calculation is a complicated one and involves the following steps:

(a) find the Total Income of husband and wife and the joint income; calculate income tax on the joint income before deducting personal allowances and apportion the tax between husband and wife in proportion to their respective individual incomes. Charges are allocated to the spouse who pays them;

(b) express personal allowances in terms of tax, giving relief for dependent relatives in priority to all others and to the individual spouse claiming. Divide the tax equivalent of the remaining allowances between the spouses in proportion to the tax as in (a);

(c) deduct the tax saving equivalent of personal allowances from the tax on incomes before giving personal allowances (as in (a)); the result is tax due on taxable income apportioned arithmetically between the spouses.

Illustration (Proforma computation - to nearest £)

Joint Liability	Total	Husband	Wife
	£	£	£
Earned income	15,000	9,000	6,000
Unearned income	8,800	5,100	3,700

		Total	Husband	Wife
		£	£	£
		23,800	14,100	9,700
Less: Interest paid (not MIRAS)		800	600	200
		23,000	13,500	9,500
Income tax:				
£				
17,200 @ 29%		4,988		
3,000 @ 40%		1,200		
2,800 @ 45%		1,260		
23,000				
(£13,500: £9,500)		7,448	4,372	3,076
Reduction of tax because of personal allowances:				
DRR (maintained by wife)				
£100 @ 45%		45		45
	£			
PA	3,655			
WEIR	2,335			
	5,990			
£	£			
2,700 @ 45%	1,215			
3,000 @ 40%	1,200			
290 @ 29%	84			
5,990 (£4,372:£3,076)	2,499	2,499	1,467	1,032
		2,544	1,467	1,077
Liability before personal allowances		7,448	4,372	3,076
Tax relief because of personal allowances (see note below)		2,544	1,467	1,077
Liability to Income Tax		4,904	2,905	1,999

Note: The wife's share of the tax benefit of the allowances must not be less than that attracted by the allowances attributable to her earned income. For this purpose WEIR is treated as saving tax at the highest rate (in this case £2,335 @ 45% = £1,051). If the wife's tax benefit of allowances had been less than this amount, a transfer from the husband's allowances would have been made to make up the difference.

Illustration

Applying the computation to the facts of Mr. and Mrs. Ford:

		Total	Mr.Ford	Mrs.Ford
		£	£	£
Earned income		24,240	18,660	5,580
Unearned income		9,909	2,509	7,400
		34,149	21,169	12,980
Less: Mortgage Interest		492	492	-
		33,657	20,677	12,980
Income Tax:				
On £33,300		12,478		
On £357 @ 55%		196		
		12,674		
Divided: (£20,677:£12,980)			7,786	4,888
Add: Tax on mortgage interest		143	143	
		12,817	7,929	4,888
	£			
Allowances:	3,655			
WEIR	2,335			
	5,990			
Reduction in tax:				
£5,633 @ 50%	2,817			
£357 @ 55%	196			
	3,013			
Divided: (£7,929:£4,888)		3,013	1,864	1,149
Tax before personal allowances		12,817	7,929	4,888
Less: Tax value of allowances		3,013	1,864	1,149
		9,804	6,065	3,739

It will be noted that the total tax borne, £9,804, is the same as resulted in the joint computation.

7.3 SEPARATE TAXATION OF WIFE'S EARNED INCOME (FA 1971,s.23)

A husband and wife who are living together may <u>jointly</u> elect that the wife's earned income shall be assessed on her as if she were a single person with no other income, her unearned income remaining that of the husband. The conditions for the election are:

(a) it must be made jointly in writing by husband and wife and continues until it is jointly revoked;

(b) it must be made within the period commencing six months before and ending twelve months after the first year of assessment to which it is to apply. It can be revoked within the same time limits.

Wife's earned income for this purpose does not include any pension or superannuation received from her husband's former employment nor any benefits under the National Insurance Acts which do not arise from her own contributions.

The detailed effects of the election are:

(a) charges are deducted from the income of the spouse who pays them;

(b) each spouse receives a single person's personal allowance; no married allowance can be claimed by the husband and no WEIR can be claimed by the wife;

(c) dependant relative relief is not available if the spouse supports an in-law as (for tax purposes) they are not related. If the wife supports her dependant relative she can claim the higher rate;

(d) any excess personal reliefs on one spouse cannot be carried over against the income of the other;

(e) loss relief is allocated in the following way:
Husband's loss - against his earned <u>and</u> his and his spouse's unearned income;
Wife's loss - against her earned income;
This may mean that there is an automatic loss of personal allowances and it may be beneficial to revoke the claim temporarily;

(f) the husband remains entitled to two £70 or one £140 exemption for a joint account in respect of income from the ordinary account in the NSB. A claim under s.23 prevents a claim for age allowance, or a claim for the additional personal allowance for looking after children.

By making a claim under s.23 savings in tax may be made in those cases where the wife has a substantial earned income.

<u>Illustration</u>
The facts are as for Mr. and Mrs. Ford, but this time a claim has been made to have Mrs. Ford's earned income separately taxed:

	Mr. Ford	Mrs. Ford
	£	£
Earned income	18,660	5,580
Unearned income	9,909	
	28,569	
Less: Mortgage interest	492	
	28,077	
Less: Personal allowances	2,335	2,335
	25,742	3,245
Income tax:		
£17,200 : 3,245 @ 29%	4,988	941
£3,000 @ 40%	1,200	
£5,200 @ 45%	2,340	
£342 @ 50%	171	
	8,699	941
Tax deducted under MIRAS	143	-
	8,842	941

The difference between the tax borne between this and joint assessment is £21, and it is therefore just beneficial to make the election.

8.0 GETTING MARRIED

In the year of marriage the income of husband and wife is not aggregated.

The husband is entitled to a married person's personal allowance scaled down by one twelfth of the difference between the married and single personal allowances for each complete tax month elapsing between 6th April and the date of marriage. A tax month commences on 6th of one month and ends on the 5th of the next month. The wife is entitled to a single person's personal allowance but no WEIR.

Non-aggregation of the wife's income in the year of marriage does not prevent the husband from offsetting excess personal allowances losses and charges against the wife's post-marriage income.

The wife can offset against her husband's income her excess personal allowances (other than her single personal allowance, age allowance, housekeeper allowance and the additional personal allowance) and charges paid on or after the date of marriage.

Illustration

Mr. & Mrs. Jones were married on 15th November 1986 and their salaries in the fiscal year 1986/87 were as follows:

	£	£
Mr. Jones		16,000
Mrs. Jones (Miss Hayden):		
to date of marriage		3,200
after date of marriage		3,250

They had no other income.

Miss Hayden/Mrs. Jones:		
Salary to date of marriage		3,200
after marriage		3,250
		6,450
Less: Personal allowance		2,335
Liable		4,115
Mr. Jones:		
Salary		16,000
Less: Personal allowance	3,655	
Less: 7/12ths of £1,320 £(3,655-2,335)	770	2,885
		13,115

Where either party had a child before the marriage it may be possible to claim in the year of marriage the additional personal allowance given to single persons claiming child allowance. In the case of a wife, the child must be living with her before the marriage; in the case of a husband it will prevent him from claiming the married personal allowance in the year of marriage.

Illustration

Mr. Kay, a widower, married Miss Ley on 24th July 1986. He claims the additional personal allowance for looking after his son Paul, aged 13.

	Claiming Married allowance	Not Claiming Married allowance
	£	£
Personal allowance	3,655	2,335
Less: 3/12ths (£3,655-£2,335)	330	
APA		1,320
	3,325	3,655
	=====	=====

For the purposes of relief under TA 1970,s.168 and CAA 1968,s.71 (surplus of agricultural buildings allowance) the wife's income from the date of marriage is available for relief.

For many couples it is important to decide whether, for tax purposes, to marry or just to co-habit. A man and woman co-habiting are treated as two separate individuals, there is no concept of the 'common law' marriage in taxation. Points to consider are:

(a) couples co-habiting can each obtain mortgage interest relief on a loan of £30,000 even if they both share the same house. Each would be able to claim the capital gains tax exemption on their respective parts of the main residence. Alternatively each could establish their own CGT free main residence;

(b) if the co-habitees have substantial unearned income non marriage will prevent the woman's unearned income being aggregated with her husband's income which normally occurs even when a s.23 FA 1971 claim is made; substantial tax savings could result;

(c) if one of the co-habitees is not working the other may transfer income to the other by means of a deed of covenant thus enabling the recipient to recover basic rate tax at no cost to the person covenanting;

(d) If there are children then the co-habitee maintaining the child could claim an additional personal allowance. If there is more than one child then both co-habitees could qualify by maintaining one each. Provided an affiliation order is obtained from the court payments may be made by the father to the children which, under revenue practice would be considered to be a charge against the income of the father and income of the children thus enabling the use of their personal allowances;

(e) Business Expansion scheme relief of up to £40,000 is available for each co-habitee; a married couple can only obtain relief for one investment of up to £40,000.

9.0 DIVORCE AND SEPARATION

When a couple are divorced or separated they will be treated as two taxable individuals as from the date of the divorce or separation. In the year of separation the husband will continue to obtain the full married allowance, thereafter it will only be available if the husband wholly maintains his wife. After the year of divorce, each automatically obtains a single person's allowance.
In the year of separation, the income of the wife will be split on the following basis:

Schedule A	-	Income entitled to be received before and after separation.
Schedule B	-	Time basis

Schedule D Cases I, II, III, IV and V	-	The assessment for the year according to the normal rules of assessment, divided on a time basis.
Schedule D Case VI	-	Actual income received.
Schedule E Dividends and other income taxed at source	-	Salary, etc. earned before and after separation. Dividends, etc. due to be received before and after separation.

After separation the wife will be entitled to a full single person's allowance.
When maintenance payments are made they can consist of two types:

(a) voluntary payments;

(b) payments made under a legal obligation.

(a) Voluntary payments have no tax effect, the payer gets no tax relief and the recipient is not liable to tax on the receipts.

(b) Payments made under a legal obligation are allowed as a deductible charge in the case of the payer and are unearned income in the hands of the recipient. Sections 52 and 53 apply to the deduction of tax from the payments unless they rank as 'small maintenance payments'. Sometimes they may be paid under deed of covenant. Where the payment is expressed as being 'free of tax' the payer is treated as having made a payment "which, after deduction of basic rate tax, leaves the 'free of tax' figure". In the case of the recipient, the payments whether small maintenance or made under deduction of tax are assessed on a current year basis.

Under normal circumstances payments made for the maintenance of children will be regarded as income of the recipient spouse. Where the payment is made to the other spouse in trust for the children it will normally be treated as having created a settlement in favour of the children and the income will be treated as that of the settlor. Where the payment is made direct to the children, it will be treated as their income provided it is made under the order of the court.

On divorce, the additional personal allowance for single persons looking after children is available.

10.0 THE SENIOR CITIZEN

If a taxpayer or his wife is over the age of 65 years at any time during the year of assessment and his total income does not exceed the following limits for 1986/87 there will be no liability to taxation:

Single taxpayer	£2,850	(£2,690 for 1985/86)
Married couple	£4,505	(£4,255 for 1985/86)

If the taxpayer's total income exceeds £9,400 (£8,800 for 1985/86) the full age allowance will be reduced by £2 for each £3 of total income over £9,400 until the allowance is reduced to the original single or married personal allowance.

Illustration

G, a widower, is 68. He receives a pension of £2,700 and dividends of £213 (excluding tax credit £87) during 1986/87.

	£
Pension	2,700
Dividends £(213 + 87)	300
	3,000
Less: Age allowance	2,850
	150
Tax thereon @ 29%	43
Less: Tax credits	87
Tax repayment	44

Illustration
H is married and aged 66. He receives a pension of £4,900 and his wife receives Schedule A income of £5,000 for 1986/87.

	£	£
Pension		4,900
Schedule A income		5,000
		9,900
Age allowance	4,505	
Less: 2/3 £(9,900 - 9,400)	333	
		4,172
		5,728
Tax thereon @ 29% on £5,728		1,661

The allowance does not affect the taxpayer's claim to other allowances, particularly WEIR.

It is important to ensure that the income of the elderly comes from the correct sources. Investments in building societies and bank deposit accounts should be avoided if there is likely to be a shortfall of income over personal allowances as the tax credits attaching to them cannot be repaid, if there is going to be a shortfall of allowances a deed of covenant could be paid to the senior citizen, the tax credits are refundable. A senior citizen without substantial income but with a house could consider a house annuity plan where the house is mortgaged to provide a capital sum to be repaid out of the proceeds of sale on death. The capital of the mortgage is used to purchase an annuity which is used firstly to pay the interest on the mortgage (allowable under MIRAS) with the excess used to provide income.

11.0 DEATH

On the death of an individual, the liability to taxation will be calculated as if all sources of income ceased on the date of death. This will involve the cessation basis being applied to certain classes of income such as Schedule D Case I and II etc. Dividends will be treated as receivable before death if they were due before the date of death. Where a widow succeeds to her husband's business on his death the Revenue will allow assessments to be continued on a preceding year basis if the widow wishes. However, losses made by the husband cannot be carried forward. This does not of course affect the widow's right to insist on a discontinuance if greater relief could be obtained. The liability to tax must be settled by the executors who are also liable to any additional tax caused by a revision of assessment on death.

The liability to tax on income received after death is that of the executors.
In the year of death, personal allowances will be given as follows:

(a) Husband's death
Full married allowance and wife's earned income relief against income to date of death; widow obtains full single personal allowance for the period from death, widow's bereavement allowance, and possibly additional personal allowance.

(b) Wife's death
Husband obtains full married allowance for year of death, and wife's earned income relief on wife's earnings up to date of death. After that year he is dealt with as a single person.

Where a man dies in a year of assessment for which he was entitled to the married person's allowance, his widow shall be entitled for that year to a further allowance of £1,320. The allowance is available both in the year of bereavement and the next following year provided that the widow has not remarried before the start of the second year.

12.0 NON-RESIDENT BRITISH SUBJECTS

With certain exceptions all income arising in the UK is liable to tax even if it is paid to a non-resident. UK residents can offset against the income their personal allowances. Non-UK residents do not qualify for personal allowances unless they fall within certain categories:

(a) British subjects;

(b) residents of the Channel Islands or the Isle of Man;

(c) missionaries or current or former Crown employees;

(d) former UK residents now living abroad for health reasons;

(e) where a double tax agreement provides.

Those within these groups qualify for a proportion of their UK allowance.
Relief is given by finding:

(a) the UK tax on the UK income after personal allowances;

(b) the UK tax on the world (or total) income after personal allowances.

For those purposes income is classified by where it arises except that income from certain Government securities - the s.99 securities, notably 3½% War Loan - is always considered to be world income. Following **CIR v. Addison 1984** the income of a wife earned through duties abroad and thus not liable to UK tax should be totally excluded.
The amount of the tax payable is the greater of:

(a) the UK tax on the UK income;

(b) the UK tax on the world income multiplied by the fraction:

$$\frac{\text{UK liable income}}{\text{World liable income}}$$

'Liable' income is income, less charges, but before personal allowances.

Illustration

Mr. and Mrs. N are British subjects who have worked in Europe for many years. Their liable income in the fiscal year 1986/87 was as under:

	£
Arising in UK:	
Rents from house	4,000
Dividends - gross	4,000
3½% War Loan Interest	500
Arising abroad:	
Salaries - Mr. N	18,000
Mrs.N	10,000
Dividends	1,000

Mr. N paid interest of £3,000 on the house to a UK bank - not under MIRAS. The couple have one child, born in 1971.

	UK Income	World Income
	£	£
Rents	5,000	5,000
Dividends	4,000	4,000
War Loan interest		500
Salary - Mr. N		18,000
Mrs.N		-
Dividends		1,000
	9,000	28,500
Less: Mortgage interest	3,000	3,000
	6,000	25,500
Less: Personal allowances		
MA	3,655	3,655
	2,345	21,845
Income tax:		
£		
2,345 @ 29%	680	
17,200 @ 29%		4,988
3,000 @ 40%		1,200
645 @ 45%		290
	680	6,478

The tax borne will be the higher of:

(a) £680 or

(b) $\frac{£\ 6,000}{£25,500}$ x £6,478 = £1,524

But if no personal allowances had been claimed the tax borne would have been:

	£		£
Rents	5,000		
Dividends	4,000		
	9,000		
Less: Charges	3,000		
	6,000	@ 29%	1,740
	=====		=====

A tax credit is not normally available to a non-resident unless he claims s.27 relief or is so entitled under the terms of a double tax agreement.

13.0 DUE DATES FOR THE PAYMENT OF INCOME TAX

The due dates for the payment of income tax are as under:

Type of Income	Due Dates Basic and Higher Rates
Income from a trade, profession or vocation (Schedule D Cases I and II Schedule D Case V - foreign businesses)	One half on 1st January in year of assessment; one half on 1st July following year of assessment
Income from employments - Schedule E	PAYE deducted from emoluments when paid
Other untaxed income	1st January in year of assessment
Other income received under deduction of tax	(Higher rates only) 1st December following year of assessment

If the assessment is issued after the due date in the table above, tax will not be due until 30 days after the date of issue of the notice of assessment.

In calculating the tax due charges may be deducted in the most beneficial way. This will normally be against investment income where the tax is due on 1st January in the year of assessment. Personal allowances are deducted primarily against earned income.

Illustration

Mr. E has the following income assessable for 1986/87:

	£
Trading profits	12,800
Rents	1,000
Dividends (net)	7,100

He is married and pays allowable interest of £600, gross.

	Schedule D I	Schedule A	Dividends
	£	£	£
Income	12,000	1,000	7,100
Add: Tax credit			2,900
			10,000
Less: Charges		600	
		400	
Less: Personal allowance	3,655	-	
	8,345	400	10,000
	£	£	£
Income tax:			
On Schedule DI/Schedule A			
@ 29% on £8,345/400	2,420	120	
Due 1.1.87	1,210	120	
1.7.87	1,210		
On Dividends			
@ 29% on £8,455			2,452
@ 40% on £1,545			618
			3,070
Less: Tax credits			2,900
Due 1.12.1987			170

14.0 INTEREST ON OVERDUE TAX

Interest is charged on overdue tax at 8.5% (11% up to 5th August 1986) per annum from the 'reckonable date'. This date will depend on whether the assessment giving rise to the tax has been appealed against. The making of an appeal against an assessment does not delay the payment of tax. This will be due on the normal due dates as above, unless an application has been made to postpone the tax payable. The balance of any postponed tax will be due 30 days after the determination of the appeal. The reckonable date for the charging of interest is found as under:

Tax not subject to appeal, the later of:

(a) the normal due date;

(b) 30 days after the date of issue of the notice of assessment.

Tax subject to appeal, the later of:

(a) the normal due date;

(b) 30 days after the date of issue of the notice of assessment;

(c) 30 days after the date of the Inspector's agreement or Commissioner's determination of any amount to be postponed.

The remainder including any increased tax liabilities are due on the later of:

(a) the due date if there had been no appeal;

(b) the later of:

(i) the date on which the tax would have become due and payable if there had been no appeal;

(ii) the earlier of:

(1) the date on which the tax becomes due and payable (see above)

(2) the appropriate date from the following table:

Type of Tax	Relevant date
Tax under Schedules A and D	1st July following the end of the year of assessment
Higher rate tax on income taxed at source	1st June following the December after the end of the year for which assessed

Illustration

A is a graphic designer assessed under Schedule D Case I. On 15th November 1986 he received an assessment for 1986/87 showing a tax liability of £30,000. On 10th December 1986 he appealed against the assessment and applied for postponement of £12,000 tax. The Inspector agreed to the postponement of £9,000 tax on 2nd January 1987. The Commissioners determined the assessment at an appeal hearing on 28th August 1987 and the final tax due was £35,000. A paid tax as under:

31st March 1987	£10,500
1st August 1987	£10,500
27th October 1987	£14,000

Interest will be charged as under:

Schedule D Case I

1st instalment	£10,500 from 1st February 1987 to 31st March 1987 (Reckonable date 30 days after Inspectors agreement)
2nd instalment	£10,500 from 1st July 1987 to 1st August 1987 (Reckonable date 1st July 1987 - normal due date)
Balance	£14,000 from 1st July 1987 to 27th October 1987 (Reckonable date 1st July 1987)

The Board of Inland Revenue may remit interest of £30.

15.0 REPAYMENT SUPPLEMENTS

A supplement will be paid to an individual taxpayer where he receives a tax repayment of not less than £25 more than twelve months after the end of the year of assessment to which the repayment relates.

The repayment supplement is calculated as interest on the amount repaid, at 8.5% (11% up to 5th August 1986) per annum from the 'relevant time' to the end of the tax month in which the repayment order is issued.

The relevant time is the later of:

(i) 5th April following the year for which repayment is made;

(ii) the end of the year of assessment in which the tax was paid.

The repayment supplement is tax free.

Illustration

K receives a repayment of tax of £1,000 in respect of 1984/85. The tax was originally paid by K on 1st July 1985. The repayment order was issued on 14th February 1988.

The relevant time is 5th April 1986.

The end of the tax month in which the repayment order is issued is 5th March 1988.

The repayment supplement will be calculated as follows:

		£
Period 6.4.86 to 5.8.86	£1,000 @ 11% p.a.	36.77
6.8.86 to 5.3.88	£1,000 @ 8.5% p.a.	134.60
		171.37

16.0 ERROR OR MISTAKE CLAIMS

If a mistake has been made in a Return or supporting document (e.g. Accounts) the taxpayer may make an error or mistake claim and reclaim any tax overpaid in respect of the previous six complete years of assessment. This relief is only available in the case of a genuine mistake by the taxpayer and no relief is available if the Return or statement is made in accordance with the law or practice applying at the time. The amount of the relief is determined by the Board of Inland Revenue with an appeal to the Special Commissioners.

11 Back Duty and Avoidance

1.0 GENERAL

When the Revenue are of the opinion that tax has been lost by the fraud, wilful default or neglect of a taxpayer they adopt a procedure for the recovery of the tax which is generally described as back duty.

The procedure can be broadly divided between the less serious aspects relating to the minor omission of income (i.e. bank deposit interest) and the making of false claims for allowances, and the understatement of business profits, which is regarded with much more gravity. The former cases are normally dealt with at district level by the appropriate inspector of taxes, whereas the second type is always dealt with by a specialist department, such as the Enquiry Branch or an investigation branch.

2.0 COMPLIANCE

s.7 TMA 1970 imposes an obligation on every person liable to income tax who has not delivered a return of income to the Inland Revenue to notify the Revenue within one year from the end of a year of assessment in which the income arises. s.10 TMA imposes a similar duty on companies with the time limit for notification being one year after the relevant accounting period. s.12 TMA contains parallel provisions for capital gains tax.

The penalty for failure to notify is £100 for each year of assessment, etc., in respect of which no notice of liability is given.

s.8 TMA requires a taxpayer to make a return of income when called upon to do so by the Inland Revenue. The time limit for compliance is 30 days from the date of issue of the notice of assessment. A return of income is treated as validly served on a taxpayer if it is delivered to him or sent to his current or last known place of residence or employment. A person who fails to make a return within the time limit is liable to a penalty of £50 together with an additional penalty of £10 for every day after default has been formally declared by the Commissioners or the Court. Additional penalties are available in s.93(2) TMA and in any case failure to submit a return promptly could constitute negligence.

There are similar provisions for requiring returns of income from a partnership or limited company.

The return made by the taxpayer to the Inland Revenue contains a declaration by him that to the best of his knowledge and belief the information contained therein is complete and correct. This is an important statement and the practitioner must point out its significance to the client before obtaining his signature to the return. s.99 TMA provides for a penalty of an amount not exceeding £500 for knowingly assisting in the making or delivery of incomplete returns or accounts. It is important therefore that when the accountant discovers irregularities these are pointed out to the client who is then advised to make full and complete disclosure to the Inland Revenue. If he refuses then the accountant cannot continue to act for the client. s.20 TMA permits an Inspector, on application to a circuit judge, to issue within 12 months a notice to any person who has acted as a 'tax accountant' and against whom a penalty under s.99 has been awarded requiring that person to deliver to the Inspector all his working papers in respect of any client for whom he has acted.

3.0 OBTAINING INFORMATION

The Inland Revenue has considerable powers of obtaining information. The major sources being:

(a) returns of employees' emoluments on forms P.35, P11D and P9D and details of casual employees.

(b) returns of fees and commissions paid;

(c) returns of interest paid.

s.20 TMA gives an Inspector or the Board of Inland Revenue powers to serve a written notice on any person to deliver up documents in his or her possession which contain information relevant to a tax liability.

s.20(3) enables an Inspector to serve a similar notice on certain third parties including spouses and children and, in respect of a business liability, to any person who is carrying on a business.

An Inspector, but not the Board, requires the consent of a Special or General Commissioner before proceeding. Penalties are required for failure to provide the information requested. Before proceeding with the notice however, an Inspector must give the taxpayer an opportunity to provide the information voluntarily.

s.20(C) TMA enables an officer of the Board of Inland Revenue, on application to a circuit judge, to obtain a warrant authorising him to enter premises and to search them and to seize any items which he believes might be required as evidence in proceedings involving tax fraud.

4.0 IN DEPTH INVESTIGATIONS

In January 1977, a new system of in depth investigation and review was introduced by the Inland Revenue. This was intended to concentrate time and expertise on those areas which based on judgement gave rise to concern. This could be evidenced by:

(a) unsatisfactory accounts; e.g. those with a qualified audit report, unusual figures for debtors and creditors, drawings etc.;

(b) low or unusual rates of gross profits;

(c) the type of trade;

(d) a bad previous history as to tax matters.

The Inspector will initially review the accounts with the aim of constructing an economic model of business. To enable him to do this, detailed notes on each type of business are prepared which give the Inspector background information on the trade and indicative gross profit percentages. Once this has been done, the Inspector will review the taxpayer individually to see whether the combination of business and personal information links up with the lifestyle and personal circumstances of the taxpayer. In doing this the Inspector might consider:

(a) the residence of the taxpayer;

(b) any chargeable assets acquired;

(c) the pattern and source of other income, etc.

He will be assisted in this by other information including returns of interest paid without deduction of tax, returns of commission, details from other Inspectors, informers' letters and other information from public sources.

After building up this economic picture of the taxpayer, the Inspector will seek to establish information on certain key points and will normally write to the accountant concerned requesting information on these points. The information given might easily clear up the matter, but if further enquiries are necessary, the Inspector might request an interview with the taxpayer and also seek discovery of books, papers, etc. Where the records are totally inadequate the Inspector might require the preparation of capital statements. These statements comprise several separate schedules as follows:

(a) a statement of the assets and liabilities at the beginning and end of the period under review and at yearly intervals in the interim;

(b) a statement of income for each year, including legacies and profits on capital transactions;

(c) a statement of expenditure for each year, including gifts and losses on capital transactions.

The details are compiled on a cash basis, any accruals only being used for the lists of assets and liabilities at the beginning and end of the whole period.

The various schedules are compiled so that Expenditure (per statement)

plus

Increase in Assets in the year

less

Income (shown on schedule)

equals

Undisclosed Income (if any).

The following is an illustration of a capital statement showing the range of enquiries necessary:

NET ASSETS

	1981	1982	at 5th April (Intervening years omitted)	1986	1987
	£	£		£	£
Dwelling house at cost	8,800	8,800		8,800	8,800
Extension thereto, at cost				2,800	2,800
Furniture, at cost	1,850	900		2,250	3,200
Country cottage, at cost		3,000		3,000	
Furniture, at cost		750		1,350	
Business assets (net)	9,000	19,000		38,000	40,000
Investments, at cost		3,000		8,000	12,000
Bank deposit accounts		2,450		8,600	15,000
Bank current accounts	350	700		600	750
	20,000	38,600		73,400	82,550
Creditors	5,000	6,500		8,600	15,200
Mortgage	6,200	5,800		1,800	1,750
	11,200	12,300		10,400	16,950
NET ASSETS	8,800	26,300		63,000	65,600
Increase in net assets (year by year)		17,500			2,600
Living expenses in year		1,800			4,600
Life assurance premiums		140			1,700
Tax Paid		3,800			13,700
Subscriptions, gifts etc.		380			1,700
		23,620			24,300
Legacies received		15,000			
Rights issue sold					600
Matured assurance policy					5,000
Investment income (net)		300			1,900
		15,300			7,500
Deposit interest		39			1,200
Profits on Stock Exchange Transactions		6,000			4,500
Football pool winnings					8,000
		21,339			21,200
Unexplained increases		2,281			3,100

The intervening years would be similarly compiled; some may show deficiencies.

The Revenue would review the taxpayer's circumstances in the light of the statements and, after making any adjustments, agree the tax lost.

5.0 CULPABILITY

In general, there are certain types of 'offence' recognised by the Taxes Acts. They fall into four broad categories:

(a) Innocent mistake

This is where a mistake is genuinely made. s.97 TMA provides that where incorrect returns of income or accounts are submitted and it comes to the taxpayer's notice that they are incorrect then he will not be treated as negligent, provided that the error is pointed out to the Inland Revenue as soon as possible.

(b) Neglect

This is defined in s.118 TMA as 'negligence or failure to give any notice, make any return or to produce or furnish any document or other information required by or under the Taxes Acts'. Negligence may be absolved by reasonable excuse. In general, it is not doing what a reasonable person would do.

(c) Wilful default

This is where a person does not do something knowing that it should have been done. It can include not making a return and accepting assessments which the taxpayer knows are less than they should be.

(d) Fraud

This is where a false representation has been made knowingly, or without belief in its truth or recklessly careless of whether it be true or not.

After the enquiry is complete, the Inspector may make additional assessments. The time limits are:

(a) Normal

Up to 6 years after the end of the chargeable period to which they relate.

(b) Negligence

Assessments may be made for the normal period of 6 years and, with the leave of a commissioner, for 6 years before the normal year. It is also possible with the leave of a commissioner to go back in 6-yearly stages from any of the earlier years in which negligence was established.

(c) Fraud and wilful default

Subject to the leave of a commissioner, the Inland Revenue can raise assessments without a time limit effectively back to 1936/37.

Assessments on a deceased person's income arising before death must be made within three years after the tax year in which he dies. Assessments for any of the six years preceding death may be made within the same time limit where the assessments are for the purpose of making good tax lost by reason of the deceased person's fraud, wilful default or neglect.

6.0 THE SETTLEMENT

Having agreed the amount of tax lost, the individual will normally be required to sign a 'certificate of full disclosure'. There are no statutory requirements to sign such a certificate but quite clearly to refuse to do so might well arouse suspicions of further matters not yet discovered. A certificate signed in cases where there has not been full disclosure may make the individual liable for fraud.

The amount of duty to be paid must then be agreed bearing in mind the respective liabilities for tax, interest on tax and penalties. The usual procedure is to agree a composite sum taking into account all three aspects, and then for the taxpayer to sign a written undertaking to pay the agreed sum, in consideration of the Revenue forbearing to pursue their rights for penalties. The Revenue may mitigate penalties where they consider it appropriate.

7.0 PENALTIES

The maximum penalties are:

(a) for fraud or wilful default are £50, plus the tax lost, plus a penalty of twice that amount;

(b) for negligence £50, plus the tax lost, plus a penalty of an amount equal to the tax lost;

<u>plus</u> in all cases interest at the following rates per annum on the tax lost.

9% from 1st July 1974 to 31st December 1979
12% from 1st January 1980 to 30th November 1982
8% from 1st December 1982 to 30th April 1985
11% from 1st May 1985 to 5th August 1986
8.5% from 6th August 1986

The following table is a summary of the other penalty provisions currently in force:

OFFENCE		PENALTY
Failure to give notice of liability to income tax within one year after the appropriate year of assessment, where no return made.		Not exceeding £100
Failure to deliver any return, statements, declaration, list or other document, to furnish any particulars, to produce any document or to make anything available for inspection, or failure to comply with a notice or precept. A partnership is not liable to penalties on any tax not chargeable on the partnership.	(a)	Not exceeding £50 and £10 a day after declaration by Court or Commissioners before whom proceedings commenced. In this case no penalty if failure remedied before proceedings started.
	(b)	If failure is in connection with person's own income, not exceeding £50 and an amount equal to the total.
Fraudulently or negligently giving information required by Taxes Management Act 1970.		Not exceeding £250, or in case of fraud £500.
Knowingly assisting in making incorrect return etc.		Not exceeding £500.

8.0 TAX AVOIDANCE

This is the process of arranging a taxpayer's affairs in such a way that he can, within the law, reduce the amount of tax payable. It differs from evasion which is knowingly breaking the law to reduce a tax liability by the deliberate concealing of income or the false claiming of allowances etc.

In **IRC v. Duke of Westminster (1936)** Lord Tomlin said:

> "Every man is entitled if he can to arrange his affairs so that the tax attaching under the appropriate Acts is less than it otherwise would be. If he succeeds in ordering them so as to secure that result, then however unappreciative the Commissioners of Inland Revenue or his fellow taxpayers may be of his ingenuity, he cannot be compelled to pay an increased tax".

In **Ayrshire Pullman Motor Services v. IRC (1929)** Lord President Clyde said:

> "No man in this country is under the smallest obligation, moral or other, so to arrange his legal relation to his business, or to his property as to enable the Inland Revenue to put the largest possible shovel into his stores".

Over the years attitudes, both judicial and public, appear to have hardened against the tax avoider. In **Latilla v. IRC (1943)** Lord Simon commented that avoiders might prepare schemes that were:

> "within their legal rights, but that is no reason why their efforts, or those of the professional gentlemen who assist them in the matter, should be regarded as a commendable exercise of ingenuity or as a discharge of the duties of good citizenship".

To combat this "digging for wealth in the subterranean passages of the Revenue" (per Lord Denning in **Griffiths v. J.P.Harrison (Watford) Ltd. (1963)**), a mass of anti-avoidance legislation has developed. Unlike some countries, there is no general anti-avoidance legislation, but a series of detailed measures designed to deal with specific instances as and when they arise. Brief details of some of the main anti-avoidance provisions are:

(a) Transactions in securities (TA 1970, ss.460-468)

Where in consequence of a transaction (or transactions) in securities, combined with any special circumstances, a person is able to obtain a tax advantage, the Revenue may make such adjustments as are necessary to correct the advantage. The Revenue must issue a notice of their intentions to correct any advantage and it is open to the taxpayer to contest the Revenue's assertions. The Revenue action will fail if the taxpayer can show that the transactions were made for bona fide, commercial reasons, or in the ordinary course of investment management, and without tax advantages being their main object, or one of their main objects.

The special circumstances referred to above are:

(i) the receipt of an abnormal amount of dividend or other distribution;

(ii) an entitlement to a deduction from profits or gains because of a decrease in the value of securities held;

(iii) the receipt of a consideration not taxable as income;

(iv) the receipt, in the form of share capital or securities, of any non-taxable consideration.

It has been held that liquidation may be a transaction in securities.

A tax advantage means any relief or repayment (or increase thereof) or avoidance or reduction of a charge or assessment to tax, whether effected by receipts accruing as non-taxable or by deduction from profits or gains.

The taxpayer may protect himself against possible action by the Revenue under these provisions by providing full details of the transactions contemplated or effected and ask for a clearance. The Revenue have 30 days to call for further information or notify their decision as to whether action will be taken.

(b) Transfer of assets abroad (TA 1970,ss.478-481)

Where as a result of a transfer of assets, or of any associated operations, an individual ordinarily resident in the UK has power to enjoy, forthwith or in the future, any income of a person resident or domiciled outside the UK which, if it had been income of that individual received by him in the UK, would have been liable to tax, it shall be deemed to be his income. These provisions will not apply if the individual can show that the purpose of avoiding tax was not the purpose or one of the purposes for which the transfer or association operations was effected or that the transfer or associated operations were bona fide commercial operations not for the purpose of avoiding liability to tax. The decision in **Vesty v IRC (1980)** illustrated that only the transferor or his spouse would be liable under these provisions and, as a result, the provisions have been amended so that a non-transferor can be liable where benefits are received and income arises after 9th March 1981.

(c) Transfer of residence (TA 1970,s.482)

Very severe penalties apply to directors and companies who knowingly, without prior Treasury consent, are party to any of the following:

(i) the transfer of the residence of a UK company abroad;

(ii) the transfer of the trade of a UK resident company to a non-UK resident;

(iii) in the case of a resident company, causing or allowing a non-resident company which it controls, to create or issue shares or debentures;

(iv) the transfer by a resident company to any person of shares or debentures owned by it in a non-resident company which it controls.

(d) Transactions between associated persons (TA 1970,s.485)

Where either the buyer or the seller (which may be a body of persons or a partnership) is controlled by the other party to the contract, or both are bodies controlled by a third person, a sale, the letting or hiring of property, the grant or transfer of a right or licence, or the giving of business facilities at a price other than market price may result in adjustment by the Revenue of that price to the open market price. This applies particularly to the transfer of stock between companies at less than the market valuation. But for these provisions a company could transfer to a subsidiary abroad stock at less than its true value thereby reducing the charge to UK tax.

(e) Capital sums received on the sale of income by an individual (TA 1970,s.487)

Where transactions or arrangements are made, having as their main object or one of their main objects, the avoidance or reduction of income tax, and which enable some other person to enjoy profits, gains, income, copyrights, licences or any other rights, deriving directly or indirectly from the personal activities, past, present or future, which an individual carries on wholly or partly in the UK and as a result that individual obtains a capital amount (i.e. not otherwise taxable) it shall be treated as the earned income of that individual assessable under Schedule D Case VI in the year in which it is receivable.

(f) Artificial transactions in land (TA 1970,s.488)

Any capital gain from the disposal of land or any part of it, which is realised by the person acquiring, holding or developing it, is treated for all tax purposes as income of the person realising the gain, assessable under Schedule D Case VI for the chargeable period in which the gain is realised, if one of the following conditions is satisfied:

(i) land (or any property deriving its value from land) is acquired with the sole or main object of realising a gain from disposing of it, or;

(ii) land is held as trading stock, or;

(iii) land is developed with the sole or main object of realising a gain from disposing of it when developed.

(g) Sale and leaseback of land (TA 1970,ss.490-494)

Where land is transferred by sale, lease, surrender or forfeiture of a lease etc. and the transferee becomes liable to pay rent or a premium treated as rent, the allowance for the rent will be restricted to the commercial rent of the land concerned. This restriction applies to situations where the rent would normally be allowable, i.e.:

(i) as a deduction from trading profits;

(ii) in computing profits or losses under Schedule D Case VI;

(iii) as a management expense;

(iv) against Schedule E emoluments;

(v) as deduction in computing profits from woodlands;

(vi) in computing profits under Schedule A.

Commercial rent means the open market rent of the land taking into account the terms and any special restrictions of the lease.

Where a lease has no more than 50 years to run, when sold, and the period for which the premises are leased back is 15 years or less, the increased rent payable, so far as it does not exceed a commercial rent, is allowable as a deduction from profits. A proportion of the consideration received by the lessee for giving up the original lease, equivalent to one fifteenth of that consideration multiplied by the number of years by which the term of the lease-back fall short of 16 years, will be treated as assessable income and not capital.

12 Introduction to Corporation Tax

1.0 A BRIEF HISTORY

Until 1965 a company was liable to income tax in the same manner as an individual trader. Corporation tax was introduced in FA 1965 but the link with income tax is retained since, unless specifically provided otherwise in the legislation, the amount of income for the purposes of corporation tax is to be computed according to income tax principles. However, the system of corporation tax, introduced by FA 1965, which was known as the classical system, tended to discriminate against the payment of dividends (since the company was required to account for income tax on any distributions made as well as accounting for corporation tax on its profits). This, among other reasons, resulted in the introduction of the imputation system of corporation tax as from 1st April 1973; this latter system is intended to be neutral on the subject of distributions.

2.0 THE IMPUTATION SYSTEM - ACT

The basis of the imputation system of corporation tax is a charge, known as advance corporation tax (ACT).

Whenever a company makes a qualifying distribution (normally by paying a dividend) the company must calculate and pay over to the Revenue an amount of ACT, based on the net distribution made. The rate of ACT is fixed for each financial year (year to 31st March) and the rates, which correspond to the basic rates of income tax, have been as follows in recent years:

FY 1984	3/7
FY 1985	3/7
FY 1986	29/71
FY 1987	27/73

Thus, a dividend of £7,100 paid on 1st September 1986 will be multiplied by 29/71 in order to determine the amount of ACT:

	£
Dividend paid to shareholder	7,100
ACT 29/71 paid to Revenue	2,900
Total cash outflow	10,000

The shareholder will be liable to tax on the gross equivalent of the dividend received. The amount of ACT is imputed to the shareholder in the form of a tax credit which satisfies the shareholder's liability to tax as the basic rate.

The amount of ACT paid by a company is treated as a payment in advance of the company's corporation tax liability on its income. The result is intended to be neutral - no matter what amount of dividend is paid the total amount of corporation tax payable should remain the same.

Illustration

A Ltd. has an income liable to corporation tax of £100,000. It distributes alternatively:

(a) 10% of net income;
(b) 100% of net income.

Take corporation tax at 50%. Distributions took place in March 1987.

	Income	Tax	Income	Tax
	£	£	£	£
Profits	100,000		100,000	
Corporation Tax @ 50%	50,000	50,000	50,000	50,000
Net Income	50,000		50,000	
Dividend paid (net)	5,000		50,000	
Retained	45,000		-	
ACT				
29/71 x £5,000		2,042		
29/71 x £50,000				20,423
Balance Payable		47,958		29,577

The balance of corporation tax payable after the offset of ACT is known as Mainstream Corporation Tax (MCT).

Tax is therefore accounted for as follows:-

	£	£
ACT	2,042	20,423
MCT	47,958	29,577
Total corporation tax paid	50,000	50,000

3.0 BODIES LIABLE TO CORPORATION TAX

With certain exceptions, corporation tax is chargeable on:

(a) All companies resident in the UK.

(b) Non-resident companies trading in the UK through a branch or agency.

The term 'company' includes not only those incorporated under the Companies Acts, but also any body corporate or unincorporated association such as a sports or social club. The profits of the latter which are classified as mutual profits, may be excluded from the charge.

A company will be resident in the UK if "central management and control" occurs within the UK (TA 1970, s.482(7); **(De Beers Consolidated Mines v. Howe (1906))** Traditionally, the control is that of the directors rather than the shareholders **(John Hood & Co. Ltd. v. Magee)**, and the place of central management has been taken traditionally to be at the place where the board of directors meets.

The case of **Unit Construction Co. Ltd. v. Bullock (1960)**, emphasised that in reviewing where control and management occurs, the courts will look to the reality of the position and not merely to the legal documentation such as the Articles of Association.

An Inland Revenue statement of practice 6/83 indicates that the Revenue will consider the following factors in determining corporate residence:

(a) Do the directors actually exercise central management and control?

(b) If so, where is this control really exercised (not merely where does the board of directors meet)?

(c) If the directors do not exercise control who does and where is it exercised?

4.0 THE ASSESSMENT OF INCOME

Companies may, subject to the rules laid down by the Companies Acts, prepare accounts for any period of time. This period is known as the period of account and can be of any length.

Companies are liable to corporation tax for an accounting period; this is the period for which the company's profits are chargeable to corporation tax. In most cases the period of account and the accounting period will be the same, however TA 1970, s.247 provides detailed rules for ascertaining the beginning and end of the accounting period.

A company's accounting period commences:

(a) when the company first becomes within the charge to corporation tax; or

(b) at the end of the previous accounting period.

A company will come within the charge to corporation tax when it becomes UK resident or first acquires a source of income, etc.

It ends on the first occurrence of any of the following:

(a) the end of the company's period of account if that is twelve months or less in length;

(b) the end of a period of twelve months from the beginning of the company's accounting period if the period of account exceeds twelve months;

(c) the company ceasing to be within the charge to corporation tax;

(d) the commencement or cessation of a trade;

(e) the commencement of a winding-up.

Illustration

B Ltd. commenced trading on 1st January 1984 and made up accounts as under:

12 months to 31st December 1984
18 months to 30th June 1986
9 months to 31st March 1987
12 months to 31st March 1988

The company went into liquidation on 30th September 1988.

Each of the above periods forms a period of account but accounting periods are:

12 months to 31st December 1984
12 months to 31st December 1985

6 months to 30th June 1986
9 months to 31st March 1987
12 months to 31st March 1988
6 months to 30th September 1988

Where the company's period of account exceeds twelve months, as in the 18 months to 30th June 1986 in this example, the first twelve months constitute one accounting period and the remaining six months another.

5.0 SPECIMEN CORPORATION TAX COMPUTATION

5.1 THE COMPUTATION OF PROFITS

Companies are liable to corporation tax on their profits. Profits are defined in TA 1970, s.238(4) as "income and chargeable gains" and include:

(a) overseas profits of a UK resident company whether remitted or not;

(b) profits arising in a winding-up;

(c) interest received from banks and building societies.

The definition of profits does not however include dividends and other qualifying distributions received from other UK resident companies (franked investment income).

A specimen corporation tax computation is as under:

	Income	Chargeable Gains
Schedule A	X	
Schedule B	X	
Schedule D	X	
Schedule E (if appropriate)	X	
UFII and Building Society interest received (gross)	X	
Capital Gains		X
Less: Capital losses		(X)
		X
Less: s.93 relief		(X)
	X	X
Less: Charges (gross)	(X)(1)	(X)(2)
	X	X
	===	===

5.2 NOTES TO THE COMPUTATION

(a) The application of income tax principles
Although a company is liable to corporation tax, in determining the income subject to tax, the same schedules and cases and the general rules of computation apply as are used for the purpose of income tax. However, provisions applying solely to individuals, e.g. the exemption of the first £70 of National Savings Bank ordinary account interest, are not available to companies. A major difference between the taxation of an individual and a company is that although the amount of profit of the company is computed by reference to income tax rules, it is charged to corporation tax on an actual basis.

(b) The treatment of capital allowances
The capital allowance computation of a company broadly follows the same general form as for an individual. Important differences are:

(i) The basis periods for capital allowances are fixed by reference to twelve month accounting periods. As there is no preceding year basis of assessment for companies, there are no problems in the opening and closing years. WDA are proportionately reduced if the accounting period is less than twelve months.

(ii) For corporation tax purposes capital allowances are treated as a trading expense in arriving at the amount which is taxable in respect of a trade. Thus for a company, trading income will mean the trading profits less capital allowances if appropriate. A balancing charge is added to the Schedule D Case I profits.

(iii) There is no private use reduction in the case of a company.

<u>Illustration</u>

A Ltd. commences trading on 1st January 1985 and makes up accounts for an 18 month accounting period to 30th June 1986. It acquires:

Plant and machinery	
1.5.1985	£6,000
1.2.1986	£6,000
Motor car	
30.5.1985	£10,000
Industrial building	
1.2.1985 (excluding land)	£40,000
The trading profits were:	£90,000

<u>AP to 31.12.1985</u>

		P & M Pool General	Cars	Industrial Building		Total
	£	£	£	£	£	£
Cost		6,000	10,000		40,000	
Allowances:						
FYA - 50%		3,000				3,000
IA - 50%				20,000		
WDA - 25%			2,000 (Rest)			2,000
- 4%				1,600	21,600	21,600
		3,000	8,000		18,400	
						26,600
						======
<u>AP to 30.6. 1986</u>						
Allowances:						
WDA - 25%		375	1,000		800	2,125
		2,625	7,000		17,600	
Additions:						
Plant	6,000					
FYA	3,000	3,000				3,000
		5,625	7,000		17,600	5,175
						======

* In each case WDA for the AP to 30.6.1986 have been reduced by six-twelfths as the AP is six months only.

The Schedule D Case I profits of the company will be:

<u>AP to 31.12.1985</u>		£
Adjusted Profits	12/18 x £90,000	60,000
Less: Capital Allowances		26,600
Schedule D Case I		33,400
		======

			£
AP to 30.6.1986			
Adjusted Profits		6/18 x £90,000	30,000
Less Capital Allowances			5,175
Schedule D Case I			24,825

(c) Stock Relief

Stock appreciation relief first appeared in FA 1974 and was originally only available to companies. It was subsequently extended and absorbed by new provisions in (No.2) FA 1975,Sch. 10.

Although amended by the provisions of FA 1976, Sch.5 the principle of the relief remained unaffected. The main change brought about by FA 1981,s.35 and Schs. 9 and 10 was the basis of calculations of the relief. While the old relief (i.e. the F(No.2) A 1975 Sch.10 and FA 1976, Sch. 5 relief) was based on the increase in the actual value of stock and work in progress during the period of account, subject to a deduction of a percentage of the relevant income, the new relief (i.e. that introduced by FA 1981) was determined by reference to movements in the 'all-stocks' index during the period of account as applied to the closing stock value of the previous period.

Stock relief has been abolished for all periods of account beginning after 12th March 1984 and equally there will be no clawback of stock relief on the cessation or deemed cessation of trade after that date.

Although FA 1984 has now abolished both stock relief and the potential clawback, provisions relating to the use of stock relief in creating losses, however, have not been abolished and notes on this appear in the chapter on loss relief.

(d) The treatment of VAT

Under most circumstances, the income and expenses of the company will be expressed exclusive of VAT. Sometimes VAT paid cannot be recovered and in these circumstances it may be treated as a trading expense or added to the capital cost of the asset, as appropriate.

(i) Non-deductible VAT

VAT which is non-deductible by effect of law, i.e. on most entertaining expenses, may be treated as a trading expense. However, UK entertaining expenditure and the associated VAT is never allowed. Where the non-deduction relates to plant and machinery etc., capital allowances may be claimed on the cost inclusive of VAT.

(ii) Partly exempt persons

Where a company is partly exempt, the proportion of VAT non-deductible may be treated as a trading expense or as an addition to the cost of the asset, as appropriate.

(iii) Persons not liable to VAT

Where a company is not liable to VAT, perhaps because the turnover is less than £20,500 per annum, the VAT suffered is allowed as a trading expense or an addition to the cost of the asset for capital allowances.

(e) The grossing up of income and charges

Certain income will be received by a company under deduction of income tax such as debenture or loan interest, patent royalties, etc. This income must be grossed up before bringing it into the corporation tax computation.

Illustration

E Ltd. received debenture interest of £710 net on 30th June 1987.

	£
Received	710
Tax deducted 29/71ths	290
Liable to corporation tax	1,000
Corporation tax thereon @ 35%	350

It will be seen however that the company will now only have £360 left out of the £710 it has received (£710 - £350). To overcome this, and to ensure that the company only pays corporation tax on its income, a credit for the income tax suffered will be given against the company's MCT. Similarly, to ensure that when a company makes an annual payment under deduction of income tax it does not receive a corresponding tax advantage, income tax deducted from annual payments must be paid over to the Revenue. The detailed procedures for doing this will be considered later, but at this stage it is sufficient to note that any excess of income tax repayable over income tax due will be offset by deduction from the mainstream corporation tax. If it exceeds the MCT any balance will be repaid in cash.

(f) Capital gains reduction (FA 1972,s.93)

Companies resident in the UK (and certain non-resident companies) are liable to corporation tax in respect of their chargeable gains. The tax payable is paid as corporation tax and not capital gains tax. It is provided that the amount of tax payable by a company must not exceed that payable as an individual, i.e. 30%. To achieve this the capital gains of a company are to be reduced by 'such a fraction as Parliament may from time to time determine'.
This has the following rates:

Years to 31.3.1983	22/52
31.3.1984	2/5
31.3.1985	1/3
31.3.1986	1/4
31.3.1987	1/7

The normal rate of corporation tax is applied to the reduced gains.

Illustration

X Ltd. makes up accounts to 31st March annually. In each of the years from March 1984 to March 1987 it makes a capital gain of £5,200. The corporation tax payable in respect of these gains will be:

Year to 31st March	1984	1985	1986	1987
	£	£	£	£
Capital Gain	5,200	5,200	5,200	5,200
Less: 2/5	2,080			
1/3		1,733		
1/4			1,300	
1/7				743
	3,120	3,467	3,900	4,457
Corporation tax at:				
50%	1,560			
45%		1,560		
40%			1,560	
35%				1,560

It should be noted that the capital gain is always reduced and taxed as shown even if the company is entitled to small companies relief.

Capital losses of the year or brought forward capital losses, must be deducted from capital gains before applying the fractional reduction.

(g) Charges on income

The charges paid by a company can be of two classes:

(i) retainable.
(ii) non-retainable.

Retainable charges include annual payments in respect of covenants, loan and debenture interest, patent royalties, etc. These will be paid under deduction of basic rate tax and will be treated as a deduction against total profits liable to corporation tax.

Non-retainable charges include interest paid to a UK bank, discount house or member of the stock exchange. These will normally be paid gross and provided the interest, etc., is incurred wholly and exclusively for the purposes of the trade it will be treated as a trade expense. Where the interest is not paid wholly and exclusively for trading purposes it will be treated as a charge against total profits **(Wilcock v Frigate Investments Ltd. (1982))**.

To be deductible as a charge, the payment must satisfy certain conditions. It must be:

(i) paid out of profits brought into charge to corporation tax in respect of a liability incurred for valuable and sufficient consideration;

(ii) borne by the company;

(iii) paid in the accounting period in which a deduction is sought.

It is possible to deduct interest from profits liable to corporation tax even when they have been charged to capital.

Despite the fact that they do not fully satisfy condition (i) above, deeds of covenant to a charity are allowed as a charge.

Where the payment is interest, then to be deductible as a charge one of the following conditions must be satisfied:

(i) the company must exist wholly or mainly for the carrying on of a trade; or;

(ii) the interest must be incurred wholly and exclusively for the purpose of the trade; or

(iii) the company must be an investment company.

Where the interest paid is treated as a trade expense rather than as a charge on total profits then the interest will be deducted on the accruals basis.

The primary rule is that charges offset against total profits are deducted:

(i) against income; then
(ii) against chargeable gains.

Illustration

X Ltd. had the following income for its accounting period to 31st March 1987:

	£
Trading profits	60,000
Rents	5,000
Capital Gains	7,000

It paid the following:

Bank interest on a business loan	2,000
Debenture interest	6,000 gross
Deed of covenant to Oxfam	1,000 gross

		I	CG
	£	£	£
Trading profits	60,000		
Less: Bank interest	2,000		
		58,000	
Schedule A		5,000	
Capital Gains			7,000
Less:s.93 Relief-1/7			1,000
		63,000	6,000
Less: Charges:			
Debenture interest	6,000		
Deed of Covenant	1,000		
		7,000	
		56,000	6,000

A UK resident non close company can make donations to charities after 31st March 1986, and treat them as charges on income. For this treatment to apply:

(i) the donations must not exceed 3% of the dividends paid on the company's ordinary shares during the accounting period in which the donations are made;

(ii) basic rate income tax must be deducted from the payments and accounted for in the normal quarterly accounting under Sch.20 FA.1972

(h) Discounts

Special reliefs were introduced in the Finance Act 1984 for discounts:

(i) Discounts suffered by a company on bills of exchange are normally allowed as a trade expense. Discount on accommodation bills which are drawn by a company, accepted by a bank and discounted by that or another bank or discount house will be allowed as a charge on income. The incidental costs of issuing such bills are allowed as a trade or management expense.

(ii) Part of the discount on an issue of deep discount securities after 13th March 1984 is allowed as a charge. A Deep Discount Security is one where there is a difference between the issue price and the amount payable on redemption excluding any interest. A deep discount is one where the discount is more than 15% of the amount payable on redemption overall or ½% per annum to the earliest possible redemption date and which is not:

(1) a share; or
(2) an index linked stock.

Broadly, the deep discount is treated as accruing evenly over the life of the security. This life is divided into income periods - successive periods of twelve months from the date of issue; however if the company pays interest, the income periods are the periods for which the company pays interest. The discount accruing in the income periods is called the 'income element'. It is calculated as under:

For the first period $$\frac{A \times B}{100} - C$$

When:

A = the issue price
B = the yield to maturity
C = the interest attributable to the income period

The yield to maturity and the income elements can be calculated at the outset.

Example

A Ltd. issues stock on 1st July 1986 in units of £100 for redemption on 30th June 1996. The redemption price is £200. Interest is 6% per annum payable half yearly on 30th June and 31st December.

Thus there will be 20 income periods of six months with the first ending on 31st December 1986.

The yield to maturity is 5.72% per income period.

For the first period:

$$\frac{£100 \times 5.72}{100} - 3 = £2.72$$

=====

this is then added to the issue price

For the second period:

$$\frac{£102.72 \times 5.72}{100} - 3 = £2.88$$

=====

etc.

The amount of the income element is allowed as a charge against the company's profits of the accounting period in which the income period ends.

Where the owner disposes of a deep discount security, the deep discount is assessed under Schedule D III for the aggregate of the income periods between acquisition and disposal. This is effectively:

Adjusted issue price	x
Less: Cost	x
	x
	===

Thus if the owner sells the security at the end of the second income period, the liability will be on:

Adjusted issue price	105.60
Less: Cost	100.00
	£ 5.60

To find any chargeable gain, the disposal proceeds are reduced by any income element taxed under D III. Thus if the disposal proceeds were £125:

Disposal proceeds	125.00
Less: Liable under D III	5.60
	119.40
Less: Cost	100.00
Capital gain (subject to indexation)	19.40

If the deep discount security qualifies as a corporate bond any capital gain will be exempt.

Provisions have been introduced in s.46 and Schedule II FA 1985 to counter the device of coupon stripping. Where this occurs the charge to tax on the holder of the deep discount securities will make him liable on the income element as it accrues rather than only on the redemption or disposal of the securities.

(i) Periods of account of more than 12 months

Where the period of account exceeds 12 months in length the profits will be apportioned into the various accounting periods as under:

(i) trading income before capital allowances are apportioned on a strict time basis;

(ii) capital allowances are calculated for the actual accounting periods;

(iii) other income is apportioned to the accounting period in which it arises or is due;

(iv) capital gains are allocated to the accounting period in which the disposal occurs;

(v) charges and dividends paid are dealt with in the accounting period in which they are paid.

6.0 THE CALCULATION OF CORPORATION TAX

6.1 GENERAL

The rates of corporation tax payable by a company are fixed for financial years. A financial year runs from 1st April to the following 31st March and is designated by the calendar year in which it begins. The financial year 1986 runs from 1st April 1986 to 31st March 1987. The rates of corporation tax for current years are as

	Normal Rate	'Small' Companies Rate
FY 1982	52%	38%
FY 1983	50%	30%

FY 1984	45%	30%
FY 1985	40%	30%
FY 1986	35%	29%

The application of the small companies rate is explained in 6.2. below.

Where a company's accounting period spans two financial years, it will be necessary to apportion the profits to the respective financial years and calculate the appropriate amounts of tax. This apportionment will be made on a strict time basis.

Illustration

C Ltd. makes up accounts for an 18 month period of account to 30th June 1986. The trading income liable to corporation tax for that period was £900,000. Assume rates of corporation tax of:

FY 1984	45%
FY 1985	40%
FY 1986	35%

The income of the period to 30th June 1986 will be divided over financial years as follows:

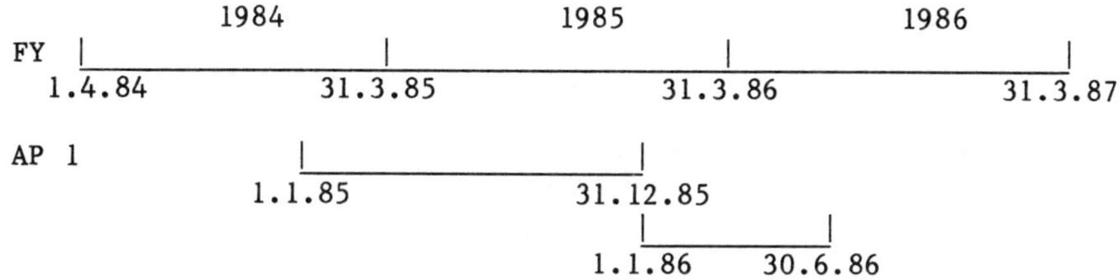

A.P. 1.1.1985 to 31.12.1985:		
12/18 x £900,000 = £600,000		
	========	
Financial year 1984	£	
3/12 x £600,000 @ 45%	67,500	
Financial year 1985		
9/12 x £600,000 @ 40%	180,000	247,500
		=======
A.P. 1.1.1986 to 30.6.1986		
6/18 x £900,000 = £300,000		
	========	
Financial year 1985		
3/6 x £300,000 @ 40%	60,000	
Financial year 1986		
3/6 x £300,000 @ 35%	52,500	112,500
		=======

6.2 SMALL COMPANIES (FA 1972, s.95)

(a) General

Where a company's Profits do not exceed certain limits its Income will bear corporation tax at 29%.

Definitions:

Income (I) All income liable to corporation tax, less charges.

Profits (P) Income (as above) plus chargeable gains plus franked investment income. Franked investment income does not include (for this purpose) dividends received from a subsidiary company, whether paid under a group election or not.

The limits known as 'the lower maximum', for recent financial years and the rates of corporation tax have been:

FY 1983	£100,000	30%
FY 1984	£100,000	30%
FY 1985	£100,000	30%
FY 1986	£100,000	29%

Illustration

K Ltd. has the following results for the year ended 31st March 1987:

	£
Trading income	20,000
Schedule A	1,000
Debenture interest paid	2,000 gross
Capital Gains	3,500
Dividends received from UK resident company on 1.12.1986	710

		I	CG	
		£	£	
DI		20,000		
Schedule A		1,000		
Capital Gains			3,500	
Less: 1/7			500	
		21,000	3,000	
Less: Charges		2,000		
		19,000 +	3,000 =	22,000
	£			
Dividends received	710			
Add: Tax credits	290			
				1,000
				£23,000P

Corporation Tax:

@ 29%	5,510	
@ 35%		1,050

Where a company's 'Profits' are greater than the lower maximum, its income will bear corporation tax at the normal rates but an abatement calculated as under, may be deducted if the 'profits' do not exceed an upper maximum:

Fraction x [(500,000 - P) x I/P]

where I and P have the meanings attributed to them as above. The upper maximum and fractions for recent financial years are:

1983	£500,000	1/20
1984	£500,000	3/80
1985	£500,000	1/40
1986	£500,000	3/200

Illustration

L Ltd. makes up accounts to 31st March 1986. It has the following income:

	£
Trading income	98,000
Schedule A income	2,000
Dividends from foreign companies (gross)	1,000
Capital gains	6,400
Capital losses brought forward	2,400
Dividends from other UK resident companies	14,000
It pays: Debenture interest (gross)	8,000

		I	CG	
		£	£	£
Schedule DI		98,000		
Schedule A		2,000		
Schedule DV		1,000		
Capital Gains			6,400	
Less: Capital losses			(2,400)	
		101,000	4,000	
Less: s.93 Relief - 1/4			1,000	
Less: Debenture interest		8,000		
		93,000	3,000	96,000
	£			
Dividends received	14,000			
Add: Tax credits	6,000			
				20,000
				116,000P
Corporation Tax @ 40%		37,200	1,200	
Less: 1/40 £[500,000 - 116,000 x 93,000/116,000]		7,697		
		29,503	1,200	

It will be appreciated that 'profits' in the small company will not be liable to corporation tax. The figure merely indicates whether a company is a small company or not.

(b) Reduction of small company limits

The small company limits of £100,000 and £500,000 referred to above will be reduced in the following circumstances:

(i) where there are associated companies;
(ii) where the accounting period is less than twelve months;
(iii) where the accounting period straddles two financial years.

(i) Associated Companies

When a company is 'associated' with other companies, the small company limits are divided equally between them. Companies are associated when one has control of the other or both are under common control. 'Control' means having or being able to acquire:

(1) more than 50% of voting power, or
(2) more than 50% of the company's income, or
(3) being entitled to more than 50% of the company's assets in a winding-up.

In this context, it is not necessary for an associated company to be resident in the UK.

Illustration

R Ltd. has two subsidiary companies. The limits for the financial year 1986 for each would be.

£500,000 ÷ 3 = £166,667
£100,000 ÷ 3 = £ 33,333

Companies are treated as associated even if they are associated for part of the accounting period only, but a company which has not carried on any trade or business during the accounting period is ignored.

To avoid effectively splitting the small company limits by subsidiary companies, it may be advantageous to use branches or operating divisions.

(ii) Accounting periods of less than twelve months

When a company has an accounting period of less than twelve months the small company limits are proportionately reduced.

Illustration

S Ltd. has an accounting period of six months. The limits for the financial year 1986 will be:

£500,000 ÷ 2 = £250,000 and
£100,000 ÷ 2 = £ 50,000

Should S Ltd. also have an associated company, the limits will be reduced further to:

£250,000 ÷ 2 = £125,000 and
£ 50,000 ÷ 2 = £ 25,000

(iii) Accounting periods straddling two financial years

Where the company's accounting period straddles two financial years, income, capital gains and profits are apportioned on a strict time basis with the appropriate small company limits applied to each.

Illustration

T Ltd. makes up accounts for the year to 30th September 1986. The results are as under:

	£	
Trading income	80,000	
Schedule A	14,000	
Patent royalties paid 30th June 1986	5,000	gross
Capital gains	5,200	
Dividends received 1st June 1986	7,100	

T Limited

	£	I £	CG £	£
Schedule DI		80,000		
Schedule A		14,000		
Capital gains:				
FY 1985.				
6/12 x 5,200	2,600			
Less:s.93 - 1/4	650		1,950	
FY 1986				
6/12 x 5,200	2,600			
Less:s.93 - 1/7	371		2,229	
		94,000	4,179	
Less: charges		5,000		
		89,000	4,179	93,179
Dividend received	7,100			
Add: Tax credit	2,900			10,000
				103,179

		£	£	£
Financial year 1985-6/12				
Income		44,500		
Chargeable gains			2,089	
Profits				51,589
Small Company Limits:				
Lower 6/12 x £100,000 =	50,000			
Upper 6/12 x £500,000 =	250,000			
Corporation Tax @ 40%		17,800	836	
Less:1/40 £[(250,000 - 51,589) x 44,500/51,589]		4,279		
		13,521	836	

	£	£	£	£
Financial year 1986-6/12				
Income		44,500		
Chargeable gains			2,090	
Profits				51,590
Small Company Limits:				
Lower 6/12 x £100,000 =	50,000			
Upper 6/12 x £500,000 =	250,000			
Corporation tax @ 35%		15,575	731	
Less: 3/200 £[(250,000 - 51,590) x 44,500/51,590]		2,567		
		13,008	731	
Combine		26,529	1,567	

7.0 INCOME TAX AND ACT

7.1 THE QUARTERLY ACCOUNTING

(a) Income Tax

A company must deduct income tax at the basic rate before making most annual payments. These include:

(i) patent royalties;
(ii) debenture and loan interest, other than that payable to a UK bank;
(iii) deeds of covenant, and qualifying donations to charities;
(iv) mortgage interest.

A company may similarly receive annual payments under deduction of income tax. These are known as 'Unfranked Investment Income' (UFII). In the corporation tax computation, unfranked investment income and annual payments are included and deducted gross.

(b) The accountability for income tax (FA 1972,Sch.20)

A company must make a return of:

(i) annual payments;
(ii) unfranked investment income.

The returns, on form CT 61, must be made for 'return periods'. These end on 31st March, 30th June, 30th September and 31st December. If the company's accounting period end is not co-terminous with one of the above dates, there must be an extra return period up to that date.

Illustration

A Ltd. makes up accounts to 30th April 1987. Its return periods are:

1st May 1986	-	30th June 1986
1st July 1986	-	30th September 1986
1st October 1986	-	31st December 1986
1st January 1987	-	31st March 1987
1st April 1987	-	30th April 1987

14 days after the end of each quarter, the company is liable to pay to the Revenue the tax deducted from annual payments, as reduced by the credit claimed for income tax deducted from unfranked investment income received in the return period. Interest will be chargeable if the payment is not made by the due date. If in a quarter a company's unfranked investment income exceeds its annual payments, the Revenue will refund the tax credit on the excess but only to the extent that the company has already paid income tax to the Revenue in the same accounting period.

Illustration

B Ltd. makes up accounts to 31st March 1987 and has the following annual payments and unfranked investment income:

2nd May 1986	Debenture interest paid	£ 6,000 (gross)
31st July 1986	Patent royalties received	£10,000 (gross)
31st October 1986	Debenture interest paid	£ 6,000 (gross)

Return period to	Annual payments	UFII	Income Tax Paid	Income Tax Repaid	Due Date
	£	£	£	£	
30.6.1986	6,000		1,740		14.7.1986
30.9.1986		10,000		1,740	on or after 14.10.1986
31.12.1986	6,000		580		14.1.1987
	12,000	10,000	2,320	1,740	
	10,000		1,740		
	2,000		580		

Notes

1 The refund of income tax in the second quarter is restricted to £1,740 as that is the amount of income tax that has been paid in the accounting period.

2 In quarter three the balance of £1,160, i.e. 29% of (£10,000 - £6,000) still owing by the Revenue is deducted from the amount due to them in that quarter.

At the end of the accounting period, there is no further liability to the Revenue.

If in the quarter to 31st March 1987 the company receives further patent royalties of £5,000 (gross) the position would be:

Return period to	Annual payments	UFII	Income Tax Paid	Income Tax Repaid	Due Date
	£	£	£	£	
30.6.1986	6,000		1,740		
30.9.1986		10,000		1,740	
31.12.1986	6,000		580		
31.3.1987		5,000		580	on or after 14.4.1987
	12,000	15,000	2,320	2,320	
		12,000			
		3,000			

Here the position is reversed. There is a surplus of UFII and a tax credit of £870 which has not been repaid to the company. This will be relieved by deduction against the MCT due by the company, and to the extent it exceeds the MCT, the balance will be repaid in cash.

Where a company received building society interest prior to 6th April 1986, the notional tax credits could not be repaid in the quarterly accounting. The notional tax credit was deducted from MCT and if the company had no MCT liability it was repaid in cash. For interest received after 5th April 1986 the tax credits on BSI received may be recovered in the quarterly accounting.

(c) <u>Distributions and Advance Corporation Tax (ACT) (s.233TA)</u>

A company may make a distribution which is defined as either a qualifying or a non-qualifying distribution. The company is only required to account for ACT on qualifying distributions.

Qualifying distributions include:

(i) dividends, including capital dividends;

(ii) interest payable on:

(1) a bonus issue of securities;
(2) an issue of securities covertible into shares, unless quoted on a recognised stock exchange or issued on terms similar to those applying to quoted securities.

(iii) interest in excess of a reasonable commercial rate;

(iv) benefits received by a member on the transfer of assets or liabilities to or from the company, unless the transfer is between members of a 51% group;

(v) the repayment of share capital preceded by a bonus issue (with certain exceptions where the bonus issue was of share capital other than redeemable share capital and the repayment takes place more than ten years after the bonus issue). The repayment is regarded as a distribution up to the amount of the bonus element;

(vi) a bonus issue preceded by a repayment of share capital (with similar exceptions as in (v) above). The bonus issue is treated as a distribution up to the amount of the repayment.

In all cases, ACT is accounted for in the normay way.

When a company makes a qualifying distribution, the term Franked Payment (FP) is applied to the amount paid plus the relevant ACT. When a distribution is received by a company, the amount received plus the tax credit is known as Franked Investment Income (FII). To qualify for the description franked investment income both recipient and paying companies must be UK resident.

Where the recipient is an individual, the gross amount (distribution plus tax credit) is treated as unearned income of the individual.

(d) Non-qualifying Distributions

There is basically only one non-qualifying distribution, namely a bonus issue of redeemable shares or securities. On the making of the bonus issue there is no liability on the company but the recipient, if an individual, is liable to higher rate taxes on the actual amount of the issue. When the issue is redeemed, this will be a qualifying distribution ((v) above) and the individual will be liable to income tax on the grossed up amount. To avoid possible double taxation, the individual can deduct from the tax due on the second event not only the basic rate credit but a credit equal to the tax paid when the bonus issue was received.

For a corporate recipient, the distribution does not rank as FII and is not liable to corporation tax in the hands of the recipient company.

The concept of a 'distribution' is wider in the case of close companies.

(e) The accountability for ACT (FA 1972,Sch.14)

The accountability for ACT is similar to that for income tax. The return periods are the same, and the return is on the same form. If at the end of the accounting period, there is a surplus of franked payments the associated ACT is available for offset against corporation tax.

Illustration

C Ltd. makes up accounts to 31st March 1987. It gives you the following information:

1st May 1986	Dividend received	£ 7,100
19th September 1986	Dividend paid	£10,650
14th October 1986	Dividend paid	£ 7,100
16th December 1986	Dividend received	£ 710
5th February 1987	Dividend received	£ 1,420

Return period to	FP	FII	ACT Paid	ACT Repaid	Due Date
	£	£	£	£	
30.6.1986	-	10,000	-	-	
30.9.1986	15,000	-	1,450	-	14.10.1986
31.12.1986	10,000	1,000	2,610	-	14.1.1987
31.3.1987	-	2,000	-	580	on or after 14.4.1987
	25,000	13,000	4,060	580	
	13,000		580		
	12,000		3,480		

Notes

1 No refund of the tax credit can be obtained in the quarter to 30th June 1986 as no ACT has yet been paid by C Ltd. in the accounting period. The credit is effectively carried forward and offset against the ACT due to the next quarter.

2 In quarter three franked payments and franked investment income in the quarter are netted before making the payment to the Revenue.

3 The company has a surplus of franked payments of £12,000 and can offset ACT of £3,480 against its liability to corporation tax.

Where at the end of the accounting period there is a surplus of franked investment income, it may be carried forward into the next accounting period and offset against future franked payments. Under normal circumstances, the tax credits on a surplus of franked investment income cannot be repaid in cash.

Illustration

If, in the previous example, the dividends received in the quarter to 31st March 1987 were £14,200 the position would be:

Return period to	FP	FII	ACT Paid	ACT Repaid	Due Date
	£	£	£	£	
30.6.1986	-	10,000	-	-	
30.9.1986	15,000	-	1,450	-	
31.12.1986	10,000	1,000	2,610	-	
31.3.1987	-	20,000	-	4,060	on or after 14.4.1987
	25,000	31,000	4,060	4,060	
		25,000			
Surplus FII		6,000			

This will be carried forward into the year to 31st March 1988. In this year, the company has:

1st June 1987	Dividend paid	£21,300
1st March 1988	Dividend received	£ 3,550

Return period to:	FP	FII	ACT Paid	ACT Repaid	Due Date
	£	£	£	£	
30.6.1987	30,000				

Return period to	FP £	FII £	ACT Paid £	ACT Repaid £	Due Date
Less: Surplus FII brought forward	6,000				
	24,000		6,960		14.7.1987
30.9.1987					
31.12.1987					
No returns required					
31.3.1988		5,000		1,450	
	24,000	5,000	6,960	1,450	
	5,000		1,450		
	19,000		5,510		

The net ACT paid of £5,510 will be offset against the corporation tax liability of the year to 31st March 1988.

Where a company receives unfranked investment income or distributions in a return period but has not made annual payments or distributions in that return period or preceding return periods (within the same accounting period), the company does not need to make a return to the Revenue.

Where there is a change in the rate of ACT and the company's accounting period straddles 5th April then that accounting period is split into two deemed accounting periods, one ending on 5th April and the other beginning on 6th April. Each of these two periods are treated as entirely separate so that ACT paid in the first period cannot be repaid against FII received in the second and FII received in the first period will be carried forward in the normal way into the second period.

Illustration

D Ltd. makes up accounts to 30th September 1986. In that year it paid and received the following:

1st November 1985	Dividend paid	£ 7,000
1st March 1986	Dividend received	£10,500
15th June 1986	Dividend paid	£35,500
18th August 1986	Dividend received	£ 7,100

Return period to	FP £	FII £	ACT Paid £	ACT Repaid £	Due Date
Deemed AP I 1.10.1985 to 5.4.1986					
31.12.1985	10,000		3,000		14.1.1986
31.3.1986		15,000		3,000	on or after 14.4.1986
5.4.1986 - no return					
	10,000	15,000	3,000	3,000	
		10,000			
Surplus FII		5,000			

Deemed AP 2 6.4.1986 to 30.9.1986					
30.6.1986	50,000				
Less: FII b/f	5,000				
	45,000		13,050		14.7.1986
30.9.1986		10,000		2,900	on or after 14.10.1986
	45,000	10,000	13,050	2,900	
	10,000		2,900		
	35,000		10,150		

The ACT of £10,150 is offset against the corporation tax liability of the 12 months accounting period to 30th September 1986.

7.2 THE OFFSET OF ACT

The basic principle is that ACT can be offset against corporation tax on income only of the accounting period in which the distribution was made. Income, for this purpose, is all income liable to corporation tax, less charges. The offset of ACT is restricted to the lower of:

(a) ACT on the surplus of franked payments for the accounting period, or

(b) basic rate income tax on the income liable to corporation tax for the accounting period.

The following are the basic rates that have applied in recent financial years.

1977	34%
1978	33%
1979 to 1985	30%
1986 onwards	29%

Illustration

X Ltd. made up accounts to 31st March 1987, and had the following income:

Trading income	£60,000
Schedule A	£10,000
Capital gains	£ 7,000

It paid the following dividends:

1.6.1986	Final 1985	£33,500
1.2.1987	Interim 1986	£37,500
1.6.1987	Final 1986	£26,800

		I	CG
	£	£	£
Schedule DI		60,000	
Schedule A		10,000	
Capital gains			7,000
Less: s.93 1/7			1,000
		70,000	6,000

	£	£	£
Corporation tax @ 29%		20,300	
@ 35%			2,100
Franked payments -			
Dividends paid in the accounting period	71,000		
ACT 29/71	29,000		
	100,000		
ACT @ 29%	29,000		
Maximum offset - 29% x £70,000	20,300	20,300	
		-	2,100
MCT		2,100	
Surplus ACT	8,700		

A surplus of ACT may be dealt with in three main ways:

(a) Carried back and offset against any liability to corporation tax on income of accounting periods beginning within the preceding six years on a LIFO basis. Priority is given to offsetting ACT of the earlier accounting period against that period's corporation tax before dealing with any carry-back of a surplus. The time limit for making a claim to carry-back surplus ACT is two years from the end of the accounting period in which the surplus arose.

(b) Surrendered to a subsidiary - this is dealt with later.

(c) Unless a claim is made for an alternative treatment, surplus ACT will automatically be carried forward and set against the corporation tax liability on income of the next accounting period, and if any is still unrelieved it can be carried forward to the next accounting period and so on, without limit. The set-off must be against the first available corporation tax liability.

In all cases the ACT (and surplus ACT) offset can never exceed the maximum found by application of the appropriate percentage.

Illustration

T Ltd. commenced trading on 6th April 1984 and has the following profits for the three years ended 5th April:

	1985	1986	1987
	£	£	£
Trading income	54,000	40,000	30,000
Case III	600	700	800
Chargeable gain (after s.93 relief)	2,000	400	1,500
Debenture interest paid (gross)	8,000	12,000	10,000

During the respective years the company made the following payments:

	Dividends	ACT	Franked Payments
	£	£	£
1985	21,000	9,000	30,000
1986	18,000	8,100	27,000
1987	29,820	12,180	42,000

Small company relief is to be ignored.

	Year ended 5th April		
	1985	1986	1987
	£	£	£
Trading income	54,000	40,000	30,000
Case III	600	700	800
Chargeable gain (after s.93 relief)	2,000	400	1,500
	56,600	41,100	32,300
Less: charges	8,000	12,000	10,000
	48,600	29,100	22,300

	Year ended 5th April		
	1985	1986	1987
	£	£	£
Corporation tax @ 45%/40%/35%	21,870	11,640	7,805
ACT paid in year	9,000	8,100	12,180
Income restriction	13,980	8,610	6,032
ACT originally utilised	9,000	8,100	6,032
MCT originally due	12,870	3,540	1,773
Less: ACT carried back	4,980	510	-
MCT ultimately suffered	7,890	3,030	1,773

Notes

1 The ACT deducted in the year ended 5th April 1987 is restricted to 29% of £20,800 - the income liable to corporation tax - and this leaves £6,148 (£12,180 - £6,032) as surplus ACT. This can be carried forward or carried back as above.

2 The ACT carried back to the year ended 5th April 1986 is restricted to the following:

	£
Year ended 5th April 1986	
Maximum ACT for set-off (30% x £28,700)	8,610
Set-off as originally paid in the accounting period	8,100
Carried back from year ended 5th April 1987	510

	£
Year ended 5th April 1985	
Maximum ACT for set-off (30% x £46,600)	13,980
Set-off as originally paid in the accounting period	9,000
Carried back from year ended 5th April 1987	4,980

3 The surplus ACT of £658 not utilised £(6,148 - 510 - 4,980) is carried forward against the corporation tax liability on income of the next accounting period.

The right to carry back surplus ACT against available corporation tax of accounting periods beginning within the six preceding years is only available for accounting periods ended after 31st March 1984. Surpluses arising in earlier accounting periods may only be carried back to accounting periods beginning within the preceding two years.

Advance corporation tax can never be carried back to a period before 1st April 1973.

Normally the rate of ACT is fixed in advance; when it is not, the old rate will continue to be used, with any adjustment made by discharge or repayment of tax or by a further assessment.

Difficulties can arise when a company's accounting period is not co-terminous with a fiscal year, and there is a change in the rate of ACT. When this occurs, the income will be apportioned over the respective fiscal years and the appropriate percentage restriction applied to each.

Illustration

Z Ltd. makes up accounts to 30th September 1986. The company has trading income of £60,000 and income from property of £20,000. It pays the following dividends:

(a) £70,000 on 1st February 1986;
(b) £35,500 on 31st August 1986.

Assume corporation tax at 50% throughout and ACT - FY 1985 3/7
- FY 1986 29/71

	£
Trading income	60,000
Schedule A	20,000
	80,000
	======

	£	£	£
Corporation tax 50%			40,000
ACT - 1st February 1986			
3/7 x £70,000		30,000	
31st August 1986			
29/71 x £35,500		14,500	
		44,500	
		======	
Maximum restricted to:			
1.10.1985 - 31.3.1986			
30% x 6/12 x £80,000		12,000	
1.4.1986 - 30.9.1986			
29% x 6/12 x £80,000		11,600	
		23,600	23,600
MCT		======	16,400
			======
Surplus ACT		20,900	
		======	

There are anti-avoidance restrictions in FA 1972, s.101 to prevent the carry-forward of surplus ACT where there has been either:

(a) within any period of three years a change in the ownership of a company coupled with a major change in the nature or conduct of a trade or business carried on by the company, or

(b) a major decline in the activity of the company and a change in its ownership, before activity revives.

7.3 USING ACT EFFECTIVELY

ACT is effectively a loan to the Inland Revenue until it is offset against a corporation tax liability. The following factors should be borne in mind to reduce the effect of this detriment:

(a) Always make a distribution (or annual payment) in a later quarter period rather than in an earlier quarter. This will postpone the payment of ACT by at least 3 months;

(b) Remember however that this must not be done for distributions made in the last quarter of an accounting period as this would defer the ACT offset against corporation tax;

(c) Try to delay paying dividends where it is known that substantial amounts of FII are likely to be received until the quarter in which they are to be received. This will avoid the loss of interest during the period that the ACT is with the Inland Revenue.

(d) In general it is always better to carry ACT back rather than to carry it forward (particularly if any of the problems in FA 1972 s.101 are likely to be encountered).

8.0 COMPREHENSIVE EXAMPLE

Papwood Ltd. was incorporated in 1963, making up accounts to 31st March. The following is a summary of the profit and loss account for the year ended 31st March 1987.

	£		£
Salaries and wages	6,003	Gross profit	194,307
Directors' remuneration	17,100	Bank deposit interest	600
Rates,electricity & insurance	620	Dividend on ordinary shares in a UK Co. (including credit)	2,000
Travelling & motor expenses	741	Profit on sales of shares	250
Repairs and renewals	480	Building Soc.interest - gross (received 1.6.1986)	100
General expenses	885		
Audit fee	719		
Debenture interest (gross) payable	6,000		
Depreciation	2,764		
Net profit	161,945		
	197,257		197,257

The general expenses consist of:

	£
Stationery,postage and telephone	362
Legal expenses: Bonus issue of shares	30
Staff service agreements	15
Deeds of covenant (gross):	
Employees' benevolent fund	200
Cathedral rebuilding fund	25
Subscription - trade association	21
Staff outing	142
Sundries (all allowable)	90
	885

Repairs and renewals are all allowable.

The debenture interest of £6,000 includes an accrual at 31st March 1987 of £2,000. The dividend was received on 15th July 1986.

Of the profit of £250 on the sale of shares, £162 is the agreed amount of the chargeable gain computed according to the capital gains tax rules after indexation allowance.

The written-down values of plant and vehicles after deducting the capital allowances for the year ended 31st March 1986 were:

	£
Pool	12,117

During the year ended 31st March 1987 the following additional plant and vehicles were bought:

	Cost £
21st November 1986 - plant	4,000
1st January 1987 - car (for use by a director, 20% privately)	2,000

Plant which was purchased in 1975 and had cost £280 was sold for £300 during the year and plant which had been bought for £500 in December 1976 was sold for £300.

Recent dividends paid by Papwood Ltd. are:

		£
1st September 1986	For the year to 31st March 1986	10,650
1st September 1987	For the year to 31st March 1987	8,978

You are required to calculate the corporation tax liability for the year ended 31st March 1987.

PAPWOOD LTD.

Computation of Corporation Tax Liability

AP to 31st March 1987

	£	I £	CG £	£
	-	+		
Net profit per accounts		161,945		
Depreciation		2,764		
Debenture interest payable		6,000		
General expenses: Bonus issue of shares		30		
Covenanted payments £(200 + 25)		225		
Capital allowances (see computation)	4,384			
Bank deposit interest	600			
Dividend from UK company	2,000			
Profit on sale of shares	250			
Building society interest	100			
	7,334	170,964		
		(7,334)		
Trading income		163,630		
Schedule D Case III -				
Bank deposit interest		600		
Building society interest - gross		100		
Chargeable gains			162	
Less: s.93 fraction 1/7			23	
		164,330	139	

Less: Charges on income				
Debenture interest paid				
£(6,000 - 2,000)	4,000			
Payments under deed of covenant	225			
		4,225		
		160,105	139	160,244
Franked Investment Income				2,000
				162,244
Corporation Tax @ 35%		56,036	48	
Less: 3/200 £[(500,000 - 162,244) x $\frac{160,105}{162,244}$]		5,000		
		51,036		
ACT				
Dividend paid	10,650			
ACT - 29/71	4,350			
	15,000			
Less: FII	2,000			
	13,000			
ACT @ 29%		3,770		
		47,266	48	
MCT		47,314		

Workings: Capital Allowances

	Pool General	Cars	Total Allowances
	£	£	£
WDV b/f at 1.4.1986	12,117		
Additions			
Car		2,000	
Plant	4,000		
	16,117		
Disposal proceeds of plant sold	580		
	15,537		
WDA - 25%	3,884	500	4,384
c/f	11,653	1,500	

There is no private use reduction on the motor car though the director may be assessed under Schedule E in respect of a car benefit.

9.0 THE DUE DATE FOR THE PAYMENT OF CORPORATION TAX

(a) Advance Corporation Tax
A company must pay over ACT to the Revenue not later than 14 days after the end of the quarter in which the distribution is made.

(b) Mainstream Corporation Tax
As already mentioned, Mainstream Corporation Tax refers to the basic liability to corporation tax, less the offset for ACT paid.

Prior to 1965, when companies were liable to income tax, the date for payment of tax on income was the same as for an individual (in those days, 1st January in the year of assessment). As a result, the date of the end of the accounting period of the company determined the time interval before the tax was payable.

Illustration
D Ltd. made up accounts alternatively as under:

Year ended 30th April 1964
31st December 1964
31st March 1965

Year ended	Year of Assessment	Due Date	Time Interval
30.4.1964	1965/66	1.1.1966	20 months
31.12.1964	1965/66	1.1.1966	12 months
31.3.1965	1965/66	1.1.1966	9 months

Where the company commenced trading after 31st March 1965, the due date for the payment of MCT is always nine months after the end of the company's accounting period. Thus if E Ltd., making up accounts to 30th June 1986 commenced trading after 31st March 1965, it will pay corporation tax on 1st April 1987.

In order not to prejudice companies existing at 31st March 1965, it is provided that where a company commenced to trade before 31st March 1965 it would retain its old time-interval for the payment of corporation tax. Thus if E Ltd. (above) making up accounts to 30th June 1986 commenced trading prior to 31st March 1965, it will pay its corporation tax on 1st January 1988.

In all cases, corporation tax is not payable earlier than 30 days after the date of issue of notice of assessment.

Where a company which commenced trading before 31st March 1965 changes its accounting date, it retains the same time interval after the end of the accounting period as was used before the change.

Illustration
F Ltd. which commenced trading before 31st March 1965, made up accounts to 30th September annually. It changed its accounting date to 31st December and made up accounts for a 15 month period from 1st October 1984 to 31st December 1985.

AP	1.10.1984 to 30.9.1985
due date of MCT	1st January 1987
i.e.a time interval of 15 months	
AP	1.10.1985 to 31.12.1985
due date of MCT	1st April 1987
still a time interval of 15 months	

10.0 INTEREST

10.1 INTEREST ON OVERDUE TAX

Interest on unpaid corporation tax is charged at the following rates:

1.1.1980 to 30.11.1982	12%
1.12.1982 to 30.4.1985	8%
1.5.1985 to 5.8.1986	11%
6.8.1986 onwards	8½%

The interest must be paid gross and is not deductible as a trade expense or as a charge. The Board of Inland Revenue may remit interest of £30 or less. Interest is charged from the reckonable date. This is the later of:

(a) the normal due date if there has been no appeal and application for postponement;

(b) if an application for postponement has been made, and agreed to, the later of:

   (i) the due date for payment under the original assessment, or

   (ii) the earlier of:
      1. 30 days after the final agreement on the tax payable, and

      2. 6 months after the normal due date.

Where an appeal is made or an application for postponement of the payment of tax is made but not agreed to by the Inspector or the Commissioners the due date for the payment of that tax is 30 days after the date of notification of that decision if that is later than the normal due date.

Where the tax due on an assessment has been increased on appeal, interest on the additional tax becomes payable from the date on which it should have been charged had it been included in the original assessment.

Illustration
X Ltd. which commenced trading in 1970, makes up accounts to 31st December 1985. On 2nd August 1986 the Inspector issues a notice of assessment showing tax due of £100,000. The company appeals on 15th August and applies for postponement of £40,000 tax. On 12th September the Inspector agrees with the company that £30,000 tax can be postponed pending the appeal hearing. The appeal was heard on 15th April 1987 and the tax due was finally determined as £110,000. The tax payments were:

£70,000 on 30th October 1986
£40,000 on 30th April 1987

Interest will be due under:

(a) On £70,000 from 11.10.1986 to 30.10.1986

(b) On £30,000 from 1.4.1987 to 30.4.1987
    On £10,000 from 1.4.1987 to 30.4.1987

Interest on unpaid ACT or income tax due under the quarterly accounting will be chargeable if payment is made later than 14 days after the end of the relevant return period. Again, the Inland Revenue may remit interest of £30 or less.

10.2 INTEREST ON DELAYED TAX REPAYMENTS

A repayment to the company by the Inland Revenue of corporation tax, ACT or the tax credit on FII, more than 12 months after the material date carries a tax-free repayment supplement at the same rates as above. The interest runs to the end of the tax month in which the repayment order is issued and starts as under:

(a)	Corporation Tax originally paid on or after the first anniversary of the material date	At the beginning of the tax month following the next anniversary of the date of the payment of the tax.
(b)	In all other cases	At the beginning of the tax month following the first anniversary of the material date.

Where tax is repaid in respect of corporation tax paid on different dates, it is allocated to that paid to a later date before an earlier one. The material date is the earliest due date for the payment of corporation tax for the appropriate accounting period.

Illustration

Y Ltd. made up accounts to 31st December 1985 and was assessed to corporation tax in the sum of £20,000 on 30th June 1986. The assessment was appealed against and the tax due was paid on the normal due date of 1st October 1986. The Commissioner's hearing took place on 1st December 1986 and agreed the tax due at £25,000. The additional tax was paid on 12th February 1987. For the year to 31st December 1986 a loss is made which is carried back under s.177(2) into 1985. This results in a repayment of tax of £8,000 which is received by the company on 30th April 1988. Originally there would have been a liability to interest on £5,000 overdue tax from:

31.12.1986 to 12.2.1987
(31.12.1986 - 30 days after the date of determination being earlier than 1st April 1987).

This will be repaid by the collector on a claim being made.
The repayment of £8,000 will be allocated as under:

(1) To the £5,000 additional payment.
Paid - 12.2.1987
Next anniversary of material date - 1st October 1987
Interest due from 6.10.1987 to 5.5.1988.

(2) To the original payment of £20,000.
Interest due from 6.10.1987 to 5.5.1988.

13 Treatment of Losses

1.0 BASIC LOSS RELIEF (s.177(1), (2) and (8))

1.1 GENERAL

A corporation tax trading loss is calculated in the same way as corporation tax trading income, i.e. after deducting capital allowances but before deducting charges paid under deduction of tax.

1.2. CARRY FORWARD TA 1970, s.177(1)

A trading loss may be carried forward and offset against the first available future trading profits of the same trade without time limit.

1.3 AGAINST OTHER PROFITS TA 1970, s.177(2)

The trading loss may be offset:

(a) against total profits of the same accounting period. Total profits means all income liable to corporation tax, and chargeable gains (after s.93 deduction), but before deduction of charges on income; and then if the company wishes;

(b) against total profits of the immediately preceding accounting period(s) of the same length as that in which the loss was incurred. A claim under (a) above must be made before a claim is made under (b).

In offsetting the loss against total profits the order of offset is:

(a) against income;

(b) against chargeable gains.

Illustration

A Ltd. makes up accounts as follows:

12 months to 31.12.1985 - Profit
9 months to 30.9.1986 - Profit
12 months to 30.9.1987 - Loss

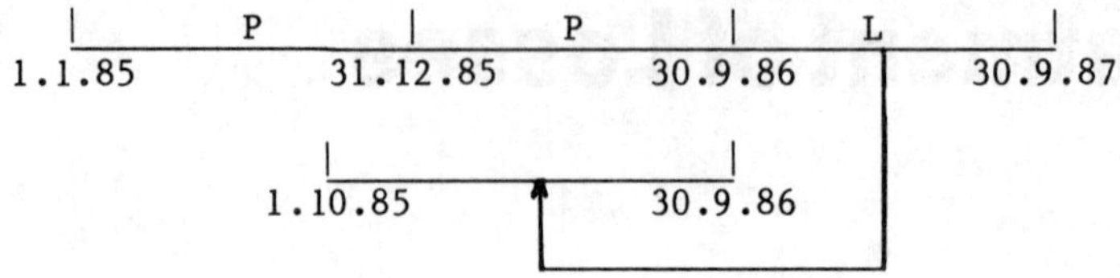

Thus the loss is carried back against the profit of:

(a) The accounting period to 30th September 1986.

(b) 3/12 of the profits of the accounting period to 31st December 1985.

All apportionments of profits are made on a strict time basis.

Before giving loss relief it is important to split any period of account into the appropriate accounting periods.

<u>Illustration</u>

B Ltd. makes up accounts as follows:

12 months to 31.12.1985 - Profit
12 months to 31.12.1986 - Profit
15 months to 31.3.1988 - Loss

In this case the 15 month period is divided up into two accounting periods:

(a) twelve months to 31st December 1987;

(b) three months to 31st March 1988

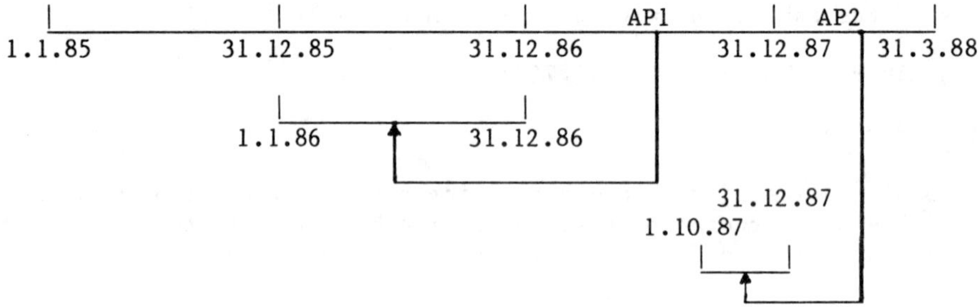

Though relief can be obtained for the loss of AP1, no relief under s.177(2) can normally be obtained for the loss of AP2 as it can only be carried back against three months of AP1 for which there is already a loss. It would, therefore, normally be carried forward.

For relief to be available under s.177(2) the company must:

(a) be trading on a commercial basis, with a reasonable expectation of profits;

(b) in the case of companies engaged in farming or market gardening, relief will not normally be available under s.177(2) if in the five preceding years there have been successive trading losses.

Relief is only available by carryback under s.177(2) if the trade producing the loss was also carried on in the accounting period(s) against whose profits the loss is being carried back.

Relief under s.177(2) is not available for Schedule D Case V or VI losses.

A claim to carry forward losses under s.177(1) must be made within six years of the end of the accounting period in which the loss occurred. A claim to deal with a loss under s.177(2) must be made within two years of the end of the accounting period in which the loss occurred.

In the case of conflict, relief is given under s.177(1) in priority to s.177(2).

Illustration

C Ltd. has the following results:

	Trading Income	Schedule A	Chargeable gains (After s.93 Relief)
	£	£	£
Year ended 31.12.1985	20,000	1,000	2,000
6 months ended 30.6.1986	6,000	500	600
Year ended 30.6.1987	(28,000)Loss	1,200	-
Year ended 30.6.1988	4,000	800	600

Show loss claims under s.177(2) and s.177(1)

	I	CG	
	£	£	£
Year ended 30.6.1987			
Trading loss			(28,000)
Schedule A	1,200		
s.177(2)	(1,200)		1,200
	Nil		(26,800)
6 months ended 30.6.1986			
Trading income	6,000		
Schedule A	500		
Chargeable Gains		600	
	6,500	600	
s.177(2)	(6,500)	(600)	7,100
	Nil	Nil	(19,700)
Year ended 31.12.1985			
Trading income	20,000		
Schedule A	1,000		
Chargeable Gains		2,000	
	21,000	2,000	
s.177(2) Relief restricted to 6/12 x £23,000	(11,500)		11,500
	9,500	2,000	(8,200)
Year ended 30.6.1988			
Trading income	4,000		
s.177(1) relief	(4,000)		4,000
	-		(4,200)
Schedule A	800		
Chargeable Gains		600	
	800	600	
Losses carried forward under s.177(1)			£(4,200)

Any apportionments of total profits or losses are made on a strict time basis.

The amount of the loss that can be carried back into 1985 is six-twelfths of total profits, i.e., income and chargeable gains. The order of offset however is:

(a) against income;

(b) against chargeable gains.

1.4 CHARGES ON INCOME (s.177(8))

So far, relief has been given for losses before the deduction of charges on income. To the extent that charges on income exceed profits, relief is available by carry forward and deduction from future trading income. This relief is only available for those charges incurred wholly and exclusively for the purposes of the trade. This effectively excludes non-trade charges such as deeds of covenant to charity, so in order to give maximum relief where there are available profits, non-trade charges should be relieved in priority to trade charges.

<u>Illustration</u>
E Ltd. has the following results:

	£
Trading income	2,000
Charges on income:	
Debenture interest	3,000
Covenant to Oxfam	500

To ensure maximum relief, charges will be deducted as under:

		£
Trading income		2,000
Less: Charges:	£	
Covenant to Oxfam	500	
Debenture interest	1,500	
		2,000
		-
Unrelieved charges		1,500

The balance of unrelieved charges, known as <u>excess charges</u>, is carried forward and relieved as a deduction against future trading income, in the same way as a s.177(1) loss.

<u>Illustration</u>
F Ltd. made up accounts as under:

	Trading Income	Schedule D Case III	Debenture interest paid (gross)
	£	£	£
Years ended:			
31.3.1985	6,000	800	1,000
31.3.1986	(20,000)	1,500	1,000
31.3.1987	8,000	900	1,000

Year ended 31.3.1986	
Trading loss	(20,000)

Schedule D Case III	1,500	
s.177(2)	(1,500)	1,500
	Nil	(18,500)
		(18,500)
(Excess charges £1,000)		
Year ended 31.3.1985		
Trading income	6,000	
Schedule D Case III	800	
	6,800	
s.177(2)	(6,800)	6,800
	Nil	(11,700)
Excess charges		
Year ended 31.3.1985	1,000	
Year ended 31.3.1986	1,000	
		(2,000)
Total loss available for carry forward		(13,700)
Year ended 31.3.1987		
Trading income	8,000	
s.177 (1)/(8)	(8,000)	
		8,000
	-	
		(5,700)
Schedule D Case III	900	
Less: Debenture interest paid	1,000	
	(100)	(100)
Total loss to be carried forward s.177(1)/(8)		(5,800)

1.5 COMPREHENSIVE EXAMPLE

X Ltd. has the following information:

	Year to 31.12.84	3 months to 31.3.85	Year to 31.3.86	Year to 31.3.87
	£	£	£	£
Trading profit	20,000		8,000	
loss		(32,000)		(9,000)
Schedule A	2,000	3,000	4,000	5,000
Schedule D III	1,000	800	600	400
Capital gains		7,000	5,600	
Capital losses	2,500			2,000
Debenture interest paid (gross)	1,000	1,000	1,000	1,000
Deed of Covenant to charity paid (gross)	200	200	200	200

	I £	CG £	£
<u>3 months to 31.3.85</u>			
Trading loss			(32,000)
Schedule A	3,000		
Schedule D III	800		
Capital gains		7,000	
Less: Capital losses b/f		(2,500)	
		4,500	
Less: s.93 relief - 1/3		(1,500)	
	3,800	3,000	
a.177(2) relief	(3,800)	(3,000)	6,800
	Nil	Nil	(25,200)
Debenture interest paid	1,000 c/f		
Deed of covenant paid	200 lost		
<u>Year to 31.12.84</u>			
Trading profit	20,000		
Schedule A	2,000		
Schedule D III	1,000		
	23,000		
s.177(2) Relief restricted to 3/12 x £23,000	(5,750)		5,750
	17,250		(19,450)
Less: Charges £(1,000 + 200)	1,200		
	16,050		
Debenture Interest 1985			(1,000)
			(20,450)
<u>Year to 31.3.86</u>			
Trading profit	8,000		
s.177(1)	(8,000)		8,000
	Nil		(12,450)
Schedule A	4,000		
Schedule D III	600		
Capital gains		5,600	
Less: s.93 relief - 1/4		1,400	
	4,600	4,200	
s.177(2) brought back	(3,600)		
	1,000		
Less: Charges - Deed of Covenant	200		
	800		
Debenture interest	800	200	
	Nil	4,000	

	I £	CG £	£
Year to 31.3.87			
Trading loss			(9,000)
Schedule A	5,000		
Schedule D III	400		
	5,400		
s.177(2) relief	(5,400)		5,400
	Nil		(3,600)
Debenture interest paid	1,000 c/f		
Deed of Covenant paid	200 lost		
s.177(2) carried back			3,600
			Nil
To carry forward therefore will be:			
Losses under s.177(1)/(8) £12,450 + £1,000			(13,450)
Capital losses		2,000	

It is important to recognise the value of the relief that has been obtained for the loss. Throughout this example, all the companies have been small and the relief obtained is as under:

Year to 31.12.84

£5,750 offset against income - 3/12 x £5,750 @ 30%
9/12 x £5,750 @ 30%

3 months to 31.3.85

£3,800 offset against income at 30%
£3,000 offset against chargeable gains at 45%

Year to 31.3.86

£11,600 offset against income at 30%

Year to 31.3.87

£5,400 offset against income at 29%

In general terms the loss should always be relieved to achieve the highest tax savings.

2.0 RELIEF UNDER s.177(3A)

Where all or part of a loss is attributable to first year allowances, that part can be carried back and relieved against total profits (as in s.177(2)) of the 36 months immediately preceding the accounting period in which the loss arose, on a LIFO basis. In order to obtain the maximum benefit under this section, a claim should be made under s.177(2), to eliminate as far as possible trading losses and writing-down allowances, followed by a claim under s.177(3A), for the first year allowances.

Illustration

D Ltd. made up accounts as under:

	Trading Income	Schedule A
	£	£
Year ended 30th June 1983	4,000	1,000
Year ended 30th June 1984	3,000	1,000
Year ended 30th June 1985	6,000	1,000

For the period ended 31st December 1985 the results were:

	£	£
Trading profits (before CA)	2,000	
Capital allowances: Writing down	8,000	
First year	20,000	
Schedule A	1,000	
Trading loss - 6 months to 31.12.1985		
Trading profits	2,000	
Less: Capital allowances	28,000	
	(26,000)	
Attributable:		
WDA	6,000	
FYA	20,000	
	(26,000)	
6 months to 31.12.1985		
Trading loss		(26,000)
Schedule A	1,000	
s.177(2)	(1,000)	1,000
		(25,000)
Year ended 30.6.1985		
Trading income	6,000	
Schedule A	1,000	
	7,000	
s.177(2) 6/12 x 7,000	(3,500)	3,500
	3,500	(21,500)

Loss relief under s.177(2) is now at an end. To the extent that the loss is attributed to first year allowances it may be carried back to the 36 months immediately preceding the 6 months to 31.12.1985.

Balance of loss attributed:

	£	
WDA	1,500	c/f s.177(1)
FYA	20,000	
	21,500	

	£	£
b/f	3,500	
Loss attributable to FYA		(20,000)
s.177(3A)	(3,500)	3,500
	Nil	(16,500)
Year ended 30.6.1984		
Trading income	3,000	
Schedule A	1,000	
	4,000	
s.177(3A)	(4,000)	4,000
	Nil	(12,500)
Year ended 30.6.1983		
Trading income	4,000	
Schedule A	1,000	
	5,000	
s.177(3A)	(5,000)	5,000
Total loss carried forward under s.177(1) £(7,500 + 1,500) = £9,000		(7,500)

Note that the s.177(2) claim is taken before s.177(3A) and is treated as being taken out of all other items, i.e. trading losses and WDA etc, first. This will give the maximum possible carryback for the FYA.

Although it appears from the legislation that a claim to relief under s.177(2) gives an automatic right to one under s.177(3A), the Revenue require a separate claim for relief to be made.

3.0 TERMINAL LOSSES (TA 1970, s.178)

When a company ceases to trade, any trading loss incurred in the last twelve months of trading that cannot be relieved under any other loss relieving section can be carried back and offset against the available trading income of the preceding 36 months, apportioned if necessary on a LIFO basis.

Section 178 provides that terminal loss relief is to be given in the last resort, after giving relief under all other loss relieving sections. It is believed that the Revenue interpret this to mean relief under s.177 only and not relief under s. 254 (relief against surpluses of franked investment income) or s.258 (group relief).

Illustration

G Ltd. ceased trading on 30th June 1987. It had the following results:

	Trading Income	Schedule A
	£	£
Year ended 31.12.1985	3,000	500
Year ended 31.12.1986	(20,000)	500
6 months ended 30.6.1987	2,000	-

Here there is the possibility of terminal loss relief as there is a loss in the last twelve months' trading. Before the amount available can be ascertained, all other loss relief must be claimed first.

Year ended 31.12.1986	£	£
Trading loss		(20,000)
Less: Relieved:		
s.177(2) of the year	500	
s.177(2) carried back	3,500	
s.177(1) carried forward	2,000	
		6,000
Loss unrelieved		(14,000)

As six months of the year ended 31st December 1986 fall into the last twelve months, terminal loss relief can be obtained for six-twelfths of the unrelieved loss, i.e. £7,000, against "available trading income" of the three years ended 30th June 1986. The balance cannot be relieved and is lost.

The term "loss" in respect of terminal loss relief includes:

(a) trading losses;
(b) excess charges on income, wholly and exclusively incurred;
(c) excess capital allowances given by discharge or repayment of tax: all of which arise wholly or partly within the last twelve months trading.

As can be seen in the example above, where an accounting period only falls partly into the last twelve months of trading, losses, etc., will be apportioned on a time basis. The term "available trading income" means the trading income of the three preceding years; apportioned if necessary on a strict time basis.

Where in those earlier periods there are trade charges, sufficient income must be retained to offset those charges. The income that is retained will be identified as:

(a) other income; then

(b) trading income;

thus giving the maximum potential relief for terminal losses.

The time limit for claiming terminal loss relief is six years from the date of cessation.

Illustration

H Ltd. ceased trading on 31st December 1987 having made up accounts to 31st December annually. Results for previous years have been as under:

	Trading Income £	Schedule A £	Debenture interest paid £
Year ended:			
31.12.1984	16,000	500	1,000
31.12.1985	8,000	2,000	1,000
31.12.1986	10,000	2,000	1,000
31.12.1987	(30,000)	2,000	1,000

	£	£
Year ended:		
31.12.1987		(30,000)
Schedule A	2,000	
s.177(2)	(2,000)	2,000
	Nil	(28,000)

	£	£
b/f		
		(28,000)
Year ended:		
31.12.1986		
Trading income	10,000	
Schedule A.	2,000	
	12,000	
s.177(~~2~~3)	(12,000)	(12,000)
	Nil	16,000
	======	======

	£
Calculation of terminal loss:	
Unrelieved trading loss of last 12 months	16,000
Excess charges of last 12 months	1,000
	17,000
	======

The excess charges of the year ended 31st December 1986 cannot be utilised and are lost.

The terminal loss can then be carried back and offset against the available trading income of the three preceding years on a LIFO basis.

	£		£	£
Terminal loss				(17,000)
Year ended 31.12.1986				
All trading income utilised under s.177(2)				
Year ended 31.12.1985				
Trading income			8,000	
Schedule A	2,000			
Retain for trade charges	1,000			
	1,000			
Terminal loss relief			(8,000)	8,000
			-	(9,000)
Liable to Corporation tax (Sch A. Balance)		1,000		
		=====		
Year ended 31.12.1984				
Trading income			16,000	
Schedule A	500			
Retain for trade charges Total £1000.	500		500	
	-		15,500	
Terminal loss relief			(9,000)	9,000
			6,500	-
Liable to Corporation tax		6,500		
		=====		

It is important to appreciate that the purpose of retaining for trade charges is to ensure that there are no unrelieved trade charges which would be incapable of carry forward.

Illustration

	Years to 31.12.83	31.12.84	31.12.85	31.12.86	9 months to 30.9.87
	£	£	£	£	£
Trading profit	6,000	4,000	2,000	1,000	(15,000)
Schedule A	600	600	600	-	600
Debenture Interest paid	1,000	400	1,000	-	-
Deed of Covenant to charity	100	100	100	-	-

9 months to 30.9.87		I £	£
Trading loss			(15,000)
Schedule A		600	
s.177(2)		(600)	600
		Nil	(14,400)
Year to 31.12.86			
Trading profit		1,000	
s.177(2) restricted to 9/12 x £1,000		(750)	750
		250	(13,650) ======
Terminal loss as above			(13,650)
Carryback period - 36 months to 30.9.1986:			
Period 1.1.1986-30.9.1986			
Terminal loss relief against balance of trading profits of year to 31.12.86 after s.177(2) relief:		(250)	250
		Nil ===	(13,400)
Year to 31.12.1985			
Trading profit	2,000		
Schedule A		600	
Retain for trade charges	400	600	
	1,600		
Terminal loss relief	(1,600)		1,600
	Nil =====		(11,800)
Deed of Covenant to charity £100 lost ====			
Year to 31.12.1984			
Trading profit	4,000		
Schedule A		600	
Retain for trade charges		400	
		200	
Terminal loss relief	(4,000)		4,000
	Nil =====		(7,800)
Less: Deed of Covenant to charity		100	
		100 ===	

	£	£	£
b/f			(7,800)
Year to 31.12.1983			
Trading profit	6,000		
Schedule A		600	
Retain for trade charges	(400)	(600)	
	5,600	-	
Terminal loss relief - restricted to 3/12 x £6,000	(1,500)		1,500
	4,100		(6,300)
Less: Deed of Covenant to charity	100		=====
	4,000		
	=====		

Note the terminal loss relief in the year to 31st December 1983 is 3/12 x £6,000 not 3/12 x £5,600.

The remainder of the terminal loss is unrelieved.

Where there have been sales of assets after cessation of trade, the normal treatment of gains and losses will be:

(a)	Sales of stock in trade, etc.	Any profits and losses are dealt with in the last period of account.
(b)	Sales of plant and other assets on which capital allowances have been claimed	Any balancing charges and allowances are dealt with in the last accounting period.
(c)	Capital gains, etc.	Assessed in the accounting period in which the asset is disposed of.

4.0 THE EXTENSION OF LOSS RELIEF WHEN THERE IS A SURPLUS OF FRANKED INVESTMENT INCOME (TA 1970, s.254)

In earlier sections the basic forms of loss relief were:

(a) under s.177(2) against total profits of the accounting period;
(b) under s.177(2) against total profits of the immediately preceding accounting period of the same length.

An extension of loss relief is available when there is also a surplus of franked investment income. Where a company has:

(a) trading losses;

(b) charges on income;

(c) management expenses;

(d) capital allowances given by discharge or repayment of tax;

(e) certain capital losses of investment companies;

and also has available a surplus of FII of the same accounting period, then the company may elect to treat that surplus of FII as if it were profits liable to corporation tax, so that the losses etc. may be relieved and the tax credit comprised in the FII repaid. Furthermore, the unrelieved losses etc., (but not management expenses or charges on income) may also be set against any surplus FII of the preceding accounting period, of the same length, and the tax credit comprised in that surplus repaid.

The order of set-off is against:

(i) total profits of the accounting period in which loss etc. arises;

(ii) total profits of the preceding accounting period;

(iii) the surplus FII of that period;

(iv) the surplus FII of the preceding accounting period.

For this relief to be claimed the claimant company must be resident in the UK and relief must be claimed:

(a) in respect of trading losses, capital allowances and the investment company's chargeable losses - within two years from the end of the accounting period in which the loss (or allowance) arose;

(b) in respect of charges on income and management expenses - within six years of the end of the accounting period in which the loss arose.

Illustration

L Ltd. is resident in the UK and has the following results:

	Years ended		
	31.3.1985	31.3.1986	31.3.1987
	£	£	£
Trading income	6,000		20,000
Trading loss		(14,000)	
Schedule A	1,000	1,000	1,000
Dividends received	3,600	2,800	2,130
Dividends paid	1,400	1,400	5,680

Show the loss claims for all years - giving relief as soon as possible.
Assume ACT at 3/7 for the financial years 1984 and 1985 and 29/71 for the financial year 1986.

	£	£	£
Year ended 31.3.1986			
Trading income			(14,000)
Schedule A		1,000	
s.177(2)		(1,000)	1,000
		Nil	(13,000)
Year ended 31.3.1985			
Trading income		6,000	
Schedule A		1,000	
		7,000	
S.177(2)		(7,000)	7,000
		Nil	(6,000)
Year ended 31.3.1986			
Dividends received	2,800		
Add: Tax credit	1,200	4,000	
Dividends paid	1,400		
Add:ACT	600	2,000	

		2,000	
s.254 claim		(2,000)	2,000
			(4,000)

Tax credit repaid - 30% x £2,000 = £600

Year ended 31.3.1985

Dividends received	3,600		
Add: Tax credit	1,543		
		5,143	
Dividends paid	1,400		
Add: ACT	600		
		2,000	
		3,143	
s.254 claim		(3,143)	3,143
		Nil	(857)

Tax credit repaid - 30% x £3,143 = £943

The effect of a claim under s.254 is to accelerate the repayment of the tax credit attached to surplus FII, thus giving a cash flow advantage. However, had the claim not been made, not only the surplus FII but also the trading loss etc. could have been carried forward for offset against future trading income. In order to put the company back in the same position as it would have been had a s.254 claim not been made, it is provided in s.254(5) that whenever in a subsequent accounting period there is a surplus of franked payments the company may treat the lower of:

(a) the amount of the surplus franked payments, or

(b) the amount of the s.254 claim

as a trading loss to be relieved against trading income as in s.177(1).

Year ended 31.3.1987	£	£	£
Trading income			20,000
s.177(1)			(857)
			19,143
Franked Payments			
Dividends paid	5,680		
Add: ACT	2,320	8,000	
FII			
Dividends received	2,130		
Add: Tax credit	870	3,000	
Surplus franked payments		5,000	
s.254(5) loss relief		(5,000)	(5,000)
			14,143
Schedule A			1,000
			15,143

Corporation tax @ 29%		4,391
ACT - 29% x £5,000	1,450	
Less: Due to Revenue on re-instatement of trading losses	1,450	-
		4,391

Notes

1. Here, the surplus franked payments are less than the amount of the s.254 claim, i.e. £5,143-£5,000 = £143. This has had the effect of reducing the amount of the surplus franked payments (and consequently ACT available for offset) to nil. The amount of £143 not relieved will be carried forward without time limit to be relieved against profits in future accounting periods.

2. The ACT that relates to the surplus of franked payments is:

   £5,000 @ 29% = £1,450

   If s.254(5) had not been claimed this amount of ACT could have been set off against the corporation tax liability on income, subject to the usual limits. However, the tax credit repaid on the original s.254 claim is now reclaimed by the Revenue, and as a result there will be no set-off of ACT. The amount of £93 (£1,543-£1,450) will be recovered by the Revenue in a future accounting period.

If the results for the year to 31st March 1988 were:

	£
Trading profits	20,000
Dividends paid	3,550

the position would be:

	£	£
Year to 31.3.1988		
Trading profits		20,000
Dividends paid	3,550	
ACT 29/71	1,450	
	5,000	
Treat the lower of £5,000 or the remaining s.254 claim of £143 as a s.177(1) loss	143	(143)
	4,857	19,857
Corporation tax @ 29%		5,759
ACT as above	1,450	
Less: Due to Revenue - balance of	93	1,357
		4,402

Thus the amount of losses received back from the Revenue and the amount of ACT restored to them precisely balance with the tax credits received from, and the losses surrendered to, the Revenue in the s.254 claim.

Does it give the same result as if no relief was obtained? If no relief under s.254 was claimed, at the end of 1985 the position would have been:

	£	
s.177(1) losses c/f		£6,000
Surplus FII		
1985	2,000	
1984	3,143	
		£5,143

In 1987 the s.177(1) claim would have been £6,000 to give trading income of £14,000 instead of £14,143 when s.254 is claimed. The surplus FII would have been offset against franked payments made in the year to 31st March 1987 and no ACT would have been payable. However, £5,143-£5,000 = £143 would be carried forward as surplus FII against future franked payments.

In essence, the claim operates by reducing the loss and releasing the tax credit under s.254 and giving back the loss and reducing the ACT available for offset under s.254(5). It is generally worth making when possible, since it means that extra money is made available straight away - a very important practical factor when a company is making a loss.

5.0 COMPANY RECONSTRUCTIONS WITHOUT A CHANGE OF OWNERSHIP (TA 1970, s.252 & s.253)

Provided certain conditions are fulfilled, where one company ceases trading and another company commences to carry on its trade, unutilised trading losses of the first company are transferred to the successor. In addition, fixed assets are transferred at their tax written-down values with no balancing adjustments and capital assets can be transferred at the price which gives neither gain nor loss.

(a) Both companies must be within the charge to UK corporation tax;

(b) At least 75% of the trade or of an interest in it (i.e. ownership of the ordinary share capital) must belong to the same persons at some time during the period commencing one year before the change, and finishing two years after it.

If relief is claimed in this way the company ceasing to trade will not be able to claim terminal loss relief.

6.0 RESTRICTIONS ON CARRY FORWARD OF LOSSES (TA 1970, s.483 & s.484)

There are anti-avoidance provisions contained in TA 1970, s.483 and s.484 prohibiting the carry forward of losses where:

(a) Within a three year period there is both a change in the beneficial ownership of the company and a major change in the nature and conduct of its trade, or

(b) at any time after a company's trading activities become small or negligible, and before they revive, there is a change in the beneficial ownership of the company.

A "major change" includes:

(a) a major change in the type of property dealt in or services or facilities provided in the trade; or

(b) a major change in customers' outlets or markets of the trade.

A change in the beneficial ownership of the company will generally occur where one or more persons acquire a majority (more than 50%) shareholding in the company concerned.

7.0 FOREIGN LOSSES AND SCHEDULE D CASE VI LOSSES

Foreign losses will be considered later, in the section on foreign income. Schedule D VI losses may only be offset against future Schedule D Case VI profits with any excess being carried forward and offset against future Schedule D Case VI profits. A claim for relief must be made within six years after the end of the accounting period in which the loss arises.

8.0 LOSSES AND STOCK RELIEF

Although stock relief has been abolished in FA 1982, the prohibitions relating to the carry forward of losses created by the new system (FA 1981) of stock relief remain.

Where stock relief for a period of account remained unused in that period of account due to, for example, an insufficiency of trading profits in that period, the surplus could be carried forward to succeeding years and utilised against profits from the same trade chargeable in those years. Provisions introduced with the new stock relief (FA 1981) restricted the carry forward of unused stock relief to a maximum of six years, i.e. unused stock relief cannot be carried forward after the termination of a six year period. The restriction only applies to stock relief given under the new provisions, in FA 1981.

Illustration

P Ltd. prepared accounts annually to 30th April. Stock relief claimed but unused for the year to 30th April 1984 cannot be carried forward beyond the year to 30th April 1990 i.e., it cannot be utilised against profits for the year to 30th April 1991 and subsequently.

For corporation tax purposes, both stock relief and, in general, capital allowances, are given as an expense in computing trading income. Where these reliefs create or enhance a trading loss, relief may be given for such loss in a variety of ways, discussed earlier. Because of the restriction on the carry forward of stock relief, where a loss is not fully utilised in a claim for the accounting period in which it occurred, or a previous period, it becomes necessary:

(a) to analyse the component parts of a trading loss into the loss excluding capital allowances (CA) and stock relief (SR), CA and SR;

(b) to determine how much of each component has been utilised by the company for the current (or preceding) accounting period;

(c) to determine, in each subsequent accounting period, how much of the component has been utilised, thereby eventually, after six years, establishing whether there is a restriction on the carry forward of the component representing stock relief.

In order to determine (b) above, the component parts are deemed to be utilised in the following order:

(a) trading loss (excluding CA and SR);

(b) capital allowances;

(c) stock relief.

Illustration

In the year to 30th September 1984, A Ltd. had a trading loss of £25,000, and was also entitled to capital allowances of £8,000 and stock relief of £6,000. A Ltd. made a claim under s.177(2) to offset the loss against the total profits of £30,000 for the year to 30th September 1983. The balance was carried forward under s.177(1).

(a) The component parts of the trading loss are:

	£
Loss (excluding CA and SR)	25,000
CA	8,000
SR	6,000
	39,000

(b) The s.177(2) claim utilises:

	£
Loss	25,000
CA (part)	5,000
	30,000

leaving a loss to carry forward under s.177(1) of £9,000 comprising:

	£
CA (balance)	3,000
SR	6,000
	9,000

Where a loss was carried forward under s.177(1) the order of utilisation of the various component parts was:

(a) capital allowances for periods of account ending on or after 14th November 1980;

(b) stock relief for the same periods (new system FA 1981 stock relief) on a LIFO basis;

(c) trading losses (other than the above) for the same periods;

(c) other losses, stock relief and capital allowances for earlier periods.

Illustration

B Ltd. prepared accounts to 31st July. For the year to 31st July 1984, B Ltd. had a trading loss of £55,000 comprising:

	£
Loss	30,000
Capital Allowances	10,000
Stock Relief	15,000
	55,000

Accumulated trading losses brought forward at 1st August 1983 totalled £30,000. The results for the year to 31st July 1985 showed trading income of £45,000.

The loss brought forward at 1st August 1984, totalling £85,000 (£30,000 + £55,000) is treated as utilised in the following order against the trading income of £45,000;

	£
CA - for year to 31.7.84	10,000
New stock relief	15,000
Losses	20,000
	45,000

The unused losses of £40,000 will be carried forward.

Where part of the loss includes first year allowances, then the procedure is to make all s.177(2) and (3A) claims in the normal way ignoring any identification of the loss. After the claims have been made identify the loss, capital allowances and stock relief utilised but in doing so <u>identify the first year allowances used in the s.177(3A) claim first before dealing with the other items</u>.

Illustration

X Ltd. is a UK resident company. It provides the following information for the years ended below:

Year ended 31st December	1981	1982	1983	1984	1985
	£	£	£	£	£
Trading profit	11,000				3,100
Trading loss		5,000	2,400	4,500	
Capital allowances:					
WDA	2,000	1,200	2,200	600	
FYA	3,300	800	3,000	1,000	
Stock relief	400	500	2,000	2,400	
Other income	15,000	2,000	6,000	2,000	2,000

Calculate the loss relief for all years. Losses are to be relieved as soon as possible.

Y/e 31.12.1981		I	CG		Loss	CA	SR
	£	£	£	£	£	£	£
TP		11,000					
CA:							
WDA	2,000						
FYA	3,300						
	5,300						
SR	400						
		5,700					
DI		5,300					
Other income		15,000					
		20,300					
s.177(2) 1982		(5,500)					
s.177(3A) 1983		(3,000)					
s.177(3A) 1984		(1,000)					
		10,800					
		======					
Y/e 31.12.1982							
TL				5,000	5,000		
CA				2,000		2,000	
SR				500			500
DI				(7,500)	(5,000)	(2,000)	(500)
Other income		2,000					
s.177(2)		(2,000)		2,000	2,000		
		Nil		5,500	(3,000)		
		====					
s.177(2) c/back				5,500	3,000	2,000	500
				Nil	Nil	Nil	Nil
				=====	====	=====	===

	I			Loss	CA	SR
	£		£	£	£	£
Y/e 31.12.1983						
TL			2,400	(2,400)		
CA			5,200		(5,200)	
SR			2,000			(2,000)
			(9,600)	(2,400)	(5,200)	(2,000)
Other income	6,000					
s.177(2)	(6,000)	(2)	6,000	2,400	2,200	1,400
	Nil		(3,600)			
S.177(3A)	====	(1)	3,000		3,000	
		c/f	(600)	NIL	NIL	(600)
			=====	=====	=====	=====

Make loss claims first ignoring identification. Then identify losses starting with FYA.

Y/e 31.12.1984						
TL			4,500	(4,500)		
CA			1,600		(1,600)	
SR			2,400			(2,400)
			(8,500)	(4,500)	(1,600)	(2,400)
Other income	2,000					
s.177(2)	(2,000)	(2)	2,000	2,000		
	Nil		(6,500)			
	=====	(1)	1,000		1,000	
		c/f	(5,500)	(2,500)	(600)	(2,400)
			=====	=====	===	=====

	I	CG		CA	SR	New Losses	Others
	£	£	£	£	£	£	£
b/forward							
1983			(600)		(600)		
1984			(5,500)	(600)	(2,400)	(2,500)	
Y/e 31.12.1985			(6,100)	(600)	(3,000)	(2,500)	
DI	3,100						
s.177(1)	(3,100)		(3,100)	600	2,500		
	Nil		(3,000)	-	(500)	(2,500)	c/f S.177(1)
Other income	2,000		=====	===	=====	=====	
	2,000						
	=====						

9.0 USING LOSSES EFFECTIVELY

A loss has been described as a negative asset; like all assets therefore it is important to use them effectively. Points to bear in mind are:

9.1 GENERAL

(a) All other things being equal, a loss should be utilised in such a way as to give the greatest tax savings. This will mean:

i) offsetting the loss against marginal profits which bear the highest effective rate of corporation tax;

ii) then offsetting the loss against profits chargeable at the normal rate;

iii) lastly offsetting the loss against profits liable at the small companies rate.

(b) Timing is important; it is generally better to obtain loss relief now rather than next year. Thus it may be better to carry the loss back rather than to carry it forward. In doing this however consider the time value of money. It might be better to carry forward a loss if the rate of relief is greater than the indexed value of the relief obtained by carrying the loss back.

(c) Where a loss is carried back (particularly under s.177(3A)) there may be the possibility of tax free repayment supplements.

(d) It is a popular misconception to believe that when a loss is offset there will be an automatic repayment of MCT. This will not always be the case, particularly if ACT has already been offset.

Illustration

A Ltd. has the following trading results:

	£
Year to 31st March 1987	30,000
Year to 31st March 1988	(40,000)

No ACT has been paid.

Before loss relief:	1987	1988
DI	30,000	(40,000)
CT @ 29%	8,700	

If s.177(2) relief is claimed:

	1987	1988
DI	30,000	(40,000)
s.177(2)	(30,000)	30,000
	Nil	(10,000)
IR repay	8,700	

If however there had been a full offset of ACT the position before loss relief in 1987 would have been:

	£
DI	30,000
CT @ 29%	8,700
ACT offset restricted to 29% of £30,000	8,700
MCT paid	-

If the loss is now carried back from 1988 there will be no repayment of corporation tax as no MCT has been paid. All the ACT offset will now be thrown into surplus but this does not guarantee a repayment if the maximum offset has already been made in the previous six years.

Where double tax relief is being claimed under the credit system, the offset of a loss may result in the loss of foreign tax credits.

9.2 TERMINAL LOSS RELIEF

In maximising this relief remember that the loss qualifying for relief is that of the last 12 months of trading. If it is desired to obtain maximum relief the temptation to "keep going for a little longer to see what the company can do" must be resisted. As there may be substantial capital gains on the disposal of assets, every effort should be made to ensure disposal before the cessation of trade so that any loss arising in the last accounting period can be offset against them.

9.3 S.254 RELIEF

Whilst relief should be claimed as early as possible it is important to remember that there is a restriction on the re-instatement of a loss - i.e. the presence of a surplus of future franked payments. Where there is unlikely to be such a surplus, possibly because of a substantial surplus of F.I.I . brought forward, it might be impossible to reinstate the loss under s.177(1) for a substantial period of time. It may be more beneficial therefore to just consider carrying the loss forward under s.177(1) where the only limiting factor is the presence of future trading profits.

14 Groups

1.0 THE TAXATION OF GROUPS - GROUP RELIEF

1.1 GENERAL - THE RECOGNITION OF A GROUP

Like many words in taxation, the word 'group' does not have a single meaning. There are different definitions of the word for separate taxation techniques and it is important initially to have a brief survey of the meanings as far as losses are concerned. Thus for loss relief under s.258-264 TA 1970 a group will exist if the holding company controls directly or indirectly at least 75% of the ordinary share capital of the subsidiary company.

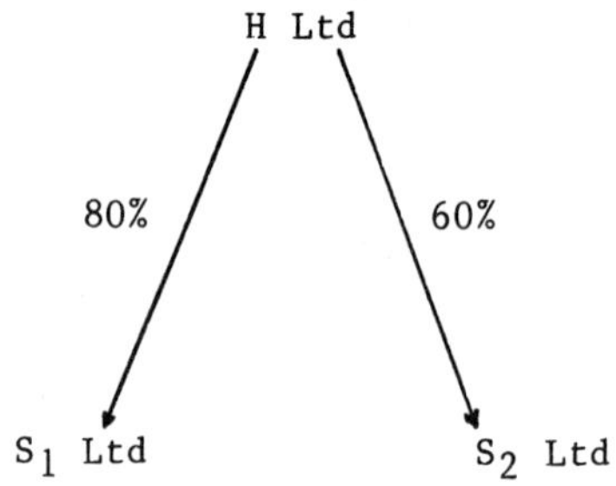

Fig. 3. Group loss relief

In this case S_1 Ltd., but not S_2 Ltd., will be a subsidiary company for group loss relief.

1.2 GROUPS AND GROUP RELIEF - DEFINITION

For group relief to be available it is necessary that two basic conditions are satisfied:

(a) all the companies concerned are UK resident;

(b) they are members of a group of companies.

(a) UK residence

TA 1970, s. 482(7) provides that a company will be considered to be resident in the UK where the central management and control of its trade or business is exercised in the UK. The traditional test of corporate residence is that it exists at the place where the board of directors meets - **(John Hood & Co. Ltd. v. Magee (1918))**. The case of **Unit Construction Co. Ltd. v. Bullock (1960)** provided that central management and control exists at the place where it actually occurs and not merely where it should occur.

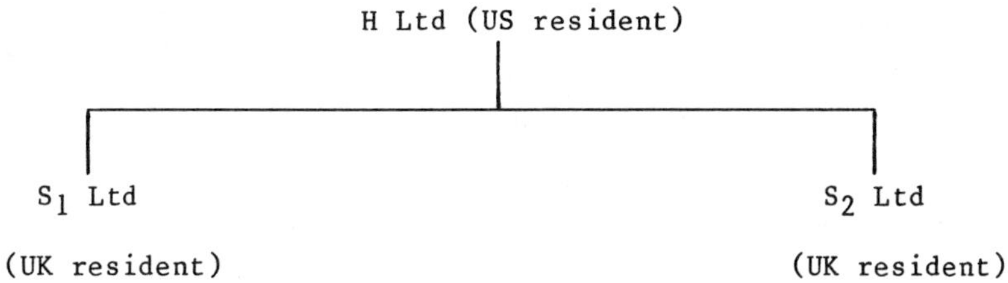

Fig.4 US residing holding company

At its most basic, a group consists of a holding company and a subsidiary company. In the above as H Ltd. is not UK resident it will not be possible for losses to be surrendered between S_1 and S_2 despite the fact that they are both resident in the UK.

To avoid this difficulty, it may be possible to interpose a UK resident intermediate holding company.

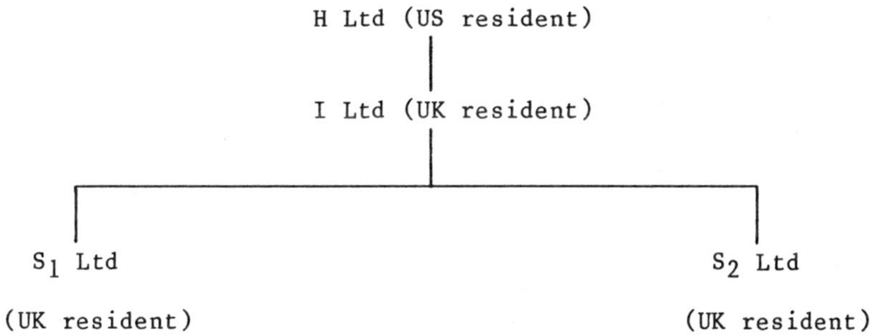

Fig. 5. US resident holding company with UK intermediary

In this case it would be possible to surrender losses between I Ltd. and S_1 and S_2 and also between S_1 and S_2 as there would now be a UK resident group of holding and subsidiary companies.

This form of structure may well be challenged by the Revenue who will try to show that I Ltd. is not truly UK resident. In particular, problems may be encountered if for example:

(i) the directors of I are the same as H Ltd.;

(ii) I Ltd. has no independent economic reason for its own existence apart from holding the shares in S_1 and S_2 and thus co-incidentally forming a UK resident group.

(b) A group of companies

For group relief purposes, companies will form a group when the holding company controls directly or indirectly at least 75% of the ordinary share capital of the subsidiary. Ordinary share capital is defined in TA 1970,S.526(5) as including all shares apart from those paying a fixed rate of dividend. It would thus include participating preference shares.

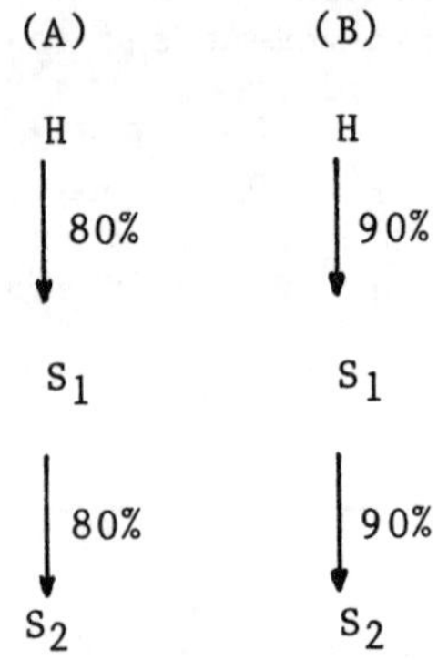

Fig. 6. Controlling interests

In Case (A), H and S_1 are within a group of companies as H controls 80% directly of S_1. Similarly, S_1 and S_2 are within a group for the same reason. H and S_2 however are not within a group as H only controls indirectly 80% x 80% = 64% of S_2. Thus losses can be transferred between H and S_1, between S_1 and S_2 but not between H and S_2. In particular it is not possible to surrender losses from H to S_1, and then on from S_1 to S_2.

In case (B), H is clearly the holding company of S_1 and S_1 the holding company of S_2. In addition H controls directly 90% x 90% = 81% of S_2. All these companies are therefore within the same group and losses may be surrendered freely between them.

Indirect holdings through non UK resident companies must be ignored, so that in (B) above, if S_1 was non UK resident S_2 would not be within a group with H.

(c) Anti-avoidance measures

FA 1973, s. 28 was introduced to deal with situations in which 'artificial groups' were created in order to utilise first year allowances. It extended the basic definition of groups, considered above, to include the following additional tests. Thus to qualify as a group the holding company should not only control at least 75% of the ordinary share capital but also:

(i) be beneficially entitled to at least 75% of the profits available for distribution to the equity holders, and,

(ii) be beneficially entitled to at least 75% of any assets of the subsidiary company available for distribution on a winding up.

1.3 ITEMS AVAILABLE FOR GROUP RELIEF S.258 TA 1970

Group relief is available for:

(a) trading losses;
(b) excess charges, including non-trade charges;
(c) excess management expenses;
(d) excess capital allowances given by discharge or repayment of tax.

Trading losses may be surrendered without any prior offset against other profits; in general the other items can only be surrendered if they exceed the other profits of the accounting period.

Losses which are caught by the provisions of TA 1970, S.180 ('hobby farming') or S.177(4) (trading not carried on on a commercial basis) are not available for group relief.

Only items of the current accounting period are available for surrender.
Once a company controls at least 75% of the OSC etc. of the owned company it is entitled to 100% of that company's losses etc.

1.4 METHOD OF GIVING GROUP RELIEF

Within the group structure there are two basic types of companies:

(a) the claimant company - the one that receives the loss, etc.;
(b) the surrendering company - the one with a loss, etc., available for surrender.

Before a loss, etc., can be surrendered by one company to another, detailed conditions must be satisfied.

(a) <u>The claimant company</u>
The claimant company may offset losses surrendered to it against total profits:

(i) against income, then,
(ii) against chargeable gains.

Before the loss is offset, however, the claimant company must offset:

(i) losses and charges brought forward under s. 177(1);
(ii) any s. 177(2) losses of the same accounting period;
(iii) charges of the same accounting period.

It must <u>not</u> however bring back losses etc. from a subsequent accounting period.

<u>Illustration</u>
J Ltd. is the 100% subsidiary of K Ltd. It provides the following information for the year to 31st March 1987:

	£
Trade loss	(1,000)
Schedule A	2,000
Capital gain	3,500
Debenture interest paid	500
Losses brought forward from 1986	(2,000)
Losses of 1988 available for carry back	(2,400)
K Ltd. has a loss of	(10,000)

	I £	CG £	 £
DI			(1,000)
Schedule A	2,000		
Capital Gains		3,500	
Less: 5.93 - 1/7		500	
		3,000	
s. 177(2)	(1,000)		1,000
	1,000		
Less: Charges	500		
	500		
	3,500 (500 + 3,000)		

3,500
=====

K Ltd. may only surrender £3,500 loss - up to the total of J Ltd.'s profits.

(b) The surrendering company

There are no specific conditions attached to the surrendering company and in general it may:

(i) surrender as much loss as it wishes to a company up to the maximum of the claimant company's own eligible profits;

(ii) spread relief over a number of companies within the group.

In considering the amount of loss that can be surrendered to another group company, the surrendering company would often consider the following factors:

(i) maximisation of loss reliefs;
(ii) effective utilisation of ACT;
(iii) timing of tax payments;
(iv) potential loss of foreign tax credits.

In deciding where to allocate a group loss, then it will often be necessary to consider a combination of the above factors. In addition possible claims under s.177(2) carry back and s.177(3A) should always be considered as a carryback claim may result in earlier relief than that available under TA 1970, s.258.

Illustration

L Ltd. is the wholly owned subsidiary of M Ltd. Both are resident within the UK. They provide you with the following information about their results:

	Year ended 31st December			
	1985	1986	1987	1988
	£	£	£	£
L Ltd.				
Trading income	1,000		4,000	
Trading loss		(4,000)		(1,000)
M Ltd				
Trading income		500		3,000
Trading loss	(1,000)		(6,000)	
Schedule A	1,500	400	500	1,200

Show suggested loss claims.

L Ltd.	£	M Ltd.	£
Year ended 31.12.1985			
Trading income	1,000	Trading loss	(1,000)
s. 177(2) c/back	(1,000)	Schedule A (s. 177(2))	1,500
	-		500
Year ended 31.12.1986			
Trading income	(4,000)	Trading Income	500
s. 177(2) c/back	1,000	Schedule A	400
	(3,000)		900
Group relief	900		(900)
C/fwd under s. 177(1)	(2,100)		-

L Ltd.	£	M Ltd.	£
Year ended 31.12.1987			
Trading income	4,000	Trading loss	(6,000)
s. 177(1) b/f	(2,100)	Schedule A (s. 177(2))	500
	1,900		(5,500)
Group relief	(1,900)		1,900
	-	C/fwd under s. 177(1)	(3,600)
Year ended 31.12.1988			
Trading loss	(1,000)	Trading income	3,000
		s. 177(1) b/f	3,000
			-
		Schedule A	1,200
Group relief	1,000		(1,000)
	-		200
		s. 177(1) loss c/f	(600)

1.5 NON CO-TERMINOUS ACCOUNTING PERIODS TA 1970, s. 261

The Companies Act provides that normally the accounting periods of all group companies shall be co-terminous. Where they are not it will be necessary to allocate the loss of the surrendering company on a strict time basis into the accounting periods of the claimant company.

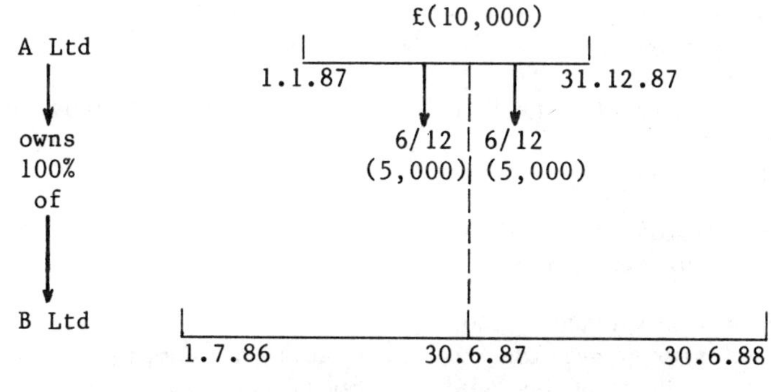

Fig. 7. Co-terminous accounting periods

It is important to remember that losses can only be surrendered if the claimant company has sufficient profits to take those losses. Where accounting periods are not co-terminous it will also be necessary to apportion the profits of the claimant company on a basis to ensure that they are sufficient to take the loss.

1.6 COMPANIES ENTERING OR LEAVING THE GROUP TA 1970, s. 262, FA 1973, s. 29

(a) Companies entering the group
When a company enters the group other than at a normal accounting date, an accounting period is deemed to end at the date on which the company enters the group. Losses, and profits if appropriate, will be apportioned using the rules given in 1.5 above.

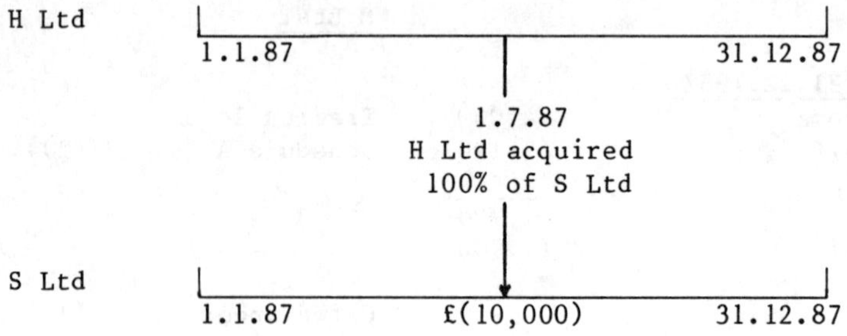

Fig. 8. Companies entering the group

In normal circumstances the loss of £10,000 will be apportioned on a strict time basis and thus six-twelfths of £(10,000) -(£5,000) would be available for surrender from S to H (subject always to H Ltd. having sufficient profits).

FA 1984 has amended this rule to deal with situations where the relief has been exploited by the utilisation of exceptional profits and losses. Where the Inland Revenue or the company consider that the application of the time apportionment rules give a result which is unreasonable or unjust then instead of the time apportionment basis, a just and reasonable method of apportioning losses and profits is to be used instead. The Inland Revenue have indicated that this will be calculated on the basis of the profits and losses of the relevant accounting periods had separate accounts been drawn up.

In certain cases, the company which it is intended to acquire will have unused tax losses or surpluses of unused ACT. TA 1970, ss. 483 and 484 and FA 1972, s. 101 contain anti-avoidance provisions designed to prevent abuse of these items. The sections provide that if:

(i) within any period of three years there is both a change in the beneficial ownership and a major change in the nature or conduct of a trade or business carried on by the company; or

(ii) at any time the trading activities of the company are small or negligible and before they revive there is a change of ownership of the company

then unused losses or ACT of the company cannot be carried forward beyond the change of ownership.

(b) Companies leaving the group

Whilst similar provisions as above apply to companies leaving the group, FA 1973, s. 29 provides that a company will not be deemed to be a group member for group relief purposes throughout any period in which arrangements exist for that company to leave the group.

The term 'arrangements' is not defined in the legislation and could be extremely wide including for example formal and informal discussions, negotiations, etc. A statement of practice (SP 5/80) gives some guidance as to what the Revenue consider to be the meaning of this term. In the case of a normal sale, it will normally be the date of the contract for sale of the subsidiary's shares or the date of the shareholders' meeting giving approval for the sale if that is required.

The effect of this will be that no group relief will normally be available in the accounting period in which the company leaves the group.

1.7 CONSORTIUM RELIEF

Consortium relief is not an independent form of relief, but merely an extension of the group provisions described above; for convenience sake however, it will be referred to as consortium relief in this section. It is important to realise that the basic principles referred to above for groups will also apply to a consortium.

(a) Recognition and definition

The definitions:
A consortium exists broadly in one of the two following circumstances:

(1) Where at least 75% of the ordinary share capital of an owned trading company is held by other UK resident companies, none owning less than 5%;
(2) Where at least 90% of the ordinary share capital of trading companies is owned by an intermediate holding and at least 75% of that company's own share capital is held by five or fewer other UK resident companies, again none owning less than 5%.

These can be expressed diagrammatically:

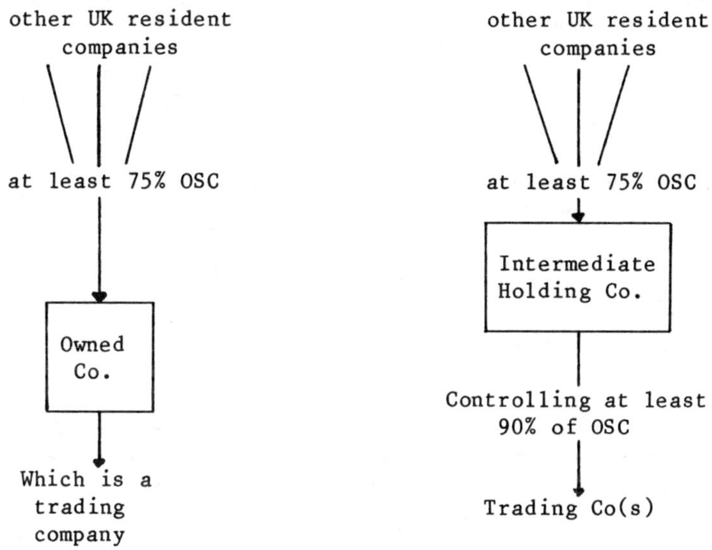

Fig. 9. Consortia

Provided that at least 75% of the OSC is held by UK resident companies then it is possible for a non-resident company or an individual to hold the remaining shares though they will not be entitled to claim any part of the owned company's losses.

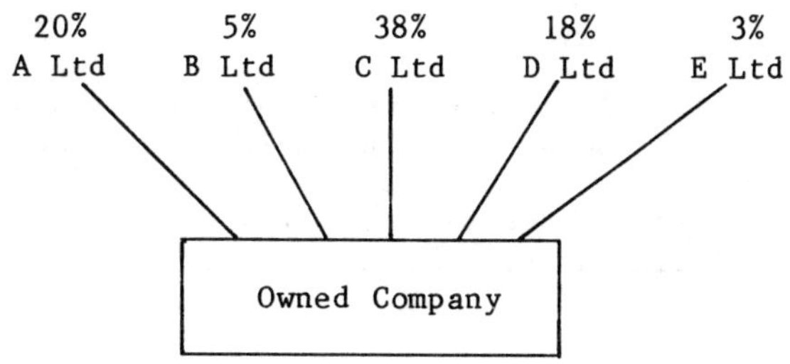

Fig. 10

The owned company is owned by a consortium of A Ltd., B Ltd., C Ltd., and

D Ltd., who control 81% of the owned company. E Ltd., because it does not control at least 5% of the OSC is not a member of the consortium.

(b) Allocation of losses, etc.

Losses, etc., of the owned company will be allocated to the members of the consortium in accordance with their interests in the ordinary share capital of that company. The loss that can be claimed will, as for groups, be restricted by the available profits of the claimant company.

Illustration

P Ltd., a trading company, has the whole of its ordinary share capital owned as under:

Q Ltd.	40%
R Ltd.	30%
S Ltd.	30%

In the year ended 30th June 1987 it made a trading loss of £10,000.
The members of the consortium can obtain relief as under:

Q Ltd.	40% of £10,000 = £4,000
R Ltd.	30% of £10,000 = £3,000
S Ltd.	30% of £10,000 = £3,000

If, in addition, Q Ltd. made up accounts to 31st December annually, its share of P Ltd.'s loss would be further divided:

Year ended 31.12.1986 - $\frac{6}{12}$ x £4,000 = £2,000

Year ended 31.12.1987 - $\frac{6}{12}$ x £4,000 = £2,000

Where a company owned by a consortium has a trading loss and other profits available in the same accounting period against which a claim could be made under s. 177(2) TA then the loss available for surrender to the consortium will be restricted on the basis that a s. 177(2) claim has been made (whether or not in reality it has). This deemed offset does not apply to group loss surrenders. Thus if P Ltd had schedule A income in the year to 30th June 1987 of £2,000 the loss available for surrender would be:

	£	£
Trading loss		(10,000)
Schedule A	2,000	
Potential s. 177(2)	(2,000)	2,000
Available for surrender		8,000

If, in fact, the s. 177(2) claim was not made, then again, only £8,000 loss could be surrendered and the balance of £2,000 would be carried forward.

As with group relief, the consortium loss that can be surrendered will be restricted by the profits of the claimant companies.

Ilustration

X Ltd. is owned as under

A Ltd 35%
B Ltd 20%
C Ltd 30%
D Ltd 15%

X Ltd. has a loss of £(10,000)

Loss allocated:

	£
A Ltd	(3,500)
B Ltd	(2,000)
C Ltd	(3,000)
D Ltd	(1,500)
	(10,000)

The loss relief may be restricted by the profits of the claimant companies:

	Profit/Loss	Loss surrendered	
	£	£	
A Ltd	50,000	(3,500)	
B Ltd	1,000	(1,000)	restricted
C Ltd	180,000	(3,000)	
D Ltd	(20,000)	NIL	restricted
		(7,500)	

It is necessary for all the members of the consortium to consent to a claim for group relief.

Losses may also be surrendered from the owning companies to the owned company. However, the loss that is surrendered may only be offset against the fraction of the owned company's profits attributable to the interests of the various owning companies.

Illustration

If X Ltd. had a profit of £10,000

		Profit/Loss	Appropriate share of profits of X Ltd	Loss surrendered	
		£	£	£	
A Ltd	35%	(25,000)	3,500	(3,500)	
B Ltd	20%	(1,000)	2,000	(1,000)	restricted
C Ltd	30%	60,000	3,000	NIL	restricted
D Ltd	15%	(30,000)	1,500	(1,500)	
				6,000	

(c) Interrelationship of group relief and consortium relief (TA 1970 s. 263)

For accounting periods beginning on or before 31st July 1985, it was provided that a loss could not be surrendered partly as group relief and partly as consortium relief. The order,in which the loss claims were made, decided the relief that was available:

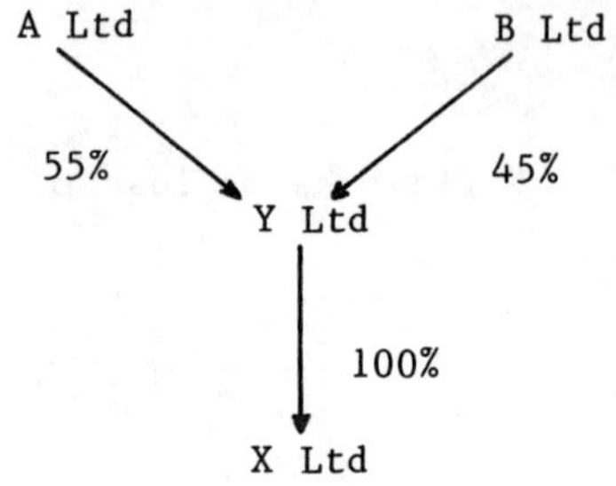

In the above Y Ltd. could give group relief for its loss to X Ltd. or consortium relief to A Ltd. and B Ltd.; it could not do both. If, however, Y Ltd. had a profit and all the other companies had losses it would be possible for Y Ltd. to take both group relief and consortium relief up to the amount of its available profits.

For accounting periods beginning after 31st July 1985 it is possible for a consortium owned company to give both consortium relief and group relief. Where consortium relief is given however the losses etc. available for surrender will be restricted by any group relief claims that have or could have been made.

<u>Illustration</u>

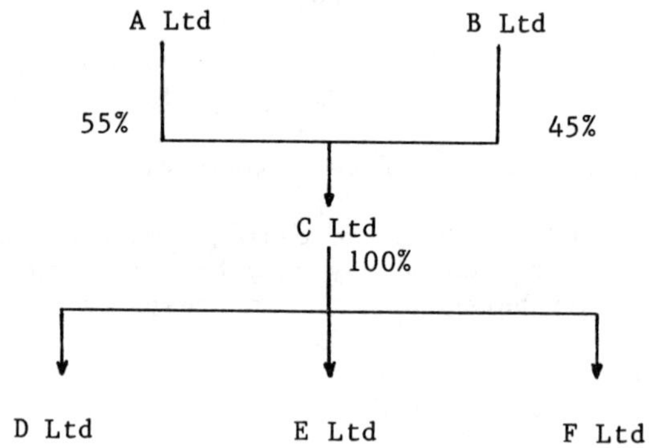

The companies have the following losses and profits:

	£
A Ltd	100,000
B Ltd	80,000
C Ltd	(20,000)
D Ltd	30,000
E Ltd	(150,000)
F Ltd	25,000

The relationships between the companies are:

(i) A Ltd. and B Ltd. are consortium owning companies of C Ltd., D Ltd., E Ltd. and F Ltd.

(ii) C Ltd., D Ltd., E Ltd. and F Ltd. are within a group of companies.

Before any consortium relief is available to A Ltd. and B Ltd. the losses of C Ltd. and E Ltd. must be reduced by any actual or potential group relief. Thus:

Losses - C Ltd.		(20,000)
E Ltd.		(150,000)
		(170,000)
Less: Potential Group Relief -		
D Ltd	30,000	
F Ltd	25,000	55,000
		(115,000)

This loss could then be split:

		£
A Ltd.	55%	(63,250)
B Ltd.	45%	(51,750)
		(115,000)

Where it is wished to surrender losses from the consortium owning company to an owned company then the profits of that latter company must be reduced in a similar way by any actual or potential group relief that might be available.

Illustration

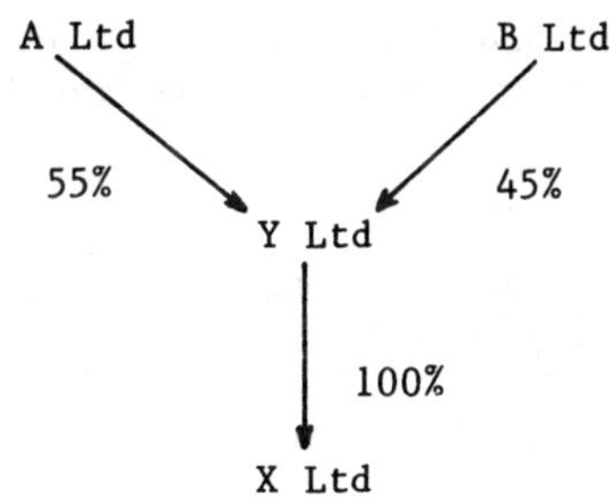

The profits and losses are:

	£
A Ltd.	(20,000)
B Ltd.	(6,000)
Y Ltd.	(4,000)
X Ltd.	40,000

	£
Profit X Ltd.	40,000
Less: Potential group relief from Y Ltd.	(4,000)
	36,000

Possible loss relief from:

A Ltd. (20,000 but restricted to 55% of £36,000)	(19,800)
B Ltd.	(6,000)

1.8 CLAIMS

A claim for group relief must have the consent of the surrendering company. It must be made within two years from the end of the relevant accounting period. It is common for a claimant company to pay the surrendering company for the loss surrendered, particularly if there is a minority interest. Provided that such payments are reasonable and do not exceed the amount surrendered they will be totally disregarded for tax purposes.

2.0 INTER GROUP PAYMENTS

2.1 DIVIDENDS - TA 1970, s. 256(1)

To avoid difficulties which could arise between a holding company and its subsidiaries it is provided that dividends (but not other distributions) may be paid without accounting for ACT when both companies are resident in the UK and either are members of the same group or the company paying the dividend is a trading or holding company owned by a consortium, the members of which include the company receiving the dividends.

A company is a member of a group for this purpose when more than 50% of its ordinary share capital is owned directly or indirectly by its parent company. Holdings through non resident companies are ignored. A company is owned by a consortium where at least 75% of its ordinary share capital is owned by other UK resident companies, none of which owns less than 5%.

The election does not cover dividends paid to minority interests, and the company must account for ACT to that extent. The election must be made jointly within three months of the first dividend to which it applies and will continue until revoked.

The dividend when paid without accounting for ACT is termed 'Group Income' of the recipient.

Making the election as such does not save tax; however,it may improve group cash flow. The paying company will not however have any ACT to offset against its corporation tax.

Illustration

D Ltd. owns all the share capital of E Ltd. They have profits of £100,000 and £40,000 respectively. E Ltd. pays D Ltd. a dividend of £14,200. D Ltd. pays a dividend of £42,600.

If no s. 256 election is applied:

		D Ltd		E Ltd
	£	£	£	£
Trading income		100,000		40,000
Corporation tax (at say 35%)		35,000		14,000
ACT on dividend paid:				
29/71 x £42,600 =	17,400			
29/71 x 14,200 =			5,800	
Tax credit on dividend received:				
29/71 x 14,200	5,800	11,600		5,800
MCT		23,400		8,200

If a s. 256 election is applied:

		D Ltd		E Ltd
Corporation tax, as above		35,000		14,000
ACT on dividend paid				
29/71 x £42,600		17,400		-
		17,600		14,000

It should be remembered that the legislation merely states that a company may pay its dividend without accounting for ACT. There are circumstances when it would be advisable for the company to pay part of the dividend after accounting for ACT and part without, for example, where the subsidiary company itself receives franked investment income. Unless it could offset the tax credit attaching thereto against its own ACT payment, the tax credit would remain unutilised. The subsidiary would therefore pay part of its dividend with ACT attaching, offset the ACT against the tax credit and thus pass it up to its parent company which could offset it against its own MCT liability on dividends to the outside shareholders.

Illustration

F Ltd. has a wholly owned subsidiary, G. Ltd. G Ltd. received a dividend of £710 from H Ltd., another UK resident company. It intends to pay a dividend of £2,840 to its parent company.

G Ltd. should pay part of its dividend with ACT as under:

	£		£
With ACT	710	ACT due 29/71	290
Without ACT	2,130		
	2,840		
Less: Tax credit on FII			290
			-

F Ltd. will now have a credit of £290 to offset against its own ACT due on dividends to outside shareholders. This will thus improve the timing of the tax liabilities of the holding company.

2.2 CHARGES - TA 1970, s. 256(2)

A similar form of election applies to group charges whereby they can be paid gross, i.e. without accounting for income tax. The conditions governing the election are the same as for group income except that the election for group charges covers not not only those paid by the subsidiary to the parent but also by the parent to the subsidiary or by one subsidiary to another. However, this extension does not apply to charges within a consortium which can only be paid gross where they pass from an owned company to the members of the consortium.

3.0 SURRENDERS OF ACT

A UK resident holding company may surrender ACT paid, in respect of dividends only, to a company which has been its subsidiary company throughout its accounting period. A company will be a subsidiary company where the holding company is entitled to more than 50% directly or indirectly of:

(a) the ordinary share capital;
(b) the profits available for distributin to the equity shareholders;
(c) the assets available for distribution on a winding up.

The ACT which can be surrendered is that of the current accounting period only. A claim to surrender ACT must be made by the surrendering company within six years from the end of the accounting period to which the claim relates and the claimant company must assent to the claim.

ACT surrendered to a subsidiary may be offset against its corporation tax liability. It is subject to the restriction of the appropriate percentage of income liable to corporation tax.

Illustration

J Ltd. owns the whole of the ordinary share capital of K Ltd. They provide you with the following information:

	£	£
J Ltd		
Trading income		80,000
Dividends paid	78,100	
Surplus ACT brought forward	6,000	
Interest paid in excess of a reasonable commercial rate - treated as a distribution	1,562	
K Ltd		
Trading income		35,000
Dividends paid	7,810	

	£	£	J Ltd £	£	K Ltd £
Trading income			80,000		35,000
			======		=======
Corporation tax (at say 35%)			28,000		12,250
ACT					
Surplus ACT brought forward		6,000			
On dividends paid:					
29/71 x £7,810				3,190	
29/71 x £78,100	31,900				
On interest in excess of commercial rate - 29/71 x £1,562	638				
	32,538				
Less: Tax credits on dividends received	3,190				
	29,348				
Surrender to K Ltd.	6,960	22,388		6,960	
		28,388		10,150	
Offset restricted					
K Ltd.: 29% x £35,000					
J Ltd.: 29% x £80,000		23,200	23,200	10,150	10,150
			4,800		2,100
			======		======

Note

It is ACT that is surrendered not surplus ACT. The amount surrendered to K Ltd. is just enough to give the maximum offset, i.e. 29% x £35,000 though it could have been up to £22,388. J Ltd. has surplus ACT of £5,188.

When the surrendered ACT exceeds the maximum offset in the subsidiary company, the excess may be carried forward and offset against future corporation tax liabilities in accounting periods of the subsidiary throughout which it remains a subsidiary of the holding company. Under no circumstances can a surplus of surrendered ACT be carried back.

Where a subsidiary company has both its own ACT and also surrendered ACT from its holding company the order of offset is:

(1) surrendered ACT;
(2) its own ACT.

Any payment made or received in return for the surrender of ACT, not being in excess of the amount of ACT surrendered, is ignored for all corporation tax purposes.

4.0 GROUPS AND CAPITAL GAINS

These are dealt with in the section on Capital Gains Tax.

5.0 SUBSIDIARIES OR OPERATING DIVISIONS

Whilst the main thrust of most of the group tax legislation is to treat the group companies as one single corporate entity, it may be more advantageous to operate through a divisional rather than subsidiary structure. Points to consider are:

a) A subsidiary structure will act to fragment the small company limits. Within a divisional structure there is only one company;

b) Many of the compliance requirements of both tax and company law will be reduced by operating through a divisional structure. The number of claims, and many of the restrictions applying to them can be avoided. Thus payments can be made between divisions without accounting for ACT or income tax and gains and losses on the disposal of capital assets will be automatically matched.

Where divisionalisation is being contemplated it would be best to centralise into the company with the longest possible period between the end of its accounting period and the date of payment of its corporation tax.

15 Tax and the Smaller Company

1.0 CHOICE OF BUSINESS STRUCTURE

One of the first major problems confronting any person intending to set up in business is to decide the type of structure within which he operates. Essentially this provides two alternatives - an unincorporated business including a partnership or a limited company. In considering this problem it must be emphasised that there is probably no structure which is going to be suitable for all or even a majority of tax payers. In coming to a conclusion the trader may be influenced by:

(a) Personal considerations - a limited company even if exempt from certain of the filing requirements of the Company's Act will inevitably require more disclosure than an unincorporated business;

(b) The type of trade - if the trade is risky or speculative then incorporation may be desirable. On the other hand, certain professions are prohibited from incorporation.

A summary of some of the major points to be considered in deciding whether or not to incorporate are:

(a) An incorporated business will pay income tax on its profits much later than a company with the same accounting date would pay corporation tax. With an accounting date of 30th April 1987 an individual would pay income tax on 1st January 1989 and 1st July 1989; a company with the same accounting date would pay corporation tax on 1st February 1988;

(b) An individual trader who makes a loss can offset it against his other income and in the case of a loss on a commencement can carry it back against the income of earlier years. A loss sustained by a company must be retained within that company;

(c) An unincorporated trader will be taxable on the entire profits that he makes even if he leaves most of the profits within the business; this could attract substantial higher rate liabilities. Within a limited company profits can be sheltered (profits up to £100,000 liable at 29% only) and be released when it is advantageous to the owners of the company;

(d) The application of the opening and closing assessment rules can mean double assessments and 'drop outs' within an unincorporated business. A company, being assessed on an actual basis, will have profits assessed once only without any 'drop outs';

(e) National insurance contributions are lower for an individual trader than for an employee of a limited company. Note however that the use of dividends may enable a limited company to distribute its profits without any national insurance liability;

(f) In an unincorporated business expenses relating wholly or partly to private purposes will be disallowed; within a company they may be allowed but assessed on the directors as a benefit. In certain cases, particularly cars, this may be more tax effective to the recipient;

(g) A trader can make retirement annuity payments to provide for his retirement. These are normally at 17½% of net relevant earnings increasing with age. Within a company far more generous contributions to a pension scheme are allowed providing that the Inland Revenue rules dealing with benefits deriving from the scheme are not breached;

(h) A trader who spends a substantial period of time abroad will get no tax relief unless he establishes non resident status. An employee or director who spends a qualifying period of 365 days abroad can obtain a deduction of 100% of assessable emoluments;

(i) Gifts of a minority interest in an unincorporated business will attract business property relief of 50%; within a limited company gifts of a minority shareholding may only attract BPR of 30%.

In general it is a useful course of action to commence as an unincorporated business and then to incorporate if conditions are favourable. If this is done then:

(a) there may be a potential 'drop out' of trading profits on the cessation of trade giving rise to tax free income;

(b) potential balancing charges on cessation can be avoided by making an election under Sch. 8 FA 1971 to transfer assets at tax written down value;

(c) unrelieved trading losses may qualify for relief against income received from the company under S.172 TA 1970;

(d) any capital gain may be deferred to the extent that the trader takes shares in the company as part of the purchase consideration.

2.0 CLOSE COMPANIES

2.1 GENERAL

A close company is a UK resident company under the control of five or fewer participators with associates or any number of directors with associates. The Inland Revenue has detailed provisions to prevent the use of such companies as vehicles to turn retained income into capital gains liable on the owners at much lower rates of tax.

2.2 DEFINITIONS

(a) <u>"Control"</u>
A number of alternative tests must be considered in order to determine whether a person, or number of persons, controls a company. <u>Any one</u> of the following

constitutes control:

(i) ability to exercise control over the company's affairs;

(ii) possession of the greater part of the total share capital or voting power of the company;

(iii) possession of rights giving entitlement to the greater part of the company's income if it were distributed;

(iv) possession of rights giving entitlement on a winding-up to the greater part of the assets available for distribution.

In each case it is also necessary to take into account any entitlement to acquire such share capital or rights. The 'greater part' means more than 50%.

In order to determine whether a number of participators have control of a company, there is attributed to a person the rights and powers of others who are:

(i) nominees of the person;
(ii) associates of the person;
(iii) companies controlled by the person or by an associate of his.

(b) "Participator"
A participator is:

(i) a person possessing or entitled to possess share capital or voting rights;

(ii) a loan creditor, other than a bank acting in the normal course of business;

(iii) a person entitled to ensure that income or assets of the company can be applied directly or indirectly for his benefit.

(c) "Associate"
An associate is:

(i) a relative, meaning: a lineal ancestor, lineal descendant, spouse, brother or sister;

(ii) a business partner;

(iii) the trustee(s) of a settlement created by the participator himself or a relative as defined in (i) above.

It should be noted that "associates" do not include associates of associates; thus the participator's wife in his associate but his wife's mother is not his associate.

(d) "Director"
A director is:

(i) a person occupying the position of director by whatsoever name called;

(ii) a person under whose instructions the directors are accustomed to act;

(iii) a manager who with associates controls 20% or more of the ordinary share capital.

Illustration

The issued capital of A Ltd. consists of 20,000 6% preference shares of £1 each, carrying no voting rights and 35,000 ordinary shares of £1 each with one vote per share.

The shareholdings are as follows:

	Preference shares	Ordinary shares
Arnold (Director)	2,000	3,000
Brian (Director)		1,500
Charles (Arnold's brother)		500
Elizabeth (Arnold's sister)		3,000
David (Director)	2,000	2,000
Fred (Director)		2,500
George	8,000	1,000
Henry		5,000
Ivan		9,000
Joan (Brian's sister)	2,000	5,500
Keith	6,000	2,000
	20,000	35,000

A Ltd is a close company because:

(1) The directors and their associates control the votes:

	Ordinary shares
Arnold + Charles + Elizabeth	6,500
Brian + Joan	7,000
David	2,000
Fred	2,500
Total possible votes = 35,000	18,000 votes

or:

(2) Five or fewer participators and their associates control the votes:

	Ordinary shares
They are:	
Ivan	9,000
Brian + Joan	7,000
Arnold + Charles + Elizabeth	6,500
Henry	5,000
Fred	2,500
	30,000

or:

(3) Five or fewer participators and their associates control the total share capital of £55,000.

	£
Ivan	9,000
George	9,000
Brian + Joan	9,000
Arnold + Charles + Elizabeth	8,500
Keith	8,000
	43,500

If Ivan had been a manager of the company, he would have been considered a director as he controls 20% or more of the ordinary share capital of the company.

Once a person has been associated with another he falls out of account and cannot be associated with anyone else.

Illustration

Two sisters B and C each own 50% of the ordinary share capital of D Ltd.

Once C has been associated with B she falls out of account, otherwise they would be deemed for tax purposes to own 200% of the share capital!

2.3 EXCEPTIONS

Certain companies are excluded from categorisation as close companies:

(a) a company controlled by the Crown;
(b) a non-resident company;
(c) a registered industrial or provident society or a recognised building society;
(d) a company controlled by one or more non-close companies.

Illustration

E Ltd. is owned as follows:

	% (1)	% (2)
F Ltd. - Non-close	40	48
G Ltd. - Non-close	15	-
Others each with 1%	45	52
	100	100

In the first case E Ltd. is not close because it is controlled by a non-close companies F & G. In the second case E Ltd. is close as it is not under the control of F Ltd., the non-close company. Thus F Ltd. is just considered to be a normal participator and with four others will control the company.

The test of closeness is made at the end of the accounting period.

2.4 QUOTED COMPANIES

A quoted company will not be a close company where:

(a) shares carrying at least 35% of the voting power, not being shares entitled to a fixed rate of dividend with no further participation, have been unconditionally allotted to or acquired by the public and are beneficially held by them, and,

(b) within the last 12 months, the shares have been quoted and dealt in on a recognised stock exchange in the UK or abroad.

"Public" specifically includes:

(i) non-close companies;

(ii) shares held by superannuation funds, retirement schemes etc., not established for the benefit of employees of the company (sometimes known as External funds).

It does not include:

(i) directors or their associates;

(ii) a company under their control or an associated company;

(iii) funds, e.g. pension funds, for the benefit of employees and directors and ex-employees and directors of the company concerned (Internal funds);

(iv) a principal member.

A principal member is a shareholder who controls more than five per cent of the voting power and who is one of the five largest shareholders.

If more than one shareholder ties for fifth place they will all be principal members.

There is an overriding proviso to this "35% public" exemption that if the principal members (including non-close companies and external funds) between them possess more than 85% of the total voting power, the "35% public" exemption cannot apply and the company will be a close company.

Illustration

F plc is owned as under; the shares are quoted and dealt in on The London Stock Exchange.

	%
A (director)	15
B (his wife)	2
C (director)	23
D (private individual)	11
E (private individual)	4
F (private individual)	3
G (private individual)	3
H Ltd. (non-close company)	21
J (pension fund for the benefit of F plc.'s employees)	6
K (pension fund for the benefit of ICI plc's employees)	12
	100

Analysis of shareholdings:

	Public	Principal members
	%	%
A & B		17
C		23
D		11
E	4	
F	3	
G	3	
H Ltd.	21	21

K - pension fund	12	12
	43	84

Since 35% or more of the voting power is held by the public, the company is not a close company.

If G sold his shares to C the company would now be close as although 35% or more of the voting power will be held by the public, the principal members would own more than 85%.

3.0 CONSEQUENCES OF BEING CLOSE

3.1 AN EXTENDED DEFINITION OF DISTRIBUTION

In addition to the distributions considered earlier, where a benefit (as defined for Schedule E) is provided for a participator or his associate but is not taxed on him under Schedule E, it will be treated as a distribution to the extent that it is not reimbursed by the participator.

The amount to be assessed will be calculated using Schedule E rules. No charge arises when the benefit is provided to the holding or a fellow subsidiary company.

3.2 LOANS TO PARTICIPATORS

Where a close company makes a loan to a participator, it must also pay over a sum equal to ACT on the loan to the Revenue. The amount is only equal to ACT and not ACT itself so that it cannot be offset against the company's corporation tax liability. It is equivalent to a compulsory loan to the Revenue.

The definition of loan is wide and includes those circumstances where:

(a) The participator, or his associate, incurs a debt to the company, except for the supply of goods in the normal course of trade unless the period of credit exceeds six months or that normally given to other customers.

(b) A debt due from a participator or his associate is assigned by the creditor to the company.

It does not however include:

(a) loans made in the normal course of business by a close company;
(b) loans made to the participator who is a director or employee of the company, and

    (i) the total loans to that person do not exceed £15,000;

    (ii) he works full time for the company;

    (iii) he does not, with associates, own more than five per cent of the ordinary share capital of the company.

On the making of the loan the company must pay over to the Revenue an amount equal to ACT at the rate in force when the loan was made. When the loan is repaid the Revenue will repay all or part of the ACT paid. A claim for repayment must be made within six years of the fiscal year in which the loan was repaid.

Illustration

H Ltd. made a loan of £7,700 to B, a participator, on 1st September 1985. He does not qualify for any of the exemptions.

A sum of £3,300, equal to ACT on the loan, must be paid 14 days after the issue of the notice of assessment. If on 30th August 1987 he repays £3,850, the Revenue will repay one-half of the amount paid over, i.e. £1,650.

If the loan is released or written off, the company forfeits the balance remaining with the Revenue and the borrower is treated as having received income equal to the grossed-up equivalent of the amount released. Grossing-up is at the rate of tax existing at the date of release.

Illustration

If, in the illustration above, the balance of the loan is waived when the basic rate of income tax is, say, 29%, the balance of tax with the Revenue of £1,650 is lost. B will be assessed on:

$$\frac{100}{71} \times £3,850 = £5,422$$

and this will be liable to higher rate taxes.

FA 1976 extended the charge to the situation where, after 16th April 1976, a loan is made, not by the close company in which the borrower is a participator, but by a company controlled by the close company or one in which the close company subsequently obtains a controlling interest.

There is no charge if it can be shown that there is no connection between the making of the loan and either:

(a) the provision of any funds by the company in which the individual is a participator to the lending company; or

(b) the acquisition of control of the lending company by the close company in which the borrower is a participator.

Where the provisions apply, the effect of the legislation is to treat the loan as being made by the company in which the borrower is a participator and not by the one making the loan.

3.3 THE APPORTIONMENT OF RELEVANT INCOME

In the absence of the apportionment provisions relating to close companies, such companies could be used to accumulate profits, thereby shielding the shareholders from higher rate tax. The apportionment provisions prevent this by requiring such companies to distribute a minimum amount of their income, determined in accordance with a formula (contained in FA 1972, Sch.16 as amended by FA 1980, Sch.9). To the extent that the company fails to satisfy the required level of distributions the company will be deemed to have made such distribution as is necessary to bring its actual distributions up to the required amount. This deemed distribution will be apportioned between the members and the tax consequences will be computed as if the deemed distribution had really been made, resulting in possible income tax liabilities in respect of the members and ACT liabilities of the company.

The required level of distribution is known as the relevant income.

(a) Specimen calculation of Relevant Income

Relevant Income	Trading Income £		Estate Income £		Investment Income £
Schedule A			X		
B			X		
Schedule D I	X				
Schedule D III					X
Schedule D IV					X
Schedule D V	X	or	X	or	X

	£		£		£
Schedule D VI			X	or	X
UFII					X
BSI					X
	X		X		X
Less: charges and losses	(X)3		(X)2		(X)1
	X		X		X
Less: corporation tax on income	(X)		(X)		(X)
	X	(T)	X	(E)	X
	===				
Distributions received and group Income (net)					X
Distributable Income			X	+	X
Less: Lower of: (a) £3,000 or (b) 10% of E + T					(X)
					X
Less: Abatement:					
$£75,000 \times \frac{E}{E + T} = a$					
$\frac{a - E}{2}$			(X)		
			X		
			===		
50% of balance of Estate Income					X
Relevant Income					X
					===

Notes

(1) Trading income is income, which if it was received by an individual would be earned income. Estate income is income arising from property assessed under Schedules A, B and D. Investment income is all other income. Chargeable gains do not have to be apportioned.

(2) Charges and losses (other than s. 177(1) losses) will be deducted:

(i) from Investment Income, then
(ii) from Estate Income, then
(iii) from Trading Income.

(3) Where the close company is a "medium" company. Then corporation tax will be apportioned across each column on a pro-rata basis.

(4) The £3,000 reduction from investment income will be reduced proportionately if the accounting period is less than 12 months. If the company is not a trading company it will be reduced to £1,000, subject to any time reduction.

(5) The £75,000 abatement figure will be reduced proportionately both if the accounting period is less than 12 months and also if there are associated companies. Abatement is not available for non-trading companies.

If the deductions in (4) and (5) above exceed the figure from which they are deductible then that figure will be reduced to nil.

Illustration

E Ltd. a trading company with an issued share capital of £12,000, had income charged to corporation tax for the year ended 31st March 1987 which comprised:

	£
Schedule A	30,000
Trading Income	64,000
Schedule A Case III	100
Capital Gains	2,100
Interest on debenture in C Ltd. another United Kingdom trading company (in which E Ltd. also held 1,800 ordinary shares out of a total of 2,000 issued)	400
Debenture interest was paid of	1,000 gross

A major shareholder received a benefit from the company of £112. He is not a director.

E Ltd. received a dividend during the accounting period of £7,677 from H Ltd. in which it held 5,000 shares out of a total of 50,000 issued.

Recent dividends paid by E Ltd. were:

Date paid	In respect of	£
5.3.1986	Year ending 31st March 1985	2,390
30.10.1986	Year ending 31st March 1986	792
1.6.1987	Year ending 31st March 1987	2,176

You are required:

(i) To calculate the amount of corporation tax payable by E Ltd. for the year ended 31st March 1987;

(ii) To show a detailed calculation of relevant income.

Ignore small company relief.

Corporation Tax payable:

		I	CG
	£	£	£
Schedule A		30,000	
Schedule D Case I		64,000	
Schedule D Case III		100	
UFII		400	
Capital Gains			2,100
Less: 1/7			300
		94,500	1,800
Less: Debenture Interest paid		1,000	
		93,500	1,800
Corporation Tax @ 35%		32,725	630

	£	I £	CG £
b/f		32,725	630
Franked payments:			
Dividends - $£792 \times \frac{100}{71}$	1,115		
Benefit to shareholder - $£112 \times \frac{100}{71}$	158		
	1,273		
FII: $£7,677 \times \frac{100}{71}$	10,812		
	NIL		
ACT		NIL	
		32,725	630
MCT		33,355	

Relevant Income:

	TI £	EI £	II £
Schedule A		30,000	
Schedule D Case I	64,000		
Schedule D Case III			100
UFII			400
	64,000	30,000	500
Less: charges		500	500
	64,000	29,500	NIL
Less: Corporation Tax	22,400	10,325	
	41,600(T)	19,175(E)	
Dividends received			7,677
Distributable Income		19,175	7,677
Less: Lower of: (a) 10% x (£19,175 + £41,600) or (b) £3,000			3,000
			4,677
Less: Abatement:			
$£37,500 \times \frac{£19,175}{19,175 + £41,600}$			
$= \frac{£11,832 - £19,175}{2}$			
		19,175	
50% thereof			9,588
Relevant Income:			14,265

A company must make distributions up to the amount of the relevant income. The following items can be taken into account in arriving at any further distribution that might be required:

(i) dividends declared for the accounting period having been paid in the period or within reasonable time after the end of it. A period of up to 18 months may be expected to be regarded as reasonable, and

(ii) other distributions made in the period, unless they relate to a previous accounting period under (i) above.

Relevant income less distributions already made is called the excess of relevant income. Thus in E Ltd.:

	£	£
Relevant income as above		14,265
Less: Dividends paid for the accounting period	2,176	
Other distributions paid in the accounting period	112	2,288
Excess of Relevant Income		11,977

(b) Apportionments

When there is an excess of relevant income, it will normally be apportioned amongst the shareholders. No apportionment will be made:

(i) When the company is a trading company or a member of a trading group, if the excess of relevant income is £1,000 or less.

(ii) When the company can justify a retention of income to meet its business requirements, i.e. planned capital expenditure or working capital. (This will be considered later.)

The amount of the excess of relevant income will be apportioned amongst the participators according to their interests in the company. A sum which is both less than 5% of the total amount to be apportioned and, inclusive of a notional amount of ACT, is less than £1,000, will not be assessed on an individual participator. The amount apportioned to an individual is treated as if it were income received on the last day of the accounting period to which it relates. The amount apportioned is grossed-up by a notional amount of ACT and is liable to higher rate taxes as though it was the highest part of the taxpayer's income.

Illustration

The shareholders in E Ltd. are:

A	20%
Mrs. A	1%
B	68%
C	1%
D Ltd. - a close company	10%
	100%

The share capital of D Ltd. is owned by E and F, as under:

E	70%
F	30%

To avoid any apportionment, a minimum dividend of £10,977 (£11,977 less £1,000) must be paid. If not, the income will be apportioned as under:

		Amount	Notional Tax credit	Gross
		£	£	£
A	- 20%	2,395	978	3,373
Mrs. A	- 1%	120	49	169
B	- 68%	8,144	3,326	11,470
C	- 1%	120	49	169
D Ltd-	- 10%	1,198	489	1,687
		11,977	4,891	16,868

No apportionment will be made on C but one will be made in respect of Mrs. A as she is associated with her husband and jointly they exceed the limits.

Where an amount is apportioned to another close company it must be sub-apportioned until it reaches the individual beneficial shareholders. Thus the amount apportioned to D Ltd. will be sub-apportioned as under:

		£	£	£
E	70%	839	343	1,182
F	30%	359	146	505
		1,198	489	1,687

Thus E will be apportioned, but F, as the amount apportioned to him does not exceed the limits, will escape.

Where an apportionment is made, the whole of the excess relevant income must be apportioned, not just enough to leave £1,000.

An appeal can be made by the company, and in certain cases the participator, against the total and division of the apportioned excess.

The participator is primarily liable for the tax due in respect of the apportioned amount.

The tax is due at the later of:

(i) 6th July following the year of assessment, or

(ii) 30 days after the issue of the notice of assessment.

If the individual does not pay the tax it may be recovered from the company.

Provisions exist to counter double taxation when in a subsequent accounting period the profits are distributed.

(c) Accounting for notional ACT

Although the company cannot avoid an apportionment of excess relevant income it can be seen that the company could possibly avoid accounting for ACT. Notional ACT will, however, be due to the Revenue in respect of the notional distribution at the end of the accounting period. The amount due may be reduced:

(i) by offset against surplus FII of the accounting period; then

(ii) by offset against available corporation tax of the accounting period subject to the appropriate percentage restriction; then

(iii) by offset against available corporation tax of accounting periods beginning in the six preceding years.

Any balance of notional ACT left is payable in cash to the Revenue. It may then be carried forward and offset against corporation tax liabilities of future accounting periods, as surplus ACT.

(d) Apportionment of other items

FA 1972, Sch. 16 provides that where a company makes annual payments not incurred wholly and exclusively for the purposes of the trade, which have been deducted as charges in the relevant income computation, they may be apportioned amongst the participators in the same way as an excess of relevant income. This will particularly apply to deeds of covenant to charity. This apportionment may be made regardless of whether there is any excess of relevant income, though, in practice, the Revenue will not make an apportionment unless the gross payments exceed £100 in an accounting period.

Illustration

X Ltd. is owned by A and B as under:

A	60%
B	40%

In the year to 31st March 1987, it makes deeds of covenant to charity of £19,000 gross.

These will be apportioned as under:

		£
A	60%	11,400
B	40%	7,600

Each of these items will be included in the personal computation of A and B though as they are in respect of charitable covenants each will be able to utilise the charity exemption against the amount apportioned. Thus, there will be no liability to tax thereon.

(e) Clearances

To avoid the uncertainty of a possible apportionment, a trading company (or any company with estate or trading income) may apply to the Inspector for a clearance, sending to him the adopted accounts, directors' report and any other relevant information. The Inspector has three months to decide whether to make an apportionment or to ask for further information. If he takes the latter course he then has a further three months after receiving the additional information before making his decision. If he does not keep to these time limits he loses his right to make the apportionment unless:

(i) the company has not fully disclosed all the material facts, or

(ii) the company ceases to trade or goes into liquidation within 12 months of the end of the accounting period.

(f) Business Requirements

As mentioned earlier, the company can avoid or reduce an apportionment if it can demonstrate the need for a higher retention of profits, by reason of its business needs. The onus is on the Revenue to show that the company can distribute its relevant income without prejudicing its requirements, but the company will need to provide evidence of its requirements. The types of requirement that would be satisfactory to the Revenue would include:

(i) a need for increased working capital;
(ii) a need to invest in business assets, such as buildings, or plant;
(iii) the purchase of another trade or business or the purchase of shares in another company in order to expand business opportunities;
(iv) the need to provide for contingent liabilities or known losses which have arisen since the year end date;
(v) the need to retain funds for research and development.

Examples of requirements which would not be satisfactory are:

(i) repayments of loans or debts incurred for less than full consideration;
(ii) artificial or fictitious transactions.

In all cases, a primary requirement in the ability to pay a dividend, is adequate resources to pay. In considering this, the Revenue would consider not only cash balances but also the possession of other liquid resources, particularly investments, which could be easily turned into cash.

Where it is possible to establish such requirements, relevant income becomes so much of the company's distributable income as can be distributed without prejudice to the requirements of the company's business. Under no circumstances can Relevant Income calculated in this way exceed that calculated in the normal arithmetic manner.

Illustration

The business requirements for E Ltd. have been agreed with the Revenue at:

(a) £15,000
(b) £10,000

The alternative calculation of relevant income will be:

	(a)	(b)
Distributable Income	26,852	26,852
Less: Business Requirements	15,000	10,000
	11,852	16,852

In case (a) the relevant income would now be reduced to £11,852, in case (b) as it exceeds the normal calculation which revealed a figure of £14,265, relevant income will remain at the lower amount.

(g) Effects of an apportionment on the capital gains tax cost of shares

Where there is an apportionment of relevant income and the tax is paid by the participator not the company, provided the profits are not subsequently distributed, the amount of the tax paid can reduce the capital gain on a subsequent disposal.

Illustration

B acquired 30% of the shares in A Ltd., a close company, on 6th April 1978 for £21,000. In 1980 there was an apportionment of relevant income on B of £4,000 gross of notional ACT, on which B was chargeable at 75%. The profits in respect of which the apportionment was made have not subsequently been distributed.

The shares were sold by B on 6th April 1987 for £30,000.
The Indexation allowance is £3,171.

	£	£
Disposal proceeds		30,000
Cost	21,000	
Tax at higher rates and investment income surcharge - £4,000 x (75-30%)	1,800	
		22,800
		7,200
Indexation		3,171
		4,029

16 Reorganisation and Special Problems

1.0 GENERAL

There are a number of areas in the corporate tax area which present specific problems. A number of these are considered in this chapter.

2.0 ACQUISITION OF A BUSINESS OR SHARES IN A COMPANY

The purchase of a business or shares in a company can present many tax problems and it is common to ask many questions of the vendors taking warranties, subject to penalty, that the information is accurate. Some of the points for consideration include:

a) tax payment date;

b) details of tax written down values of assets for capital allowance purposes, and their current values. Details of assets transferred intra group and of assets on hire purchase;

c) details of items giving rise to a timing difference;

d) details of any group structure, details of loss transfers and group elections made etc, the CGT costs of all group assets with details of transferred assets, depreciatory transactions etc.

e) details of any rolled or held over gains etc.

f) whether the target of the acquisition has complied with its taxation obligations including:

   i) VAT registration and documentation requirements;
   ii) PIID, dispensations and Schedule E obligations;
   iii) back duty or accounts investigations;
   iv) s.485 obligations

3.0 MANAGEMENT BUYOUTS

3.1 GENERAL

A management buyout is the situation where a holding company wishes to dispose of a subsidiary and offers it to its management and employees. The latter would buy the assets of the organisation or alternatively buy the shares in the company using, in both cases, a mixture of their own funds and external financing.

3.2 TYPES OF BUYOUT

Whilst there are many forms of buyout, there are two common types:

a) Type 1 - in this case the management intending the buyout establish a company - NEWCO providing initial finance in consideration of a share issue. NEWCO then acquires further capital by issues of shares or loan stocks either to individuals or financial institutions. NEWCO then acquires the existing trade from the vendor with the consideration being either cash or a mixture of cash and loan stocks. It can be illustrated as under.

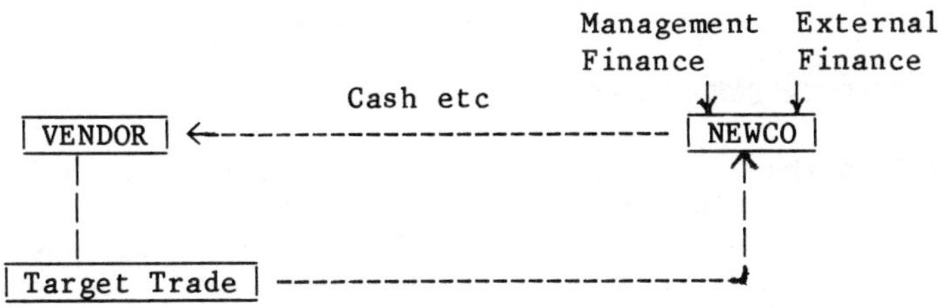

The taxation implications of this type of buyout are:

i) As the vendor will be disposing of assets this will give rise to:

   a) Balancing charges or allowances on the plant, industrial buildings, patents etc transferred;

   b) Capital gains or losses.

ii) The possible loss of unused trading losses relating to the transferred trade.

The vendor company would be able to use the trading losses against any balancing charges and possibly roll over any capital gains against the cost of any qualifying assets it might acquire.

NEWCO will be able to claim capital allowances on the plant etc transferred. In the case of industrial buildings a reduced tax life could result in accelerated allowances.

b) Type 2 - in this type, NEWCO acquires the share capital of the company carrying on the target trade. It can be illustrated as under:

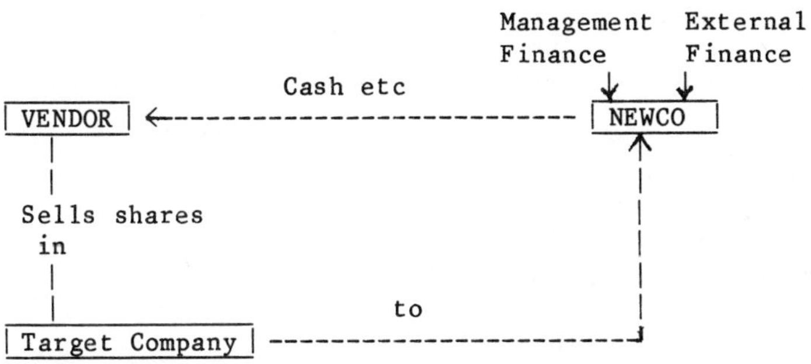

The sale of shares by the vendor may result in a liability to tax on any capital gains.

As far as NEWCO is concerned it will be buying shares rather than assets. This will mean that the acquired company will continue as before subject to:

a) the change of ownership, coupled with any changes in trade could affect the carry forward of any trading losses or surpluses of ACT;

b) there may be latent tax liabilities eg: capital gains rolled over, assets transferred intra group within the preceding 6 years which could affect the purchase price;

c) there will be no balancing charges, in respect of plant and machinery, industrial buildings etc. as the assets have not been sold by the company leaving the group.

4.0 COMPANIES PURCHASING THEIR OWN SHARES

Legislation was provided in the 1981 Companies Act which enabled companies to purchase back their own shares. The tax position relating to this was formalised in FA 1982 and broadly allowed any gain in such a purchase to be treated as a capital, rather than a revenue, gain to the shareholder whose shares were being purchased subject to the detailed conditions in Sch 9 FA 1982 being complied with:

a) the company whose shares are being purchased must be a trading company and be unquoted (shares dealt in on the USM are not regarded as being quoted);

b) the shareholder must be resident and ordinarily resident in the UK;

c) the shares must normally be held by the shareholder for at least 5 years prior to the purchase. Where the shares have been inherited, the period of ownership is restricted to 3 years, including any period of ownership by the deceased;

d) the shareholder must either sell the whole of his shareholding or it must be materially reduced. It will be so reduced where the proportion of the company's issued share capital held after the purchase does not exceed 75% of that held just before the purchase.

Illustration

The issued share capital of A Ltd is:

10,000	£1 Preference Shares
20,000	£1 Ordinary Shares
£ 30,000	
======	

B owns 3,000 Preference Shares and 9,000 Ordinary Shares. A Ltd is proposing to purchase from him

i) 3,000 Ordinary Shares, or
ii) 8,000 Ordinary Shares

B's interest in the share capital before the purchase is

$$\frac{3,000 + 9,000}{30,000} \times 100 = 40\%$$

after repurchase it is:

i) $\frac{3,000 + 6,000}{27,000} \times 100 = 33.33\%$

ii) $\frac{3,000 + 1,000}{22,000} \times 100 = 18.2\%$

Thus in case (a) the holding is not materially reduced and thus any purchase would be a qualifying distribution. In case (b) the reduction is material.

(e) In addition to (d) above the person selling shares must also suffer a material reduction (measured as above) in his entitlement to share in profits. Thus the proportion of the company's profits to which the vendor is entitled after the purchase does not exceed 75% of that held just before the purchase.

The profits available for distribution follow the definitions in the Companies Act plus:

a) £100 and
b) any fixed distributions - eg preference dividends for one year.

In the above the distributable reserves are £80,000 and the preference shares have a dividend paid annually of 12%.

Before the purchase:

		B's entitlement
Reserves, and	80,000	36,000
Preference Dividend	1,200	360
and	100	45
	81,300	36,405
		44.78%

Assuming in part (b) of the illustration above that the 8,000 Ordinary shares are purchased for £30,000, the position would be:

		B's entitlement
Reserves, and	50,000	4,167
Preference dividend	1,200	360
and	100	8
	51,300	4,535
		8.84%

Again a substantial reduction.

The shareholder's interest in both (d) and (e) must include that of his associates, broadly his spouse and minor children.

f) the purpose of the purchase must be for the benefit of the trade carried on by the company and not part of a scheme for the avoidance of tax.

The company may apply for a clearance prior to the purchase, which must be made out of reserves available for distribution.

Where shares of the same class are acquired at different times, disposals to the company are identified on a FIFO basis to determine the qualifying period of ownership.

5.0 DEMERGERS

The basic purpose of a demerger is to enable trades formerly carried on together by one company to be managed and owned independently. The intention is that this independence would stimulate the activities of the various parts.

The mechanics of a demerger can take several forms:

(a) a transfer to any or all of the members of a company of the shares of a 75% subsidiary;

(b) a transfer of a trade by one company to another or the transfer to that company of shares in a 75% subsidiary followed in both cases by the issue of shares in the transferee company to the shareholders of the transferor company.

The members of a company are holders of the ordinary share capital of that company.

Where there is a valid demerger:

(a) the demerger will not be treated as a distribution in the hands of the transferor company and no ACT will be due; and

(b) there will be no CGT liability; and

(c) no stamp duty will be charged on the demerger documents.

The conditions that must be satisfied are:

(a) The transferor company, any 75% subsidiaries and any recipient company must be UK resident;

(b) The transferor company must be a trading company or a member of a trading group, this must also apply to any 75% subsidiaries;

(c) The distribution must be made wholly or mainly for the benefit of trading activities previously carried on by the transferor company and which are now to be carried on by the recipient company;

(d) The distribution must not be part of a scheme or arrangement for the avoidance of tax, the making of any chargeable payments or for the future cessation of all or part of the trade after the distribution.

There are elaborate provisions designed to deal with avoidance devices. Companies contemplating a demerger may obtain a clearance from the Revenue.

6.0 COMPANY RECONSTRUCTIONS

The reconstruction of a company or the amalgamation of two or more companies may have complex taxation consequences not only for the companies themselves but also for those who are shareholders in those organisations. The terminology is not clear. **In Wilde v. South African Supply and Cold Storage Co.** a reconstruction was considered to be a corporate reorganisation under substantially the same ownership whilst an amalgamation involved "... a blending of two undertakings...". Essentially a reconstruction or amalgamation can consist of one of the following events:

(a) The transfer to the shareholders of a company of shares owned in a subsidiary company - a demerger;

(b) The amalgamation of companies, perhaps by the setting up of a holding company to acquire the shares of the companies joining together. The shareholders in the old companies would exchange their shares for shares in the new company;

(c) The transfer of a trade from one company to another.

When any scheme of reconstruction or amalgamation is being considered it is essential to apply to the Revenue for clearance especially in view of the penal provisions of TA 1970, s.460. In general this will be given if the Revenue is satisfied that:

(a) the scheme is being arranged for bona fide commercial reasons; and

(b) its main purpose is not the avoidance of taxation.

The demerger has already been considered, the other two main instances are described below.

6.1 COMPANY MERGERS

In this case, provided that the company issuing the new shares controls as a result of the merger more than 25% of the ordinary share capital (it will normally be 100%), then the issue of shares in the acquiring company to the shareholders in the amalgamating companies will simply be treated as a share for share exchange. No disposal will be treated as having occurred for CGT purposes. This may then be followed by a transfer of the trades of the (now) subsidiary companies to the new holding company. This will be particularly important in the case of the situation where the holding company is a close company.

There may be restrictions on the carry forward of losses and ACT. TA 1970, s.483 provides that where within any period of three years there is both a change in the ownership of a company and a major change in the nature or conduct of its trade or, where at any time after the company's trading activities have become small or negligible and before revival there is a change in ownership of the company, then:

(a) unrelieved losses may not be carried forward under s.177(1) to accounting periods after the change:

(b) surpluses of ACT arising before the change may also not be carried forward.

For these purposes an accounting period is deemed to end at the date of the change in ownership.

6.2 THE TRANSFER OF A TRADE

Where a company's business is transferred to another company, there will normally be a disposal of assets and the cessation of a trade. The consequences of this may be avoided and no change of ownership will be deemed to have occurred provided:

(a) both companies are within the charge to corporation tax; and

(b) within the period commencing 12 months before and ending 24 months after the cessation of the trade by the transferor company, at least 75% of the trade is owned by the same persons.

Ownership of the trade is measured by interests in the ordinary share capital of the company and to establish beneficial ownership it may be necessary to pierce the veil of trusts and companies holding shares.

If the conditions are satisfied, then important reliefs are available:

(a) unused trading losses may be carried forward to the successor company to be offset against income of the same trade;
(b) assets on which capital allowances have been claimed may be transferred across at tax written-down value.

It it impossible to transfer across capital losses or surpluses of ACT or FII and if the trade is the sole asset of the transferor company it may mean that these items will be lost. Consideration should therefore be given to their utilisation before cessation of trade.

In the case of capital allowances, relief will be given up to the date of transfer to the transferor company and thereafter to the successor. Writing-down allowances will be apportioned for periods of less than 12 months.

TA 1970, s.273 will provide relief for CGT as the transferor and successor companies will normally both be within the same 75% group. There will be a charge under s.278 if the acquiring company leaves the group within six years.

Terminal loss relief is not normally available to the transferor company.

7.0 INVESTMENT COMPANIES

7.1 GENERAL

An investment company is any company whose business consists wholly or mainly in the making of investments and the principal part of whose income is derived therefrom.

The calculation of profits liable to corporation tax proceeds in the normal way. Dividends received from other UK companies are not liable to corporation tax. A particular element in the computation is likely to be income from property assessable under Schedule A or Schedule D Case VI.

From the income liable to corporation tax there can be deducted management expenses. These are normally of three main types:

(a) pure management expenses which are not specific to any particular type of income, eg directors' salaries;

(b) annual charges;

(c) capital allowances which are not given specifically against one class of income.

These are aggregated and offset against total profits. Any unrelieved balance may be carried forward.

A particular feature of this sort of company is that it is likely to have a large amount of franked investment income. To the extent that there is a surplus thereof, the unrelieved management expenses can be the subject of a s.254 claim.

Illustration

A Ltd. is an investment company making up accounts to 31st December annually. It provides you with the following information in respect of the year ended 31st December 1987.

	£
Rents	5,000
Bank deposit interest	500
Dividends received	7,100
Expenses:	
Repairs to property	1,200
Rent collection charges	400
Office salaries	4,000
Directors' salaries	1,000
Debenture interest paid (gross)	200
Dividends paid	2,840

	£	£	£
Schedule A			
Rents		5,000	
Less: Expenses:			
Repairs	1,200		
Rent collection	400		
		1,600	
			3,400
Schedule D Case III			500
			3,900
Management expenses:			
Office salaries		4,000	
Directors' salaries		1,000	
Debenture interest		200	
		5,200	
Offset		3,900	3,900
		1,300	Nil

The excess management expenses can either be carried forward and treated as expenses of the next Accounting period or, as there is a surplus of FII, made the subject of a s.254 claim.

	£		
Dividends received		7,100	
Add: Tax credit		2,900	
		10,000	
Dividends paid	2,840		
Add: Tax credit	1,160		
		4,000	
		6,000	
s.254		1,300	(1,300)
Surplus FII c/f		4,700	Nil

Repay tax credits
29% of £1,300 = £377

7.2 RELEVANT INCOME

"Relevant Income" for an investment company is the lower of:

(a) so much of the estate of trading income (if any) as could be distributed without prejudice to the business requirements, so far as concerned with the activities or assets giving rise to that income, plus the remainder of the distributable income, and

(b) the distributable investment income plus 50% of the estate income. "Distributable investment income" means investment income less charges and corporation tax, plus dividends received and group income, after deduction of the lower of £1,000 or 10% of estate and trading income.

There is no abatement for investment companies.

Illustration
B Ltd., an investment company, provides you with the following information for the year ended 31st March 1987:

	£
Schedule A	10,000
Schedule D Case III	4,000
Schedule D Case VI - furnished lettings	2,000
Management expenses	6,000
Dividends received	6,900

The company can justify a retention of £4,000 for business requirements.

(a) Assuming no retention

	Estate Income £	Investment Income £
Schedule A	10,000	
Schedule D Case III		4,000
Schedule D Case VI	2,000	
	12,000	4,000
Less: Management expenses	2,000	4,000
	10,000	-
Less: Corporation tax	2,900	
	7,100	-
Dividends received	-	6,900
Distributable income	7,100	6,900
Less: Lower of 10% x £7,100 or £1,000		710
Distributable investment income		6,190
50% of £7,100		3,550
		9,740

(b) Assuming a retention of £4,000

	Estate Income £	Investment Income £
Estate income	7,100	
Less: Business requirements	4,000	3,100
		6,900
Remainder of distributable income		10,000

Relevant income will be the lower of (a) and (b), i.e. £9,740.

Note: Management expenses, like charges and losses, are deducted first form investment income then from estate income, and finally from trading income if there is any.

7.3 LOSSES ON UNQUOTED SHARES IN TRADING COMPANIES

If an investment company makes a loss on shares which it has subscribed for in an unquoted trading company it may treat that loss as a revenue loss and offset it as in section 1.1 above. The offset will be against the other profits of the same accounting period and then carried back against total profits of previous accounting periods ended within the previous twelve months, though if one straddles the beginning of that period only, the profits which fall within the twelve month period (apportioned on a strict time basis) will qualify for relief.

Relief is given after any relief for earlier losses but before deductions for charges and management expenses.

To obtain relief the investment company making the loss must normally have traded for six years and must not control or be associated with the company in respect of which the loss has been sustained.

As an alternative, relief under s.254 is available.

8.0 COMPANIES IN LIQUIDATION

On the passing of a resolution for the winding-up of a company, an accounting period ends and a new one commences. Thereafter accounting periods are made up for periods of twelve months with a final period to the completion of the winding-up. To avoid delay because the rate of corporation tax is fixed in arrears, the rate of corporation tax to be used for the company's final accounting period is normally that fixed for the last financial year.

Where a close company ceases to trade or goes into liquidation, the relevant income for its last accounting period and for any other which ends in the last twelve months preceding liquidation or cessation is 100% of its income. There can be no business requirements as it is becoming non-existent and normally relevant income will only be reduced should the creditors of the company be prejudiced. The 100% requirement also applies to accounting periods ending during the process of winding-up.

Where applicable, abatement and the reduction of investment income will be available.

Illustration

C Ltd., a close company, went into liquidation on 31st December 1985. It previously made accounts up to 30th June, and had results as under:

	£
Year ended 30th June 1985	
Trading income	40,000
Schedule A	50,000
Schedule D III	3,000
Six months ended 31st December 1985	
Trading income	5,000

Schedule A	30,000
Schedule D III	12,000

As the year ended 30th June 1985 ended within twelve months of liquidation the 100% requirement will apply to both accounting periods.

	Trading Income £	Estate Income £	Investment Income £
Year ended 30.6.1985	40,000	50,000	3,000
Less: Corporation tax @ 30%	12,000	15,000	900
	28,000	35,000	2,100
Less: the lower of:			
(1) £3,000 or			
(2) 10% of £28,000 + £35,000			3,000
			NIL
Less: abatement:			
$£75,000 \times \frac{£35,000}{£28,000 + £35,000} =$	41,667		
$\frac{£41,667 - £35,000}{2}$		3,333	
Relevant income		31,667	
6 months ended 31.12.1985	5,000	30,000	12,000
Less: Corporation tax thereon @ 30%	1,500	9,000	3,600
	3,500	21,000	8,400
Less: the lower of			
(1) $£3,000 \times \frac{6}{12}$ or			
(2) 10% of £3,500 + £21,000			1,500
Less: abatement:			
$£37,500 \times \frac{£21,000}{£3,500 + £21,000} = 32,143$			
$\frac{£32,143 - £21,000}{2}$		5,572	
Relevant income		15,428	6,900

Income during the liquidation period would be charged to tax in the normal way and if the company is a close company it may be apportioned amongst the participators.

17 Overseas Matters

1.0 STATUS IN THE UK

The taxation status of an individual is of great importance in determining his liability to income tax. In general a person will only be liable to UK tax if he is either:

(a) resident in the UK, or

(b) has a UK source of income.

To determine liability certain terms need to be defined.

1.1 RESIDENCE

There is no statutory definition of residence and in practice it may be a difficult thing to determine. An Inland Revenue booklet - IR 20 - states the Revenue's view though it must be pointed out that it is selective in its approach and bases its conclusions on those parts of the legislation and case law which favour the Revenue whilst ignoring those which favour the taxpayer.

It is possible to be resident in the UK without having a place of residence, thus a tramp who spent all his life in the UK would be resident even though he had no home in the material sense. Similarly it is not necessary that the taxpayer should intend to be resident in the UK. He may be resident if required to be here because of military service - **IRC v. Inchiquin (1948)** or attendance at school - **Miesagaes v. IRC (1957)**. A person in jail would also be resident in the UK. In deciding whether a person is resident the court would consider:

(a) nationality

(b) physical presence

(c) past history as to residence

(d) family and business ties

(e) the maintenance of a place of abode.

It is important to appreciate that,

"Residence is not a term of invariable elements, all of which must be satisfied in each instance. It is highly flexible and its many shades of meaning vary not only in the contexts of different matters but also in different aspects of the same matters".
per Rand J in **Thomson v. Minister of National Revenue (1946)**

In general the Revenue in IR 20 propose three basic tests of residence:

(a) presence in the UK for six months in the fiscal year,

(b) habitual and substantial visits,

(c) the maintenance of a place of abode.

(i) Presence in the UK for six months in the fiscal year

A person who is physically present in the UK for six months (equated by the Revenue to 183 days) in the fiscal year will be resident for that year. TA 1970,s.51 provides that a person will not however be resident if he is in the UK for some temporary purpose only and not with any intention to become resident. The corollary of this appears to be that if a person enters the UK with the intention of becoming resident then he will be resident even if physically present for less than one-half of the fiscal year.

(ii) Habitual and substantial visits

Where a person is not resident under (i) above, he may be so if he visits the UK year after year and the visits are habitual and substantial.

In **Levene v. IRC (1928)** the taxpayer left the UK in 1919 to stay abroad. He did not acquire a place of abode but instead lived in hotels or with friends. He also paid substantial visits to the UK amounting to an average of five months per year between 1919 and 1925 when he acquired a flat abroad. During his visits to the UK he visited his relatives, obtained medical treatment and dealt with personal affairs. Held that he was resident in the UK. His visits were so habitual and substantial as to show that he still was resident here. Per Lord Sumner,

"He changed his sky but not his home".

In **IRC v. Lysaght (1928)** Mr. Lysaght had worked for many years in the UK as a director of a family business but in 1919 he partially retired to Ireland to live on the family estate. He sold his property in the UK and had no place of abode in the UK. He continued however to attend board meetings of the company and for that purpose he visited the UK every month staying each time for about a week. During this period he stayed in hotels and in no year was he present in the UK for more than 101 days. Held that he was resident in the UK.

In considering the above two cases it is important to note that the question of residence was found as a matter of fact by the Commissioners and the courts were not prepared to overturn their findings.

The Revenue equate habitual and substantial to visits of an average period of three months over four fiscal years. Normally the taxpayer would only become resident from year five though if he has the intention of following this pattern of visits he will be treated as resident from the beginning.

(iii) The maintenance of a place of abode

Where an individual maintains a place of abode in the UK then he will be treated by the Revenue as resident if he visits the UK at any time in the fiscal year. This principle is based on the case of **Cooper v. Cadwallader (1904)**.

In this case an American attorney leased a hunting lodge in Scotland and visited it for two months each year. During the rest of the time it remained empty apart from two servants. Held that he was resident in the UK in each year in which he visited Scotland.

TA 1970,s.50 provides however that where a person carries on a trade, profession, vocation or employment wholly outside the UK then the question of residence will be decided without considering the existence of a place of abode in the UK. Thus in these circumstances the individual will only be resident if either test (i) or (ii) are satisfied. The word 'wholly' is interpreted strictly.

In **Robson v. Dixon (1972)** the taxpayer was an airline pilot working for KLM and based in the Netherlands. He had a place of abode in the UK. He normally flew from the Netherlands to South America but on a limited number of occasions he landed at Heathrow en route either to or from Amsterdam. Held that there was a substantial performance of duties in the UK.

A UK citizen going abroad will be regarded as still being resident in the UK if his absence is purely temporary. In practice temporary can extend to a period of up to one year. It is up to the taxpayer to establish non-residence though in the case of a person going abroad permanently he may be regarded as absent ab initio.

In the year that an individual leaves the UK for permanent residence abroad or enters the UK for permanent residence, the Inland Revenue will normally split his income as under:

(a) in the period of residence - all income will normally be assessed;

(b) in the period of non-residence - only the UK arising income will be liable to UK tax.

In the year of leaving or becoming resident in the UK, the full personal allowances are available.

The residence of companies has been discussed in the section on corporation tax and unlike individuals depends not on physical presence but the wider concept of central management and control s.482(7) TA 1970.

1.2 ORDINARY RESIDENCE

Ordinary residence denotes greater permanence than 'residence'. Using the dicta of Lord Cave in **Levene v. IRC** it denotes residence with 'some degree of continuity' and that of Lord Buckmaster in **Lysaght v. IRC** it

> "means ... that the residence is not casual and uncertain but that the person held to reside does so in the ordinary course of his life".

1.3 DOMICILE

The term domicile denotes as the place of abode of an individual, the country which he regards as his natural home. On birth a person acquires a domicile of origin (normally from his father but from his mother if he is illegitimate). This lasts until the age of 16 when a child is capable of establishing his own independent domicile. This independent domicile, known as the domicile of choice, can be established by the individual abandoning his domicile of origin. Abandonment of the domicile of origin is not an easy thing to establish; it is proved by definite action by the individual to renounce his domicile of origin; he could do this by:

(a) severing all contact with the country in which he is presently domiciled; selling all property there and closing all bank accounts etc.;

(b) showing himself as subject to the laws of the new domicile; taking nationality in the new country, making a will according to its laws;

(c) establishing a presence in the new country; buying a residence there or even a burial plot!

From 1st January 1974 a wife does not automatically take the domicile of her husband upon marriage, but can establish her own independent domicile. Women married on 1st January 1974 retain their husband's domicile until they take positive action to change. Whilst a person can be resident or ordinarily resident in more than one country, it is only possible to have one domicile for income tax purposes.

1.4 APPEALS

Appeals against the decision of the Revenue on the question of residence, ordinary residence and domicile can be made to the Special Commissioners and then to the courts.

2.0 LIABILITY UNDER SCHEDULE D CASES IV AND V

2.1 INCOME ASSESSABLE

Schedule D Case IV - Interest received from foreign securities such as mortgages and debentures.

- Deep discount foreign securities.

Schedule D Case V - Income from foreign possessions such as foreign dividends and rents. Foreign pensions and the profits of foreign businesses controlled from abroad are also liable under Case V. Salaries and wages from abroad are liable under Schedule E.

2.2 BASIS OF ASSESSMENT

The basis of assessment is normally the same as Schedule D Case III i.e. the income arising in the preceding year of assessment whether remitted or not with the same rules for the commencement and cessation of a source. In two cases however the basis of assessment is the remittances made in the preceding year of assessment. This basis, known as the 'Remittance Basis', applies to:

(a) persons not domiciled in the UK;

(b) British subjects not ordinarily resident in the UK.

In calculating the amount assessable on the 'arising' basis certain deductions may be made from the assessable income:

(a) In the case of a foreign trade deduction of twelve and a half per cent for 1984/85 was made from the assessable profits calculated in accordance with the provisions of Schedule D Cases I or II. For 1985/86 and on no deduction is available.

(b) In the case of foreign pensions a deduction of ten per cent is made. Pensions received as a victim of Nazi persecution are exempt.

<u>Illustration</u>
From the details below calculate the amount assessable under Schedule D Cases IV or V for the fiscal year 1986/87:

		1985/6 £	1986/7 £
A -	A British subject resident and domiciled in the UK but not ordinarily resident		
	Interest on a mortgage of property in France.		
	Received in the years	40	50
	Remitted in the years	10	40
	Alternatively, assume he was also ordinarily resident.		
B -	A French citizen temporarily resident in the UK.		
	Share of profits from the Paris partnership.		
	Received in the years	1,000	2,000
	Remitted in the years	500	1,000
C -	A Dutch citizen resident, but not domiciled, in the UK. Income from a pension derived from his former employment in Holland.		
	Received in the years	600	900
	Remitted to the UK	700	400
	Alternatively, assume the recipient was a British citizen domiciled, resident and ordinarily resident in the UK.		

A	(1)	£ 10	D IV
	(2)	£ 40	D IV
B	(1)	£500	D V
C	(1)	£700	D V
	(2)	£600 - 10% = £540	D V

Where there is an overseas loss it will be available for relief under s.168 or s.171. When relief is given under s.168 it is only against other foreign income as under:

(a) foreign profits,

(b) foreign pensions,

(c) foreign emoluments assessed under Schedule E.

Illustration

A provides you with the following information: he is resident, ordinarily resident and domiciled in the UK.

Foreign Trade:

Year ended	31.3.85	£ 6,000 profit
Year ended	31.3.86	£10,000 loss

Foreign Pension:

	£
1985/86	2,000
1986/87	3,000

UK Dividends:

1985/86	4,500 (gross)
1986/87	7,000 (gross)

Relief for the overseas loss is to be claimed as early as possible.

1985/86

		Income Earned	Income Unearned
	£	£	£
D V - Foreign trade		6,000	
D V - Foreign pension	2,000		
Less: 10%	200		
		1,800	
UK Dividends			4,500
		7,800	4,500
D V - Foreign loss - Year to 31.3.86	(10,000)		
s.168 relief	7,800	(7,800)	
	(2,200)	NIL	
Total Income: 1985/86		4,500	

1986/87

	£	£	£	£
D V - Foreign trade			NIL	
D V - Foreign pension	3,000			
Less: 10%	300			
			2,700	
UK Dividends				7,000
s.168 relief		2,200		
			(2,200)	
			500	
Total Income: 1986/87			7,500	

The costs of travel to and from the place where the assessee's trade is carried on is treated as a S.130 deduction. Similar provisions as for employees apply to the travel expenses of a spouse and member of the family.

2.3 UNREMITTABLE INCOME

Where overseas income is termed 'unremittable', it may be omitted from assessments if the tax paying company gives written notice to the Inspector before such assessments become final(TA 1970,s.418). Unremittable income is defined as:

(a) such income as cannot, despite reasonable endeavour, be remitted to the UK by reason of the laws of the overseas country, executive action of its Government or the impossibility of obtaining foreign currency, and
(b) such income as the taxpayer has not realised outside the overseas territory for sterling or an unblocked currency.

Where the Revenue consider that these conditions are no longer satisfied, i.e. that the income is no longer unremittable, the income becomes assessable.

2.4 CONSTRUCTIVE REMITTANCES

A person assessed on the remittance basis may possibly avoid taxation by, for example, obtaining a loan abroad, remitting the proceeds of the loan and using the overseas income to clear the loan. Thus there would be a remittance of capital (non-taxable) rather than income (taxable). TA 1970,s.122 provides that income arising outside the UK shall be treated as having been remitted, and therefore liable to tax if it is applied towards the satisfaction of:

(a) a loan received in the UK,

(b) a loan received outside the UK, the proceeds of which are remitted to the UK.

3.0 SPECIFIC PROBLEMS RELATING TO TRADING

3.1 THE PROBLEM OF TRADING WITHIN AS DISTINCT FROM TRADING WITH THE UK

TA 1970,s.108 provides that a non-resident will be liable to UK tax on the profits of trading within as distinct from trading with the UK.

Trading within the UK was defined by Brett, L J in **Erichsen v. Last (1881)**;

> "Whenever profitable contracts are habitually made in England by or for a foreigner ... such foreigners are exercising a trade in England even though everything done or supplied by those persons to fulfil the contract is done abroad."

The mere purchase of goods in the UK for export or resale abroad is not trading within the UK, **Sulley v. Attorney General (1860).**

The place of the contract is determined according to UK law and is the place where the acceptance of the offer is communicated; thus if acceptance is made by the overseas party by letter that acceptance is abroad. If communication is by telex, acceptance may be within the UK.

The fact that the foreigner has an employee or representative in the UK will not mean that he carries on a trade here provided that the contracts are concluded abroad, **Greenwood v. Smidth (1922).**

In **Grainger & Son v. Gough (1896)**, a French champagne house canvassed orders for champagne through the firm of Grainger and Son who would pass on all orders and money received from UK customers to the French company in Rheims. The contracts for sale were made in France and the risk passed there. It was held by the House of Lords that the French company was not trading within the UK.

In **Pommery and Greno v. Apthorpe (1886)**, the London agents of Pommery held stocks of wine in the UK and these were used to satisfy all but large orders. The money collected was paid into Pommery's bank account in the UK. Held that he was trading within the UK.

Although the place of acceptance of the contract was held by Lord Esher in **Werhle v. Colquhoun (1888)** as being the "... foundation of the trade ...", Lord Cave in **Maclaine v. Ecott (1926)** said that there were other factors to be taken into account and disclaimed any exhaustive test. In **Greenwood v. Smidth**, Atkin, LJ asked:

> "Where do the operations take place from which the profits in substance derive?"

In **Firestone Tyre and Rubber Co. v. Llewellin (1957)**, an American company had a subsidiary of the same name in Brentford, UK. The subsidiary made tyres in the UK and on the directions of its parent supplied them to foreign dealers. The House of Lords held that the American parent was trading within the UK as also was the subsidiary. The location of the master sales agreement in America which governed the trade between the parent and the subsidiary was not conclusive.

The UK tax principles are often affected by the provisions of a double tax convention. Under Article 5 of the OECD draft double taxation agreement, a country cannot impose tax unless the trader is carrying on a business within a territory through the medium of a permanent establishment there. This is broadly defined as a fixed place of business through which the operations of the enterprise are wholly or partly carried on. The term includes a place of management, branch, office, factory or workshop together with an agent with authority to, and who habitually does, conclude contracts in the name of the enterprise. It does not include facilities for the storage, display or delivery of goods or the maintenance of a stock of goods for these purposes.

The profits to be taxed will be limited under Article 7 OECD to those which the enterprise would have been expected to make if it was:

(a) a distinct and separate enterprise;

(b) engaged in the same or similar activities;

(c) under the same or similar conditions;

(d) dealing independently of the enterprise of which it is a permanent establishment.

This may be more favourable than the provisions for establishing the profits of a branch laid down in TMA 1970,s.79 where the amount assessable would be the amount of profit arising directly or indirectly through or from the branch agency.

TMA 1970,s.81 however provides that on election the branch or agency may be charged to tax on the profits which might reasonably be expected to be earned by a merchant who had bought from the manufacturer or producer direct.

3.2 THE CHOICE OF BUSINESS STRUCTURE

The profits of a trade carried on wholly abroad are assessed under Schedule D Case V. If part of the trade is carried on in the UK the liability will be under Schedule D Case I.

It is very difficult for a sole trader resident in the UK to show that he is trading wholly abroad. Even though he does not take any part in managing his business in the UK, the mere fact that he could have done so if he wished is enough to show that the trade is not carried on wholly abroad **Ogilvie v. Kitten (1908).**

Mr. Ogilvie was a manufacturer in Aberdeen and acquired a wool warehousing business in Canada. The Canadian enterprise was operated entirely under local management and Mr. Ogilvie never interfered with the conduct of the business. It was held that the profits were assessable under Schedule D Case I because he had the power to manage the business if he had wished and that was enough to show that the operations were not conducted wholly abroad.

Where it is desired to carry on business abroad, a UK trader can do so by either:

(a) exporting directly;

(b) licensing an overseas trader to act on his behalf;

(c) setting up a subsidiary company;

(d) establishing an overseas branch.

The fundamental difference between an overseas subsidiary and an overseas branch is that the former is a separate legal person from the UK person who creates and owns it. Thus if the overseas operation is likely to be successful, it may be better to set up a subsidiary as that freedom is maintained over the remittance of profits by way of dividend, subject to the company not contravening the controlled foreign company legislation. This however will only be so if it is possible to show that the subsidiary is not UK resident and therefore care must be taken at its establishment to ensure that it is not controlled and managed from within the UK. Conversely, if the overseas operation is likely to produce a loss, then the attraction of a branch is that under the **Ogilvie v. Kitten** principle it will be a mere extension of the UK trade and that the losses will be allowable as a deduction from the UK income. This could of course be achieved via the medium of an overseas subsidiary provided that it was UK resident, however when operations become profitable it would then be desirable to change the UK residence to a non-UK one to preserve the non-assessability of profits to UK tax. This would require:

(a) Treasury permission under TA 1970,s.482;

(b) a very strong case to satisfy the Revenue that residence had truly changed and that control and management were genuinely abroad. (Remember the principle laid down in **Unit Construction v. Bullock (1960)** that control is at the place where it actually occurs and not where it should occur).

In summary therefore the UK tax implications of branches and subsidiaries will be:

(a) overseas branch of a UK company: the trading profits of such a branch form part of the total profits of the UK company subject to UK corporation tax. As a result:

  (i) branch profits are taxed in the UK whether or not remitted to the UK;

  (ii) relief is available in the UK for branch losses;

  (iii) capital allowances may be claimed in respect of the branch, if appropriate;

(b) overseas subsidiary: the trading profits of a subsidiary are subject to UK tax only when a dividend is receivable from the subsidiary. As a result:

  (i) unremitted profits are normally free from UK tax;

  (ii) there is no relief in the UK for the subsidiary's trading losses;

  (iii) no UK capital allowances are available in respect of the subsidiary's activities.

The optimum business structure therefore appears to be that it would be advantageous to start business with an overseas branch (to obtain maximum relief for initial losses, capital expenditure etc.) and later when matters become profitable to incorporate the branch into a foreign subsidiary;

this however will result in the following difficulties:

  (i) s.482(1)(b) requires Treasury consent for the transfer of the trade or business or any part of a trade or business from a UK resident body corporate to another person who is not a UK resident;

  (ii) the transfer will trigger balancing charges;

  (iii) the transfer of assets to a non-UK resident company, even though wholly owned is a disposal outside the group and will thus result in potential chargeable gains. Relief may be obtained under CGTA 1979,s.115 (roll-over) if other qualifying UK assets are acquired or relief may be claimed under the provisions of TA 1970,s.268(A). Under this latter section any chargeable gains may be taken out of account where:

    (1) a company transfers the whole or part of its overseas trade to a non-resident company (domestication), and

    (2) the consideration consists wholly of shares or loan stock in the overseas company, and

    (3) after the issue of shares, the UK company holds at least 25% of the ordinary share capital of the overseas company.

  Where the shares or loan stock received form less than 100% of the consideration, the deferred gain is reduced proportionately.

If these conditions are satisfied, the UK company may claim that the net gains on domestication are to be left out of account. If only part of the consideration consisted of securities, only that part of the net gain represented by the proportion:

$$\frac{\text{market value of securities at date of domestication}}{\text{market value of total consideration at that date}}$$

may be left out of account, the balance being taxed in the normal way.

The deferred gain is brought into account if the securities in the non-resident company are disposed of. If only part of the securities received as consideration are disposed of, only part of the gain is brought into account, based on the proportion:

$$\frac{\text{market value of securities disposed of}}{\text{market value of consideration securities held immediately before disposal}}$$

The deferred gain is also brought into account if within six years of domestication the non-resident company disposes of any of the transferred assets, other than to other group members. The amount of gain to be brought into account is determined as the proportion:

$$\frac{\text{gross chargeable gain on domestication on assets now disposed of}}{\text{gross chargeable gain on domestication on all assets held immediately before disposal}}$$

Illustration

Brett Ltd. a UK resident company, carries on business in South Africa through a branch there. In 1985, Brett Ltd. is required by the local government to incorporate a company, Brett SA, to carry on the activities previously undertaken by the branch.

Brett Ltd. obtains s.482 consent and the local government takes up 70% of the shares in Brett SA, for which Brett Ltd. receives considerations of £1,200,000; the 30% holding of Brett Ltd. in Brett SA is valued at £400,000.

The assets of the branch, together with their cost and market value at the time of transfer, were as follows:

	Cost	MV
	£	£
Goodwill	-	900,000
Factory 1	180,000	200,000
Factory 2	70,000	100,000
Stock	50,000	80,000
Plant and Machinery	200,000	150,000
Patents and know-how	75,000	100,000
Net working capital	70,000	70,000
	645,000	1,600,000

In 1987 Brett SA disposed of factory 1 for £320,000.

In 1989 Brett Ltd. was required to transfer all its shares in Brett SA to the local government. Brett Ltd. received compensation of £500,000.

Calculate the capital gains tax position. (Ignore Indexation)

1985

Chargeable gain on transfer

Chargeable assets	Cost	MV	Chargeable gain
	£	£	£
Goodwill	-	900,000	900,000
Factory 1	180,000	200,000	20,000
Factory 2	70,000	100,000	30,000
Patents and know-how	75,000	100,000	25,000
			975,000

The amount of gain which may be deferred on the transfer of the branch is:

$$£975,000 \times £ \frac{400,000}{1,200,000 + 400,000} = £243,750$$

The balance of the gain, £731,250, is brought into charge in 1985.

1987

As factory 1 has been sold within six years of domestication part of the deferred gain will be assessed.

$$£243,750 \times \frac{20,000}{975,000} = £5,000$$

1989

As all the shares have now been sold, the balance of the deferred gain will be brought into charge to tax.

	£
Disposal proceeds	500,000
Market value on domestication	400,000
	100,000
Balance of deferred gain £(243,750 - 5,000)	238,750
	338,750

In establishing any business outside the UK there are important non-fiscal matters to be taken into account:

(a) a branch entails the loss of legal liability and some privacy;

(b) it also lacks flexibility for mergers etc.;

(c) the setting-up expenses of a branch and the administration costs often tend to be more expensive than those of a subsidiary;

(d) a subsidiary may be more satisfactory as regards nationalist sentiments.

3.3 REPATRIATION OF FUNDS/TRANSFER PRICING

(a) Repatriation of funds

The following constitute the main methods of repatriation to the UK of profits arising from overseas activities:

(i) dividends

(ii) interest

(iii) rents

(iv) royalties

(v) management charges

(vi) licence fees.

(b) Liability to UK taxation on repatriated funds
Companies or individuals resident in the UK are subject to UK tax on their world-wide income, irrespective of where those profits arise:

(i) trading profits of a branch established in an overseas country are charged under Schedule D Case I on an arising basis, regardless of whether the profits are remitted to the UK. Exceptionally, trading profits of an overseas branch could be taxed under Schedule D Case V if it could be shown that the trade of the branch was carried on, i.e. managed and controlled, overseas;

(ii) management expenses charged to an overseas operation are charged to tax under Schedule D Case I;

(iii) interest, royalties etc., are charged under Schedule D Cases IV or V, on an arising basis, regardless of whether the profits are remitted to the UK;

(iv) the sale of know-how, manufacturing rights, selling rights, patents etc. for a lump sum and/or royalties or licence fees result in the lump sum or royalties being taxed under Schedule D Cases I or V (TA 1970,ss.380 and 386);

(v) the trading profits of an overseas resident company are not within the charge to UK tax until a dividend is paid by the overseas company to the UK company; a dividend so paid is charged under Schedule D Case V.

With the exception of management charges, these forms of repatriation will generally be subject to a withholding tax in the overseas country. Since management charges are not generally subject to a withholding tax, the imposition of management charges is frequently viewed with disfavour by overseas tax authorities, who consider the use of such charges as a method of extracting profits from their jurisdiction. This may result in management charges being disallowed for tax purposes in the overseas country or alternatively redesignated as a distribution to which a withholding tax may be applied.

(c) Transfer pricing
Where trading transactions between connected parties are undertaken at other than market price, the price may be adjusted by the Revenue to market price (TA 1970,s.485). In particular where either the buyer or the seller (being a company or a partnership) is controlled by the other party to the contract, or both are controlled by the same persons, any transaction at other than market price can be adjusted so that:

(i) if the price is below market price, market price is substituted in computing the seller's profit (unless the buyer is a UK resident trader and is entitled to deduct the price paid in computing his own profits;

(ii) if the price is above market price, market price is substituted in computing the buyer's profits (unless the seller is a UK resident trader who would thus bring in as a trade receipt the price received).

For this purpose 'control' means the power of a person to secure, by shareholding or voting power (either directly or through another company) or under articles of association, that the company's affairs are conducted according to that person's wishes.

The transactions which are brought within the provisions of this section include not only sales, but also 'the letting and hiring of property, grants and transfers of rights, interests or licences and the giving of business facilities of whatever kind'.

As detailed above, the provisions of s.485 apply particularly in connection with transactions between a UK resident company and an overseas company over which it has control (or which are under common control). It is advisable for such transactions to be at arm's length, since otherwise a notional amount may be assessed on one party without any corresponding adjustment to the amount assessed by the overseas tax authorities on the other party to the transaction, and this may be so despite the provisions of a DTA between the two countries. It is also relevant to note that there are provisions similar to s.485 within the tax legislation of several other countries.

Article 9 OECD Draft Double Taxation agreement provides:

ASSOCIATED ENTERPRISES

1 Where

(a) an enterprise of a contracting State participates directly or indirectly in the management, control or capital of an enterprise of the other contracting State, or

(b) the same persons participate directly or indirectly in the management, control or capital of an enterprise of a contracting State and an enterprise of the other contracting State, and

conditions, in either case, are made or imposed between the two enterprises in their commercial or financial relations which differ from those which would be made between independent enterprises. Any profits which would have accrued to one of the enterprises, but, by reason of those conditions, have not so accrued, may be included in the profits of that enterprise and taxed accordingly.

2 Where a contracting State includes in the profits of an enterprise of that State - and taxes accordingly - profits on which an enterprise of the other contracting State has been charged to tax in that other State and the profits so included are profits which would have accrued to the enterprise of the first-mentioned State if the conditions made between the two enterprises had been those which would have been made between independent enterprises, then that other State shall make an appropriate adjustment to the amount of tax charged therein on those profits. In determining such adjustment, due regard shall be had to the other provisions of this convention and the competent authorities of the contracting States shall if necessary consult each other.

This is wider than UK legislation as it extends to management control or capital without specifying degrees of control. Paragraph 2 refers to the warning in an earlier paragraph. If an adjustment is made by one State to the profits of an enterprise then it is reasonable that the other State makes a corresponding adjustment. The treaty states that the other State shall make an appropriate adjustment. 'Shall' does not of course mean 'will' and 'appropriate' depends on the individual perception of those concerned.

3.4 FOREIGN BORROWING ARRANGEMENTS

(a) Payment of interest

When borrowing from overseas, a UK resident company or individual must be aware of the requirements concerning the payment of interest; a tax deduction for the interest payments must also be assured.

A UK resident company paying annual interest on a borrowing is normally required to deduct income tax at the basic rate from the interest payments (TA 1970,s.54). This deduction is not required in certain circumstances:

(i) where the interest is payable in the UK on an advance from a bank carrying on a bona fide banking business in the UK; or

(ii) where the interest is payable to a non-UK resident person, who is resident in a country with which the UK has concluded a DTA which provides that the amount of tax to be deducted from the interest be reduced; or

(iii) where the interest is of foreign source (so that the interest is not within Schedule D Case III, a requirement for s.54 to apply).

Circumstances (ii) and (iii) are relevant when considering a foreign borrowing. For (ii) to apply, i.e. for interest payments to be paid with income tax deducted at a reduced or nil rate, permission has to be obtained from the Inspector of Foreign Dividends. Frequently, even where a DTA is available, foreign lenders are not prepared to follow the procedures necessary to obtain permission for deduction at a reduced rate or alternatively to accept interest payments which are other than gross; this may be because the lender is not in a position to obtain relief for the income tax deducted against its own tax liability. If such is the case, it is necessary to arrange for the interest to be of foreign source, i.e. (iii) above.

There are various procedures which if adopted will generally establish that the interest is of foreign source; these include making the loan document subject to non-UK law, drawing it under seal outside the UK, retaining the document outside the UK. It is advisable to confirm with the Revenue that a proposed loan document will constitute a foreign source.

(b) Charges on income

The UK resident company will be concerned to obtain a tax deduction for the interest payments. In order to obtain such a deduction, the interest must qualify as a charge on income (TA 1970,s.248). The definition 'charge on income' broadly covers yearly interest, other annual payments, and interest payable in the UK on an advance from a bank carrying on a bona fide banking business in the UK, and there are conditions regarding such interest payments which must be satisfied in order for payments to qualify as charges on income (s.248(5) and (6)).

Where interest is paid to a non-UK resident, it will not qualify as a charge on income unless the paying company is UK resident and one of three conditions is satisfied, namely:

(i) income tax is deducted under s.52 (this condition is satisfied if the tax is deducted at a reduced or nil rate under the terms of a DTA), or

(ii) the conditions of s.249 are satisfied; the conditions set out in TA 1970,s.249 are:

(1) the interest must be paid by a UK resident company carrying on a trade;

(2) the loan agreement must specify that the interest is to be paid, or may be required to be paid, outside the UK;

(3) the interest must be paid outside the UK.

(c) Foreign Lending Arrangements
Where a UK resident company makes a loan to an overseas subsidiary, the UK company must ensure that the interest charged on the loan represents a commercial return; failure to do so could lead to an adjustment under TA 1970,s.485. If the loan agreement could be regarded as a debenture issued by the subsidiary, it will be necessary to obtain Treasury consent under TA 1970,s.482(1)(c).

3.5 TREASURY CONSENT UNDER ICTA 1970, s.482

Under s.482 it is necessary to obtain Treasury consent before undertaking any of the transactions detailed in (a) to (d) below. There is specific provision with this section for the imposition of penalties of up to two years' imprisonment and/or a fine up to £10,000 where a UK resident company fails to obtain Treasury consent when it is required under the section. As far as is known there have been no prosecutions under s.482. However, a failure to obtain consent for a relevant transaction could cause enquiry and possible delay in subsequent dealings with the Treasury or Revenue.

Treasury consent is required:

(a) where a UK resident company ceases to be UK resident; or

(b) where a UK resident company transfers its trade or business or any part thereof to a non-UK resident person; or

(c) where a UK resident company causes or permit a non-UK resident company over which it has control to create or issue any shares or debentures; or

(d) except for the purposes of enabling a person to be qualified to act as a director, where a UK resident company transfers to any person, or causes or permits to be transferred to any person, any shares or debentures of a non-UK resident company over which it has control, being shares or debentures which it owns or in which it has an interest.

Applications for consent are required in a format laid down by the Treasury, requiring certain information. In giving consent the Treasury will be concerned to ensure that there is not a loss of UK tax as a result of the transaction, and accordingly if not satisfied to this effect, the Treasury may impose conditions in giving consent, such as the 100% repatriation of profits to the UK.

A number of general consents have been published; if a transaction falls within one of these general consents, specific Treasury consent need not be applied for.

4.0 DOUBLE TAX RELIEF

4.1 GENERAL

Double tax relief is available to individuals and companies, it is given to ensure that where a UK resident, individual or company receives income from abroad it is not disadvantaged by being taxed twice, once in the country of origin and again in the UK. Relief can be in one of two forms:

(a) Treaty Relief TA 1970,s.497
This relief is given in accordance with the terms of a double taxation agreement negotiated between the UK and another sovereign State. The Organisation for Economic Co-operation and Development has produced a draft double tax agreement which is commonly used as a basis for the drawing up of detailed treaties.

(b) Unilateral Relief TA 1970,s.498
This is relief given by the UK Government when there is no double taxation agreement in existence, or it does not provide relief for a particular class of income.

4.2 TYPES OF RELIEF

There are three basic types of relief:

(a) the foreign tax is deducted from the gross foreign income and the net amount is assessed to UK tax (TA 1970,s.516). This method may be disadvantageous and is not normally claimed, unless loss relief is required;

(b) the gross amount of the foreign income is charged to tax in the UK. The amount of foreign tax is allowed as a tax credit against the UK tax chargeable on the foreign income. For the purpose of this relief the foreign income is treated as the top slice of the individual's income; the amount of relief is the lower of the foreign tax credit or the UK tax borne. The only foreign tax credits that can be used for relief are those suffered for direct foreign tax; such direct taxes are often known as withholding tax. No relief is available to an individual for foreign indirect, or 'underlying' tax (the credit system);

(c) the foreign income is exempted from tax in the country of origin (exemption).

Methods (b) and (c) above are specifically referred to in Article 23 OECD. UK practice is to grant exemption from UK tax to a number of sources of UK income including:

(a) commercial profits not derived from a permanent establishment;

(b) payments received from overseas by a foreign student;

(c) certain interest and dividends derived from UK sources by a foreign resident;

(d) pensions derived from UK sources by foreign residents.

4.3 TYPES OF OVERSEAS TAX

(a) withholding (direct) tax - tax which is directly deducted from a foreign source of income;

(b) underlying (indirect) tax - tax on the profits of which a foreign dividend forms a part.

4.4 METHOD OF RELIEF - INDIVIDUALS

CALCULATION OF RELIEF UNDER THE CREDIT SYSTEM

As already mentioned, under the credit system, the overseas income is grossed by the overseas tax before being charged to UK tax. In order to ensure the maximum relief for the overseas tax credit, the taxpayer may treat the overseas income as the 'top slice' of the taxable income. No relief is available to an individual for underlying tax.

Illustration

Mr A is married. In the year 1986/87 he is assessable on:

	£
DI Profits	20,300
Dividends from Ruritania	600 (net)

The dividends had suffered foreign tax of £400 (credit relief is claimed).

DI	20,300
DV - dividend £(600 + 400)	1,000
	21,300
Less: Personal allowance	3,655
	17,645

Income tax:

£	
17,200 @ 29%	4,988
445 @ 40%	178
17,645	5,166

The credit for the foreign tax is the lower of:

(a)	Foreign tax		£400	
(b)	UK tax assuming the foreign dividend to be the top slice of taxable income			
	£445 @ 40%	178		
	£555 @ 29%	161		
			£339	339
	UK tax payable			4,827

Where there are several amounts of foreign income, the taxpayer can rank them in such a way as to obtain the greatest relief.

Illustration

Mr B receives the following UK income for 1986/87:

	£
Salary	20,000
Schedule A - Rents	6,000

He also receives the following foreign income:

Dividends from Ruritania	600 (Ruritanian Tax Credit £400)
Dividends from Amazonia	450 (Amazonian Tax Credit £550)

He pays allowable interest of £2,500 gross and is entitled to personal allowances of £4,000.

To obtain the greatest advantage it is important to regard the income that has suffered the greatest amount of foreign tax as the highest slice of income, so that the greatest possible amount of UK tax is available to offset the overseas tax.

	£	£
Salary		20,000
Schedule A	6,000	
Schedule DV:		
Ruritanian Dividend £(600 + 400)	1,000	
Amazonian Dividend £(450 + 550)	1,000	
		8,000
		28,000
Less: Charges		2,500
		25,500
Less: Personal allowances		4,000
		21,500

Income tax:

£		£
17,200 @ 29%		4,988
3,000 @ 40%		1,200
1,300 @ 45%		585
21,500		6,773

Tax credit relief:

Amazonian Dividend

Taxable income £20,501 - £21,500

Taxed: £1,000 @ 45% = £450

Foreign tax £550		
Tax credit given	450	

Ruritanian Dividend

Taxable income £19,501 - £20,500

Taxed:	£300 @ 45%	135
	£700 @ 40%	280
		£415

Foreign tax £400		
Tax credit given	400	
		850
		5,923

Where foreign dividends are paid through a UK paying agent, the UK agent must, under s.159 TA, deduct UK tax at a basic rate before paying it over to the recipient. Where foreign withholding tax has been deducted the paying agent will normally deduct UK tax at such a rate as will give a total deduction of the UK basic rate. All foreign dividends paid through a UK paying agent are assessed on a current year basis.

	£
Gross dividend	1,000
Less: Withholding tax - 15%	150
	850
Less: UK tax deducted by paying agent - 14% (making 29% in all)	140
Paid to Mrs C	710
	=====

Mrs C will include £1,000 gross in her personal computation with a tax credit of £290, of which only £140 is available for any repayment to which she may be entitled.

4.5 METHOD OF RELIEF - COMPANIES

Foreign income received by a UK resident company normally arises under one of three heads:

(a) Schedule D Case I - Income from a trade carried on abroad through a branch etc. by a UK resident company;

(b) Schedule D Case IV - Income from foreign securities such as loans and debentures;

(c) Schedule D Case V - Income from foreign possessions such as royalties, rents, dividends etc.

If a non-resident company carries on business in the UK through a branch or agency then it will be liable to UK corporation tax on:

(a) trading profits derived from the branch or agency;

(b) income from property owned by the branch or agency;

(c) chargeable gains on assets situated in the UK used for the purposes of the branch or agency.

THE APPLICATION OF THE CREDIT SYSTEM

The overseas income will be grossed-up by the foreign withholding tax and the gross assessed to UK corporation tax. The foreign tax is then treated as a credit against the UK corporation tax on the foreign income.

Illustration

D Ltd. receives a dividend from Ping-Pong Incorporated of £5,500. This has borne a withholding tax of 15%.

Net amount received	£5,000
	======
Gross for withholding tax - $£5,000 \times \frac{100}{85}$ =	£5,882
	======

	£
UK corporation tax @ 50%	2,941
Credit for withholding tax	882
UK corporation tax payable	2,059

Underlying tax is the foreign equivalent of corporation tax. It is the tax payable on the profits of which the dividend forms a part. It is only of relevance when considering dividend payments. Relief for underlying tax is limited to UK resident companies which control, directly or indirectly, at least 10% of the voting power of the company paying the dividend.

If in the above illustration D Ltd. controls 10% of the voting power of Ping-Pong Incorporated, and Ping-Pong has borne underlying tax at 25%, the gross amount to include in the corporation tax computation is computed as:

Dividends grossed-up for withholding tax £5,882

Grossed-up for underlying tax -

$$£5,882 \times \frac{100}{75} = £7,843$$

	£	£
UK Corporation tax @ 50%		3,921
Less: Credit for underlying tax	1,961	
withholding tax	882	
		2,843
UK corporation tax payable		1,078

As has been illustrated, to avoid double taxation, the amount of the foreign tax borne can be treated as a credit against UK corporation tax on the foreign income. However, the amount of the credit cannot exceed the UK corporation tax borne.

Illustration

B Ltd. is a large multinational company which bears corporation tax at 50% on its income. It receives a dividend from a foreign investment of £36,000. The amounts of foreign tax borne are:

(a) £64,000

(b) £24,000

	(a) £	(b) £
Dividend received	36,000	36,000
Foreign tax	64,000	24,000
	100,000	60,000
Corporation tax @ 50%	50,000	30,000
Less: Foreign Tax credits	64,000	24,000
Corporation tax payable	NIL	6,000
Foreign tax credits lost	14,000	

Where the amount of underlying tax is not given, it will be necessary to calculate it using the principles in **Bowater Paper Corporation v. Murgatroyd (1969).** The formula for calculating the tax is:

$$\text{Overseas corporation tax actually paid on foreign profits} \times \frac{\text{Dividend gross of withholding tax}}{\text{Profits available for distribution per the accounts}}$$

Illustration

F plc is a large UK multinational company. It controls directly 40% of the voting power of Wong Inc. a company resident in Hong Kong. The profit and loss account of Wong Inc. converted into sterling for the year to 31st March 1987 is:

	£	£
Trading profits		600,000
Taxation:		
On current profits	210,000	
Transferred to deferred taxation account	40,000	
	250,000	
Overprovision 1986	20,000	
		230,000
		370,000
Dividends:		
Paid to shareholders	200,000	
Local Income Tax	100,000	
		300,000
Retained profits		70,000

The Hong Kong corporation tax actually paid for the year to 31st March 1987 was £190,000.

The underlying tax credit will be:

$$£190,000 \times \frac{£80,000 + 40,000}{370,000} = £61,622$$

The amount chargeable under Schedule D Case V will be:

	£	£
Dividend received		80,000
Foreign tax credits:		
Withholding	40,000	
Underlying	61,622	
		101,622
		181,622

For accounting periods ended on or before 31st March 1984 it was necessary to deduct ACT before relieving foreign tax credits. For accounting periods ended after that date it is now possible to reverse that order, thus giving a greater possibility of receiving foreign tax credits.

To maximise the utilisation of the foreign tax credits FA 1982,s.100 provides that charges on income, management expenses and other items capable of offset against profits of more than one description may be allocated as the company thinks fit. This will normally be:

(a) against chargeable gains;

(b) against UK income;

(c) against foreign income.

It also provides that the maximum ACT offset against my class of income will be an appropriate percentage - presently 29% of that income.

Illustration

F Ltd. a UK resident company, has the following income for the year ended 31st March 1987:

	£	£
Schedule D Case I		35,000
Schedule A		5,000
Capital Gains		3,500
Foreign dividend received	22,000	
Foreign tax credits	8,000	
		30,000

The company paid dividends of £35,500 in the accounting period and also paid debenture interest of £4,000 gross.

Corporation Tax Computation	I	CG
	£	£
Schedule D Case I	35,000	
Schedule A	5,000	
Schedule D Case V	30,000	
Chargeable gains		3,500
Less: s.93 - 1/7		500
	70,000	3,000
Less: Debenture Interest	4,000	
	66,000	3,000
Corporation Tax thereon	19,800	1,050

Calculation of double tax relief:

	UK Income	Overseas Income	
	£	£	£
Schedule D Case I	35,000		
Schedule A	5,000		
Schedule D Case V		30,000	
Chargeable gains after s.93			3,000
	40,000	30,000	3,000
Less: Debenture interest	1,000		3,000
	39,000	30,000	-

	£	£	UK Income £	Overseas Income £	£
Corporation tax as above apportioned £39,000:£30,000			11,785	9,065	
Less: Foreign tax credits				8,000	
				1,065	
ACT paid: 29/71 x £35,500		14,500			
Maximum offsets -					
Against UK income: 29% x £39,000	11,310				
Against overseas income: 29% x £30,000	1,065	12,375	11,310	1,065	
MCT			475	NIL	
Surplus ACT		2,125			

As an alternative to the credit system the company may claim relief under TA 1970,ss.511-516. If this is done, the foreign tax will be deducted from the foreign income and only the net amount will be charged to UK tax. This is not normally advantageous as it means that no relief at all will be received for the foreign tax credits; however, it may be used where the company has a loss.

5.0 CONTROLLED FOREIGN COMPANIES

Legislation was introduced in FA 1984 to prevent avoidance of tax by the use of UK companies maintaining subsidiaries in tax haven countries. By this means it is possible to keep profits outside the UK jurisdiction and to subject them to reduced or possibly nil rates of tax. Where the Inland Revenue directs, the chargeable profits of a CFC will be imputed to a UK company which satisfies certain conditions. The chargeable profits will not include any capital gains.

The conditions that will trigger an apportionment are that:

(a) the CFC is in a low tax area;

(b) it is controlled by UK resident persons;

(c) the UK company must, together with associates, be entitled to at least 10% of the profits of the CFC.

An area will be a low tax area if the tax paid by the CFC in its country of residence is less than 50% of the UK tax that would be payable on the equivalent profits.

The provisions of FA 1984 will not be applied where:

(a) the CFC engages in exempt activities; these are broadly where the company has a real presence in the country in which it is resident and its main activities are not those of leasing or dealing in securities; or

(b) the profits of a CFC for a 12 month period are less than £20,000; or

(c) the CFC remits by way of dividend enough of its profits to satisfy an 'acceptable distribution' test.

If these conditions are not satisfied then there may be an apportionment.

18 Introduction to Capital Gains Tax

1.0 WHEN CAPITAL GAINS TAX STARTED

A comprehensive capital gains tax was introduced in FA 1965 to apply with effect from 6th April 1965 and subsequent amendments have been made by later Finance Acts. These have now been consolidated into the Capital Gains Tax Act 1979 and further amendments have been made since then.

2.0 WHO IS LIABLE? (CGTA 1979, s.2)

All persons (including companies) resident or ordinarily resident in the UK are liable to tax on the disposal of any asset whether situated in the UK or not, but see later for a list of exempt assets. If an individual is not of UK domicile, but resides in the UK, he will only be liable on gains arising in the UK or remitted to this country. A person who is neither resident nor ordinarily resident in the UK but who carries on business in the UK through a branch or agency is liable to CGT on disposals of the assets of that branch or agency.

Where foreign assets are disposed of outside the UK and the proceeds are incapable of remittance to the UK because of executive action abroad, exchange control restrictions etc., then assessment will be deferred until the proceeds can be remitted. The whole gain will be assessed in the year in which the restrictions are lifted, there is no relating back into the year in which the gain arose.

3.0 WHAT IS A DISPOSAL?

A disposal of an asset, for CGT purposes, does not just mean a sale but also includes the following:

(a) a gift;

(b) loss or destruction of an asset;

(c) provision of use of an asset e.g. the granting of a lease;

(d) compensation for damage or injury;

(e) compensation for forfeiture of rights;

(f) compensation for not exercising a right.

In addition , where an asset has become of negligible value, the owner may claim to be treated as having disposed of the asset and immediately reacquired it at its present value. This will enable loss relief to be claimed.

In general terms, an asset is disposed of when an unconditional contract is made for its disposal and not when the proceeds are received. If the contract is conditional, disposal will occur when the conditions are satisfied (**Stanton v. Drayton Commercial Investments Co. Ltd (1982)**). Where a capital sum is received e.g. as compensation, the disposal occurs when the sum is received.

4.0 BASIS OF ASSESSMENT

The basis of assessment is the actual gains made during the year of assessment or accounting period for a company. Thus, if an individual taxpayer sells an asset on 10th January 1987 he will be liable to tax on any gain he makes in 1986/87 subject to the exempt amount for that year.

5.0 DUE DATE OF PAYMENT

CGT is payable on 1st December following the end of the year of assessment to which it relates or within 30 days of the issue of the final assessment, whichever is later.

6.0 PAYMENT BY INSTALMENTS

Where the disposal proceeds are to be paid by instalments over a period exceeding 18 months and the taxpayer can satisfy the Inland Revenue that it would cause him hardship to pay the tax at the normal due date, then the tax may be paid by instalments over a period not exceeding 8 years, or the period covered by the instalments if shorter.

19 Method of Calculation

1.0 CALCULATION OF GAIN

The gain arising on the disposal of a capital asset is in general calculated by deducting from the proceeds of sale the allowable costs.

2.0 ALLOWABLE DEDUCTIONS

Those expenses which are available for deduction from the proceeds of sale in order to arrive at the capital gain are as follows:

(a) cost of the asset;

(b) incidental costs of acquisition (e.g. advertising for a seller, stamp duty, commission, etc.)

(c) costs of improving the asset, provided the expenditure is reflected in the nature of the asset at the time of sale;

(d) costs of defending title to the asset;

(e) incidental costs of disposal.

For disposals after 5th April 1982 the allowable deductions may be increased by an "indexation allowance".

2.1 COMPUTATIONS

There are two major principles of computation:

(a) time apportionment;

(b) partial disposal.

2.2 TIME APPORTIONMENT

Where the asset was acquired before 6th April 1965, the chargeable gain is deemed to arise on a strict time basis evenly over the period of ownership of the asset. Only the gain arising after 6th April is liable to CGT. Calculations may generally be made to the nearest month in practice.

Illustration

A bought property on 6th April 1950 for £1,000. It was sold on 6th April 1987 for £20,000.

		£
Disposal proceeds		20,000
Cost		1,000
		19,000
Chargeable	$\frac{6.4.65-6.4.87}{6.4.50-6.4.87} = \frac{22}{37}$	11,297

Where the asset was acquired before 6th April 1945, the gain will be time apportioned only from that date. The gain will, however, still be calculated from the original cost.

Illustration

B bought a property on 1st January 1930 for £1,000. It was sold on 6th April 1987 for £25,000.

		£
Disposal proceeds		25,000
Cost		1,000
		24,000
Chargeable	$\frac{22}{42}$	12,571

As an alternative to time apportionment, the taxpayer may elect to calculate the gain by reference to the value of the asset at 6th April 1965. This election, made under CGTA 1979, Sch.5, para. 12, must be made within two years of the end of the fiscal year (accounting period in the case of a company) in which the disposal occurs. Once the election has been made, it is irrevocable.

Illustration

In the above illustration, the 6th April 1965 valuation was £14,000.

	£
Disposal proceeds	25,000
6.4.1965 valuation	14,000
	11,000

B would therefore elect to utilise 6th April 1965 valuation.

Use of this valuation can be made to reduce a gain but it cannot be used to turn a gain into a loss.

Illustration

C bought an asset on 6th April 1960 for £1,000 and sold it on 6th April 1987 for £21,000.

	£
Disposal proceeds	21,000
Cost	1,000
	20,000

Time apportion	$\frac{22}{27}$	£16,296

If the 6th April 1965 valuation was £25,000, and the Sch.5, para.12 election was made, the position would be:

	£
Disposal proceeds	21,000
6.4.1965	25,000
	(4,000)

The election should be made, but it will not produce a loss. It will simply produce a no gain no loss situation.

If the overall result is a loss it will be time apportioned like a gain. Where the use of 6th April 1965 valuation gives a greater loss than the time apportioned loss, then the former loss may be claimed. No loss is available, however, which exceeds the actual loss suffered.

Illustration

D bought an asset on 6th April 1960 for £21,000 and sold it on 6th April 1987 for £1,000. The 6th April 1965 valuation was:

(a) £18,000

(b) £28,000

Time apportioned loss:

		£
Disposal proceeds		1,000
Cost		21,000
		(20,000)
Time apportion	$\frac{22}{27}$	(16,296)

If Sch.5, para 12 election is made:

	(a)	(b)
	£	£
Disposal proceeds	1,000	1,000
6.4.1965 valuation	18,000	28,000
	(17,000)	(27,000)

In situation (a) the allowable loss will be increased to £17,000. In situation (b), however, the loss available will be restricted to £20,000, the actual loss suffered in respect of the asset.

2.3 PARTIAL DISPOSAL

Where part of an asset is sold, it is necessary to find the cost to be used in the CGT computation by the use of the part disposal formula. This is:

$$\text{Cost} \times \frac{\text{Disposal proceeds}}{\text{Disposal proceeds} + \text{Market value of the remainder at the date of disposal}}$$

Illustration

E bought a property in 1970 for £24,000. It was divided into two flats and he sold one on 6th April 1987 for £18,000, when the value of the other flat was £20,000.

	£
Disposal proceeds	18,000
Cost £24,000 x $\frac{18,000}{18,000 + 20,000}$	11,368
	6,632

If the asset had been acquired on 6th April 1960, this gain would be time apportioned.

$$\text{Gain } £6,632 \times \frac{21}{26} = £5,356$$

If the 6th April 1965 value of the property had been £30,000 this would again have the part disposal formula applied to find the value to be used in the computation.

	£
Disposal proceeds	18,000
6.4.1965 valuation	
£30,000 x $\frac{18,000}{18,000 + 20,000}$	14,210
	£3,790

The part disposal formula may only be applied to common costs. Costs which are specifically attributable to one part of the asset or to another must be allocated to that part. If in the above illustration additional costs were:

(a) common conversion costs £2,000;

(b) cost of an extension to the flat sold £1,200

the revised gain would be:

	£	£
Disposal proceeds		18,000
Costs - Building	24,000	
Conversion	2,000	
	26,000	
£26,000 x $\frac{18,000}{18,000 + 20,000}$	12,316	
Cost of extension	1,200	
		13,516
		4,484

2.4 IMPROVEMENT EXPENDITURE

Where there has been improvement expenditure on an asset it is necessary to calculate the gain on the various parts separately.

Provided the asset was acquired after 6th April 1965 no further problems arise.

If, however, the asset was purchased before 6th April 1965, thereby exempting part of the gain by means of time apportionment, a further calculation is necessary. The theory is that part of the gain must arise because of the enhancement expenditure which, if incurred after the acquisition, must give a different time span over which to spread that part of the capital gain. Thus, before applying time apportionment it is necessary to allocate the capital gain to the various items of expenditure after which the relevant proportion can be time apportioned using its own time span. The method of allocating the gain is somewhat arbitrary: it is done in the ratio of the actual expenditure.

Illustration

D purchased a house on 6th April 1956 for £3,000. On 6th April 1964 he incurred improvement expenditure of £1,000 and on 6th April 1970 he further improved the property at a cost of £2,000. On 6th April 1986 he sold the whole property for £36,000.

Calculate the chargeable gain if the market value at 6th April 1965 was £22,000.

D

1986/87

		£	£
Sale proceeds	6.4.86		36,000
Less: Cost of purchase	6.4.56	3,000	
(1) Improvements	6.4.64	1,000	
(2) Improvements	6.4.70	2,000	
			6,000
Capital gain			30,000

Proportion of capital gain applicable to:

		£
Original property	$\frac{£3,000}{£6,000} \times £30,000$	15,000
Improvement (1)	$\frac{£1,000}{£6,000} \times £30,000$	5,000
Improvement (2)	$\frac{£2,000}{£6,000} \times £30,000$	10,000
		30,000

Chargeable gain:

Period of ownership:

Original property:	6.4.56 to 6.4.86 - 30 years
Improvement (1)	6.4.64 to 6.4.86 - 22 years
Improvement (2)	As this expenditure was incurred after 6.4.65 the whole of this part of the gain is chargeable.
Chargeable period:	6.4.65 to 6.4.86 - 21 years

		£
Original property	$\frac{21}{30} \times £15,000$	10,500
Improvement (1)	$\frac{21}{22} \times £5,000$	4,772
Improvement (2)	whole gain	10,000
Chargeable gain		25,272

However, election can be made ot use market value at 6th April 1965 if this is beneficial and as improvement expenditure (2) was incurred after that date it must be added to that value thus:

			£	£
Sale proceeds				36,000
Less:	Market value	6.4.65	22,000	
	Improvement (2)	6.4.70	2,000	
				24,000
Chargeable gain				12,000

The market value election is clearly beneficial.

3.0 BASIC RATE OF TAX

Limited companies pay corporation tax on their capital gains and CT applies to individuals only, but includes individuals acting as executors or trustees. The basic rate of tax has remained at 30% since its introduction in 1965.

4.0 THE TAXABLE AMOUNT

The "taxable amount" of an individual must be established for a year of assessment. The taxable amount is the net chargeable gain, i.e. chargeable gains less all allowable losses, arising from disposals made in the year.

5.0 CALCULATION OF CGT PAYABLE

For 1986/87 the first £6,300 (1985/86 £5,900) of the taxable amount of an individual is exempt from CGT; the balance is chargeable at 30%. For trustees, in respect of settled property, the exemption is £3,150 (1985/86 £2,950).

6.0 TREATMENT OF LOSSES

If a taxpayer makes losses on the disposal of capital assets he can only obtain relief by deducting them from capital gains. Except in exceptional circumstances, capital losses can never be set against income or trading profits. Likewise, except for companies, trading losses can never be set against capital gains.

Unutilised allowable losses brought forward may be deducted from the taxable amount. However, the taxable amount need not be reduced by such losses below £6,300 and thus sometimes all or part of the losses brought forward may be preserved for carry forward to some future year assessment.

Illustration

	A £	B £	C £
Unutilised losses at end of 1985/86	(3,000)	(3,000)	(3,000)
1986/87			
Chargeable gains	12,000	5,900	7,500
Less: Allowable losses	1,000	1,000	1,000
Taxable amount	11,000	4,900	6,500
Deduct losses brought forward	(3,000)	nil	(200)
Taxable amount	8,000	4,900	6,300
Less: First £6,300	6,300	6,300	6,300
	1,700	nil	nil
CGT thereon	510	nil	nil
Losses carried forward	nil	nil	2,800

20 Indexation Allowance

1.0 INTRODUCTION

FA 1982, brought in measures designed to give relief from the effects of inflation where a chargeable gain arose on an asset held for more than twelve months. The relief took the form of an allowance (known as the 'Indexation Allowance') which was deducted from the gross gain. The allowance was computed by uplifting allowable deductions other than disposal costs by the increase in the retail price index from March 1982 onwards, or the anniversary of the incidence of the relevant allowable expenditure, if later.

Provisions have been introduced in FA 1985 to amend and extend the original indexation allowance. In particular it will now be possible for disposals occurring after 5th April 1985 (31st March 1985 for companies) to:

(a) obtain relief for increases in the RPI from the date of acquisition (or March 1982 if later) without waiting for 12 months;

(b) use the indexation allowance to create or augment a loss;

(c) apply the allowance to the value of assets at 31st March 1982 rather than to original cost if that is advantageous.

2.0 METHOD OF GIVING THE INDEXATION ALLOWANCE

(a) The indexation allowance is given as a deduction from the gross gain before time apportionment.

(b) Where the market value on 6th April is taken on a CGTA 1979,Sch.5,para 15, election, the indexation allowance is calculated on a 6th April 1965 valuation or the value at 31st March 1982 if desired.

3.0 METHOD OF CALCULATING THE INDEXATION ALLOWANCE

(a) The indexation allowance is the total of the 'indexed rise' in each element of 'relevant allowable expenditure'.

(b) 'Relevant allowable expenditure' is any item of expenditure taken into account in computing the overall gross gain excluding generally costs of disposal.

(c) The 'indexed rise' in an element of allowable expenditure is computed by multiplying that item by the decimal equivalent of:

$$\frac{(RD - RI)}{RI}$$

RD = The retail prices index (RPI) for the month in which the disposal occurs.

RI = The RPI for March 1982 or if later, the month in which the allowable expenditure was incurred.

The indexed rise is normally calculated to three places of decimals. The indexed rise in an item of relevant allowable expenditure will be nil whenever RD is less than or equal to RI.

Illustration

S sells an antique sofa for £43,800 on 6th June 1986. The sofa had originally cost £15,000 on dates given below:

(i) August 1985

(ii) October 1982

(iii) January 1979

(iv) February 1960.

Compute the chargeable gains arising in respect of each of the above acquisition dates on the assumption that the RPI was as follows:

March 1982	313.4
October 1982	359.0
August 1985	400.1
June 1986	419.2

		£
(i)	Disposal proceeds	43,800
	Less: Cost	15,000
	Gross gain	28,800
	Less: Indexation allowance	
	$\frac{RD - RI}{RI}$ x cost	
	$\frac{419.2 - 400.1}{400.1}$ x £15,000 =	720
	Chargeable gain	28,080

		£
(ii)	Disposal proceeds	43,800
	Less: Cost	15,000
	Gross gain	28,800
	Less: Indexation allowance	
	$\frac{419.2 - 359.0}{359.0}$ x £15,000 =	2,520
	Chargeable gain	26,280

		£
(iii)	Disposal proceeds	43,800
	Less: Cost	15,000
	Gross gain	28,800
	Less: Indexation allowance	
	$\frac{419.2 - 313.4}{313.4} \times £15,000 =$	5,070
	Chargeable gain	23,730

		£
(iv)	Disposal proceeds	43,800
	Less: Cost	15,000
	Gross gain	28,800
	Indexation allowance as in (iii)	5,070
	Capital gain	23,730
	Chargeable gain = $£23,730 \times \frac{21\ 2/12}{26\ 4/12} =$	19,074

If in the above illustration the sofa has been acquired during October 1982:

(i) For £46,000

(ii) For £42,000

the result would now be as under:

		£
(i)	Disposal proceeds	43,800
	Less: Cost	46,000
		(2,200)
	Indexation allowance:	
	$\frac{419.2 - 359.0}{359.0} \times £46,000$	7,728
	Allowable loss	(9,928)

		£
(ii)	Disposal proceeds	43,800
	Less: Cost	42,000
		1,800
	Indexation allowance:	
	$\frac{419.2 - 359.0}{359.0} \times £42,000$	7,056
	Allowable loss	(5,256)

Where assets acquired before 1st April 1982 have been disposed of after 5th April 1985 (31st March 1985 for companies), the taxpayer may claim that the indexation allowance be calculated on the value of the asset at 31st March 1982. The election which is irrevocable, must be made within two years from the end of the tax year or accounting period in which disposal occurred.

If, in the above example, the sofa had been acquired in January 1979 and the value at 31st March 1982 was agreed to be £30,000, the revised gain would be:

	£
Disposal proceeds	43,800
Cost	15,000
	28,800
Indexation: $\frac{419.2 - 313.4}{313.4} \times £30,000$	10,140
Gain	18,660

Where the market value on 6th April 1965 is used under Para 12 5th Schedule the indexation allowance will be applied between March 1982 and the time of disposal. The indexation allowance calculated is once more deducted from the gross gain. It may be based on the 6th April 1965 value or on the value at 31st March 1982.

Illustration

N purchased an investment property on 6th April 1950 for £20,000. She sold the property on 6th April 1986 for £180,000. The property was valued at £90,000 on 6th April 1965. The RPI for March 1982 was 313.4 and for April 1986 360.3.

The chargeable gain under time apportionment is calculated as follows:

Chargeable gain	£
Disposal proceeds	180,000
Less: Cost	20,000
Gross gain	160,000
Less: Indexation allowance	
$\frac{360.3 - 313.4}{313.4} \times £20,000$	3,000
Capital gain	157,000
Chargeable gain = $£157,000 \times \frac{21}{36}$	91,583

If an election is made under Schedule 5,para 12, CGTA the position would be:

	£
Disposal proceeds	180,000
6.4.1965 valuation	90,000
	90,000
Indexation: $\frac{360.3 - 313.4}{313.4} \times £90,000$	13,500
	76,500

If a claim had been made to base the indexation allowance on the 31st March 1982 valuation, the position, assuming an agreed value of £150,000, would be:

	£	£
Disposal proceeds	180,000	180,000
Cost	20,000	
6.4.1965 valuation		90,000
	160,000	90,000
Indexation:		
$\frac{360.3 - 313.4}{313.4} \times £150,000$	22,500	22,500
	137,500	67,500
Time apportion $\frac{21}{36}$	£80,208	

Where there has been improvement expenditure, the indexation allowance will be deducted from the gross gain before dividing the net gain over the various components of cost and time apportionment, if appropriate.

Illustration

B purchased a property on 6th April 1960 for £22,500. He subsequently incurred expenditure on carrying out improvements on the following dates:

6th April 1970	£6,000
24th May 1982	£2,500

The property was sold on 5th April 1987 for £60,000.
The retail prices index was:

March 1982	313.4
May 1982	322.0
April 1987	370.9

No claim is made to use the value at 31st March 1982 for indexation purposes.

	£	£
Disposal proceeds		60,000
Cost 1960	22,500	
Improvements 1970	6,000	
1982	2,500	
		31,000
		29,000
Indexation:		
On cost and 1970 improvements:		
$£28,500 \times \frac{370.9 - 313.4}{313.4}$	5,215	
On 1982 improvements:		
$£2,500 \times \frac{370.9 - 322.0}{322.0}$	380	
		5,595
		23,405

Chargeable gain:

		£
Cost	$£23,405 \times \frac{£22,500}{£31,000} \times \frac{22}{27}$	13,842
Improvement 1	$£23,405 \times \frac{£\ 6,000}{£31,000}$	4,530
Improvement 2	$£23,405 \times \frac{£\ 2,500}{£31,000}$	1,888
		20,260

21 Exempt Assets

1.0 SUMMARY OF EXEMPT ASSETS

Set out below is a brief list of those assets which are exempt or partly exempt and in the following paragraphs some of these are considered in greater depth:

(a) the taxpayer's own home;

(b) tangible movable property (chattels) sold for £3,000 or less;

(c) government securities and qualifying corporate bonds disposed of after 2nd July 1986;

(d) private motor vehicles;

(e) securities issued under the National Savings Movement (e.g. National Savings Certificates);

(f) gains on death;

(g) life assurance policies, unless the person disposing is not the original beneficial owner;

(h) betting winnings;

(i) awards for valour, unless purchased;

(j) foreign currency for personal use of taxpayer outside the UK;

(k) gifts for charity;

(l) gifts to the nation;

(m) cash (sterling);

(n) tangible movable property which is a wasting asset.

2.0 PRIVATE RESIDENCE

The taxpayer is not liable to CGT on any gains arising from the disposal of his own home, known as his 'only main residence'. As this implies, the taxpayer can only claim this exemption for one home: if he in fact occupies two, say a town house and a country cottage, he can nominate whichever he prefers as qualifying for the exemption. The election must generally be made within two years of acquiring the second residence.

A CGT exemption is also available to a taxpayer on the disposal of a residence occupied rent free by a dependent relative of the taxpayer or his wife. Not more than one house may qualify for relief under the 'dependent relative' provisions at any one time.

If the area of land occupied by the residence and garden exceeds one acre then a proportion of the gain may be liable to tax. Likewise, if any part of the residence is used exclusively for a purpose other than the taxpayer's home this will also give rise to a liability.

Further, if the taxpayer uses the property as his home for part only of the period of ownership then the gain will be apportioned on a time basis to determine how much is chargeable. Provided the taxpayer has physically occupied the property for some time during ownership however the last two years will always be treated as exempt irrespective of the use to which the property was put during those two years.

Illustration

W purchased a house on 1st July 1974 for £5,000 and lived in it until 1st July 1977 when he purchased another house and let his son live in the first. On 1st July 1987 he sold the first house for £17,000 net. A claim is made for the indexation allowance to be calculated on the March 1982 value of £12,000.

RPI	March 1982	313.4
	July 1987	370.6

	£
Disposal proceeds	17,000
Less: Cost	5,000
	12,000
Indexation $\frac{370.6 - 313.4}{313.4} \times £12,000$	2,196
	9,804

Period of ownership		
1.7.74 to 1.7.87	=	13 years
Exempt period		
1.7.74 to 1.7.77 (actual residence)		3 years
2.7.85 to 1.7.87 (last two years)		2 years
		5 years

	£
Gain as above	9,804
Less: Exempt $\frac{5}{13} \times £9,804$	3,770
Chargeable gain	6,034

(a) In addition to the last two years there are other periods of temporary absence during which the taxpayer will be treated as if he had resided in the property, provided:

(i) he actually resided there both before and after the period of temporary absence;

(ii) he had no other property which would qualify for exemption if he so chose.

Where the period of absence is because of employment abroad or work elsewhere in the UK, then, it will not be necessary for the taxpayer to return and reside in the house to validate the last period of absence (Extra-statutory Concession D4).

(b) The periods of temporary absence are:

(i) any period or periods which do not in total amount to more than three years;

(ii) any period or periods which do not in total exceed four years if the taxpayer has been forced to move elsewhere in the UK because of his employment;

(iii) any period if the taxpayer has gone abroad because of his job.

The Revenue take the view that if these time limits are exceeded, then only the first three or four years as appropriate will be treated as a period of residence with the balance of the gain chargeable.

Illustration

S acquired a house in Croydon in June 1972 at a cost of £4,500 and lived in it until July 1973 when he left for reasons of employment and lived in rented accommodation in Huddersfield where he remained until March 1977. He then went to work abroad for three years. He returned to the house in March 1980 and resided there until May of that year when he acquired another residence. In September 1986 the first house was sold for £21,500. No claim is made to base indexation on the March 1982 value.

RPI	March 1982	313.4
	September 1986	371.3

	£
Disposal proceeds	21,500
Cost	4,500
	17,000
Indexation $\frac{371.3 - 313.4}{313.4}$ x 4500	833
	16,167

June 1972 to July 1973	-	exempt as own residence
August 1973 to March 1977	-	exempt as temporary absence

(three years for any reason
four years for reason of employment in the UK)

April 1977 to March 1980	-	exempt as temporary absence

(any length of period for reason of employment abroad)

April 1980 to May 1980	-	exempt as own residence
October 1984 to September 1986	-	exempt as last two years of ownership and the property has been the taxpayer's only or main residence for some period.

Thus, the only chargeable period is June 1980 to September 1984, i.e. 52 months out of a total period of ownership of 171 months, and the chargeable gain is therefore:

$$\frac{52}{171} \times £16,167 = £4,916$$

Where the property is let during any periods of absence, then this will not result in the loss of any periods of exemption. Indeed, the provisions of FA 1980,s.80, as amended by FA 1984,s.63(3), allow a further deduction from the assessable gain equal to the lower of:

(a) the gain attributable to actual or deemed occupation;

(b) the chargeable gain;

(c) £20,000.

Thus, in the above illustration, if the property had been let throughout all the periods of absence the result would be:

		£	£
Gain as above			4,916
Less: lower of:			
(i)	gain attributable to owner occupation (£16,167 - £4,916)	11,251	
(ii)	chargeable gain	4,916	
(iii)	the first	20,000	4,916
			NIL

The relief would also be available if a part of the property had always been sub-let.

Illustration

J bought a house in December 1971 for £20,000 and sold it in December 1987 for £56,000. During the whole of this period he has let one-third of the house on a commercial basis. (Ignore indexation).

The gain is £36,000, of which £12,000 is potentially chargeable.

The rule in FA 1980,s.80 exempts the £12,000 to the extent of the lower of:

(a) £24,000

(b) £12,000

(c) £20,000

The chargeable gain is therefore £12,000 - £12,000 = NIL.

When a taxpayer owns a residence and is employed or self employed and lives in other 'job related' accommodation, any gain made on the residence will be exempt so long as he intends to occupy the accommodation as his only or main residence in due course.

Where a lodger occupies part of the taxpayer's residence living as a member of the family by sharing facilities and taking meals with them, etc., then there will be no assessable gain.

The exemptions above not only apply to houses and flats but also to static caravans together with the land that they occupy **Makins v. Elson (1973).**

In **Batey v. Wakefield (1980)** buildings appurtenant to the residence qualified for the exemption. Thus it was held that the disposal of a caretaker's cottage occupied rent free and situated within the curtilage of the main dwelling house was not liable to CGT.

It has already been mentioned that where the grounds attached to a residence exceed one acre the excess may be liable to CGT unless the Revenue are satisfied that a larger area should qualify for relief having regard to the size and character of the house etc. Any exemption attaching to the garden or grounds will be lost where the garden is retained after disposal of the house - **Varty v Lynes (1976).** The Revenue have indicated however that they will only take this point where the land retained had development value.

A married couple can only have one residence between them. If ownership of a property has passed between spouses e.g. on marriage or death then the respective periods of occupation are aggregated in considering the relief available to the spouse disposing of the property.

Where there is the breakdown of a marriage, then one spouse, normally the husband, will leave the matrimonial home. Provided that the remaining spouse continues to occupy the property as his or her main residence then continuity of exemption can be claimed by that spouse. In the case of a divorce, then each person will be treated as an independent taxpayer and may qualify for an individual residence exemption. In the case of a separation, difficulties may be experienced where the spouse leaving the property elects for some other house to be considered as his or her principal residence.

3.0 TANGIBLE MOVABLE PROPERTY (CHATTELS)

Tangible movable property can be defined for the purpose of this chapter as any asset which can be touched or moved. If an asset within this category is sold and the disposal proceeds (before expenses) do not exceed £3,000 there is no liability to CGT.

Illustration

X bought a ring for £1,000 and sold it for £1,800.

	£
Disposal proceeds	1,800
Cost	1,000
	800

Not liable to CGT.

Where the disposal proceeds exceed £3,000 the full gain is liable to CGT but the chargeable gain must not exceed:

5/3 (Disposal proceeds - £3,000)

Illustration

Y bought an antique clock for £2,200 in March 1982. It was sold on 6th April 1987 for either:

(a) £3,300

(b) £5,300

RPI	March 1982	313.3
	April 1987	360.7

	(a)	(b)
	£	£
Disposal proceeds	3,300	5,300
Cost	2,200	2,200
	1,100	3,100
Indexation $\frac{360.7 - 313.4}{313.4}$	332	332
	768	2,768
Gain restricted to:		
5/3 (£3,300 - 3,000)	£500	
5/3 (£5,300 - 3,000)		£3,833

In the case of (a) the maximum assessable gain is £500 and in the case of (b) £2,768.

Where the chattel is sold for less than £3,000 and cost £3,000 or less then no capital loss will be allowable. Where the chattel cost more than £3,000 and was sold for less than £3,000 then an allowable loss is available but the disposal proceeds are deemed to be £3,000.

Illustration

An antique coffee pot was sold for £2,600 having cost £3,400 in 1969. Although the taxpayer has incurred an actual loss of £800 (£3,400 - £2,600), the loss for capital gains tax purposes will only be £400 calculated as follows:

	£
Deemed disposal proceeds	3,000
Cost	3,400
Allowable capital loss	(400)

This will be increased by any available indexation allowance.

The exemption for gains arising on the sale of tangible movable property where the consideration does not exceed £3,000 would be open to abuse, where sets of articles are concerned, but for anti-avoidance provisions. These require a set to be treated as one asset when disposed of to the same person or to connected persons. Thus it is not possible to sell parts of a set at different times for less than £3,000 and avoid capital gains tax. However, at no stage in the legislation is 'set' identified which, in practice, makes the provisions difficult to enforce.

Illustration

A bought a set of 2 chairs on 1st September 1982 for £700. He sold one on 6th April 1986 to B for £2,200 and the other to B's wife on 6th April 1987 for £2,400. On 6th April 1986 the value of the other chair was £2,300.

RPI	September 1982	329.1
	April 1986	358.3
	April 1987	360.7

1986/87

	£
Disposal proceeds	2,200
Cost £700 x $\frac{2,200}{2,200 + 2,300}$	342
	1,858
Indexation $\frac{358.3 - 329.1}{329.1}$	30
	1,828

Restricted to:

5/3 £ $\left[2,200 - 3,000 \times \frac{2,200}{2,200 + 2,300} \right]$	£1,222

1987/88

	£
Disposal proceeds	2,400
Cost £(700 - 342)	358
	2,042
Indexation $\frac{360.7 - 329.1}{329.1}$	34
	2,008

Restricted to:

5/3 £(4,600 - 3,000)	2,666
Less: Already assessed	1,222
	1,444

Specifically excluded from the definition of chattels are commodities dealt with on terminal markets and currency. Plant and machinery can be included (see later).

4.0 GOVERNMENT SECURITIES

No chargeable gain or allowable loss arises when selling marketable government securities, provided those securities have been owned for at least one year (a sale on the anniversary of purchase is exempt). Disposals on or after 2nd July 1986 are exempt irrespective of the period of ownership.

Illustration

	Treasury Stock (a)		(b)	
Date of purchase	1.10.83	for £1,000	1.10.84	for £1,000
Date of sale	2.1.86	for £2,000	2.1.86	for £2,000
Chargeable gain		None		None

Where there have been several acquisitions there are rules of identification of disposals. Where government securities are sold for cash settlement (the normal treatment), disposal proceeds will be identified:

(1) with purchases on the preceding business day;

(2) with purchases on the same day;

(3) with purchases during the preceding twelve months, FIFO;

(4) with earlier acquisitions (no liability to CGT as outside twelve months).

Illustration

C bought 3½% War Loan as under:

		£
16.11.1980	£5,000 stock cost	2,200
1.5.1985	£3,000 stock cost	1,000
30.12.1985	£2,000 stock cost	900
16.4.1986	£4,000 stock cost	2,100

He sold £10,000 stock on 16th April 1986 for £4,800.
Identification of disposals:

		£	£
(1)	purchases on the same day:		
	Disposal proceeds		
	£4,000/10,000 x £4,800	1,920	
	Cost 16.4.1986	2,100	
			(180)
(2)	acquisitions within previous twelve months:		
	FIFO		
	Disposal proceeds		
	£3,000/10,000 x £4,800	1,440	
	Cost 1.5.1985	1,000	
			440
	Disposal proceeds		
	£2,000/10,000 x £4,800	960	
	Cost 30.12.1985	900	
			60
	Chargeable gain		320

There is no identification with the 1980 acquisition as this is more than twelve months from disposal. There is no indexation allowance on disposal of government securities.

Special rules apply to deal with losses on disposals of government securities where there has been a deemed reacquisition within a short period of the disposal. There are two situations:

(a) Bed and Breakfasting

(b) Double Banking

(a) Bed and Breakfasting

Where an allowable loss is established on a disposal of government securities and the same securities are reacquired within one month (six months if other than through a stock exchange) then the losses may not be offset generally but only against any future gains on the reacquired securities.

Illustration

D bought £20,000 3½% War Loan for £6,000 on 16th February 1984. He sold it on 14th November 1984 for £5,000 and reacquired the stock on 1st December 1984 for £5,200. The reacquired stock was sold for £7,000.

(i) on 30th June 1985

(ii) on 30th April 1986

	£
Disposal proceeds 14.11.1984	5,000
Cost	6,000
Allowable loss	(1,000)
	=====

As the stock has been reacquired within one month the loss may only be carried forward and offset against the gains on the reacquired stock.

	(a)	(b)	
	£	£	
Disposal proceeds	7,000	7,000	
Cost	5,200	5,200	
	1,800	1,800	Not assessable: balance of loss of £1,000 lost.
Loss brought forward	1,000		
Assessable	800		
	=====		

(b) Double Banking

This occurs when an additional holding of government securities is acquired within one month (six months if other than through a stock exchange) before a disposal of securities of the same kind. Again any loss on disposal can only be carried forward and offset against gains on the double-banked securities.

On the nationalisation of companies, shares and securities are acquired by the Government in exchange for Government Stock. To avoid a possible avoidance procedure whereby the taxpayer could hold the Government Stock for a year and then claim that there was no liability to CGT, it is provided that where gilt edged securities are received in exchange for shares or securities in companies acquired by nationalisation, any gain arising on the shares up to the date of nationalisation will be calculated but assessment will be deferred until the compensation securities are disposed of. Similarly any losses will be calculated but not allowed until disposal. On receipt of the Government compensation securities the normal rules will apply and if they are retained for at least twelve months any gain arising on them will be exempt from CGT.

Illustration

A owned 6,000 £1 shares in B Ltd which cost him £9,000 in 1966. In November 1985, B Ltd was nationalised and A received £16,000 9% Treasury Stock in compensation. This had a market value of 75 on the date of nationalisation.

A alternatively:

(a) kept the stock for six months and sold at a profit of £4,000;

(b) kept the stock for six months and sold at a loss of £5,000;

(c) kept the stock for two years and sold at a profit of £4,000;

(d) kept the stock for two years and sold at a loss of £4,000.

On nationalisation there will be a chargeable gain.

	£
Value of Treasury Stock	12,000
Cost of shares in B Ltd	9,000
Gain	3,000

This will be deferred until the sale of the Stock.

		£	
(a)	Profit	4,000	
	Gain deferred	3,000	
		7,000	
(b)	Loss	(4,000)	
	Gain deferred	3,000	
	Allowable loss	(1,000)	
(c) & (d)	Profit/Loss	-	Exempt
	Gain deferred	3,000	
		3,000	

5.0 QUALIFYING CORPORATE BONDS

Capital gains made on certain qualifying corporate bonds are exempted from CGT if they are owned for more than twelve months before disposal or disposed of on or after 2nd July 1986 irrespective of the period of ownership.

The exemption is applicable to bonds, debentures, debenture stock or loan stock which are:

(a) quoted on a recognised UK stock exchange or dealt in on the USM or were issued by a company with some of its shares or securities so quoted; and

(b) are a normal commercial loan; and

(c) are expressed in sterling and which are incapable of conversion into another currency.

A qualifying corporate bond is a corporate bond which was:

(a) issued after 13th March 1984, or

(b) issued before 14th March 1984 but acquired after 13th March 1984 unless it was acquired as a gift or by another no gain, no loss transaction and was not a qualifying corporate bond prior to the disposal.

22 Quoted Shares and Securities

1.0 GENERAL

Unlike most other assets, the market value of quoted shares can be easily ascertained. They are an exception to the time apportionment principle.

2.0 CALCULATION OF MARKET PRICE

The method of calculating market price of quoted shares is as follows:

(a) At 6th April 1965 the higher of:

(i) a figure halfway between the two prices in The London Stock Exchange Official Daily List quotation, or

(ii) a figure halfway between the highest and lowest prices of recorded bargains.

(b) At all other times the lower of:

(i) a figure one-quarter up from the lower of the two prices in the quotation, or

(ii) a figure halfway between the highest and lowest price of recorded bargains.

3.0 IDENTIFICATION OF DISPOSALS

3.1 OLD RULES I - DISPOSALS ON OR BEFORE 5TH APRIL 1982 (COMPANIES 31ST MARCH 1982)

Disposals are identified with acquisitions as under:

(a) with acquisitions on the same day;

(b) with acquisitions before 6th April 1965, FIFO;

(c) with acquisitions after 5th April 1965, in the pool.

Where the liability is being calculated on pre-6th April 1965 acquisitions, it is necessary to compare disposal proceeds firstly with the cost and secondly with the

6th April 1965 value.

Where there are two gains, the lower is assessed and where there are two losses again the lower is relieved. Where there is one gain and one loss then it is taken as no gain and no loss (NGNL) and no gain is assessed nor loss allowed.

In the case of shares acquired post-5th April 1965, they are pooled together and treated as one combined holding of shares. Where shares are sold, a proportionate amount of cost will be taken from the pool.

Illustration

A taxpayer has the following holding in Bounce plc, a listed company:

600 shares purchased 1.10.66	cost	£ 700
800 shares purchased 1.5.68	cost	£2,000
200 shares purchased 13.12.71	cost	£ 350

800 shares were sold in 1981/82 for £1,600.

The chargeable gain would be as follows:

		£	
	600 shares cost	700	
	800 shares cost	2,000	
	200 shares cost	350	
1,600		3,050	
800		1,525	(800 / 1,600 x £3,050)
800		1,525	
=====		=====	
	Proceeds	1,600	
	Cost (as above)	1,525	
	Chargeable gain	75	
		=====	

The combined effect of the old rules is as under:

B acquired the following shares in Gowns plc, a listed company:

Year of Purchase	Shares	Cost £
1961	300	475
1963	500	500
1964	200	280
1966	400	600
1970	300	500
1972	100	120
1973	200	240

Market value at 6th April 1965 - 120p per share.

She sold 400 shares for £600 in 1977/78 and 800 for £1,200 in 1981/82.

Calculate the chargeable gains arising on these disposals.

GOWNS PLC

			Cost		Market Value 6.4.65	Gain or Loss
			£		£	£
(a)	**1977/78 sale**					
(i)	Acquisition in 1961:					
	Proceeds $\frac{300}{400}$ x £600		450		450	
	Cost		475			
	Market value				360	
		Loss	25	Gain	90	NGNL
(ii)	Acquisition in 1963:					
	Proceeds $\frac{100}{400}$ x £600		150		150	
	Cost $\frac{100}{500}$ x £500		100			
	Market value				120	
	(leaving 400 shares for disposal later)	Gain	50	Gain	30	30
	Chargeable gain for 1977/78					30
(b)	**1981/82 sale**					
(i)	Acquisition in 1963:					
	Proceeds $\frac{400}{800}$ x £1,200		600		600	
	Cost $\frac{400}{500}$ x £500		400			
	Market value				480	
		Gain	200	Gain	120	120
(ii)	Acquisition in 1964:					
	Proceeds $\frac{200}{800}$ x £1,200		300		300	
	Cost		280			
	Market value				240	
		Gain	20	Gain	60	20
(iii)	Post-6.4.65 acquisitions:					
	Cost					
	1966 400 shares		600			
	1970 300 shares		500			
	1972 100 shares		120			
	1973 200 shares		240			
	1,000		1,460			
	Sold 200 $\frac{200}{1,000}$ x £1,460		292			
	800		1,168			
	Proceeds $\frac{200}{800}$ x £1,200		300			
	Cost as above		292			8
	Chargeable gain 1981/82					148

3.2 THE CGTA 1979, SCH.5, PARA 4 ELECTION

Clearly, if the original cost of quoted shares is not known, it is impossible to complete the normal two computations and, in such a case, the Revenue will adopt the circumstances most disadvantageous to the taxpayer. However, there is an election available under CGTA 1979, Sch.5,para.4 to ignore cost altogether and assume that pre-6th April 1965 acquisitions were acquired on 6th April 1965 at the market value on that date, and as a result these shares will be pooled with subsequent acquisitions.

The election must be made within two years of the end of the year of assessment in which the first relevant disposal after 19th March 1968 takes place. There are two elections available:

(a) In respect of quoted fixed interest securities and preference shares, and/or

(b) In respect of other quoted investments, i.e. ordinary shares.

Once an election is made it is irrevocable and will apply to all quoted shares and securities of whatever company which were held on 6th April 1965 and had not been disposed of prior to 19th March 1968.

A CGTA 1979,Sch.5,para.4 election cannot have the effect of reducing gains and where the market value as at 6th April 1965 was lower than the original cost, it will increase them. It may, however, increase the amounts of allowable losses, or produce such losses in situations where, without the election, a 'no gain, no loss' situation would arise.

It must be emphasised that a Sch.5,para.4 election can only apply to quoted investments and quoted securities. In the case of unquoted investments and securities and other assets held on 6th April 1965 the only election available is under CGTA 1979,Sch.5,para 12.

If the election had been made for the shares of Gowns plc, the position would be:

			£
Pre 6th April 1965 acquisitions:			
1961	300	shares	
1963	500	shares	
1964	200	shares	
	1,000	@ 6.4.1965 value	1,200
1966	400	Cost	600
1970	300	Cost	500
1972	100	Cost	120
1973	200	Cost	240
	2,000		2,660
Sold 1977/78	400	400/2,000 x £2,660	532
	1,600		2,128
Sold 1981/82	800	800/1,600 x £2,128	1,064
	800		1,064

1977/78	
Disposal proceeds	600
Cost	532
Chargeable gain	68

1981/82	£
Disposal proceeds	1,200
Cost	1,064
Chargeable gain	136

In this case, it would have been disadvantageous to make the election.

It must be appreciated that the election covers all the quoted shares in either of the two categories. It cannot be made on a piecemeal basis.

3.3 OLD RULES II - DISPOSALS BETWEEN 6TH APRIL 1982 AND 5TH APRIL 1985 (COMPANIES 1ST APRIL 1982 TO 31ST MARCH 1985)

Disposals are identified with acquisitions as under:

(a) transactions in the same Stock Exchange account are matched;

(b) sales are matched with shares acquired in the previous twelve months, on a 'first in first out' (FIFO) basis;

(c) sales are then matched with shares acquired more than twelve months before disposal but after 5th April 1982 on 'last in first out' (LIFO) basis;

(d) acquisitions in the pool purchased between 6th April 1965 and 5th April 1982;

(e) shares acquired before 6th April 1965 are identified on a LIFO basis.

Indexation will be available where appropriate.

Illustration

B acquired ordinary shares in Golf plc as follows:

September 1982	500
October 1982	1,000
November 1982	500
January 1983	500
March 1983	1,000
December 1983	1,500

In December 1983 he sold 3,500 shares in Golf plc in the same Stock Exchange account as his purchase of 1,500 shares.

The 3,500 shares sold in Golf plc will be identified as under:

1 Firstly with the 1,500 shares purchased in December 1983; account bargains. No indexation.

2 Then with the 500 shares purchased in January 1983 - no indexation.

3 Then with the 1,000 shares purchased in March 1983 - no indexation.

The purchases in January 1983 and March 1983 were both in the previous twelve months and are dealt with on a FIFO basis.

4 Then with 500 shares purchased in November 1982. As this acquisition took place outside the previous twelve month period, it is identified on a LIFO basis.

Indexation will be from November 1983, the twelfth month after that in which the shares were purchased.

Illustration

C sold 2,500 shares in ICI plc on 31.12.1983 for £15,000. His holding had been acquired as under:

		£
1.10.1960	600 share cost	2,900
12.7.1964	500	2,100
15.11.1970	1,200	8,000
7.12.1980	300	2,000
1.11.1982	100	500
19.4.1983	200	900
30.10.1983	500	2,900

The 6th April 1965 value of the shares was £4.50 each.

RPI	March 1982	313.4
	November 1983	381.7
	December 1983	400.8

Shares sold are identified as under:

(1) Acquisitions within the preceding twelve months, FIFO:

	£	£
Disposal proceeds		
200/2,500 x £15,000	1,200	
Cost 19.4.1983	900	
		300
Disposal proceeds		
500/2,500 x £15,000	3,000	
Cost 30.10.1983	2,900	
		100
		400

(2) Acquisitions after 5th April 1982 but outside the last twelve months. LIFO:

	£	£
Disposal proceeds		
100/2,500 x £15,000	600	
Cost	500	
	100	
Indexation $\frac{400.8 - 381.7}{381.7}$	25	
		75
c/f		475

		£	£	£
		b/f		475
(3)	Pool			
	1970 1,200 Cost	8,000		
	1980 300 Cost	2,000		
	1,500	10,000		
	Sold 1,500	10,000		
	-	-		
	Disposal proceeds			
	1,500/2,500 x £15,000		9,000	
	Cost		10,000	
				(1,000)
	(No indexation)			
(4)	Pre 6th April 1965 acquisitions, LIFO:			
	Disposal proceeds			
	200/2,500 x £15,000	1,200	1,200	
	Cost: 200/500 x £2,100	840		
	6.4.1965 value - 200 x £4.50		900	
		360	300	
	Indexation $\frac{400.8 - 313.4}{313.4}$	234	251	
		126	49	49
				(476)

If C had elected under CGTA 1979,Sch.5,para 4 the position would be:

			£
1960	600	shares	
1964	500	shares	
	1,100	@ 6.4.1965 value of £4.50	4,950
1970	1,200	cost	8,000
1980	300	cost	2,000
	2,600		14,950
Sold	1,700	(1,700/2,600 x £14,950)	9,775
	900		5,175

The position on the post-5th April 1982 acquisitions will be the same:

Shares bought	19.4.1983	300
	30.10.1983	100
	1.11.1982	75
	c/f	475 gain

		£
	b/f	475
	£	
Disposal proceeds		
1,700/2,500 x £15,000	10,200	
Cost as above	9,775	
	425	
Indexation $\frac{400.8 - 313.4}{313.4}$	2,726	NIL
Chargeable gain		475

3.4 NEW RULES - DISPOSALS AFTER 5TH APRIL 1985 (COMPANIES AFTER 31ST MARCH 1985)

The Finance Act 1985 provides for pooling to be re-introduced for shares and securities of the same class in the same company. The new provisions cover shares and securities which are either:

(a) acquired after 5th April 1982 (31st March 1982 - companies) and which are still held at 5th April 1985 (31st March 1985 - companies);

(b) acquired after 5th April 1985 (31st March - companies).

The method of pooling is dealt with in accordance with the following steps:

(a) ascertain the number and cost of the shares acquired after 5th April 1982 (31st March 1982 - companies) and which are still held at 5th April 1985 (31st March 1985 - companies). Find the indexation allowances thereon from acquisition to 5th April 1985 (31st March 1985 - companies). The indexation allowance is not restricted to three decimal places. The computation then starts with the following format:

Shares	Cost	Indexed Cost
	£	£
x	x	x

(b) Every time there is an operative event increase the indexed cost by the indexation allowance between April 1985 (March 1985 - companies) or the most recent operative event (if later) using the formula:

$$\text{Value brought forward in indexed pool} \times \frac{RE - RL}{RL}$$

where RE is the RPI for the month in which the operative event occurs and RL is the RPI for the month in which the most recent operative event occurred;

(c) If the operative event is an acquisition, the cost is added to the cost and to the indexed pool;

(d) If the operative event is a disposal, a proportionate amount of both cost and the indexed pool is removed using the part disposal formula;

(e) The indexation allowance on a disposal is the difference between the amount removed from the cost and indexed pool columns.

(f) In practice, of course, the cost column may be completely ignored; the chargeable gain (or allowable loss) is simply the difference between the proceeds and the amount removed from the indexed pool column.

As mentioned above all indexation in the post 5.4.1982 pool is not restricted to three decimal places.

Illustration

X bought shares in ICI plc as under:

7th December 1983	2,000	Cost £7,000
19th July 1984	1,200	Cost £5,100
11 June 1985	600	Cost £2,450

On 30th September 1985 he sold 1,400 shares for £6,000.

RPI	December 1983	329.3
	July 1984	340.7
	April 1985	346.9
	June 1985	350.1
	September 1985	352.7

	Shares	Cost £	Indexed Cost £
7th December 1983			
Cost	2,000	7,000	7,000
Indexation to April 1985 $\frac{346.9 - 329.3}{329.3} \times £7,000$			374
19th July 1984			
Cost	1,200	5,100	5,100
Indexation to April 1985 $\frac{346.9 - 340.7}{340.7} \times £5,100$			93
	3,200	12,100	12,567
11th June 1985			
Indexation to June 1985 $\frac{350.1 - 346.9}{346.9} \times £12,567$			116
			12,683
Cost	600	2,450	2,450
	3,800	14,550	15,133
30th September 1985			
Indexation to September 1985 $\frac{352.7 - 350.1}{350.1} \times £15,133$			112
			15,245
Sale of 1,400 shares	(1,400)		
Cost: £14,550 x 1,400/3,800		(5,360)	
Indexed cost: £15,245 x 1,400/3,800			(5,617)
	2,400	9,190	9,628

If the following transactions then took place:

6th April 1987	800 shares	Cost	£3,600
30th November 1987	1,000 shares were sold for		£5,000
RPI April 1987		360.7	
November 1987		370.3	

the position would be:

	Shares	Cost	Indexed Cost
		£	£
Brought forward	2,400	9,190	9,628
6th April 1987			
Indexation to April 1987 $\frac{360.7 - 352.7}{352.7} \times £9,628$			218
			9,846
Cost	800	3,600	3,600
	3,200	12,790	13,446
30th November 1987			
Indexation to November 1987 $\frac{370.3 - 360.7}{360.7} \times £13,446$			358
			13,804
Sale	(1,000)		
£12,790 x 1,000/3,200		(3,996)	
£13,804 x 1,000/3,200			(4,314)
	2,200	8,794	9,490

The chargeable gains would be:

	£
Disposal proceeds 30.9.85	6,000
Cost and indexation	5,617
	383
Disposal proceeds 30.11.87	5,000
Cost and indexation	4,314
	686

3.5 ORDER OF IDENTIFICATION

The basic order of identification is that disposals are identified as under:

(1) with acquisitions on the same day;

(2) with acquisitions in the previous 9 days on a FIFO basis;

(3) with the pool of acquisitions after 5th April 1982;

(4) with the pool of acquisitions between 6th April 1965 and 5th April 1982 (the frozen pool);

(5) with acquisitions pre 6th April 1965 on a LIFO basis.

Acquisitions in (1) and (2) above are not pooled and for (2) no indexation allowance is given.

Illustration

Y bought shares in ICI plc as under:

			£
19th June 1958	600	cost	900
30th December 1963	200	cost	400
11th January 1970	500	cost	1,650
2nd April 1980	1,100	cost	4,000
1st March 1983	400	cost	1,800
31st December 1985	700	cost	3,600
6th April 1987	100	cost	550

The 6th April 1965 value was £2.50 per share and the value at 31st March 1982 was £4.00 per share. He sold 3,000 shares on 6th April 1987 for £18,000.

RPI	March 1982	313.4
	March 1983	330.1
	April 1985	346.9
	December 1985	355.0
	April 1987	360.7

An election is made to base the indexation allowance on the 31st March 1982 value when appropriate. The disposals are identified as under:

		£	£
(1)	With acquisitions on the same day		
	Disposal proceeds 100/3,000 x £18,000	600	
	Cost	550	
	Chargeable gain	50	50

		Shares	Cost	Indexed Cost
(2)	With post 5.4.1982 pool		£	£
	1st March 1983 Cost	400	1,800	1,800
	Indexation to April 1985 $\frac{346.9 - 330.1}{330.1} \times £1,800$			92
				1,892
	Indexation to December 1985 $\frac{355.0 - 346.9}{346.9} \times £1,892$			44
				1,936
	Cost 31st December 1985	700	3,600	3,600
	c/f	1,100	5,400	5,536

		£	£	£
b/f	1,100	5,400	5,536	50
Indexation to April 1987				
$\frac{360.7 - 355.0}{355.0}$ x £5,536			89	
			5,625	
Sold 6th April 1987	(1,100)	(5,400)	(5,625)	
	=====	=====	=====	
Disposal proceeds:				
1,100/3,000 x £18,000			6,600	
Cost			5,400	
			1,200	
Indexation £(5,625 - 5,400)			225	
Chargeable gain			975	975
(3) <u>With 'frozen pool' of shares acquired between 6.4.1965 and 5.4.1982</u>				
Disposal proceeds:				
1,600/3,000 x £18,000			9,600	
Cost				
1970	500	1,650		
1980	1,100	4,000		
	1,600	5,650		
Sold	1,600	5,650	5,650	
			3,950	
Indexation				
$\frac{360.7 - 313.4}{313.4}$ x £(1,600 x 4.00)			966	
			2,984	2,984
			=====	
(4) <u>With pre-6.4.1965 acquisitions LIFO</u>				
Disposal proceeds:				
200/3,000 x £18,000		1,200	1,200	
Cost		400		
6.4.1965 value			500	
		800	700	
Indexation				
$\frac{360.7 - 313.4}{313.4}$ x £(200 x 4.00)		121	121	
		679	579	579
				4,588
				=====

Where shares have been disposed of during the period 6.4.1982 to 5.4.1985 they will be identified under the old rules.

<u>Illustration</u>
Z bought shares in ICI plc as under:

1st June 1983	600
19th December 1983	1,000
15th April 1984	300

1,500 shares were sold on 31st December 1984.

The shares sold will be identified using the rules existing between 1982 and 1985 (old rules II - see above).

(1) with acquisitions in the previous 12 months FIFO - 300 in April 1984;

(2) with acquisitions outside the last 12 months LIFO - 1,000 in December 1983 and then 200 from June 1983.

Thus, 400 shares will be left which will be indexed, on disposal from June 1983 to April 1985, to form a new pool.

The election under Para 4,5th Schedule CGTA has already been introduced in section 3.2. For most pre 6.4.1965 holdings the time limit for the election had expired many years ago. A second opportunity has now been provided in FA 1985. As before it covers:

(a) fixed interest securities and preference shares;

(b) equities

and must be made for <u>all</u> securities in one or both of those classes. The shares covered by the election will enter the 'frozen pool' as they are now deemed to have been acquired on 6th April 1965 at their values on that date. The time limit for making the election is two years from the end of the chargeable period (year of assessment or accounting period) in which the first disposal of any shares in either category occurs after 5th April (31st March) 1985. A group election by the principal company of a group binds that company and all members of the group.

Thus the position if a claim under Para 12 5th Schedule was made for Y's holding above would be:

				£	£
Identifications 1 and 2					
Gains as before 50 + 975					1,025
Frozen pool:					
Pre 6.4.1965 acquisitions:					
1958	600				
1963	200				
	800	@ 6 4/65 value		2,000	
1970	500	cost		1,650	
1980	1,100	cost		4,000	
	2,400			7,650	
Sold	1,800	1800/2400 x 7,650		5,738	
	600		c/f	1,912	
	=====			=====	

		£	£
	c/f		1,025
Disposal proceeds 1,800/3,000 x £18,000		10,800	
Cost		5,738	
		5,062	
Indexation $\frac{360.7 - 313.4}{313.4}$ x £(1,800 x 4)		1,087	3,975
			5,000

Thus it would not be advantageous to make an election in this particular instance.

4.0 BONUS ISSUES AND RIGHTS ISSUES - ITEMS OF THE SAME CLASS

A bonus issue or rights issue is deemed to have been acquired at the same date as the shares, etc., from which it was derived.

4.1 BONUS ISSUES

There will be no increase in the total cost of the holding but on a unit basis the cost per share will be reduced.

Illustration

		£	Unit cost
X bought	2,000 ICI plc shares for	4,000	£2.00
Bonus Issue 1:2	1,000	-	
	3,000	4,000	£1.33

If the shares were acquired before 6th April 1965, the value on this date will also be reduced on a unit basis.

Illustration
As above except that the shares were acquired in 1960 and the 6th April 1965 value was £5.00 per share.

	£	Unit value
Original 6th April 1965 value		
2,000 shares at £5.00	10,000	£5.00
1,000 Bonus Issue	-	
3,000	10,000	£3.33

The revised unit 6th April 1965 value is often referred to as the 'adjusted 6th April 1965 value'.

It is important when considering a bonus or rights issue to ensure that it is properly attributed to the shares to which it relates.

Illustration
F bought shares in ICI plc as under:

			£
1.9.1962	1,000	cost	3,000
6.10.1971	500	cost	1,900
9.12.1980	800	cost	3,700
7.6.1986	200	cost	690

On 1.12.1986 there was a bonus issue of 1 for 4. F sold 2,400 shares on 6th April 1987 for £12,000. The value of the shares in issue on 6th April 1965 was £4.00 and at 31st March 1982 £4.50.

RPI	March 1982	313.4
	June 1986	358.3
	April 1987	360.7

A claim was made to base the indexation allowance on the value at 31st March 1982.

Schedule of acquisitions	September 1962		1982 Pool		New Pool June 1986	
	Shares	£	Shares	£	Shares	£
1962	1,000	3,000				
1971			500	1,900		
1980			800	3,700		
1986					200	690
	1,000	3,000	1,300	5,600	200	690
Bonus Issue	250		325		50	
	1,250		1,625		250	
Sold	(525)	(1,260)*	(1,625)	(5,600)	(250)	(690)
Retained	725	1,740	-	-	-	-
	=====	=====	=====	=====	=====	=====

$* \frac{525}{1,250} \times £3,000$ = £1260.

	£	£	£
Disposal proceeds: 250/2,400 x £12,000	1,250		
Cost - 1986	690		
	560		
Indexation $\frac{360.7 - 358.3}{358.3} \times £690$	5		555
Disposal proceeds: 1,625/2,400 x £12,000	8,125		
Cost - pool	5,600		
	2,525		
Indexation $\frac{360.7 - 313.4}{313.4} \times £(1,300 \times 4.50)$	883		1,642
		c/f	2,197

= 5850

1625 x (4.50 / 1.444)

1625 x 3.60 = 5850

Correct way

		£	£	£
			b/f	2,197
Disposal proceeds:				
525/2,400 x £12,000		2,625	2,625	
Cost - 1962		1,260		
6.4.1965 value	£			
Original - 1,000 @ £4	4,000			
Bonus Issue 250	-			
1,250	4,000			
Per share 4,000/1,250	3.20			
525 x £3.20 (£4/1¼ = £3.20)			1,680	
		1,365	945	
Indexation $\frac{360.7 - 313.4}{313.4}$ x £(525 x 3.60)* (= 1890.)		285	285	
		1,080	660	660
				2,857

* 31.3.1982 Value	£
Original - 1,000 @ £4.50	4,500
Bonus Issue 250	-
1,250	4,500
Per share £4,500/1,250	3.60

4.2 RIGHTS ISSUE

If there is a rights issue, there will be an addition to both the number of shares held and also to the original cost and 6th April 1965 value if appropriate. Although the rights are deemed to have been acquired at the same time as the shares from which they derive, for indexation purposes, the cost of the rights will only be indexed from the date on which it was due or paid whichever is the later.

Illustration
Facts as in the previous illustration except that instead of the bonus issue there was a rights issue of 1 for 4 at £6.00.

RPI	March 1982	313.4
	June 1986	358.3
	December 1986	359.0
	April 1987	360.7

No claim is made to base indexation on the 1982 values.

Schedule of acquisitions

	September 1962		1982 Pool		New Pool June 1986	
	Shares	£	Shares	£	Shares	£
Cost as before	1,000	3,000	1,300	5,600	200	690
Rights Issue	250	1,500	325	1,950	50	300
250 @6						
	1,250	4,500	1,625	7,550	250	990
Sold	(525)	(1,890)	(1,625)	(7,550)	(250)	(990)
Retained	725	2,610	-	-	-	-

Disposal proceeds:		£	£	£
250/2,400 x £12,000			1,250	
Cost - 1982			990	
			260	
Indexation $£690 \times \frac{360.7 - 358.3}{358.3}$		5		
$£300 \times \frac{360.7 - 359.0}{359.0}$		1	6	254
Disposal proceeds:				
1,625/2,400 x £12,000			8,125	
Cost - pool			7,550	
			575	
Indexation $£5,600 \times \frac{360.7 - 313.4}{313.4}$		846		
$£1,950 \times \frac{360.7 - 359.0}{359.0}$		10	856	(281)
Disposal proceeds:				
525/2,400 x £12,000		2,625	2,625	
Cost - 1962		1,890		
6.4.1965 value:	£			
Original - 1,000 @ £4	4,000			
Rights 250 @ £6	1,500			
1,250	5,500			
Per share £5,500/1,250	£4.40			
525 x £4.40			2,310	
c/f		735	315	(27)

		£	£	£
c/f		735	315	(27)
Indexation				
Breakdown of cost:	£			
Original 525/1,250 x £3,000 =	1,260			
Rights 525/1,250 x £1,500 =	630			
	1,890			
£1,260 x $\frac{360.7 - 313.4}{313.4}$	190			
£ 630 x $\frac{360.7 - 359.0}{359.0}$	3	193		
Breakdown of 6.4.1965 value				
Original 525/1,250 x £4,000 =	1,680			
Rights 525/1,250 x £1,500 =	630			
	2,310			
£1,680 x $\frac{360.7 - 313.4}{313.4}$	254			
£ 630 x $\frac{360.7 - 359.0}{359.0}$	3		257	
		542	58	58
				31

5.0 BONUS ISSUES AND RIGHTS ISSUES - ITEMS OF A DIFFERENT CLASS

The basic principle of share pooling is that items may only be pooled together where they are identical. Where this is not so it will be necessary to split up both cost and 6th April value, if appropriate. This division will be made by reference to the market values of the various items on the first day of dealing in the new issue.

Illustration

G bought 2,000 £1 ordinary shares in ICI plc on 16th December 1970 for £5,200. On 19th July 1980 there was a rights issue of 1 for 2 debentures at 88. The market value of the various items on the first day of dealing in the new debentures were:

Shares	£5 each
Debentures	£90

The debentures were redeemed at par on 6th April 1987

RPI	March 1982	313.4
	April 1987	360.7

The value of the various items at 31st March 1982 were:

Shares	£6 each
Debentures	£92

and a claim was made to use the values on that date for indexation.

Cost of holding:	£
2,000 £1 shares cost	5,200
1,000 debentures - rights issue	880
	6,080

Thus the combined holding of 2,000 shares and £1,000 debentures is deemed to have been acquired on 16th December 1970 at a combined cost of £6,080.

Split by reference to market values:

	£
Shares 2,000 x £5	10,000
Debentures £1,000 @ 90	900
	10,900
Shares $6,080 \times \frac{10,000}{10,900}$	5,578
Debentures $6,080 \times \frac{900}{10,900}$	502
	6,080
Debentures redeemed at	1,000
Cost	502
	498
Indexation $\frac{360.7 - 313.4}{313.4} \times (£1,000 \times 92)$	139
Chargeable gain	359

If the shares had originally been acquired before 6th April 1965, it would also be necessary to adjust and split 6th April 1965 value. This is done in the same way.

Illustration

Facts as before except that the shares had been acquired in 1960. The unadjusted 6th April 1965 value was £3 each.

	£	£	£
Disposal proceeds		1,000	1,000
Cost		502	
6.4.1965 value:			
Original 2,000 @ £3 =	6,000		
Cost of Rights Issue of debentures	880		
	6,880		
Split over shares and debentures:			
Shares 6,880 x 10,000/10,900	6,312		
Debentures 6,880 x 900/10,900	568		568
	6,880		
		498	432
Indexation (360.7 - 313.4)/313.4 x (£1,000 x 92)		139	139
		359	293
Take the lower gain			293

A bonus issue of items of a different class would be treated in exactly the same way except that there would be no addition to cost or 6th April 1965 valuation.

6.0 SALE OF RIGHTS NIL-PAID

This is treated as a part disposal. However, where the proceeds are small then they may be deducted instead from cost and 6th April 1965 value if appropriate. This will defer any gain until a subsequent disposal. The proceeds will be regarded as small where they do not exceed 5% of the ex rights price of the holding from which they derive.

Illustration

H bought 1,000 shares in ICI plc on 2nd January 1970 for £4,000. On 6th April 1987 there was a rights issue of 1:2 shares at £3. She did not take up the rights and sold them alternatively:

(a) for £2 per share

(b) for 20p per share.

Market values of the shares were:

After receipt of rights		£5.50
At date of disposal		£6.00
RPI	March 1982	313.4
	April 1987	360.7

No claim is made to base indexation on the March 1982 value.

(a) Sale at £2 per share

	£
Disposal proceeds 500 x £2	1,000
This is material as it exceeds	
5% x (1,000 x £5.50) = £275	
therefore there is a part disposal.	
Cost £4,000 x $\frac{1,000}{1,000 + (1,000 \times £6)}$	571
	429
Indexation $\frac{360.7 - 313.4}{313.4}$ x £571	86
Chargeable gain	343
The cost to carry forward will be £4,000 - £571	3,429

(b) Sale at 20p per share

	£
Disposal proceeds 500 x 20p	100
This is immaterial as it does not exceed £275 and it will be deducted from cost.	
Cost	4,000
Less: Disposal proceeds of rights	100
Cost carried forward	3,900

If the shares were originally acquired in 1960 and the 6th April 1965 value was £5 per share, the position would be:

(a) If proceeds material:

	£	£
Disposal proceeds	1,000	1,000
Cost	571	
6.4.1965 value £5,000 x $\frac{1,000}{1,000 + 6,000}$		714
	429	286
Indexation $\frac{360.7 - 313.4}{313.4}$	86	108
	343	178
Take lower gain		178
Cost carried forward	3,429	
6.4.1965 value carried forward £5,000 - £714		4,286

(b) If proceeds immaterial, the carry forwards would be:

	£	£
Cost	4,000	
6.4.1965 value		5,000
Less: Disposal proceeds of rights	100	100
	3,900	4,900

Where the disposal proceeds are small and are deducted from cost and 6th April 1965 valuation, then the calculation of the indexation allowance on a subsequent sale would be:

Indexation uplift on original cost etc. before reduction	x
Less: Indexation uplift on disposal proceeds deducted assuming it to be expenditure incurred on the date the proceeds were received	(x)
Deduct from gross gain	x

Illustration

Following from the previous example, assume:

(a) the proceeds of the rights were small and deducted from cost etc.;

(b) the ICI shares were sold in April 1988 for £9,000.

RPI	March 1982	313.4
	April 1987	360.7
	April 1988	372.1

	£	£
Disposal proceeds		9,000
Cost		3,900
		5,100
Indexation:		
On gross cost $£4,000 \times \frac{372.1 - 313.4}{313.4}$	748	
On disposal proceeds of rights $£100 \times \frac{372.1 - 360.7}{360.7}$	(3)	745
		4,355

The same procedure would be applied to the 6th April 1965 value.

Where a capital repayment is received, it is dealt with in the same way as a sale of rights 'nil paid'.

7.0 TAKEOVERS AND REORGANISATIONS

These fall into two main categories:

(a) paper for paper;

(b) cash for paper.

Where the transaction is paper for paper, i.e. a share exchange, there will normally be no liability to CGT as none of the gain has been realised.

Where the transaction is cash for paper, then there may be an immediate liability to CGT in respect of the cash received.

In both cases it will be necessary to split cost and 6th April 1965 value, if appropriate. This will be done by reference to the market values of the various items received immediately following the successful takeover bid.

Illustration

J bought 3,000 shares in ICI plc in 1966 for £8,000. On 6th April 1987 it was taken over by Emile Woolf (International) plc on the following terms:

2 Emile Woolf (International) plc shares

£3 Emile Woolf (International) plc debentures

£4 cash

for every 3 ICI shares held.

The market values of the Emile Woolf shares and debentures on the first day of dealing following the successful takeover were:

Shares	£4
Debentures	90

RPI	March 1982	313.4
	April 1987	360.7

The value of the ICI shares at 31st March 1982 was £4 each and a claim was made to base the indexation allowance on this value.

Items received following the takeover:	£
EW shares 2,000 @ £4 each	8,000
EW debentures £2,000 @ 90	1,800
Cash	4,000
	13,800
	=====

Split cost pro rata to these values:	£
EW shares $\frac{8,000}{13,800}$ x £8,000	4,638
EW debentures $\frac{1,800}{13,800}$ x £8,000	1,043
Cash $\frac{4,000}{13,800}$ x £8,000	2,319
	8,000
	=====

As the gain attributable to the cash element has been realised, there will be an immediate assessment.

	£
Cash received	4,000
Cost	2,319
Gain before indexation	1,681
	=====

As the indexation allowance is being based on the values of the ICI plc shares at 31st March 1982, it will be necessary to split that also in the same way as cost.

	£
EW shares $\frac{8,000}{13,800}$ x (3,000 x £4)	6,957
EW debentures $\frac{1,800}{13,800}$ x £12,000	1,565
Cash $\frac{4,000}{13,800}$ x £12,000	3,478
	12,000

Gain as above	1,681
Less: Indexation $\frac{360.7 - 313.4}{313.4}$ x £3,478	525
Chargeable gain	1,156

The EW shares and debentures will now be carried forward as separate 1982 pools.

Where the cash received is less than five per cent of the value of the shares acquired immediately prior to the date of the takeover then there will not be a part disposal computation in respect of the cash element. Instead the cash received may be deducted from cost and 6th April 1965 valuation, if appropriate. The net amount will then be split pro rata to the values of the other items received.

For indexation purposes, there will be a calculation similar to that on the disposal of shares where an earlier rights issue had been sold nil paid for a small amount.

Illustration

Facts as in the previous illustration except that:

(a) the cash received was only £400.

(b) the value of the ICI shares prior to takeover was £3.30 each.

The debentures were redeemed in April 1988 at par.

RPI	April 1987	360.7
	April 1988	372.1

Received on takeover:

	£
EW shares 2,000 @ £4 each	8,000
EW debentures £2,000 @ 90	1,800
Cash	400
	10,200

Market value of ICI shares prior to takeover:

	£
3,000 @ £3.30	9,900
	£
5%	495

As the cash element is less than £495 it may be deducted from cost.

	£
Cost of ICI shares	8,000
Less: Cash	400
	7,600

Split over:

EW shares $\frac{8,000}{9,800} \times £7,600$	6,204
EW debentures $\frac{1,800}{9,800} \times £7,600$	1,396
	7,600

	£	£
Redemption proceeds of debentures		2,000
Cost		1,396
		604
Indexation:		
31st March 1982 value of debentures:		
$£12,000 \times \frac{1,800}{9,800}$	2,204	
Less: Cash received $£400 \times \frac{1,800}{9,800}$	73	
	2,131	
On March 1982 value:		
$\frac{372.1 - 313.4}{313.4} \times £2,204$	412	
Less: Indexation on cash received		
$\frac{372.1 - 360.7}{360.7} \times £73$	(2)	410
Chargeable gain		194

8.0 UNIT TRUSTS

Disposals of units will be dealt with in a similar way to quoted shares.

1 unit = 1 share.

23 Unquoted Shares and Securities

1.0 GENERAL

Many of the calculations relating to disposals and unquoted shares and securities are similar to those on the disposal of quoted shares and securities.

2.0 MARKET VALUE

In finding market value, there is deemed to be a transaction between a willing buyer and a willing seller. CGTA 1979,s.152 provides that a purchaser is deemed to have available all the information that a prudent purchaser is likely to require.

3.0 CALCULATION OF THE GAIN OR LOSS

The principles of time apportionment and separate election for 6th April 1965 valuation under CGTA 1979,Sch.5,para 12 apply to unquoted shares. For the purpose of an election for 6th April 1965 valuation, every unquoted share is deemed to be a separate asset, and this will mean that an election made for one share will not bind future disposals of the same shares in the same company. In practice, when unquoted shares are taken from a pool, the Revenue will often insist on the part disposal formula being applied strictly. However, in examinations this may not be so strictly applied and costs on a part disposal can often be calculated in the same way as for quoted shares.

The rules of identification of disposals follow broadly the same rules as for quoted shares. As regards disposals made after 5th April 1985 (31st March 1985 for companies, they are as under:

(a) with acquisitions on the same day or in the previous 9 days;

(b) with acquisitions in the post-5th April 1982 pool (31st March 1982 for companies);

(c) with the pool of acquisitions between 6th April 1965 and 5th April 1982 (31st March 1982 for companies) (the frozen pool);

(d) with pre-6th April 1965 acquisitions (LIFO).

Illustration

A bought shares in Unquoted Ltd. as under:

			£
6.10.1960	800	Cost	2,400
6.4.1963	200		1,400
6.11.1972	300		1,700
13.7.1980	100		500
19.6.1982	150		700

1,000 shares were sold on 6th April 1987 for £6,000. The agreed 6th April 1965 valuation was £5 per share for a holding of that size or smaller.

RPI	March 1982	313.4
	June 1982	320.3
	April 1987	360.7

Election has been made to base, where appropriate, the indexation allowance on the value of the shares at 31st March 1982, which was agreed to be £5 per share.

	£	£	£
Disposal proceeds:			
150/1,000 x £6,000		900	
Cost - 1982		700	
		200	
Indexation $\frac{360.7 - 320.3}{320.3} \times 700$		88	112

Frozen Pool:

		£
1972	300 shares cost	1,700
1980	100 shares cost	500
	400	2,200
Sold	400	2,200
	-	-

	£	£	£
Disposal proceeds:			
400/1,000 x £6,000		2,400	
Cost - pool		2,200	
		200	
Indexation $\frac{360.7 - 313.4}{313.4}$ x £2200 - original cost higher.		332	(132)
Disposal proceeds:			
200/1,000 x £6,000	1,200	1,200	
Cost - 1963	1,400		
6.4.1965 value		1,000	
	(200)	200	
Indexation $\frac{360.7 - 313.4}{313.4}$ x ① £1,400 = 211 ② 1,000 = 151	211	151	
	(411)	49	
Time apportion 22/24	(377)		(377)

Do not elect for 6.4.1965 value.

	c/f	(397)

	£	£	£
Disposal proceeds:		b/f	(397)
250/1,000 x £6,000	1,500	1,500	
Cost 250/800 x £2,400	750		
6.4.1965 value		1,250	
	750	250	
Indexation $\frac{360.7 - 313.4}{313.4}$ x (250 x £5)	189	189	
	561	61	
Time apportion 22/26½	465		
Elect			61
			(336)

4.0 BONUS ISSUES AND RIGHTS ISSUES - ITEMS OF THE SAME CLASS

These are dealt with in the same way as for quoted shares.

5.0 REORGANISATIONS INCLUDING TAKEOVERS AND BONUS ISSUES AND RIGHTS ISSUES OF ITEMS OF A DIFFERENT CLASS

There are basically three types:

(a) a reorganisation etc., of shares acquired after 5th April 1965;

(b) a reorganisation etc., before 6th April 1965 of shares acquired before 6th April 1965;

(c) a reorganisation etc., after 5th April 1965 of shares acquired before 6th April 1965.

(a) Type 1

In this case there will be no immediate computation, unless part of the gain is realised by the receipt of cash. Where part of the new holding is sold, an appropriate amount of cost is taken using the part disposal formula.

Illustration

B bought 2,000 £1 shares in Unquoted Ltd. on 1st January 1973 for £5,000. On 30.6.1980 there was a rights issue of 1:2 debentures at 90. £500 debentures were sold at par on 6th April 1987 when the value of the shares was £4 each.

RPI	March 1982	313.4
	April 1987	360.7

The value of the shares on 31st March 1982 was only £2 each and the debentures 50. No claim was therefore made to base indexation on the values of the assets at that date.

The debentures are deemed to have been acquired at the same time as the holding of shares from which they derive. Thus, on 1st January 1973, B is treated as having acquired:

	£
2,000 shares	5,000
£1,000 debentures @ 90	900
	5,900

The combined cost of £5,900 will not be split immediately as with quoted shares. When the debentures are sold part of the overall cost will be taken using part disposal.

	£
Disposal proceeds	500
Cost 5,900 x $\frac{500}{500 + (500 + 8,000)}$	328
	172
Indexation $\frac{360.7 - 313.4}{313.4}$ x £328	50
Chargeable gain	122
	=====

The market value of the remainder is:

	£
2,000 shares @ £4	8,000
£500 debentures at par	500
	8,500
	=====

The cost to be carried forward is £5,900 - £328 = £5,572. This is the combined cost of the remaining 2,000 shares and £500 debentures.

If on 6th April 1988 B sold 900 shares for £3,000 when the value of the remaining shares was £6,100 and the debentures were at 105 the position would be:

RPI April 1988 372.1

	£
Disposal proceeds	3,000
Cost £5,572 x $\frac{3,000}{3,000 + (6,100 + 525)}$	1,737
	1,263
Indexation $\frac{372.1 - 313.4}{313.4}$	325
Chargeable gain	938
	=====

The cost to be carried forward is now £3,835 (£5,572 - 1,737). This is the cost of the remaining 1,100 shares and £500 debentures.

(b) Type 2

In this case, cost will be completely ignored and 6th April 1965 value only used in the computation. Concessional relief may be given where the 6th April 1965 value is less than the original cost.

Illustration

C bought 1,000 shares in Unquoted Ltd. on 6th April 1960 for £3,000. On 6th April 1963 there was a reorganisation and C received 3,000 new shares and £1,000 debentures in exchange for his existing shareholding. The values of these items at that date were:

New shares	£1.80 each
Debentures	80 each

The 6th April 1965 values were:

Shares	£2.00 each
Debentures	90 each

On 6th April 1987, 1,400 shares were sold for £5,000 when the market value of the remainder was £7,000 and the debentures were valued at par.

RPI	March 1982	313.4
	April 1987	360.7

The values at 31st March 1982 were:

Shares	£3.00 each
Debentures	£92

and a claim was made to base the indexation allowance on those values.

		£
Disposal proceeds		5,000
6.4.1965 value		
$£6,000 \times \frac{5,000}{5,000 + 7,000}$		2,500
		2,500
Indexation		
31.3.1982 value		
$£9,000 \times \frac{5,000}{5,000 + 7,000}$	= £3,750	
$£3,750 \times \frac{360.7 - 313.4}{313.4}$		566
Chargeable gain		1,934

Much of the information given in the above illustration is irrelevant. It is important that in this type of situation the student is capable of distinguishing the relevant from the irrelevant information.

(c) Type 3

In this situation, the calculation is made in two parts:

(i) Find the gain or loss from acquisition to reorganisation, time apportioning or using 6th April 1965 valuation as appropriate. Any gain or loss so found will be deferred, unless it has been partly realised by the receipt of cash.

(ii) On disposal find the gain or loss from reorganisation to disposal, then bring into charge all or part of the gain deferred in (i).

Illustration

D bought 2,000 shares in Unquoted Ltd. on 6th April 1960 for £5,000. On 6th April 1975 the entire share capital of Unquoted Ltd. was acquired by CAC plc on the following terms:

3 CAC Shares
£4 CAC Loan Stock
£4 Cash

for every two Unquoted Ltd. shares held. The market values of the items in CAC plc at the date of the takeover were:

Shares	£2 each
Debentures	80

The 6th April 1965 value of the Unquoted Ltd. shares was £4 each.
On 6th April 1987 D sold all the debentures at par and 1,000 shares for £5,000, when the market value of the remaining shares was £17,000.

RPI	March 1982	313.4
	April 1987	360.7

No claim was made to base indexation on the March 1982 values.

(a) Position up to reorganisation:

	£	£
Value of items received on takeover:		
£3,000 CAC shares @ £2	6,000	
£4,000 Debentures @ 80	3,200	
£4,000 Cash	4,000	
	13,200	

Value of items received as above	13,200	13,200
Cost of Unquoted Ltd. shares	5,000	
6.4.1965 value		8,000
	8,200	5,200
Time apportion 10/15	5,466	
Elect to use 6th April 1965 value - lower gain		5,200

Split the gain over the various items received in CAC plc pro rata to values at reorganisation:

CAC shares $£5,200 \times \frac{6,000}{13,200}$ £2,364

CAC debentures $£5,200 \times \frac{3,200}{13,200}$ £1,260

Cash $£5,200 \times \frac{4,000}{13,200}$ £1,576

The gain of £1,576 attributable to the cash received will be immediately assessed, the remaining gains will be deferred.

(b) Position from reorganisation to disposal:

	Shares	Debentures
	£	£
Disposal proceeds	5,000	4,000
Values at reorganisation:		
Shares $£6,000 \times \frac{5,000}{5,000 + 17,000}$	1,364	
Debentures		3,200
c/f	3,636	800

		£	£
	b/f	3,636	800
Indexation $\frac{360.7 - 313.4}{313.4}$		206	483
		3,430	317
Deferred gains:			
Shares £2,364 x $\frac{5,000}{5,000 + 17,000}$		537	
Debentures			1,260
Chargeable gains		3,967	1,577

24 Wasting Assets

1.0 GENERAL

A wasting asset is one with a predictable useful life of less than 50 years. Land is specifically excluded from the definition.

2.0 TANGIBLE MOVABLE PROPERTY

Where the wasting asset is tangible movable property, there will be no liability to CGT on a disposal. Thus gains will not be assessed nor losses allowed.

An exception to this rule is plant and machinery in respect of which capital allowances have been or could have been given. These will produce a capital gain in the normal way without any wasting away of cost if the disposal proceeds exceed cost unless they would fall under the chattels rules. In the case of disposal at a loss, any capital allowances claimed are to be excluded from the cost of the plant.

3.0 INTANGIBLE PROPERTY

This type of property is liable to CGT and the cost must be depreciated generally speaking to take account of the reduction in cost prior to sale. Assets which fall into this category will include:

(a) Options

(b) Copyrights

(c) Trademarks

(d) Certain patents

(e) Life interests in settled property where the expected life of the life tenant is less than 50 years.

(f) Short leases (treated separately below)

In all cases, apart from certain options, the cost of the asset must be reduced by the fraction:

$$\frac{\text{Remaining life of the asset}}{\text{Original life of the asset}}$$

thus writing off the cost on a strict time basis evenly over the life of the asset. Where the asset has a residual value, this will be deducted from cost before making any calculations. Indexation is always calculated on the reduced cost.

Illustration

D acquired the copyright to a book on 6th April 1971. It had 30 years to run at the date of acquisition and cost £24,000. It was assigned to B on 6th April 1987 for £19,000. No election is made to base the indexation allowance on the 31st March 1982 value.

RPI	March 1982	313.4
	April 1987	360.7

	£
Disposal proceeds	19,000
Cost £24,000 x $\frac{14}{30}$	11,200
	7,800
Indexation $\frac{360.7 - 313.4}{313.4}$ x £11,200	1,691
	6,109

If the copyright had been acquired before 6th April 1965 the gain would have been time apportioned.

Where the asset is an option, the calculations can be divided into two types:

(a) traded options;
(b) other options.

3.1 TRADED OPTIONS

These are options which are quoted on The Stock Exchange or in the London International Financial Futures Exchange or on certain overseas exchanges. They are not treated as wasting assets if the option is abandoned, the cost of the option will constitute an allowable loss. If the option is bought and subsequently sold there will be a chargeable gain or allowable loss according to the rules for quoted shares, etc.

3.2 OTHER OPTIONS

These are normally treated as wasting assets. When an option is granted, the grantor is assessed on the full consideration received. The grantee may add the cost of the option on to the cost of the asset to be aquired but if the option is abandoned there will not be an allowable loss. If the option is acquired and subsequently sold it will be necessary to waste away the cost over the life of the option using only the residual cost in the CGT computation.

4.0 SHORT LEASES

Unlike other assets, a short lease is deemed to waste away on a curved line basis. This will mean that each year is given an actuarial value using the tables contained in CGTA 1979, Sch.3. This is given below:

CGTA 1979, SCH.3
SHORT LEASES PERCENTAGE TABLE

Years	Percentage	Years	Percentage
50 (or more)	100	25	81.100
49	99.657	24	79.622
48	99.289	23	78.055
47	98.902	22	76.399
46	98.490	21	74.635
45	98.059	20	72.770
44	97.595	19	70.791
43	97.107	18	68.697
42	96.593	17	66.470
41	96.041	16	64.116
40	95.457	15	61.617
39	94.842	14	58.971
38	94.189	13	56.167
37	93.497	12	53.191
36	92.761	11	50.038
35	91.981	10	46.695
34	91.156	9	43.154
33	90.280	8	39.399
32	89.354	7	35.414
31	88.371	6	31.195
30	87.330	5	26.722
29	86.226	4	21.983
28	85.053	3	16.959
27	83.816	2	11.629
26	82.496	1	5.983
		0	0

Disposal of a leasehold interest can take two forms:

(a) an assignment,
(b) a granting.

4.1 ASSIGNMENTS

Where a lease is assigned, the vendor disposes of his entire interest in the lease. It is therefore a disposal. As with other wasting assets it will be necessary to reduce cost by the fraction:

$$\frac{\text{Remaining life of the lease on disposal}}{\text{Life of the lease on acquisition}}$$

but before applying it to the cost, it must be converted to the Sch.3 values.

Illustration

B acquired a lease with 35 years to run for £10,000 on 1st May 1977. He sold it for £11,000 on 1st May 1987. No claim is made to base indexation on the March 1982 value.

RPI	March 1982	313.4
	May 1987	366.5

			£
Disposal proceeds			11,000
Cost £10,000 x	$\left[\frac{25}{35}\right.$	$\left.\frac{81.100}{91.981}\right]$	8,817
			2,183
Indexation	$\frac{366.5 - 313.4}{313.4} \times £8,817$		1,490
			693
			=====

If the duration of the lease is not in complete years, the table value can be found as under:

(a) eliminate days by rounding to the nearest month, odd days of 14 or more being rounded up;

(b) add to the table value for the last full year, one twelfth of the difference between that figure and the next higher in the table for each complete month.

Illustration

A lease has a duration of 34 years 7 months and 25 days. The Sch.3 value is:

$$\underset{91.156}{\text{34 years}} + \frac{8}{12}\left[\underset{91.981}{\text{35 years}} - \underset{91.156}{\text{34 years}}\right] \text{ rounding 25 days upwards} = 91.706$$

Where the lease was acquired before 6th April 1965, the gain will be found in the normal way and then time apportioned.

Illustration

C acquired a 40 year lease on 6th April 1963 for £30,000. He assigned it on 6th April 1987 for £26,000. No claim is made to base indexation on the March 1982 value.

RPI	March 1982	313.4
	April 1987	360.7

			£
Disposal proceeds			26,000
Cost £30,000 x	$\left[\frac{16}{40}\right.$	$\left.\frac{64.116}{95.457}\right]$	20,150
			5,850
Indexation	$\frac{360.7 - 313.4}{313.4} \times 20,150$		3,043
			2,807
			======
Time apportion 22/24			2,573
			======

If an election is made under CGTA 1979, Sch.5, para.12 to use 6th April 1965 valuation, the lease will be deemed to have been acquired on that date at its value at that date. This will mean that the duration of the lease will be taken to be the period from 6th April 1965 to the date of expiry of the lease. Thus, if in the above example, the lease had a 6th April 1965 valuation of £29,000, it would have to be reduced on the assumption that it was the "cost" of a lease with a life of 38 years commencing on 6th April 1965 and ending on 5th April 2003.

	£
Disposal proceeds	26,000
6.4.1965 valuation £29,000 x $\left[\frac{16}{38}\right] \frac{64.116}{94.189}$	19,741
	6,259
Indexation $\frac{360.7 - 313.4}{313.4}$ x 19,741	2,981
	3,278

Election is thus not beneficial.

Where there has been improvement expenditure, then each part of the original cost and improvement expenditure must be reduced assuming that it was incurred on the first day of a lease which began on the date that the expenditure was incurred and ended on the date that the main lease expired. The overall gain will then be apporitoned over the various parts on the basis of the reduced costs and time apportioned as appropriate.

Illustration

D acquired a 45 year lease of a property on 6th April 1953 for £20,000. He improved it as under:

Extension	6.4.1963	Cost	£10,000
Extension	6.4.1973	Cost	£8,000

The lease was assigned on 6th April 1987 for £45,000.

RPI	March 1982	313.4
	April 1987	360.7

No claim is made to base indexation on the March 1982 value.

		£	£
Disposal proceeds			45,000
Costs:			
	Original property £20,000 x $\left[\frac{11}{45}\right] \frac{50.038}{98.059}$	10,206	
	Extension 1 £10,000 x $\left[\frac{11}{35}\right] \frac{50.038}{91.981}$	5,440	
	Extension 2 £8,000 x $\left[\frac{11}{25}\right] \frac{50.038}{81.100}$	4,936	
			20,582
			24,418
Indexation $\frac{360.7 - 313.4}{313.4}$			3,108
			21,310

Apportion pro rata to cost and then time apportion:

		£
Original property	$£21,310 \times \frac{10,206}{20,582} \times \frac{22}{34}$	6,837
Extension 1	$£21,310 \times \frac{5,440}{20,582}$	5,163
Extension 2	$£21,310 \times \frac{4,936}{20,582}$	5,111
		17,111

Where the lease is a long lease on disposal it will not be necessary to use the Sch.3 tables and the gain or loss will be calculated as though it were the normal disposal of an asset.

Illustration

E bought a 99 year lease for £50,000 on 1st April 1972. It was assigned on 6th April 1987 for £68,000. The value at 31st March 1982 was £64,000 and a claim was made to use this in the calculation of the indexation allowance.

RPI	March 1982	313.4
	April 1987	360.7

	£
Disposal proceeds	68,000
Cost	50,000
	18,000
Indexation $\frac{360.7 - 313.4}{313.4} \times 64,000$	9,664
Chargeable gain	8,336

If the lease is a long lease on acquisition but a short lease on disposal, the calculation will be as for the disposal of a short lease.

Illustration

F bought a 60 year lease on 1st April 1963 for £20,000 and sold it on 1st April 1987 for £28,000. A claim was made to base the indexation allowance on the March 1982 value of £25,000.

RPI	March 1982	313.4
	April 1987	360.7

Ignore 6.4.1965 value.

	£
Disposal proceeds	28,000
Cost $£20,000 \times \left[\frac{36}{60}\right] \frac{92.761}{100.00}$	18,552
	9,448
Indexation $\frac{360.7 - 313.4}{313.4} \times \left[25,000 \times \left[\frac{36}{41}\right] \frac{92.761}{96,041} \right]$	3,646
	5,802
Time apportion 22/24	5,318

4.2 GRANTINGS

A granting is the creation of a subsidiary interest out of a superior interest, it is therefore a part disposal. There are three types of grantings:

(i) the grant of a short lease out of another short lease;
(ii) the grant of a long lease out of a freehold or another long lease;
(iii) the grant of a short lease out of a freehold or a long lease.

(a) <u>The grant of a short lease out of another short lease</u>
This will normally give rise to two tax liabilities:

(i) a liability to income tax under Schedule A on the grant of the short lease.

(ii) a liability to CGT on the grant of the right

The CGT liability is calculated as under:

Disposal proceeds		x
Cost x $\dfrac{\text{Duration of headlease on grant of sublease} - \text{Duration of headlease at end of sublease}}{\text{Duration of the headlease when originally acquired}}$		x
		x
<u>Less:</u> Indexation		x
Chargeable gain		x
<u>Less:</u> Assessable Premium:		
Premium	x	
Less: 2 $\left\{ \text{Duration of sublease in years} - 1 \right\}$ % thereof	x	x
Balance of gain assessable		x

The assessable premium will be liable in full even if it exceeds the chargeable gain. If it does, then the chargeable gain will be reduced to nil, it will not turn it into a loss.

<u>Illustration</u>
G acquired a 40 year lease on 6th April 1973 for £30,000. On 6th April 1987 he granted a 20 year sublease for a premium of £28,000 and a rent of £1,000 per annum. No election is made to index using the March 1982 value.

RPI		
	March 1982	313.4
	April 1987	360.7

		£
Disposal proceeds		28,000
Cost £30,000 x $\left[\dfrac{26 - 6}{40}\right]$ x $\dfrac{82.496 - 31.195}{95.457}$		16,123
	c/f	11,877

		£
	b/f	11,877
Indexation $\frac{360.7 - 313.4}{313.4}$		2,435
Chargeable gain	£	9,442
Assessable premium:		
Received	28,000	
Less: 2(20 - 1)% x £28,000	10,640	
		17,360
Chargeable gain assessed		Nil

No capital loss

(b) The grant of a long lease out of another long lease or a freehold

As the lease granted is long there will be no Schedule A liability. The gain will be calculated using the normal part disposal formula in which the market value of the remainder will be made up of two elements:

(i) the capital value of the rents to be received measured at the date of granting;

(ii) the value of the reversionary interest.

Illustration

H bought a 125 year lease on 6th April 1960 for £25,000. He granted a 60 year lease to J on 6th April 1987 for £30,000 and a rent of £1,000 per annum. The capital value of the rents was calculated at £17,641 and the value of the reversionary interest was fixed at £22,000. No claim is made to index using the March 1982 value.

RPI	March 1982	313.4
	April 1987	360.7

Ignore 6th April 1965 valuation.

	£
Disposal proceeds	30,000
Cost £25,000 x $\frac{30,000}{30,000 + (17,641 + 22,000)}$	10,770
	19,230
Indexation $\frac{360.7 - 313.4}{313.4}$ x 10.770	1,626
Chargeable gain	17,604
Time apportion 22/27	14,344

(c) The grant of a short lease out of a long lease or a freehold

Again there will be a liability to Schedule A on the premium. The calculation of the chargeable gain will be:

	£
Premium	x
Less: 2[years of duration of lease - 1] % thereof	x
Liable under Schedule A	x
	===
	£
Disposal proceeds	x
Cost x Disposal proceeds / (Total Premium + Capital value of the rents and Value of the reversionary interest)	x
	x
Indexation	x
Chargeable gain	x
	===

Illustration

K acquired a freehold property on 19th June 1975 for £40,000. He granted to L a 21 year lease on 6th April 1987 for a premium of £18,000. The value of the reversionary interest was £16,000 and the capital value of the rents was estimated at £28,000. The value at 31st March 1982 was £50,000 and a claim was made to base indexation on this figure.

RPI	March 1982	313.4
	April 1987	360.7

	£
Premium	18,000
Less: 2(21 - 1)% x £18,000	7,200
	10,800
	======
Disposal proceeds	7,200
Cost £40,000 x $\frac{7,200}{18,000 + (16,000 + 28,000)}$	4,645
	2,555
Indexation	
Value at 31.3.1982 £50,000	
£50,000 x $\frac{7,200}{62,000}$ = 5,806	
£5,806 x $\frac{360.7 - 313.4}{313.4}$	877
Chargeable gain	£1,678
	======

(d) Relief for premiums paid

In all the above examples, the method of acquiring the lease was left open. When a person acquires a lease it may be either by assignment from an earlier owner or by the grant of a new lease or sublease. Where a short lease has been granted then the landlord will be assessed under Schedule A and the grantee will be able to obtain relief for the chargeable amount of the premium paid by deduction from either:

(i) trading profits
(ii) rent received from the grant of a sublease

The method of giving relief is calculated by the following formula:

$$\frac{\text{Chargeable amount assessable on landlord}}{\text{Duration of lease}}$$

The amount of relief given as above will reduce cost on a subsequent disposal.

Illustration

L granted to M a 40 year lease for a premium of £30,000 on 1st January 1981. On 31st December 1987 M assigned the lease to N for £38,000. M was a trader and prepared accounts to 31st December annually. No claim is made to index the value at March 1982.

RPI	March 1982	313.4
	December 1987	368.4

		£	£
Disposal proceeds			38,000
Cost £30,000 x $\left[\frac{33}{40}\right]\frac{90.280}{95.457}$		28,372	
Relief for premium paid to L:	£		
Premium paid	30,000		
Less: 2(40 - 1) % x £30,000	23,400		
	6,600		
Annual relief 6,600/40 = £165 pa			
Relief already obtained £165 x 7		1,155	
			27,217
			10,783
Indexation $\frac{368.4 - 313.4}{313.4}$			4,763
Chargeable gain			£ 6,020

25 Business Problems

1.0 RETIREMENT RELIEF

Where taxpayer aged over 60 has a material disposal of business assets which include:

(a) the whole or part of a business;

(b) shares or securities in a family company (which can either be a trading company or the holding company of a trading group)

then 'retirement' relief may be available. The relief is a maximum of £100,000, provided that the person retiring:

(a) is aged over 60;

(b) has a qualifying period for relief of at least ten years.

It is not necessary to retire to qualify for relief, so long as the person disposing of the asset is aged over 60 he may retain his business interests.

Illustration

O, aged 64 years, retired and sold his business premises for £194,000. The premises had cost him £10,000 in 1968. His chargeable gain (ignoring indexation) will be:

	£
Disposal proceeds	194,000
Less: Cost	10,000
	184,000
Less: Retirement relief	100,000
Chargeable gain	84,000

Where the qualifying period is less than ten years the amount of retirement relief will be proportionately reduced.

Illustration

M, aged 64, retired from his business after eight years. He sold the goodwill for £100,000. It had cost him £10,000 eight years ago. (Ignore indexation)

	£
Disposal proceeds	100,000
Less: Cost	10,000
	90,000
Less: Retirement relief £100,000 x 8/10	80,000
Chargeable gain	10,000

No retirement relief is available unless the qualifying period is at least one year.

Where the taxpayer retires before the age of 60, retirement relief may still be available provided the retirement was due to ill-health. This will be decided by the Inland Revenue subject to appeal to the Special Commissioners.

A qualifying period is one during which the taxpayer was either:

(a) in business; or

(b) owned shares in, and was a full time working director of, a family company.

1.1 DISPOSAL OF A BUSINESS OR AN INTEREST IN A BUSINESS

Relief will be given on the disposal of business assets. For this purpose, these may consist of all or part of a business and an interest in a partnership. The calculation of the relief is as under:

Gains, less losses on chargeable business assets	x
Less: Retirement relief	x
	x

A chargeable business asset is an asset (including goodwill but not including shares, securities or other assets held as investments) which is used for the purpose of a trade, profession or vocation carried on by the individual concerned. For full relief the taxpayer must have traded for a qualifying period of at least 10 years.

Illustration

Y had been trading since 6th April 1940 as a sole trader in a grocery business. On 6th April 1987 he retired, aged 62, and sold his entire business as a going concern to Z. The assets sold were:

	Cost	Date of acquisition	6.4.65 value	Disposal proceeds
	£		£	£
Land and buildings	10,000	6.4.1950	34,000	150,000
Leasehold shop	30,000	6.4.1984 (40 year lease)		45,000
Goodwill	-	-	14,000	60,000
Plant	12,000	6.4.1971		6,000
Debtors				15,000
Stock				32,000
Cash				19,000

In addition, creditors of £14,000 were taken over by Z.

RPI	March 1982	313.4
	April 1984	328.3
	April 1987	360.7

Y elected to claim an indexation allowance based on the values at 31st March 1982. They were agreed with the Inland Revenue at:

	£
Land and buildings	100,000
Goodwill	30,000

<u>Chargeable Business Assets sold</u>	£	£	£
Land and buildings:			
Disposal proceeds	150,000	150,000	
Cost	10,000		
6.4.1965 valuation		34,000	
unindexed gain.	140,000	116,000	
Indexation $\frac{360.7 - 313.4}{313.4} \times 100,000$	15,100	15,100	
	124,900	100,900	
87-65 → 22/37 - 87-50 = 37.	74,265		
No election under Sch.5, para 12.			74,265
Leasehold shop:			
Disposal proceeds		45,000	
Cost £30,000 x $\left[\frac{37}{40}\right]$ $\frac{93.497}{95.457}$		29,384	
		15,616	
Indexation $\frac{360.7 - 328.3}{328.3} \times 29,384$		2,909	
			12,707
Goodwill:			
Disposal proceeds	60,000	60,000	
Cost	-		
6.4.1965 valuation		14,000	
	60,000	46,000	
Indexation $\frac{360.7 - 313.4}{313.4} \times 30,000$	4,530	4,530	
	55,470	41,470	
22/42	29,056		
No election			29,056
			116,028
Less: Retirement relief			100,000
			16,028 + other gains.
Less: annual exemption			x.
			x

The goodwill is deemed to have been acquired for nil consideration and built up over the period of ownership of the business.

1.2 DISPOSAL OF SHARES IN A FAMILY COMPANY

To obtain relief:

(a) the company must be a trading company or the holding company of a trading group; a company will be a trading company if it exists wholly or mainly for the purpose of carrying on a trade;

(b) the taxpayer must be a full-time working director of the company. A full-time working director is one who is required to devote all, or substantially all, of his time to the company in a managerial, supervisory or technical capacity;

(c) the company must be a family company. This is one in which:

  (i) the taxpayer controls at least 25% of the voting power personally, or

  (ii) he controls at least 5% of the voting power personally and more than 50% of the voting power is held by members of the family including him.

Family includes the husband or wife of an individual, and a relative of the individual or of the individual's husband or wife. A relative means brother, sister, ancestor or lineal descendant.

Calculation of the relief:

(1)	Find the gains on the shares disposed of	x (A)
(2)	Find the gain attributable to the chargeable business assets:	
	Gains on shares x Chargeable business assets / Total chargeable assets	x (B)

Chargeable Assets are all the company's assets except those which would not be liable to CGT (i.e. cash, stocks, debts, etc.).

Chargeable Business Assets are all assets, including goodwill, (but not including shares or securities or other assets held as investments), which are used for the purposes of the company's trade and are chargeable assets.

(3)	Deduct Retirement Relief	x
		x
(4)	Assess the remainder of the gain (A - B)	x
		x

For full relief the conditions in (a),(b) and (c) above must all be satisfied for a qualifying period of at least 10 years.

Illustration

X retired on 6th April 1987 and sold all his shares in his family trading company for £50 each. He had acquired his shares as under:

16.12.1936	1,000 shares cost	£1,000
6.4.1960	1,000 shares cost	£2,000
6.4.1976	1,000 shares cost	£3,000

The balance sheet of the company at 6th April 1987 was:

	£		£
Share Capital 10,000 shares of £1	10,000	Freehold property	80,000
Profit and Loss account	200,000	Goodwill	20,000
		Plant and machinery	15,000
	210,000	Motor cars	8,000
Creditors	12,000	Stock	12,000
		Debtors	30,000
		Investments	40,000
		Cash	17,000
	222,000		222,000
	=======		=======

It was agreed that all the assets were valued at proper market values apart from the freehold property which was worth £100,000.

X was aged 61 years at the date of his retirement.

RPI	March 1982	313.4
	April 1987	360.7

Ignore an election under CGTA 1979,Sch.5,para.12. The values at 31st March 1982 are not used for indexation.

Gains on shares:	£	£
Disposal proceeds	50,000	
Cost 6.4.1976	3,000	
	47,000	
Indexation $\frac{360.7 - 313.4}{313.4}$ @ 3000.	453	46,547
Disposal proceeds	50,000	
Cost 6.4.1960	2,000	
	48,000	
Indexation $\frac{360.7 - 313.3}{313.4}$ @ 2000.	302	
	47,698	
	======	
22/27		38,865
Disposal proceeds	50,000	
Cost 16.12.36	1,000	
	49,000	
Indexation $\frac{360.7 - 313.4}{313.4} \times 1000$.	151	
	48,849	
	======	
22/42		25,587
		110,999
		======

Attributable to Chargeable Business Assets:

& Market Values.

	£
$£110,999 \times \dfrac{100,000 + 20,000 + 15,000}{100,000 + 20,000 + 15,000 + 40,000}$	85,627
Less: Retirement relief	100,000
	NIL
Remainder of gain (110,999 - 85,627)	25,372
	25,372
Less: annual exemption	x
	x

Where an individual has been involved in two or more businesses, then provided that the relevant conditions are fulfilled, the qualifying periods may be aggregated in order to determine the amount of retirement relief due, provided that any gap between them does not exceed 2 years.

Retirement relief is also available in certain circumstances on disposals by trustees and by directors or employees of assets held for the purposes of his office or employment.

2.0 TRANSFER OF A BUSINESS TO A LIMITED COMPANY

On the transfer of the business of a sole trader or a partnership to a limited company there will often be a transfer of business assets (e.g. land, building and goodwill) which is a chargeable event for CGT purposes.

Relief is given for this gain provided that:

(a) the business is transferred as a going concern together with all its assets, or all assets other than cash;

(b) the business is transferred wholly or partly for shares issued by the company to the transferor;

(c) the transferor is not a company.

If the transfer is for shares only, the total gain is deferred until the shares are finally sold. This gain is brought into charge at the date of sale by reducing the cost of shares by the amount of the gain.

The calculation of the deferral will be:

(1)	Find gains on assets transferred	x
(2)	Defer the amount of the gain, found by the fraction:	
	$\text{Gains on assets} \times \dfrac{\text{Value of shares}}{\text{Value of total consideration}}$	x
	Assess	x

Illustration

Assume the facts of Y above except that instead of retiring, Y transferred his entire business to Y Ltd for a consideration of:

£50,000 cash
150,000 £1 Ordinary Shares fully paid

	£
Gain on assets transferred	116,028
Deferred 263,000 / 313,000 (313K less 50K cash)	97,493
Immediate Assessment	18,535

Note: The value of the assets transferred is the total value of assets less the creditors.

The deferred gain will be deducted from the value of the shares:

	£
Value of shares 150K Nominal Sh	263,000
Less: Gain deferred	97,493
Revised cost	165,507

Base value of shares.

3.0 ROLL-OVER RELIEF

If a taxpayer disposes of a business asset and replaces it within the period commencing one year before the date of the disposal and ending three years after that date, he is permitted to deduct the chargeable gain made on the disposal from the cost of the replacement asset thereby postponing the chargeable gain until a subsequent disposal. This procedure can be repeated for as long as one business asset is replaced with another asset provided the assets are within the following categories:

(a) Land and buildings. Furnished holiday lettings under FA 1984,s.50 are also eligible for roll-over relief where the new asset is disposed of after 5th April 1982.

(b) Fixed plant.

(c) Ships.

(d) Aircraft.

(e) Goodwill.

(f) Hovercraft.

The first asset does not have to be replaced by a similar asset. Thus a ship can be sold and the gain rolled-over against the purchase of, say, goodwill.

The first asset and the replacement asset must be used for the purposes of the taxpayer's trade. If the taxpayer, either successively or at the same time, carries on two or more trades, those trades are treated as a single trade for the purposes of this relief.

Illustration

Charles Wilson sold his freehold factory (which cost £30,000 in 1968) for £40,000 on 1st June 1979 and invested the whole amount in the freehold of a similar factory which he acquired on 1st January 1980. He sold the factory for £48,000 on 1st December 1985 and did not reinvest the proceeds. The capital gains tax position, assuming roll-over relief is claimed, will be:

On disposal of factory 1

	£
Sale proceeds	40,000
Less: Cost	30,000
Chargeable gain	10,000

As the proceeds of sale were fully reinvested within three years of disposal by purchasing an eligible asset, the chargeable gain may be rolled-over and deducted from the cost of the new asset so that the gain on the disposal of that asset will be correspondingly increased, thus, assuming RPI for December 1985 to be 341.3, and that indexation is not based on the value of the asset at March 1982, the position will be:

	£
Cost of factory 2	40,000
Gain rolled-over	10,000
Revised cost for CGT purposes	30,000
Disposal proceeds factory 2	48,000
Cost	30,000
	18,000
Indexation $\frac{341.3 - 313.4}{313.4}$ £30,000.	2,670
Chargeable gain	15,330

Where the taxpayer does not reinvest all the disposal proceeds, there will be an immediate liability to CGT on the non-reinvested gain equal to the proceeds not reinvested. The balance of the gain may then be rolled-over. Thus, if in the above illustration, factory 2 cost £37,000 instead of £40,000 the position would be:

	£	£
Immediate assessment:		
Disposal proceeds		40,000
Less: Cost of factory 2		37,000
		3,000
Disposal proceeds factory 2		48,000
Cost	37,000	
Less: Balance of gain rolled-over	7,000	
		30,000
		18,000
Indexation		2,670
Chargeable gain		15,330

If the asset was acquired before 6th April 1965 then part of any gain will not be assessed because of theoperation of the time apportionment rules. When this occurs then any immediate assessment on the non-reinvested gain will be restricted by the formula:

Gain not reinvested x $\frac{\text{Chargeable Gain}}{\text{Total Gain}}$

Illustration

Y bought a freehold factory on 6th April 1958 for £20,000 and sold it on 6th April 1984 for £80,000. On December 1st 1986 he spent £70,000 of the proceeds in acquiring a new factory. RPI April 1984 - 350.6.

	£
Disposal proceeds	80,000
Cost	20,000
	60,000
Indexation $\frac{350.6 - 313.4}{313.4}$	2,380
	57,620
Time apportionment 19/26	42,106

The gain not reinvested is £80,000 - £70,000 = £10,000.

The immediate assessment will be:

£10,000 x $\frac{42,106}{57,620}$ = £ 7,307

The CGT cost of factory 2 will be:

	£
Cost	70,000
Less: Gain rolled-over £(42,106 - 7,307)	34,799
	35,201

Where an election is made under CGTA 1979, Sch.5, para 12 to use 6th April 1965 valuation, the above restriction will not be applied to the proceeds not reinvested, which will be charged in full. Thus, if in the above illustration 6th April 1965 valuation was £45,000, the position would be:

	£
Disposal proceeds	80,000
6.4.1965 valuation	45,000
	35,000
Indexation $\frac{350.6 - 313.4}{313.4}$	5,355
	29,645

Gain not reinvested, and therefore assessed £10,000.

The balance of the gain available for roll-over will be £19,645.

Where part of the asset is not used for trading purposes, then the gain attributable to that part will not qualify for roll-over relief.

Illustration

A bought a freehold factory on 1st January 1983 for £200,000. He used 90% of it in his manufacturing business and sublet the remainder. He sold it on 6th April 1987 for £400,000 and immediately reinvested £350,000 in another freehold factory.

RPI	January 1983	326.3
	April 1987	360.7

	£	£
Sale of Factory 1:		
Disposal proceeds	400,000	
Cost	200,000	
	200,000	
Indexation $\frac{360.7 - 326.3}{326.3}$	21,000	
	179,000	
Analysis of gain:		
Available for roll-over 90%	161,100	
Immediately assessed 10%	17,900	17,900
	179,000	
Assessment of proceeds not reinvested:		
Proceeds	400,000	
Less: 10%	40,000	
	360,000	
Reinvested	(350,000)	10,000
Immediate assessment		27,900
Cost of second factory	350,000	
Less: Gain rolled-over	151,100	
Revised CGT cost	198,900	

Capital allowances (if appropriate) will be available on the full purchase cost less non-qualifying expenditure.

Where the replacement asset is a depreciating asset, the rolled-over gain is not deducted from the cost of the replacement asset since this cost is depreciated and it would therefore effectively mean that the postponed gain is depreciated. The charge to CGT on the gain deferred is postponed until the earliest of the following events:

(a) the passing of ten years from the date of acquisition of the replacement asset;

(b) the sale of the replacement asset;

(c) the cessation of trade, or the cessation of the use of the asset in the trade.

The postponed gain will be deemed to arise during the year of assessment (or accounting period) in which the earliest of these events takes place and the capital gains tax will be calculated according to the rates ruling in that year of assessment etc.

A depreciating asset is one with a predictable life of less than 50 years or one which will have a life of less than 50 years at any time within ten years of acquisition. Instead of roll-over the term hold over is applied to this situation.

Illustration

Z bought a freehold factory in June 1983 for £30,000. He sold it on 19th June 1987 for £40,000 and immediately reinvested £36,000 in ~~fixed~~ plant. This was sold on 6th April 1999 for £70,000.

depreciating asset.

RPI	June 1983	326.3
	June 1987	370.1
	April 1999	600.0

	£	£
1987/88		
Sale of factory:		
Disposal proceeds		40,000
Cost		30,000
		10,000
Indexation $\frac{370.1 - 326.3}{326.3}$		4,020
		5,980
← if you don't re-invest all of the proceeds.		
Immediate assessment on: 40,000 - 36,000		4,000
Cost of plant		36,000
Gain held over 10 yrs from Acq date of replacement asset. (5980 - 4000)	1,980	
1997/98		
Held over gain assessed at expiration of 10 years from acquisition	1,980	
1999/2000		
Disposal proceeds of plant		70,000
Cost. June 87		36,000.
		34,000
Indexation $\frac{600.0 - 370.1}{370.1}$		22,356
Chargeable gain		11,644 + 1980.

Where, within the hold-over period, the taxpayer acquires a non-depreciating asset he may elect to substitute the hold-over claim for a roll-over claim against the cost of the non-depreciating asset. This will have the effect of converting a temporary deferral into one which is semi-permanent. To obtain full relief the cost of the non-depreciating asset should be at least equal to the disposal proceeds of the first asset. If this is not so, then only part of the held-over gain can be converted.

4.0 RELIEF IN RESPECT OF LOANS TO TRADERS

Where a loan has been made to a trader after 11th April 1978, and that loan later becomes irrecoverable, then any loss will be treated as an allowable loss for CGT purposes. To obtain relief, the loan must be a qualifying loan which is one where:

(a) the money lent is used by the borrower for the purpose of carrying on a trade other than the trade of moneylending;

(b) the borrower is UK resident;

(c) the debt is not a debt on security.

The Revenue must be satisfied that the debt is irrecoverable.

Relief will be obtained in the fiscal year or accounting period in which the claim for relief is made. It is, however, possible to backdate the claim for up to two years provided that at that time the debt was irrecoverable.

If the debt is recovered either wholly or partly, there will be a chargeable gain equal to the amount recovered which will be assessed in the year of recovery.

The relief also applies to payments made under a guarantee.

5.0 PARTNERSHIPS AND CAPITAL GAINS

Dealings in partnership assets are treated as those of the individual partners and not those of the firm. The CGT liability will be assessed on the partners individually. The treatment of partnership gains is set out in a Revenue press release of January 1975, as amended by other statements of practice.

5.1 NATURE OF THE ASSET LIABLE TO TAX

As far as the partnership assets are concerned, each partner is treated as owning a fractional share of each asset. Where it is necessary to find the value of a partner's share in an asset for CGT purposes, it will be taken as a fraction of the value of the total partnership interest in the asset with no discount for the size of the share. When a new partner joins the partnership, he will be treated as acquiring a share in the partnership assets from the other partners.

Illustration

A was a sole trader. On commencement of trade in 1969 he acquired goodwill for £20,000. In 1982 he took B into partnership at which time the goodwill was valued at £30,000. The partnership business was sold in 1987, goodwill realising £50,000.

The agreement between A and B provided that profits and losses were to be shared equally. Ignore indexation.

In 1982, A will be treated as having sold one-half of the goodwill to B.

	£
Disposal proceeds	
$\frac{1}{2}$ x £30,000	15,000
Cost - $\frac{1}{2}$ x £20,000	10,000
Chargeable gain	5,000

In 1987, each partner will be treated as having sold his share of the goodwill:

	A	B
Disposal proceeds	25,000	25,000
Cost	10,000	15,000
Chargeable gain	15,000	10,000

To give a liability to CGT, there must normally be a disposal. A mere revaluation of assets with a credit to the partners' capital accounts in profit sharing ratio will not constitute a disposal. Where, on the admission of a partner, there is no revaluation of assets, then there will not normally be any liability to CGT as the incoming partner will only be paying the other partners an amount equal to their share of the cost of the asset.

Thus, if in the above illustration, the goodwill was not revalued on the admission of B, the position would be:

On admission of B:	£
Disposal proceeds	
½ x £20,000	10,000
Cost - ½ x £20,000	10,000
	-

On sale of the goodwill:	A	B
Disposal proceeds	25,000	25,000
Cost	10,000	10,000
Chargeable gain	15,000	15,000

A liability to CGT will also arise when there is a change in partnership profit sharing ratios including changes arising from a partner joining or leaving the partnership. In these circumstances, a partner who reduces or gives up his share in asset surpluses will be treated as disposing of part of the whole of his share in each of the partnership assets and a partner who increases his share will be treated as making a corresponding acquisition. The normal disposal consideration will be a fraction of the current balance sheet value of each chargeable asset. Where no upward revaluation is made of the asset values, there will only be an adjustment to the original cost of the asset.

Illustration

A, B and C have been in partnership for many years sharing profits in the ratio 3:2:1. As from April 6th 1987 they decide to share profits equally. All the assets of the partnership are properly valued apart from the freehold premises which cost £50,000 and which are presently worth £110,000. It has been decided not to make an upward revaluation.

	A	B	C
Current profit sharing ratio	50%	33 1/3%	16 2/3%
New ratio	33 1/3%	33 1/3%	33 1/3%
Increase/(decrease)	(16 2/3)	-	16 2/3

Chargeable gain - A		£
Disposal proceeds	16 2/3% x £50,000	8,333
Cost	16 2/3% x £50,000	8,333
		Nil

Adjustments to cost:	A	B	C
	£	£	£
Original	25,000	16,667	8,333
Disposal	(8,333)		
Acquisition			8,333
	16,667	16,667	16,666

If the revaluation were made:

Chargeable gain - A		
Disposal proceeds	16 2/3% x £110,000	18,333
Cost	16 2/3% x £ 50,000	8,333
Chargeable gain		10,000

Adjustments to cost:	A	B	C
	£	£	£
Original	25,000	16,667	8,333
Disposal	(8,333)		
Acquisition			18,333
	16,667	16,667	26,666

Where an asset is disposed of by the partnership to a third party each of the partners will be treated as disposing of his fractional share of the asset. Similarly, if a partnership makes a part disposal of an asset, each partner will be treated as making a part disposal of his fractional share. In finding gains and losses, disposal proceeds will be allocated between the partners in the ratio of their shares in asset surpluses at the time of the disposal. Expenditure on the acquisition of assets by the partnership will be allocated between the partners in the same way at the time of acquisition. This allocation may require adjustment, as above, if there has been a subsequent change in the partnership sharing ratios.

Illustration

D, E and F have been in partnership for many years sharing profits 5:4:3 throughout. In 1974 the firm acquired a freehold office block for £210,000 and sold it on 6th April 1987 for £480,000. The value at March 1982 was £400,000 and a claim is made to base indexation on this figure.

RPI	March 1982	313.4
	April 1987	360.7

	D (5)	E (4)	F (3)
	£	£	£
Disposal proceeds	200,000	160,000	120,000
Cost	87,500	70,000	52,500
	112,500	90,000	67,500
Indexation $\frac{360.7 - 313.4}{313.4} \times 400{,}000$	25,167	20,133	15,100
	87,333	69,867	52,400

Illustration

G, H and J are in partnership sharing profits 3:2:1. In 1970 the firm acquired a property for £30,000 and sold it on 6th April 1987 for £90,000. In 1978 J had been admitted as a partner in place of I who had retired. The profit sharing ratio as between G, H and I was maintained on the admission of J. J paid £10,000 to I in 1978 for his share of the property. (Ignore indexation).

	G	H	I	J
1970	£	£	£	£
Cost of property	15,000	10,000	5,000	
1978				
Disposal proceeds/cost to J			10,000	10,000
Chargeable gain				
			5,000	
1987				
Disposal proceeds	45,000	30,000		15,000
Chargeable gain	30,000	20,000		5,000

6.0 COMPANIES

6.1 GENERAL

Where a company disposes of a capital asset, the same rules of computation apply as for an individual in determining the amount of the chargeable gain or allowable loss. Reliefs specifically applying to individuals (e.g. the £6,300 annual exemption) are ignored.

Instead of CGT, a company pays corporation tax on the chargeable gain as reduced by a fraction. This fraction is one-third, one-quarter and one-seventh for the financial years 1984, 1985 and 1986 respectively.

Illustration

A Ltd. disposes of an asset in the year to 31st March 1987 realising a capital gain of £70,000. The amount brought into charge to corporation tax is:

	£
Capital gain	70,000
Less: £70,000 x 1/7	10,000
	60,000

The tax payable on the gain is £60,000 x 35% = £21,000. This amount is the same as tax at a rate of 30% on the chargeable gain.

Chargeable gains, after deducting allowable (capital) losses of the current period and any unrelieved capital losses brought forward, and after reduction by the specified fraction, form part of the total profits of the company subject to corporation tax. As such, chargeable gains may be used to relieve a trading loss where claims under TA 1970,ss.177(2),(3a),258 are made. Capital losses may not be offset against trading profits.

6.2 GROUPS AND CAPITAL GAINS

(a) Definition. A group is one consisting of a principal company and all its 75% subsidiaries. If a subsidiary has its own 75% subsidiary, then the latter company will also be a member of the group. Thus, if the following arises:

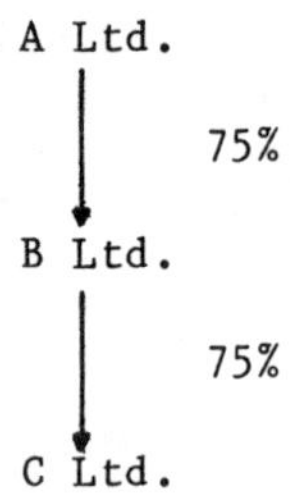

all the companies will be within a group. Holdings are still relevant if held through a non-resident company. Within a group, assets will be transferred at such a price as will give neither gain nor loss. This will normally be the cost plus any indexation allowance. For the calculation of any subsequent allowances, the date of acquisition of the transferor will be deemed to be that of the transferee. Thus a capital gain will normally only arise where the asset is disposed of outside the group. Where the holding company owns less than 75% of the ordinary share capital of the subsidiary, any transfer of an asset is deemed to be at market value.

Where an election is made to base indexation on the value of an asset at 31st March 1982, the acquiring company will base future indexation calculations on original cost plus indexation calculated on the March 1982 value.

(b) Companies leaving the group. Where a group member leaves the group, and within the six years prior to leaving has acquired an asset from another group member at original cost, then the company leaving will be deemed to have made a chargeable gain equal to the difference between the cost and market value of the asset at the date of the original transfer. Not the date on which the company left the group.

Illustration

A Ltd. acquired a building for £50,000 in 1970. In 1981 it was transferred to B Ltd., another group company, when its market value was £90,000. In 1984 B Ltd. was sold to another group and in April 1988 it sold the building for £130,000.

RPI	March 1982	313.4
	April 1988	397.5

Liabilities:

1981 A Ltd. No effect; transferred at original cost.

1984	B Ltd.	At the time of leaving the group a gain equal to the difference between the original cost and its value at the date of transfer to B Ltd. is deemed to be made and treated as a gain of 1979.

	£
Market value	90,000
Cost to A Ltd.	50,000
	40,000

1988 B Ltd.

Disposal proceeds	130,000
Deemed acquisition cost	90,000
	40,000
Indexation $\frac{397.5 - 313.4}{313.4}$	24,120
	15,880

(c) Depreciatory Transactions. Where the value of a subsidiary's share is materially reduced as a result of a depreciatory transaction, any capital loss arising on the subsequent disposal of the subsidiary's shares may be reduced. A depreciatory transaction can include:

(i) intragroup disposals of assets at less than market value;

(ii) any other intragroup transaction.

<u>Illustration</u>

C Ltd. acquired 100% of the share capital of D Ltd. for £100,000. The major asset of D Ltd. was a freehold property which cost £20,000. After acquisition, D Ltd. transferred the property to C Ltd. at cost, when its market value was £75,000. One year later C Ltd. sold the shares of D Ltd. for £30,000. Ignore indexation.

The transfer of the property to C Ltd. is a depreciatory transaction to the extent of:

	£
Value at transfer	75,000
Consideration	20,000
	55,000

The loss on the disposal of the shares in D Ltd. will be restricted by this amount:

	£
Disposal proceeds	30,000
Cost	100,000
	(70,000)
Less deducted as above	55,000
Allowable loss	15,000

As the amount of the loss on disposal of D Ltd.'s shares has been reduced by £55,000, it follows that double taxation could occur if on disposal of the property by C Ltd. the cost was taken as £20,000. To avoid this, an equivalent deduction is made in calculating any chargeable gain of C Ltd.

(d) Group Roll-Over. It is possible to roll-over gains on the disposal of qualifying assets by one group company against the cost of assets acquired by another.

Illustration

D Ltd. and E Ltd. are members of a group of companies. D Ltd. disposes of a factory for £100,000 on 1st July 1985, realising a gain of £20,000. E Ltd. acquires a light aircraft on 30th September 1987 for £95,000.

(i) the replacement asset has been acquired within the 3-year period commencing 1st July 1985, so that hold-over relief is available;

(ii) not all the proceeds of disposal have been reinvested, so only a portion of the gain may be held-over:

£95,000 - (£100,000 - £20,000) = £15,000

The balance of D Ltd.'s gain, £5,000, is chargeable in D Ltd.'s accounting period which includes 1st July 1985;

(iii) the asset acquired by E Ltd. is a wasting asset, and thus the held-over gain of £15,000 will crystallise on the earliest of:

1 the cessation of E Ltd.'s trade;

2 the disposal of the aircraft;

3 ten years from acquisition of the aircraft, i.e. 30th September 1997.

(e) Trading Stock. When an asset is transferred by one group company to another which appropriates it as trading stock, the asset passes at cost and then the acquiring company is treated as appropriating it into stock at market value. The gain or loss may be either:

(i) assessed or relieved in the normal way; or

(ii) be deducted from the 'cost' of the stock in the case of a gain, or added to 'cost' in the case of a loss. Thus, effectively, the assets are being taken into stock at their original cost plus indexation allowance to the transferor company.

(f) Group Relief for Capital Losses. There is no group relief for capital losses. Thus it is important to match gains and losses by either holding assets within one company or transferring assets to one company before they are sold.

(g) Non-Resident Companies. A company not resident in the UK is not within the charge to corporation tax unless it is carrying on a trade in the UK through a branch or agency. In such a case it will be liable to corporation tax on chargeable gains on the disposal in the UK of assets used in the trade.

(h) Close Companies. Where there is an apportionment of relevant income which has resulted in a liability to higher rate taxes or investment income surcharge, the tax thus paid will be allowable as a deduction in finding the gain on a subsequent disposal of shares.

Illustration

B acquired 30% of the shares in Alpha Ltd., a close company on 6th April 1983 for £21,000. On 6th April 1987 he sold them for £30,000. In 1984 there was an apportionment of relevant income on B of £4,000 gross of notional ACT, on which B was chargeable at 75%. The profits subject to the apportionment have not subsequently been distributed.

RPI	April 1983	329.7
	April 1987	360.7

	£	£
Disposal proceeds		30,000
Cost	21,000	
Tax at higher rates and investment income surcharge on apportionment £4,000 x (75% - 30%)	1,800	
		22,800
		7,200
Indexation $\frac{360.7 - 329.7}{329.7}$ x £21,000		1,974
		5,226

If a close company transfers an asset to any person at a value less than its market value and the person receiving the asset is not liable either under Schedule E or on a qualifying distribution, i.e. as an employee or as a share-holder, then the amount of the undervalue will be apportioned amongst the participators and will reduce the cost of their shares for CGT purposes.

Thus, if Alpha Ltd. had previously transferred a property worth £25,000 to the friend of one of the shareholders for £15,000 then the amount of the undervalue of £10,000 would be apportioned between the participators and B would have to deduct from the cost of his shares 30% x £10,000 - £3,000 so reducing his cost down to £18,000.

7.0 RELIEF FOR LOSSES ON SHARES IN UNQUOTED TRADING COMPANIES

FA 1980,s.37 provides that where a person subscribes for shares in an unquoted trading company and makes a capital loss on disposal it is possible to offset that loss against income.

The loss is calculated as for CGT purposes and may be offset against any income in the fiscal year in which disposal takes place and/or the next fiscal year.

The order of offset is as for s.168; however, s.37 takes priority over s.168.

A qualifying trading company is an unquoted company which:

(a) is a trading company at disposal or which ceased to be such a company not more than three years before the disposal;

(b) is resident in the UK;

(c) has traded for at least six years prior to the date of disposal, subject to certain conditions.

Companies which do not trade on a commercial basis or which trade in stocks and shares, land or commodity or financial futures are not eligible for relief. The disposal must be at arm's length or by way of distribution in a winding-up or by a deemed disposal under CGTA 1979,s.22.

If the subscriber for shares is an investment company, then it may offset the loss against the other income in the same way as a loss under s.177(2).

If relief cannot be claimed under s.37, then normal CGT relief is available.

Where there are several acquisitions of shares of the same class some by subscription and some by purchase for s.37 purposes any disposal is identified on a LIFO basis.

Illustration

X acquired shares in Alpha Ltd. an unquoted trading company as under:

15.6.1980	1000 shares purchased for	£3,000
15.10.1982	2000 shares subscribed for at £4 each	£8,000
19.12.1984	1500 shares purchased for	£3,700

On 6th April 1987 2,500 shares were sold for £3,000.

RPI	March 1982	313.4
	October 1982	320.1
	December 1984	340.9
	April 1985	350.6
	April 1987	360.7

For CGT purposes the disposal is identified in the normal way, in this case with the post 5.4.1982 pool.

		Shares	Unindexed cost	Indexed cost
		£	£	£
15.10.1982	Subscription	2,000	8,000	8,000
	Indexation to April 1985 $\frac{350.6 - 320.1}{320.1}$			762
19.12.1984	Purchase	1,500	3,700	3,700
	Indexation to April 1985 $\frac{350.6 - 340.9}{340.9}$			105
		3,500	11,700	12,567
	Indexation to April 1987 $\frac{360.7 - 350.6}{350.6}$			362
				12,929
6.4.1987	Sale	(2,500)	(8,357)	(9,235)
		1,000	3,343	3,694

Disposal proceeds	3,000
Cost and indexation	9,235
Capital loss	(6,235)

For s.37 purposes the disposal is identified on a LIFO basis:

(1) with 1,500 shares purchased in 1984

(2) with 1,000 shares subscribed for in 1982.

On the latter the loss would be:

		£
Cost		4,000
Indexation to April 1985	$\frac{350.6 - 320.1}{320.1}$	381
		4,381
Indexation to April 1987	$\frac{360.7 - 350.6}{350.6}$	126
		4,507
Disposal proceeds 1,000/2,500 x £3,000		1,200
Available for s.37 relief		3,307
		=====

The remainder of the loss of £6,235 - £3,307 qualifies for capital loss relief.	£2,928
	=====

26 Miscellaneous Matters

1.0 COMPENSATION AND INSURANCE PROCEEDS

Where an asset is destroyed, this will be a disposal for CGT purposes. Where compensation is received, then a gain or loss must be calculated in the normal way. Where, however, the whole of the compensation is applied within twelve months of receipt, or such longer period as the Revenue may direct, towards the acquisition of a replacement asset then any gain may be deducted from the cost of the replacement asset.

Illustration

A bought a piece of jewellery on 1st April 1975 for £20,000. It was stolen and on 6th April 1987 insurance compensation of £28,000 was received. This was used to acquire a replacement piece on 1st June 1987 which cost £34,000. No claim was made to base the indexation allowance on the value at March 1982.

RPI	March 1982	313.4
	April 1987	350.6

	£
Compensation received (deemed disposal proceeds.)	28,000
Cost	20,000
	8,000
Indexation $\frac{360.7 - 313.4}{313.4}$	3,020
Chargeable gain	4,980
Cost of replacement asset	34,000
Less: gain deferred	4,980
Revised cost (Base cost of asset)	29,020

Where the asset has been damaged and compensation is received which is wholly applied towards restoration of the asset, then there will be no assessment of any gain.

Illustration

B bought a painting for £8,000. It was later damaged by fire and compensation of

£2,500 received. The cost of restoration was £3,000.

	£
Original cost	8,000
Cost of restoration	3,000
	11,000
Less: Compensation	2,500
Revised cost	8,500

Where compensation is received, but not all of it is spent on restoration, there will be a part disposal computation. If the amount not spent is small then it will be deducted from cost, and 6th April 1965 value if appropriate, thus deferring any gain. 'Small' in this context means less than 5% of the compensation received.

Illustration

C bought a Chippendale commode for £18,000 in 1970. It was damaged and compensation of £8,000 was received. The amount spent on restoration was:

(a) £7,700

(b) £6,000

The value of the commode after restoration was £23,000. (Ignore indexation)

	(a) £	(b) £
Compensation received	8,000	8,000
Amount spent	7,700	6,000
	300	2,000

5% of compensation = £400

Thus in (a) , the amount not spent is small. It is less than 5% of the compensation. The position will be:

	(a) £
Cost	18,000
Spent on restoration	7,700
	25,700
Compensation received	8,000
Revised cost	17,700

In the case of (b) however the amount not spent is substantial and there will be a part disposal computation.

	£
Amount not spent	2,000
Cost £18,000 x $\frac{2,000}{2,000 + 23,000}$	1,440
Chargeable gain	560

The cost to be used in any future computation will be:

	£
Cost	18,000
Less: used in part disposal	1,440
	16,560
Spent on restoration	6,000
	22,560
Less: Compensation received	6,000
(£8000 less amount subject to part disposal).	
	16,560 ← revised base cost.

2.0 RELIEF FOR GIFTS FA 1980,s.79

A gift is deemed to be made at market value for CGT purposes and this may result in a liability to tax on the donor. Where, however, both donor and donee are individuals and the donee is resident or ordinarily resident in the UK, then relief may be claimed. The relief is given by allowing the chargeable gain arising on the disposal to the donee to be deducted from the donee's cost for CGT purposes. This will defer possible assessment of the gain until a future disposal by the donee.

Illustration

A bought a ring on 1st January 1970 for £10,000. He gave it to B on 6th April 1984 when its market value was £25,000. Ignore 31st March 1982 valuation.

RPI	March 1982	313.4
	April 1984	329.3

		£
Market value on disposal		25,000
Cost		10,000
		15,000
Indexation $\frac{329.3 - 313.4}{313.4}$		510
Chargeable gain	s.79 deferral	14,490

The cost to B would be:

		£
Market value on acquisition		25,000
Less: A's gain deferred	s.79.	14,490
		10,510 base cost.

This will be the cost used on a subsequent disposal. Indexation will be available from the date of the gift. Thus if B sold the ring on 6th April 1987 for £40,000, the position would be:

RPI	April 1987	360.7

	£
Disposal proceeds	40,000
Cost	10,510

	£
	29,490
Indexation $\frac{360.7 - 329.3}{329.3} \times £10,510$	998
Chargeable gain	28,492

The gain that may be deferred will be the final chargeable gain, i.e. after applying time apportionment and after deducting retirement relief etc.

Illustration

C retired on 6th April 1987 as a full-time working director in a qualifying trading company. He was aged 63 and had satisfied all the conditions for a full amount of retirement relief. On retirement he gave his shares to his son D. The cost of the shares on 6th April 1960 was £10,000 and the market value on 6th April 1987 was £200,000. (Ignore 6th April 1965 valuation) The value of the shares at 31st March 1982 was £150,000.

RPI	March 1982	313.4
	April 1987	360.7

	£
MV of shares	200,000
Cost	10,000
	190,000
Indexation $\frac{360.7 - 313.4}{313.4} \times £150,000$	22,650
	167,350
Time apportionment 22/27	136,359
Less: Retirement relief	100,000
Chargeable gain	36,359
Cost to D:	
MV of shares	200,000
Less: gain deferred	36,359
	163,641

Where any part of the gain is realised, there will be an immediate liability to CGT on that amount and only the balance of the gain may be deferred. Thus, if in the above illustration of A's gift to B, A had instead sold the ring to B for £14,000 the position would be:

	£
Chargeable gain as before	14,490
Amount realised:	
Disposal proceeds	14,000
Cost	10,000
Immediate assessment	4,000

The balance of the gain may be deferred.
The cost to B would be:

	£
Market value of ring at date of acquisition	25,000
Less: Gain deferred £(14,490 - 4,000)	10,490
	14,510

If the sale at an undervalue is of an asset in respect of which retirement relief has been claimed then there will only be an assessment if the realised gain exceeds the retirement relief given. Thus, if in the illustration of C and D above, C had, instead of giving the shares to D, sold them to him for:

(a) £ 90,000

(b) £145,000

the position would be:

	(a) £	(b) £
Disposal proceeds	90,000	145,000
Cost	10,000	10,000
Realised gain	80,000	135,000
Less: Retirement relief	100,000	100,000
Immediate assessment	NIL	35,000
Original gain	36,359	36,359
Assessed as above	NIL	35,000
Available for deferral	36,359	1,359

Where there was also a CTT liability in respect of the gift, then the donee's cost on a subsequent disposal will be increased by the amount of the CTT paid (whether by transferor or transferee). The addition of the CTT can result in a smaller gain but cannot turn a gain into an allowable loss.

Illustration

E gave to F a property on 6th April 1984 when its value was £50,000. It had cost £12,000 on 6th April 1962. The CTT paid on the transfer was:

(a) £50,000

(b) £90,000

F sold the asset on 6th April 1987 for £80,000.

RPI	March 1982	313.4
	April 1984	360.7
	April 1987	381.4

(Ignore 6th April 1965 valuation)

	£
MV of property at date of gift	50,000
Cost	12,000
	38,000

Indexation $\frac{360.7 - 313.4}{313.4}$	1,812	
	36,188	
Time apportion 19/22	31,253	

Cost to F:

	£
Market value	50,000
Less: Gain deferred	31,253
	18,747

On the sale by F:

		(a)		(b)
	£	£	£	£
Disposal proceeds		80,000		80,000
Cost	18,747		18,747	
Indexation $\frac{381.4 - 360.7}{360.7}$	1,069		1,069	
	19,816		19,816	
CTT paid on gift	50,000		90,000	
		69,816		109,816
Chargeable gain		10,184		NIL

Deferral is also available when an individual transfers assets into a settlement, and also when assets are transferred out of a settlement by the trustees to the beneficiary. In all cases, a joint election is required except for transfers into a settlement.

Where deferment has been claimed and the donee ceases to be resident or ordinarily resident within six years of the claim for relief, there will be a clawback of the relief given immediately before the donee ceases to be resident or ordinarily resident in the UK.

A similar form of relief is available for gifts or sales at an undervalue of business assets by an individual to any person (e.g. a company) resident or ordinarily resident in the UK. (CGTA 1979,s.126)

To qualify, the gift must be:

(a) an asset used in the trade or profession of the transferor or of his family company;

(b) shares or securities of a trading company which is the transferor's family company.

Family company is defined in the same way as for retirement relief.

The calculations are made in the same way as for s.79 relief except that no adjustment will be made for any CTT paid.

3.0 TRUSTEES

Where assets are transferred into a settlement there will be a disposal at market value by the settlor. It is possible to defer the gain if relief is claimed under FA 1980,s.79. If the trustees dispose of trust assets in the normal course of administration then they will be liable to CGT in the normal way but gains of only £3,150 will normally be exempt. Where assets are transferred out of the settlement to a beneficiary, then, again provided that joint election is made under s.79, any gains on the transfer of the assets at market value may be deferred, by deduction from the cost to the beneficiary.

Where after 5th April 1982, the life tenant of the settlement dies the assets will pass to the trustees at market value. There will be no liability to CGT unless s.79 relief had previously been claimed on the transfer of the assets into the settlement; if it had previously been claimed it will crystallise on death. The assets will normally pass to the beneficiaries at the value at which they pass to the trustees.

4.0 FOREIGN CURRENCY DEPOSIT ACCOUNTS

With effect from 6th April 1983, a foreign bank account belonging to a non-UK domiciled person is treated as located outside the UK. Gains on withdrawals (after 5th April 1983) are therefore exempt if the cash remains abroad, but losses are not allowable.

5.0 HUSBAND AND WIFE

Transfers between husband and wife living together are treated as being made at such a value as gives no gain and no loss.

Where an asset originally acquired before 31st March 1982 is transferred after that date, the acquiring spouse may elect to calculate the gain or loss (on a disposal to a third party) by reference to the original cost and to base the indexation allowance on the 31st March 1982 market value. In other cases, the acquiring spouse's gain or loss, and indexation allowance, will be based upon the original cost plus indexation allowance up to the month of the transfer.

The acquiring spouse will be treated as having acquired the asset for time apportionment purposes at the original date of acquisition of the other spouse. Indexation is available to the acquiring spouse from the date of the transfer.

Where the spouse acquiring the asset appropriates it as trading stock, the transfer will be treated as being made at market value and any subsequent gain on disposal will be liable under Schedule D Case I or II.

The gains and losses of each spouse will be aggregated and the combined amount will be liable to CGT. There is only one annual exemption available to a married couple and this will be apportioned between them pro rata to their respective net gains.

Illustration

Mr. and Mrs. A have the following gains and losses for 1986/87.

		Mr.A	Mrs.A
	£	£	£
Gains		5,600	3,900
Losses		600	400
Mr. A			
Gains	5,600		
Less: Losses	600		
		5,000	
Mrs.A			
Gains	3,900		
Less: Losses	400		
			3,500
Annual exemption £6,300 dividend 5,000:3,500		3,706	2,594
		1,294	906
Tax @ 30%		388.20	271.80

In the year of marriage, the spouses are treated as though they were separate individuals in the same way as for income tax.

In the year of separation, husband and wife are treated as one person up to the date of separation. After separation, the wife will be treated as a separate taxable person. Up to the date of separation, the annual exemption will be apportioned between husband and wife in proportion to the husband's total gains in the fiscal year and the wife's gains up to the date of separation. After separation, the wife will be treated as a separate taxable person with her own annual exemption.

6.0 DISPOSALS TO CONNECTED PERSONS

Where a disposal is made to a connected person which is not on an arm's length basis, then the market value of the asset will be substituted for the consideration (if any).

Connected persons are broadly speaking:

(a) a person's spouse or relative (brother, sister, lineal ancestor or descendant) or a relative of the spouse, separated spouses are connected, divorced spouses are not;

(b) the trustees of a settlement set up by the person;

(c) persons in partnership with that person;

(d) a company controlled by that person or that person and other persons connected with him or her.

If the disposal to the connected person at market value results in a loss, that loss may only be offset against future gains on other disposals to the <u>same</u> connected person.

When assets which form part of a set are disposed of within a 6 year period to a connected person, then the value of the assets transferred will be the greater of:

(a) a proportion of the market value of the total of the assets transferred in the series (taken at the end of the series);

(b) the value of each asset if taken together they exceed the value in (a).

Subject to certain transitional provisions, these new rules cover transactions made after 19th March 1985.

Illustration

X purchased a set of two candelabra on 1st July 1983 for £22,000. He sold one candelabra to his son on 6th April 1986 for £18,000 which was agreed to be its market value. The value of the other was agreed to be £15,000. He sold the other to his son on 6th April 1987 for £17,000 which was again agreed to be its market value. The value of the set to the son at 6th April 1987 was agreed to be £45,000.

RPI	July 1983	329.7
	April 1986	350.6
	April 1987	360.7

First disposal:

	£
Disposal proceeds	18,000
Cost £22,000 x $\frac{18,000}{18,000 + 15,000}$	12,000
	6,000
Indexation $\frac{350.6 - 329.7}{329.7}$ x £12,000	756
	5,244

Second disposal:

	£
Disposal proceeds	17,000
Cost (£22,000 - £12,000)	10,000
	7,000
Indexation $\frac{360.7 - 329.7}{329.7}$ x £10,000	940
	6,060

However, as the total value to the son is £45,000 at 6th April 1987 and this exceeds £35,000 (£16,000 + £17,000) the Inland Revenue will require the gains to be recalculated using total disposal proceeds of £45,000. These will be split on a just and reasonable basis.

First disposal - gain recalculated:

	£
Deemed disposal proceeds - say	22,500
Cost £22,000 x $\frac{22,500}{22,500 + 15,000}$	13,200
	9,300
Indexation $\frac{350.6 - 329.7}{329.7}$	832
	8,468

Second disposal - gain recalculated:

	£
Deemed disposal proceeds	22,500
Cost £22,000 - £13,200	8,800
	13,700
Indexation $\frac{360.7 - 329.7}{329.7}$	827
	12,873

27 Introduction

1.0 GENERAL PRINCIPLES

Value Added Tax (VAT) is chargeable on the supply of goods or services in the UK where that supply is a taxable supply made by a taxable person in the course or furtherance of any business carried on by such a taxable person. In addition, tax is chargeable on the importation of goods and some services.

The basic principle of VAT is fairly simple - a supplier of chargeable goods or services adds VAT at 15% to the price he charges to customers and pays the total tax added over to the Commissioners of Customs and Excise (CCE) quarterly. This VAT is known as output tax. In making the payment to CCE, the supplier is entitled to deduct the VAT he has suffered on chargeable goods and services supplied to him. This VAT is known as input tax. Thus each quarter the supplier is paying to CCE his output tax minus his input tax.

As chargeable goods move from manufacturer to wholesaler to retailer to ultimate consumer, each trader in the chain pays input tax when he buys and charges output tax when he sells. The ultimate consumer pays the tax when he buys and has no one to pass the tax on to, and so finally bears the burden of the tax.

Illustration

A Ltd. manufacturers a sewing machine and sells it to:

B Ltd., a wholesaler, for £100 plus 15% VAT	=	£115
B Ltd. sells it to C Ltd. for £140 plus 15% VAT	=	£161
C Ltd. sells it to D, the final consumer for £200 plus 15% VAT	=	£230

The effect on each of them is shown in the following table:

Transaction	Input Tax	Output Tax	Paid to CCE	Ultimate effect
	£	£	£	
A Ltd. sale to B Ltd.				
A Ltd.		15	15	A Ltd. - nil
B Ltd.	15			
B Ltd. sale to C Ltd.				
B Ltd.		21	6	B Ltd. - nil
C Ltd.	21			
C Ltd. sale to D				
C Ltd.		30	9	C Ltd. - nil
D	30			D suffers the £30

It can be seen that A Ltd. collects £15 from B Ltd. and pays it over to CCE (no effect on A). B Ltd. suffers that £15 but collects £21 from C Ltd., and pays the difference of £6 to CCE (no effect on B). C Ltd. suffers the £21 but collects £30 from D, and pays the difference of £9 to CCE. D suffers the £30 and stays suffering.

2.0 SOURCES OF THE LAW AND ITS INTERPRETATION

VAT was introduced by FA 1972 and came into force on 1st January 1973. Since that time the tax has been amended and the legislation has been consolidated in the Value Added Tax Act 1983 (VATA 1983), although further amendments have been enacted by subsequent Finance Acts.

All statutory references are to the VATA 1983, unless otherwise stated.

VAT is administered by HM Customs and Excise.

Unlike other taxes, many detailed rules have been subordinated to Orders, Rules and Regulations in the form of Statutory Instruments.

In addition, the Acts and the Regulations frequently provide for the Customs and Excise to be provided with a discretion **(J.H. Corbitt (Numismatist) Ltd. v. CCE)** in their implementation.

An indication of the likely attitude of the Customs and Excise can be obtained from the various notices and leaflets published by them and obtainable from their offices.

With certain exceptions (e.g. Notice 727 (Special schemes for retailers)), these notices have no legal effect and should not be relied on when considering the application of the law to specific transactions.

It must also be borne in mind that in certain cases EEC law may prevail where there is a conflict between that and UK law.

28 Registration

1.0 INTRODUCTION

A person who is or who ought to be registered as a taxable person and taxable supplies made by that person carry with them the obligation to charge and account for VAT. Unless registration is actually effected VAT cannot be charged so that the VAT to be accounted for is determined by treating the consideration for the supplies as inclusive of VAT.

It is therefore advisable that the regulations regarding the requirements for registration are considered carefully.

Where the supplies are zero-rated the Customs and Excise have discretion to exempt the person from having to register.

A person's liability to register dates from the time that he should have registered rather than the time he actually does register.

2.0 REGISTRATION LIMITS

A person is liable to register for VAT if his taxable turnover exceeds certain limits specified in Schedule I. These are, if the turnover (exclusive of VAT) exceeds:

(a) £7,000 for the last calendar quarter; or

(b) £20,500 for the last four calendar quarters.

A person is also required to register if there are reasonable grounds for believing that the taxable turnover for the next twelve months will exceed £20,500. Exempt supplies (see later) do not count towards the limit.

A person includes a self employed individual, limited company, partnership, club etc., who carries on a business activity, profession or vocation.

It is the person who is to be registered and not the business (**CCE v. Glassborrow**), accordingly it is the aggregate supplies of all businesses carried on by a person that is considered for registration purposes, restriction on input tax credit due to exempt supplies, etc.

It is not possible to transfer registration from one person to another, although when a business is transferred to a limited company, it is possible to transfer the same registration from the business to the limited company.

Partnership registration is in the name of the partnership.

A person liable to register must obtain form VAT I and submit it to the CCE no later than 10 days after the end of the relevant quarter. Registration will then be effective from the 21st day of the next quarter or from such other date as is agreed with the CCE. Advance registration is allowed provided that the person can satisfy the CCE that his future turnover will exceed the registration limits.

3.0 VOLUNTARY REGISTRATION (Sch.I,para 11)

Registration may be effected voluntarily at the discretion of HM Customs and Excise even though the turnover limits have not been exceeded. This will be desirable where, for example, the customers are all registered persons able to reclaim the VAT charged on any supplies. Inability to register in such circumstances would mean that the actual cost to customers may be increased as the supplier's costs will include VAT for which no relief is available.

Voluntary registration, once granted will normally be effective for at least 2 years.

4.0 GROUP REGISTRATION

Companies resident in the UK who are members of a group may elect to be treated for VAT purposes as a single person. The registration need not cover all of the companies in the group and provides opportunities for tax planning. The principal advantages relate to reduction of administration, possible avoidance of restrictions on input, tax credit due to the making of exempt supplies and in cash flow.

The representative member is responsible for maintaining records, making returns, etc., but the responsibility for the tax due is a joint and several liability.

The application for group registration must be made at least 90 days before the date on which it is to have effect although the Customs and Excise do have discretionary power to accept a late claim.

Registration takes effect from the beginning of the prescribed accounting period and any changes in the group must be notified within 21 days of the change.

A claim for group treatment means that:

(a) Intra group supplies of goods or services can be disregarded;

(b) any other supply of goods or services to or from a group member is deemed to be made to or from the representative member only and that this member is also liable for any tax payable on the importation of goods.

Companies will be within a group where the holding company controls more than one half of its ordinary share capital.

5.0 DEREGISTRATION

A person may deregister for VAT on either of the following grounds:

(a) that the expected total of taxable supplies in the next 12 month period will not exceed £19,500.

(b) that for the two years period ended with the date of the last quarter, the turnover in both years has not exceeded £20,500 in each of those years and that it is unlikely to do so in the next year.

A person who ceases to make taxable supplies must notify CCE within 10 days and the CCE will deregister him. Application for deregistration is not compulsory and a taxpayer may retain his registration if he wishes.

On deregistration VAT is due on any retained stocks of goods for resale and equipment. This must be accounted for on the last VAT return. VAT is due on all sales up to deregistration in the normal way. Normally no VAT is due on goods in respect of which no VAT has been reclaimed. VAT due on deregistration is remitted if it is £250 or less.

6.0 CHANGES IN REGISTRATION

The following changes in registration particulars must be notified to the local VAT office within 21 days:

(a) changes in the trading name of the business and any changes in names and addresses of any partners in the business;

(b) changes in the address of the principal place of business;

(c) changes in trade classification;

(d) changes in bank accounts.

29 Output Tax

1.0 GENERAL

Tax chargeable on supplies is known as Output Tax. There are currently two rates of tax - the standard rate of 15% and the zero rate.

2.0 SUPPLY

Supplies of goods or services made in the UK are liable to tax. The UK comprises England, Wales, Scotland, Northern Ireland and the territorial sea of the UK.

As from 1st April 1980 the Isle of Man and the UK form a single VAT area although the Isle of Man provides for its own collection and administration.

The term includes:

(a) sales, whether made directly or by an agent, on hire purchase, auction, cash or credit sale;

(b) hiring, leasing, rental loan or exchange of goods;

(c) goods provided as gifts or as promotional items

and as far as services are concerned any service provided for money or money's worth.

Certain events are or may be deemed to be supplies:

(a) Self supplies: where a person acquires or produces goods or does anything for the purpose of that business which would be a supply of services if made for a consideration - those goods or services are deemed to have been both supplied to and by him. Orders have been made in respect of printed material and cars;

(b) The private use or disposal of assets is deemed to be a supply of services or goods respectively;

Certain supplies are not considered to be supplies for VAT purposes:

(a) the sale of certain repossessed goods;

(b) transactions within a VAT group of companies;

(c) goods lost or destroyed (this does not cover the situation where cash is stolen as the supply will already have occurred).

The recission of a voidable contract **(HB Litherland & Co. v. CCE)** annuls the supply. However, the disposal of stolen goods **(CCE v. Oliver)**, or sale subject to reservation of title **(Vermitron v. CCE)**, are considered to be supplies.

3.0 THE TIME OF THE SUPPLY - TAX POINT

The obligation to account for VAT on a supply is determined by the prescribed accounting period in which the tax point falls.

For VAT purposes the time when a supply of goods or services takes place can have far-reaching effects not only because it may determine whether a person is liable to register himself, but also because it helps to dictate the amount of VAT he must pay in a particular period. The time at which a supply of goods or services is deemed to take place is known as the 'tax point', i.e. the point at which VAT becomes chargeable.

There are special rules governing the time of supply. Subject to certain alternative rules (which are described below), the supply of goods will be treated as taking place:

(a) if the goods are removed at the time of the removal;

(b) if the goods are not removed at the time when they are made available to the person to whom they are supplied.

A supply of services will be treated as taking place when the services are performed.

The 'basic tax point' above will be overridden in the following circumstances:

(a) if before the time of supply mentioned above, the person making the supply issues a tax invoice in respect of it, the supply will, to the extent covered by the invoice, be treated as taking place when the invoice was issued;

(b) if before the time of supply mentioned above, the supplier receives a payment, the supply will, to the extent covered by the payment, be treated as taking place at the time the payment is received;

(c) if the supplier issues a tax invoice within a period of fourteen days following
the date otherwise applicable in (a) and (b) above, the supply will be treated as taking place at the time the invoice is issued. Customs and Excise can extend the fourteen day period (e.g. monthly invoicing).

Where goods are supplied on hire, it is provided generally that the supply will be treated as having taken place when a payment under the agreement is received.

4.0 VALUE OF SUPPLY

Where no mention of VAT is made the consideration is deemed to be VAT inclusive. In particular where:

(a) Consideration is in the form of money: the value of the supply is that amount which together with VAT thereon at the appropriate rate (governed by the rate applicable at the tax point), amounts to the consideration.

(b) Consideration is not or not wholly in money: the value is taken as its market value.

Where discounts are offered, the consideration is taken to be the amount reduced by the available discount whether or not, in fact, it is taken. If discount is available at varying rates the lowest discounted value is to be taken:

Illustration

A supplies goods to B at a price of £5,000 + VAT. A discount is available of 5% for payment within 30 days. Whether or not the discount is taken, the VAT due is:

	£
Price	5,000
Less: 5% discount	250
	4,750
VAT @ 15%	712
Consideration	5,462

5.0 SPECIAL TYPES OF OUTPUTS

5.1 MOTOR CARS

Where a motor car has been used in a business no VAT is due on a disposal where the disposal proceeds are less than the purchase price. Where they exceed the purchase price VAT is due in respect of the margin which is regarded as being VAT inclusive.

Illustration

B acquired a motor car for use in his trade as a manufacturer. The cost in 1980 was £8,000 and because of a demand for that particular model it was resold in 1987 for £11,200. VAT is due on the margin as under:

£11,200 - £8,000 = £3,200 x 3/23 = £417

5.2 GIFTS

A gift of business assets is a supply of goods and VAT is due on the cost of those goods. No VAT will normally be due where the gift is:

(a) of goods costing less than £10 not forming part of a series of gifts to the same person;

(b) free meals to employees.

Gifts to charities are normally exempt. The provision of trade samples would not normally be considered to be a gift and thus would not normally be liable to VAT. Prizes of goods are treated as gifts.

Gifts of services are not liable to VAT.

5.3 PRIVATE USE

Where the proprietor of the business or an employee takes goods out of the business for personal use there is a supply and VAT will be due on the cost of those goods.

5.4 LOSS, THEFT ETC.

No VAT is chargeable where the trader can satisfy CCE that goods which belong to him have been accidentally lost or destroyed. Where goods have been sold and the cash stolen VAT will still be due.

Where goods are stolen or obtained by fraud, the trader may be able to claim relief provided that:

(a) the theft is reported to the police, and

(b) a conviction is obtained.

5.5 SALARIES AND WAGES

These are not liable to VAT.

5.6 SALES ON HIRE PURCHASE

These are supplies of goods and tax is due in the normal way. The hire purchase finance charge is exempt. Where goods are repossessed because of the default of the purchaser this is not treated as a supply of goods. A sale of repossessed goods by the person who repossessed them is generally a supply of goods and VAT will be due unless:

(a) the goods are covered by one of the secondhand schemes eg. cars, antiques, caravans etc., and

(b) the goods are sold by the repossessor in substantially the same condition as when they were acquired.

If these conditions are satisfied then the disposal will be outside the charge to VAT.

6.0 LOCAL AND NATIONAL AUTHORITIES

Goods and services supplied to a national or local authority are liable to VAT in the normal way. Where such an authority provides goods or services liable to VAT then the tax must be charged and a VAT invoice provided in the normal way.

7.0 EXPORTS

Exports are zero rated, and thus no VAT will be chargeable. The exporter will need to satisfy CCE that export has occurred. This can be done by producing when required:

(a) the customer's order;

(b) the exporter's copy invoice;

(c) copies of the airfreight documents or bill of loading for sea freight etc.;

(d) evidence of payment by the customer.

Exports on sale or return or transfers of goods by a UK trader to a place of business abroad are not taxable supplies.

A retail export scheme is available for overseas visitors who purchase goods in the UK and who intend to leave the UK within 3 months of purchasing the goods and who have not been in the UK for more than 365 days out of the two years preceding the purchase of the goods. Certain goods are not eligible including motor cars, motor cycles and motor caravans; to qualify for zero rating these must be exported direct. To qualify, the visitor must be asked to provide evidence that he qualifies for zero rating - normally by producing his passport. Once the supplier is satisfied he will charge VAT in the normal way but provide the visitor with VAT form 407 describing with registration or identification marks the goods purchased. When the visitor leaves the UK, he will produce the form and goods to customs at the port of embarkation who will certify it. The form will then be returned to the supplier who will refund the VAT charged.

8.0 RELIEF FOR BAD DEBTS

Relief for bad debts can be claimed if the customer has been made bankrupt or entered into a scheme of arrangement.

The goods and services supplied must not have been supplied for more than market value, and the supplier must have accounted for the output tax.

In making the calculation:

(i) specific payments on account are allocated to the invoices to which they relate;

(ii) general payments on account are allocated to earlier debts rather than to later debts;

(iii) amounts due to the customer are set off against amounts due from him.

Illustration

An individual has made standard and zero rated supplies to XYZ Ltd. XYZ Ltd. has recently gone into liquidation and will be unable to pay its creditors.

Invoices have been issued as follows:

Tax Point	Net £	VAT Rate	Gross £
17th April 1986	25,000	nil	25,000
11th May 1986	12,234	15%	14,069
19th August 1986	18,197	15%	20,926
7th November 1986	11,500	nil	11,500

XYZ Ltd. has made a payment of £3,000 on account of the invoice dated 19th August 1986, and general payments on account of £17,000 and £9,600. On a separate contract, the individual owes XYZ Ltd. £1,056.

	Total Debt £	Specific Allocation £	General Allocation £	Amount Unpaid £	VAT Rate	VAT Repayment Claim £
17.4.86	25,000		25,000	-	Nil	
11.5.86	14,069		2,656	11,413	15/115	1,489
19.8.86	20,926	3,000	-	17,926	15/115	2,338
7.11.86	11,500			11,500	Nil	
	71,495	3,000	27,656	40,839		3,827

	£
Amount received	17,000
Amount received	9,600
Set-off	1,056
	27,656

	£
Claim from Customs & Excise	3,827
Claim from liquidator	37,012
	40,839

Note: It is not possible to reduce the amount of outstanding debt by the issue of credit notes.

Where a dividend is subsequently received there are no provisions to claw back any of the VAT recovered.

In the case of an overseas bad debt then the VAT charged cannot be recovered.

30 Input Tax

1.0 INTRODUCTION

Input tax is the tax on the supply to a taxable person, of goods or services and on the importation of any goods used or to be used for the purposes of any business carried on or to be carried on by him.

Relief is granted to taxable persons for input tax, primarily by set off against VAT to be accounted for on supplies made.

Where the input tax exceeds the output tax in any prescribed accounting period the excess is refunded to the taxable person.

Although it is any taxable person who is entitled to relief, not just registered persons, claims by non-registered persons are likely, in practice, to be met with resistance.

Section 23, however, provides for relief to be granted to a person carrying on a business in the EEC but not in the UK whereas s.21 provides for relief to do-it-yourself house-building ventures.

VAT on non-business goods or services received will not be recoverable. This will include items acquired for private use or supplied to the trader for the use of another person. Where there is partial private use CCE will restrict the recovery of input tax.

Illustration

C incurs repairs on a building used partly for his residence and partly for business. The agreed ratio is 40:60. The repair bill is £1,000 + VAT.

The recoverable VAT will be

1,000 x 15% = £150 x 60% = £90
===

2.0 IRRECOVERABLE INPUT TAX

Certain input tax suffered is irrecoverable whether or not the expense relates to the business; it includes:

(a) Business entertaining:
VAT suffered on entertaining is always disallowed unless it relates to:

(i) overseas customers, or potential customers;

(ii) staff.

An overseas customer is one who is not ordinarily resident in the UK and who is not carrying on a business in the UK. A deduction can also be obtained for entertaining an agent who is himself not ordinarily resident of a customer as above.

VAT on subsistence costs incurred by the employer's staff is deductible.

(b) Motor Cars:
Tax on private cars, but not on vans, lorries, London taxis etc., cannot be recovered. If the vehicle is a private car then no recovery is permissible even if the vehicle is wholly used for business purposes. VAT on repairs and maintenance can be reclaimed in full even if the car is used partly for private motoring.

VAT may be recovered on petrol relating to business journeys. Where employees are reimbursed for petrol costs then input tax may be reclaimed where mileage allowances are paid to employees using a car for business purposes then the employer can recover as input tax 3/23 of the mileage allowance provided:

(i) detailed records are kept of business mileage, type, model and cc of the car, rate of allowance paid etc.;

(ii) the allowance paid must relate closely to the cost of the petrol, where it does not the allowance will have to be apportioned before applying the 3/23 fraction.

As from 6th April 1987, traders can recover all the input tax on petrol irrespective of business or private use. Instead the petrol used by the proprietor or employee will be deemed to be a supply to him and VAT will be due. For 1987/88 the deemed value of the supplies of fuel will be:

	Value of supply		VAT Due	
cc of vehicle	Quarterly	Monthly	Quarterly	Monthly
	£	£	£	£
Up to 1400 cc	120	40	15.65	5.21
1401 - 2000 cc	150	50	19.56	6.52
2001 cc and over	225	75	29.34	9.78

Where business mileage exceeds 4500 per quarter or 1500 per month the value is reduced by one half.

Where VAT cannot be recovered it will increase the revenue or capital cost which may then be treated as a trade expense or qualify for capital allowances as appropriate.

3. IMPORTS

VAT on importation is chargeable and payable as if it were a customs duty. Prior to 1st October 1984 a registered taxable person could adopt a postponed accounting system whereby the VAT is shown on the return in which that VAT is claimed - it is treated as both an output and an input. Effectively therefore, VAT was not paid until the goods were sold, when VAT on the full consideration was accounted for. Since 1st October 1984, VAT must be paid on imports and the postponed accounting system has been abolished.

A number of reliefs are available:

(a) where goods would otherwise be zero rated (s.16);

(b) where Customs and Excise legislation in respect of Customs duties is extended by s.24;

(c) by Treasury Orders and Regulations (in respect of goods used for demonstration, personal goods of small value imported from the Isle of Man or the EEC).

After 31st May 1985, provided ownership is not transferred to the processor, taxable persons need not pay VAT on importation in respect of

(a) goods temporarily imported for repair or renovations and re-exported with the same identity (i.e. goods restored to their original condition); and

(b) goods temporarily imported for modifications or processing and re-exported with the same identity. The relief will not apply to materials for manufacture into other goods or goods imported only for warehousing, or minor handling such as re-packing.

Also from 1st June 1985, goods which have been temporarily exported and are re-imported after repair, process or adaptation will bear VAT only on the value of the repair etc., plus freight and insurance, provided the goods are re-imported by, or on behalf of, the original exporter and property in the goods has not been transferred.

31 Exemption and zero rating

1.0 EXEMPTION

Certain supplies are either exempt or zero rated.

If a trader's supplies are totally exempt then he is not liable to register for VAT irrespective of the size of his turnover. As he is not registered however he will not be able to reclaim input tax. The main categories of exempt supplies are:

(a) Land - the grant, assignment or sale of land or of an interest in land is exempt. This will not cover the provision of accommodation in a hotel etc., holiday accommodation, car parking fees etc.;

(b) Insurance;

(c) Postal services provided by the Post Office;

(d) Betting, gaming and lotteries;

(e) Finance charges;

(f) Education provided by schools, universities and other non-profit making bodies;

(g) The provision of health care by a registered medical practitioner or in certain hospitals etc. The provision of certain goods and appliances;

(h) Burial and Cremation, the funeral of a pet is not exempt;

(i) Subscription to professional bodies, learned societies, trades unions and trade associations.

(j) Certain disposals of heritage property where not CTT or CGT is chargeable

2.0 PARTIAL EXEMPTION

Where a person makes both taxable - normal or zero rate - and exempt supplies then he may not be able to recover all the input tax suffered. The normal calculation for finding the deductible input tax is:

$$\frac{\text{tax exclusive value of all taxable supplies}}{\text{total tax exclusive value of all supplies}} \times 100$$

Illustration
X Ltd has the following:

Value of standard rated supplies	400,000
Value of zero rated supplies	300,000
Value of exempt supplies	300,000
Purchases - all standard rated	300,000

(all figures are VAT exclusive).

The recoverable input tax is (300,000 x 15%) = £45,000
=======

$$\left[\frac{400,000 + 300,000}{400,000 + 300,000 + 300,000}\right] = 70\% \times 45,000 = £31,500$$
=======

At the end of each tax year the annual percentage will be calculated and annual adjustments made. A tax year will end on 31st March, 30th April or 31st May depending on the date to which the VAT returns are made up.

Where a taxable person makes both exempt and taxable supplies, his supplies will all be deemed to be taxable (and thus he will be able to recover all his input tax) where the value of the exempt supplies is less than:

(a) £200 per month on average, or

(b) both £8,000 per month on average and one half of the value of all supplies;

(c) both £16,000 per month on average and one quarter of the value of all supplies; or

(d) 1% of the value of all supplies.

3.0 ZERO RATING

A person making zero rated supplies is a taxable person if his turnover exceeds the registration limits and will be liable to register despite the fact that no VAT is chargeable on his outputs. This will be advantageous to him because he can now recover VAT on inputs.

The major zero rated supplies are:

(a) Food and Drink - This is zero rated if it is provided for human consumption unless it is supplied in the course of catering, for consumption on the premises where the supply was made or is hot take away food. Sweets, crisps, alcoholic and many non-alcoholic soft drinks are standard rated. Animal feeding stuffs, but not pet food, is zero rated;

(b) The provision of water and sewerage services;

(c) Books, newspapers, maps, music etc.;

(d) Talking books and wireless sets, and recording apparatus for the blind;

(e) Fuel and power other than petrol;

(f) The sale of land and the construction of new buildings other than professional fees, hire of goods etc. Repairs are generally standard rated unless they relate to a protected building;

(g) Passenger transport in a ship, vehicle or airplane designed to carry 12 or more persons. Commercial freight services outside the UK or transport to or from a place outside the UK;

(h) Mobile caravans and houseboats;

(i) Gold and bank notes;

(j) Drugs, medicines and certain supplies made to a sick or disabled person;

(k) Certain imports and exports;

(l) Certain supplies to charities;

(m) Clothing and footwear for young children and certain protective clothing;

(n) Certain commodity transactions on a terminal market.

32 Special schemes for retailers

1.0

Normally a taxable person has to account for VAT each time he supplies goods or services to a customer. This is called output tax. To account for output tax in the normal VAT way, the taxable person needs to have a record of every separate transaction. Most retailers cannot keep a record of that kind for all their sales, because they do not usually issue invoices to their customers or make any written record at the time when a sale takes place. The special schemes for retailers allows retailers to calculate output tax (or most of it) in other ways, which vary according to the particular scheme.

A retailer for this purpose can include anybody whose business consists mainly of supplying goods or services direct to the public without tax invoices.

There are nine different schemes for retailers to choose from. Some of them are suitable only for certain types of business and some have conditions or limits in them which mean that not every retailer is allowed to use them.

Details of three common schemes are:

SCHEME A

This scheme calculates output tax on supplies of goods or services which are all subject to the same rate of tax. For this scheme it is necessary to keep a record of daily gross takings for those supplies, as well as the record of inputs and the VAT account.

Calculation of the output tax:

Total of daily gross takings for the tax period	£ =======
Scheme output tax - daily gross takings multiplied by VAT fraction	
$\frac{15}{115}$ for 15% rate	£ =======

SCHEME B

This is a scheme for calculating output tax on supplies of goods at no more than two different rates of tax (zero counting as a separate rate). It is a condition of the scheme that the takings for goods sold at the lower of the two rates must not amount to more than half of the other takings. It must be possible to record the total

VAT-inclusive amounts realisable from selling those goods subject to the lower of the two rates. This amount is then subtracted from gross takings and the remainder is then assumed to be the value of the supplies of goods at the other rate.

Calculation of the output tax:

Gross takings total for the tax period		£_______
The amounts, including VAT, expected to be realised (after allowing for losses, goods sold by wholesale, special offers, etc.) for goods at the lower rate of VAT	Subtract	£_______
Estimated higher rate takings total		£_______
Estimated higher rate takings total x VAT fraction = Output tax at higher rate		£_______

If the lower rate is the zero rate there is no VAT fraction to apply. If the lower rate is not zero but another rate, multiply the estimated value of the lower rate supplies by the appropriate VAT fraction, like this:

Estimated lower rate takings total x VAT fraction = Output tax at lower rate	£_______

SCHEME C

This scheme is intended for the very small retailer of goods, whose total taxable turnover for the whole of his business in a year does not exceed £50,000, and who sells goods at two or more rates of tax (zero counting as a separate rate). It is limited to businesses whose trade-classification, shown on their certificate of registration, is from 8201 to 8239. To use this scheme, a record must be kept of the VAT inclusive prices which have to be paid to suppliers for the goods bought for re-sale. A separate column is needed for each of the tax rates. At the end of the tax period, the columns must be totalled and a fixed mark-up added to the total of each positive rate column. Output tax is then calculated by applying the correct VAT fraction to each result. The fixed mark-up will depend upon the kind of business, e.g. whether a grocer, a florist etc.

Calculations of the output tax:

Total cost, including VAT of all goods received for retailing in the tax period at:

	The Standard rate £	Positive rate "a" £	Positive rate "b" £
VAT-inclusive amounts			
Add the amount of your fixed mark-up for your trade classification	_______	_______	_______
Total assumed retail value	_______	_______	_______

To arrive at the Scheme C output tax for each rate of tax, multiply each of the total assumed retail values by its own VAT fraction, like this:

Total assumed retail value at the standard rate	x	VAT fraction for the standard rate	=	£ ====	Output tax
Total assumed retail value at positive rate "a"	x	VAT fraction for positive rate "a"	=	£ ====	Output tax
Total assumed retail value at positive rate "b"	x	VAT fraction for positive rate "b"	=	£ ====	Output tax

33 Administration

1.0

The Board of Commissioners - a Chairman, two Deputy Chairmen and Commissioners - are responsible for the management, administration and collection of VAT.

The local VAT offices are in direct contact with taxable persons. Control visits are made every two to three years, usually by prior appointment.

The VAT (General) Regulations make provisions obliging taxable persons to notify the Customs and Excise of changes in their circumstances. Customs and Excise are empowered to request any information they may require about any goods and supplies of goods or services such as the consideration or the name and address of the recipient of the supply.

Samples may be taken (Sch.7), books and documents may be removed and Customs and Excise are empowered to require security before a supply can be made where, for example, they have reason to believe that VAT will not be accounted for.

Customs and Excise are empowered to exchange information with the Revenue.

In extreme cases the Customs and Excise have the power of entry and search (Sch.7, para.10) and to distrain goods and chattels where tax has not been paid after it had been demanded by the Collector.

2.0 RETURNS

At regular intervals a taxable person must render accounts of input and output tax and return them to the Revenue on Form VAT 100. This will show the net amount of VAT payable by or repayable to him. The period for which a return is made is known as the tax period and the standard period is three months. Where, however, a taxable person expects his input tax to regularly exceed his output tax, he may have a tax period of one month. In order to spread the flow of returns evenly over the year, the three-month return periods are staggered. Where the net tax payable is £1 or more, the full amount must be paid at the same time that the return is made. Similarly, when the net tax repayable is £1 or more the Customs and Excise will make a refund of the amount due. If the tax due or repayable is under £1 then a return must still be made, but the payment or repayment is waived. If a registered person fails to make a return when it is due, or if he makes an incomplete return the Customs and Excise have power to make estimated assessments. These will be made under Schedule 7, in the following circumstances.

(a) the absence of proper information;

(b) failure to make returns;

(c) failure to keep proper records;

(d) where it appears to the Customs and Excise that a submitted return is incomplete or incorrect.

The time limits for the making of estimated assessments are:

(a) two years after the end of the prescribed accounting period, or

(b) one year after the evidence of facts sufficient in the opinion of the Customs and Excise to justify the making of the assessment, comes to their knowledge.

Further assessments may be made if an estimated assessment proves to be insufficient, so long as they are based on further information that has come to light.

The normal time limit for the making of assessments is six years after the end of the prescribed accounting period. In the case of fraud, wilful default or neglect, the assessment can, with the leave of the VAT Tribunal, be made at any time. An appeal to a VAT Tribunal can be made against any assessment.

In winding-up or bankruptcy proceedings, VAT limited to that which has become due within a period of twelve months ending at the relevant date, enjoys the same priority as other taxation liabilities.

Distress may be levied on a trader's goods under a warrant signed by a collector of Customs and Excise if the trader refuses or neglects to pay any actual or estimated amount of tax due from him.

Records

Every taxable person must keep such records as the Commissioners of Customs and Excise may require (currently for six years). These will consist of the following:

(a) tax invoices relating to inputs;

(b) evidence of tax on imported goods;

(c) copies of tax invoices attributable to outputs;

(d) details of credits allowed to customers and received from suppliers;

(e) details of errors and adjustments requiring collection;

(f) details of any self supplies.

Special requirements are provided by the Value Added Tax General Regulations 1980, as to the issue and content of VAT invoices. As a general requirement a taxable person when making a taxable supply to another taxable person must supply him with a tax invoice. The invoice must include all the following items, although the exact order and layout are immaterial:

(a) the name, address and VAT registered number of the supplier;

(b) the date of the supply;

(c) the number of the invoice;

(d) the name and address of the person to whom the goods or services are supplied;

(e) the type of supply;

(f) a description sufficient to identify the goods or services supplied ;

(g) the amount payable before VAT for each of the descriptions;

(h) the rate of any discount offered;

(i) the rate and amount of tax chargeable.

In the case of retailers it is recognised that the task of making out separate tax invoices would be extremely burdensome. It is provided therefore that such a person is not generally required to provide a tax invoice. If, however, he is requested to do so, and the value of the supply is under £50 inclusive of VAT, then the tax invoice need only contain the following details:

(a) the name, address and registration number of the retailer;

(b) the date of the supply;

(c) a description sufficient to identify the goods or services supplied;

(d) the total amount payable including tax;

(e) the rate of tax in force at the time of making the supply.

The tax invoices do not have to accompany the VAT return but must be kept available for inspection for six years,

If, in addition to supplies taxable at one or more positive rates of tax, a tax invoice includes zero rated or exempt supplies, it will be necessary to show clearly which items bear no VAT charge.

Special rules apply to traders who adapt the till rolls produced by their cash registers to serve as tax invoices.

3.0 COMPUTERS

Taxable persons are able to forego the need to provide tax invoices and instead for the necessary information to be recorded in a computer and to be transmitted to the customer electronically (directly from computer to computer).

It is a condition of the legislation that the Customs and Excise be given at least one month's notice for the person to comply with any conditions that the Customs and Excise might impose. In this respect it should also be noted that all records may be maintained on a computer provided it can be readily converted into a form capable of inspection by the Customs and Excise on request.

The Customs and Excise should be consulted at the design stage when considering using computer-based accounting systems for VAT.

4.0 ACCOUNTS

It will be necessary to summarise taxable transactions and record the VAT in an appropriate account. This is to enable the Customs and Excise officers to check the accuracy of the returns. The Commissioners of Customs and Excise require records to be kept for such period as they may require. This is normally six years. The records may be kept in bound books or by such other means (i.e. in a computer) as the Commissioners may approve. An example of a specimen VAT Account may appear as follows:

SPECIMEN VAT ACCOUNT FOR FULLY TAXABLE PERSONS

Input Tax (inclusive of tax on imported goods and goods from bonded warehouses):	£	£	Input Tax	£	£
August	849.10		August		1,199.00
September	870.30		September		1,096.10
October	816.90		October		932.90
		2,536.30			3,228.00
			Tax due on imported goods and goods from bonded warehouses:	£	
			August	70.20	
			September	40.30	
			October	72.80	
					183.30
Overdeclaration and/or overpayments of tax in respect of previous periods:			Underdeclarations and/or underpayments of tax in respect of previous periods:		
Notified by Customs and Excise	Nil		Notified by Customs and Excise	Nil	
Other	271.60		Other	213.70	
		271.60			213.70
TOTAL TAX DEDUCTIBLE		2,807.90			
By credit transfer TAX PAYABLE		817.10			
		3,625.00	TOTAL TAX DUE		3,625.00

The officers of the Customs and Excise have considerable powers as to the obtaining of information, copies of records and samples of goods. In the obtaining of these items, the officers may at any reasonable time enter the premises used in connection with the carrying on of a business. Powers of forcible entry, seizure and search are available on the granting of a warrant by a Justice of the Peace.

Where an authorised person removes any documents, etc., he must, on request, provide a record of what has been removed. The officer in overall charge of the investigation must, on request, allow access to such documents, etc., and allow them to be photocopied unless he has reasonable grounds for believing that to do so would prejudice any investigation or criminal proceedings.

5.0 PENALTIES

Criminal penalties involving fines and imprisonment are available for certain tax offences including:

(a) Fraudulent evasion of tax;

(b) furnishing or producing with intent to deceive false documents or making knowingly or recklessly false statements;

(c) making false returns;

(d) dealing in goods or services which tax has not been paid.

Civil penalties are also chargeable in addition to those above for a number of offences including:

(a) tax evasion involving dishonesty;

(b) serious misdeclarations or neglect resulting in understating tax due or overclaiming recoveries;

(c) failure to notify a liability to register;

(d) the unauthorised issue of VAT invoices;

(e) breaches of regulations.

A taxable person who fails to submit a return or pay the tax shown on a return within the required time is in default. If the default continues to subsequent return periods then the CCE may serve a surcharge liability.

The liability surcharge is the greater of:

(a) £30; and

(b) 5% of the outstanding tax for the first default period, 10% for the second default period up to a maximum of 30% for the sixth and any later period.

No civil penalty under (b) - (c) above arises where the person satisfies CCE or a tribunal that there is reasonable excuse for his conduct. A tribunal has no general power to vary the amount assessed as a penalty.

6.0 REPAYMENT SUPPLEMENTS

A repayment supplement of 5% of the amount repaid or £30 whichever is the greater will be applied to repayments provided the return is received by CCE no later than 2 months after the end of the prescribed period.

7.0 APPEALS

7.1 GENERAL

Appeals can be made against decisions of the Commissioners of Customs and Excise in respect of the following:

(a) registration or cancellation of registration;

(b) assessments;

(c) tax chargeable;

(d) tax deductible; and certain other items;

(e) civil penalties.

On an appeal against an assessment to a penalty, etc., the burden of proof that tax has been evaded and conduct involves an element of dishonesty lies upon the Commissioners.

An appeal will not normally be entertained until a taxpayer is up to date on all returns and tax payable by him. In the case of items (b) and (c) above, the Commissioners may require that part or all of the tax due must be paid over before the appeal can commence. If it is subsequently discovered that it is not due then it will be repaid with interest.

Provisions similar to s.54 TMA 1970 are made for the Commissioners and an applicant or his agent to settle appeals by agreement, subject to repudiation by the appellant within 30 days.

Where an appellant notifies the Commissioners of his intention of withdrawing his appeal, unless the Commissioners object to the withdrawal within 30 days, the parties are treated as having agreed that the decision under appeal should be upheld without variation.

7.2 VAT TRIBUNALS

To hear VAT appeals VAT Tribunals have been set up in major cities in the UK. Unlike certain tribunals, they have been brought under the direct supervision of the Council on Tribunals. This has the effect of ensuring that all alterations in the workings of the Tribunal can only be made with the approval of the Council.

7.3 STAFF

The executive head of the Tribunals is the President. He is appointed by the Lord Chancellor and must be a solicitor or barrister of at least ten years' standing. The President may retire at any time, and can be removed by the Lord Chancellor for incapacity or misbehaviour. His remuneration is fixed by the Treasury.

The other members of a Tribunal consist of Chairman and members. Both are chosen from a panel. The quorum for a tribunal is normally three but where only two members are present the chairman has a casting vote. Chairmen are normally full-time and paid a salary. Other members are normally part-time and paid a fee only.

7.4 CONDUCT OF AN APPEAL

To be effective a notice of appeal must be served at the appropriate tribunal centre. It must be served by or on behalf of the appellant and must be signed by him or his agent. Inter alia it must state:

(1) His name and business address.

(2) The grounds of the appeal.

The normal time limit for the making of an appeal is 30 days after the date of a letter from the Commissioners containing the disputed decision. This may be extended in certain cases. When an appeal is received at the Tribunal Centre an acknowledgement will be sent.

Within 21 days of the notification of the appeal the Commissioners of Customs and Excise must serve at the Tribunal Centre a copy of the disputed decision and their reasons for making it. A copy of these reasons will be forwarded to the person making the appeal. If the Commissioners consider that an appeal does not lie they once again must serve a notice of their reasons at the appropriate Tribunal Centre and a copy must once again be sent to the appellant. Each party to the appeal must within 21 days of the date of the service of the appeal, deliver to the Tribunal Centre a list of the documents that he intends to produce at the hearing together with a list of the witness statements. He must indicate a reasonable time and place for the inspection of these documents by the opposing party. All the documents must be available at the Tribunal hearing. The witness statements must contain details of the evidence proposed to be given by any witness together with his name, address and description. If a witness is unwilling to come forward then a summons may be issued requiring his attendance.

The appeal will normally be held in public unless the Tribunal decides that all or part of it would be best held in private.

The taxpayer or any person whom he may appoint for the purposes is entitled to conduct his case at the hearing. A similar right applies to the Commissioners.

Where on the hearing of an appeal, no party is represented, the Tribunal may dismiss the appeal. If only one party is present then the Tribunal may proceed in the absence of the other party. In both cases the Tribunal is empowered to reinstate the appeal or set aside their decision on such terms as may be just.

7.5 PROCEDURE

The procedure before the Tribunal is for the appellant to address the Tribunal and to call and examine witnesses. The opposing party can also address the Tribunal and call and examine witnesses. Both sides have the opportunity of cross-examination. Witnesses before a Tribunal are examined under oath or affirmation.

7.6 DECISION

At the end of a hearing the decision may be announced by the Chairman. In all cases however a written notice of the decision is sent to both parties. This is signed by the Chairman and contains all findings of fact and the reasons for the decision.

7.7 COSTS

Costs may be awarded by the Tribunal. These normally follow the event.

7.8 APPEALS FROM THE TRIBUNAL

Under the Tribunals and Inquiries Act 1971, a party dissatisfied with a decision of the Tribunal on a point of law may appeal to the High Court, or under certain cases direct to the Court of Appeal.

7.9 PENALTY FOR FAILURE TO COMPLY WITH DIRECTIONS, ETC., OF TRIBUNALS FA 1985

A person who fails to comply with a direction or summons issued by a VAT Tribunal is liable, subject to appeal, to a penalty not exceeding £1,000.

34 Inheritance Tax

1.0 INTRODUCTION

For many years, the major charge to tax on transfers of capital was Estate Duty. Introduced in 1894, this was widely regarded as an "avoidable tax" as careful estate planning coupled with gifts made many years before death could easily result in no charge to tax.

FA 1975 introduced capital transfer tax (CTT) to bring into taxation both lifetime and death transfers of property, thereby replacing the old estate duty legislation which was essentially a tax on death transfers only. The FA 1976 made substantial changes to the legislation, and the FA 1981 altered the future basis of charge. Other enactments have introduced minor alterations and increases in the CTT rates.

The Capital Transfer Tax (Consolidation) Act 1984 brought together all the legislation enacted.

FA 1986 introduced major changes to the legislation; the tax has now been renamed Inheritance Tax and the CTTA has been renamed the Inheritance Tax Act 1984. The major change introduced by IHTA has been to remove most lifetime transfers of goods or property from the charge to IHT provided that they are made more than 7 years before death.

2.0 LIABILITY TO TAX

2.1 GENERAL

IHT is chargeable whenever a chargeable transfer of value has been made. A transfer of value is any disposition which results in a loss in value to the transferor's estate and which is not an exempt transfer.

2.2 SCOPE OF THE TAX

If the transferor is domiciled in the UK, he is liable to IHT on transfers of assets made anywhere in the world. If he is not domiciled in the UK, he is only liable on transfers of assets situated in the UK.

(a) Situation of property: Subject to any double-taxation agreements the following rules apply to determine where property is situated:

(i) tangible property is situated where it is physically located. (Note: a work of art in the UK solely for public examination, cleaning or restoration will not be treated as situated in the UK if it is normally kept outside the UK);

(ii) land, whether freehold or leasehold, is situated where it is physically located;

(iii) registered shares and securities are situated in the country where they are registered, i.e. where the register is required to be kept;

(iv) bearer securities are situated where the document of title is located at the time of transfer;

(v) bank accounts are situated at the branch where the money is payable;

(vi) business assets (including goodwill) are situated where the business is carried on (this includes an interest in a partnership);

(vii) debts are situated in the country where the debtor resides;

(viii) life policies are situated in the country where the proceeds are payable;

(ix) currency is situated where it is physically located, not in the country of issue;

(x) trust property is situated according to the above rules, regardless of the appropriate trust law or the residence of the trustees.

(b) Domicile: The general definition applies (i.e. a person's domicile is the place in which he has his fixed and permanent home, and to which, whenever he is absent, he has the intention of returning).

However, for IHT purposes a person will also be deemed to be domiciled in the UK, if at the time of a transfer:

(i) he was domiciled in the UK on or after 10th December 1974 and at any time within the three years immediately preceding the transfer; or

(ii) he was resident in the UK for tax purposes on or after 10th December 1974 and in at least seventeen of the twenty years of assessment ending with the year of assessment in which the transfer is made.

3.0 EXEMPT, CHARGEABLE AND POTENTIALLY EXEMPT TRANSFERS

3.1 GENERAL

IHT is chargeable when a person makes a chargeable transfer of value. A transfer of value is any disposition which reduces the transferor's estate. A chargeable transfer of value is a transfer of value which is not an exempt transfer. The measure of a transfer of value is the loss to the transferor's estate; not necessarily the gain to the transferee.

The new IHT regime divides transfers into three main categories:

(a) exempt transfers;

(b) chargeable transfers;

(c) potentially exempt transfers.

3.2 EXEMPT TRANSFERS

Certain transfers, provided that they satisfy the appropriate conditions will be exempt from IHT.
They include:

3.2.1 Normal expenditure out of income

Where lifetime gifts are made out of income they are wholly exempt from IHT provided that the transferor can show that:

(a) the transfer was part of his normal expenditure. Normal is equivalent to typical or habitual and would entail such expenditure recurring for at least three years. However, the first payments on a life assurance policy or a deed of covenant are treated as normal, and retrospective exemption may be given for other gifts once normality is established; and

(b) taking one year with another the gift was made out of income. "Income" is net income after income tax and the exemption is not lost merely because of fluctuations in yearly income; and

(c) he was left with sufficient income to maintain his usual standard of living; this being the personal standard normally maintained by the transferor himself.

In practice, a transferor with an established pattern of gifts (of say £1,000 per annum) is likely to be able to claim the exemption in respect of such gift even if it is made to a new transferee.

3.2.2 Small gifts

Outright lifetime gifts are exempt from IHT provided they do not exceed £250 to any one individual in any one tax year. A transferor may, thus, make any number of gifts below £250 (say fifty gifts of £200 each) to different donees, and each of them would be exempt.

3.2.3 Transfers on marriage

Gifts in consideration of marriage are exempt from IHT up to a limit which is dependent on the relationship between the transferor and the parties to the marriage. The gifts (whether outright or settled) must be made or promised before and in consideration of a particular marriage, which must take place. The exemptions are:

(a) £5,000 if the transferor is a parent of one of the parties to the marriage;

(b) £2,500 if the transferor is a grandparent or remoter ancestor of one of the parties to the marriage;

(c) £2,500 if the transferor is one of the parties to the marriage;

(d) £1,000 if the transferor is any other person.

The exemption is given to each transferor in respect of any one particular marriage, and so the four parents of the bride and groom (if alive) can each give an exempt £5,000. If an individual gift is over £5,000, the annual exemption might be applied to all or part of the balance. Where the gift is made into a marriage settlement, the beneficiaries must be limited to the parties to the marriage, their issue, and any spouses of the issue. By concession, a spouse may put his partner in sufficient funds to enable both parents to claim the £5,000 exemption without the associated operations provisions being revoked.

3.2.4 Annual Transfers up to £3,000

Lifetime gifts, which are not exempted or relieved under any other provision, are exempt up to a total of £3,000 per transferor in any one tax year. Where the gifts in any tax year exceed the exemption limit, they are counted towards the limit in chronological order, the later gifts receiving less or no exemption allowance. If the gifts in any tax year are below the exemption limit, the unused balance may be carried forward into the following year, but no further. The current year's exemption allowance must be fully utilised before any brought-forward allowance can be used.

Illustration

Calculate the transfers in respect of the following gifts made by Edward:

June 1986	£200 to his friend Alice
November 1986	£6,000 to his daughter on her marriage
January 1987	£1,500 to his niece
July 1987	£3,200 to his now closer friend Alice

		£	£
June 1986	Gift to Alice		200
	Less: small gift exemption		200
			—
November 1986	Gift to daughter		6,000
	Less: marriage exemption	5,000	
	annual exemption 86/87	1,000	
			6,000
			—
January 1987	Gift to niece		1,500
	Less: annual exemption 86/87		1,500
			—
July 1987	Gift to Alice		3,200
	Less: annual exemption 87/88	3,000	
	annual exemption 86/87	200	
			3,200
			—

(Note: The unused annual exemption of £300 from 1986/87 is lost.)

Where a transferor makes more than one gift on the same day the exemption is apportioned between them in proportion to the amounts that would otherwise be chargeable to tax.

Illustration

Assuming that on 10th June 1987 Edward made three more gifts to each of his grandchildren, of £1,000, £3,000 and £6,000 respectively, the transfers would be:

	£	Chargeable Transfer £
Gift 1	1,000	
Less: annual exemption $\frac{1,000}{10,000} \times £3,000$	300	700

		£	Chargeable Transfers £
Gift 2		3,000	
Less: annual exemption	$\frac{3,000}{10,000}$ x £3,000	900	2,100
Gift 3		6,000	
Less: annual exemption	$\frac{6,000}{10,000}$ x £3,000	1,800	4,200

If in the same year there is a potentially exempt transfer and a chargeable transfer, the latter is always deemed to be made first and will thus take the annual exemption.

3.2.5 Gifts Between Husband and Wife

A husband and wife are each entitled to the various exemptions and reliefs in their own right (i.e. each party can claim the £3,000 annual exemption etc.), and in general, transfers between them are completely exempt from IHT. However, if the transferee is not UK domiciled, the exemption is limited to a cumulative total of £55,000. This prevents the transfer of UK property to a non-UK domiciled person and so creating excluded property. Where both spouses are UK domiciled or where both are non-UK domiciled the full exemption applies.

3.2.6 Gifts to Charities

Outright gifts (and gifts in trust subject to anti-avoidance provisions) to UK charities are wholly exempt from IHT.

3.2.7 Gifts to Political Parties

Outright gifts to political parties are wholly exempt from IHT if made more than one year before the transferor's death. Bequests on death and gifts made within one year of death are exempt up to a total of £100,000.

In order to qualify for the exemption a political party must either:

(a) have had two members elected to the House of Commons at the last general election before the gift; or

(b) have had one member elected and 150,000 votes cast for all its candidates.

3.2.8 Gifts for National Purposes

Gifts of funds or property to national institutions which exist wholly or mainly for the purpose of preserving (for the public benefit) any collection of scientific, historic or artistic interest and which are approved by the Treasury, are exempt. Such institutions include:

(a) the National Gallery;

(b) the British Museum;

(c) other approved art galleries and museums;

(d) the National Trust;

(e) the Nature Conservancy Council;

(f) any library serving the needs of teaching and research at a UK university;

(g) any local authority;

(h) any UK university or university college;

(i) any government department.

The exemptions considered above are available on lifetime and death transfers as under:

	Lifetime	Death
Normal Expenditure	✓	
Small gifts	✓	
Marriage	✓	
Annual transfers up to £3,000	✓	
Gifts between husband and wife	✓	✓
Gifts to charities	✓	✓
Gifts to political parties	✓	✓
Gifts for national purposes	✓	✓
Gifts for the public benefit	✓	✓
Transfers into employee trusts	✓	✓

3.3 CHARGEABLE TRANSFERS

All other transfers which are neither exempt nor potentially exempt are chargeable transfers. These will need to be included in the IHT computation when they are made and tax calculated thereon. These transfers could include:

(a) transfers to trustees, if not exempt; e.g. a transfer into a discretionary settlement;

(b) a transfer involving a company, e.g. a transfer of an asset at an undervalue by a close company.

3.4 POTENTIALLY EXEMPT TRANSFERS

A potentially exempt transfer (PET) is a transfer of value made by an individual which, if certain conditions apply, might be exempt from IHT. They broadly comprise three main types of transfers:

(a) to another individual;

(b) to an accumulation or maintenance trust;

(c) to a disabled trust.

A PET will become a chargeable transfer if the donor dies within 7 years of making it and IHT may be charged, subject to tapering relief. If the donor survives for 7 years after making the PET it will become an exempt transfer. Under normal circumstances the tax on a PET becoming chargeable will be due from the donee, subject to a right of recovery from the personal representatives of the deceased. The tax due when a PET becomes chargeable will be that which applies at the date of death of the donor, less the tapering relief given in the following table:

Years between date of PET & date of death	%age of tax charged
0 - 3	100%
3 - 4	80%
4 - 5	60%
5 - 6	40%
6 - 7	20%

3.5 DISPOSITIONS WHICH ARE NOT TRANSFERS OF VALUE

Subject to the various conditions being met certain transfers, which are not exempt, will not be considered to be transfers of value. These will include:

3.5.1 Gifts for Family Maintenance

Lifetime gifts for the maintenance of family dependants are exempt from IHT in certain circumstances:

(a) a gift for the maintenance of a spouse or former spouse is unconditionally exempt;

(b) a gift for the maintenance, education or training of a child of either party to the marriage is exempt up to the age of eighteen or until the completion of full-time education if later. This exemption is also available for any child not in the care of its parents or who is illegitimate, adopted or a step-child;

(c) a gift to make reasonable provision for the care and maintenance of a dependant relative of the transferor or his spouse is exempt if the relative is incapacitated by old age or infirmity from maintaining herself/himself (or is the widowed, divorced or separated mother of the transferor or his wife, whether incapacitated or not).

3.5.2 Gifts in the Course of Trade

Gifts made in the course of trade, such as Christmas gifts to staff, small gifts to customers, ex gratia retirement pensions to ex-employees, are exempt from IHT provided that they are an allowable deduction in arriving at the adjusted profit for income tax purposes.

3.5.3 Waivers of Dividends and Remuneration

A person who waives any dividend within twelve months before any right to the dividend has accrued is not treated as making a transfer of value. A general waiver of all future dividends is only effective for dividends payable within twelve months after the waiver.

A waiver of remuneration is not a transfer of value where, had the remuneration not been waived (or repaid), it:

(a) would have been assessable to Schedule E income tax;

(b) would have been deductible in computing the employer's profits for tax purposes.

3.5.4 Gifts for the Public Benefit

Gifts of certain national heritage property to a non-profit organisation are exempt from IHT where approved by the Treasury. This exemption applies to property comprised in a settlement as well as assets owned by individuals and covers:

(a) land of outstanding scenic, historic or scientific interest;

(b) buildings approved for preservation as being of outstanding historic, architectural or aesthetic interest, together with the cost of preservation;

(c) land used as the grounds of any building within (b), and any object which is normally kept in and which is given with, a building within (b);

(d) any print, picture, book, manuscript, work of art or scientific collection which is of national, scientific, historic or artistic interest;

(e) property given to be a source of income for the upkeep and maintenance of any of the above to the extent that it produces no more income than is required.

If necessary, undertakings to ensure reasonable public access and the preservation of the property may have to be given.

3.5.5 Transfers into Employee Trusts

A lifetime or death transfer of shares in a company by an individual into a trust for the benefit of the employees of that company is exempt from IHT provided that:

(a) the shares are held on trust for the benefit of the majority of all employees of the company;

(b) any participator who is entitled to five per cent or more of any class of shares in the company or to five per cent or more of its assets on a winding-up, cannot benefit under the trust;

(c) at or within twelve months of the transfer, the trustees hold more than half of the ordinary shares in the company and have voting control of the company.

3.6 GIFTS WITH RESERVATION

A person may make a transfer of value and yet retain some interest in the property transfered. A common example would be the gift of a taxpayer's residence to his children subject to retaining the right to live there for the remainder of his or her life. This type of transfer is called a gift with reservation.

S.102 IHTA provides that a gift with reservation is one where the individual makes a gift and either:

(a) possession and enjoyment of the property is not bona fide assumed by the donee at or before the beginning of the relevant period, or

(b) at any time in the relevant period, the property is not enjoyed to the entire exclusion or virtually to the entire exclusion, of the donor and of any benefit to him by contract or otherwise.

The relevant period is the seven years prior to the death of the donor.

If the gift is subject to the provisions, the asset will be taxed as though it was still beneficially held by the donor.

The provisions may be avoided where:

(i) In the case of a chattel or land, the donee pays a market rent for the enjoyment of the asset, or

(ii) the occupation by the donor was unforseen and was brought about by his old age, infirmity or otherwise and is a reasonable provision for his maintenance.

3.7 EXCLUDED PROPERTY

Certain assets are ignored for IHT purposes and do not enter any IHT computation. Such excluded property includes:

(a) property situated outside the UK if the person beneficially entitled to it is domiciled outside the UK;

(b) settled property situated outside the UK provided the settlor was domiciled outside the UK at the time of making the settlement. This exclusion applies even when the beneficiaries of the trust property are UK domiciled on death;

(c) certain Government securities which are exempt from income tax if owned by a person neither domiciled nor ordinarily resident in the UK (the deemed domicile provisions are ignored). Such securities comprised in a settlement also qualify as excluded property if the person beneficially entitled to an interest in possession in them is neither domiciled nor ordinarily resident in the UK.

Tax free Government securities include certain issues of:

(i) 3½% War Loan;

(ii) Funding Loan;

(iii) Treasury Loan;

(iv) Convertible Stock;

(v) Exchequer Stock;

(d) certain savings held by a person domiciled in the Channel Islands or the Isle of Man. These savings are:

(i) War savings certificates;

(ii) National savings certificates;

(iii) Premium savings bonds;

(iv) Deposits with the National Savings Banks or with a Trustee Savings Bank;

(v) Certified contractual savings schemes (e.g. SAYE);

(e) assets of a member of the armed forces passing as a result of death from wounds, accident or disease while on active service (or in Northern Ireland). Although technically an exemption, this provision is included here for convenience;

(f) emoluments and tangible moveable property of members of visiting forces and staff of allied headquarters posted to the UK;

(g) cash options under approved retirement annuity schemes;

(h) foreign currency accounts at UK banks (or the Post Office) owned by a person neither domiciled, resident nor ordinarily resident in the UK at the time of his death;

(i) a reversionary interest in settled property. A reversionary interest is a future interest in trust property, such as that of the remainderman of a trust. Although a reversionary interest could be valued actuarily, it is excluded for IHT purposes, provided that:

(i) it has not been acquired at any time for a valuable consideration;

(ii) neither the settlor nor his spouse is or has been beneficially entitled to the reversionary interest at any time.

3.8 OMISSIONS TO ACT

Where a person's estate is reduced in value while another's estate is increased in value as a result of the former's deliberate omission to exercise a right, he is treated as having made a transfer of value at the latest time that he could have exercised the right. An omission benefiting a discretionary trust will also be treated as a transfer of value. This provision is designed to prevent, for example, shareholders with control from surrendering control by failing to take up rights issues (and so reducing the value of their holdings for IHT purposes).

4.0 CALCULATION OF THE TAX

4.1 Rates of Inheritance Tax

Death Scale

Cumulative chargeable transfers (gross)	Rate %	IHT on band	Cumulative IHT	Rate on net
0 - 71,000	NIL	-	-	-
71,001 - 95,000	30	7,200	7,200	3/7
95,001 - 129,000	35	11,900	19,100	7/13
129,001 - 164,000	40	14,000	33,100	2/3
164,001 - 206,000	45	18,900	52,000	9/11
206,001 - 257,000	50	25,500	77,500	1
257,001 - 317,000	55	33,000	110,500	1 2/9
over 317,001	60			1 1/2

Chargeable lifetime transfer scale

Cumulative chargeable transfers (gross)	Rate %	IHT on bond	Cumulative IHT	Rate on net
0 - 71,000	NIL	-	-	-
71,001 - 95,000	15	3,600	3,600	3/17
95,001 - 129,000	17½	5,950	9,550	7/33
129,001 - 164,000	20	7,000	16,550	1/4
164,001 - 206,000	22½	9,450	26,000	9/31
206,001 - 257,000	25	12,750	38,750	1/3
257,001 - 317,000	27½	16,500	55,250	11/29
over 317,001	30			3/7

Where a chargeable lifetime transfer is made, the person with primary liability to pay IHT is the transferor. As the measure of the transfer is the reduction in value of his estate as the result of making the transfer it will be gift plus the tax. To find the tax it is necessary to gross up the transfer.

Illustration

A makes a transfer to a discretionary trust on 30th June, 1986 of £100,000. (Ignore any exemptions).

This is a "net" transfer and it is necessary to gross up. Using the net cumulative chargeable transfers in the lifetime table, find the net amount nearest beneath the transfer:

91,400 net =		95,000 gross
8,600 difference		
100,000		

The difference is grossed up as though it had suffered tax at the rate applying to net transfers between

£91,400 and £119,450

$$£8,600 \times \frac{100}{100 - 17\frac{1}{2}} \qquad 10,424$$

105,424 gross

The IHT payable is

£105,424 - 100,000 = £ 5,424

An alternative method of finding the tax is

Tax on	£91,400 net is	3,600
on	£ 8,600 x 7/33 is	1,824
		5,424

If, alternatively, the transfer was made into the discretionary trust on the understanding that the trustees would bear the IHT themselves, the reduction in value of the transferor's estate would be only £100,000. This would be a "gross" transfer and tax could be found on the £100,000 directly without any grossing up.

Tax on	£95,000	3,600
on	£ 5,000 @ 17½%	875
		4,475

On death, the value of the estate increases the amount of the chargeable lifetime transfers. Tax is calculated using the rates on death.

Illustration

A died on 31st July 1990. The value of his estate was £200,000.

			£
Transfers within the previous 7 years			105,424
Value of the estate			200,000
			305,424
IHT payable using death scale:			
	On £257,000		77,500
	£ 48,424 @ 55%		26,633
			104,133
	Less: IHT on transfers within the previous 7 years on death scale - £105,424		
	on £95,000 @ 30%	7,200	
	£10,424 @ 35%	3,648	
			10,848
	Payable by executors		93,285

As A has died within 7 years of the earlier transfer, additional tax is due. This will be the difference between the IHT (if any) already paid on the transfer and the tax chargeable on it using the IHT rates at the date of death. The tax found will then be reduced by tapering relief as under:

Years between date of earlier transfer and date of death	%age of tax charged
0 - 3	100%
3 - 4	80%
4 - 5	60%
5 - 6	40%
6 - 7	20%

	£
Tax on death scale	10,848
Less: tax paid when transfer made	5,424
	5,424
60% thereof	£3,254

Where a potentially exempt transfer has been made, no calculation takes place during lifetime when the transfer was made. On a death within 7 years, tax will be calculated in the same way as before and abated by tapering relief at the appropriate rate.

Illustration

On 1st January 1987 B gave £110,000 to her son on his marriage. She had not made any earlier transfers. On 15th April 1990, B died, her estate was valued at £100,000.

The transfer to B's son was a potentially exempt transfer. Its value on 1st January 1987 was:

	£	£
Gift		110,000
Less: Marriage exemption	5,000	
Annual exemption -		
1986/87	3,000	
1985/86 b/f	3,000	
		11,000
		99,000

On B's death the tax will be calculated as under:

	£
Transfer within previous 7 years	99,000
IHT thereon at death rates -	
on £95,000	7,200
£ 4,000 @ 35%	1,400
	8,600
Payable by B's son - 80% thereof	6,880

IHT on estate:

Transfers within previous 7 years as above	99,000
Value of estate	100,000
	199,000

	£
IHT thereon -	
on £164,000	33,100
£ 35,000 @ 45%	15,750
	48,850
Less: IHT on £99,000	8,600
Payable by personal representatives	40,250

Frequently there will be a number of previously chargeable or partly exempt transfers, and it will be necessary to calculate the IHT payable in respect of each of them.

Illustration

C died on 31st December 1992. He had made the following transfers during his lifetime:

30th June 1986	to a discretionary trust	£100,000
30th June 1987	to his daughter on her marriage	£ 50,000
15th December 1988	to his son	£ 25,000

The value of his estate on death was £150,000.

The schedule of transfers made within the 7 years before death will appear as under:

			£
30th June 1986	to trustees		100,000
	Less: Annual exemption -		
	1986/87	3,000	
	1985/86	3,000	
			6,000
			94,000
	IHT thereon		
	on £91,400		3,600
	£ 2,600 x 7/33		552
			4,152

This was a net transfer as the trustees have not paid the tax themselves.

The gross transfer is thus £ 98,152

			£	£
30th June 1987	Daughter		50,000	
	Less: Marriage exemption	5,000		
	Annual exemption - 1987/88	3,000		
			8,000	
				42,000 PET
15th December 1988	Son		25,000	
	Less: Annual exemption - 1988/89		3,000	
				22,000 PET

On the death within 7 years additional tax will be due on the chargeable transfer into the discretionary trust, and the potentially exempt transfers will become chargeable.

		£	£	£
Transfer to discretionary trust			98,152	
IHT - on £95,000		7,200		
on £ 3,152 @ 35%		1,103		
	£98,152	8,303		8,303
			98,152	8,303
Transfer to daughter			42,000	15,258
			140,152	23,561
IHT - on £129,000		19,100		
on £ 11,152 @ 40%		4,461		
	£140,152	23,561		
Transfer to son			22,000	8,800
			162,152	32,361
IHT - on £129,000		19,100		
on £ 33,152 @ 40%		13,261		
	£162,152	32,361		

The IHT payable will be:

Trustees	£8,303 x 20%	1,661
	Paid already	4,152
	To pay	£ NIL

Daughter	£15,258 x 40%		£6,103
Son	£8,800 x 60%		£5,280

The tax payable on the estate would be:

	£
Total chargeable transfers	162,152
Value of estate	150,000
	312,152
IHT - on £257,000	77,500
on £ 55,152 @ 55%	30,334
£312,152	107,834
Less: IHT on £162,152	32,361
	75,473

Although only transfers made within the preceding 7 years enter into the computation to find the IHT on the value of the estate, in finding the tax on transfers made within the 7 year period before death, the rates of IHT will be charged on the value of the gift at its place in the table at the time the gift was made. This will mean that the gift will be aggregated with any other transfers made within the 7 years prior to it, despite the fact that they will have dropped out by the time death occurs to make those later gifts chargeable.

Illustration

D transfers £110,000 into a discretionary trust on 31st December 1986. The trustees pay any IHT thereon. He transfers £50,000 to his son on 31st December 1989 and dies on 30th June 1994 leaving an estate of £79,000. (Ignore any exemptions)

IHT on gift to son:

	£	£		
Transfer to son		50,000		
Transfers within previous 7 years		110,000		
		160,000		
IHT - on £129,000		19,100		
on £ 31,000 @ 40%		12,400		
£160,000		31,500		
Less: IHT on £110,000				
on £95,000	7,200			
on £15,000 @ 35%	5,250	12,450		
		19,050	x 60%	£11,430

IHT on estate:

	£
Transfer within 7 years of death	50,000
Value of estate	79,000
	129,000
IHT thereon	19,100
Less: IHT on £50,000	NIL
Due from personal representatives	19,100

4.2 QUICK SUCCESSION RELIEF (QSR)

Where a person's estate is increased by a transfer received and not more than five years later IHT arises as a result of a second transfer made, then a proportion of the IHT or CTT on the first transfer will be allowed as a credit against the IHT on the second transfer. The relief will only apply where the second transfer occurs on death, or is of settled property in which the transferor is entitled to an interest in possession.

The IHT payable on death is reduced by a percentage of part of the tax payable on the earlier transfer received, the percentage varying according to the time period between the two transfers:

Not more than 1 year	100%
More than 1 year but not more than 2 years	80%
More than 2 years but not more than 3 years	60%
More than 3 years but not more than 4 years	40%
More than 4 years but not more than 5 years	20%

The relevant percentage is applied to the IHT attributable to the Net Value of the property which had increased the deceased's estate. In other words:

$$QSR = \text{tax paid on first transfer} \times \frac{\text{net gift}}{\text{gross gift}} \times \text{relevant percentage.}$$

The relief is given whether or not the particular property which had been received is owned by the deceased on his death. If it is owned, then its value on that death is completely irrelevant. If there is more than one transfer subsequent to the original chargeable transfer (e.g. two deaths in "quick succession"), the credit will be given against the earliest of these. However, if the whole of the tax credit is not used, subsequent transfers may benefit - so long as they fall within the five year period.

Illustration

In June 1983, Justin (gross chargeable transfers of £116,000) gave Mary shares worth £10,000 (no exemptions being available). Mary died in August 1986 and included in her estate were the shares, now worth £12,000.

Assuming that Mary had paid the CTT due in 1983 (i.e. £10,000 @ 20% = £2,000), QSR would be:

$$£2,000 \times \frac{8,000}{10,000} \times 60\% = £960$$

Assuming that Justin had paid the CTT due in 1983 (i.e. $£10,000 \times \frac{20}{80} = £2,500$), QSR would be:

$$£2,000 \times \frac{10,000}{12,000} \times 60\% = £1,200$$

The QSR is deducted from IHT chargeable on Mary's death, and if not fully used may still be available if the shares are again transferred on the death of Mary's beneficiary (within five years of the first transfer). The credit is calculated by deducting the QSR used on the second transfer from the QSR available on the third.

4.3 LIABILITY TO PAY IHT

The Inland Revenue can collect IHT from a number of people, some of whom have a primary liability to pay the tax while others have a secondary liability (and are only approached on the default of a person with a primary liability):

Chargeable event	primary liability on	secondary liability on
Chargeable transfers	the transferor	(i) the transferee (ii) any other person in whom the property has become vested.
Additional IHT on chargeable transfers (within seven years of death)	the transferee	the personal representatives and any other person in whom the property has become vested.
Free estate (passing on death)	the personal representative	any person in whom the property is vested after death.
Potentially exempt transfers	the transferee	the personal representatives and any other person in whom the property has become vested.
Settled property (on the termination of an interest in possession)	the trustee(s)	(i) any person with an interest in possession (ii) any person to whose benefit the property (or income) is applied (iii) if the termination (or transfer) is during his lifetime - the settlor

It is also necessary to distinguish between who pays the tax (i.e. as shown above) and who actually bears it (i.e. the person whose property is reduced by the payment). In the case of:

(a) lifetime gifts, the IHT is borne by the person responsible for the payment;

(b) the free estate:

(i) the IHT on personalty is paid out of the residue of the estate, and so is effectively borne by the residuary legatees (whose benefit is reduced);

(ii) the IHT on realty is borne by the residuary legatees.

Naturally, a deceased person's will may indicate responsibility for bearing IHT other than that prescribed by law (e.g. a legacy of shares subject to any IHT attributable to the gift);

(c) settled property, the IHT is paid out of the trust capital and is therefore borne by the remaindermen.

Where IHT is not paid on land and certain other property an Inland Revenue charge will attach thereto until the tax is paid.

5.0 VALUATION

5.1 INTRODUCTION

The value of property for IHT purposes is determined by the amount the transferor's estate is reduced by the transfer. In effect his estate should be valued immediately before and immediately after the transfer, and the difference is the transfer of value. However, as this is both impractical and unnecessary,

> "the value at any time of any property shall for the purposes of IHT be the price which the property might reasonably be expected to fetch if sold in the open market at that time; but that price shall not be assumed to be reduced on the ground that the whole property is to be placed on the market at one and the same time."

The valuation must be at the price which would be negotiated between unconnected persons seeking to strike an arm's length bargain, producing the best possible price for the vendor. Regard must be had to any other property comprised in the transferor's estate which, if sold together with the property under consideration, would enhance its price. If there are any restrictions on the freedom to dispose of property (e.g. limitations on the transferability of shares or the disposal of a share in a partnership), the value of that property may be reduced. Another consideration is the possibility of property values being affected by the existence of related property, and before dealing with specific items, it is necessary to explain the meaning of this term.

5.2 RELATED PROPERTY

The value of any property in a person's estate is found by taking <u>related property</u> into account where by so doing a higher value for all or part of the property in his estate would be obtained. Property is related to that in a person's estate if:

(a) it is comprised in the estate of his spouse (including trust property in which either party has an interest in possession); or

(b) it has been transferred by either spouse, within the previous five years, to become the property of a charity, charitable trust or one of the political, national or public bodies to which exempt transfers may be made.

The related property provisions may apply, for example, to the joint ownership of a house by the husband and wife, or to valuable chattels whose ownership is divided (e.g. a set of five rare prints may be worth more collectively than the sum of the values of two prints owned by the husband and three prints owned by the wife when valued separately). However, the most important aspect of the related property provisions is in respect of shares in private companies.

Illustration

The shares in a private company are held as follows:

Mr. D	40%
Mrs. D	35%
Junior D (their son)	20%
Charity (shares given by Mrs. D three years ago)	5%

Mr. D transfers 50% of his holding to his son, the estimated values for different levels of holdings being:

	£
5%	5,000
20%	23,000
35%	45,500
40%	52,000
60%	86,000
80%	120,000

The transfer of value by Mr. D is not £23,000, or even £29,000 (i.e. the difference between the value of a 40 per cent holding and a reduced holding of 20 per cent), as related property must be taken into account.

The related property before the transfer amounts to a holding of 80 per cent (i.e. 40% + 35% + 5%) valued at £120,000, while after the transfer it amounts to 60 per cent (i.e. 20% + 35% + 5%) valued at £86,000. The transfer of value by Mr. D is calculated as follows:

		£
Holding before the transfer:		
$\frac{40}{80}$ x £120,000	=	60,000
Holding after the transfer		
$\frac{20}{60}$ x £86,000	=	28,667
Transfer of value (loss to transferor's estate)		31,333

If Mr. D had gifted all his shares, or they had passed on his death, their value would have been £60,000.

The value of property passing on death is usually increased as a result of the related property provisions. If, within three years of death, the whole or part of that property is sold by the personal representative or beneficiary at arm's length to an unconnected person (with no right of repurchase) for a lower price, a claim for relief may be made. The relief is given by revaluing the property sold as at the date of death ignoring the related property provisions; then recomputing the IHT payable, and reclaiming any overpaid IHT. For example, if the 40% of shares owned by Mr. D passed on his death (at a value of £60,000 - see above), and were sold within three years by his PR for £55,000, relief could be claimed. The shares would be revalued at £52,000 (the value ignoring related property provisions) and the IHT recomputed. However, where this relief is claimed, there may also be a reduction in the amount of business property relief or agricultural relief available. The adverse effects of this may make it worthwhile not to claim for the reduced valuation.

5.3 UNLISTED INVESTMENTS

Unlisted shares and securities are valued at the price they would fetch in the open market in an arm's length transaction between a willing buyer and a willing seller. The prospective purchaser is assumed to have available all the information that a prudent purchaser might reasonably require (e.g. prospective take-over bids, flotations etc). To some extent, this is an artificial basis of valuation as, of course, there is no open market in unlisted investments and agreement must be reached with the Inland Revenue.

5.4 LISTED INVESTMENTS

Listed shares and securities are valued at the lower of:

(a) one-quarter up on the difference between the lower and higher closing prices on the Stock Exchange (the <u>quarter-up rule</u>); or

(b) halfway between the highest and lowest recorded (<u>or marked</u>) bargains for the day.

Units in an approved unit trust scheme are valued at the manager's buying price, which is the lower of the two prices published.

Where the transfer takes place on a day the Stock Exchange is closed, the valuation is made using the prices quoted or bargains marked on the day previous, or the day following the transfer, whichever produces the lowest result on the property transferred.

<u>Illustration</u>

E transferred 1,000 ordinary shares in Rolltic plc to his son on Saturday 25th June. On Friday 24th June the shares were quoted at 150-158 with recorded bargains of 150, 151, 152 and 156. On Monday 27th June the shares were quoted at 150-156 with recorded bargains of 151, 154 and 156. The four valuations, in the order given, are:

1	1,000	@	152	=	£1,520
2	1,000	@	153	=	£1,530
3	1,000	@	151½	=	£1,515
4	1,000	@	153½	=	£1,535

The value of the PET is, therefore, based on the quotations for Monday 27th June.

5.5 ACCRUED INCOME AND PAYMENTS IN ADVANCE

Regular income such as rent, or interest accrued to the deceased's date of death, is included in a person's estate with apportionment being made to the nearest day (including the date of death). Adjustments are not usually made for rent paid in advance, although accrued liabilities may be deducted. For examination purposes apportionment is usually made to the nearest month.

As regards listed investments:

(a) if the quotation is cum div accrued income is already included in the valuation;

(b) if the quotation is ex div the whole amount of the next impending dividend (or interest net of tax) must be added to the ex div price. For example, if on Herbert's death, £2,000 10% National Stock in his estate was quoted 80-84 ex div (interest payable half yearly), the IHT valuation would be:

	£	£
£2,000 10% National Stock @ 81		1,620
Interest - ½ x 10% x £2,000	100	
Less: income tax @ 29%	29	
		71
		1,691

This calculation is only made in respect of transfers on death as the interest will form part of the deceased's estate when received.

The statutory apportionment of dividends or interest for executorship or trust purposes has no effect on the IHT valuation of the listed investments. However, if the deceased was a life tenant of a trust, care must be taken to include any income accrued up to the date of his death in the free estate and not as part of the settled property. Although the total IHT liability in respect of his death remains the same, more tax will be borne by the free estate and less by the settled property.

5.6 FALL IN VALUE OF LISTED INVESTMENTS

Where qualifying investments are included in a deceased person's estate and are sold (by the PR or any other person responsible for paying the IHT on them) within twelve months after death for a price lower than the valuation at death, relief may be available. Qualifying investments include shares and securities quoted on the Stock Exchange, holdings in authorised unit trusts, and shares in a common investment fund (e.g. managed by the Public Trustee). The gross sale prices (before deduction of expenses) may be substituted for the death valuations, but all investments sold within the period must be revalued in this way and not just those which have fallen in value. The reduction in value of the listed investments does, of course, reduce the total value of the estate passing on death, thereby reducing the IHT rate applicable to other property.

The relief is restricted if listed investments are purchased between the date of death and two months after the last sale in the twelve month period. The loss on sale is reduced by the fraction:

$$\frac{\text{total purchase prices}}{\text{total sale prices}}$$

- the expenses of sale or purchase being excluded.

Illustration

F died on 1st January 1987 leaving an estate valued at £110,000, including quoted investments valued at £50,000. Eight months after F's death his PR sold the investments for £40,000, but within two months of the sale purchased other quoted investments for £30,000.

The revised IHT computation at death would include the listed investments valued as follows:

		£	£
Other property			60,000
Listed investments:			
Value for probate		50,000	
Proceeds for sale		40,000	
Loss on sale	c/f	10,000	

		£	£
	b/f	10,000	60,000
Less: $\frac{30,000}{40,000}$ x £10,000		7,500	
		2,500	
New valuation £(50,000 - 2,500)			47,500
			107,500

Note that the computation is laid out to show the allowable fall in value as a deduction from the original probate value of the investment.

5.7 LAND AND BUILDINGS

Land and buildings, like other property, have to be valued at an open market price. The transferor, or his PR, would normally employ a professional valuer and ultimately reach agreement with the Inland Revenue's own district valuers. When valuing agricultural estates, any farm cottages occupied by agricultural workers are valued as agricultural cottages and not as potentially more valuable second homes etc.

Where land and buildings are included in a deceased person's estate and are sold within three years after death, relief may be available. The gross sale proceeds, if lower, may be substituted for the value at the date of death, but all sales of land by the person(s) acting in a particular capacity must be revalued in this way and not just those which have fallen in value.

No claim can be made where the difference between the two values is less than the lower of £1,000 or five per cent of the value on death, and also where the sale is to a beneficiary or one of his near relatives. The relief is restricted if land is purchased between the date of death and four months after the last sale in the three years period. The loss on sale is reduced by the fraction:

$$\frac{\text{total purchase prices}}{\text{total sale prices}}$$

- the expenses of sale or purchase being excluded.

Illustration

G died on 30th April 1987. His total estate was £250,000 and included the following:

	£
Property A	15,000
B	28,000
C	47,000

The properties were sold on 30th June 1987 to pay IHT and realised:

	£
Property A	14,500
B	20,000
C	50,000

The loss on Property A can be ignored as the loss is lower than the smallest of:

(a) £1,000; or

(b) 5% x £15,000 = £750

The loss and gain on Properties B and C are both material and so the value of the estate would be reduced by:

	£
Loss on Property B	(8,000)
Gain on Property C	3,000
	(5,000)

The IHT chargeable, assuming no previous transfers, would be:

	£
Initial value of estate	250,000
Less: reduction in value	(5,000)
	245,000
IHT on £206,000	52,000
on £ 39,000 @ 50%	19,500
	71,500

5.8 LIFE ASSURANCE POLICIES, ANNUITIES AND PENSIONS

Where a life policy matures on a person's death and the proceeds are payable to his PRs, the actual proceeds received are the value for IHT purposes. Where the life policy is part of a deceased person's estate, but does not in fact mature until another person's death, its value for IHT is the open market value. An annuity or pension which ceases on death is ignored for IHT purposes, but one which continues after death is valued on the basis of the balance due, unless it arises under an Inland Revenue approved retirement contract. Even if the deceased had the option for a lump sum to be paid to his PR (and where it is payable to his dependants) the value does not have to be brought into account.

Where the transfer of a life policy or annuity is made during a person's lifetime (e.g. where he assigns the policy in favour of someone else) the transfer of value is the greater of:

(a) the market value of the policy, usually the surrender value; or

(b) the premiums or other consideration already paid, less any sum paid out under the policy. (Note: Where life policies are linked to unit trust units, the value based on premiums paid is reduced by any depreciation in the value of the underlying units after they have been allotted to the policy.)

The usual exemptions may be applied (as relevant) to arrive at the amount of the transfer, including the marriage exemption, the transfer between spouses exemption, the annual exemption and (in the case of low values) the small gifts exemption.

When a life policy is assigned, or is written out in trust from the outset (e.g. a policy on a person's life for another's benefit), the proceeds which arise on a person's death are not paid into his estate but to the assignees or named beneficiaries. The proceeds do not, therefore, form part of the deceased's estate for IHT purposes. If the assignor or policyholder continues to pay the premiums on the policy after assignment or writing it out in trust, then each premium paid constitutes a transfer of value. However, the relevant exemptions (e.g. the normal expenditure out of income exemption, the transfers between spouses exemption, the annual exemption) may be applied to reduce or completely cover the amounts paid. This is a very important means of integrating potential IHT liability but still providing any dependants etc. with a capital sum on death.

If an annuity is purchased and the income produced by it is used to pay the premiums on a life policy written out in trust (a back-to-back operation), the Inland Revenue may assume (until it is shown otherwise) that the scheme falls under the associated operations provisions and the normal expenditure exemption cannot be applied. Furthermore, the purchase of the annuity may also be treated as a transfer of value.

5.9 OTHER PROPERTY

The position as regards the valuation of certain other items of property may be summarised:

(a) amounts due. A debt payable either on demand or at a future date is assumed to be payable in full at the appropriate time. However, if at the date of valuation it can be shown that the full recovery of the debt is impossible or impractical (e.g. because of the debtor's insolvency or refusal to comply with Court orders), the actual amount recoverable (if any) may be accepted provided that the transferor had not himself contributed to the irrecoverability;

(b) goodwill. When valuing a business, goodwill has to be taken into account as one of the business's assets;

(c) leases for life. Where a lease of property is granted for the life or lives of any persons, or for a period determinable by someone's death, it is treated as a settlement (unless it is granted for full consideration). The value of the leased property is divided into two parts, the lessor's interest forming part of his estate while the lessee's interest becomes chargeable under the trust provisions;

(d) options. Where property is transferred subject to an option purchase, the option is ignored unless it was granted in exchange for consideration of money or money's worth;

(e) property owned in joint names. Where property is held under a joint tenancy, then on the death of one party his share passes to the survivor automatically. However, where the property is held by tenants in common, the deceased party could leave his share to any other person. In both cases the value of the deceased's share is included in his estate (even though in a joint tenancy he has nothing to pass on). The related property provisions may have some relevance in the valuation of joint owned property.

5.10 LIABILITIES ON LIFETIME TRANSFERS

A transferor's general liabilities are not normally relevant to the valuation of property transferred during his life, the valuation being the asset transferred. However, there may be liabilities arising from the transfer itself, for example:

(a) incidental expenses, such as costs of valuation, transfer costs, stamp duty, etc;

(b) capital gains tax on the "disposal".

Where liabilities are paid by the transferor, they are ignored for IHT purposes and there is no grossing-up of them (even though they reduce the value of his estate). However, if these liabilities are paid by the transferee, they are allowed as a deduction from the value transferred (as the payment by the transferee effectively lessens the reduction in the transferor's estate). Note that when capital gains tax on a transfer is deferred until a subsequent disposal (under s.79 FA 1980) is made by the transferee, any IHT paid on the transfer is added to the base cost of the asset in the CGT computation.

5.11 LIABILITIES ON DEATH

General liabilities, if incurred by the deceased for full consideration, are deductible from estate property; primarily from general personalty although debts specifically attached are deducted from the relevant asset (e.g. a mortgage on a house is deducted from the realty, a loan secured by shares is deducted from the value of those shares). The position regarding liabilities may be summarised as follows:

(a) debts not enforceable by law (e.g. gambling or prostitution debts) cannot be deducted even if paid by the PR (but statute-barred debts can be deducted if actually paid);

(b) debts not falling to be paid until some future date are deductible, but at a discounted amount which takes into account the future date of payment;

(c) rent accrued to the date of death may be deducted, as can rates made and payable before death;

(d) taxation liabilities assessed up to the date of death are deductible if payable out of the estate (e.g. income taxes due);

(e) reasonable funeral expenses paid by the PR are allowed as a deduction (which is not affected by any death grants received). What is reasonable depends on the deceased's station in life, and the cost of a tombstone;

(f) foreign debts should be used to reduce the value of property situated abroad, as far as is possible. Provided the debts are recoverable in the UK any balance remaining may be deducted from general personalty.

5.12 NATIONAL HERITAGE PROPERTY - CONDITIONAL EXEMPTION

Gifts of property of national, historic or scientific interest to museums, art galleries etc. are exempt. However, even where such property is not transferred to an approved body or organisation, a conditional exemption may still be claimed. This exemption applies to all transfers on death, and to those lifetime transfers where the property has been owned by the transferor or his spouse for the previous six years. (The six years limit does not apply where the property was inherited on a death to which the conditional exemption had applied.)

The property must be designated by the Treasury as being in one of the following categories:

(a) works of art etc. of national, historic, scientific or artistic interest;

(b) buildings of outstanding historic or architectural interest, together with any amenity land or objects of historic associations;

(c) land of outstanding scenic or historic or scientific interest.

The conditions are that undertakings are given in relation to preservation and maintenance, while affording reasonable access to the public, and that the property will remain permanently in the UK except for a purpose and period approved by the Treasury.

Provided all requirements in respect of the transfer and the designation of the property are satisfied, and the undertakings are made, the property transferred is exempt (i.e. not included in any IHT computation) and no IHT liability arises.

5.13 NATIONAL HERITAGE PROPERTY - CHARGEABLE EVENTS

A sale of the conditionally exempted property, or a breach of the undertakings, will give rise to a charge to IHT based on the net sale proceeds or on the market value (in circumstances other than a sale).

The rate of IHT will be based on the circumstances of the person who last made a conditionally exempt transfer of the property. This person is known as the "relevant person".

If the relevant person is still alive when the breach occurs, the lifetime rate of tax will be applied as though a transfer had been made when the chargeable event occurred. If the relevant person has died IHT will be charged as though the transfer was a marginal addition to his estate. If the conditionally exempt transfer was made during his lifetime the lifetime rates will be used. If it was made on death, the death rates will be applied.

5.14 BUSINESS PROPERTY RELIEF

Where there is a transfer of value and the whole or part of the value transferred is attributable to the value of any business property, the whole or part is reduced by an appropriate percentage. The property to which the relief applies may be any:

(a) property consisting of a business (e.g. as a sole trader) or an interest in a business (e.g. share in a partnership);

(b) shares in or securities of a trading company which (either by themselves or together with other such shares or securities owned by the transferor) gave the transferor control of the company immediately before the transfer;

(c) shares (but not securities) of a trading company not included in (b) above and which are not listed on a recognised stock exchange (i.e. a minority holding in an unquoted company);

(d) land or buildings or machinery or plant which, immediately before the transfer, was used wholly or mainly for the purposes of a business carried on by a company of which the transferor then had control, or by a partnership of which he then was a partner, or if part of settled property, was used by the life tenant for his business.

The definition of business includes a business carried on in the exercise of a profession or vocation, but does not include a business carried on otherwise than for gain. Plant and machinery in general will mean those assets which would normally be eligible for capital allowances.

The value transferred of property falling into categories (a) and (b) is reduced by fifty per cent, while for categories (c) and (d) the reduction is thirty per cent.

In general, the property must have been owned by the transferor for at least 2 years before the transfer. Special rules apply to replacement assets.

Business property relief does not apply to:

(a) shares or securities of companies dealing in land or buildings, stocks, shares or securities (except for stock jobbers and discount houses in the UK), or holding companies of one or more companies whose business is dealing in land etc;

(b) shares or securities in companies in liquidation;

(c) business property where there is a binding contract of sale, except where this is to a company formed to take them over in exchange mainly for shares or securities, or where the sale is made for the purposes of reconstruction or amalgamation.

Where property qualifying for relief has passed as a PET or chargeable transfer no relief will be available to reduce the tax or additional tax payable on a death within 7 years unless the original property has been held by the transferee from the date of the transfer to the death of the transferor. Partial relief will be available where only part of the original property is still held by the transferee.

Illustration

On 31st December 1986, K gave to his daughter:

(a) his greengrocery business valued at £80,000;

(b) 30% of his shares in Beta Ltd, an unquoted trading company valued at £70,000.

He had made no other transfers during his lifetime and died on 31st May 1991 leaving an estate valued at £150,000. The business and shares were still owned by his daughter at the date of K's death.

The transfer during his lifetime would have been a PET. On his death, the value transferred would be calculated as:

		£	£	£
Business			80,000	
Less: 50% BPR			40,000	
				40,000
Shares			70,000	
Less: 30% BPR			21,000	
				49,000
				89,000
Less: Annual exemption	1986/87	3,000		
	1985/86	3,000		
				6,000
				83,000
Value of estate				150,000
				233,000
IHT on £206,000		52,000		
on £ 27,000 @ 50%		13,500		
				65,500
Less: IHT on PET payable by donee:				
on £71,000		NIL		
on £12,000 @ 30%		3,600		
				3,600
Payable by executors				61,900

The final IHT payable by K's daughter will be:

Tax as above	£3,600
	======
60% thereof	£2,160
	======

5.15 AGRICULTURAL PROPERTY RELIEF

Agricultural property relief gives relief by reducing the value transferred of agricultural property by an appropriate percentage. Other exemptions and reliefs may then be applied. No claim is necessary as the relief is given automatically if the necessary conditions are satisfied.

For this purpose agricultural property means agricultural land or pasture and includes woodlands and any building used in connection with the intensive rearing of livestock or fish, and such cottages, farm buildings and farm houses (together with the land occupied with them) as is of a character appropriate to the property. Land and buildings used for the purpose of a stud farm are also treated as agricultural property.

The relief extends to that part of a transfer of value which is attributable to the agricultural value of the property, this being the value that would be given to the property if immediately before the transfer it had been subject to a perpetual covenant prohibiting its use for anything other than agriculture. Any part of the transfer of value that is not agricultural value will normally qualify for business property relief at the appropriate rate.

Note that personal property, livestock, deadstock and agricultural plant and machinery do not qualify for agricultural property relief (although growing crops do). However, business property relief may be available.

The property qualifies for relief where the transferor has occupied the land for the purposes of agriculture throughout the period of two years prior to the transfer. If the property is not occupied by the transferor relief will only be available where it is owned by him throughout the period of seven years prior to the transfer, and was during that time occupied (by him or someone else) for the purpose of agriculture. Occupation by a company over which the transferor has control is treated as occupation by the transferor.

The minimum period of occupation is deemed to be satisfied where the property transferred replaced other property and both in aggregate had been occupied by the transferor for two out of the five years immediately preceding the transfer. Similarly, the minimum period of ownership is deemed to be satisfied where the property transferred replaced other property and both in aggregate had been owned for seven out of the immediately preceding ten years, by the transferor and occupied (whether by him or someone else) for the purpose of agriculture during that period.

For agricultural property transferred after 9th March 1981 the percentage reduction applied to the transfer of value (or agricultural value) is:

(a) fifty per cent where the transferor has vacant possession of the agricultural property (or the right to obtain it within twelve months) at the time of the transfer;

(b) thirty per cent where the vacant possession qualification is not satisfied but the other qualifications are.

Illustration

W, a farmer in Hampshire, owned two farms:

(a) Greenacre: 700 acres, was acquired by him in 1964 and farmed by him alone since that date. Market value (vacant) £250,000, agricultural value £150,000;

(b) Whiteacre: 800 acres, was acquired by him in May 1981 and farmed under tenancy with his brothers in partnership. Tenanted value £350,000, agricultural value £195,000.

Transfers of value: (Lifetime or Death)

	£	£
(a) Greenacre		
(vacant possession; current rates apply)		
Development value £(250,000 - 150,000)		100,000
Agricultural value	150,000	
APR 50%	75,000	
		75,000
		175,000

Note: Business property relief may be available at 50% (asset of a sole trader) on the non-agricultural value of the property (i.e. on the £100,000). Any available general exemptions (e.g. the annual exemption) may then be applied.

	£	£
(b) Whiteacre		
Development value £(350,000 - 195,000)		155,000
Agricultural value	195,000	
APR 30%	58,500	
		136,500
		291,500

Note: Business property relief at 30% may be available on £155,000. If the land had not been farmed by Winston in partnership, but by another person(s), then the tenanted farm would not be qualifying business property eligible for business property relief.

5.16 FARMING COMPANIES

Where a transfer of shares in, or securities of a company occurs then agricultural property relief will be available if:

(a) agricultural property forms part of the company's assets and part of the value of the shares, etc, can be attributed to the agricultural value of that property; and

(b) the shares, etc, gave the transferor control of the company immediately before the transfer.

Control for this purpose means more than fifty per cent of the voting power with or without the inclusion of related property.

The condition for ownership and occupation must be satisfied by the company, and for this purpose any period of occupation by a person who subsequently controls the company will be deemed to be occupation by the company itself. In addition, the transferor must have owned the shares, etc, throughout the periods of either two or seven years, as appropriate. The company must also be able to satisfy the conditions to claim either the fifty per cent or thirty per cent relief that apply to individuals.

Illustration

T Ltd has owned a farm valued at £300,000 with an agricultural value of £240,000 for many years. Mr. T owns 20,000 out of the 30,000 £1 ordinary shares in issue and has farmed the property for eight years. On 6th April 1987 he transfers his holding of shares to his son, having used up the previous year's annual exemption. The shares are valued at £13 per share.

Mr. T dies on the 16th December 1993.

At death within seven years the value of the initial PET will be:

	£	£
Value of shares transferred (20,000 @ £13)		260,000
Agricultural property relief:		
Agricultural value attributable to shares transferred = £240,000 x $\frac{20,000}{30,000}$ =	160,000	
Relief at 50%		(80,000)
Business property relief:		
Value not qualifying for agricultural property relief = £260,000 - £160,000 =	100,000	
Relief at 50%		(50,000)
		130,000
Annual exemption 1987/88		3,000
		127,000
Lifetime transfer		127,000
IHT on £95,000	7,200	
on £32,000 @ 35%	11,200	
		18,400
20% thereof		3,680

5.17 WOODLANDS RELIEF

The IHT liability arising on growing timber on a transfer on death may be deferred until the timber is sold either felled or still growing, providing a claim is made in writing within two years of death. This relief also applies to the underwood but not the land, and will only apply if the woodland does not already fall within the relief for agricultural property.

The deceased must have held beneficial ownership of the woodland for at least five years prior to death or, if he held the woodland for a shorter period, he must have acquired it by gift or inheritance. Holding the controlling shares in a company which holds the woodland is not sufficient.

The relief is given by simply excluding the value of the growing timber from the IHT computation at death, so effectively reducing the IHT rate applicable to the rest of the estate.

Liability to IHT will arise when the trees are either sold or become the subject of a lifetime gift, but the tax will be calculated not by reference to the value at the date of death but by reference to the net sale proceeds or the net market value at the time of the gift. In addition, the rate of tax to be used is that applicable as if the net sale proceeds or market value formed the top-slice of the estate at the immediately previous death. The rate of IHT to be used is that at the time of sale. Once the timber has been transferred again on another death no tax is chargeable on subsequent disposals by reference to the first death. The tax due is payable within six months after the end of the month in which the disposal took place, and is payable by the person benefiting from the sale proceeds or by the legatee who is now disposing of the timber.

When calculating the net sale proceeds or net market value the following expenses (provided they are not allowable for income tax) may be deducted from the sale proceeds or market value:

(a) expenses of disposing of the trees and underwood;

(b) expenses of replanting within three years of disposal or such longer time as the Inland Revenue may allow;

(c) expenses of replanting because of a previous disposal, insofar as such expenses were not deducted from the earlier disposal.

Woodlands forming part of a business may qualify for business property relief on a lifetime or death transfer if the usual conditions for receiving that relief are satisfied. If election is made for woodlands relief, business property relief may be due on the value attributable to the rest of the business, including the land on which the trees are growing.

Illustration

H dies on 16th March 1987 leaving an estate of £387,000 which included commercial woodland worth £150,000 of which £40,000 is attributable to land and £110,000 to growing timber. H had made no chargeable lifetime transfers. By will he left the whole of his estate to his daughter Rosemary, who elected for the woodlands relief.

On 25th August 1989 Rosemary (who had continued the timber business) sold the timber, receiving net proceeds of £200,000.

Assume BPR is available.

IHT payable on H's death on 16th March 1987

	£	£
Chargeable estate excluding woodlands (£387,000 - £150,000)		237,000
Land (on which there is growing timber)	40,000	
Business property relief @ 50%	(20,000)	
		20,000
Chargeable estate at death		257,000
IHT on £257,000		77,500

Note: Business property relief may also apply to other business assets, but no details are given.

IHT payable on sale on 25th August 1989

	£	£
Chargeable estate at death		257,000
Net sale proceeds	200,000	
Business property relief @ 50%	(100,000)	
		100,000
		357,000
IHT payable by Rosemary		57,000

Note: Business property relief is available as the property would have qualified for it on H's death.

6.0 PLANNING POINTS

6.1 GENERAL

There are essentially two types of gift: gifts of income, and gifts of capital.

Gifts of income can be very efficient as they may attract total exemption from IHT, either through the small gift or annual exemptions or through the exemption for normal expenditure out of income. A particularly efficient method is the use of a deed of covenant. This will be effective where it is used by a parent to pass income either to an adult (aged over 18), or to a child or by a remoter relative - e.g. grandfather or grandmother to pass income to a child of any age.

Illustration

A wishes to give his grandson £2,000 per annum gross under deed of covenant.

	£
Net cost to grandfather £2,000 - 30% =	1,400
	=====
Received by grandson	1,400
Add: Tax credit	600
	2,000
Less: Personal allowance 1986/87	2,335
	-
Income tax recovered by grandson	600
	=====

This should be covered by the normal expenditure out of income exemption.

Gifts of income, whether or not under deed of covenant, could be made to beneficiaries under a will in order to provide for potential IHT liabilities on death.

The normal expenditure exemption could also be used to fund an interest-free loan. In this case a wealthy (say 60%) taxpayer could lend a capital sum to a relative, child etc. It would be supported by a written agreement stating that it is repayable on demand and could be secured on the borrower's house. This could then be used by the borrower to produce income.

Illustration

B makes an interest-free loan of £50,000 to C, his son. B pays income tax at 60% but his son is a basic rate taxpayer. The sum is invested by his son in securities producing 12% gross.

	£
Loss to B:	
Potential Income - £50,000 x 12%	6,000
Less: Income tax @ 60%	3,600
	2,400
	=====

	£
Gain to C:	
Income	6,000
Less: Income tax @ 29%	1,740
	4,260
Net income savings	1,860

Gifts of capital should be made in a tax advantageous way by reviewing both the future performance of the asset, and the availability of reliefs.

In general gifts should be made of assets which are likely to appreciate. These could consist of:

(a) shares in a family company or other investments;

(b) property with an existing tenant who might die or vacate the property.

Obviously these should be given as early as possible so that the 7-year chargeable period can elapse. Any capital gain should be deferred under s.79 FA 1980.

If the donee requires income then income-producing assets, debentures or preference shares should be given.

Wherever possible gifts should be made of assets which would qualify for the additional business property or agricultural property reliefs.

The identity of the donee is important; there is little benefit in passing property to a son or daughter who then passes it on to a grandchild. The property should be given to the grandchild directly. In addition, where substantial gifts of shares in a family company or an interest in a family business are being contemplated it may be possible to equalise estates by transfers of shares to a spouse or by making the spouse a partner before the gift is made, taking obvious note of the related property provisions and the restrictions on associated operations.

Where, on a death, there are substantial insurance benefits to be received from an employer's insurance scheme they should be nominated to children or other relatives rather than paid into the estate.

Illustration

A dies leaving an estate of £500,000 to his wife. His employers had insured his life for £150,000.

If this was paid to his wife it could possible bear an IHT charge of 60% - £90,000 on her death if she passed it to their children. It should be agreed with the trustees that this sum should be paid direct to his children or grandchildren, this will not be a chargeable transfer of value and considerable tax savings could result.

7.0 VARIATION OF DISPOSITIONS ON DEATH

It is possible to undertake a number of transactions or arrangements after the death which can nonetheless be treated as occurring on the death itself and therefore not give rise to a separate chargeable transfer. These include:

(a) any Deed of Family Arrangement or similar instrument which alters or varies the provisions either of a will or the provisions arising on an intestacy, providing such arrangements are made within two years of death;

(b) a disclaimer of any legacy or interest in the deceased person's estate if made within two years of the death;

(c) a disclaimer of an interest in settled property whether or not the interest arises on a death, but does not apply where the deceased merely had an interest in possession;

(d) a transfer of property by the legatee to other persons under a direction in the will, provided the transfer is made within two years of the death.

Sections 17 and 142 IHTA 1984 allow these variations of dispositions on death, so that the IHT on death is computed as if the deceased had made the variations (so possibly reducing the IHT liability) and the variation itself is not treated as a transfer of value.

It does not matter that assets are redirected to persons other than members of the family or persons mentioned in the will.

These provisions will not apply to any variation or waiver which is made for consideration in money or money's worth, unless the consideration is made in return for some other variation etc. in respect of the same estate. To take advantage of the provisions, the persons making the deed or instrument must submit a written notice of election to the Inland Revenue within six months of the date of the instrument (or such longer time as the Revenue may allow) which itself must be made within two years of the person's death.

The use of these provisions can provide substantial tax savings.

Illustration

X died leaving an estate of £164,000 to his wife. His wife died 6 months later leaving this estate, together with property of her own worth £153,000, to their children.

At present the position would be:

	£
IHT on husband's death (estate passes to wife)	NIL
IHT on wife's death on estate of (£164,000 + £153,000) = £317,000	110,500

If the terms of the husband's will were varied so that his estate was left to his children the position would be:

	£	£
IHT on husband's estate		33,100
on wife's estate		
on £129,000	19,100	
on £ 24,000 @ 40%	9,600	
		28,700
		61,800
Potential savings		48,700

8.0 CLOSE COMPANIES

Although only individuals can make chargeable transfers of value, where a close company makes such a transfer it will be apportioned amongst the participators with each being deemed to have made a transfer of the amount apportioned to him. These rules will not apply where the transfer is subject to tax elsewhere:

(a) under Schedule E where the shareholder is a director or employee;

(b) as a dividend in the hands of any other shareholders.

The amount apportioned to each shareholder will be included as a chargeable transfer in their individual computations and the IHT calculated as if they had made a net gift of the amount apportioned to them. The annual exemption may be deducted but not the small gift, marriage or normal expenditure exemptions. Where, however, the amount apportioned to any shareholder does not exceed five per cent of the total, although the IHT will be calculated by reference to the previous chargeable transfers of the shareholder, the amount apportioned will not be included in the IHT computation.

The liability to pay the IHT is that of the company but if it does not pay then there will be a liability on:

(a) the shareholders;

(b) the recipient of any benefit.

However, where the amount apportioned does not exceed five per cent of the total, the individual will escape any liability on the non-payment by the company.

Note also that there is a CGT implication in that the amount of the undervalue will reduce the base cost of the shares in the close company.

Changes in the voting rights of different classes of shares may give rise to a IHT liability.

9.0 ASSOCIATED OPERATIONS

A deemed transfer can arise where there has been a series of transactions which fall into the definition of associated operations. This is an anti-avoidance provision intended to prevent value being transferred between individuals in such a manner that value is passed from one person to another avoiding the normal liability for straightforward transfers.

Associated operations can be defined as two or more operations any of which affect the same property, or one of which affects one property and the other(s) affects property which represents that property. The definition also includes any two operations, of which one is effected with reference to the other, or with a view to enabling the other to be effected. An omission to exercise a right may be regarded as an operation. It does not matter that the operations concerned are not effected by the same person or whether or not they are simultaneous.

There are two exceptions to the associated operations provision. The granting of a lease for a full consideration is not to be taken to be associated with any operation effected more than three years after the grant, and no operation effected after the 27th March 1974 can be taken as associated with anything effected before that date.

Where a transfer of value is made by associated operations carried out at different times it is to be treated as made at the time of the last of them. However, if any one or more of the earlier operations also constitutes a transfer of value made by the same transferor, the value transferred by the earlier operation(s) is treated as reducing the value transferred by all the operations taken together. An exception to this rule arises where the transfer constituted by the earlier operation was exempt as a result of a transfer to a spouse, but the operations overall do not represent a transfer to a spouse, and are therefore not exempt as such.

10.0 FOREIGN PROPERTY AND DOUBLE TAX RELIEF

10.1 GENERAL

As already mentioned, where the transferor is domiciled or deemed to be domiciled in the UK, a charge to IHT will arise on his world-wide property. Where he is not UK domiciled a liability will only arise on UK situated property.

10.2 DOUBLE TAX RELIEF

Foreign death duties equivalent to IHT (or indeed taxes on lifetime transfers) may be payable on property situated in a foreign country. Where relief is not available under double-taxation agreements, the foreign transfer tax is allowed as a credit against the UK IHT liability on the relevant foreign property.

Illustration

X died on 1st January 1987 with an estate of £200,000, on which IHT of £80,000 was due. Included in his estate was a property in Spain valued at £50,000 on which foreign IHT was paid as follows: (1) £15,000, (2) £23,500.

	(1) £	(2) £
Value of property	50,000	50,000
	======	======
UK share of IHT $\left(\frac{80,000}{200,000}\right)$ = 40%	20,000	20,000
(1) Foreign tax paid £15,000 - no restriction	15,000	
(2) Foreign tax paid £23,500 - restricted to		20,000
UK IHT payable	5,000	Nil
	======	======

Where foreign transfer taxes as well as UK IHT are payable on property situated in both countries or in a third country, credit is given for a proportion of the foreign tax. The amount of credit is calculated by using the formula:

$$\frac{\text{IHT}}{\text{IHT + foreign tax}} \times \text{the lower of IHT or foreign tax}$$

10.3 EXPENSES

Costs of administration are not deductible. However, the additional costs of administering and realising property situated abroad will be allowed as a deduction from the value of the foreign property, but only up to five per cent of the value of that property.

11.0 ADMINISTRATION

11.1 GENERAL

The administration of IHT is in the hands of the Capital Taxes Office under the general direction of the Commissioners of Inland Revenue.

11.2 DATES OF PAYMENT OF IHT

Payment of IHT chargeable on lifetime transfers:

(a) made between 6th April and 30th September (inclusive) is due on the following 30th April;

(b) made between 1st October and 5th April (inclusive) is due six months after the end of the month in which the transfer was made.

The additional IHT payable on transfers made within three years before death or the IHT due when a PET becomes chargeable is due six months after the end of the month in which the death occurs.

Payment of IHT on death (by the PRs) is due on submission of their account (by law twelve months is allowed for the submission of the account to obtain probate). In practical terms the personal representatives must submit a form of account and pay the IHT before probate will be granted, the result being that the tax will often be paid before the due date.

11.3 INTEREST ON IHT

Where IHT is not paid on the due dates interest will be charged at:

(a) eleven per cent on other transfers;

(b) nine per cent on death transfers, including Pets.

11.4 IHT PAID BY INSTALMENTS

IHT may be paid in ten equal annual instalments if election is made by the taxpayer and liability arises because the transfer is of the following types of property:

(a) land of any description, wherever situated;

(b) shares and securities of any limited company which give control to the donor immediately prior to transfer;

(c) unlisted shares and securities which do not give control where the tax arises on a transfer on death and where the IHT represents at least twenty per cent of the total tax arising on that chargeable event, or where the payment of the IHT in one amount would cause undue hardship;

(d) unlisted shares and securities which do not give control but their value, exclusive of IHT, exceeds £20,000 and they represent at least ten per cent of the nominal value of the company;

(e) a business or an interest in a business;

(f) growing timber

In order to qualify to pay IHT by instalments the chargeable transfer must arise on the death of the donor, or on a lifetime gift where the IHT is paid by the recipient of the gift (except in the case of woodlands).

It is only possible to pay the IHT due on a PET where the transferee has retained the property transferred.

11.5 INTEREST ON IHT PAID BY INSTALMENTS

Interest attributable to land which does not qualify for agricultural relief and to shares in an investment or property company, is payable on the outstanding balance of the total IHT due at each interest date.

Where the IHT is attributable to any of the property listed above (other than land which does not qualify for agricultural relief and shares in an investment or property company), instalments are interest free if paid on time (i.e. interest is only charged while the instalments are in arrear).

12.0 TRUSTS

12.1 Whilst, in many cases, an outright gift of property is the easiest way of passing down assets, a transfer into trust can provide the settlor with the ability to influence investment and distribution policy, particularly as regards younger children.

There are three main types of settlement:

(a) those with an interest in possession;

(b) accumulation and maintenance settlements;

(c) those with no interest in possession (discretionary settlements).

In addition to the above, there is the base trust. In this case the assets are held by the trustees effectively as nominees for the beneficiary as he or she has the absolute right to receive both capital and income. Thus a transfer into such a settlement is really an outright gift of assets.

12.2 SETTLEMENTS WITH AN INTEREST IN POSSESSION

A person with an interest in possession in a settlement is considered to be beneficially entitled to the property contained within the settlement. If several people have an interest, each will be treated as owning his or her appropriate share of the property. Thus a life tenant in such a settlement would be treated as being the effective owner of the underlying assets which provide the income.

Lifetime transfers into such a trust will be chargeable lifetime transfers and thus will attract an immediate liability to IHT.

Illustration

On 30th June 1986, A transfers quoted shares worth £100,000 into a trust, the terms of which are that his brother receives the income for life and on his death the property should pass to his sister. (Ignore possible exemptions and reliefs.)

On the transfer of the property into trust the IHT would be:

		Gross	IHT
	£	£	£
Transfer		100,000	
IHT - on £95,000	3,600		
on £ 5,000 @ 17.5%	875		
	____		4,475

On the cessation of the interest in possession either by:

(a) the death of the life tenant; or

(b) the termination of the interest at a specific earlier date; or

(c) the gift or sale of the interest,

there will again be a charge to IHT.

If the interest is terminated during the lifetime of the beneficiary he will be treated as having made a chargeable lifetime transfer (not a PET). Where appropriate, the annual exemption, spouse exemption and relief for agricultural and business property are available.

On the death of the life tenant, the value of the assets contained within the settlement will be added into his estate. The IHT payable on the total of estate and trust assets will be apportioned rateably and the tax on the trust assets paid by the trustees of the settlement.

Illustration

B died on 31st October 1988. On her death she left the following:

	£
Greengrocery business worth	70,000
Residence	30,000
Personal effects	10,000

She was entitled to one half share in the income of the Alpha settlement. On her death the assets of the settlement were valued at £90,000.

She had made no earlier lifetime transfers.

	£	£
Value of estate		
Greengrocery business	70,000	
Less: 50% BPR	35,000	
		35,000
Residence		30,000
Personal effects		10,000
		75,000
One half share of assets of Alpha settlement		45,000
		120,000
IHT thereon:		
on £95,000		7,200
on £25,000 @ 35%		8,750
		15,950

Effective estate rate = $\frac{£15,950 \times 100}{120,000}$ = 13.29%

Payable by trustees of Alpha settlement	
45,000 x 13.29%	5,981
By executors	9,969
	15,950

If the beneficiary's spouse takes a life interest in the property on his death, or if the property reverts back to the settlor, there will be no IHT charge on the death of the beneficiary.

Where the beneficiary originally has a life interest in the settlement and then later on the property contained in the settlement passes to him absolutely there will be no liability to IHT on the termination of the settlement as he is already deemed to own the assets by being entitled to the income.

12.3 An accumulation and maintenance settlement is one where:

(a) One or more beneficiaries will acquire settled property either absolutely or at least an interest in possession at an age of not more than 25, and

(b) there is no interest in possession and the income of the settlor is to be accumulated or applied for the maintenance, education or benefit of a beneficiary.

Transfers into an A & M settlement are potentially exempt transfers and there will thus be no IHT liability unless the settlor dies within seven years of making the transfer. There will be no 10 year periodic charge, neither will there be a charge to IHT when the beneficiary takes his interest in the settlement.

Within the settlement income wil be liable at 45% (29% + additional rate tax of 16%) and must be accumulated by the trustees whilst the child is unmarried or under the age of 18. The income of the settlement will not be income of the settlor and the accumulated income can be distributed to the child after the age of 18 as capital.

These settlements can provide the trustees with considerable control over the assets in the settlement. As long as the child beneficiary receives an interest in the settlement (i.e. a settlement in the income) by the age of 25, he may not be entitled to receive the capital of the settlement until some time later.

Settlements with no interest in possession or discretionary trusts are the most flexible of all settlements. They will allow a settlor to put capital into a settlement and within limits leave the trustees totally free to determine how and when capital and income of the settlement will be distributed.

Capital introduced into a discretionary settlement is a chargeable lifetime transfer and IHT will be due on the "lifetime" scale. Additional IHT may be payable if the settlor dies within seven years.

On each tenth anniversary of the creation of the settlement there will be a liability to IHT. Broadly this will be equal to 30% of the IHT, calculated on lifetime rates, applied to the value of the trust property at the anniversary date accumulated with the value of the chargeable transfers made by the settlor within seven years before the creation of the settlement. Taking a maximum "lifetime" rate of IHT this would give a maximum rate of charge of 30% x 30% = 9%.

A further charge to IHT will apply when the assets leave the settlement.

Income accumulating within the settlement will be liable to income tax at 45%.

Appendix 1 Examination Questions

The following are provided to enable you to practise answering examination questions under examination conditions. Many of the problems have been taken from actual papers and our thanks must go to the ACCA, the ICAEW and the ICMA for allowing us to reproduce their question material here.
The questions will each require knowledge of several areas of the ACCA Level 3 syllabus. It would therefore be misleading to attempt to subdivide them into particular subject areas.

1 The employment of Mountain, who was sales manager of Alban plc, was terminated during July 1985. As a result of the termination he received a compensation payment of £60,000 from Alban plc.

Mountain died on 30th September 1986. By his Will he left £50,000 in trust for his two children, born in 1968 and 1970, with the residue of his estate absolutely to his wife.

The total amount of Mountain's salary, benefits and pension from Alban plc between 6th April 1986 and 30th September 1986 was £18,920. After his death the company paid a pension to his widow, the amount up to 5th April 1987 being £9,545.

Mrs Mountain, who was born in 1940, had commenced an interior design consultancy business on 1st December 1984, not having worked previously since the first child was born. Profits of the business, as adjusted for income tax, have been agreed as follows:

	£
Period ended 31st May 1985	3,278
Year ended 31st May 1986	7,804
Year ended 31st May 1987	9,472

There are no capital allowances for her business.

An election for separate taxation of Mrs Mountain's earnings has been in force since 1981/82, and you need not consider the possibility of withdrawal of the election for 1986/87.

The other income and outgoings of Mr and Mrs Mountain during the year ended 5th April 1987 were as follows:

	Mountain	Mrs Mountain	
	6.4.86 to 30.9.86	6.4.86 to 30.9.86	1.10.86 to 5.4.87

	£	£	£
Dividends from UK companies and tax credits	6,510	2,235	2,905
Dividends from foreign company - amount received after deduction of withholding tax 15% and UK income tax 14%			795
Income from Mountain's estate (gross)			5,840
Interest on mortgage of £22,000 obtained to buy their house (gross)	1,480		1,235
Covenanted payments to charity (gross)		120	260

Mrs Mountain has not made any provision for a pension based on her own earnings, and she asks you to advise her in connection with tax relief on premiums paid for this purpose.

You are required to:

(a) calculate the income tax chargeable on the compensation payment made to Mountain; (7 marks)

(b) calculate the income tax payable by Mrs Mountain for 1986/87 on her income as a widow; (10 marks)

(c) list the points that you would discuss with Mrs Mountain on the tax relief available on self-employed pension premiums. (4 marks)

(Total 21 marks)

2 Roberts, a married man, is employed as a sales manager by Spionkop plc, from whom he received salary and commission totalling £19,850 for the year ended 5th April 1987.

The company provides him with a BMW car (cost £17,600 in March 1986) and pays for all expenses and fuel, with the sole exception that Roberts has to pay for any fuel purchased on holiday abroad; the 1986/87 tables show a scale benefit of £1,320 and a fuel benefit of £900 for this car. During the year Roberts used the car for 19,500 business miles and 8,500 private miles, including a holiday in Europe during which he spent £215 on petrol.

Mrs Roberts had not worked for many years before 1st December 1985 when she commenced a business providing a travelling accounting service for farmers. Her first accounts were made up to 31st December 1986 and showed a profit, as adjusted for income tax, of £7,176.

The only asset on which capital allowances are claimed is her car, which had been bought for £4,400 on 3rd January 1985 and used privately before business commenced. On 1st December 1985 the car had a market value of £3,600 as certified by the dealer who had supplied it; the Inspector of Taxes has agreed that 75% of the use of the car is for business.

Mrs Roberts also owns 3 properties (A, B and C) which she has let unfurnished at full rents payable in advance on the usual quarter days:

A Rent £2,000 per annum under a lease for seven years expiring in 1988. Tenant is responsible for all repairs.

B Rent £2,200 per annum under a lease for five years which expired on 25th December 1986. Empty until 25th March 1987, when let on a lease for five years at rent of £2,600 per annum. Mrs Roberts is responsible for all repairs.

C Used as a holiday home by Mr and Mrs Roberts until 31st August 1986. Empty until 29th September 1986, when let for three years at a rent of £1,000 per annum. Mrs Roberts is responsible for all repairs.

Her expenditure on these properties during 1986/87 was as follows:

	A	B	C
	£	£	£
Agents' commission	117	130	190
Advertising for tenants		205	40
Ground rent	48		
Repairs - while let		980	730
- while empty		840	550

During 1986/87 Roberts received dividends from UK companies totalling £7,445 (including tax credit) and paid interest under the MIRAS scheme on a £15,000 mortgage on their residence, the actual amount paid to the Building Society being £1,221. Mrs Roberts paid £426 (net) under four-year convenants in favour of charities.

Mr and Mrs Roberts have not previously elected for separate taxation of her earnings, but ask you to advise them whether they should do so for 1986/87. Mrs Roberts, who is aged 41, also asks you for advice on providing for a retirement annuity based on her earnings; she would like to obtain the maximum relief against 1986/87 earnings if this is possible.

You are required to:

(a) prepare computations (ignoring the possible payment of a retirement annuity premium) of the total income tax payable by Mr and Mrs Roberts for 1986/87 in order to advise them whether a wife's earnings election should be made; (14 marks)

(b) state your advice on connection with the retirement annuity premium. (4 marks)

(Total 18 marks)

3 Valentine resigned from his partnership in a firm of stockbrokers in December 1984. On 1st July 1985 he purchased a small estate in Kent and commenced farming; the purchase price was £1,450,000, made up of £1,320,000 for land and buildings and £130,000 for livestock.

None of the farm machinery was purchased, and Valentine has leased all the machinery used since 1st July 1985.

The farm accounting date is 31st March and his first two accounts have produced the following agreed figures for income tax purposes:

	Profit
	£
Period ended 31st March 1986	29,250
Year ended 31st March 1987	62,600

Profits for the year ending 31st March 1988 are expected to show a substantial increase.

The previous owner of the farm had incurred the following qualifying expenditure on agricultural buildings since 31st March 1975:

	£
In year ended 31st March 1976	11,800
In year ended 31st March 1977	nil
In the 7 years from 1 April 1977 to 31 March 1984	114,600
In the year ended 31st March 1985	6,700
From 1st April 1985 to 30th June 1985	nil

Valentine spent £28,400 on an extension to his milking parlour in March 1986.

On 7th April 1986, Valentine married a widow with a child aged eleven. Mrs Valentine was employed as a buyer by Harry Elliott plc and she continued her employment after marriage. Her salary has been £7,944 per annum since 1st March 1986 and she has also received the following amounts from the company:

Date received	For year ended	Commission	Dividend (cash amount)
		£	£
17th July 1986	31st March 1986	1,235	3,820
30th June 1987	31st March 1987	1,646	3,802

In June 1983 Harry Elliott plc provided a car for Mrs Valentine, paying all expenses and petrol, including private use. The car, for which the normal scale benefit for 1986/87 is £450 and in respect of which the normal fuel benefit for 1986/87 is £450, was sold on 31st January 1987 and Mrs Valentine used a pool car for business journeys until a further car was provided on 15th April 1987. Her business mileage from 6th April 1986 to 31st January 1987 was 2,300.

Other information on the form P11D for Mrs Valentine for 1986/87 was as follows;

	£
Travelling on the company's business	2,540
Medical insurance - BUPA subscription	134
- policy providing cover while travelling abroad on business	465

Her duties involve regular overseas visits, and during the year ended 5th April 1987 she spent 41 qualifying days outside the UK.

Although Mrs Valentine has been resident in the UK for several years she has retained her domicile of origin in a foreign country. She is entitled to income from a trust in that country, the income (after deduction of foreign tax at 20%) being paid into her bank account in that country. Until recently no income was remitted to the UK, but from May 1985 remittances have been made.

The amounts of her trust income and remittances in recent years have been as follows:

	Paid into foreign bank	Remitted to UK
	£	£
Year ended 5th April 1985	2,180	nil
1986	3,065	350
1987	4,150	1,000

No initial allowance was claimed on any expenditure up to 31.3.1984.

<u>You are required to:</u>

(a) calculate the net Schedule D assessments on Valentine's farming business for the years 1985/86 to 1987/88, assuming all possible reliefs are claimed;

(10 marks)

(b) calculate the income tax borne by Mrs Valentine for 1986/87. (8 marks)

(Total 18 marks)

4 R Robb is appointed Sales Director of the Wirral Widget plc, a UK registered company, on 1st April 1986 at a salary of £20,000 per annum. The Company also provided him with:

(a) a new company car, a 2,500 cc model, costing £10,000; his normal mileage is 25,000 miles of which 20% is non-business: total annual expenditure for the car, paid by the company is £2,800, including fuel;

(b) a company-owned new TV Video System in his house costing £800.

On 1st July 1986 he flew from London to Egypt on the first stage of a sales visit from which he returned to London on 12th September 1986. For the month of August 1986 he was joined by his wife Sally and their younger son. The company reimbursed Robb £1,600 for their fares and £1,000 for their accommodation. He contributes 4% basic salary to an approved superannuation scheme. Following his return from overseas, the company transferred him to its headquarters outside London. Robb sold his dwelling house in London for £55,000: he had bought it for £62,500 three years ago: under the company's housing scheme, the company compensated him in full for his loss on this sale. It also made him a loan of £25,000 at 5% per annum payable monthly from 1st November 1986 to assist his purchase of a new house: he has no other mortgage.

Robb has a pension of £750 per annum from a German company for whom he worked in Africa for ten years.

During the year, Mr Robb's wife subscribed for 10,500 £1 ordinary shares at issue of the Rose Boutique Ltd, a trading company owned equally by five unconnected individuals: she has no other connection than as shareholder: she borrowed £8,000 from the Bank at 12% per annum, payable quarterly in arrears, on 1st October 1986.

Required

Compute R. Robb's taxable income for 1986/87. (Do not calculate tax payable but comment very briefly on your treatment of benefits in kind). (15 marks)

5 Jerry has been appointed by the Board of his company, XYZ (Surrey) Ltd to be the next managing director from March 1987. His present salary of £25,000 will then be doubled: he is married. He calls at your office to discuss the following proposals for reducing his income tax liability:

(a) to increase his provision for retirement pension by membership of an additional scheme that the company is developing for senior executives. Presently his contribution is 4%. He would be permitted to contribute a further £4,500 per annum and the company would pay in £7,500 on his behalf;

(b) to purchase 40 acres of rough land for £10,000 in August 1987 and develop a woodland scheme calling for development expenditure of £8,000 per annum in 1987/88 and the three following years;

(c) to arrange a 'golden handshake' of £75,000 on retiring in ten years;

(d) to invest £5,000 per annum in 'gilt-edged' securities.

Required:

(a) Comment briefly upon his proposals. (14 marks)

(b) Ilustrate their combined effect for 1987/88, assuming that existing personal allowances and tax rates continue to apply. (5 marks)
(Total 19 marks)

6 Walters and Mitchell have been in partnership as public relations consultants since 1974. On 31st July 1986 Walters retired from the firm on reaching the age of 70; on the next day Barnett, who was the firm's manager, was admitted as a partner.

The partnership profit-sharing arrangements before and after the change are summarised below:

	Walters	Mitchell	Barnett
Up to 31st July 1986:			
Annual salaries	£3,000	£7,500	
Share of profit or loss	55%	45%	

	Walters	Mitchell	Barnett
From 1st August 1986			
Annual salaries		£6,000	£6,000
Share of profit or loss		60%	40%

Under the terms of the partnership agreement the partners in the new firm convenanted on 1st August 1986 to pay Walters an annuity of £5,000, payable quarterly commencing on 31st October 1986.

Accounts have always been made up to 31st July and recent results, as adjusted for income tax, have been as follows:

Year ended 31st July 1983	Profit £16,200 and Capital Allowances £2,600
Year ended 31st July 1984	Loss £2,850 and Capital Allowances £15,450

The profit and loss account for the year ended 31st July 1985 was as follows:

	£	£
Fees receivable		48,700
Depreciation	1,630	
Salaries - staff	8,740	
- manager (Barnett)	6,800	
- partners (Walters and Mitchell)	10,500	
Other expenses (all allowable)	17,020	44,690
Net profit		4,010

There was no capital allowances based on the year ended 31st July 1985.

Notice of election for the continuing basis has been properly given by the partners.

Walters and Mitchell both wish to claim relief for the loss for the year ended 31st July 1984 and related capital allowances as soon as possible, but do not wish to include their wives' incomes for this purpose.

Walters had private investment income of £2,425 for 1984/85 and £2,760 for 1985/86. Mitchell had no private income in either year; he pays £4,000 per annum as maintenance under a court order in favour of his previous wife.

You are required to:

(a) show the amounts to be included in the total income of Walters, Mitchell and Barnett for 1986/87 in respect of the partnership, assuming that there are no further changes in the partnership by 5th April 1987; (12 marks)

(b) outline the effect of the annuity payments on the income tax liabilities of Walters and the continuing partners; (5 marks)

(c) explain how the Finance Act 1985 has changed the basis of taxation of partnerships. (6 marks)

(Total 23 marks)

7 A partnership of Alex, Bert and Charles distributes irrigation equipment throughout the world. Profits/losses are shared: Alex 50%, Bert 30%, Charles 20%. Schedule D, Case I computations have been agreed by HM Inspector of Taxes as follows:

	£
Year to 31st July 1985	3,300
Year to 31st July 1984	16,480
Year to 31st July 1983	10,340
Year to 31st July 1982	11,240
Year to 31st July 1981	15,000

Owing to political disturbances in a number of market areas, the partnership made a loss, adjusted for tax purposes, of £26,280 in the period ending 31st January 1986. Alex retired at this date. The business was taken over by Aquamove Ltd, incorporated on 1st February 1986, whose ordinary £1 share holdings are divided; Bert 40,000, Charles 35,000, Powerpumps plc (a company quoted on the Stock Exchange) 25,000.

For the year to 31st January 1987 Aquamove's Corporation Tax profit was £20,000: it paid an interim dividend of 15% on 22nd December 1986: directors' salaries included £10,000 each for Bert and Charles.

Alex, Bert and Charles are all married. Alex's savings account with the Bank of Wessex shows interest credited, 1st November 1982, £350; 1983, £402; 1984, £416; 1985, £605; 1986, £700; 1987, £527. The account was opened in the early 1970s.

Bert pays £1,500 and Charles £1,150 interest each year to the building society on their principal private residences.

Required:

Compute the loss relief claims most advantageous to the partners and explain the reasons for your choice.

Note

For purposes of answering this question the married personal allowance for earlier years can be taken as:

1986/87	£3,655
1985/86	£3,455
1984/85	£3,155
1983/84	£2,795
1982/83	£2,445
1981/82	£2,145

(23 marks)

8 John, Bob and Steve were equal partners for many years in a manufacturing business. Steve retired on 30th September 1985, Tom joined the partnership on 1st October 1985. The accounts have been prepared to 3rd May each year and this date has been retained: no accounts were prepared at 30th September 1985. The following information is derived from the partnership accounts:

Year to 3rd May	1986	1987	1988
Adjusted tax profit on accounts before any relief	57,218	66,184	77,424
Plant/Machinery purchased - 30.4.86	6,250		
- 30.4.87	-	3,128	
Building for developing and testing new design projects - completed 27th April 1986	7,250	-	-

For many reasons all partners agreed that an election under TA 1970, s.154(2) would not be made on the change of partnership.

When the Schedule D, Case I assessments for the old partnership (John, Bob and Steve) were amended, the following were unutilised for 1984/85:

	Losses	C/A
	£	£
John	4,145	1,863
Bob	1,262	3,492

The new partnership (John, Bob and Tom) agreement:

(a) provides for annual salaries - John £8,000; Bob £5,000;

(b) determines share of profit - John 25%; Bob 35%; Tom 40%;

(c) grants a specified annuity to a retired partner, all existing partners contributing. Steve qualifies for £4,200 pa gross from the date of retirement. In this respect, this repeats the terms of the old partnership agreement. The annuity is paid monthly under deduction of tax;

(d) allows Tom to absent himself from the UK for up to 100 days in any period of 18 months to engage in a mineral exploration partnership (set up in 1973) with his brother who lives in Australia. This partnership operates from Adelaide, South Australia and has no interest nor contacts whatsoever outside Australia. Tom's share of the Australian profit for the year to 31st December 1984 was £8,000 - to 31st December 1985, £10,000 and to 31st December 1986, £8,500. Tom remits only £1,000 a year to the UK. He departed for Australia on 1st March 1986 and returned on 1st May 1986. (Ignore Australian Tax.)

John is married and has grossed UK dividends of £10,000 pa. Neither Bob nor Tom is married and neither has any other income.

Required:

(a) Compute Schedule D, Case I assessments for the new partnership, together with capital allowances for all relevant years of assessment. (13 marks)

(b) Compute the taxable income of the new partners for 1985/86 and 1986/87. (Do not compute tax chargeable.)

(12 marks)
(Total 25 marks)

9 Charles Redd and Tom Wood, who trade as Redwood Furniture, are thinking about forming a new company, Redwood Decor Ltd, to take over their partnership business from 1st April 1987. In their partnership, which commenced on 1st April 1967, profits and losses are shared equally.

Various details are shown below:

	Cost		Estimated value at 1st April 1987
	£		£
Freehold factory	27,000	(1.4.1969)	149,000
Plant etc.	44,000	(various dates)	32,000
Goodwill	-		46,000
Stock in trade	72,000		72,000
Trade debtors	32,000		32,000
Trade creditors			51,000
			280,000

At 31st March 1982 the marked value of the factory was agreed to be £100,000, and that of the goodwill £30,000. The tax written-down values for capital allowances at 6th April 1986 were - Factory nil; plant etc £10,000. The partnership proposes to purchase a new machine costing £25,000 on 4th February 1987 (which is included in the estimated value above).

Adjusted trading profits have been agreed with HM Inspector of Taxes as follows:

Year to 31st March 1986 - £150,000
Year to 31st March 1985 - £120,000
Year to 31st March 1984 - £100,000

Year to 31st March 1983 - £ 80,000

The projected profit for the year to 31st March 1987 - £160,000.

It is suggested that the new company would acquire the partnership business in exchange for 280,000 £1 Ordinary Shares. Redd prefers the exchange to be 200,000 £1 Ordinary Shares and to put £80,000 on loan account with the company for Wood and himself as directors.

Your tax partner asks you to outline for him the tax difficulties which may arise in these proposals, but not yet to prepare alternative plans.

The Retail Price Index may be taken to be:

April 1969	102.3
March 1982	313.4
March 1987	420.3

Required:

Prepare in outline your commments with illustrative figures regarding the implications for:

(a) Income tax, and capital allowances. (10 marks)

(b) Capital gains tax (5 marks)
(Total 15 marks)

10 Solomon Matthews, a chartered surveyor, receives an estimated assessment dated 15th October 1986 in respect of his practice profits for 1986/87 of £30,000, with tax charged at £14,000. He appeals against the assessment on 11th November 1986, and applies for postponement of £5,000 of tax. The Inspector of Taxes agrees his postponement application on 27th January 1987.

The final assessment figures are determined by the Commissioners on 11th August 1987, showing tax due of £17,000.

Required:

(1) State the due dates of payment of the tax.

(2) State the reckonable dates in respect of the interest on overdue tax incurred.

(3) Assuming that Matthews settles the full liability on 1st October 1987, calculate the interest on overdue tax incurred.

(Assume interest on overdue tax is charged at 8.5%) (13 marks)

11 Mr Van Rijn was born in the Netherlands in April 1917 and educated there. He is the managing director of a Netherlands electronics company in Amsterdam. In 1939 he came to the UK and joined the Royal Air Force. From 1945-49 he studied engineering at London University and then returned to the Netherlands where he has lived since. His wife is English and though they visit the UK regularly they have never previously done so in two consecutive years of assessment and never for longer than two months. The following points arise:

(a) Mr Van Rijn visited the UK with his wife from 22nd April - 24th June 1986. During his visit, he was engaged as a consultant on several research projects of a UK supplier company: he was paid £5,000.

(b) He and his wife own four cottages in the UK which produce £750 each per half-year, net of expenses.

(c) Mrs Van Rijn inherited a farm in the UK from her father on his death in 1975. It was rented and when the tenant farmer died on 2nd April 1987 it was sold for £135,000 (after expenses). At her father's death, the probate value was £92,500.

(d) For many years Mr and Mrs Van Rijn have derived an income from £10,000 3½% War Loan and £12,000 15½% Treasury Loan 1998.

Required:

Discuss these points, explaining whether or not UK tax will arise. (15 marks)

12 Pierre Gaston was born in France in August 1928. He qualified as an engineer and worked for a major French company until 31st December 1963. On 1st Janury 1964 he came to the UK, at the request of the French company, to set up a UK subsidiary operation. Prior to coming to the UK, he married a French girl, Monique, and she came to the UK with him.

It has always been the intention of Pierre and Monique Gaston to return to France in their later years and spend the rest of their lives there.

The following points arise:

(a) Pierre wishes to sell a large shareholding in a French company, and with the proceeds purchase a villa in the South of France. He will go there for occasional holidays and during the rest of the year he will let it for a substantial rent.

(b) Monique's mother, who had been living in France, has recently died leaving her an expensive painting. Monique is thinking of gifting the painting to her old art teacher in France. The painting has always been held in France.

(c) Monique's mother has also left her a bank account of £100,000. Monique would like to leave the money to earn interest in France, but would occasionally like to bring over sums of money to the UK for her own use.

Required:

Discuss these points, explaining whether or not UK tax will arise. (Ignore any possible French taxation.) (15 marks)

13 **THE OLIVIA AERO ENGINE CO LTD**

Profit and Loss Account for the 65 weeks ended 31st March 1986 (i)

	£	£
Turnover		1,262,000
Net trading profit after charging:		351,500
Directors' remuneration	42,000	
Auditors' fees and expenses	4,600	
Hire of plant and machinery	5,400	
Depreciation of fixed assets (ii)	31,400	
Amortisation of 50-year lease of premises	6,500	
Patent royalties (gross) (iii)	16,000	
Provision for bad debts through insolvency of major customer	25,000	
Income from investments:		
Dividends from UK companies (iv)	17,080	
Rents received (v)	24,250	41,330
	c/f 172,230	c/f 392,830

	b/f	172,230	b/f 392,830
		£	£
Net profits before interest, taxation and extraordinary items			392,830
Interest payable: On bank overdraft		6,100	
On debentures repayable August 1990		10,500	(16,600)
Corporation tax		110,000	
Less: Over-provided in 1984		4,500	(105,500)
			270,730
Extraordinary items:			
Surplus on sale of shares held as an investment (vi)			13,520
Payment for infringement of patent (iii)			(4,500)
Capital sum to establish profit-sharing scheme for employees (vii)			(18,900)
Expenses of loan stock issue (viii)			(1,224)
Net profit for the accounting period			259,626
transferred to reserve to redeem 9% Debenture Stock			(10,000)
Dividends paid and proposed (ix)			(72,670)
Unappropriated profit carried forward			176,956
			=======

Notes

(i) The company's accounting date was changed to be more in accord with its pattern.

(ii) Depreciation -

	£
Plant and machinery	16,400
Buildings (including sales office not qualifying for capital allowances £1,950)	15,000

(iii) Patent royalities are calculated on certain sales. Owing to a legal dispute payment for the twelve months to 31st December 1984 (£9,000) was withheld and paid on 1st September 1985. The payment for the period to 31st August 1985 (a total of £4,600) was made on 31st January 1986. Royalties due at 31st March 1986 (£11,400), though not yet paid, have been reserved in the profit and loss account.

On 1st July 1985 OAEC Ltd paid £4,500 as a penalty for an infringement of the UK patent.

(iv) Dividends received:

- from ordinary shares £6,650 on 31st May 1985
- from 9% cum. pref. shares £10,430 on 15th November 1985.

The cumulative preference dividend represented arrears unpaid for 1983 and 1984.

(v) Rental income includes:

(a) rents from residential properties let to tenants on a 14 year lease at £10,800 per year payable quarterly until 1989. Rent owing from a previous tenant of £2,500, which was written off in 1978, was received from his executors on 1st December 1985 and is included in the accounts. Relevant allowable expenditure, £800 per quarter, has already been charged in the trading account of OAEC Ltd.

(b) The remaining rent is received on a monthly basis.

(vi) Shares in the Tornado Engine Co plc, acquired for £10,500 on 7th April 1965, were sold on 8th April 1985 for £24,020 (net of incidental expenses) to provide cash as working capital. Their market value at 31st March 1982 was £15,000.

(vii) The company's profit-sharing scheme was given Revenue approval on 6th April 1985. The fund was formally set up on 6th May 1985.

(viii) On 31st March 1986 the company made an issue of £30,000 loan stock at 12 %, redeemable in 1990 or convertible into ordinary shares at that time. Included are secretarial and printing costs £364, solicitor's fees £410, stamp duty £450.

(ix)

Dividends	£	Declared	Paid
Preference shares	6,300	20.12.84	2.1.85
Ordinary shares (final 1984)	37,500	28. 2.85	6.6.85
Ordinary shares (interim 1985/86)	53,500	31.10.85	1.3.86
Preference shares	6,300	21.12.85	4.1.86
Ordinary shares (final 1985/86)	12,870	10. 4.86	31.5.86

(x) The following information appears in the notes to the balance sheet at 31st March 1986:

Fixed assets - additions:			
Machinery	12.1.85	38,000	
Machinery	29.4.85	25,500	(see note (v)(b))
Machinery	15.1.86	1,206	
Buildings	21.3.85	25,200	
(Extension to research laboratory)			
Motor cars 30.3.85:			
Managing Director		12,000	
3 sales representatives		18,000	

(The capital allowance written-down value for plant/machinery, other than that shown above, is £26,000: for cars £4,280 (bought June 1983) at 31st December 1984.

Debenture interest (£8,400 pa) is paid on 15th December annually. The company is not a close company for corporation tax. The company commenced to trade on 1st January 1934.

RPI	March 1982	313.4
	April 1985	373.9

Required:

Compute the mainstream corporation tax payable by the company and state when it is payable. (29 marks)

14

(a) Q Ltd which commenced to trade on 1st December 1984, is a wholly-owned subsidiary of T Ltd. Trading results are as follows:

	Q Ltd	T Ltd
	£	£
Year to 30.11.84		(5,000)
Trading profit (loss)	-	
Year to 30.11.85		
Trading profit (loss)	(12,000)	10,000
Bank interest received	-	5,000
Debenture interest (gross) paid	-	2,000
Year to 30.11.86		
Trading profit (loss)	(5,000)	(10,000)
Bank interest received	-	5,000
Debenture interest (gross) paid	-	2,000

Required:

Ilustrate how loss relief is claimed and why you make your particular form of claim in these circumstances. Explain how unrelieved losses and charges may be dealt with. (9 marks)

(b) The issued share capital of Z Ltd is 80,000 £1 ordinary shares. 48,000 are owned by A Ltd, 24,000 by B Ltd and 8,000 by C Ltd. Trading results of all companies, which are resident in the UK, for the year to 30th June 1986 are:

		£
Z Ltd	profit	50,000
A Ltd	profit	40,000
B Ltd	loss	(60,000)
C Ltd	profit	10,000

Explain fully how and in what conditions B Ltd's loss may be relieved.

(6 marks)
(Total 15 marks)

15 Bandroyal Limited has the following sources of income for the year ended 31st March 1986:

	£
Schedule D, Case I	400,000
Rental income	40,000
Dividend from overseas subsidiary	see below
Capital gains (before reduction)	40,000

It paid debenture interest of £50,000 on 1st August 1985, and a dividend of £441,000 on 1st January 1986.

During the year, Bandroyal received a dividend from its wholly-owned subsidiary in Ruritania amounting to £144,000, after withholding-tax of 10% had been deducted by the Ruritanian tax authorities.

The subsidiary company had paid 20% tax on its profits as they arose.

Required:

Calculate the Mainstream Corporation Tax payable by Bandroyal Limited for the year ended 31st March 1986, clearly showing the utilisation of foreign tax and ACT paid.

Corporation tax	40%
ACT	3/7ths
Capital Gains Reduction Fraction	1/4th

(10 marks)

16 A Ltd has the following results for the year ended 31st March 1986:

Trading Income	50,000
Bank interest received	20,000
Rental income less outgoings	10,000
Capital gains (before reduction)	12,000
Dividends received (net)	1,400
Charges paid (gross)	16,000
Dividends paid (net)	58,800

The company has also received a dividend of £10,800 from its wholly-owned subsidiary in Ruritania (a foreign country). The dividend has suffered withholding-tax of 10%. The rate of tax paid on corporate profits in Ruritania is 40%.

Calculate the company's liability for Mainstream Corporation Tax, for the year ended 31st March 1986, indicating clearly the amount of foreign tax wasted and ACT carried forward.

Assume:	Corporation tax	40%
	ACT	3/7ths

(15 marks)

17 Verity Spinners Ltd is a close company engaged in the textile industry; it also owns residential properties which are let. The company owns 60% of the ordinary share capital of Langridge Ltd, which operates retail shops.

For many years Verity Spinners Ltd has made up accounts to 31st March, and in the year ended 31st March 1985 the company incurred a loss of £96,100 (including capital allowances) in its trade. Claims for relief were made against the profits of that year and the previous year, the amount of loss so used being £47,448.

The profit and loss account for the year ended 31st March 1986 may be summarised as follows:

	£
Profit on trading	102,846
Rental income (net of related expenses)	13,220
Investment income	9,290
Surplus on a sale of a residential property	16,130
	141,486

Items charged in arriving at the profit on trading include the following:

	£
Depreciation (including amortisation of lease)	20,800
Patent royalties (gross)	7,850
Repairs at Kirkstall Mill:	
Alterations to accommodate new machinery	3,200
Replacement of fencing	6,970

The patent royalties were payable under an agreement entered into in August 1985. The amount charged in the accounts includes £1,440 accrued, but not yet paid, at 31st March 1986.

The investment income, which was all received during the accounting period, consists of the following items:

	£
Interest on bank deposit	2,340
Dividend from Langridge Ltd (paid under a group election to pay dividends without accounting for advance corporation tax)	5,250
Dividends from other UK companies (including tax credit)	1,700
	9,290

The surplus on sale of a residential property relates to a house sold for £42,350 on 16th February 1986; the house had been bought for £26,220 in 1970. The Retail Price Index was 313.4 for March 1982 and 410.4 for February 1986. The market value of the house at 31st March 1982 was £35,000.

The main premises of Verity Spinners Ltd are at Kirkstall Mill, which has been occupied since 1st May 1979 under a lease for 20 years; a premium of £55,000 was paid for the lease. The lessor had acquired the land for £9,000 in 1970 and completed construction of the mill on 1st January 1974 at a cost of £124,500. In February 1981, with the permission of the lessor, Verity Spinners Ltd incurred expenditure of £31,600 on an extension to the building for the purpose of storing raw materials.

On 1st June 1985 the company purchased Park Mill in order to increase production capacity, paying £115,000 (including £17,500 for land) to another company which had used the building continuously as a mill since construction was completed on 1st June 1972. The original cost was £10,000 for land and a further £62,650 for construction.

On 10th March 1986 Verity Spinners Ltd paid £26,500 for the erection of a small laboratory in the grounds of Park Mill for the purposes of technical research into matters connected with the trade.

The pool value of the company's plant and machinery on 1st April 1985 was nil. During the year ended 31st March 1986 purchases of new machinery totalled £58,500 and sales realised £6,100; no item was sold for more than it cost.

The last dividend paid by Verity Spinners Ltd was in August 1984.

<u>You are required to calculate:</u>

(a) the corporation tax payable by Verity Spinners Ltd for the year ended 31st March 1986; (15 marks)

(b) the maximum amount of income which may be apportioned to the members for the year. (7 marks)

(Total 22 marks)

18

(a) The ordinary share capital of North Yorkshire Plastics Ltd is acquired by the Mendips Investment plc in July 1987. NY Plastics operated specialist manufacturing processes. Owing to changes in market patterns its trade had begun to diminish from about 1984. By July 1985 it had unrelieved corporation tax losses of £420,000, surplus ACT of £75,000 and losses for CGT of £36,000. Mendips Investment plc contemplates extending the design function of NY Plastics for use by other companies within its group and to diversify somewhat the range of NY Plastics' manufacturing activities. Four of the seven directors of NY Plastics will retire.

You are required to comment on any taxation difficulties that may arise from this proposal.

(7 marks)

(b) Recent legislation (FA 1980, s.117) introduced 'demerger' provisions to make easier the splitting of a larger unit into smaller units.

<u>Required</u>

Explain:

(i) what are the two principal problems which caused obstacles to demergers?

(ii) what solutions are contained in the 1980 legislation?

(iii) what are the main conditions for exemption under the legislation?

(8 marks)

(Total 15 marks)

19 Jardine, who was born on 23rd October 1917, is resident and ordinarily resident in the UK. During the year ended 5th April 1987 he carried out the following capital transactions, none of which was with a connected person.

(a) On 1st December 1986 he sold 3,000 unquoted ordinary shares in Townsend Ltd for £13,500.

Before the sale he owned 4,000 shares, which he had bought as follows:

8th June 1956	1,500 shares for	£4,200
3rd April 1962	2,500 shares for	£12,800

You are informed that in both 1963 and 1964 Townsend Ltd suffered substantial losses and accordingly it is likely that the market value of the shares on 6th April 1965 was only about £2 each.

(b) On 3rd April 1987 he sold all his unquoted ordinary shares in Clark (Winchester) Ltd for £20,700. Jardine had been a full-time director of the company, which sells video equipment, since he bought the shares for £11,500 on 29th June 1985, and his holding carried 10% of the voting rights. The other voting rights were exercisable 10% by Jardine's sister, 35% by his son and 45% by a merchant bank.

The market values of the company's assets on 3rd April 1987 were agreed as follows:

	£
Freehold premises	95,000
Goodwill	64,500
Investments	5,500
Stock, debtors and bank balance	48,400
	213,400

(c) Jardine made the following sales of 10% Treasury Stock 1992, which is included in Capital Gains Tax Act 1979, Sch. 2 as being exempt from capital gains tax in certain circumstances:

9th May 1986	£8,000 stock for	£6,850
21st December 1986	£20,000 stock for	£17,360

His purchases of this stock were as follows:

6th October 1985	£6,000 stock for	£4,420
8th December 1985	£9,000 stock for	£7,065
17th March 1986	£14,000 stock for	£13,540
1st February 1987	£5,000 stock for	£4,150

All transactions in Treasury Stock were carried out through the Stock Exchange.

Retail Price Index figures include the following:

March 1982	313.4	December 1986	361.9
June 1985	358.3	April 1987	372.3

Jardine also asks for your advice in connection with potential liability to capital gains tax and capital transfer tax on a house with a current market value of about £50,000 which he bought for £8,000 in 1968. It has never been his residence, having been let throughout his ownership, and has no development value.

He wishes to transfer the house early in 1988 to trustees for the benefit of his infant grandchildren. He has made no gifts since 26th March 1974.

You are required to:

(a) prepare a statement showing Jardine's capital gains tax position for 1986/87 (12 marks)

(b) list the points relating to capital gains tax that you would bring to his attention in connection with the proposed transfer of the house. (4 marks)
(Total 16 marks)

20 Your diary contains an appointment to meet Sutton, a client who has retired from full-time work, in order to discuss capital gains tax on certain recent transactions and possible future transactions. His file shows the following facts:

(a) On 16th January 1987 he sold 6,000 quoted ordinary shares in Sillitoe plc for £9,570. Before the sale his holding was 12,000 shares which had been bought as follows:

25th June 1972	3,000 shares for £2,650
18th March 1975	7,000 shares for £4,080
2nd August 1986	2,000 shares for £1,660

The Retail Price Index is assumed to be 313.4 for March 1982, 340 in May 1986, 350 in August 1986, and 363.8 for January 1987.

(b) In May 1986 he paid £8,000 for a painting which was professionally valued at £15,000 in December 1986. In January 1987 the painting was damaged and in March 1987 Sutton received £9,000 from his insurers; he subsquently used this sum to restore the painting to its original condition.

(c) He has recently received an offer of £190,000 from a developer who wishes to acquire a seaside house which Sutton bought for £42,500 in March 1977; the house has never been his main residence and has never been let. No improvements have been carried out during Sutton's ownership.

(d) He holds 12,000 shares in O'Reilly plc which cost £10,700 in 1972, when the shares were quoted. The quotation was suspended in 1973, since when the shares have had only a minimal value.

You are required, in preparation for your meeting with Sutton, to:

(a) calculate his capital gains tax payable for 1986/87 if no claims for relief are made. (6 marks)

(b) list the reliefs that can be claimed and your recommendations in this connection, and (4 marks)

(c) calculate, assuming that Sutton accepts the offer for the house, the gross gain for capital gains tax before deducting the indexation allowance.
(4 marks)
(Total 14 marks)

21 Tom and Dick have been in partnership as consulting architects since 1st April 1950. As Tom, who celebrated his 62nd birthday on 1st April 1986, wishes to retire in a few years they decide to offer their young manager, Harry, a partnership from

1st October 1986. They estimate their partnership goodwill to be worth £250,0000. (An insurance valuation of assets in June 1965 then regarded the value of their professional goodwill to be £108,000). They incorporate this valuation into the partnership accounts at 1st October, 1986. Harry buys a 20% share in this asset and will receive 25% of the profits of the firm. Tom and Dick will continue to share the balance equally in both assets and profits/losses.

Retail Price Index may be taken as:

1982:	March	313.4
1986:	March	345.1
	April	349.7
	October	368.6

Required:

Explain, with any necessary calculations, the partners' position for 1986/87 in regard to capital gains tax. (8 marks)

22. Hans Schmidt, an Austrian national, aged 36, has approached you for tax advice regarding a large legacy he has recently inherited in the UK. The legacy comprises a plot of land with substantial development value, and various bank and building society accounts. The following points arise:

(a) He is thinking of disposing of the plot of land with substantial development value to a property developer in the near future. Hans wishes to ascertain what taxes may be payable as a result of the sale.

(b) He would like to retain some of the moneys in the UK in his own name for possible use in the future, but is concerned about the adverse impact of IHT in the event of his early death. He wishes to know whether he can minimise his exposure to IHT.

Required:

Draft short notes for your discussions with Hans Schmidt. (15 marks)

23. The share capital of Hallsvalla Ltd, a trading company, is owned as follows:

	Shares
John Stephens	630
Mary Stephens (John's wife)	140
Jim Stephens (John's brother)	230
	1,000

The shares have been held for many years.

John's son, Philip, joined the business on 17th May 1986 and on that date John gifted Philip 280 shares in the company. Jim gifted Philip 140 shares.

The Revenue have agreed the following share valuation:

75 - 100%	£53 per share
50 - 74%	£37 per share
26 - 49%	£23 per share
10 - 25%	£11 per share
0 - 9%	£ 4 per share

Calculate the value of the potentially exempt transfer made by both John and Jim on the gift of the shares.

(Ignore capital gains tax) (13 marks)

24 Nichols died on 8th February 1987. He was a widower, domiciled in England, and his assets were valued for probate as follows:

	£
Freehold house in Essex	86,500
Foreign assets	31,900
Quoted investments	261,690
Personal chattels	18,100
Bank balance	33,600

The debts due by Nichols at the date of his death amounted to £6,850 and funeral expenses were £490. The foreign duty on the foreign assets is £3,833.

His wife had died in 1971 leaving her entire estate in trust to Nichols for life with remainder to their only child, a son, born in 1960. The total value of the trust fund on 8th February 1987 was £178,450.

Nichols was also life tenant of a family trust in which his interest had commenced on the death of an aunt on 15th March 1986 when the value of the trust fund was £41,800; inheritance tax of £7,420 was payable by the trustees as a result of the aunt's death. The value of the fund on 8th February 1987 was £37,350.

By his Will, Nichols made charitable bequests totalling £30,000. The residue of his estate was left in trust for his son, who was to become absolutely entitled to the capital of the estate on reaching the age of 25.

During his lifetime, Nichols had made chargeable transfers of value totalling £21,400. No tax was payable on these transfers.

All the IHT payable as a result of the death of Nichols was paid on 30th September 1987, no claim for deferment of any tax being made.

On 19th October 1987, his executors purchased UK Government Stock for £7,440. They still own this stock.

Since obtaining probate the executors have made the following sales of quoted investments owned by Nichols at the time of his death:

	Probate value	Gross proceeds	Selling expenses	Net Proceeds
	£	£	£	£
21st October 1987	160,500	142,800	1,150	141,650
14th November 1987	41,800	43,200	450	42,750

The remaining quoted investments which were owned by Nichols at the time of his death are still owned by the executors on 15th December 1987 and all have current values higher than probate values.

You are required to:

(a) Calculate the total IHT payable as a result of the death of Nichols. (7 marks)

(b) Calculate the potential repayment of IHT resulting from the transactions in quoted investments. (3 marks)

(c) List the points relating to IHT that you would bring to the attention of the executors in connection with any future transactions in quoted investments. (3 marks)

Total (13 marks)

Appendix 2 Suggested Answers to Examination Questions

1 **MOUNTAIN**

(a) Income tax chargeable on compensation payment

Income excluding compensation:		£	£
Earned income: Schedule E			18,920
Investment income: UK dividends - Mr Mountain		6,510	
	Mrs Mountain	2,235	
		8,745	
Less: mortgage interest		1,480	
			7,265
			26,185
SPA			23,351
Taxable income ignoring compensation			23,850
Compensation received			60,000
Less: exempt			25,000
Taxable			35,000
Tax on first £25,000			£
25,400 - 23,850 =	1,550 x 45% x 50%		348.75
	7,900 x 50% x 50%		1,975.00
	7,900 x 55% x 50%		2,172.50
	7,650 x 60% x 50%		2,295.00
	25,000		
Tax on remainder	10,000 x 60% x 75%		4,500.00
Tax chargeable on compensation payment			11,291.25

(b) Mrs Mountain

Income tax payable

1st October 1986 to 5th April 1987	£	£	£
Earned income			
Business profits {6/12 x [3,278 + (6/12 x 7,804)]}			
Pension			3,590
			9,545
			13,135
Investment income:			
UK dividends		2,905	
Foreign dividends	795		
UK and foreign taxes deducted (21/71)	325	1,120	
		4,025	
Estate of Mountain deceased		5,840	
		9,865	
Less: Loan interest and charges paid -			
interest	1,235		
covenant	260	1,495	8,370
Statutory Total Income			21,505
Personal allowance		2,335	
Additional personal allowance		1,320	
Widows' Bereavement allowance		1,320	4,975
Taxable Income			16,530

Basic and Higher Rates

	£	£
16,530 @ 29%		4,793.70
Add: Basic rate on charges:		
Mortgage interest £1,235 x 29%	358.15	
Deed of covenant £260 x 29%	75.40	433.55
Income Tax Payable (before tax credits)		5,227.25

(c) Points for discussion with Mrs Mountain on the tax relief available on Self Employed Pension Premiums.

(i) As Mrs Mountain was born in 1940 tax relief on previous tax paid is limited to 17½% of her net relevant earnings.

(ii) Relief is obtained in the year in which a premium is paid.

(iii) An election can be made to treat a premium paid as having been paid in the previous tax year.

(iv) Unused relief can be carried forward for six years and utlised on the FIFO basis in a year when the premium paid exceeds the maximum for that year.

(v) The maximum amount payable for 1986/87 is £2,895 calculated as follows:

Year of Assessment	Calculations	Net relevant earnings £	£
1984/85	Actual: $\frac{4}{6}$ x £3,278		2,185
1985/86	1st 12 months:		
	6 months	3,278	
	6 months $\frac{6}{12}$ x £7,804	3,902	7,180
1986/87	1st 12 months:		7,180
			16,545
	17½% thereof		2,895

(vi) Because of the wife's earnings election and the effect of the year of husband's death on Mrs Mountain's income tax liability, relief will be obtained on the premium paid in 1986/87 at the rate of 29%.

It is likely that Mrs Mountain will pay tax at a higher rate in 1987/88 than 1986/87 so that a premium paid in that year will attract relief at those higher rates. The premium paid in that year can absorb all of the unused relief brought forward from 1984/85 to 1985/86.

To be relieved in 1987/88, the premium should be paid in that year or it can be paid in 1988/89 with an election for the premium to be treated as paid in 1987/88.

2 ROBERTS

(a) Computation showing effect of Wife's Earnings Election 1986/87

		Total £	Mr Roberts £	Mrs Roberts £
Mr Roberts: Schedule E		20,960	20,960	
Mrs Roberts:				
Schedule D Case II	6,624			
Capital allowances	619	6,005		6,005
		26,965	20,960	6,005
Unearned Income				
Mr Roberts: Dividends		7,445	7,445	
Mrs Roberts: Schedule A		1,835	1,835	
		36,245	30,240	
Charges				
Mortgage £(1,221 x 100/71)		(1,720)	(1,720)	
Deeds of Covenant £(426 x 100/7)		(600)		
Allowances				
MA		3,655		
WEIR		2,335		
SPA			2,335	2,335
Taxable Income		27,935	26,185	3,070

	Total	Mr Roberts	Mrs Roberts
	£	£	£
Basic and Higher Rates			
£			
17,200 x 29%/3,070 x 29%	4,988.00	4,988.00	890.30
3,000 x 40%	1,200.00	1,200.00	
5,200 x 45%	2,340.00	2,340.00	
2,535 x 50%/785 x 50%	1,267.50	392.50	
Income Tax Borne	9,795.50	8,920.50	890.30
Add:			
Basic Rate on charges			
Mortgage £1,720 x 29%	498.80	498.80	
Deed of Covenant			
£600 x 29%	174.00		174.00
Income tax payable	10,468.30	9,419.30	1,064.30

Mr Roberts + Mrs Roberts: £10,483.60

The wife's earnings election will result in an increase in income tax payable of £15 and should not be made.

(b) Advice in connection with the Retirement Annuity Premium

(i) As Mrs Roberts is aged 41, she can pay a retirement annuity premium of up to 17½% of her net relevant earnings, and have the payment allowed against her marginal rate of tax.

(ii) Unused relief can be carried forward for up to six years and utilised on a FIFO basis in a year when the premium paid for that year exceeds the limit for that year.

(iii) The maximum retirement annuity premium payable by Mrs Roberts for 1986/87 is £1,398, calculated as follows:

	Schedule D Case II	Capital Allowances	Net Relevant Earnings	17½%
	£	£	£	£
1985/86	2,208	225	1,983	347
1986/87	6,624	619	6,005	1,051
Maximum RAP payable				1,398

(iv) The payment of the retirement annuity premium for 1986/87 will have an effect on the wife's earnings election as follows:

	Total	Mr Roberts	Mrs Roberts
	£	£	£
Income tax payable (as before)	10,468.30	9,419.30	1,064.30

	Total	Mr Roberts	Mrs Roberts
	£	£	£
Retirement Annuity Premium:			
1,398 x 50%	(699.00)		
1,398 x 29%			(405.42)
	9,769.30	9,419.30	658.88
		£10,078.18	

Hence it would be beneficial not to have a wife's earnings election.

(v) There is no tax saving achieved by making a wife's earnings election in 1986/87. It will, also not be beneficial to make one in 1987/88 considering the likely increases in allowances and indexation of tax bands, and thus the marginal rate of tax will be 50%.
Accordingly, Mrs Roberts may consider carrying forward the unused relief at 5th April 1987 and making a larger payment in 1987/88 thereby obtaining relief at possibly 50% in that year.

Mr Roberts
Schedule E

	£	£	£
Salary			
Car benefit	1,320		19,850
Less: 50%	660	660	
Fuel benefit	900		
	450	450	1,110
			20,960

Mrs Roberts
Schedule D Case II
1985/86 first year

1986/87 first 12 months = $\frac{12}{13}$ x 7,176 = £6,624

Capital Allowances

	£	
Purchase of car		
Open market value	3,600	
1985/86 WDA 25% x $\frac{4}{12}$	300 x 75% =	£225
	3,300	
1986/87 WDA 25%	825 x 75% =	£619
	2,475	

Rental Income	TRL A £	LFR B £	LFR C £
24th June 1986	500	550	-
29th September 1986	500	550	250
c/f	1,000	1,100	250

		TRL A £		LFR B £		LFR C £
b/f		1,000		1,100		250
25th December 1986		500		-		250
25th March 1987		500		650		250
		2,000		1,750		750
Expenses	£		£		£	
Agents' Commission	117		130		190	
Advertising	-		205		40	
Ground Rent	48		-		-	
Repairs - while let			980		730	
- while empty	-		840		-	
		165		2,155		960
		1,835		(405)		(210)

The loss on an LFR cannot be set against the profit on a TRL.

Note:

Repairs while empty not allowed on 'C' as this was not a void period within the required definition.
It is assumed that the repairs are of a revenue nature, in spite of their relative size.

3 **VALENTINE**

(a) Schedule D assessments for 1985/86 to 1987/88

	1985/86 £	1986/87 £	1987/88 £
Schedule D Case I (working 1)	29,250	44,900	62,600
Averaging adjustment (working 1)		6,150	(6,150)
	29,250	51,050	56,450
Less: Agricultural buildings allowances (working 2)	9,982	20,650	14,970
Net Schedule D Assessments	19,268	30,400	41,480

Workings

(1) Opening year assessments and averaging adjustment

	£
1985/86 Actual	29,250
1986/87 First twelve months (£29,250 + 3/12 x £62,600)	44,900
1987/88 PY - year ended 31.3.87	62,600

(Valentine will not elect under s.117 as profits are rising)
Although the first year cannot enter an averaging claim such a claim is available for 1986/87 and 1987/88.

44,900 > 70% of £62,600
< 75% of £62,600

Therefore marginal relief applies.

Averaging adjustment 3(H-L) - 75% H
= 3(62,600 - 44,900) - 75% (62,600) = £6,150

(2) Agricultural buildings allowances

	1985/86 (restricted to 9/12)	1986/87	1987/88
	£	£	£
Year ending			
31.3.76 £11,800 x 10% WDA	885	-	-
31.3.78 to 31.3.84			
£114,600 x 10%	8,595	11,460	11,460
31.3.85 £6,700 x 30%/10%	502	670	670
31.3.86 £28,400 x 30%		8,520	2,840
	9,982	20,650	14,970

(b) Mrs Valentine - Income Tax Borne 1986/87

		£	£
Earned income:			
Schedule E: Salary			7,944
Commission			1,646
Benefits in kind: Travelling			2,540
	Car benefit £450 x 10/12		375
	Fuel benefit £450 x 10/12 (not insubstantial as 2,300 > 2,500 x 10/12)		375
	BUPA subscription		134
			13,014
Less: s.189 relief			2,540
			10,474
Unearned Income:		£	
UK dividends £3,820 x 100/71		5,380	
Schedule D V (remittance basis - 2nd year actual) 1,000 x 10/8		1,250	6,630
STI			17,104
Less: Personal allowances			
SPA		2,335	
APA		1,320	4,655
Taxable income			12,449
Tax borne: £12,449 x 29%		3,610.00	
Less: DTR		250.00	
UK income tax borne		3,360.00	

4

R ROBB

Taxable Income 1986/87

	£	£	£
Schedule E - Salary			20,000
Less: Superannuation (4%)			800
			19,200
Benefits in kind:	900		
Less 50%	450	450	
Fuel	900		
	450	450	
Less 50%			
TV - Video (20% x £800)		160	
Foreign accommodation		1,000	2,060
Schedule E			21,260
Schedule D Case V (750 x 90%)			675
Less:			21,935
Mortgage interest £25,000 x 5% x $\frac{5}{12}$		520	
Interest (Rose Boutique Ltd) £8,000 x 12% x $\frac{6}{12}$		480	1,000
Less Personal Allowances:			
Marriage allowance		3,655	20,935
Business expansion scheme		10,500	14,155
Taxable income			6,780

(1) Car Benefit
The car benefit is the scale figure, less 50% as business mileage is more than 18,000 miles per year.

(2) Fuel Benefit
The fuel benefit is per table, less 50% reduction as business mileage is more than 18,000 miles year.

(3) TV-Video
The benefit is 20% of market value at the time it is first provided by the employer for the employee.

(4) Foreign Accommodation
Reimbursed expenses for travel are allowable where the employee is performing the duties of his employment outside the UK for a period of not less than 60 consecutive days. Accordingly, only the accommodation is a chargeable benefit.

(5) Housing Scheme
It was held in **Hochstrasser v. Mayes (1960)** that for a benefit to be taxable, it must be made by reason of the duties of the employment rather than just because he is an employee. Accordingly, a compensation for the loss in value of the house was held not to be taxable.

(6) Beneficial Loan
As the loan is for a qualifying purpose, no benefit-in-kind arises on the beneficial loan.

(7) Business Expansion Scheme
The investment in Rose Boutique Ltd qualifies for relief under the Business Expansion Scheme.

5 **JERRY**

(a) (i) Retirement Provision
So long as the pension scheme is approved by the Revenue, payments made by Jerry are deductible from his Schedule E income and payments by the employer are fully allowable and are not treated as a benefit.

If the scheme is not approved, no deduction is available to the employee and the employer's payment is assessable as a benefit in kind.

(ii) Woodlands
The normal basis of assessment in respect of the owner of woodlands managed on a commercial basis is Schedule B, when the basis of assessment is one third of the annual value of the land.

An election can be made to be assessed under Schedule D Case 1 and this will normally be beneficial in the early years of the development when expenditure is high and thus loss relief is available against other income. No deduction is available in respect of the cost of the land.

When the woodlands start to show profit it would be beneficial to be assessed under Schedule B. No election can be made from Schedule D Case 1 to Schedule B.

Accordingly, Jerry could sell the woodlands to a partnership or company, causing a cessation of the old business; the new owners can then be assessed under Schedule B.

(iii) Golden Handshake
For the favourable rules on termination payments to be applied the payment must not be remuneration for services past, future or present.

It is likely that the Revenue would argue that the entitlement to the 'golden handshake' (e.g. in the employee's contract or under the company's Articles of Association) will be treated as ordinary Schedule E remuneration.

If there is no contractual right to the payment, special rules apply in taxing the payment. The first £25,000 is exempt; the next £25,000 is taxed at 50% of normal rates; the next £25,000 is taxed at 75% of normal rates; the excess is taxable in full.

(iv) 'Gilt-Edged Securities'
The income from the gilt-edged securities will be liable to UK income tax - no exemption from income tax can be claimed whilst Jerry is resident and ordinary resident in the UK.

If the interest payments are made gross (e.g. War Loan) the assessment will be under Schedule D Case III (on a preceding year basis). If the interest payments are made net, the assessment will be on an actual basis.

No relief is available on the capital cost of the security against the individual's income tax liability.

When the gilt-edged securities are sold any capital gain made is exempt from tax. Conversely any loss is not allowable.

5(b) 1986/87

	£	£	£	£
Salary		50,000		50,000
Less: Pension contribution	2,000		2,000	
Additional	-		4,500	
Woodlands (s.168)	-		8,000	
		2,000		14,500
		48,000		35,500
Marriage allowance		3,655		3,655
Taxable Income		44,345		31,845

Basic and Higher Rates:

£		
17,200 x 29%	4,988.00	4,988.00
3,000 x 40%	1,200.00	1,200.00
5,200 x 45%	2,340.00	2,340.00
7,900 x 50%/6445 @ 50%	3,950.00	3,222.55
7,900 x 55%	4,345.00	
3,145 x 60%	1,887.00	
44,345	18,710.00	11,750.50
	11,750.50	
Tax saving	6,959.50	

6 WALTERS, MITCHELL AND BARNETT

(a) Amounts to be included in total income in respect of the partnership for 1986/87.

	Total £	Walters £	Mitchell £	Barnett £
Net profit for year to 31.7.85	4,010			
Add back: depreciation	1,630			
drawings	10,500			
Schedule D Case I	16,140			
6.4.86 to 31.7.86 (4 months) =				
$\frac{4}{12}$ x 16,140	5,380			
Salaries (4/12)	3,500	1,000	2,500	
PSR 55:45	1,880	1,034	846	
	5,380	2,034	3,346	

	Total	Walters	Mitchell	Barnett
	£	£	£	£
1.8.86 to 5.4.87 (8 months) =				
8/12 x 16,140	10,760			
Salaries (8/12)	8,000		4,000	4,000
PSR 60:40	2,760		1,656	1,104
	10,760		5,656	5,104
Total	16,140	2,034	9,002	5,104
Less: TA 1970 s.171		(2,034)	(565)	
			8,437	
Annuity received/paid: (2 payments in year) 60:40		2,500	(1,500)	(1,000)
Amounts to be included in income		2,500	6,937	4,104

Calculation of loss available under s.171

		Total	Walters	Mitchell
(1)	Allocation of loss 1984/85	£	£	£
	Loss of year to 31.7.84	2,850		
	Add: Capital allowances	15,450		
		18,300		
	Salaries	10,500	3,000	7,500
	PSR 55:45	(28,800)	(15,840)	(12,960)
		18,300	12,840	5,460
(2)	Assessments for 1984/85 and 1985/86			
	1984/85 Schedule D I (y/e 31.7.83)	16,200		
	Less: Capital allowances	2,600		
		13,600		
	Salaries	10,500	3,000	7,500
	PSR 55:45	3,100	1,705	1,395
		13,600	4,705	8,895
	Add: Investment income		2,425	
	Deduct: Maintenance			(4,000)
	Income		7,130	4,895
	Less: TA 1970 s.168		(7,130)	(4,895)
	1985/86 Investment income		2,760	
	Less: TA 1970 s.168		(2,760)	

(3) Summary of Loss Utilisation

	Total	Walters	Mitchell
	£	£	£
Loss for the year 1984/85		12,840	5,460
Less: s.168 relief: 1984/85		(7,130)	(4,895)
1985/86		(2,760)	
Carried forward under s.171		2,950	565

Note: Walters wastes £916 of the loss relief (£2,950 - £2,034 in 1986/87)

(b) Effect of Annuity Payments on Income Tax Liabilities of Walters and the Continuing Partners

(i) Annuities are accounted for on a paid basis; no accruals are brought into the calculations.

(ii) The annuity payments are not an expense within Schedule D Case I; they are added back and allowed in each partner's computation.

(iii) Under FA 1974, S.16, so long as a partner retires through age or ill health and payments are made under a partnership agreement for his benefit then up to a certain limit, the annuity will be treated as earned income in the hands of the recipient (Walters) and as a deduction from the earned income of the paying partners.

The limit referred to is 50% of the average of the partner's share of the profits for the best three out of the last seven years in which the partner worked for the partnership (including 1985/86 in the case of Walters).

The profit shares are indexed by the retail prices index in December of each year to December in the year of retirement.

The yearly limit is also indexed by the retail prices index in December prior to the year of payment to December in the year of retirement.

(iv) The annuity is paid net of basic rate income tax; higher rate relief is given in the paying partners' personal computations.

(c) On the change in the personnel of an existing partnership, the assessment for the tax year of the change and the following three years are to be on actual profits. The options normally available in the second and third years of a new business will apply to the fifth and sixth years. The new rule applies to partnership changes occurring from 20th March 1985. The option to elect within two years of the date of the change for the continuation basis remains in force.

7 **ALEX, BERT AND CHARLES**

Each partner can deal with his share of the loss in the manner most beneficial to him.

Alex (£12,590)

The options available to Alex are:

s.168 (set-off against total income)
s.174 (terminal loss relief)

As Alex's other income in 1985/86 is £605, this is covered by his personal allowance for the year. Hence, there is no advantage in making a claim under s.168.

Accordingly, the only claim that can beneficially be made by Alex is under s.174.

The claim would be:	1982/83 £	1983/84 £	1984/85 £	
Original Schedul D Case I Assessments	7,500	7,216	3,846	
Terminal Loss Relief	(1,528)	(7,216)	(3,846)	= £(12,590)
Revised Assessments	5,972	-	-	

Bert and Charles (£7,554 and £5,036)

The options available to Bert and Charles are:

s.174 (terminal loss relief)
s.172 (carry forward against income from company)

As most of the trading profits assessable on Bert and all of the assessable profits on Charles for 1982/83 to 1984/85 are covered by charges and personal allowance, a terminal loss relief claim will be wasted:

	1982/83 £	1983/84 £	1984/85 £
Bert			
Schedule D Case I	4,500	4,330	2,308
Charges	(1,500)	(1,500)	(1,500)
Allowances	(2,445)	(2,795)	(3,155)
Effective TLR	555	35	-
Charles			
Schedule D Case I	3,000	2,887	1,539
Charges	(1,150)	(1,150)	(1,150)
Allowances	(2,445)	(2,795)	(3,155)
Effective TLR	-	-	-

Accordingly, Bert and Charles should claim relief under s.172 against the income derived from the company instead (so long as the company continues the same trade and Bert and Charles continue to own the shares).

The relief would be:

	Bert (7,554)		Charles (5,036)	
	1985/86 £	1986/87 £	1985/86 £	1986/87 £
Schedule E	1,666	8,334	1,666	8,334
s.172	(1,666)	(5,888)	(1,666)	(3,370)
	-	2,446	-	4,964

Loss incurred in 1985/86

	£
6.4.85 - 31.7.85 = $\frac{4}{12}$ x 3,300 =	1,100
1.8.85 - 31.1.86 = $\frac{6}{6}$ x 26,280 =	(26,280)
	(25,180)

The loss is shared by Alex, Bert and Charles in their profit-sharing ratio,

i.e. Alex	£12,590
Bert	£ 7,554
	£ 5,036
	£25,180

Schedule D Case I Assessments

	Normal	s.118		
1985/86	Nil	Nil		
1984/85	£	£		£
PY - y/e 31.7.83	10,340			
Actual 6.4.84 - 5.4.85:				
6.4.84 - 31.7.84		$\frac{4}{12}$ x £16,480 =	5,493	
1.8.84 - 5.4.85		$\frac{8}{12}$ x £3,300 =	2,200	7,693
1983/84				
PY - y/e 31.7.82				
Actual 6.4.83 - 5.4.84	11,240	$\frac{4}{12}$ x £10,340 =	3,446	
6.4.83 - 31.7.83		$\frac{8}{12}$ x £16,480 =	10,987	14,433
	21,580			22,126

The Revenue will revise the assessments to atual under TA 1970, s.118.

Division of assessments between partners:

	Total £	Alex £	Bert £	Charles £
1985/86 None	-	-	-	-
1984/85 (Actual)	7,693	3,846	2,308	1,539
1983/84 (Actual)	14,433	7,216	4,330	2,887
1982/83 (PY)	15,000	7,500	4,500	3,000

JOHN, BOB AND TOM

(a) Schedule D Case I Assessments and Capital Allowances for new Partnership

Schedule D Case I
1985/86

	£	£
Actual 1.10.85 to 5.4.86 = $\frac{6}{12}$ x £57,218		28,609
	c/f	28,609

		£	£
		c/f	28,609
1986/87			
Actual 6.4.86 to 3.5.86 = $\frac{1}{12}$ x £57,218 =		4,768	
4.5.86 to 5.4.87 = $\frac{11}{12}$ x £66,184 =		60,669	65,437
1987/88			
Actual 6.4.87 to 3.5.87 = $\frac{1}{12}$ x £66,184 =		5,515	
4.5.87 to 5.4.88 = $\frac{11}{12}$ x £77,424 =		70,972	76,487
1988/89			
Actual 6.4.88 to 3.5.88 = $\frac{1}{12}$ x £77,424 =		6,452	
4.5.88 to 5.4.89 = $\frac{11}{12}$ x £60,012 =		55,011	61,463

Capital Allowances

Basic Periods
1985/86: 1.10.85 - 5.4.86
1986/87: 6.4.86 - 5.4.87
1987/88: 6.4.87 - 5.4.88
1988/89: 6.4.88 - 5.4.89

		Plant	Scientific Research	Allowances
		£	£	£
1985/86				None
1986/87				
Purchase		6,250	7,250	
WDA (25%)		1,563		1,563
	c/f	4,687		
Scientific Research (100%)			7,250	7,250
			-	8,813
1987/88				
Purchase		3,128		
		7,815		

		Plant	Scientific Research	Allowances
		£	£	£
WDA (25%)		1,954		1,954
	c/f	5,861		
1988/89				
WDA (25%)		1,465		1,465
	c/f	4,396		

(b) Taxable Income of John, Bob and Tom 1985/86 and 1986/87

	Total	John	Bob	Tom
	£	£	£	£
1985/86				
Schedule D Case I	28,609			
Salaries $\frac{6}{12}$	6,500	4,000	2,500	
Profits	22,109	5,527	7,738	8,844
	28,609	9,527	10,238	8,844
Less: Capital Allowances b/f		(1,863)	(3,492)	
Losses b/f		(4,145)	(1,262)	
		3,519	5,484	8,844
Schedule D Case V				8,000
Dividends		10,000	-	-
		13,519	5,484	16,844
Less: Charges $\frac{6}{12}$ x 4,200 = 2,100		(525)	(735)	(840)
Allowances		(3,455)	(2,205)	(2,205)
		9,539	2,544	13,799
1986/87				
Schedule D Case 1	65,437			
Capital Allowances	8,813			
	56,624			
Salaries	13,000	8,000	5,000	-
Profits (25:35:40)	43,624	10,906	15,268	17,450
	56,624	18,906	20,268	17,450

	Total	John	Bob	Tom
	£	£	£	£
Schedule D Case V (no deduction)				10,000
Dividends £(7,100 + 2,900)		10,000		
		28,906	20,268	27,450
Less: Charges £4,200		(1,050)	(1,470)	(1,680)
Allowances		(3,655)	(2,335)	(2,335)
Taxable income		24,201	16,463	23,435

9 **CHARLES REDD AND TOM WOOD**

(a) Income Tax

The transfer of the business to a limited company causes a cessation of the partnership.

(i) TA 1970, s.118

1986/87	Normal	s.118
	£	£
Actual	160,000	160,000
1985/86		
PY - y/e 31st March 1985	120,000	
Actual - y/e 31st March 1986		150,000
1984/85		
PY - y/e 31st March 1984	100,000	
Actual - y/e 31st March 1985		120,000
	220,000	270,000

The Revenue will revise the assessments for 1984/85 and 1985/86 to actual.

(ii) Capital Allowances

A balancing charge will arise on the transfer of the factory and plant to the limited company. The balancing charge will be calculated by taking market value of the asset at date of transfer (subject to this value not exceeding cost) over the tax written down value.

However, an election can be made under FA 1971, Sch. 8, para. 13 for the assets to be transferred at the tax written down value, as the buyer (the company) and seller (the partnership) are connected persons.

When such an election is made, the partnership can claim first year allowances in the final year of trading.

(b) Capital Gains Tax

(i) A charge to capital gains tax will arise on the sale of the chargable assets of the partnership to the new company.

	Factory	Goodwill	
	£	£	
Consideration	149,000	46,000	
Cost	27,000	-	
Gross gain	122,000	46,000	
Indexation (based on 31.3.82 market values)			
$\frac{£100,000}{£30,000} \times \frac{420.3 - 313.4}{313.4}$	34,100	10,230	
	87,900	35,770	= 123,670

(ii) As all the assets of the business are being transferred to the company, an election can be made under CGTA 1979, s.123 to deduct the chargeable gain arising on the transfer from the cost of the shares acquired, to the extent that the consideration is satisfied by shares.

	£	£
Chargeable gain	123,670	123,670
Transfer wholly for shares	123,670	
Transfer partly for shares		
Relief limited to $\frac{£200,000}{£280,000} \times 123,670$		88,336
Chargeable to CGT (1986/87)	Nil	35,334
Market value of shares transferred	280,000	200,000
Gain rolled over (CGTA 1979 s.123)	123,670	88,336
	156,330	111,664

10 **SOLOMON MATTHEWS**

(a) The due dates are:

(i) £4,500 (first instalment) (½ x 9000)
later of 1st January 1987
26th February 1987

i.e. 26th February 1987

(ii) £4,500 (second instalment)
later of 1st July 1987
26th February 1987

i.e. 1st July 1987

(iii) £8,000 (balance) 12th September 1987

(b) The reckonable dates are:

(i)	£4,500 (first instalment)	26th February 1987
(ii)	£4,500 (second instalment)	1st July 1987
(iii)	£8,000 (balance)	1st July 1987

(c) Interest on overdue tax is:

		£
(i)	£4,500 x 8.5% x $\frac{217 \text{ days}}{365 \text{ days}}$ =	227.40
(ii)	£4,500 x 8.5% x $\frac{92 \text{ days}}{365 \text{ days}}$ =	96.41
(iii)	£8,000 x 8.5% x $\frac{92 \text{ days}}{365 \text{ days}}$ =	171.39
Total interest on overdue tax		495.20

11 MR AND MRS H VAN RIJN

The pattern of visits to the UK suggests that under normal Revenue practice, Mr and Mrs Van Rijn are not resident and not ordinarily resident in the UK.

As regards domicile, Mr Van Rijn would appear to have a domicile of origin in the Netherlands with no indication that this has changed. Mrs Van Rijn is also almost certainly domiciled in the Netherlands either by the domicile of dependence rule (marriage prior to 1st January 1984) or by her acquiring a domicile of choice in the Netherlands.

(a) Consultancy Engagement

It is necessary to determine whether the consultancy engagement was an employment or self-employment. If this was an employment (a contract of service), it will be liable to UK income tax under Schedule E Case II.

If this was a self-employment (a contract for services), it will be liable under Schedule D Case II or possibly Case VI.

(b) Rental Income

Mr Van Rijn is assessable under Schedule A in respect of the rents arising in the UK.

(c) Sale of Farm

As Mrs Van Rijn is neither resident or ordinarily resident in the UK, and the farm was not being used for trade being carried on by her (through a branch or an agency in the UK), there is no liability to UK capital gains tax.

The rental income from the farm would have been assessed under Schedule A.

(d) Government Securities

Under TA 1970, s.99, where certain British Government securities are beneficially owned by persons not ordinarily resident in the UK, income arising thereon is exempted from UK income tax.

Both the 3½% War Loan and the 15½% Treasury Loan 1998 are such British Government securities.

12 PIERRE AND MONIQUE GASTON

It is clear that Pierre and Monique Gaston are resident and ordinarily resident in the UK. It is also almost certain that in view of their intentions to return to France, they have remained domiciled in France.

(a) Sale of Shares in France and Purchase of Villa

As Pierre is resident and ordinarily resident in the UK, he is liable to capital gains tax on gains made anywhere in the world.

However, when an individual is not domiciled in the UK a gain made on an overseas asset is only chargeable if it is remitted to the UK.

Accordingly, as Pierre is not domiciled in the UK and the overseas gain is not being remitted to the UK, no liability to capital gains tax arises.

(Note: it has been held that income or gains do not lose their character by being invested overseas and then remitted to the UK. Accordingly, if Pierre subsequently sells the villa and then remits the proceeds to the UK, he will have remitted the original gain on the sale of shares and will pay tax accordingly.)

Income tax will be due on the rental income under Schedule D Case V. As Pierre is not domiciled in the UK, he will be liable only on a remittance basis.

(b) Gift of Painting

Although Monique is not domiciled in the UK, as she has been resident in the UK for 17 out of the previous 20 tax years, she is deemed to be domiciled for inheritance tax purposes and may be liable to Inheritance Tax on worldwide transfers if she dies within 7 years.

Accordingly, although the painting is an overseas asset, Monique will be making a transfer on the gift to her art teacher.

She may be able to utilise her annual exemptions for the current year and the previous year if these have not yet been utilised.

Any chargeable transfer must be reported to the Revenue.

(c) Bank Accounts

The interest on the bank accounts will be assessable under Schedule D Case V. As Monique is not domiciled in the UK, she will be liable only on a remittance basis.

Where some remittances are made out of a mixed capital and income source, the Revenue will argue that remittances are made first out of income (which are liable to UK tax) and then out of capital (which are not liable to UK tax).

As Monique intends making occasional remittances, she would be best advised to have the capital of £100,000 kept in one bank account, with the interest earned being credited to a separate bank account. Any remittance can then be made out of the capital account and can clearly be demonstrated not to have been a remittance of income.

13 **THE OLIVIA AERO ENGINE CO LTD**

Mainstream Corporation Tax Liability

		12 months to 31.12.1985		3 months to 31.3.1986
	£	£	£	£
Schedule D Case I (W1)		254,251		76,545
Schedule A (W4)		14,200		3,550
		268,451		80,095
Less: Charges paid:				
Patent Royalties	9,000		4,600	
Debenture interest	8,400	17,400	-	4,600
		251,051		75,495
Corporation tax (W6)		101,347		28,960
Less: ACT (W3)		14,431		22,649
Mainstream Corporation Tax Liability		86,916		6,311
Due Date		1.1.1987		1.4.1987

Workings

(1) Adjustment of profit for 15 months period of account to 31.3.1986

			£
Net profit per accounts			259,626
Add:	Depreciation		31,400
	Amortisation		6,500
	Patent royalties		16,000
	Debenture interest		10,500
	Corporation tax		105,500
	Capital costs of setting up profit sharing scheme		18,900
	Stamp duty on loan stock issue		450
	Payment for infringement of patent		4,500
	Rented property expenses		4,000
			457,376
		£	
Deduct:	UK dividends	17,080	
	Rental income	14,250	
	Surplus on investment	13,520	
			54,850
Adjusted trading profit before capital allowances			402,526

CAP	y/e 31.12.85	3 mths to 31.3.86
	£	£
Profits	322,021	80,505
Less: Capital allowances (Note 2)		
on plant	(42,570)	(3,960)
on research equipment	(25,200)	-
	254,251	76,545

(2) Capital allowances

(i) On plant used in the trade

	Expensive car	Car Pool	Pool	Capital allowances
	£	£	£	£
CAP y/e 31.12.85				
Tax WDV b/f	-	4,280	26,000	-
Additions not qualifying for FYA	12,000	18,000		
		22,280		
WDA @ 25% (max)	(2,000)	(5,570)	(6,500)	14,070
FYA 12.1.85 £38,000 x 75%			38,000	28,500
			(28,500)	
				42,570
CAP 3 months to 31.3.86				
Tax WDV	10,000	16,710	29,000	
WDA @ 25% x 3/12 (max)	(500)	(1,044)	(1,813)	3,357
FYA 15.1.86 £1,206 x 50%			1,206	603
			(603)	
Tax WDV c/f	9,500	15,666	27,790	3,960

(ii) On expenditure for scientific research
CAP y/e 31.12.85 100% relief on research laboratory expenditure
£25,200
=======

(3) Advance Corporation Tax

			£
CAP y/e 31.12.85			
Dividends paid: 2.1.85			6,300
6.6.85			37,500
			43,800
		£	
Less: Dividends received:	31.5.85	6,650	
	15.11.85	10,430	
			17,080
			26,720
ACT thereon @ $\frac{3}{7}$			11,451
Surplus ACT from 3 months to 31.3.86 carried back (see below)			2,980
			14,431
CAP 3 months to 31.3.86			
Dividends paid: 1.3.86			53,500
4.1.86			6,300
			59,800
ACT thereof @ $\frac{3}{7}$			25,629
Maximum set-off 30% x 75,495			22,649
Surplus ACT c/back			2,980

(4) Rents from property/leasing

	12 months to 31.12.85	3 months to 31.3.86
	£	£
Rents	10,800	2,700
Less: Expenses	3,200	800
	7,600	1,900
Other Rent	6,600	1,650
	14,200	3,550
	£	£
Leasing charges	6,000	2,250
Less: FYA (Note 2)	6,000	2,250

(Note Rents recovered of £2,500 will normally be assessed in the year they were receiveable though where accounts are prepared the IR may accept recovered rents as assessable in the AP in which received.

(5) Capital Gains

Investments sold 8.4.85

	£	£
Proceeds		24,020
Less: Cost		10,500
Gross gain		13,520
Less: Indexation allowance £15,000 x 0.193		2,895
Chargeable gain		10,625
FYA 1984 $\frac{3}{12}$ =	2,656	
Less: $\frac{1}{3}$ =	885	1,771
FYA 1985 $\frac{9}{12}$ =	7,959	
Less: $\frac{1}{4}$	1,992	5,977
		7,748

(6) Year ended 31.12.85

		Total	FY 1984 3/12	FY 1985 9/12
		£	£	£
Income		251,051	62,763	188,288
Capital gains (W5)		7,748	1,937	5,811
		258,799	64,700	194,099
FII	17,080 x $\frac{10}{7}$	24,400	6,100	18,300
		283,199	70,800	212,399

	£	£
FY 1984: £62,763 @ 45%	28,243	
Less: Small companies relief		
$\frac{3}{80}$ (125,000 - 70,800) $\frac{62,763}{70,800}$	1,802	
	26,441	
£1,937 @ 45%	871	
FY 1985: £188,288 @ 40%	75,315	
Less: Small companies relief		
$\frac{1}{40}$ (375,000 - 212,399) $\frac{188,288}{212,399}$	3,604	
c/f	71,711	27,312

		£	£
	b/f	71,711	27,312
£5,811 @ 40%		2,324	74,035
			101,347

3 months ended 31.3.86

	£	
Income: 75,495 @ 40%	30,195	
Less: Small companies relief 1/40 (125,000 - 75,495)	1,238	28,960

14

(a) Q Ltd

Group relief can be surrendered in the same period in which the loss is incurred.

Group relief is claimed after all other reliefs (including charges except for reliefs due from a later accounting period (e.g. ss.177(2), (3a)).

T Ltd

Year to 30.11.1984

Loss can be carried forward under s.177(1).

Year to 30.11.1985

	£
DI	10,000
Less: s.177(1)	(5,000)
	5,000
DIII	5,000
	10,000
Less: Charges paid	2,000
	8,000
Group Relief (s.258)	8,000
	-

Year to 30.11.1986

	£
DI (Loss)	(10,000)
DIII (s.177(2)).	5,000
	(5,000)

The loss of £5,000 is carried forward against future profits of the same trade under s.177(1).

The debenture interest of £2,000 is also carried forward against future profits of the same trade (under s.177(8)).

Q Ltd

Year to 30.11.1985

DI (loss)	(12,000)
Surrendered to T Ltd	8,000
	(4,000)

The loss of £4,000 must be carried forward against future profits of the same trade under s.177(1).

Year to 30.11.1986

	£
DI (loss)	(5,000)

The loss of £5,000 must be carried forward against future profits of the same trade under s.177(1).

(b) Z Ltd

Z Ltd is owned by a consortium, as all the companies resident in the UK are, and at least 75% is owned by UK resident companies.

Since 1981, consortium relief can pass in either direction pro rata to the shareholding.

Accordingly, B Ltd can set part of its loss against the profits of the consortium company.

The relief is limited to the lower of proportionate share of profits and proportionate share of losses.

	£
Profit share $\frac{£24,000}{80,000} \times £50,000$	15,000
Loss $\frac{£24,000}{80,000} \times £60,000$	(18,000)
Maximum relief is	15,000

B Ltd

	£
Loss	(60,000)
Consortium relief (as above)	15,000
	(45,000)

The loss of £45,000 must be carried forward against future profits of the same trade in B Ltd under s.177(1).

The claim for consortium relief must be made with the written consent of the corsortium members within two years of the end of the surrendering company's accounting period to which the claim relates.

15 BANDROYAL LTD

Year ended 31st March 1986

Mainstream Corporation Tax Payable

		DI	A	DV	Chargeable gains
		£	£	£	£
		400,000	40,000	200,000	30,000
Charges		20,000	-	-	30,000
	c/f	380,000	40,000	200,000	-

	DI £	A £	DV £	Chargeable gains £
Corporation tax @ 40%	133,000	14,000	70,000	
DTR	-	-	56,000	
	133,000	14,000	14,000	
Less: ACT set-off (restricted)	114,000	12,000	14,000	
	19,000	2,000	-	

The Mainstream Corporation Tax Liability is £42,000.

ACT carried forward

	£
ACT paid £441,000 x $\frac{3}{7}$ =	189,000
ACT utilised	140,000
ACT carried forward	49,000

Calculation of Schedule D Case V and Foreign Tax

	£	Foreign Tax £
Dividend received	144,000	
Withholding tax $\left(\frac{10}{90}\right)$	16,000	16,000
	160,000	
Underlying tax $\left(\frac{20}{80}\right)$	40,000	40,000
Schedule D Case V	200,000	56,000

16 A LTD

(a) Mainstream Corporation Tax Liability Year Ended 31st March 1986

	Source £	Charges £	Net £	CT @ 40% £	DTR £	ACT £	MCT £
DI	50,000		50,000	20,000		15,000	5,000
DIII	20,000		20,000	8,000		6,000	2,000
A	10,000	7,000	3,000	1,200		900	300
DV	20,000		20,000	8,000	8,000		-
Gain	9,000	9,000	-				
				37,200	8,000	21,900	
Mainstream Corporation Tax Liability							7,300

(b) Schedule D Case V and Foreign Tax

	£	Foreign Tax £
Dividend received	10,800	
Withholding tax $\frac{(10)}{(90)}$	1,200	1,200
	12,000	
Underlying tax $\frac{(40)}{(60)}$	8,000	8,000
Schedule D Case V	20,000	
Total foreign tax available		9,200
Utilised		8,000
Foreign tax relief wasted		1,200

(c) ACT Carried Forward

	£
Dividends received	1,400
Dividend paid	58,800
Net	57,400
ACT at $\frac{3}{7}$	24,600
Utilised	21,900
	2,700

17 VERITY SPINNERS LTD

(a) Corporation Tax Payable Year Ended 31st March 1986

	£	
Schedule D Case I (Schedule 1)	76,102	
Less: B/f (s.177(1)) £(96,100 - 47,448)	48,652	
	27,450	
Schedule A	13,220	
Schedule D Case III	2,340	
	43,010	
Less Charges:		
Patents Royalties £(7,850 - 1,440)	6,410	
Income chargeable to corporation tax	36,600	(I)
Add: Chargeable gains	3,960	
Profits chargeable to corporation tax	40,560	
FII	1,700	
Profits for Small Companies' Rate (less than £50,000 - £100,000 ÷ 2)	42,260	

		£
Corporation tax on income	£36,600 x 30%	10,980
Corporation tax on chargeable gains	£3,960 x 40%	1,584
Corporation Tax Payable		12,564

(b) Maximum Amount of Income for Apportionment Year Ended 31st March 1986

	Trading Income £	Estate Income £	Investment Income £
Schedule D Case 1	27,450		
Schedule A		13,220	
Schedule D Case III			2,340
	27,450	13,220	2,340
Less: Charges		4,070	2,340
	27,450	9,150	-
Corporation tax @ 30%	8,235	2,745	
	19,215 (T)	6,405 (E)	
Dividends £1,700 x70%			1,190
Group Income			5,250
			6,440
Less: Lower of (1) £3,000 (2) 10% of £(19,215 + 6,405)			2,562
Less: Abatement			
$\pounds \frac{\left[75,000 \times \frac{1}{2} \times \frac{6,405}{25,620}\right] - \pounds 6,405}{2} =$		1,485	
		4,920	
50% thereof		2,460	2,460
Maximum amount of Income for Apportionment			6,338

SCHEDULES

Year ended 31st March 1986

(1) Schedule D Case I

	£	£
Trading profits		102,846
Add: Depreciation	20,800	
Patent Royalties	7,850	
Alterations	3,200	
		31,850
		134,696
Less: Capital allowances (Schedule 2)	56,889	
Lease amortisation	1,705	58,594
Schedule D Case I		76,102

		£	£
(2)	**Capital Allowances**		
	(a) IBA on Park Mill = £62,650 / 14 yrs.		4,475
	(b) IBA on Extension at Kirkstall Mill = £31,600 x 4%		1,264
	(c) Scientific Research 100% x £26,500		26,500
	(d) Plant: Balancing charge	(6,100)	
	FYA £(58,500 + 3,200) x 50%	30,750	24,650
			56,889

		£
(3)	**Relief for Lease Premium Paid**	
	Premium	55,000
	Less: 2% (20 - 1) x £55,000	20,900
	Schedule A	34,100
	Annual Equivalent £34,100 / 20	1,705

		£
(4)	**Chargeable Gain on Sale of House**	
	Consideration	42,350
	Cost	26,220
	Gross Gain	16,130
	Indexation $\frac{410.4 - 313.4}{313.4}$ = 0.310 x £35,000	10,850
		5,280
	Less: $\frac{1}{4}$ (FA 1972, s.93)	1,320
	Chargeable Gain	3,960

18

(a) North Yorkshire Plastics Ltd

A company is a distinct legal entity; hence normally there is no effect on the corporation tax position of the company if the ownership of the company changes.

However, the following points should be noted in connection with the change:

(i) Trading Losses

Under TA 1970, s.177(1), a trading loss can be carried forward against future profits of the same trade. So long as the same trade is being continued by the company (a question of fact), loss relief will not be denied.

However, where there is both a change in ownership and a major change in the nature of conduct of the trade (including the type of property dealt in, customers, outlets or markets), or within a period of three years a company's trade has become negligible and before there is a considerable revival of the trade, there is a change in the ownership of the company, loss relief under s.177 can be withheld (TA 1970, s.483).

(ii) Advance Corporation Tax

Under FA 1972, s.101 the carry forward of ACT can be restricted in the same circumstances.

(iii) Capital Losses

There is no statutory provision restricting the amount of capital loss available to be carried forward against future gains of the company.

It is, however, worth pointing out that under the House of Lords' decision in the **Ramsay** case, the **Burmah** case and **Furniss v. Dawson (1983)**, if the transactions are carried out purely for tax avoidance purposes with no commercial reason for the transactions, loss relief can be denied.

(iv) Retirement of Directors

The retirement of the directors on its own does not have any adverse tax effect. If the company is to make compensation payments, it will have to demonstrate that these are wholly and exclusively for the purposes of the company's trade for them to be an allowable deduction.

(b) Demergers

(i) The two principal problems which caused obstacles to demergers were (1) on division of the group or company, a distribution took place, with adverse income tax and ACT consequences, and (2) a disposal or part disposal took place for capital gains tax purposes.

(ii) Under FA 1980, s.117, so long as the demerger was an exempt distribution, no income tax or ACT arose and the shareholder was exempted from any CGT liability in a reorganisation, at the point of transferring the shares.

(iii) The main conditions for exemption are:

(1) The transaction must be one which would otherwise be a distribution within TA 1970, s.233.

(2) The company making the distribution must be a trading company (or a member of a trading group).

(3) The transaction must be wholly or mainly to benefit some or all of the trading activities involved in the demerger.

(4) It is intended that the newly demerged trade should be left free to operate under its new independent management - quite separate from the former parent.

(5) All the companies involved must be resident in the UK at the time of the distribution.

(6) The demerger must not be part of a scheme or arrangements for the avoidance of tax.

(7) If the transfer is of shares, these must not be redeemable, and the shares constitute substantially the whole of the distributing company's holding and voting rights in the 75% subsidiary's share capital.

(a) <u>Statement of capital gains tax position for 1986/87</u>

	£	Gains/ losses £
(1) 1.12.86 Sale of unquoted shares in Townsend Ltd		
(1) Sale of 3.4.62 holding:		
Proceeds 25/30 x £13,500	11,250	
Less: Cost	12,800	
Loss:	(1,550)	
Indexation 12,800 x $\frac{361.9 - 313.4}{313.4}$	(1,984)	
	(3,534)	
Time apportion: $\frac{21\frac{8}{12}}{24\frac{8}{12}}$	(3,104)	(3,104)

(By comparison, BDV would produce a gain. Thus no election should be made for BDV.)

	£	
(2) Sale of 500 shares out of 8.6.56 holding:		
Proceeds 5/30 x £13,500	2,250	
Less: Cost 5/15 x £4,200	1,400	
Gross gain	850	
Less: Indexation:		
£1,400 x $\frac{361.9 - 313.4}{313.4}$ = 0.155	217	
	633	
Time apportion: $\frac{21\frac{8}{12}}{30\frac{6}{12}}$	4,491	4,491
		(2,655)
Compare to BDV:		
Proceeds	2,250	
Less: BDV 500 x £2	1,000	
Gross gain	1,250	
Less: Indexation: £1,000 x 0.155	155	
	1,095	

Hence BDV not beneficial and no election is made.

	£
(ii) 3.4.87 Sale of shares in Clark (Winchester) Ltd:	
Proceeds	20,700
Less: Cost 29.6.85	11,500
Gross gain c/f	9,200

		£	Gains/ losses £
	b/f	9,200	
Less: Indexation:			
£11,500 x $\frac{372.3 - 358.3}{358.3}$		449	
Net chargeable gain		8,751	

Less: Retirement Relief:
As Jardine has been a full-time working director for 1 3/4 years the maximum retirement relief available to him is:

$$\frac{1\frac{3}{4}}{10 \text{ years}} = 17.5\% \times £100{,}000 = £17{,}500$$

Gain Eligible for Retirement Relief

£8,751 x $\frac{£95,000 + £64,500}{£95,000 + £64,500 + £5,500}$ =	8,458	293

(iii) (1)	9.6.86 Sale of 10% Treasury Stock 1992 identified on a FIFO basis:		
	6.10.85 Proceeds £6,850 x $\frac{6,000}{8,000}$	5,137	
	Less: Cost 6,000	4,420	
		717	717
	8.12.85 Proceeds $\frac{2,000}{8,000}$ x £6,850	1,713	
	Less: Cost $\frac{2,000}{9,000}$ x £7,065	1,570	
	Chargeable gain	143	143
			(1,503)
(2)	Second disposal not liable to ACT as made after 2.7.86	(1,388)	
	Overall allowable loss for 1986/87		(1,503)

(b) Points to note in connection with proposed transfer of house:

Capital gains tax

The transfer of the house to trustees is a chargeable disposal for capital gains tax. The gain will be computed as the difference between its market value and original cost with relief for indexation from March 1982 to the month of transfer. The chargeable gain may be held over by election under FA 1980, S.79 (as extended by FA 1982. s.82 to gifts from individuals to UK trustees). The election must be made within six years of the year of assessment in which the transfer is made but need only be signed by

Jardine, the settlor. The gain is held over by reducing the trustees' base cost for subsequent disposals by the gain held over.

If Jardine still has an unused nil band for 1987/88 he could sell the house to the trustees for its original cost (£8,000) plus his unused nil band. The part of the full chargeable gain represented by the proceeds surplus, to cost could not be held over but would instead be chargeable in 1987/88 and covered by his nil band. To achieve this he would have to first settle sufficient cash on the trustees. The benefit would accrue to the trustees thereby having a higher base cost since less of the gain is held over.

20 SUTTON

(a) Capital gains tax payable for 1986/87 if no claims for relief are made.

(i) 16.1.87 Sale of 6,000 shares in Sillitoe plc

	£	Gains £
Identify with 2,000 shares bought 2.8.86		
Sale proceeds $\frac{2,000}{6,000}$ x £9,750	3,190	
Less: Cost	1,660	
Gross gain	1,530	
Less: Indexation allowance:		
£1,660 x $\frac{363.8 - 350}{350}$	65	1,465
Identify with pool of 10,000 shares costing £6,730:		
Sale proceeds $\frac{4,000}{6,000}$ x £9,750	6,380	
Less: Cost $\frac{4,000}{10,000}$ x £6,730	2,692	
Gross gain	3,688	
Less: Indexation allowance:		
£2,692 x $\frac{363.8 - 313.4}{313.4}$ = 0.161	433	3,255

(ii) Jan 1987 Painting Damage

	£	Gains £
Insurance proceeds	9,000	
Less: Portion of cost £8,000 x $\frac{9,000}{15,000}$	4,800	
Gross gain	4,200	
Less: Indexation allowance:		
£4,800 x $\frac{363.8 - 340}{340}$	336	3,864
		8,584
Less: Exempt		6,300
		2,284
Capital gains tax at 30%		685.20

(b) Reliefs Available and Recommendations

(1) Insurance Proceeds re Damaged Painting.

An election can be made for the insurance proceeds to be deducted from the cost of the painting as all the insurance proceeds were used to restore the painting.

Sutton is recommended to make the election as this will reduce the chargeable gain on the painting to nil and eliminate the capital gains tax for the year.

(2) Negligible Value of Shares in O'Reilly plc

If the Revenue accept that shares are of negligible value by the end of the year for which the loss is being claimed Sutton could claim constructive loss relief for the fall in value of the shares in O'Reilly plc.

It was held in **Williams v. Bullivant (1983)** that the date on which the claim is made should be used to establish the time of disposal.

In practice, the Revenue allows a claim to be made within two years of the end of the year of assessment for which the relief is claimed.

Sutton is not recommended to make the claim for 1986/87 as his liability has already been eliminated by claiming the relief in respect of the painting ((a) above).

Sutton should review his capital gains tax position in 1987/88 and consider making a claim for that year if this will be beneficial.

(c) Gross Gain for Capital Gains Tax on Sale of House

	£
Consideration	190,000
Less: Cost	42,500
Gross gain before indexation	147,500

21 **TOM, DICK AND HARRY**

(a) Capital Gains Tax 1986/87

	Tom £	Dick £
(i) Time Apportionment Basis		
Value of Goodwill Disposal (20%) x 250,000 = 50,000	25,000	25,000
Cost (1 April 1950)	Nil	Nil
	25,000	25,000
(No indexation as cost is nil)		
Time Apportionment Gain		
$\frac{6.4.65 - 1.10.86}{1.4.50 - 1.10.86} = \frac{258 \text{ mths}}{438 \text{ mths}}$	14,726	14,726
(ii) 6.4.65 Value Basis	£	£
Value of Goodwill Disposal (20%)	25,000	25,000
Value at 6.4.65 (20%) x 108,000 = 21,600	10,800	10,800
Gross Gain	14,200	14,200
Indexation: $\frac{368.6 - 313.4}{313.4}$	1,901	1,901
Indexed Gain	12,299	12,299

Tom and Dick will make an election under CGTA 1979, Sch. 5, para 12 to substitute market value at 6th April 1965.

	£	£
Gain (as above)	12,299	12,299
Retirement relief (full £100,000 available)	12,299	
	-	
Annual exemption		6,300
Chargeable at 30%		5,999
CGT @ 30%		£1,799.70

22 Hans Schmidt is almost certainly not resident nor ordinarily resident nor domiciled in the UK.

(a) Capital Gains Tax

As Hans Schmidt is neither resident or ordinarily resident in the UK, he is not liable to capital gains tax.

If he uses the asset in a trade carried on by him through a branch or agency in the UK, he will be liable to capital gains tax.

(b) Retention of Assets in the UK

To minimise his exposure to inheritance tax on moneys retained in the UK, Hans could consider the following:

(i) Excluded Property

Certain Government securities (e.g. 3½% War Loan) are 'excluded property' if owned by an individual who is non-domiciled and non-ordinarily resident in the UK.

Excluded property does not attract a charge to inheritance tax if given away during lifetime or on death.

(ii) Foreign Currency Bank Accounts

When an individual who is not resident, not ordinarily resident and not domiciled in the UK dies owning a foreign currency bank account in the UK, it is 'left out of account' - in the estate of the deceased person. Hence no IHT will be payable on such an account.

23 HALLSVALLA LTD

John Stephens

Gift in May 1986

	£
Estate before:	
630 x £53	33,390
(related property = 770 shares)	
Estate after:	
350 x £23	8,050
(related property = 490 shares)	
	25,340
Less: BPR 50%	12,670
Transfer of value	12,670

Jim Stephens
Gift in May 1986

	£
Estate before: 230 x £11	2,530
Estate after 90 x £4	360
	2,170
Less: BPR 30%	651
Transfer of value	1,519

24 NICHOLS

(a) Inheritance tax paid on death of Nichols

Date of Death 8th February 1987.

Estate	£	£
Freehold house		86,500
Foreign assets		31,900
Quoted investments		261,690
Personal chattels		18,100
Bank balances		33,600
		431,790
Less: Debts	6,850	
Funeral expenses	490	
		7,340
		424,450
Less: Charitable bequests		30,000
		394,450
Life interest in family trust		37,350
Estate on Death		431,800

	Gross £	IHT £
Chargeable lifetime transfers (at death rates)	21,400	-
Estate on death	431,800	192,220
	453,200	192,220

	£
IHT on death estate	192,220 (estate rate 44.52%)
Less: Quick succession relief on trust:	
100% x £7,420 x 34,380 / 41,800	(6,103)
c/f	186,117

		£
	b/f	186,117
Less: Double taxation relief		(3,833)
(foreign tax rate = $\frac{3,833}{31,900}$ = 12.02% which is less than estate rate, hence all can be offset)		182,284
		=======

(b) Potential repayments of inheritance tax through transactions in securities

Net loss on sale within 12 months:

	Probate Value £	Gross Proceeds £
12th October 1987	160,500	142,800
14th November 1987	41,800	43,200
	202,300	186,000
	186,000 ←	
Net Loss on Sale	(16,300)	
Reinvestment Restriction:		
$\frac{7,440}{142,800 + 43,200}$ x 16,300 =	652	
Reduction in Estate	(15,648)	
	=======	
IHT Marginal Rate 60%	9,389	
	=======	
Potential Repayment of IHT	9,389	
	=======	

(c) Points in connection with future transactions in quoted investments

(i) No further sales should be made of quoted securities showing a profit over their probate value until 9th February 1988.

(ii) No further purchases of quoted securities should be made within two months of the last sale. (If no further sales are made, this date is 14th January 1988.)

(iii) The securities purchased in October 1987 can be sold by the executors, with no further effect on the relief.

Index